1996

Concepts and C

Concepts and Cultures

A Reader for Writers

Martin Itzkowitz

Rowan College of New Jersey

Allyn and Bacon

Boston   London   Toronto   Sydney   Tokyo   Singapore

Editor in Chief, Humanities: Joseph Opiela
Editorial Assistant: Brenda Conaway
Marketing Manager: Lisa Kimball
Production Administrator: Rowena Dores
Editorial-Production Service: Tara M. Padykula
Text Designer: Pat Torelli
Composition Buyer: Linda Cox
Manufacturing Buyer: Louise Richardson
Cover Administrator: Linda Knowles

Library of Congress Cataloging-in-Publication Data
Concepts and cultures: a reader for writers / [edited by] Martin
  Itzkowitz.
     p.   cm.
   Includes index.
   ISBN 0-205-15279-1
   1. College readers. 2. English language—Rhetoric.
 I. Itzkowitz, Martin.
 PE1417.C643 1995
 808'.0427—dc20   94-28818
                                                  CIP

This textbook is printed on
recycled acid-free paper.

Acknowledgments
Chapter 1
    Pliny, the Younger. "The Eruption of Vesuvius," reprinted by permission of the publishers
and the Loeb Classical Library from *Pliny's Letters and Panegyrics*, Letters xvi and xx, trans. Betty
Radice. Cambridge, Massachusetts: Harvard University Press.

Acknowledgments continued on page 554, which constitutes an extension of the copyright page.

Printed in the United States of America

10 9 8 7 6 5 4 3 2 1   97 96 95 94

Contents

> *Ashes were already falling, hotter and thicker as the ships drew near, followed by bits of pumice and blackened stones, charred and cracked by the flames: then suddenly they were in shallow water and the shore was blocked by the debris from the mountain.*

> *As he walks along, he passes a house with an open lattice. He is on his way to report for official duty, but cannot help stopping to lift up the blind and peep into the room.*

> *Rather the ice than their way: to take what is mine by single strength, theirs by the crookedness of their law. But they have marked me—even to myself.*

CHAPTER 2 **Description** 69

KAMO NO CHŌMEI   **The Hut Ten Feet Square**   84

Now that I have reached the age of sixty, and my life seems to evaporate like the dew, I have fashioned a lodging for the last leaves of my years. It is a hut where, perhaps, a traveler might spend a single night; it is like the cocoon spun by an aged silkworm.

Views of the Galapagos Islands   90

HERMAN MELVILLE   **The Isles at Large**   90

However wavering their place may seem by reason of the currents, they themselves, at least to one upon the shore, appear invariably the same; fixed, cast, glued into the very body of cadaverous death.

CHARLES DARWIN   **The Galapagos**   94

This archipelago is situated under the Equator, at a distance of between five and six hundred miles from the west coast of South America. It consists of five principal islands, and of several small ones. . . . They are all volcanic.

MARGARET MEAD   **A Day in Samoa**   101

As the dawn begins to fall among the soft brown roofs and the slender palm trees stand out against a colourless, gleaming sea, lovers slip home from trysts beneath the palm trees or in the shadow of beached canoes. . . . Cocks crow, negligently, and a shrill-voiced bird cries from the breadfruit trees.

DYLAN THOMAS   **Quite Early One Morning**   105

Quite early one morning in the winter in Wales, by the sea that was lying down still and green as grass after a night of tar-black howling and rolling, I went out of the house . . . to see if it was raining still, if the outhouse had been blown away, potatoes, shears, rat-killer, shrimpnets, and tins of rusty nails aloft in the wind, and if all the cliffs were left.

KHUSHWANT SINGH   **The Haunted Simla Road**   111

Many years ago the bells of St. Crispin woke up the people of Mashobra on Sunday mornings. We threw open our windows and let the chimes flood into the room along with the sunlight. . . . The bells of St. Crispin do not toll any more.

DORIS LESSING   **The Sun Between Their Feet**   114

Sacred beetles these, the sacred beetles of the Egyptians, holding the symbol of the sun between their busy stupid feet. Busy, silly beetles, mothering

---

CHAPTER 4 **Process Analysis**   181

CHAPTER 5   **Comparison-Contrast and Analogy**   229

Buddha taught that a man who takes liquor and forces another to drink will be reborn five hundred times without hands.

Though liquor is as loathsome as I have described it, there are naturally some occasions when it is hard to dispense with.

I now understood what had been to me a most perplexing difficulty—to wit, the white man's power to enslave the black man. It was a grand achievement, and I prized it highly. From that moment, I understood the pathway from slavery to freedom.

After great pain, a formal feeling comes—
The Nerves sit ceremonious, like Tombs—

Impulsively he said, "Are you lonely, miss? I too am lonely. I am always lonely. My whole life long I have been lonely."

Who had killed these men of the bogs? Why in winter, or early spring? Why should they—apparently—have led privileged lives? And why the same kind of meals before their sudden ends?

PLATO   **Crito**   488

[T]he only question which remains to be considered is, whether we shall do rightly, I by escaping and you by helping me . . . ; or whether in reality we shall not do rightly; and if the latter, then death or any other calamity which may ensue on my remaining quietly here must not be allowed to enter into the calculation.

LUCIUS ANNAEUS SENECA   **On Crowds**   500

To consort with the crowd is harmful; there is no person who does not make some vice attractive to us, or stamp it upon us, or taint us unconsciously therewith.

Shepherd Versus Nymph   505

CHRISTOPHER MARLOWE   **The Passionate Shepherd to His Love**   505

Come live with me, and be my love.

SIR WALTER RALEIGH   **The Nymph's Reply to the Shepherd**   506

If all the world and love were young,
And truth in every shepherd's tongue,
These pretty pleasures might me move
To live with thee and be thy love.

THOMAS JEFFERSON   **The Declaration of Independence**   509

[T]o secure these rights, Governments are instituted among Men, deriving their just powers from the consent of the governed. . . .

Thematic Table of Contents

HUMOR

LANGUAGE, LEARNING, AND COMMUNICATION

MANNERS, MORES, MORALS

MEN AND WOMEN

RITUAL: SECULAR AND SACRED

SCIENTIFIC INQUIRY

THE STATUS OF WOMEN

Preface

Concepts and Cultures unites current pedagogic concerns with traditional writing principles. Using rhetorical patterns as guides, it introduces a wide range of readings from diverse cultures. Selections include work from Africa, Asia, and Latin America, as well as writing by Americans and Europeans with varied backgrounds. Several pieces are cross-cultural (Sam Gill's "Disenchantment") or deal with an aspect of non-Western civilization (S. Robert Ramsey's "China, North and South"). Such material and selections from writers whose traditions differ from that of the Anglo-American mainstream comprise about a third of the readings.

Writing from the Western tradition blends the classical and the contemporary. Plato (*Crito*) and Pliny the Younger ("The Eruption of Vesuvius") are included, as are Doris Lessing ("The Sun Between Their Feet") and Susan Sontag ("TB and Cancer as Metaphor"). The abundance of unusual selections is complemented by a number of more familiar ones (Rachel Carson's "The Gray Beginnings," Desmond Morris's "Territorial Behaviour," and the Declaration of Independence) long established as useful in writing courses. Such diversity is also reflected in the multidisciplinary character of the writings, with the humanities and social sciences especially well represented.

References within the text are also eclectic, ranging from Georgia O'Keeffe and Angkor Wat to the Three Stooges and Axl Rose. The tone is often upbeat, conversational, even humorous at times, all in an effort to engage the student. Each introduction includes a section demonstrating the use of the rhetorical type in various academic disciplines and, by way of summary, a section guiding students in its use.

A novel feature of the apparatus is a group of provocative questions called "Considerations" that challenge students to consider, for themselves personally and for their culture(s), the implications of ideas, attitudes, or circumstances presented by the readings. In addition to encouraging such intimate and intellectual engagement, these questions regularly include related suggestions for writing—writing that is most often not pattern-specific, since this need is fulfilled by a supplementary list of suggested topics at chapter's end.

Given the inclusive nature of the selections here, it should not be surprising that several are translations. Many of these are by such widely recognized figures as Benjamin Jowett and Donald Keene, and all necessarily stand as examples of English prose in their own right. As a matter of chance (and British colonialism), the readings from India and all but one from Africa are English originals.

The vast majority of readings here are presented in their entirety. In some instances, as in the pieces by Levi and Sontag, they are self-contained portions of longer works. In rare cases where deletions have been made, selections nevertheless retain their essential integrity. One of them, in fact, Twain's "The Lowest Animal," is regularly published in its present abbreviated form.

Two features of the rhetorical arrangement are unusual. Chapter 5 includes analogy with comparison-contrast. The rationale for this is twofold: first, analogy itself is a type of comparison, and second, it is rather too specialized a structural pattern to justify a separate chapter. Including analysis with division-classification in chapter 6 is perhaps more radical. The intellectual processes involved here are quite similar, however, as the discussion itself points out. In addition, like the arrangement in chapter 5, the fusion of strategies suggests that rhetorical patterns are interdependent.

ACKNOWLEDGMENTS

Regardless of the single name that appears on the title page, this text is the result of the resources, energy, and encouragement of many others. Part of the writing and research was funded by grants awarded by the faculty and administration of Rowan College. My department head, David Cromie, provided convenient schedules that enabled me to work on the text in optimum blocks of time without compromising my teaching or other faculty responsibilities. Many other of my supportive colleagues regularly inquired about my progress.

Laura Kaighn was an eager and tireless research assistant in the early stages of the project, and M. Patricia Kemery helped greatly with correspondence, particularly in regard to securing permissions. My wife, Ann, worked on final manuscript preparation, my son Job on word processing, my son Seth—resident computer guru—on word processing and electronic troubleshooting.

To continue in a nepotistic vein, my brother Joel B. Itzkowitz of Wayne State University provided valuable comments on the headnotes to the Greek and Roman writers and clarified some points of translation. Advice and assistance on various matters, occasionally unwitting, were supplied by Jim Grace, Gary Hunter, Tom Kloskey, and Linda McMenamin, all of Rowan College.

Most of the research was conducted at the Van Pelt Library of the University of Pennsylvania and the Savitz Library at Rowan College. The staffs of both institutions were most helpful. I am particularly obliged to Karl Kahler of the Van Pelt Library for his recommendations in regard to the treatment of Chinese and Japanese names. In addition, Toni Libro of Rowan College and Dan Walsh provided material from their personal libraries for my perusal and consideration.

Joseph Opiela, English editor for Allyn & Bacon, who showed great faith in the text from the start, helped me to guard against excesses in scope and style and (with the aid of his reviewers) to shape the text to the needs of its intended audience. His assistant, Brenda Conaway, provided ready answers to my many questions about the publication process and related procedures.

I am also indebted to the following reviewers for their suggestions and criticisms of the manuscript drafts: Christopher Burnham, New Mexico State University; Peter Carino, Indiana State University; Duncan Carter, Portland State University; Stephen Hahn, William Paterson College; Douglas Krienke, Sam Houston State University; William Lalicker, Murray State University; Joel Nydahl, Babson College; Eugene Young, Sam Houston State University; and Randy Woodland, University of Michigan.

To these people and to any others I might have inadvertently omitted I extend my deepest thanks.

Concepts and Cultures

Introduction:
Reading, Writing, and This Text

READING AND WRITING

The old "Pogo" comic strip sometimes featured an irate weevil who once exclaimed that if he could write, he would write a letter to the mayor—if *he* could read. Part of the humor here lies in the separation of two activities— reading and writing—that are, in fact, inseparable. Although both statements must be qualified, "You are what you eat" and "You write what you read" are quite nearly parallel.

Without question, effective writers draw upon their own experience. But part of that experience is literary—that is, it involves the choice and combinations of words, arrangement of sentences and ideas, approaches and attitudes toward subjects, even the punctuation, found in the writing of others. Through reading, we are exposed to myriad ways in which the written word may be used, and if we read enough, we are certain to make some of these ways our own. Of course, if we read nothing but first-grade primers we are likely to produce variations of "See Spot run." For example,

> My college writing teacher is Professor Ellis. She seems all right. We have our first paper due on Tuesday. The topic is "The Limits of Language." I hope to do well.

If you are more venturesome and include "Batman" comics, the daily horoscope in the local paper, "Dear Abby," and *People* magazine, you might avoid old Spot, which is all to the good; but to deal comfortably, or even uncomfortably, with complex ideas you will need to reach out in your reading toward new levels of stylistic and structural sophistication. Since you are more widely read than the unfortunate writer quoted above, you have probably developed more flexible and varied writing options. Still, all of us need to "pump paper" regularly to give our writing muscle, shape, and tone.

1

The fact is, however, that in this age of image and instant communication, people tend to read less—and less well—than they used to, a reality that necessarily affects their writing. Some written forms, like the personal letter, have—thanks to the telephone—all but disappeared. And there is no doubt that television has rechanneled the course of the written word. But someone still writes the TV script or the news, and nearly all academic courses, occupations, and trades require, even demand, effective writing.

If, as suggested, effective reading will produce more effective writing, you will find it useful—as well as interesting and informative—to regularly read material more challenging than that to which you are accustomed. If you currently read nothing but class assignments, you might begin with a major daily newspaper—including lengthier news articles and syndicated columns on the op-ed page. You might also consider reading a weekly news magazine from cover to cover over seven days. If you already read *Time* and the *Daily Planet,* you might like some of the more specialized magazines devoted to politics, science, or the arts. Many of these are available in your college library as well as at newsstands and bookstores. Browse.

As for books, if your inclination runs to titles like *Passion on the Half Shell,* you need not give up the vice—in moderation, junk reading, like junk food, might be pleasurable—but you might also explore a biography like *Lust for Life,* or a social analysis like *Sexual Politics* (*not* an exposé of elected officials). Since learning and developing skills are ideally lifelong processes, your search for variety, novelty, and appropriate complexity in what you read and write should be ongoing. Browse again.

Of course, although what you read contributes to how you express yourself and how you think about what you express, your writing is ultimately your own—no matter how much you have learned from a Hemingway or a Huxley, an Alice Walker or an Oscar Wilde. That "own," however, will have been favorably affected by the quality, range, and quantity of your reading experience.

This book assumes that you are well beyond "See Spot run." It also assumes that you are sensitive enough to language to have recognized the wordplay four paragraphs back and perhaps to have judged it (according to the length of your groan) somewhere between highly questionable and downright wretched. Finally, it assumes that through reading and using this text—not as a paperweight or doorstop but for the purposes intended—your critical sense will be heightened and your writing appreciably improved.

SOME WRITING STRATEGIES

Although you might get useful suggestions from classmates and in some cases work cooperatively with one or more partners, most of your writing will be the result of your individual effort. Despite pauses in the process of composing to ask for advice or reactions from professors or peers ("Hey, listen to this paragraph"), the writer's usual condition is one of purposeful solitude.

What, then, do you do after turning on the computer or getting your pad of paper and arranging your twice-sharpened pencils on the desk, placing the coffee cup or soft-drink can within easy reach, and fine-tuning the radio? Having established a comfortable working environment, you can begin the part of the writing process known as **invention.** In this stage you discover what it is you have to say.

There are several ways to make the discovery. One is to ask questions. You might apply to your topic the *who, what, when, where, why,* and *how* of the journalist to generate some basic, preliminary information. Suppose you were writing about campus crime. You might ask who the victims and perpetrators have been, what crimes have been committed, where on campus they occurred, and at what times of day, and how and why they happened. Perhaps you have answers to these questions; if not, you will have to do some research. Alternatively, you can ask the sort of question that will result in your writing in a particular mode.

How were the crimes carried out? (process)

What kinds of crime occurred? (division and classification)

What were the consequences for the victim and the college? (cause and effect)

What can be done to prevent or curb campus crime? (analysis or argument/persuasion)

Even if the questions do not at first lead to specific answers, at least they will have stimulated your thinking and provided some directions for further exploration.

Especially for topics that do not require research, you might try **brainstorming** followed by **clustering.** When brainstorming, you jot down words or phrases pertinent to your topic—as many as you can think of and in no particular order. If you were to brainstorm on the topic "Crime at Dismal State," you might come up with a list that after twenty minutes or so looked like this:

mugging   Gina's purse stolen   arson—wastebasket in Admin. bldg.

campus police asleep   college policies   bicycles stolen near library

Huntz Hall vandalism   security inept

petty theft—hair dryers, hot plates, loose change

my tires slashed   reflection of general environment

rape (date)   judicial process   student carelessness

open doors   walking alone late at night

damage to trees—knives   town rowdies
swiped silverware in cafeteria   immaturity of student body
cars left unlocked   damage to cars by students
broken windows in Union bldg.   drunk and disorderly
Brian's car broken into   understaffed local police
drug and alcohol offenses

While nothing is coherent yet, certain patterns begin to emerge. Once related items are clustered, the patterns become clearer still. For instance, "walking alone late at night," "student carelessness," "open doors," and "cars left unlocked" seem to go together. So do "security inept," "campus security asleep," and "understaffed local police"—as possible reasons for lack of control. The individual crimes themselves form a large group. Here, however, a further clarification might be made by separating mugging, rape, and perhaps some drug offenses from the others, which are relatively petty. Other combinations are possible too.

It is also possible that some items might relate to no other. "Campus policies," "town rowdies," and "judicial process" are examples of this. Since you have produced little material about these phrases, you might well eliminate them from consideration.

After clustering, you have two or three options. You might write about the reasons why crime is prevalent, in terms of security or of student attitudes and general behavior. At present, however, you don't seem to have enough data about either of these topics. You could continue to brainstorm about each in order to generate more material, or you might combine them. If so, you would eventually get to the **thesis** (central idea): "Campus crime proliferates because of student laxity and lapses in security." Another possibility might be to focus on the crimes themselves. Some of these seem to be petty mischief, others low-level crimes against property; a few are much more serious. A careful evaluation might lead to the following conclusion: "Although a few major crimes have occurred, offenses at Dismal State are generally petty, involving chiefly minor theft and vandalism."

A paper devoted to this idea will then draw upon the data from which it was derived for its support—for instance, Gina's stolen purse, Brian's broken window, your slashed tire. You might, however, have to discover additional specific instances. In general, it is best to generate more material than you can use easily. Doing so permits you to see a larger picture and to select the most relevant illustrative details.

As you may have gathered by now, the goal of asking questions, brainstorming, and clustering is to discover the main point of what you have to say and to assemble details through which to say it convincingly. But there is another popular means to the same end, **freewriting,** which depends less on these rational processes than on associations. Freewriting's primary purpose is to find material, but it may also be used as a warm-up exercise and as a means of overcoming writer's block. In an unfocused freewrite you write whatever comes to mind, usually for about ten to fifteen minutes, keeping the pen or pencil constantly in motion and following your thoughts wherever they may lead—even to a temporary obstacle. Here is an abbreviated version of one such exercise:

> It's late. I want to go home. Can't leave yet. Nearly six. Too bad the traffic is so lousy. Public transportation is the anser—But I have to drive. Drive. Drive. Endless, monotonous. Driving rain—that sort of whether doesn't help any either. Still ten minutes to go. Clock moves slowly. Itch scratch. Ah—feel's good. Now what? Who's out there—oh—just wind. Oh well. What to do. What to do. Keep writing. Old man river, just keeps rolling along. Five, four three two one. Kaboom. Quite a thunder-clap. Roads will be flooded there's never any drainage on route 644. Just have to wade through with the old boat or sink. Man found dead in his old Taurus. No bull. . . .

Notice that there is nothing consistent here. The mind wanders. Some passages, like the countdown, say nothing but simply mark time. Grammatical lapses and spelling errors go uncorrected. Nothing is censored. At the same time, two topics seem to recur: the lateness of the hour and the prospect of the drive home—to both of which the mind of the writer repeatedly turns.

In a focused freewrite, the writer proceeds in much the same way, but with a topic fixed in mind. The purpose again is to discover ideas and supporting details. Here is one you might have done based on the crime problem at Dismal State:

> Crime isn't to bad here. Lots of vandalism though. Smashed car windows. Brian for instance. Damaged tires—mine got slashed last week. Dumb kids steal silverware from the cafeteria. They'll wind up eating from a trough—pigs. What else? Else? Else? Oh yeah, Gina's purse got swiped. Not to much of that. Two muggings though last year. A rape this fall. But I don't know—pretty unusual for this place. Some petty stuff. missing hairdryers, radios and things. No stereos though. Part of the problem are the kids—leaving doors open to rooms and dorms. They walk alone late at night too looking for trouble. Trouble. Security not worth a damn. Town police are even worse. Couldn't even catch some-one who ripped off a a bicycle. Maybe serves those ecology nerds right. well not really. Let them breathe smoke. Now what about other crimes. Drunk and disorderly one or a two a weekend. Drinking in the dorms; once in a while there's a drug bust. No hard stuff though. The place all in all seems pretty safe. You gotta be careful though.

This contains some of the elements of the unfocused freewrite—the associa-tive **style,** the lack of complete sentences at times, the lack of correction or censorship, the marking of time ("Else?"). But because it has a focus, this freewrite generates much of the same material as the brainstorm. If there is enough to work from, you might develop a thesis similar to that derived from the brainstorm above. If not, freewriting further on some specific aspect of the focused freewrite, such as vandalism, might be in order:

> Vandals, goths, visigoths. They are running rampant. Cutting gashes into trees and not just hearts and initials. Some of the dumpsters behind the Union have been overturned in the wee hours. Students regularly pull fire alarms. One day someone will die from ignoring them. Too many cries of wolf. What more—uh—the un-let me see, breaking of the wooden sheep pen at the aggie campus, someone also made off with some hog slop. God knows why. Well it beats what you get on the meal plan. That's another thing. Kids taking trays as well as silverware. What do they do with them. Hang them in the dorm—oh and all that loose change taken from bureau tops. Good thing you don't leave wallets around.

This has produced additional specifics to add to those in the original focused freewrite. You might keep the process going until you are satisfied that there is enough material to work with.

Just as all roads were said to lead to Rome, each of these methods is perfectly acceptable if it leads to solidly supported papers. Depending on background, training, personal preference, results, even brain function, you might be happier with one technique than another. Experiment freely.

A paper concerning crime on campus might be written on the basis of personal experience, research, or both. Unless your instructor limits or specifies these options, the choice is yours. The tendency in much academic writing is away from the personal, experiential **essay,** in favor of the third-person, objective, researched paper. Where there is greater emphasis on self-expression or on the writer's participation in a process or events, however, the personal mode might prevail. Although you might not be the ultimate source of information or authority for a given topic, you may well be a primary one. You have had nearly two decades of life experience, at the very least, as well as twelve years of formal education. Within the limits of the topic or conditions of your assignments, draw upon it as freely as you can.

Having limited your topic, discovered your central and subordinate ideas, and generated the details necessary to support them, you are ready to write. If you prefer, you can work up an informal outline as a guide to organization before you begin. Some writers do this after completing their first drafts to check whether what they have produced is structurally sound. If the paper is to be fairly brief, say two to four pages, you might try to write the first draft at a single sitting. As in the case of the freewrite, do not censor yourself or stop to make corrections. Let it flow. Relieve any blockage that may occur by freewriting, skipping to another part of the paper, or taking a short break.

Although your final version will have a beginning, middle, and end, you need not worry excessively about sequence at this point. Instead of laboring over the introduction, for instance, focus on the heart of the paper. You can work on the introduction (and conclusion) afterward, with your purpose and main ideas now clarified by what you have written.

Once the first draft is completed, set it aside for a day or two if possible. When you return to it, do not faint, panic, or in disgust tear it literally to shreds. Most first drafts are not pretty sights. Calm restored, begin draft two. Perhaps with the help of an outline, work on major problems of gross organization—including the positioning of paragraphs, the elimination of useless sentences, and the addition of significant ideas or supporting details. You might have to eliminate whole passages or rewrite them completely as well as compose new passages altogether. If the first draft was a lump of clay, the second, when completed, should have some shape and perhaps a few ill-defined features. Set draft two aside as well.

If something strikes you as seriously amiss after you have reread the second draft, you should of course correct it before proceeding with the third. However, the third draft should be devoted primarily to refinement. Improve **transitions** between and within paragraphs. Fix awkward sentences. Replace dull words with vivid, vigorous ones. Rearrange sentences. Alter, add, or eliminate details.

Make sure that the introduction not only presents the perspective and attitude of the paper but "grabs" the reader as well. Two phrases that are certain to get the reader's attention are "According to Webster's dictionary" and "In this paper I will"—they scream "Boredom ahead!" Try instead an anecdote; a shocking or surprising fact or opinion; or a significant and attractive quotation. Similarly, although the conclusion should remind the reader of the essay's main concerns and position, "In this paper I have shown" and "To repeat what was said above" will not rouse the sleeper from the slumber that such writing earlier in the paper will have induced. While most conclusions announce "Exit—stage right," effective ones do it with a flourish and grace.

At this point you are ready to edit, a process that is far more technical, even mechanical, than drafting or rewriting. It is a matter of crossing t's and dotting i's, almost literally, since spelling should now be among your present concerns. Check the paper for grammar and mechanics: Do subjects agree with verbs, pronouns with antecedents? Are there any fragments? Do they need to be complete sentences? Do I mean *its* or *it's, amount* or *number?* Are there periods at the ends of sentences, capitals at beginnings, apostrophes to show possession? Pay particular attention to any points that you have found troublesome in the past. When you have made all necessary corrections, write the "all-but-final" draft.

You are not quite through. Having put this last version aside for a day or so, return to it once more. Make corrections as necessary (minor, one hopes) and prepare a clean copy for submission. When the paper is returned, read the grade, weeping or exulting appropriately. Then complete the learning process for this assignment by reading your instructor's comments and considering them along with any you might have received from other students.

Why Rhetorical Patterns

Tradition has recognized four general types of writing: narration, description, argumentation, and, in its various forms, **exposition**—writing that explains. Each of these modes has its own broad but flexible rhetorical patterns. There are also degrees of overlap. You can't write a convincing argument, for instance, without explaining your ideas. And although you know from experience that stories and arguments differ greatly, you might not have realized that narratives may be used to advocate a specific position or point of view. In *The Jungle* (1906), for example, Upton Sinclair presents a fiction intended to promote socialism. Instead, because the novel exposed unsanitary practices in the meat-packing industry, it motivated the passage of the Pure Food and Drug Act (1906), which is still in force today. Nevertheless, the examination of both primary rhetorical patterns and writing in which they appear is a useful way to begin the formal study of composition.

It is true that professional or other experienced writers do not sit down and ask themselves "Shall I write a definition? Shall I do a process analysis? Should I divide and classify topic X?" One of the reasons they don't is that they are professional or experienced. Their use of such rhetorical types has become second nature to them, a conditioned, if not instinctive, reflex. They know when illustrations, descriptions, or comparisons are needed, just as painters know about perspective, the nature of various paints, and the types of brushes and strokes, and just as carpenters know about drill bits, chisels, and awls. They know, in short, the "tools" of their trade.

Since your writing experience is probably somewhat limited, the text introduces you to some of the "tools" used in writing and allows you to gain experience with them through your instructor's assignments (some possibilities for which appear in the text) and your own experimentation. The writings you produce, however, should be more than mere exercises; they should be pieces to be valued in their own right. For example, when James Abbott McNeill Whistler painted *Arrangement in Gray and Black, No. 1: The Artist's Mother,* he was primarily interested in experimenting with the effects of juxtaposed shades of color. But the result—going well beyond this concern with technique—was a significant portrayal of character. You probably know the piece as Whistler's Mother.

Roughly speaking, you will be in the position of the third-year dental student who is just beginning to work with live patients. Under the guidance of professors, the dentist in training selects an anesthetic and syringe—but perhaps misses numbing the desired nerve; ultimately chooses the proper instrument but slips and inadvertently cuts the patient's gum; mixes the amalgam in faulty proportions and has to repeat the process. But the dental student's assessment of problems, and skill in dealing with them, will improve with practice. As a writer, you also must develop skills through practice and repetition. The rhetorical pattern provides controlled conditions for doing so. With these, your instructor's guidance, the advice of your fellow students, and your own best effort, you should succeed.

Although the patterns themselves (and the readings that illustrate them) present models for writing, they need not be followed slavishly. First of all, most writing includes a variety of approaches. The readings here are no exception. They have been assigned to particular chapters, however, according to their predominant pattern. For instance, Marianne Moore's essay "What There Is to See at the Zoo" (chapter 3) contains many examples, but most of these are highly descriptive. In addition, an implied comparison underlies the essay, as does perhaps an argument. Second, even when using a particular dominant pattern you will have choices to make—depending on your subject, audience, and purpose. In a comparison-contrast essay, for example, you will need to decide if similarities or differences are more significant, or if similarities are more important in some cases, and differences in others. Given answers to these questions, you will need to determine the order in which the material will be presented. This settled, you will have to judge whether your points have been illustrated to best advantage and presented fluently. There is great room for creativity here.

On the other hand, in an age that still values "doing your own (if nameless) thing" perhaps direct imitation has been unduly de-emphasized. In times past, it was central to a classical education. But some forms of imitation are still crucial to what and how we learn—in the acquisition of language, for instance. Occasionally, imitation might be useful in discovering what makes a piece of writing "tick" or how a writer achieves a particular effect. The pragmatic Benjamin Franklin, who was largely self-taught, explains in his autobiography how he learned to write by reworking essays from an early eighteenth-century journal, written principally by Joseph Addison and Sir Richard Steele:

> About this time I met with an odd volume of the Spectator. . . . I bought it, read it over and over, and was much delighted with it. I thought the writing excellent, & wish'd if possible to imitate it. With that view, I took some of the papers, & making short hints of the sentiment in each sentence, laid them by a few days, and then without looking at the book, try'd to compleat the papers again, by expressing each hinted sentiment at length & as fully as it had been express'd before, in any suitable words that should come to hand.
>
> Then I compar'd my Spectator with the original, discover'd some of my faults & corrected them. But I found I wanted a stock of Words

or a readiness in recollecting & using them, which I thought I should have acquir'd before that time, if I had gone on making verses [an activity Franklin describes earlier], since the continual occasion for words of the same import but of different length, to suit the measure, or of different sound for the rhyme, would have laid me under a constant necessity of searching for variety. . . . Therefore I took some of the tales & turn'd them into verse: and after a time, when I had pretty well forgotten the prose, turn'd them back again. I also sometimes jumbled my collections of hints into confusion, and after some weeks, endeavour'd to reduce them into the best order, before I began to form the full sentences & compleat the paper. This was to teach me method in the arrangement of thoughts. By comparing my work afterwards with the original, I discover'd many faults and amended them; but I sometimes had the pleasure of fancying that in certain particulars of small import, I had been lucky enough to improve the method or the language and this encourag'd me to think I might possibly in time come to be a tolerable English writer, of which I was extreamly ambitious.

Occasional writing assignments in this book provide opportunities for creative imitation, sometimes in the form of parody. Whether imitation is the sincerest form of flattery may be debatable, but when we imitate, even in writing, we are probably responding to something significant, unusual, or valuable in the substance or style of the original. How often, for example, have you encountered parodic imitations of Edgar Allan Poe's *The Raven*? A quick riffle through a few issues of *Mad* magazine is likely to turn one up. And perhaps you have written one yourself. Acknowledging virtues in the writing of others and attempting to acquire them should be a source of embarrassment or obstacle to your own creativity—"Nevermore!"

HOW TO USE THE TEXT

The chapters in this text are arranged according to the rhetorical types mentioned above, with exposition presented through several distinct patterns. Each chapter begins with a discussion of the pattern under consideration and includes illustrations that range in length from a brief paragraph to that of a typical student essay. This discussion also offers examples of the pattern's function in academic writing and suggestions for using it in your own.

A group of readings follows. These professional selections illustrate the pattern at length, but they should also stimulate your thinking about a wide variety of topics. The majority of the readings are by American and British writers, many of them contemporary. Others are by writers from a number of different cultures: classical Greek, Roman, Chinese, Japanese, Latin American, and African, among others. Often these readings will provide insight into subjects and ways of life with which you might (for now) be unfamiliar. Beyond helping you to develop your writing, the essays collectively suggest something of the breadth of human experience.

Four groups of questions follow each reading. "Thesis and Thought" contains questions to check your general comprehension. "**Structure**" examines how the rhetorical pattern under consideration is used and explores other matters relevant to the organization of the piece. "Style" addresses such topics as sentence patterns and variety, **diction** (word choice and phrasing), imagery, and tone. "Considerations" asks you to explore your own thinking and experience in relation to the issues raised by the selection and suggests writing topics specifically based upon the reading. A supplementary list of topics geared to the particular rhetorical pattern being examined appears at the end of each chapter.

Your instructor is likely to present suggestions, guidance, or requirements for using these questions. The general advice offered here is to ignore the questions altogether until you have read the selection once, leisurely and for pleasure. At that point, you might check your understanding of the reading by attempting to answer the questions in "Thesis and Thought." Then reread, keeping an eye out for answers to those questions you might have missed, and perhaps making marginal notes and highlighting or underscoring passages you think significant. Then repeat the process with the other sets of questions, and read the piece for the third time—particularly in the case of longer, more complex selections. Reading simply with an eye toward answering the questions, however, would be foolish and counterproductive.

Conduct a dialogue with the text. Notes such as "disagree with this" (along with reasons why), "weak example," "effective image," "sums up my life OK," "what about other government programs?" and so on, are useful in establishing your comprehension, improving your sensitivity to the writing techniques, and developing your critical faculties.

As a student, you are neither an empty vessel waiting to be filled, nor a sponge passively soaking up the pooled knowledge of the centuries. You are an active participant in your own education. If you bring to this text (and the course for which it is used) a desire and willingness to read, write, and learn, you should achieve the satisfaction that derives from labor that has led to accomplishment. And you might well have had some fun—of a cerebral sort—along the way.

1

Narration

A good tale ill told is a bad one.

JOHN RAY, *English Proverbs*

One day in the Neander valley two hunters, Grik and Greb, left their cave in pursuit of game. Hours later, Grik returned with four rabbits and a small deer. As she took the kill from him, one of the cave dwellers looked up and uttered, "Greb?"

Grik seated himself before the fire and sighed with pleasure as he replied haltingly, "Eat howl dog many Greb."

The woman paused, flint knife poised in midair. Then with a guttural grunt of comprehension, she resumed her skinning.

However slight, this anthropological travesty is a narrative. It presents a series of events, explaining who was involved and how the action occurred. We might even see a touch of sophistication in how it depicts the detachment of the surviving parties.

But does the dialogue itself constitute narrative? Loosely translated from cartoon Neander, it runs as follows:

"Where is Greb?"
"He was eaten by wolves."

Although the response describes an action, we think very little of it as a story. Isolated, the action lacks context and continuity. It is perhaps an ingredient of narration—not narration itself. For, in the overwhelming majority of instances, what Aristotle said twenty-four hundred years ago about the plot of a play also holds true for narration: it requires a beginning, a middle, and an end. Potentially the dialogue may be any of these (you could use "Greb was eaten by wolves" to begin or end a narrative), but it functions here as part of the middle of the story of Grik, Greb, and the nameless woman, which, however skimpily, includes the three necessary elements.

Simply multiplying the number of events will not create cohesion. You might recall the nursery rhyme and game "This little piggy went to market," in which someone touches, in turn, each of the digits of a child's hand or foot and concludes by tickling the listener after reciting these lines as each finger or toe is touched:

> This little piggy went to market.
> This little piggy stayed home.
> This little piggy ate roast beef.
> This little piggy had none.
> And this little piggy cried, "Wee, wee, wee," all the way home.

We have in the five "piggies" five actions but no narrative. "And" in the final line suggests a shift in emphasis or contrast, though what is to be emphasized or contrasted is never made clear. On the other hand, the story "The Three Little Pigs" supplies the heroes with a purpose (seeking their fortune), an enemy (the wolf) whose behavior creates conflict, and after adversity (two destroyed houses), a clever, dramatic, and successful resolution (one boiled wolf—unless you've read the expurgated version).

A working definition of narrative, then, is purposeful writing that presents a series of related actions that has, for the most part, an apparent or reconstructible chronological order, including a clear beginning, middle, and end.

NARRATIVE IN FICTION:
PLOT, CHARACTER, POINT OF VIEW

In fiction, as you know, the sequence of action is called the plot. In children's stories, such as "The Three Little Pigs," plots are often of the "sandwich" variety—with "once upon a time" and "happily ever after" as the usual slices of bread and with fillings (in which our interest chiefly lies) that are rather more diverse. Between the slices we can, for example, find a range of bears—from the mythical one that first lost its tail, to the three porridge-eaters of Goldilocks fame, to Pooh, Paddington, and Corduroy—who have either a single adventure (with clearly marked stages) or a series of them.

Despite other complexities, some adult fiction also has such simple plots. Cervantes' *Don Quixote* is a prime example. It consists of a group of isolated incidents, which attain their minimal **unity** principally because the title character and his "squire," Sancho Panza, are involved in them all. Swift's *Gulliver's Travels* is constructed in similar fashion. It was not until the nineteenth century that the plot **structure** of novels—in English at least—achieved consistently greater sophistication.

Whether episodic or intricate, plots present conflict. Three types are generally recognized:

1. struggle between the principal character (protagonist) and an adversary (antagonist)
2. struggle between the character and the environment
3. an internal psychological or spiritual struggle

These are often combined, although one may tend to dominate.

Adventure stories are most likely to be of the first or second type. The most active portions of Michael Crichton's *Jurassic Park* (novel and film) clearly involve conflict with the environment. So does Juan Bosch's "The Woman," to be found later in this chapter, although in this story the physical and emotional environments are fused.

Psychological turmoil dominates such works as Feodor Dostoyevsky's *Crime and Punishment,* in which the criminal Raskolnikov wrestles mightily with both his guilt and depression. In another vein, spiritual struggle pervades Hermann Hesse's *Siddhartha,* which is based upon the awakening and evolution of the Buddha. Maria Luisa Bombal focuses on the interior life of her narrator in "Sky, Sea and Earth" (chapter 6), and in "Davud the Hunchback" (chapter 7) Sadeq Hedayat fixes on the emotional state of his title character.

Although, strictly speaking, narrative pertains most directly to plot, actions certainly reveal character as well. This is perhaps especially significant in short fiction, in which the plot may focus on little more than a single incident. "The Woman" in this chapter is illustrative in this regard. Similarly, in Dorothy Parker's "The Waltz" (chapter 5), the central figure is defined both by what she says and does, and by what she thinks but does not say or act upon.

The perspective the narrator assumes in regard to the actions of the plot or to the actors within it is known as **point of view.** There are several possibilities. In first-person narration, the narrator uses the personal pronoun *I* and may be either a major or minor character in the story being told. Frequently, the reader becomes sympathetic to such a narrator, thus running the risk of accepting the perspective as "truth" instead of as one version of it. The first-person narrator, however, may be as limited and biased a witness as any.

The stories by Bombal and Parker cited above are first-person narratives presented by the major character, whereas Arthur Conan Doyle's "The Adventure of the Blue Carbuncle" (chapter 9) is told by the minor character Dr. Watson (which is the case in all but two of the Sherlock Holmes adventures). Although frequently an active participant, Watson is essentially an observer of the methods and actions of his consulting detective friend. Although the question of bias does not arise in "The Waltz," the issue of limited vision does: in Parker's narrative, "reality" exists exclusively through the perceptions and speech of her nameless heroine. We have no sense of what others, particularly her partner, are experiencing.

Third-person point of view is of three principal sorts: omniscient, limited omniscient, and objective. In omniscient third person, the narrator literally sees all and knows all—the unexpressed thoughts and feelings of all the characters as well as their histories. In limited-omniscient third person, the narrator may present thoughts and motives, but only as they appear to and through one of the characters. Objective point of view is restricted in a somewhat different manner. Here the narrator is a nonjudgmental reporter who presents impartially only what is visible. Among the stories in this text, Stephen Crane's "The Upturned Face" (chapter 4) is omniscient, whereas the Bosch piece in this chapter approaches objectivity.

In some twentieth-century literature, particularly in response to growing awareness of how the mind works, a technique called "stream of consciousness" is used. Instead of linear chronology and logical arrangement, the author attempts to reproduce the thoughts, feelings, and perceptions of characters as they occur, which is often randomly and associatively; but because the writer is in control, patterns begin to emerge. A prime example of stream-of-consciousness writing is James Joyce's *Ulysses;* its hundreds of pages present twenty-four hours in the mental life of the central character, Leopold Bloom. In this chapter, William Carlos Williams employs elements of the method in his account of "Red Eric." If you have done any freewriting (see p. 46), you too have used stream of consciousness—although probably without the extensive reworking necessary to produce a finished product that preserves the illusion of spontaneity.

NONFICTION NARRATIVE

Our principal concern in this text is with narrative nonfiction. Such narrative does not exist primarily for art's or entertainment's sake but to support or illustrate an idea. Its forms may range from the briefest of anecdotes to a full-blown account developed elaborately and at length. Although you might not be very familiar with such extensive nonfiction narratives, you certainly have had experience with more limited forms. Consider, for example, the following brief narration:

> Taking out the trash the other night, Tony missed the last step and fell face first on the walk. He picked himself up, but instead of calmly placing the trash in the can, he decided to test his jump shot. He missed, of course, and the bag burst open, scattering half-rotted peels, used Kleenex, and stale pork rinds all over the place. By the time Tony cleaned up the mess, he was so furious that he slammed the trash-can lid closed—catching and cutting three fingers. His departing kick broke

two toes. Bleeding and in pain, he hopped up the stairs on one leg, lost his balance, and struck his head on the door, raising a huge lump and causing a mild concussion. He's resting quietly now.

While we recognize the passage as narrative, the writer has not yet told us what to make of it. Here are some possibilities:

1. Tony has two left feet; the rest of him is all thumbs.
2. Tony had a terrible time last night.
3. If you're Tony, taking out the trash may be hazardous to your health.
4. Never take out the trash.

With some modification, the anecdote could well illustrate any of the first three points. Indeed, although the events may have led the writer to one of these conclusions, the actual writing is more likely to have begun with the idea either expressed immediately or held firmly in mind. Tony's story probably exists as a narrative example solely to explain or clarify what the writer means.

The point is that narrative used in expository writing must be integral to the thesis it is attempting to help establish. Here, for example, the anecdote is inadequate to support the broad fourth statement, "Never take out the trash." A difficult proposition at best, such an idea would require far more elaboration and support before a reader could accept it. Even the more limited "Tony should never take out the trash" would pose problems. (Perhaps if he were more careful and controlled his temper, Tony could remove trash efficiently.)

Of the three acceptable propositions above, the second and third are rather well supported by the anecdotal evidence. No one reading it can doubt that Tony's night was painful or that at least on this occasion his health was affected adversely. The proposition that Tony is clumsy, however, might require additional support, because it assumes something chronic or habitual in his behavior. To satisfy skeptics you might have to include other information about Tony's clumsiness, which could take the form of additional anecdotes. You might go on to tell the tale of the chowder spilled on Dr. Pazic's new suit, or the episode of the three stepped-on cats, or the adventure of the motorcycle and the maples—as many as necessary to show that Tony's behavior last night is typical.

Although each of these anecdotes might be as fully developed as the trash episode, you might also present them in abbreviated form—perhaps in a single summary paragraph:

But last night's comedy of errors is nothing new for Tony. Babysitting for his cousin one night, he stepped into a dark room and managed to tread on the tails of all three household cats in a matter of seconds.

They returned the favor by drawing blood. Serving at last year's honors dinner, he missed the soup bowl and ladled chowder into the lap of Dr. Cynthia Pazic—the guest of honor. More harrowing was the time he failed to take "Dead-Man's Curve" on his Harley (his helmet had fallen over his eyes) and wound up in a maple tree—no one is quite sure how—with multiple bruises, a sprained neck, and a cracked rib. The bike was fine.

Together with the elaborated anecdote of the trash, this might be sufficient to make the case for left feet and thumbs. More generally, whether you use developed anecdotes, synopses, or a combination of both will depend on how extensively you need to clarify, illustrate, or support your statements. This, in turn, will depend on the complexity of your subject and the nature of the audience to which your writing is addressed.

What then constitutes sufficient evidence? It might be clear from the qualifications in the previous paragraph that there are no formulas, no hard and fast rules. In part, deciding that you have provided enough is a matter of judgment based on experience. There are, however, a few guidelines. Put yourself in the reader's place. For example, how much evidence would it have taken to convince you that any of the statements concerning Tony is true? At least until you gain more experience, err on the side of too much support rather than too little. If necessary, you can eliminate some of it on revision. Supplementing inadequate evidence is likely to send you back to square one in the process of generating material. You might also examine chapter 3, in which the question of support is discussed at length.

There are several writing situations in which narrative, even of a single action or event, becomes the dominant means of exposition. Some of these involve the use of fiction for expository purposes. Forms such as the beast fable or the parable (some examples of which you will find in the readings for this chapter) depend on story to vivify the moral, ethic, or precept that is at the heart of the piece. Aesop's fable of the tortoise and the hare, although amusing in itself, derives meaning only from the conclusion drawn from it: "Slow and steady wins the race." Hypothetically, at least, the emphasis in such fables is on the instruction rather than the tale. Similarly, the parable is presented not for any intrinsic action, but for the lesson to be derived from it.

You are more likely to be involved with reality than fantasy in any extensive narrative you attempt. The autobiographical sketch, such as the one you might have written when applying to college, is one example. And it will be far better if the experiences you report go beyond a mere chronicle of events, to reveal your character or some aspect of it. A statement such as, "My life has been shaped primarily by the fact that my parents are Korean immigrants," will put any subsequent narrative accounts of cultural conflict or accommodation, racial hostility, efforts to attain the American dream, or adjustments to American reality into a comprehensive perspective that a mere listing of events would lack. Professional biographies are similarly interpreted narratives of their subjects' lives.

The personal essay provides similar narrative scope. Topics such as "My Most Memorable/Horrifying/Embarrassing/Joyful/Exciting Experience"— though well worn—nevertheless call for complete narrative treatment to fully reveal the horror, joy, and so on. But you needn't have been a teenage werewolf to have something intrinsically interesting to tell. More plausibly, an account of your sister's birth, the first wake or funeral you attended, your encounter with a rabid raccoon, your experiences working in a nursing home or at McDonald's, provided they have human appeal or application beyond the events themselves, may be suitable topics for the personal narrative essay. Here is one such possibility:

> I was in my senior year when the campaign started, thinking vaguely about law school and a possible career in politics myself. The city had been falling apart—literally—streets going unrepaired, bridge supports crumbling. The underpass beneath Pershing Boulevard had collapsed. Poverty and crime, however, were on the rise. A GM assembly plant had just closed to the tune of fourteen hundred lost jobs, bringing the total during the past three years to more than four thousand. Daylight robberies were nearly as frequent as nocturnal break-ins. My own brother had been mugged. Through all this, Mayor Froehling had been useless. The IRS was now investigating his tax returns, and his brother, the commerce commissioner, had taken off for Venezuela to avoid being tried for accepting bribes.
>
> Perhaps it was this bleak background that made candidate Norman Bartlett especially attractive to me. He had ideas—a jobs program tied to repairing the infrastructure, a package of incentives to keep businesses in the city and lure others to it, changes in police administration to deploy personnel more efficiently. But most of all he seemed to be the great democrat—a man of the people despite his corporate enterprises, the kind who went to ball games, bought his lunch from street vendors, took the bus to work. And his team seemed inclusive without pandering as usual to ethnic, gender, and racial voting blocks. Some of his "best friends" literally seemed to be blacks, Armenians, Jews, and Puerto Ricans. And he had pledged to appoint women to cabinet posts beyond the nominal one to Human Services. Full of ideas and enthusiasm, I decided to volunteer.
>
> Twenty minutes after I arrived at ward headquarters, I began talking with the assistant campaign director. "Bob, listen. if Norman includes playground rehab in the jobs program we might—"
>
> "Right," Bob interrupted, thumbing through his wallet. He handed me a fifty. "Pick up the sandwiches from the luncheonette, will ya? Get something for yourself too."
>
> He brushed past me, leaving me to stare at Grant's impassive face.

After lunch I tried again. "If Bartlett raised his proposed break on corporate taxes to six percent from four, he—"

"Mindy—"

"Mandy."

"Mandy. Me talk; you listen." Bob thrust a huge batch of flyers toward me. "Here's a route map. Hit every mailbox."

Resigned to my fate, I ran errands for a few days and worked the phones. The cause was worth it. Maybe I'd get to talk with Bartlett himself later on.

On Friday morning Bob called to me, "Wendy—got something for you to deliver."

"Mandy."

"Oh, right—grab a cab and take this envelope to Dorothy Lorenzon's place."

Lorenzon was a columnist for the *Herald* and a strong Bartlett backer, as was her husband, Eldon Mann, TV-station owner and patron of the arts. I arrived at their uptown brownstone and rang the bell. A maid, complete with apron and cap, answered. Stepping into the vestibule, I explained my business. She took the envelope and started to leave. When I followed, she turned, stopping me with a laser stare. "Please wait here," she said icily.

I checked the soles of my shoes. Nothing. I looked around. There were small paintings on the vestibule walls, a small table atop which stood a jade sculpture. Ahead, I could see the Persian rug and oversized white sofa of the living room.

The maid returned. "No message," she said and showed me out.

"Not exactly grass roots," I thought to myself.

I took a bus back downtown.

The following Monday morning ward headquarters was agog with the news that Bartlett himself would be stopping by. His limousine pulled up at noon. Bartlett emerged, silk suit glinting in the sunlight. He waved to the gathered crowd, smiling broadly, then made his way inside.

"We've got a problem, Mr. B."

"What's that, Bill?"

"Bob, Mr. B." He went on as Bartlett grimaced. "Fuselli just released this."

He handed Bartlett the press notice that I had already seen. It reproduced a Bartlett memo, written prior to his entering the race, which included plans for relocating his corporate offices to the suburbs. It also contained a list of a dozen slum properties Bartlett owned through a dummy corporation, and another list giving an ethnic breakdown of Bartlett corporate management. The numbers and distribution were less than impressive.

Bartlett riffled through the pages grimly. "Damn wop," he muttered, then shoved the release at his press director and bellowed, "Darren, take care of this!"

Regaining composure, he put on his public face to address the "troops." There was something about "all the people," "working for change," "ending dishonesty and corruption," but by this time I wasn't paying much attention.

As it turned out, Froehling settled with the IRS, got his brother to come back and face the music, and was reelected. I graduated from college later that year. I never went to law school but took a Ph.D. in political science instead. I wrote my dissertation on municipal campaign operations. If I can show people the difference between political theory and political practice, I'll be doing something more valuable and more rewarding than being Norman Bartlett's gofer.

The narrative here does not simply exist for its own sake but to illustrate Mandy's disillusion with part of the political process and to suggest how that disillusion helped determine her professional career.

Had she chosen to, Mandy might have subordinated the autobiographical elements in her account so that the narrative attacked political corruption and deceit more directly. In such an event, her first-person narrative would have been used as a means of argument or persuasion. George Orwell, author of *1984*, regularly takes this approach in his autobiographical essays.

It is also possible to cast personal experience in third person. This method might readily deflect attention from the actor to the action, from the performer to the process. Altering the point of view as it does, such a technique affects not only the way you approach your material as a writer but its impact on the audience as well. Here, for example, is a paragraph from the essay above redone in third person:

Mandy checked the soles of her shoes. Nothing. She looked around. There were small paintings on the vestibule walls, a small table atop which stood a jade sculpture. Ahead, she could see the Persian rug and oversized white sofa of the living room.

In this version, we no longer see through Mandy's eyes but through those of a remote other. Whether such distancing is useful, however, depends on the writer's purposes and emphases. What (and how) you wish your own audience to perceive or discover will determine, of course, the perspective you employ.

NARRATION IN ACADEMIC WRITING

Since most writing in academic subjects tends to be expository, analytical, or argumentative, narration (although often used in conjunction with other techniques) is not usually the writing pattern of choice. The chief exception is history, which is narrative in its recounting of events—but even here the historian may be more concerned with the *how* and *why* of occurrences and use the *what* simply as the raw material of interpretation or explanation. For example, George Roux provides a narrative summary of seventy years of ancient Eastern history, a series of events he goes on to analyze in the remainder of the chapter:

> In 612 B.C., less than thirty years after Ashurbanipal celebrated his triumph, the palaces of Nineveh collapsed in flames, and with them collapsed the Assyrian state. The Chaldean kings of Babylonia, responsible with their allies the Medes for this sudden violent and radical destruction, remained sole masters in Mesopotamia. Their rule witnessed a colossal amount of building work in southern Iraq, and Babylon—now the largest, most beautiful city in the Near East—became the centre of a movement of architectural, literary, and scientific renaissance. It looked as though another Nineveh had been born, and indeed the campaigns of Nebuchadrezzar II in the west suggest that a Babylonian empire was on the verge of replacing the Assyrian empire. But the brilliant "Neo-Babylonian period" was short-lived. The last great Mesopotamian monarch was succeeded by weak, irresponsible princes incapable of resisting the new, formidable enemy that had risen in the East. In 539 B.C. Babylon fell without resistance into the hands of the Persian conqueror Cyrus.
>
> *Ancient Iraq,* p. 338

Such is also the case in other studies treated historically—in literature, art, music, science, and philosophy—especially in regard to the history of ideas. Philosopher Bertrand Russell, for example, discussing the rise of modern scientific thought, recounts the perhaps familiar story of Galileo and his confrontation with the orthodoxies of his day:

> In astronomy, Galileo adopted the heliocentric theory and went on to make a number of important discoveries. Perfecting a telescope that had lately been invented in Holland, he observed a number of facts that once and for all destroyed the Aristotelian misconception about the heavenly regions. The Milky Way turned out to consist of vast numbers of stars. Copernicus had said that in his theory the planet Venus must show phases, and this was now confirmed by Galileo's telescope. Likewise, the telescope revealed the satellites of Jupiter, and it was shown that these move round their parent planet in accordance with [Johannes] Kepler's laws. All these discoveries upset long-cherished prejudices and led orthodox scholastics to condemn the telescope which had thus undermined their dogmatic slumbers. . . .
>
> Sooner or later Galileo was bound to fall foul of orthodoxy. In 1616 he was condemned in a closed session of the Inquisition. But his behavior seemed to remain too unsubmissive, so that in 1633 he was once more dragged before court, this time in public. For the sake of peace he

recanted and promised henceforth to abandon all thoughts of the earth moving. Legend has it that he did as he was bidden but mumbled to himself "and yet it moves." His recantation was of course only for show, but the Inquisition had succeeded in stamping out scientific enquiry in Italy for several centuries.

Wisdom of the West, pp. 246–47

Elements of Russell's sympathies are implicit in his account.

Taking quite another tack, art historian Heinrich Zimmer supplies the mythological background for the work he wishes to discuss, a relief sculpture that depicts the Hindu god Siva as an archer:

> [I]t is related . . . that Siva once annihilated and simultaneously redeemed the universe with a single shaft. The demons, titans or antigods . . . , who are half-brothers and eternal rivals of the gods, had contrived to gather to themselves the reins of cosmic government. They had been led in this enterprise by an austere and crafty tyrant named Maya, who, when he had driven the deities from their seats, constructed three strongholds, one in the firmament, one on earth, and a third in the atmosphere between. All were invincible; and by a feat of magic he then amalgamated them into one prodigious center of demon chaos and tyrannical world rule. A prophecy made it known that if this incredibly powerful keep were pierced by a single arrow the rule of the antigod would end. But who among the gods could deliver such a blow? Not Indra, the rain and thunder king; not Agni, the deity of fire; not Vayu, the deity of wind. These were . . . heavenly specialists, but no match for such a cosmic assignment. Indeed, none of the radiant refugees from Mount Sumeru, the central mountain of the universe (the Indian counterpart of the Greek Olympus) . . . , could muster the power to rive Maya's defenses. Therefore they all turned in hopeful prayer to Siva, the god beyond gods, and he, with his bow, flying in his chariot, performed the deed with ease.

The Art of Indian Asia, 2nd ed. vol. I, p. 11

Narrative also has its place in the social sciences. The clinically oriented psychologist might present the narrative of a case, the sociologist or anthropologist an account of behavior typical (or atypical) of a group. The anthropologist might also record narratives of nonliterate cultures studied—their history, legends, and myths. In *Gods, Graves, and Scholars*, C. W. Ceram includes several narratives of major archaeological discovery. One of them recounts Heinrich Schliemann's search for the historical Troy, site of most of the action in Homer's *Iliad*:

> Carrying his belief in Homer before him like a banner, in his forty-sixth year the millionaire Heinrich Schliemann set forth directly for the kingdom of the Achaeans, not even bothering, en route, to

explore modern Greece. It is of symbolic interest that almost the first native Greek he got to know was an Ithacan blacksmith whose wife was introduced to him as Penelope, his sons as Odysseus and Telemachus. We can only imagine how he must have been fired by this auspicious omen.

Gods, Graves, and Scholars, p. 32

Schliemann, of course, knew Odysseus both as a central figure in the *Iliad* and prime focus of the *Odyssey*. Penelope and Telemachus are, respectively the Homeric hero's wife and son.

Although studies in the natural sciences are less likely to use narration, it sometimes occurs, particularly in anecdotal form. Here, for example, Isaac Asimov recounts (with measured skepticism) the story of how Archimedes, Greek mathematician of the third century B.C., came to discover the principle of buoyancy that bears his name:

> The story is that King Hiero of Syracuse, having received a gold crown from the goldsmith, suspected graft. The goldsmith had, the king felt, alloyed the gold with cheaper silver and . . . pocketed the difference. Archimedes was asked to tell whether this had been done, without, of course, damaging the crown.
>
> Archimedes knew that a gold-silver alloy would have a smaller density than would gold alone, but he was at a loss for a method for determining the density of the crown. He needed both its weight and its volume for that, and while he could weigh it easily enough, he could not estimate the volume without pounding it into a cube or sphere or some other shape for which the volume could then be worked out by the geometry of the time. . . .
>
> The principle of buoyancy is supposed to have occurred to Archimedes when he lowered himself into a full bathtub and noted the displaced water running over the sides. He ran naked through the streets of Syracuse (so the story goes) shouting, "Eureka! Eureka!" ("I've got it! I've got it!"). By immersing the crown in water and measuring the new weight together with the rise in water level, and then doing the same for an equal weight of pure gold, he could tell at once that the density of the crown was considerably less than that of the gold. The goldsmith was suitably punished. . . .

The History of Physics, pp. 123–24

At times, like the confluence of rivers, academic interests converge. In the following passage Jürgen Thorwald prefaces an account of medical practices in ancient Mexico with some historical background of anthropological interest:

> In 1562 the second bishop of Yucatan, Diego de Landa, had all the books of the Mayas in the city of Mani put on a great pyre and publicly

burned. Thus he destroyed all historical records. The three books which escaped his zeal contained astronomical and religious matters.

In his old age Landa realized the folly of his action. With the aid of a surviving Maya king he tried to record at least the hieroglyphs the Mayas had used, along with their meanings in Spanish. Among other things he succeeded in preserving the signs for the days and months. But this late work of his continued to be ignored, for lack of texts, until it suddenly acquired importance in the nineteenth and twentieth centuries. For long ages additional tokens of magnificent early Central American culture slumbered in the forests of Yucatan, where lush jungle closed ever more densely around incomparable works of architecture.

Science and Secrets of Early Medicine, p. 255

USING NARRATION

Purpose

A narrative essay will have a point even if it is not explicitly expressed as a thesis statement. Keep the purpose of your narrative firmly in mind as you write. Select only those incidents and details that help fulfill your intention.

Suppose you were writing about a confrontation with a salesclerk and began as follows:

> The day started well enough. My friend Shelley and I met for breakfast and spent half an hour catching each other up on the latest. Afterward, on the bus downtown the driver smiled, and my seatmate and I struck up a pleasant conversation. The three-block walk to Carswell's from where the bus left me off was invigorating on a bright sixty-two-degree morning. But whatever cheerfulness had evolved between eight-thirty and ten o'clock was about to be extinguished. Adelaide Baumgartner would see to that.
>
> Ms. Baumgartner first appeared after I had been browsing in "Petites" for about ten minutes. She looked me over once or twice and asked, "Are you sure you have the right department?"
>
> I returned the favor of sizing her up. Her thick bovine build made her a likely candidate for Holstein of the month.
>
> "Perfectly sure," I replied.
>
> "Many of our garments can easily be altered," she informed me in sweet condescension, and withdrew—for five minutes.
>
> When she returned, we began round two. . . .

Here the opening paragraph provides background and contrast for what ensues. It also suggests that the narrator was hardly in a confrontational mood before entering the store. The ensuing paragraphs suggest that the remainder of the piece will zero in on the conflict and on the destruction of what started out to be a pleasant day.

However, the writer might easily have gone astray. For example, she might have reported some of the conversation with Shelley—the trouble her friend was having with Frank, her own mother's recovery from recent surgery, the menu of the new restaurant over on Fourth. And she might have gone on to compound the felony by telling us about her seatmate's grandchildren, the open hydrant that the bus drove past, and how she stopped at a construction site on the way to Carswell's. None of these, however, would have enhanced the setting of the opening paragraph; all would have been distracting and tangential to the main action.

Chronology

Make sure that your chronology is clear. You will usually present events in the order in which they occurred, taking care to use appropriate transitions that will guide your reader in following the events described.

If you choose to begin in the middle and flash back (and perhaps forward again), take your reader with you:

> It was three in the morning and pouring rain. And there I was, stranded on a highway forty miles from Boise. The feeling of isolation and helplessness was overwhelming but not altogether unfamiliar. I had experienced it many times before—when I had my tonsils out—with Shag—when I got Joanne's "Dear Chuck" letter at boot camp. . . .
>
> I was only four when I had my tonsils out and had not been well prepared. . . . Waking up alone in recovery was worst of all.
>
> Now, here I was again, not in a starkly lit, whitewashed room, but in the dark interior of a crippled van. Between the darkness and the rain, visibility was all but nil. It was getting colder. I grabbed the emergency blanket and wrapped it around me, holding myself tight. It didn't seem to help.
>
> Hugging Shag the night he died had seemed equally futile. He lay in my arms like a rag doll, the wind blowing his long hair every which way. Mom and Dad were gone for the evening. Brian was off at college, and Leora at the movies with her friends. I had let the dog loose and gone out back to look for him ten minutes later when he failed to return whining and scratching at the door as usual. Finding him lying motionless in the far corner of the yard, I knew at once. I sat beside him, lifted him into my lap. He was warm but lifeless. As I cradled him, my chest heaved with sobs and my tears blinded me to all but the reality of his loss.
>
> The rain fell more heavily, beads and sheets blurring all but the occasional headlight from across the highway and diffusing even that. . . .

And so on—alternating between the more recent predicament and remote situations. In accord with the pattern established so far, you can project the narrator's recounting the incident involving Joanne and a final return to the highway. One possible ending would be the arrival of a highway-patrol car or emergency vehicle (since the narrator is telling us about the past, he must have survived being stranded) and comparing it with the resolution of the other crises—the family reunion after surgery, the puppy that he was given six months after Shag's death, and the girlfriend that followed Joanne.

Even if you use stream of consciousness you must be in sufficient control of the material to allow the reader to follow your thread through the associative maze. Your purpose, after all, is to communicate—not simply express.

Point of View

Decide on your point of view. First-person narrative, as in the two writing examples above, is a likely choice for presenting your own experience. But even here, third person may be an option. It is possible, for example, that an objective approach might have underscored Ms. Baumgartner's rudeness.

If you are a reporter rather than a participant, you are almost certain to write in third person, unless you have a particular purpose in calling attention to yourself. Since journalistic accounts typically have "angles," however, such writing will also have a thesis. A sports reporter, for instance, might not write a play-by-play or score-by-score account, but provide the plays or scores while focusing on the sloppiness of the team's performance.

Be aware that narration may be useful to you even when the principal purpose of your writing or its primary structure is not narrative. Anecdotes, summaries of events, or even protracted accounts may be useful for everything from providing examples to establishing an argument.

Pliny, the Younger

(Rome; ca. 62–ca. 113)

A government official like his uncle, Pliny the Elder, Pliny the Younger studied law, rose to the position of consul, and ultimately became governor of two provinces in Asia Minor. The uncle wrote an influential natural history; the nephew was, literally, a man of letters.

It is chiefly through his letters that Pliny is remembered. Deliberately crafted, they rise beyond simple transmission of information to the level of literary art. Pliny's topics vary, although many relate to his profession of politics. Some are addressed to the emperor Trajan, whose replies we also have, since Pliny published much of his correspondence. Other letters, of a private nature, provide glimpses of Roman life in the first century.

Tacitus, to whom the letters reproduced below are written, was a major Roman historian. However, the portion of his work that would have incorporated Pliny's account of the eruption has not survived.

Vesuvius erupted on August 24 in A.D. 79, burying such communities as Pompeii and Herculaneum for more than sixteen centuries until excavations—still ongoing—were begun in 1709. Small comfort to its victims, the catastrophe preserved these two towns nearly intact and provided posterity with considerable information about Roman architecture, civic planning, and daily life.

The Eruption of Vesuvius

XVI

To Cornelius Tacitus

THANK YOU FOR ASKING ME to send you a description of my uncle's death so that you can leave an accurate account of it for posterity; I know that immortal fame awaits him if his death is recorded by you. It is true that he perished in a catastrophe which destroyed the loveliest regions of the earth, a fate shared by whole cities and their people, and one so memorable that it is likely to make his name live for ever: and he himself wrote a number of books of lasting value: but you write for all time and can still do much to perpetuate his memory. The fortunate man, in my opinion, is he to whom the gods have granted the power either to do something which is worth recording or to write what is worth reading, and most fortunate of all is the man who can do both. Such a man was my uncle, as his own books and yours will prove. So you set me a task I would choose for myself, and I am more than willing to start on it.

My uncle was stationed at Misenum,[1] in active command of the fleet. On 24 August, in the early afternoon, my mother drew his attention to a cloud of unusual size and appearance. He had been out in the sun, had taken a cold bath, and lunched while lying down, and was then working at his books. He called for his shoes and climbed up to a place which would give him the best view of the phenomenon. It was not clear at that distance from which mountain the cloud was rising (it was afterwards known to be Vesuvius); its general appearance can best be expressed as being like a pine rather than any other tree, for it rose to a great height on a sort of trunk and then split off into branches, I imagine because it was thrust upwards by the first blast and then left unsupported as the pressure subsided, or else it was borne down by its own weight so that it spread out and gradually dispersed. Sometimes it looked white, sometimes blotched and dirty, according to the amount of soil and ashes it carried with it. My uncle's scholarly acumen saw at once that it was important enough for a closer inspection, and he ordered a boat to be made ready, telling me I could come with him if I wished. I replied that I preferred to go on with my studies, and as it happened he had himself given me some writing to do.

As he was leaving the house he was handed a message from Rectina, wife of Tascus, whose house was at the foot of the mountain, so that escape was impossible except by boat. She was terrified by the danger threatening her and implored him to rescue her from her fate. He changed his plans, and what he had begun in a spirit of inquiry he completed as a hero. He gave orders for the warships to be launched and went on board himself with the intention of bringing help to many more people besides Rectina, for this lovely stretch of coast was thickly populated. He hurried to the place which everyone else was hastily leaving, steering his course straight for the danger zone. He was entirely fearless, describing each new movement and phase of the portent to be noted down exactly as he observed them. Ashes were already falling, hotter and thicker as the ships drew near, followed by bits of pumice and blackened stones, charred and cracked by the flames: then suddenly they were in shallow water, and the shore was blocked by the debris from the mountain. For a moment my uncle wondered whether to turn back, but when the helmsman advised this he refused, telling him that Fortune stood by the courageous and they must make for Pomponianus at Stabiae.[2] He was cut off there by the breadth of the bay (for the shore gradually curves round a basin filled by the sea) so that he was not as yet in danger, though it was clear that this would come nearer as it spread. Pomponianus had therefore already put his belongings on board ship, intending to escape if the contrary wind fell. This wind was of course full in my uncle's favour, and he was able to bring his ship in. He embraced his terrified friend, cheered and encouraged him, and

---

[1]The northern arm of the Bay of Naples (Capo Miseno). [Tr.]   [2]Stabiae was four miles south of Pompeii. [Tr.]

thinking he could calm his fears by showing his own composure, gave orders
that he was to be carried to the bathroom. After his bath he lay down and
dined; he was quite cheerful, or at any rate he pretended he was, which was
no less courageous.

Meanwhile on Mount Vesuvius broad sheets of fire and leaping flames
blazed at several points, their bright glare emphasized by the darkness of
night. My uncle tried to allay the fears of his companions by repeatedly
declaring that these were nothing but bonfires left by the peasants in their
terror, or else empty houses on fire in the districts they had abandoned. Then
he went to rest and certainly slept, for as he was a stout man his breathing
was rather loud and heavy and could be heard by people coming and going
outside his door. By this time the courtyard giving access to his room was full
of ashes mixed with pumice-stones, so that its level had risen, and if he had
stayed in the room any longer he would never have got out.[3] He was wakened,
came out and joined Pomponianus and the rest of the household who had sat
up all night. They debated whether to stay indoors or take their chance in the
open, for the buildings were now shaking with violent shocks, and seemed to
be swaying to and fro as if they were torn from their foundations. Outside on
the other hand, there was the danger of falling pumice-stones, even though
these were light and porous; however, after comparing the risks they chose
the latter. In my uncle's case one reason outweighed the other, but for the
others it was a choice of fears. As a protection against falling objects they put
pillows on their heads tied down with cloths.

Elsewhere there was daylight by this time, but they were still in darkness,   5
blacker and denser than any night that ever was, which they relieved by
lighting torches and various kinds of lamp. My uncle decided to go down to
the shore and investigate on the spot the possibility of any escape by sea, but he
found the waves still wild and dangerous. A sheet was spread on the ground
for him to lie down, and he repeatedly asked for cold water to drink. Then
the flames and smell of sulphur which gave warning of the approaching fire
drove the others to take flight and roused him to stand up. He stood leaning
on two slaves and then suddenly collapsed, I imagine because the dense fumes
choked his breathing by blocking his windpipe which was constitutionally
weak and narrow and often inflamed. When daylight returned on the 26th—
two days after the last day he had seen—his body was found intact and
uninjured, still fully clothed and looking more like sleep than death.

Meanwhile my mother and I were at Misenum, but this is not of any
historic interest, and you only wanted to hear about my uncle's death. I will
say no more, except to add that I have described in detail every incident
which I either witnessed myself or heard about immediately after the event,
when reports were most likely to be accurate. It is for you to select what best
suits your purpose, for there is a great difference between a letter to a friend
and history written for all to read.

[3]Hence the many bodies found in the excavations at Pompeii. [Tr.]

XX

TO CORNELIUS TACITUS

So the letter which you asked me to write on my uncle's death has made you eager to hear about the terrors and also the hazards I had to face when left at Misenum, for I broke off at the beginning of this part of my story. "Though my mind shrinks from remembering . . . I will begin."[4]

After my uncle's departure I spent the rest of the day with my books, as this was my reason for staying behind. Then I took a bath, dined, and then dozed fitfully for a while. For several days past there had been earth tremors which were not particularly alarming because they are frequent in Campania: but that night the shocks were so violent that everything felt as if it were not only shaken but overturned. My mother hurried into my room and found me already getting up to wake her if she were still asleep. We sat down in the forecourt of the house, between the buildings and the sea close by. I don't know whether I should call this courage or folly on my part (I was only seventeen at the time) but I called for a volume of Livy and went on reading as if I had nothing else to do. I even went on with the extracts I had been making. Up came a friend of my uncle's who had just come from Spain to join him. When he saw us sitting there and me actually reading, he scolded us both—me for my foolhardiness and my mother for allowing it. Nevertheless, I remained absorbed in my book.

By now it was dawn,[5] but the light was still dim and faint. The buildings round us were already tottering, and the open space we were in was too small for us not to be in real and imminent danger if the house collapsed. This finally decided us to leave the town. We were followed by a panic-stricken mob of people wanting to act on someone else's decision in preference to their own (a point in which fear looks like prudence), who hurried us on our way by pressing hard behind in a dense crowd. Once beyond the buildings we stopped, and there we had some extraordinary experiences which thoroughly alarmed us. The carriages we had ordered to be brought out began to run in different directions though the ground was quite level, and would not remain stationary even when wedged with stones. We also saw the sea sucked away and apparently forced back by the earthquake: at any rate it receded from the shore so that quantities of sea creatures were left stranded on dry sand. On the landward side a fearful black cloud was rent by forked and quivering bursts of flame, and parted to reveal great tongues of fire, like flashes of lightning magnified in size.

At this point my uncle's friend from Spain spoke up still more urgently: "If your brother, if your uncle is still alive, he will want you both to be saved; if he is dead, he would want you to survive him—so why put off your escape?" We replied that we would not think of considering our own safety as long as 10 we were uncertain of his. Without waiting any longer, our friend rushed off and hurried out of danger as fast as he could.

Soon afterwards the cloud sank down to earth and covered the sea; it had already blotted out Capri and hidden the promontory of Misenum from sight. Then my mother implored, entreated, and commanded me to escape as best I could—a young man might escape, whereas she was old and slow and could die in peace as long as she had not been the cause of my death too. I told her I refused to save myself without her, and grasping her hand forced her to quicken her pace. She gave in reluctantly, blaming herself for delaying me. Ashes were already falling, not as yet very thickly. I looked round: a dense black cloud was coming up behind us, spreading over the earth like a flood. "Let us leave the road while we can still see," I said, "or we shall be knocked down and trampled underfoot in the dark by the crowd behind." We had scarcely sat down to rest when darkness fell, not the dark of a moonless or cloudy night, but as if the lamp had been put out in a closed room. You could hear the shrieks of women, the wailing of infants, and the shouting of men; some were calling their parents, others their children or their wives, trying to recognize them by their voices. People bewailed their own fate or that of their relatives, and there were some who prayed for death in their terror of dying. Many besought the aid of the gods, but still more imagined there were no gods left, and that the universe was plunged into darkness for evermore. There were people, too, who added to the real perils by inventing fictitious dangers: some reported that part of Misenum had collapsed or another part was on fire, and though their tales were false they found others to believe them. A gleam of light returned, but we took this to be a warning of the approaching flames rather than daylight. However, the flames remained some distance off; then darkness came on once more and ashes began to fall again, this time to heavy showers. We rose from time to time and shook them off, otherwise we should have been buried and crushed beneath their weight. I could boast that not a groan or cry of fear escaped me in these perils, had I not derived some poor consolation in my mortal lot from the belief that the whole world was dying with me and I with it.

At last the darkness thinned and dispersed into smoke or cloud; then there was genuine daylight, and the sun actually shone out, but yellowish as it is during an eclipse. We were terrified to see everything changed, buried deep in ashes like snowdrifts. We returned to Misenum where we attended to our physical needs as best we could, and then spent an anxious night[6] alternating between hope and fear. Fear predominated, for the earthquakes went on, and several hysterical individuals made their own and other people's calamities seem ludicrous in comparison with their frightful predictions. But even then, in spite of the dangers we had been through and were still expecting, my mother and I had still no intention of leaving until we had news of my uncle.

---

[6]25–26 August. [Tr.]

Of course, these details are not important enough for history, and you will read them without any idea of recording them; if they seem scarcely worth even putting in a letter, you have only yourself to blame for asking for them.

Translated by Betty Radice

THESIS AND THOUGHT

1. What are the stated purposes of Pliny's two letters? (You may wish to reread paras. 1 and 7.) What implicit purpose does he have in the first?
2. Describe the character of the elder Pliny as revealed by the first letter. Using both letters, what do you deduce about the character of the author?
3. Taking the letters as your source and using strictly chronological order, write a paragraph in which you summarize the physical events of the eruption and its aftermath.

STRUCTURE

1. What is the purpose of Pliny's disclaimer in paragraph 13? In what sense might its inclusion be appropriate to the letter as a form?
2. Explain what changes, if any, might be necessary to transform the letters into essays.
3. Examine the transitions in the series of paragraphs following paragraphs 2 and 7; then explain how they establish sequence and changes of scene.

STYLE

1. At the end of paragraph 6 Pliny writes that "there is a great difference between a letter to a friend and history written for all to read." How might a history book have dealt with the eruption differently? Consider both subtopics and language. Be prepared to support your response specifically.
2. What is the contrast that Pliny attempts to establish in paragraph 4 ("They debated whether to stay indoors . . . " etc.)? How is it related to Pliny's general intention in this letter? Do you think the attempt is successful?
3. Which of the two letters strikes you as more graphic? What might account for any difference in this regard between the two?

CONSIDERATIONS

1. In paragraph 6 Pliny says of the first letter that what he did not witness himself he "heard about immediately after the event, when reports were most likely to be accurate." Do you agree that immediate reports concerning

disasters tend to be more accurate than those rooted in subsequent investigation? Base your answer on specific disasters—local, national, or global—including but not limited to fires, floods, tornadoes, bombings, mass murders, or power failures.

2. Apart from his uncle's behavior and his own, Pliny describes a range of responses to the eruption and its effects. In your experience, how do people respond to perilous situations? How widely do their reactions vary? How do you explain the differences?

3. Write a narrative essay in which you recount someone's (or some group's) reaction to either a natural disaster or one caused by human action.

Sei Shōnagon
(Japan; ca. 966–ca. 1017)

Daughter of a well-known poet, Shōnagon spent the decade beginning in 991 at the court of Empress Sadako, where Murasaki Shikibu (Lady Murasaki), author of the classical Japanese novel The Tale of Genji (Genji Monogatari), *was among her aristocratic peers. After her mistress died in 1000, she traveled extensively, possibly having taken religious orders.*

It is through her stay at court, however, that Shōnagon is best and most clearly known. While there, she compiled The Pillow Book (Makura no Sōshi), *a miscellany containing poems, prose fragments that are sometimes little more than lists, and critical, witty observations about the manners and arts of her time. The book provides considerable insight into the life of the aristocracy during part of the Heian period of Japanese history (794–1185).*

As you read Shōnagon's account of romantic dalliance, observe the differences between the mores and manners of tenth-century imperial Japan and those of our own day, whether in actuality or as depicted in either popular literature or the mass media.

Morning Interlude

IT IS SO STIFLINGLY HOT in the Seventh Month that even at night one keeps all the doors and lattices open. At such times it is delightful to wake up when the moon is shining and to look outside. I enjoy it even when there is no moon. But to wake up at dawn and see a pale sliver of a moon in the sky—well, I need hardly say how perfect that is.

I like to see a bright new straw mat that has just been spread out on a well-polished floor. The best place for one's three-foot curtain of state is in the front of the room near the veranda. It is pointless to put it in the rear of the room, as it is most unlikely that anyone will peer in from that direction.

It is dawn and a woman is lying in bed after her lover has taken his leave. She is covered up to her head with a light mauve robe that has a lining of dark violet; the colour of both the outside and the lining is fresh and glossy. The woman, who appears to be asleep, wears an unlined orange robe and a dark crimson skirt of stiff silk whose cords hang loosely by her side, as if they have been left untied. Her thick tresses tumble over each other in cascades, and one can imagine how long het hair must be when it falls freely down her back.

Near by another woman's lover is making his way home in the misty dawn. He is wearing loose violet trousers, an orange hunting costume, so lightly coloured that one can hardly tell whether it has been dyed or not, a white robe of stiff silk, and a scarlet robe of glossy, beaten silk. His clothes, which are damp from the mist, hang loosely about him. From the dishevelment of his side locks one can tell how negligently he must have tucked his hair into his black lacquered head-dress when he got up. He wants to return and write his next-morning letter before the dew on the morning glories has had time to vanish; but the path seems endless, and to divert himself he hums "the sprouts in the flax fields."

As he walks along, he passes a house with an open lattice. He is on his 5 way to report for official duty, but cannot help stopping to lift up the blind and peep into the room. It amuses him to think that a man has probably been spending the night here and has only recently got up to leave, just as happened to himself. Perhaps that man too had felt the charm of the dew.

Looking round the room, he notices near the woman's pillow an open fan with a magnolia frame and purple paper; and at the foot of her curtain of state he sees some narrow strips of Michinoku paper and also some other paper of a faded colour, either orange-red or maple.

The woman senses that someone is watching her and, looking up from under her bedclothes, sees a gentleman leaning against the wall by the threshold, a smile on his face. She can tell at once that he is the sort of man with whom she need feel no reserve. All the same, she does not want to enter into any familiar relations with him, and she is annoyed that he should have seen her asleep.

"Well, well, Madam," says the man, leaning forward so that the upper part of his body comes behind her curtains, "what a long nap you're having after your morning adieu! You really are a lie-abed!"

"You call me that, Sir," she replied, "only because you're annoyed at having had to get up before the dew had time to settle."

Their conversation may be commonplace, yet I find there is something 10 delightful about the scene.

Now the gentleman leans further forward and, using his own fan, tries to get hold of the fan by the woman's pillow. Fearing his closeness, she moves farther back into her curtain enclosure, her heart pounding. The gentleman picks up the magnolia fan and, while examining it, says in a slightly bitter tone, "How stand-offish you are!"

But now, it is growing light; there is a sound of people's voices, and it looks as if the sun will soon be up. Only a short while ago this same man was hurrying home to write his next-morning letter before the mists had time to clear. Alas, how easily his intentions have been forgotten!

While all this is afoot, the woman's original lover has been busy with his own next-morning letter, and now, quite unexpectedly, the messenger arrives at her house. The letter is attached to a spray of clover, still damp with dew, and the paper gives off a delicious aroma of incense. Because of the new visitor, however, the woman's servants cannot deliver it to her.

Finally it becomes unseemly for the gentleman to stay any longer. As he goes, he is amused to think that a similar scene may be taking place in the house he left earlier that morning.

Translated by Ivan Morris

Thesis and Thought

1. Explain whether the narrative has any point other than possible amusement. Consider the piece as it is presented but also the conditions under which it was written, that is, as an entry in a miscellaneous journal.

2. Describe the costume, architectural detail, decor, and etiquette of tenth-century Japan to the extent it is recorded by the selection.

Structure

1. How useful are paragraphs 1, 2, and 10 in introducing and advancing the narrative? If you were editing this text, would you retain them as is, eliminate them, or revise? Explain your response.

2. What are the sources of conflict in Shōnagon's account? How intense is the conflict?

Style

1. Characterize the tone of the dialogue in paragraphs 8, 9, and 11.

2. What effect do Shōnagon's elaborate descriptions in paragraphs 3, 4, and 6 have on narrative development?

3. Identify any comic elements in the selection.

CONSIDERATIONS

1. Do you share the author's obvious amusement with her story? Explain why.

2. Drawing upon your knowledge of history, including any gained through films or television, speculate on whether a similar scene might have taken place in any European nation. If you think it might have, where and in what era? In either case, explain why you think so.

3. How might the action begun in paragraph 5 play out in a contemporary American setting? Present your answer in the form of a brief narrative.

William Carlos Williams
(United States; 1883–1963)

For most of his adult life, Williams was a practicing pediatrician in Ruther-ford, New Jersey, his hometown. At the same time, however, he was building his reputation as an essayist, novelist, and poet, working particularly with American themes.

In the American Grain (1925), for example, is a collection of essays in which aspects of the American character are revealed through presentations based on historical personalities. Similarly, the five-volume continuing poem Paterson (1946–1958) is rooted in a northern New Jersey city not far from Rutherford and depicts the intricacies of modern urban life in the United States, although its implications are global. Here and elsewhere, Williams's poetry frequently depends on his perception of everyday scenes, sights, and sounds.

Whatever universality is latent in Williams's local subjects and scenes may derive in part from his heritage as the son of a British father and Puerto Rican mother. Study in Switzerland and Germany, both before and after he received his medical degree from the University of Pennsylvania, also provided cultural perspective.

In 1963 Williams was awarded a posthumous Pulitzer Prize for Pictures from Brueghel and Other Poems.

As you read "Red Eric," ask yourself who is narrating to whom, and where the narration essentially takes place.

Red Eric

RATHER THE ICE than their way: to take what is mine by single strength, theirs by the crookedness of their law. But they have marked me—even to myself. Because I am not like them, I am evil. I cannot get my hands on it: I, murderer, outlaw, outcast even from Iceland. Because their way is the just way and my way—the way of the kings and my father—crosses them: weaklings holding together to appear strong. But I am alone, though in Greenland.

The worst is that weak, still, somehow, they are strong: they in effect have the power, by hook or by crook. And because I am not like them—not that I am evil, but more in accord with our own blood than they, eager to lead—this very part of me, by their trickery must not appear, unless in their jacket. Eric was Greenland: I call it Greenland, that men will go there to colonize it.

I, then, must open a way for them into the ice that they follow me even here—their servant, in spite of myself. Yet they must follow.

It was so from the beginning. They drove me from Jaederen, my father and me. Who was this Christ, that he should come to bother me in my own country? His bishops that lie and falsify the records, make me out to be what I am not—for their own ends—because we killed a man.

Was he the first man that was ever killed, that they must sour over it?   5
That he was important to their schemes, that he meant much to them—granted: one of their own color, we who altered him must be driven from Norway. Their courts and soft ways. Not that we killed him. One or the other of us had to die, under the natural circumstance. He or we. But that if we had been killed, would he then have been driven from his country? They would have made him Archbishop.

To Iceland, then. Forget Norway. What there? My father dead. Land to the north cleared. A poor homestead. Manslaughter had driven me there. Then I married Thorhild, removed from the north and cleared land at Haukadal. Must I be meek because of that? If my slaves cause a landslide on Valthioff's farm and Valthioff's kinsman slays them, shall I not kill him? Is it proper for me to stand and to be made small before my slaves? I am not a man to shake and sweat like a thief when the time comes.

Rather say I killed two men instead of the one. They tried me among themselves and drove me out once more. To the north, then. Iceland wilderness.

There Thorgest comes to me and asks if I will lend him my outer dais-boards: ready to take me at a loss. Why else? For Eric the Red is a marked man, beyond the law, so it would seem: from that man one steals at will—being many in the act against his one. Thorgest keeps the decorated woodpieces. I go to his house and remove my property. He gives chase and two of his sons are killed in the encounter.

This time they have done the thing. They search for us among the islands—me and my people.

This is the way of it, Thorhall, this has always been the way with me from   10
the first. Eric loves his friends, loves bed, loves food, loves the hunt, loves his sons. He is a man that can throw a spear, take a girl, steer a ship, till the soil, plant, care for the cattle, skin a fox, ring, dance, run, wrestle, climb, swim like

a seal. A man to plan an expedition and pay for it, kill an enemy, take his way through a fog, a snowstorm, read a reckoning by the stars, live in a stench, drink foul water, withstand the fierce cold, the black of winter and come to a new country with a hundred men and found them there. But they have branded me. They have separated murder into two parts and fastened the worse on me. It rides in the air around me. What is it to be killed? They have had their fling at me. Is it worse, so much worse, than to be hunted about the islands, chased from Norway to Iceland, from south to north, from Iceland to Greenland, because—I am I, and remain so.

Outlaws have no friends. Murderers are run down like rabbits among the stones. Yet my ship was built, fitted, manned, given safe conduct beyond the reefs. To Thorbiorn I owe much. And so to Greenland—after bitter days fighting the ice and rough seas. Pestilence struck us. The cattle sickened. Weeks passed. The summer nearly ended before we struck land. This is my portion. I do not call it not to my liking. Hardship lives in me. What I suffer is myself that outraces the water or the wind. But that it only should be mine, cuts deep. It is the half only. And it takes it out of my taste that the choice is theirs. I have the rough of it not because I will it, but because it is all that is left, a remnant from their coatcloth. This is the gall on the meat. Let the hail beat me. It is a kind of joy I feel in such things.

Greenland then. So be it. Start over again. It turns out always the one way. A wife, her two sons and a daughter. So my life was split up. The logic of it also. This is my proof. We lived at our homestead, well rid of the world. Traders visited us. Then Lief, Eric's son, sails to Norway, a thousand miles, in one carry. But on his return, Lief the Lucky, he is driven westward upon a new country, news of which he brings to Brattahlid. At the same stroke he brings me back pride and joy-in-his-deed, my deed, Eric moving up, and poison: an edict from Olaf—from my son's mouth—solid as an axe to cut me, half healed, into pieces again.

Not that it was new. Only that here in Greenland I had begun to feel that I had left the curse behind. Here through the winters, far to the west, I had begun to look toward summer when I should be whole again. My people at work, my wife beside me, the boys free from my smear, growing in strength and knowledge of the sea. Here was an answer to them all: Thorstein and Lief Erickson, sons of Red Eric, murderer! Myself in the teeth of the world.

So they chopped me up. The Pope wins Olaf. Lief at court—Olaf commissions him to carry the thing back to Greenland. It grows like fire. Why not? Promise the weak strength and have the strength of a thousand weak at your bidding. Thorhild bars me, godless, from her bed. Both sons she wins to it. Lief and Thorstein both Christians. And this is what they say: Eric, son of evil, come and be forgiven.—Let her build a church and sleep in it.

With the years there began to be much talk at Brattahlid of Vinland the   15
Good that Lief had first seen, that it should be explored. And so Karlsefni and Snorri fitted out a ship. Eric, too old to go with them, watches the ship depart.

But Eric is in the ship, with the men, Eric the bedless, the sonless. Fate has pulled him out at the holes of his eyes and flung him again to sea as the ship steers southward. Now the glass darkens as the sea takes them to the New World.

They found wild rice, they built booths and palisades. First they traded with the Skrellings, whose cheekbones were high, whose eyes wide, then fought them. Whereas Karlsefni and his men had shown white shields before, now they took red shields and displayed them. The Skrellings sprang from their canoes and they fought together. Karlsefni and Snorri were beaten. They fell back. Then it was that Freydis, Eric's natural daughter, came out from her cabin. Seeing that the men were fleeing, she cried; Why do you flee from these wretches, when ye should slaughter them like cattle? Had I a weapon I would fight better than any of you.

Lagging behind the rest as they ran, because of her belly, she being with child, she found a dead man in front of her. It was Snorri's son, with his head cleft by a stone, his naked sword beside him. This she took up and prepared to defend herself. The Skrellings then approached her, whereupon she stripped down her shirt and slapped her breast with her bare sword. At this the Skrellings were terrified and ran down to their boats.

So, thinning out, more and more dark, it ran: Eric in Freydis' bones: Freydis now, mistress of her own ship, persuades two brothers, Helgi and Finnbogi, to sail with her again to Vinland; all to share equally the good things that might there be obtained. Lief to lend her his house there. Two ships, each to have thirty able-bodied men besides the women, but at the start Freydis violated the compact by concealing five men more. Karlsefni feared her.

Now they put out to sea, the brothers in one ship and Freydis and Karlsefni in the other, having agreed that they would sail in company. But although they were not far apart from each other the brothers arrived somewhat in advance and carried their belongings up to Lief's house. Freydis comes and does the same. The brothers withdraw and build a new house nearby. Within a month, the two houses are at odds and winter comes on.

Spring. Freydis, one night, after long thinking, arose early from her bed   20
and dressed herself, but did not put on shoes and stockings. A heavy dew had fallen. She took up her husband's cloak, wrapped it about her and walked in the dark to the brothers' house and up to the door, which had been only partly closed by one of the men, who had gone out only a short time earlier. She pushed open the door and stood silently in the doorway for a moment. Finnbogi was awake and said: What dost thou wish here, Freydis? She answered: I wish thee to arise and go with me for I would speak with thee. They walked to a tree which lay close by the wall of the house and seated themselves upon it. How art thou pleased here, she said. He answered that he was well pleased with the place, except for the quarrel which had come up between them. They talked.

It was the brothers' boat—it seemed—she wanted, larger than her own. Finnbogi slow, thickheaded, or asleep, consents to let her have it. Freydis, split with anger or bad blood, returns home and Finnbogi to his bed.

The woman climbed into bed and awakened her husband with her cold feet. Why so cold and wet? I have been to the brothers to buy their ship, but they refused and beat me!

Thorvard roused his men. They went to the brothers' house, took them and all their people, and slaughtered them one by one as they were brought from within. Only the women were left. These no man would kill. What? said Freydis. Hand me an axe! This done, she fell upon the five women and left them dead.

In Greenland, Lief, now head of the family, has no heart to punish his sister as she deserves: But this I predict of them, that there is little prosperity in store for their offspring. It came to pass that no one from that time forward thought them worthy of aught but evil. Eric in his grave.

THESIS AND THOUGHT

1. Identify the following based solely on what you can gather from the narrative: Thorhall (para. 10), Olaf (para. 12), Brattahlid (para. 15), Skrellings (para. 16), Thorvard (para. 23).

2. Describe (in several sentences) the nature of the conflict between Eric and his fellow Norwegians.

3. Is the behavior of Freydis consistent with that of her father? Can you detect any differences? Does Eric?

4. Write a third-person summary of the events covered in paragraphs 1–14. Follow strict chronological order.

5. The historical figure on whom Williams bases the narrative is usually known as Eric the Red—a reference to his coloring. Does Williams's choice of "Red Eric" for his title have any greater significance?

STRUCTURE

1. Do we have one narrative here or two? Defend both positions.

2. What is the difference in narrative point of view between paragraphs 1–14 and paragraphs 15–24 ? Why does Williams make the change? Is paragraph 24 consistent with this apparent shift?

3. Although Eric nominally addresses Thorhall, to whom is he primarily speaking in paragraphs 1–14? Where does the narrative process (as opposed to the content) take place? How is paragraph 6 typical of Williams's narrative technique in this section?

STYLE

1. After examining the contexts in which they appear, explain the following phrases and sentences:
    a. "in their jacket." (para. 2)
    b. "They have separated murder into two parts and fastened the worse on me." (para. 10)
    c. "This is the gall on the meat." (para. 11)
    d. "Myself in the teeth of the world." (para. 13)
    e. "So they chopped me up." (para. 14)
    f. "Fate has pulled him out at the holes of his eyes and flung him again to sea as the ship steers southward." (para. 15)
    g. "So, thinning out, more and more dark, it ran: Eric in Freydis' bones. . . ." (para. 18)

2. Explain the **paradox** of paragraph 3. How is it significant to Eric's issues of power and independence?

3. Williams frequently has Eric speak in fragments and short, staccato sentences. The beginning of paragraph 12 is typical. How are these a function of the point of view and a reflection of Eric's character?

4. By contrast, fragments and short sentences are greatly reduced in paragraphs 15–24. (See, for example, any para. but 23.) Suggest reasons for this stylistic change.

CONSIDERATIONS

1. "Red Eric" is part of a collection called *In the American Grain,* which includes essays on various historical figures, such as Abraham Lincoln, whose history and values have affected American civilization. What in Eric's behavior or character, if anything, strikes you as especially "American"? Elaborate in an essay, which treats his behavior or one of his traits as an aspect of the American character. (If you have found none, choose a trait or behavior that seems antithetical to the American character, and explain why you think that is the case.)

2. Write an essay narrating an event or series of events in which you were a participant for part of the time but thereafter were either absent or merely an observer.

3. Write an essay in which you attack or defend the idea that either Eric or Freydis is a role model for our time.

4. Taking either Eric or Freydis as your focus, imagine what Hollywood might do with this story. Write a scenario suggesting how it might be handled by one of your favorite directors; or, if you have none, by someone whose work you know (e.g., George Lucas, Steven Spielberg, Woody Allen, Spike Lee); or by you as screenwriter/director.

Mulk Raj Anand

(India; b. 1905)

Although the subjects of Anand's writing include art, cooking, and even the history of India's postal service, he is primarily a novelist, short-story writer, and essayist, whose work is highly sensitive to the plight of India's underclasses. The titles of two of his earliest novels, Untouchable *(1935) and* Coolie *(1936), suggest as much. Indeed, Anand describes himself as "a veteran novelist of India, who left teaching philosophy to write fables, stories, and fictions about human relations" and his writings as "marked by [a] sense of compassion for suffering people, especially in the obscure corners of India, in the tradition of Mahatma Gandhi, whose Talisman for those who despair was to go to the needy." A veteran as well of India's independence movement, he has long been active in the struggle for social and economic reform.*

Anand's later career has focused, although not exclusively, on The Seven Ages of Man, *a projected seven-volume autobiographical novel of which five have been published to date. The selection that follows is taken from the first of the series,* Seven Summers.

Seven Summers *is set in colonial India. The child who is its central figure and narrator lives in moderately comfortable circumstances. But as he matures and explores his world, he learns other, more discomfiting lessons than that roses have thorns.*

The Road

SUNSHINE SCATTERS LIKE GOLD DUST. A buzz in the air, as though the pinpoints of gold are flying hither and thither. The green trees of the grove spread the shadow of their protection on the white-bearded spirit of Mian Mir which, mother has told me, lives in the Persian wheel well. On one side of our house are the straight barracks, where soldiers live, on the other side are the bungalows of the Sahibs, with their gardens, white-washed and still, and hazy with their mysteries before my eyes. Dividing the barracks and the bungalows is the road, lined with casuarina trees, which stretches from end to end of the horizon. I stand for a long while with my thumb in my mouth wondering where it comes from and where it goes. Then I run round in circles on the little clearing under the grove surrounding the Persian wheel well in a wild delirium of movement, oblivious of the past and the future, excited by my own happiness at finding myself wandering freely in the wide open world . . .

That is one of my first vivid memories.

I run round in circles in the grove, because mother has said I can go out and play so long as I don't cross the road.

This road, on which caravans of camels and donkeys and horses and men are always passing, is the first hurdle that must be crossed.

The gardener calls me: "Son, come here."   5

I heed him not and go on describing circles. Then, suddenly, I fall across the stub of the root of the huge banyan tree and begin to cry.

The gardener comes and picks me up, consoling me the while with queer, affecting sounds from under his full mustachio and throwing me up in the air. I am still sobbing. So he puts me astride his neck and prances like a horse. And, with the jolting of his body and with the precarious movement of mine, holding on to his head with tight fists, there arises a hilarious atmosphere. And though I cry, "Put me down, put me down!" I am happy. Of course, when I am actually brought down and placed square on my sturdy little legs by the place where the gardener is cutting grass, I want to be picked up again. But as the gardener starts to work I become fascinated by the way he cuts grass with a flat khurpi while he hums a tune in his throat.

"Sing to me," I say to him.

"Go, budmash,[1] your mother is calling," he answers.

"Where is my mother?" I say and look towards the door of our house.   10

Mother is not there. I know she is having her siesta, with my little brother, Prithvi, by her side. I insist, "Sing to me."

The gardener smiles and begins to hum his tune loudly, moving his head the while.

I too move my head.

Then I hear the sound of tinkling bells on the road and I drift thither. A row of camels passing, tied nose to tail, tail to nose, and the drivers seated on their backs sway up and down as the mountainous backs of the camels advance. I involuntarily put my finger in my mouth and stand watching the caravan pass, amazed at the long legs of the camels, my body rapt in the sound of their tinkling bells. Whence they come and where they go, that is what I want to know. But mother has said, "Krishna, you are not to go on the road."

Some sepoys are coming up from the direction in which, I have been   15
told, lies the Sadar Bazaar. They salute, looking the while to their left.

A shape passes, a pink man in khaki clothes, a shape which takes the form of a Sahib. I know he lives in that bungalow opposite our house, across the road. He whirs past on his bicycle.

Now that the fearsome person is gone, there can be no danger in going to his garden.

And there is a violent urge in me to cross the road.

I look back to see if my mother is about. Also, I sweep the grove by the well to make sure that the gardener is not looking. And, without pausing for breath, I rush blindly across the barrier, the limit of all my previous truancies.

---

[1]**budmash:** "mischievous one" (Hindi). [Ed.]

Once across, I rush into the bowers of the garden. And quickly, breath-   20
lessly, with the panorama of the green orchards hanging over my eyes, though
not in them, I attack the nearest rosebud on a bush before me. The panic of
my mother's voice fills me. And I am oblivious of the thorns on the stem. I
suddenly feel a shooting pain in my fingers, but I pull with all my might. The
rosebud without the stem comes into my hand. And, without looking back at
the silent bungalow or at the shimmering, buzz-punctured air before me, I run,
my torso further forward than my legs.

I have darted back across the road. But in the wild happiness of having
the flower in my hand, I mix up my steps. My legs get intertwined and I fall.

A shriek comes involuntarily out of my throat. And I weep with fear as
I lie on the warm earth. The sun is moving towards me and I cry more
persistently to be heard. I have the taste of dust in my mouth. And the sweat
is pouring down my cheeks, I am hot with frustration. Then I hear steps.

It is the gardener.

"Aré, budmash!" he says scoldingly.

I shut my hand tight where I hold the flower, for he is the gardener and   25
he does not like anyone plucking flowers.

He picks me up in his arms and, swaying me from side to side, tries to
drown my weeping with words and whispers and snatches of nonsense
rhymes.

My mother, who has heard my cries, stands at the door.

"Where has he been?" she asks.

"He fell down, playing," says the gardener.

"What, in that dirty ditch? Has he been on the road?" she says in a panic.   30

I am still sobbing.

"Never mind, son, you have only killed some ants," the gardener says,
metaphorically.

"Show me your leggies," mother says. And she takes me in her arms.

There is a sweet smell about her neck and her face, like milk and sugar.
She kisses my knees, saying: "That will make them better." And she puts me
down on the bed by Prithvi and lies by my side, hugging me.

I am not sobbing any more, only whimpering. Soon sleep, the sleep of   35
fatigue, steals into my eyes.

When I wake up in the arms of my father in the afternoon, the rosebud
is still clutched tight in my fist, and the scratches of the thorns tell the whole
story.

Thesis and Thought

1. Although "The Road" is the title of a greater portion of *Seven Summers* than
   is reproduced here, explain why it is appropriate to the present selection.

2. Explain what is meant by, "The road . . . is the first hurdle that must be crossed" (para. 4).

3. Summarize both the exterior and psychological action of the narrative; then explain the interdependence of the two.

STRUCTURE

1. At one level, paragraphs 1, 14, and 17–21 comprise the central narrative but less than half of the writing. To what is the rest of the piece devoted? How is the whole unified?

2. Explain how the child's relationships with the three adults (mother, gardener, father) contribute to establishing and resolving the external and interior conflicts.

STYLE

1. Does Anand recount the events through the mind and eyes of a child or through those of an adult attempting to recapture and recreate the experience of childhood? Explain your answer thoroughly.

2. "The Road" is written in first person. What, if anything, does Anand gain by choosing this point of view? Similarly, is anything gained by the use of present tense? Rewrite paragraph 7 or 20 using third person, then again using third person and past tense. Describe the differences in effect you find between the original and your two versions.

3. Assess the role of descriptive language in creating the tone of the narrative and in advancing it. (You might want to read pages 75–79 in chapter 2.)

4. Although the narrative is autobiographical, is the road in any sense a **symbol**?

CONSIDERATIONS

1. Recall a "road" of your own childhood and write a narrative essay in which you present the conflict you experienced and its resolution.

2. In paragraph 7, the narrator says about the gardener, "I become fascinated by the way he cuts the grass with a flat khurpi while he hums a tune in his throat." If you have had a similar fascination with the skill and manner with which someone else works, write a substantial paragraph describing both the labor and your response. If you do not recall such an experience, do some "field work" before writing the paragraph.

3. Making allowances for setting and local details such as the procession of camels, is the quality of childhood Anand describes either desirable or possible in the United States today? Write an essay explaining your response.

Mark Mathabane

(South Africa; b. 1960)

Mark Mathabane is known for his two autobiographical volumes, Kaffir Boy *(1986) and* Kaffir Boy in America *(1989). The first, from which the present excerpt is taken, is the story of his childhood and adolescence in South Africa; the second, a record of his first decade in the United States, where he now resides.* Kaffir *is an Arabic word meaning "infidel" that is used by white South Africans as a derogatory term equivalent to* nigger.

Eldest of seven children, Mathabane grew up ten miles north of Johannesburg in Alexandra township. His childhood was marked by the oppression, poverty, and degradation—including police raids and assaults—typically suffered by blacks under apartheid. An avid reader, Mathabane long desired to study in the United States. But it was his tennis skills that brought him to the attention of some white South Africans and, in turn, to tennis champion Stan Smith. It was Smith, later best man at his wedding, who arranged a tennis scholarship for Mathabane at a small American college.

Once in the United States, however, Mathabane attended several schools before being graduated from Dowling College, where he was a student activist and editor of the college paper. He went on to graduate study in journalism at Columbia University.

Eighteen when he left South Africa, Mathabane was not at the forefront of political movements. He participated, however, in the Soweto riots of 1976 and angered the South African government sufficiently for it to revoke his passport. He has been critical of the political passivity and conservatism of American students.

The Shit-Men

AS I WANDERED ABOUT the kitchen I suddenly smelled feces and urine. The stench came from outside. I closed the door but the insufferable stench persisted. It was night soil collection night, the once-in-two-weeks night on which the shit-men—belligerent immigrant workers who, because of the work they did, were looked down upon by many black people—went about the communal lavatories picking up buckets of excrement.

Unable to take the stench any longer, I left the house for the streetcorner, where I knew a group of boys would be assembled—as they always did on such a night—to sing ditties denigrating the shit-men. I found about ten boys pacing excitedly about the dimly lit corner.

We waited, rehearsing our mean ditties. A while later the shit-men came down the road, trotting powerfully behind the night soil truck, dirty handker-

47

chiefs over their mouths and noses like cowboys during a stickup, dirty, thick plastic aprons about their thighs and savage-looking, gleaming metal hooks in their hands. They had no shirts or gloves on. The truck slowed down to a cruise to allow the shit-men time to go into the yards and come out with dripping buckets atop their powerful, bare shoulders. As the truck neared, we ran up to a ridge a few yards from the street and started throwing stones at the shit-men while gesturing obscenely, and singing tauntingly:

> *The shit-men feast on our feces*
> *They love to do so, just look at their faces*
> *Eat shit-men eat good my feces*
> *For they'll make good your kisses.*

The shit-men were in no mood for our mean ditties. The truck suddenly screeched to a halt abreast the ridge, and the driver signalled the shit-men to go after us. Caught unaware, we scattered in all directions, the shit-men hot on our heels, screaming like cannibals chasing a white man lost in a jungle. "Mbambe! Mbambe! Mbambe, loyo mfana! (Grab! Grab! Grab that brat!)" I stumbled over an unseen pothole, and two of the shit-men nabbed me. I bawled with terror, trying to tear myself away, as they dragged me back toward the truck. But the shit-men's hands were like a vise.

"Where's your home, boy!" the truck driver hissed as the two shit-men   5
brought me before him.

I was paralyzed with fear and couldn't answer.

"I said, where's your home, boy!" the driver repeated.

"TALK, BOY!" one of the two shit-men said fiercely as he savagely twisted the metal hook in my face, a hook he used to haul buckets from beneath the privies.

"I didn't mean any harm," I begged, making piteous gestures. "Please le' me go."

"I said where's home, boy!" the driver said irately. His eyes grew fierce   10
with anger.

"Over there," I pointed with a trembling hand.

The fuming driver ordered the two shit-men to take me home and confront my parents. They dragged me to the door.

"Who's in there!" the shorter of the shit-men bellowed. The door was slightly open.

"No one," I whimpered.

"You lying, boy. Who's in there?"   15

"No one. I swear."

The door being slightly open, the shorter shit-man peeped inside.

"There's no one," he told his comrade.

They looked at each other, like cannibals ogling a plump victim. To my utter horror, they ordered me to take my clothes off. I hesitated, remembering the Mpandhlani episode. But one of the shit-men made my mind up for me: he brandished the metal hook in my face. As I began undressing, the taller shit-man left for the gate. Still horrified I stood there naked and perspiring, wishing that the other shit-man would go away too. Suddenly, the taller shit-man came strutting back with a bucket brimming with excrement upon his right shoulder. He set it before me.

"Get in there, boy!" he bellowed, pointing to the bucket with his metal hook. 20

I was speechless. His voice came floating like an echo from a distant mountain so that I thought I was having a nightmare.

"Get in there, boy!" the order was repeated, louder than before, and I jolted back to reality. However, I did not move; I could not do so.

The taller shit-man advanced toward me, twisting his metal hook menacingly. "Jump in there before we make you!" he snapped.

Thinking that he probably was going to disembowel me if I didn't obey, I slowly lifted my legs and gingerly dipped them into the bucket. My body shuddered as the feces, urine and paper squished under my feet. The shit-men, watching me teeter as I attempted to secure my balance, broke into peals of maniacal laughter. Several people walking up and down the street stopped momentarily to witness the spectacle, but no one came to my rescue, for they knew the savage reputation of the shit-men. Meantime, I was knee-deep in the bucket. The shorter shit-man ordered me to march in place inside the bucket. I obeyed, and the gooey, reeking mess splattered all over my naked body. Some drops even fell on my face and lips. As I grimaced, the shit-men convulsed with laughter.

After a while, the taller shit-man rasped, "Let's make him eat some, maybe that'll teach him a lesson." 25

"I think he's learned his lesson," replied the comrade; and, turning to me, he bellowed, "Haven't you, boy!"

I nodded my head so vigorously in affirmation that I lurched forward, nearly pitching over. They ordered me out of the bucket. I got out. They spilled the contents right at our door and left, guffawing like madmen. Smelling like a cesspool, I staggered into the house and took pieces of rags, doused them in water and wiped myself, but the stench remained. My mother came back later, and I tearfully explained to her what had happened.

"Don't you ever make fun of those people again, you hear?" she rebuked me. She then went to Mrs. Munyama and borrowed a washtub and a thistle-brush and a dose of laundry detergent. As she scrubbed me, she lectured me: "These men do unpleasant jobs, and many of our people hate them for that. They themselves don't like their jobs; but they have no choice. Taunting them is bad. You're lucky they didn't make you eat the stuff."

Following that harrowing incident, I was sure of one thing: never again would I jeer at the shit-men, nor at anyone, for that matter.

THESIS AND THOUGHT

1. According to Mathabane, what is the point of the narrative? What other message, if any, do you draw from it?
2. Why is the reaction of the "shit-men" so intense?

STRUCTURE

1. What other conflicts underlie the immediate one between Mathabane and his antagonists?
2. Here, for comparison, is a revised narrated version of the dialogue in paragraphs 5–18:

> The driver asked me where I lived, repeating himself because I was too paralyzed with fear to answer. Under threat of the metal hook, I finally told him. Ignoring my pleas to be let go, the others dragged me to the door. One of them, skeptical of my denial that anyone was home, peered inside to confirm it.

Is the revision or the original more successful in creating tension? Why?

STYLE

1. Compare Mathabane's use of the word *shit* with its customary use in American vocabulary. Do you find its employment at all at odds with the euphemistic *night soil*?
2. The word *ditties* is rarely seen or heard in the United States. What substitute would be appropriate in American English?
3. Mathabane uses *ditties* three times in paragraphs 2–4 and *bucket* three times in paragraph 24 alone. Would the writing in these passages be improved by eliminating such repetition either through omission or the use of synonyms and pronouns?
4. Find evidence, among the similes in paragraphs 3, 4, and 19, of Mathabane's possible exposure to American popular literature or films.

CONSIDERATIONS

1. The opening paragraph describes the shit-men as "immigrant workers." Does this fact at all explain their occupation?
2. Write a brief narrative essay in which you recount your own story of taunting and reprisal.

3. In *1984*, George Orwell conceived of room 101, a torture chamber in which victims are confronted with their worst nightmares. Mathabane's experience might qualify as one of them—for others as well as himself. Write a paragraph in which you describe a possible humiliating or horrifying ordeal that you fear greatly.

– An Album of Short Narrative Forms –

This section will introduce you to four short narrative forms: the parable, the folktale, the ballad, and the modern short story. With the exception of the last, these are not especially common in typical literary or academic contexts. The structures of the parable and folktale, however, offer guidance in using narrative within broader rhetorical environments, and the ballad provides experience at reading between the narrative lines.

PARABLES

You have perhaps encountered parables in any exposure you might have had to biblical literature, but the form is by no means the special province of ancient Hebraic culture. One of the five to follow is Chinese, and two others are modern European, although its author, Kierkegaard, is steeped in Christian tradition. As you read, ask yourself what the parables have in common structurally.

Chuang Tzu

(China; ca. fourth century B.C.)

A Taoist opponent of Confucianism, Chuang Tzu and his disciples wrote the book that bears the master's name as title. The work consists of parables and other stories of philosophical import. To oversimplify, followers of the tao, or "way," believed that nature, rather than rigidly prescriptive rational systems, was the source of spiritual development and moral authority.

Chuang Tzu and the King's Officials

ONCE WHEN Chuang Tzu was fishing in the P'u River, the king of Ch'u sent two officials to go and announce to him: "I would like to trouble you with the administration of my realm."

Chuang Tzu held on to the fishing pole and, without turning his head, said, "I have heard that there is a sacred tortoise in Ch'u that has been dead for three thousand years. The king keeps it wrapped in cloth and boxed, and stores it in the ancestral temple. Now would this tortoise rather be dead and have its bones left behind and honored? Or would it rather be alive and dragging its tail in the mud?"

"It would rather be alive and dragging its tail in the mud," said the two officials.

Chuang Tzu said, "Go away! I'll drag my tail in the mud!"

Jesus of Nazareth

(Judea; ca. 4 B.C.–ca. A.D. 29)

The gospels contain many instances of Jesus teaching by parable. In some instances, parables presented in one gospel reappear, with some modification, in another. The two printed below are, respectively, among the briefest and the most elaborate.

The selections are from the King James Version, but punctuation and capitalization have sometimes been altered. In two instances, two verses have been fused.

Wheat and Tares

ANOTHER PARABLE put he forth unto them, saying, The kingdom of heaven is likened unto a man which sowed good seed in his field.

But while men slept, his enemy came and sowed tares among the wheat, and went his way.

But when the blade was sprung up, and brought forth fruit, then appeared the tares also.

So the servants of the householder came and said unto him, "See, didst not thou sow good seed in thy field? From whence then hath it tares?"

He said unto them, "An enemy hath done this." The servants said unto   5
him, "Wilt thou then that we go and gather them up?"

But he said, "Nay, lest while ye gather up the tares, ye root up also the wheat with them. Let both grow together until the harvest. And in the time of harvest I will say to the reapers, 'Gather ye together first the tares, and bind them in bundles to burn them. But gather the wheat into my barn.'"

Matthew 13:24–30

The Good Samaritan

AND BEHOLD, a certain lawyer stood up and tempted him, saying, "Master, what shall I do to inherit eternal life?"

He said unto him, "What is written in the law? How readest thou?"

And he answering said, "Thou shalt love the Lord thy God with all thy heart, and with all thy soul, and with all thy strength, and with all thy mind, and thy neighbor as thyself."

And he said unto him, "Thou hast answered right. This do, and thou shalt live."

But he, willing to justify himself, said unto Jesus, "And who is my 5 neighbor?"

And Jesus answering said, "A certain man went down from Jerusalem to Jericho, and fell among thieves, which stripped him of his raiment, and wounded him, and departed, leaving him half dead.

"And by chance there came down a certain priest that way; and when he saw him, he passed by on the other side.

"And likewise a Levite, when he was at the place, came and looked on him, and passed by on the other side.

"But a certain Samaritan, as he journeyed, came where he was. And when he saw him, he had compassion on him, and went to him, and bound up his wounds, pouring in oil and wine, and set him on his own beast, and brought him to an inn, and took care of him.

"And on the morrow when he departed, he took out two pence, and gave 10 them to the host, and said unto him, 'Take care of him; and whatsoever thou spendest more, when I come again I will repay thee.'

"Which now of these three, thinkest thou, was neighbor unto him that fell among the thieves?"

And he said, "He that showed mercy on him." Then said Jesus unto him, "Go, and do thou likewise."

Luke 10:25–37

Søren Kierkegaard
(Denmark; 1813–1855)

A theologian and philosopher, Kierkegaard anticipated twentieth-century ex-istentialist thought, in which the central issue is the fate of the isolated individual in a seemingly indifferent or amoral universe. Although he maintained religious fervor, Kierkegaard was strongly opposed to institutionalized Christianity, which he saw as an impediment placed between adherents and the spiritual sources of their faith.

The Happy Conflagration

What happens to those who try to warn the present age?

IT HAPPENED THAT A FIRE broke out backstage in a theater. The clown came out to inform the public. They thought it was just a jest and applauded. He repeated his warning; they shouted even louder. So I think the world will come to an end amid general applause from all the wits, who believe that it is a joke.

from Either/Or

The Wager

How much moral and spiritual vitality remains in the "heroics of modernity"?

IT IS SAID THAT two English noblemen were once riding along a road when they met a man whose horse had run away with him and who, being in danger of falling off, shouted for help. One of the Englishmen turned to the other and said, "A hundred guineas he falls off." "Taken," said the other. With that they spurred their horses to a gallop and hurried on ahead to open the tollgates and to prevent anything from getting in the way of the runaway horse. In the same way, though without that heroic and millionaire-like spleen, our own reflective and sensible age is like a curious, critical, and worldly-wise person who, at the most, has vitality enough to lay a wager.

from The Present Age

FOLKTALES

Each civilization, literate or otherwise, produces stories of its own—whether to amuse or to explain the cosmos as a whole or in part. While there are longer, more involved stories than the ones presented here, folktales tend to brevity and, perhaps more than fiction created by professionals, reflect the culture from which they emerge and by which they have been adopted. As you read, observe these cultural elements, particularly the expectations and ideals.

A Legend of Multnomah Falls

A tribe of the Pacific Northwest, the Multnomahs, from whom this tale derives, has all but disappeared. The story has familiar elements of death, rebirth, and the sacrificial virgin, though here the sacrifice is voluntary.

MANY YEARS AGO the head chief of the Multnomah people had a beautiful young daughter. She was especially dear to her father because he had lost all his sons in fighting, and he was now an old man. He chose her husband with great care—a young chief from his neighbors, the Clatsop people. To the wedding feast came many people from tribes along the lower Columbia and south of it.

The wedding feast was to last for several days. There were swimming races and canoe races on the river. There would be bow-and-arrow contests, horse racing, dancing, and feasting. The whole crowd was merry, for both the maiden and the young warrior were loved by their people.

But without warning the happiness changed to sorrow. A sickness came over the village. Children and young people were the first victims; then strong men became ill and died in one day. The wailing of women was heard throughout the Multnomah village and the camps of the guests.

"The Great Spirit is angry with us," the people said to each other. The head chief called together his old men and his warriors for counsel and asked gravely, "What can we do to soften the Great Spirit's wrath?"

Only silence followed his question. At last one old medicine man arose.   5 "There is nothing we can do. If it is the will of the Great Spirit that we die, then we must meet our death like brave men. The Multnomah have ever been a brave people."

The other members of the council nodded in agreement—all except one, the oldest medicine man. He had not attended the wedding feast and games, but he had come in from the mountains when he was called by the chief. He rose and, leaning on the stick, spoke to the council. His voice was low and feeble.

"I am a very old man, my friends; I have lived a long, long time. Now you will know why. I will tell you a secret my father told me. He was a great medicine man of the Multnomah, many summers and many snows in the past.

"When he was an old man, he told me that when I became old, the Great Spirit would send a sickness upon our people. All would die, he said, unless a sacrifice was made to the Great Spirit. Some pure and innocent maiden of the tribe, the daughter of a chief, must willingly give her life for her people. Alone, she must go to a high cliff above Big River and throw herself upon the rocks below. If she does this, the sickness will leave us at once."

Then the old man said, "I have finished; my father's secret is told. Now I can die in peace."

Not a word was spoken as the medicine man sat down. At last the chief   10 lifted his head. "Let us call in all the maidens whose fathers or grandfathers have been headmen."

Soon a dozen girls stood before him, among them his own loved daughter. The chief told them what the old medicine man had said. "I think his words are the words of truth," he added.

Then he turned to his medicine men and his warriors, "Tell our people to meet death bravely. No maiden shall be asked to sacrifice herself. The meeting has ended."

The sickness stayed in the village, and many more people died. The daughter of the head chief sometimes wondered if she should be the one to give her life to the Great Spirit. But she loved the young warrior—she wanted to live.

A few days later she saw the sickness on the face of her lover. Now she knew what she must do. She cooled his hot face, cared for him tenderly, and left a bowl of water by his bedside. Then she slipped away alone, without a word to anyone.

All night and all the next day she followed the trail to the great river. At sunset she reached the edge of a cliff overlooking the water. She stood there in silence for a few moments, looking at the jagged rocks far below. Then she turned her face toward the sky and lifted up her arms. She spoke aloud to the Great Spirit. 15

"You are angry with my people. Will you make the sickness pass away if I give you my life? Only love and peace and purity are in my heart. If you will accept me as a sacrifice for my people, let some token hang in the sky. Let me know that my death will not be in vain and that the sickness will quickly pass."

Just then she saw the moon coming up over the trees across the river. It was the token. She closed her eyes and jumped from the cliff.

Next morning, all the people who had expected to die that day arose from their beds well and strong. They were full of joy. Once more there was laughter in the village and in the camps of the guests.

Suddenly someone asked, "What caused the sickness to pass away? Did one of the maidens—?"

Once more the chief called the daughters and granddaughters of the headmen to come before him. This time one was missing. 20

The young Clatsop warrior hurried along the trail which leads to Big River. Other people followed. On the rocks below the high cliff they found the girl they all loved. There they buried her.

Then her father prayed to the Great Spirit, "Show us some token that my daughter's spirit has been welcomed into the land of the spirits."

Almost at once they heard the sound of water above. All the people looked up to the cliff. A stream of water, silvery white, was coming over the edge of the rock. It broke into floating mist and then fell at their feet. The stream continued to float down in a high and beautiful waterfall.

For many summers the white water has dropped from the cliff into the pool below. Sometimes in winter the spirit of the brave and beautiful maiden comes back to see the waterfall. Dressed in white, she stands among the trees at one side of Multnomah Falls. There she looks upon the place where she made her great sacrifice and thus saved her lover and her people from death.

The Mountain Where Old People Were Abandoned

This story may be read as an explanation of how the Japanese came to venerate the aged, but the abandonment, here rejected, also has an historical basis. Like most tales, this has its counterparts in other traditions.

LONG AGO when people had reached the age of sixty and were unable to do anything, they were thrown into a mountain canyon. This was known as "sixty canyon abandonment."

In a certain village there was a farmer who became sixty years old. Since the lord of the country had commanded it, the time had arrived for him to be thrown into the mountain canyon. The man's son took him on his back and set off for the mountains. They continued farther and farther into the mountains. As they went along, the old man, riding on his son's back, broke off the tips of tree branches in order to mark the trail. "Father, father, what are you doing that for? Is it so you can find your way back home?" asked the son.

"No, it would be too bad if you were unable to find your way home," replied the father, "so I am marking the trail for you."

When he heard this the son realized how kindhearted his father was, and so he returned home with him. They hid the old man under the porch so that the lord would know nothing about it.

Now the lord of the country sometimes commanded his subjects to do   5
very difficult things. One day he gathered all the farmers of the village together and said, "You must each bring me a rope woven from ashes."

All the farmers were very troubled, knowing that they could not possibly weave a rope from ashes. The young farmer whom we just mentioned went back home, called to his father under the porch, and said, "Today the lord commanded that everyone bring a rope woven from ashes. How can we do this?"

"You must weave a rope very tightly, then carefully burn it until it turns to ashes; then you can take it to the lord," said the old man.

The young farmer, happy to get this advice, did just as he was told. He made a rope of ashes and took it to the lord. None of the other farmers were able to do it, and so this farmer alone had carried out the lord's instructions. For this the lord praised him highly.

Next the lord commanded, "Everyone must bring a conch shell with a thread passed through it."

The young farmer went to his father again and asked him what he should   10
do. "Take a conch shell and point the tip toward the light; then take a thread and stick a piece of rice on it. Give the rice to an ant and make it crawl into the mouth of the shell; in this way you can get the thread through."

The young farmer did as he was told, and so got the thread through the conch shell. He took the shell to the lord, who was much impressed. "How were you able to do such a difficult thing?" he asked.

The young farmer replied: "Actually I was supposed to throw my old father down into the mountain canyon, but I felt so sorry for him that I brought him back home and hid him under the porch. The things that you asked us to do were so difficult that I had to ask my father how to do them. I have done them as he told me, and brought them to you," and he honestly told what had happened.

When the lord heard this he was very much impressed and realized that old people are very wise and that they should be well taken care of. After that he commanded that the "sixty canyon abandonment" be stopped.

The Seal's Skin

An Icelandic tale, this story is current among other northern peoples as well. Ultimately unable to live a human life, the seal is nevertheless torn between her two worlds. This is somewhat reminiscent of mermaids and mermen who, despite their physical duality, are essentially sea creatures. The conflict is well presented in an early twentieth-century play by Jean Giraudoux called Ondine.

THERE WAS ONCE SOME MAN from Myrdal in Eastern Iceland who went walking among the rocks by the sea one morning before anyone else was up. He came to the mouth of a cave, and inside the cave he could hear merriment and dancing, but outside it he saw a great many sealskins. He took one skin away with him, carried it home, and locked it away in a chest. Later in the day he went back to the mouth of the cave; there was a young and lovely woman sitting there, and she was stark naked, and weeping bitterly. This was the seal whose skin it was that the man had taken. He gave the girl some clothes, comforted her, and took her home with him. She grew very fond of him, but did not get on so well with other people. Often she would sit alone and stare out to sea.

After some while the man married her, and they got on well together, and had several children. As for the skin, the man always kept it locked up in the chest, and kept the key on him wherever he went. But after many years, he went fishing one day and forgot it under his pillow at home. Other people say that he went to church one Christmas with the rest of his household, but that his wife was ill and stayed at home; he had forgotten to take the key out of the pocket of his everyday clothes when he changed. Be that as it may, when he came home again the chest was open, and both wife and skin were gone. She had taken the key and examined the chest, and there she had found the skin; she had been unable to resist the temptation, but had said farewell to her children, put the skin on, and flung herself into the sea.

Before the woman flung herself into the sea, it is said that she spoke these words:

> *Woe is me! Ah, woe is me!*
> *I have seven bairns on land,*
> *And seven in the sea.*

It is said that the man was broken-hearted about this. Whenever he rowed out fishing afterwards, a seal would often swim round and round his boat, and it looked as if tears were running from its eyes. From that time on, he had excellent luck in his fishing, and various valuable things were washed ashore on his beach. People often noticed, too, that when the children he had had by this woman went walking along the seashore, a seal would show itself near the edge of the water and keep level with them as they walked along the shore, and would toss them jellyfish and pretty shells. But never did their mother come back to land again.

The Dogs Hold an Election

Told by Lame Deer at the Rosebud Indian Reservation (Sioux) in 1969 and obviously contemporary in tone, this tale attests to the vitality of folk traditions.

WE DON'T THINK MUCH of the white man's elections. Whoever wins, we Indians always lose. Well, we have a little story about elections. Once a long time ago, the dogs were trying to elect a president. So one of them got up in the big dog convention and said: "I nominate the bulldog for president. He's strong. He can fight."

"But he can't run," said another dog. "What good is a fighter who can't run? He won't catch anybody."

Then another dog got up and said: "I nominate the greyhound, because he sure can run."

But the other dogs cried: "Naw, he can run all right, but he can't fight. When he catches up with somebody, what happens then? He gets the hell beaten out of him, that's what! So all he's good for is running away."

Then an ugly little mutt jumped up and said: "I nominate that dog for 5 president who smells good underneath his tail."

And immediately an equally ugly mutt jumped up and yelled: "I second the motion."

At once all the dogs started sniffing underneath each other's tails. A big chorus went up:

"Phew, he doesn't smell good under his tail."

"No, neither does this one."

"He's no presidential timber!" 10
"No, he's no good, either."
"This one sure isn't the people's choice."
"Wow, this ain't my candidate!"
When you go out for a walk, just watch the dogs. They're still sniffing underneath each other's tails. They're looking for a good leader, and they still haven't found him.

THE BRITISH BALLAD

In Great Britain the folk song has often been a folktale in verse—set to music, of course—and often told with greater subtlety than its prose counterparts. The English and Scots folk ballad is a particular type of story song that evolved in the late medieval and early modern period. It is typically written in four-line stanzas (quatrains), with the verses alternating between four stresses and three and rhyming in an *abcb* pattern.

Though long passed down through oral tradition, songs such as these began to be collected and transcribed in the eighteenth and nineteenth centuries, as the romantic movement in Europe encouraged looking to the natural wisdom of the common people. We owe, for example, the fairy tale collection of the brothers Grimm to this impetus. "Sir Patrick Spens" and "Get Up and Bar the Door" are taken from the landmark collection of Francis James Child, *The English and Scottish Popular Ballads*, although the spelling and vocabulary have been modernized where possible.

As you read "Sir Patrick Spens," account for what seem to be gaps or unexplained action in the narrative. "Get Up and Bar the Door" records a rather straightforward domestic squabble, the stuff of which a modern television sitcom might be made.

Sir Patrick Spens

The king sits in Dumferling town,
    Drinking the blood-red wine:
"O where will I get a good sailor,
    To sail this ship of mine?"

Up and spake an eldern knight, 5
    Sat at the king's right knee:
"Sir Patrick Spens is the best sailor
    That sails upon the sea."

The king has written a broad letter,
 And signed it with his hand,
And sent it to Sir Patrick Spens,
 Was walking on the sand.

The first line that Sir Patrick read,
 A loud laugh laughed he;
The next line that Sir Patrick read,
 The tear blinded his ee.[1]

"O who is this has done this deed,
 This ill deed done to me,
To send me out this time o' the year,
 To sail upon the sea!

"Make haste, make haste, my merry men all,
 Our good ship sails the morn:"
"O say not so, my master dear,
 For I fear a deadly storme.

"Late late yestreen[2] I saw the new moon,
 With the old moon in her arm,
And I fear, I fear, my dear master,
 That we will come to harm."

O our Scots nobles were right loath
 To wet their cork-heeled schoone;
But long owre[3] all the play were played,
 Their hats they swam aboone.[4]

O long, long may their ladies sit,
 With their fans into their hand,
Or e'er they see Sir Patrick Spens
 Come sailing to the land.

O long, long may the ladies stand,
 With their gold combs in their hair,
Waiting for their own dear lords
 For they'll see them no mair.

Half o'er, half o'er to Aberdour,
 It's fifty fathom deep,
And there lies good Sir Patrick Spens,
 With the Scots lords at his feet.

10

15

20

25

30

35

40

---

[1]**ee:** eye. [Ed.] [2]**yestreen:** yesterday evening. [Ed.] [3]**owre:** after. [Ed.]
[4]**aboone:** above. [Ed.]

Get Up and Bar the Door

It fell about the Martinmas[1] time,
    And a gay time it was then,
When our goodwife got puddings to make,
    And she's boiled them in the pan.

The wind so cold blew south and north,   5
    And blew into the floor;
Quoth our goodman to our goodwife,
    "Go out and bar the door."

"My hand is in my hussyfskap,[2]
    Goodman, as ye may see;   10
An[3] it should not be barred this hundred year,
    It's no be barred for me."

They made a paction tween them twa,[4]
    They made it firm and sure,
That the first word whoe'er should speak,   15
    Should rise and bar the door.

Then by there came two gentlemen,
    At twelve o'clock at night,
And they could neither see house nor hall,
    Nor coal nor candle-light.   20

"Now whether is this a rich man's house,
    Or whether is it a poor?"
But ne'er a word would one o' them speak,
    For barring of the door.

And first they ate the white puddings,   25
    And then they ate the black;
Though much thought the goodwife to herself
    Yet ne'er a word she spake.

Then said the one unto the other,
    "Here, man, take ye my knife;   30
Do ye take off the old man's beard,
    And I'll kiss the goodwife."

"But there's no water in the house,
    And what shall we do than?"
"What ails ye at[5] the pudding-broo,   35
    That boils into the pan?"

[1]**Martinmas:** feast day of St. Martin of Tours, November 11. [Ed.]   [2]**hussyfskap:** housework.
[Ed.]   [3]**An:** if. [Ed.]   [4]**twa:** two. [Ed.]   [5]**"What ails ye at":** (idiomatically) "what's wrong
with" or "why not use." [Ed.]

O up then started our goodman,
    An angry man was he:
"Will ye kiss my wife before my een,[6]
    And scald me with pudding-bree?"

Then up and started our goodwife,
    Gave three skips on the floor:
"Goodman, you've spoken the foremost word,
    Get up and bar the door."

40

CONSIDERATIONS

1. What makes a parable? Write one.

2. Write a tale that explains a natural phenomenon or social custom or that illustrates a cultural ideal.

3. Write a summary of the action in "Sir Patrick Spens"—including what the ballad does not express directly.

4. Write a ballad that presents either a personal or collective disaster (as in "Sir Patrick Spens") or a public event such as an assassination or execution. If you omit steps, be sure that readers can follow the narrative. If you are able to compose, you might want to set the piece to music.

5. Discuss what vitality "Get Up and Bar the Door" retains after five hundred years. Why?

THE MODERN SHORT STORY

Developed more recently than the novel, the modern short story emerged in the nineteenth and early twentieth centuries through the work of such influential writers as Poe and Anton Chekhov. Although its scope is more limited than that of the novel, the short story is often more intense, with its characters, their motivations, and conflicts often revealed in a single concentrated incident or action. This tendency is apparent to varying degrees in the stories included in subsequent chapters. "The Adventure of the Blue Carbuncle" (chapter 9), occupied as it is with detection, displays it least. "Davud the Hunchback" (chapter 7) and the following story display it most intensely.

---

[6]**een:** eyes. [Ed.]

Juan Bosch

(Dominican Republic; b. 1909)

Although his literary achievements have been recognized, Bosch is probably far better known as a political leader. In opposition to the dictatorship of Rafael Trujillo, Bosch left the Dominican Republic in 1937 and began a self-imposed twenty-four-year exile. Abroad in Latin America, he helped found the Dominican Revolutionary party (PRD) and disseminated its populist and socialist views throughout the region.

After Trujillo's assassination, Bosch, having returned, was elected president by a landslide vote in 1962. However, he was still opposed by industrialists, the church, and the United States, which was smarting from a disastrous attempt at the Bay of Pigs to oust Cuba's Fidel Castro. Bosch was overthrown by military coup in 1963.

His supporters' attempted countercoup two years later was suppressed, partly through U.S. military intervention. Nevertheless, Bosch returned from a second exile to continue in Dominican politics. In 1973 he resigned from the PRD and formed the Dominican Liberation Party (PLD), persisting in his efforts to diversify and democratize the Dominican political process.

As you read "The Woman," consider to what extent the characters are products of their environment.

The Woman

THE ROAD IS DEAD. Nobody nor anything will bring it back to life. Long, infinitely long, not even its gray skin betrays any sign of life. The sun killed it; the steel sun, glowing red-hot—a red that turned to white. Later the white steel became transparent, and there it remains, on the road's back.

Many centuries must have passed since its death. Men with pickaxes and shovels dug it up. They sang and dug; there were some, however, who neither sang nor dug. All that took very long. You could tell they came from far away; they sweated and stank. In the afternoon, the white steel would turn red; then a very small bonfire would flare up behind the pupils of the men who were digging up the road.

Death crossed the savannas, and the hills and the winds covered her with dust. Later the dust also died and it came to rest on the gray skin.

Along the sides there are thorny bushes. Often the eye grows sick from so much vastness. But the plains are bare. Scrubland in the distance. Perhaps birds of prey crown the cactus. And the cactus are out there, farther off, stuffed into the white steel.

There are huts too, almost all of them low and made of mud. Some are painted white and cannot be seen under the sun. Only the coarse roof stands out, dry, eager to be burned day after day. Gray hairs emanated from those roofs down which water never rolls.

The dead road, totally dead, lies there, dug up, gray. The woman first looked like a black dot, then like a stone that someone might have left on the long mummy. There she lay, without a breeze to stir her rags. The sun did not burn her; only the screams of her child made her feel pain. The child was bronzed, tiny, with his eyes full of light, and he grasped at his mother trying to pull her with his little hands. Soon the road would burn the tiny body, at least the knees, of that naked and screaming child.

The house was nearby, but could not be seen.

As he advanced, what seemed like a stone thrown in the middle of the great dead road grew. It continued to grow, and Quico said to himself: "A calf, no doubt, run over by a car."

He looked around: the plain, the savanna. A distant hill covered with brush, as if that hill were only a little mound of sand piled up by the winds. The bed of a river; the dry jaws of the earth which held water a thousand years ago. The golden plain cracked and split under the heavy transparent steel. The cactus, crowned with birds of prey.

Now closer, Quico saw that it was a person. He distinctly heard the 10 screams of the child.

Her husband had beaten her. He chased her through the only room of the hut, which was hot like an oven, pulling her by the hair and pounding her head with his fists.

"You slut! You slut! I'm going to kill you like a lousy bitch!"

"But nobody came by, Chepe; nobody came by!" she tried to explain.

"No, eh? Now you're going to see!" And he beat her again.

The child clutched at his father's legs. He saw the woman bleeding 15 through the nose. The blood didn't frighten him, no, it only made him want to cry and scream a lot. Mommy would die for sure if she kept on bleeding.

It was all because the woman didn't sell the goat's milk as he had ordered her to do. When he returned from the hills, four days later, he didn't find the money. She said the milk had gone sour; the truth was that she had drunk it, preferring not to have a few coins rather than let the child suffer from hunger for so long.

Later he told her to leave with her son: "I'll kill you if you come back to this house!"

The woman lay sprawled on the earth floor, bleeding a lot, hearing nothing. Chepe, in a frenzy, dragged her to the road. And there she lay, half dead, on the back of the great mummy.

Quico had water for two more days of travel, but used almost all of it to sprinkle the woman's forehead. He took her to the hut, by having her lean on his arm, and he considered ripping his striped shirt to wipe off her blood. Chepe came in through the backyard.

"I told you I didn't want to see you here again, damn you!" 20

It seems that he had not seen the stranger. That white transparent steel had surely turned him into a beast. His hair was bleached stiff and his corneas were red.

Quico shouted at him, but he, half-crazed, once more threatened his victim. He was about to hit her. That was when the fight broke out between the two men.

The child, tiny, so tiny, began to shout again: now he wrapped himself in his mother's skirt.

The fight was like a silent song. They didn't say a word. Only the screams of the child and the violent steps could be heard.

The woman saw how Quico was choking Chepe: his fingers hooked onto   25
her husband's throat. The latter's eyes began to close; his mouth was opening, and the blood was rushing to his face.

She didn't know what happened, but nearby, next to the door there was a rock; a rock like a hunk of lava, rough, almost black, heavy. She felt a brutal force growing within her. She raised it. The blow sounded dull. Quico first let go of the other's throat, bent his knees, then opening his arms wide, he fell backward, without complaining, without a struggle.

The earth of the floor absorbed that blood which was so red, so abundant. Chepe could see the light shimmering on it.

The woman's hands twitched over her face, all her hair loose and her eyes straining to pop out. She ran. She felt weak in all her joints. She wanted to see if someone was coming; but on the big dead road, totally dead, there was only the sun which killed her. In the distance, beyond the plain, the hill of sand which the winds piled up. And the cactus, stuffed into the steel.

Translated by Gustavo Pellón

THESIS AND THOUGHT

1. Summarize or list the events of the story in the chronological order in which they occur.
2. What are the causes of the woman's drinking the goat's milk? Quico's helping the woman? The fight between the two men?
3. Why does the woman kill Quico instead of Chepe? Why is she nameless?
4. What forces seem to control the lives of the characters?

STRUCTURE

1. When you answered question 1 above, you almost certainly realized that Bosch does not present the action in chronological order but flashes back

(paras. 11–18), then forward again (paras. 19–28). What has he gained by this approach? Explain whether straightforward chronology would have been as effective.

2. Dominating the first six—perhaps nine—paragraphs and reappearing at the end, the road and its surroundings frame the central action. How do they offset, augment, or otherwise relate to the events narrated in paragraphs 11–27? Does the exterior scene complement or contrast with the interior action?

STYLE

1. A literary motif is a recurring pattern, whether of language, imagery, or thought. The road, for instance, may be considered a motif here. Another, associated with it to be sure, is death. Cite instances of the various ways in which Bosch presents the deadliness of the environment he describes.

2. Which colors predominate here? How do they serve Bosch's purposes? Are they (individually or collectively) another motif?

3. Although punctuated by complex or compound sentences, the simple sentence seems to dominate here:

"The road is dead." (para. 1)
"But the plains are bare." (para. 4)
"He distinctly heard the screams of the child." (para. 10)
"The child clutched at his father's legs." (para. 15)
"He was about to hit her." (para. 22)
"She ran." (para. 28)

What is the overall effect of such sentences, particularly in regard to Bosch's **point of view** and to establishing **tone**?

4. Despite the presence of the road, no one leaves. Explain how this is an example of **irony.**

CONSIDERATIONS

1. We have learned that people who have been abused often absolve their abusers, taking upon themselves responsibility for the brutality and maintaining the bond with the perpetrator. Discuss whether this psychological mechanism is at work in the story.

2. In "Neutral Tones," poet Thomas Hardy writes, "The smile on your mouth was the deadest thing / Alive that had strength to die." Discuss the lives of Bosch's characters in terms of this quotation.

3. Write an essay in which you explore the role of environment in shaping one's destiny.

Suggestions for Writing: Narration

Write a narrative essay on one of the topics below. Decide what the purpose of your account is—to inform, to explain, to persuade, to advocate—before settling on your narrative point of view.

—a competitive edge

—the other driver

—a case of pollution

—lost in _____

—a crisis of conscience

—fulfilling a desire or meeting a need

—adventure on _____ Street

—just an accident

—choices

—a lack of faith

—living an ideal

—eating crow

2

Description

"It was a dark and stormy night . . . "

EDWARD BULWER-LYTTON, *Paul Clifford*

. . . with relentless rain pounding on the roofs of cars or the tops of air conditioners, which jutted like metallic warts from the sentinel facades of uniform apartment buildings; and wind, thrashing or rippling as it rose and fell, the standing pools before the glutted drains. A night of sounds: muffled cymbal clash of rain on glass or steel, low vibrations or piercing whines as the wind funneled through broad or narrow alleys, the odd sharping of car brakes or discordant horns—but mostly the steady drumming, drumming of the rain like a malevolent heartbeat. A night of smells, thick with the musk of refineries and landfills, of microbic offal swirled from gutters and weedy dog-defiled lots. The air tasted of cigar stubs three days old, the dregs of yesterday's coffee—tepid, laced with grounds—the breath of carnivores. And all about, the night clung like the wet fur of some extinct species, oil expressed from a primitive gland to float heavily upon the surface; or billowed in the wind, a mastless sail drawing all slowly, slowly to the depths of dark.

Desolate, the furtive streets fell to the irregular patrol of rats, their needle noses piercing the gloom, guiding them unerringly toward miscellaneous leavings to be speared with long incisors honed on sewer pipe, cement, the bones of sleeping children. . . .

Had enough? Perhaps the following will be more to your liking:

Borrower does hereby mortgage, grant, and convey to Lender the following described property located in the County of Philadelphia, State of Pennsylvania:

All that certain lot or piece of ground with the three-story brick messuage or tenement thereon erected, described according to a Plan and Survey made thereof on November 14, 1922 . . . as follows, to wit:

Situate on the Northwest side of Bryson Avenue at the distance of ninety feet Northeastwardly from the Northeast side of Navarre Street in the 44th ward of the City of Philadelphia.

Containing in front or breadth on the said Bryson Avenue, eighty feet, and extending of that width in length or depth Northwestwardly between parallel lines at right angles with the said Bryson Avenue, two-hundred-four feet.

Being known as premises No. 1122 Bryson Avenue.

Not exactly interesting reading, is it?

One major problem with each of these passages is that as reader, you haven't the faintest idea of their purpose. In the second, the writer might have given additional details about the "messuage" or other appurtenances to the property; measured its distance form Montpelier, Missoula, or Mars; or pinpointed its position on a galactic map with equal or perhaps even less effectiveness. Likewise, the author of the first passage might have added other ingredients to the adjectival stew or metaphorical soup without improving its palatability. The point is that a description, of whatever type, rarely functions independently. Except as an exercise, it is usually a means to a rhetorical end, almost never an end in itself.

Description is nevertheless an invaluable writing tool. As you perhaps have realized from the previous chapter, it is essential to narration, and as you will see in the chapters to come, it is extremely useful for expository writing as well. How easily, for instance, can you provide an example without describing its subject or action? Or compare without delineating the items of the comparison? Something as simple as a children's book will distinguish between the *kind, little blue* engine that could and the *dingy, rusty old* engine that couldn't. And since argument and persuasion employ exposition in achieving their ends, they are likely to use description as well. Persuasive writing especially, which is often dependent upon emotional appeals, frequently includes carefully chosen, highly charged descriptive language to make its case.

OBJECTIVE AND IMPRESSIONISTIC DESCRIPTIONS

Description can be classified as objective (or quantitative) and impressionistic (or subjective). The goal of objective description is to offer information or data without interpretation. It presents measurements that are easily verifiable or uses descriptive words—adjectives and adverbs—as unadorned as Pilgrim dress. (It would tend, for instance, not to have employed the simile in the previous sentence.) Such description is very much matter of fact, pragmatic, clinical, or scientific. The earlier passage about a piece of property is an example of objective description. Its intention is to identify the location and boundaries of the property for legal purposes. The author has no interest whatsoever in whether the neighbors are pleasant, or how lovely the roses on the front lawn are this time of year, or whether the house sparkles with its fresh coat of white paint. Such matters are the province of the real-estate agent who attempts to persuade potential customers to buy the property objectively described above.

Objective description need not be so formal as the passage taken from a property deed. If you were giving directions to a party at Lola's, you might say, "Her house is the fourth from the corner of Willow, on the right as you drive west along Ellington." Number, location, and geographic direction figure here as well but in a far more conversational tone. Similarly, in the Presleyan admonition "Don't you step on my blue suede shoes," *blue* and *suede* are descriptive but merely identify the items—without blame, praise, or other judgment.

Although objective descriptions are often found in professional or scientific contexts, the degree of their detachment or austerity may vary significantly, as this passage by geologist John A. Shimer illustrates:

> The Painted Desert of Arizona lies in one of the lower and dryer parts of the region. Here layers of soft crumbling shale with vividly bright colors have been uncovered by erosion. Iron-stained, red, orange, and yellow rocks contrast with light gray and white layers. Since there is no vegetation to cover up the land the colored rocks stand out in all their rainbow brilliance in the bright sunshine. Petrified tree trunks are found in some of the layers; a few are now completely exposed to view looking like trunks of trees which have just been felled. The illusion that this is someone's axework is increased by the way in which the petrified wood has broken into small slivers looking like chips from a log, chips which are found to be . . . hard silica which through geologic time has replaced the wood.
>
> *This Sculptured Earth: The Landscape of America*, p. 98

While essentially factual, the passage contains some of Shimer's reaction to what he sees: "vividly," "rainbow brilliance," and "the illusion that this is someone's axework" are not, strictly speaking, objective.

In his description of April's flora and fauna, however, journalist and naturalist John Kieran is far less restrained:

> It's a cantankerous month of good, bad, and indifferent days, but snow and ice are quickly put to rout. Spring begins to assert itself. The Red Maples are in colorful bloom and Marsh Marigolds open to pave the floor of the swamp with gold. The lake now harbors a pair of Wood Ducks, a Coot, two male Ring-necked ducks, three Pied-billed Grebes,

and a pair of Pintails of aristocratic bearing. The Horsetail stalks stand
a foot high along the railroad track and a little Garter Snake, moving
among them, pauses to stick out its tongue at us. No offense is intended
on either side.

A Natural History of New York City, p. 402

We get the facts here but they are often adorned with images of Kieran's
invention. Even the sentence that lists the birds includes the human attribute
aristocratic.

Although directed as Kieran's is to a lay audience, the prose of entomolo-
gist George Ordish is far more reserved:

> The furniture beetle, or *Anobium*, is a small light-brown insect
> which varies in length from one tenth to one quarter of an inch. The
> freshly emerged insect is covered with a light, yellow down which
> becomes worn as it ages. The wing cases have a number of rows of
> pinspots on them (giving rise to the Latin specific name of *punctatum;*
> the generic name—*Anobium*—arises from its habit of shamming dead)
> running the length of the body. The head is curious in being shielded
> by a hard hood or lump on the insect's thorax, the middle segment of its
> body. . . .

The Living American House, pp. 50–51

In contrast with these essentially objective descriptions, especially that
of the furniture beetle, impressionistic description is intensely expressive of
feeling or mood and heavily dependent on sensory image. We may have no
idea of the writer's purpose in describing the dark and stormy night at the
beginning of this chapter, yet we understand that the night is ominous,
perhaps frightening, certainly unpleasant, and decidedly negative.

But those who write impressionistically usually have a clear purpose in
mind. In the case of a real-estate agent, the purpose is to sell property.

> For sale: Newly redecorated 4 bdr. beauty on tree-lined street. Large
> front yard planted with prizewinning roses. Warm, friendly neighbors.
> Convenient to shops, schools, major highways. A gem! Asking: 1 arm,
> 1 leg.

But impressionistic description is not the exclusive preserve of commercial-
ism—crass or otherwise. Such descriptions express feeling or create the tone
of a piece of writing, as in the following excerpt from Poe's "The Fall of the
House of Usher":

> During the whole of a dull, dark, and soundless day in the autumn
> of the year, when the clouds hung oppressively low in the heavens, I had
> been passing alone, on horseback, through a singularly dreary tract of

country, and at length found myself, as the shades of the evening drew on, within view of the melancholy House of Usher. I know not how it was—but, with the first glimpse of the building, a sense of insufferable gloom pervaded my spirit. . . . I looked upon the scene before me—upon the mere house, and the simple landscape features of the domain—upon the bleak walls—upon the vacant eye-like windows—upon a few rank sedges—and upon a few white trunks of decayed trees—with an utter depression of soul. . . . There was an iciness, a sinking, a sickening of the heart—an unredeemed dreariness of thought which no goading of the imagination could torture into aught of the sublime. . . .

Doom and gloom are clearly pervasive here, but of course the mood need not be so grim.

Poe's direct appeal to the reader's senses is rather typical of impressionistic description. At times, however, an impression built upon images latent in the reader's experience may, like a genie, be almost conjured to appear. But as novelist Toni Morrison demonstrates, it is the writer's hand that rubs the lamp:

He just did it. One man. One defenseless girl. Death. A sample-case man. A nice, neighborly, everybody-knows-him man. The kind you let in your house because he was not dangerous, because you had seen him with children, bought his products, and never heard a scrap of gossip about him doing wrong. Felt not only safe but kindly in his company because he was the sort women ran to when they thought they were being followed, or watched, or needed someone to have the extra key just in case you locked yourself out. He was the man who took you to your door if you missed the trolley and had to walk night streets at night. Who warned young girls away from hooch joints and the men who lingered there. Women teased him because they trusted him. He was one of those men who might have marched down Fifth Avenue—cold and silent and dignified—into the space the drums made. He knew wrong wasn't right, and did it anyway.

Jazz, pp. 73–74

As we have already seen in the selection from Kieran, impressionistic description occurs in nonfiction as well, though usually with greater restraint than in imaginative writing. Here is a passage that provides atmospheric background for the dancing performed in a section of New Orleans:

Boudoum, boudoum! The giant hollow drums reverberated through the Sunday stillness, played by men who sat astride them and pounded with hands and feet. The sound of sticks hitting smaller drums, the clanging of triangles, and the thudding, pounding echo of hundreds of bare feet slapping the hard earth; these sounds, intermixed with the roar of a wounded bull, the screech of circus baboons; the panting dissonance

of the Indians playing a wild game of racquette; these were the sounds
of Congo Square.

LYNNE FAULEY EMERY, *Black Dance: From 1619 to Today,* 2nd rev. ed., p. 154

The following extract from the autobiography of American dance and cultural revolutionary Isadora Duncan is even more intense:

> That evening there was in the audience calling aloud with the
> rest, a young Hungarian of god-like features and stature, who was to
> transform the chaste nymph that I was, into a wild and careless Bac-
> chante. Everything conspired for the change. The spring, the soft moon-
> light nights, and, when we left the theatre, the scent of the air, heavy
> with the perfume of the lilacs. The wild enthusiasm of the audience
> and the first suppers that I had ever eaten in company with abso-
> lutely care-free and sensual people, the music of the gypsies; the Hun-
> garian goulasch, flavoured with paprika, and the heavy Hungarian
> wines—it was, indeed, the first time in my life that I was nourished,
> over-nourished and stimulated with an abundance of food—all brought
> about the first awareness of my body as something other than an instru-
> ment to express the sacred harmony of music. My breasts, which un-
> til then had been hardly perceptible, began to swell softly and astonish
> me with charming but embarrassing sensations. My hips, which had
> been like a boy's, took on another undulation, and through my whole
> being I felt one great surging, longing, unmistakable urge, so that I
> could no longer sleep at night but tossed and turned in feverish, painful
> unrest.

My Life, pp. 100–101

As a species of narrative, biography might tend quite naturally to use the
devices we associate with fiction, particularly in the hands of a dramatic and
dynamic personality like Duncan.

What all these impressionistic descriptions have in common, to varying degrees, is their dependence on the senses. Poe's introduction to "The
Fall of the House of Usher" emphasizes the spiritual or psychological significance of what is seen, but relies first on literal vision. Despite its shortcomings, the "dark and stormy night" passage at the beginning of this chapter
attempts to use all five senses—for example, in the appearance of the air
conditioners, the sounds of the rain, and the stench, taste, and wet-fur-feel of
the stale night air.

Because we are visual creatures primarily, most of our imagery will be
drawn from the sense of sight. But the word *imagery* is applied broadly to
information derived from or addressed to the other senses as well. The lines
from Isadora Duncan contain more imagery pertinent to smell, taste, and
touch than to sight; the imagery that describes Congo Park is predominantly
auditory.

DESCRIPTIVE TECHNIQUES AND FIGURATIVE LANGUAGE

Creating Descriptions

Descriptions are usually created in three ways: through the use of (1) adverbs and adjectives, (2) strong verbs, and (3) figures of speech:

1. Resolute, with fierce eyes staring straight ahead, Chang made his rapid way across the traffic-filled street.
2. Chang dashed across the street oblivious to traffic.
3. Crossing the street, Chang paid no more attention to the traffic than a foxhound to a fallen tree.

There are two potential risks in using these. First, you might be inclined to adjectival or adverbial overkill. Too many descriptive words tend to call attention to themselves rather than to the nouns or verbs they modify. Item 1 is in danger of this error if not already guilty of it. Another is using figures of speech when the image might not register with your audience, as in item 3. How many of us, after all, have seen foxhounds in pursuit? Perhaps one of the following **analogies** might have been more effective:

... than an 8:00 A.M. class to a lecture on the sleep cycle.

... than a smoker to a surgeon general's warning.

... than a neutered dog to a spayed bitch.

But only if the context makes humor appropriate and if readers are likely to find the brand of humor acceptable. If not, you will need to be more reserved:

... than a felon to the law.

... than a saint to adversity.

... than a carpenter to a countersunk nail.

Item 2 avoids both pitfalls, carried by the forcefulness of the verb *dashed* (others such as *sped, raced,* and *darted* would also have served) and using only one modifier, *oblivious.*

Combinations among the three approaches are possible. For instance, here is a revised version of item 3:

> Oblivious to danger, Chang charged across the street like a Rough Rider up San Juan Hill.

Descriptive words are minimal here, the verb strong, and the image reinforcing—although it depends on the reader's catching the **allusion** to Theodore Roosevelt's troops and the Spanish-American War.

You are likely to have had sufficient (even excessive) experience in using adjectives and adverbs in description, and with a little effort you are likely to come up with verbs that show specific intensities in the actions they communicate rather than some generic behavior. (Try, for example, to find more precise and vivid alternatives for the following verbs: *eat, talk, look, hit, walk.*) Finding appropriate figures of speech, however, might be more challenging.

Figures of Speech

The figures of speech in item 3 and its suggested substitutes are examples of **simile.** They compare two phenomena by use of the word *like* or *as*—explicitly in the Rough Rider simile, implicitly in the others. (Chang was *like* a foxhound, *as* indifferent as a saint.) **Metaphor** also compares, but in such a way as to make the two elements of the comparison identical; it uses neither *like* nor *as* directly or by implication:

> A Rough Rider charging up San Juan Hill, Chang dashed across the street oblivious to danger.

This is a metaphorical construction because Chang and the Rough Rider are not merely similar but are interchangeable. Chang is not *like* a Rough Rider; he *is* one.

Metaphor, of course, is a familiar poetic device. A poem, in fact, may be "governed" by a single extended or elaborated image. This sort of consistency and cumulative effect, however, is also useful in creating a **dominant impression** in prose. The passage from Poe earlier in the chapter suggests as much, but the technique is by no means exclusive to fiction:

> Ah! that hot, wide plain of East St. Louis is a gripping thing. The rivers are dirty with sweat and toil and lip, like lakes, along the low and burdened shores; flatboats ramble and thread among them, and above the steamers bridges swing on great arches of steel, striding with mighty grace from shore to shore. Everywhere are brick kennels,—tall, black and red chimneys, tongues of flame. The ground is littered with cars and iron, tracks and trucks, boxes and crates, metals and coal and rubber. Nature-defying cranes, grim elevators rise above pile on pile of black and grimy lumber. And ever below is the water,—wide and silent, gray-brown and yellow.
>
> W. E. B. DU BOIS, *Darkwater: Voices from Within the Veil*, p. 90

In their totality the harsh images here suggest the starkness of danger and decay—an impression borne out in succeeding pages.

In addition to simile and metaphor, **personification, hyperbole,** and **understatement** are among the figures of speech you might consider using. In personification, human qualities are attributed to other species, inanimate objects, or even abstractions:

> Glazed eyes heavily lidded with ancient draperies, the house sagged weary and disconsolate.

Houses have eyes (whether here or in the House of Usher) only metaphorically and they are incapable of experiencing either weariness or consolation.

> Fig Newton frolicked in her goldfish bowl, turning gleeful somersaults in and out of her plastic castle.

Fish fry, yes; fish frolic, no—except as a personification. And as for glee, it is clearly attributed to the somersault (and fish) by the human observer. Such description communicates the writer's perception rather than any literal experience of what is observed. The naming of animals, whether fish, fowl, or feline, is also a means of personifying them. So are attributes of "family" life—as in mother hens, baby hamsters, or daddy longlegs—and domestic constellations such as those in *Bambi, The Tale of Peter Rabbit,* or the movie *Beauty and the Beast,* in which "living" utensils are prominent. Popular entertainment for children often depends heavily on this device, using everything from dishes running off with spoons (there is little new under the sun) to Alvin harmonizing nasally with his brother chipmunks. Carefully used, however, personification may be quite effective in adult nonfiction:

> The sun rose this morning, grinning hideously, to begin the ninth straight day of record-breaking heat.

Such a sentence is expressive and also hearkens back to tendencies in civilizations worldwide to animate and personify, even deify, natural forces.

Hyperbole is a form of exaggeration. For example, the tall tales of extraordinary achievement concerning figures such as Paul Bunyan and Pecos Bill are hyperbolic. Closer to home—literally—parents are often good sources:

> Why were you out till dawn? (You were really back by 1:15 and do not live in the land of the midnight sun.)
> Your clothes are all over the place. (It's really only a sweatshirt over a chair and a pair of jeans on the bed—oh, and a couple of odd socks on the floor.)

Accuracy aside, the exaggerated message makes it clear that the topics are of great importance to Mom or Dad. But hyperbole need not involve potential confrontation. If someone says that Big Lenny sits down to a ton of potatoes afloat in fifty gallons of gravy, we know that his appetite is large. Quite large. Extremely large. The extremity is true of other exaggerations as well, from the "monster" head cold to the grade-point average so minuscule that it can be read only with an electron microscope.

Understatement does the opposite of hyperbole. By describing Scotland's highest mountain as "a considerable protuberance," Samuel Johnson reduced the 4,406-foot Ben Nevis to the geographic equivalent of a wart or mole. Since it minimizes significance, understatement is often useful for calming what others perceive as crises or for otherwise taking winds out of sails. Suppose a resident of your dorm came into your room screaming something about a fire, which, it turns out, is a few scraps of paper burning at the bottom of a metal wastebasket. "Where do you keep the marshmallows?" might be an appropriate understated response—as you douse the flames with what's left of your Coke.

Such **irony**, however, might be both more sophisticated and purposeful. In "A Modest Proposal," for example, Jonathan Swift attempts to call attention to the misery of the Irish masses and appeal for their relief. But instead of ranting, he presents his economic solution in a cool, rational manner designed to underscore the urgency of the situation by strategically understated detachment:

> I shall now therefore humbly propose my own thoughts, which I hope will not be liable to the least objection.
>
> I have been assured by a very knowing American of my acquaintance in London, that a young healthy child well nursed is at a year old a most delicious, nourishing, and wholesome food, whether stewed, roasted, baked, or boiled, and I make no doubt that it will equally serve in a fricassee, or a ragout.
>
> I do therefore humbly offer it to public consideration, that of the hundred and twenty thousand children already computed, twenty thousand may be reserved for breed, whereof only one fourth part to be males, which is more than we allow to sheep, black-cattle, or swine. . . . That the remaining hundred thousand may at a year old be offered in sale to the persons of quality, and fortune, throughout the kingdom, always advising the mother to let them suck plentifully in the last month, so as to render them plump, and fat for a good table. A child will make two dishes at an entertainment for friends, and when the family dines alone, the fore or hind quarter will make a reasonable dish, and seasoned with a little pepper or salt will be very good boiled on the fourth day, especially in winter.

Swift maintains his mock benevolence to the last, concluding as follows:

> I profess in the sincerity of my heart that I have not the least personal interest in endeavouring to promote this necessary work, hav-

ing no other motive than the public good of my country, by advancing our trade, providing for infants, relieving the poor, and giving some pleasure to the rich. I have no children by which I can propose to get a single penny; the youngest being nine years old, and my wife past child-bearing.

Determining the Amount of Description

You will have to choose not only your means of description but also its extent. Topic and audience help determine this, but elaboration or its opposite is partly a matter of taste, fashion, or *zeitgeist*—the spirit of the age. As a product of your time ("postmodern," according to many), but not exclusively so, you are likely but not compelled to write relatively unadorned prose. But the amount of description you use ultimately depends on well exercised judgment and on the answer to this question: What are the most efficient and effective means of expressing what I have to say?

DESCRIPTION IN ACADEMIC WRITING

Writing on academic themes is as likely to be as descriptive as any other, although the description must be tailored to the nature of the topic and the expectation of the discipline. Criticism in the arts, for example, is likely to be more impressionistic than a sociological, economic or scientific study. A statement such as the following might be acceptable in an interpretive account of a painting and its psychological effects:

> The dot of brilliant blue, just off center in a white field, inevitably draws viewers' eyes, creating tension between its placement and conventional ideas of balance.

However, you would not write this in your lab report for chemistry:

> The solution turned the color of Tiffany's eyes.

Personal associations have little place in the objective description required in this case.

The following passages, from various disciplines, provide an indication of the descriptive range typical of academic writing and suggest what may be appropriate for each field and its near relations. Commenting on American advertising in general, literary scholar and critic Leo Spitzer paints a verbal picture of a particular advertisement as a prelude to his analysis:

> [O]n a high mountain range, covered with snow that glistens in the bright sunshine, furrowed by vertical gullies, towering over a white

village with its neat, straight rows of orange trees, there rests a huge
orange-colored sun, inscribed with the word "Sunkist." In front of this
vista, set squarely in the midst of the groves, is a glass of orange-juice
which rises to the exact height of the mountain range and whose color
exactly matches that of the sun ball. Next to this gigantic glass of juice
is a smaller one of the same color, and next to that, a fruit-squeezer on
which lies the orange to be squeezed. . . .

   [T]his [depiction] . . . represents a highly poetic procedure, since,
thereby . . . on our routine reality there is superimposed another, dream-
like, reality: the consumer may have the illusion, for a moment, of
drinking nectar at the source. And the public accepts willingly the
hypocrisy of the artist. It is as though this manifestation of commercial
self-expression were denying its essential purpose, that of selling and of
profit-making. . . . In the city drugstore, over whose counter this sunny
picture shines, the wall opens up before us like a window on Nature.
Business becomes poetic because it recognizes the great grip which
poetry has on the modern unpoetic world. . . . And the modest way in
which the business firm hides its own tremendous activity behind
anonymous Nature will impress us favorably.

Essays on English and American Literature, pp. 251–53

The nature of the advertisement is clear from the description in the first
paragraph and the basis of its appeal, as Spitzer sees it, through the interpre-
tative critique in the second.

   On the other hand, with the possible exception of the opening sentence,
James Stuart Olson's description of the camps in which Japanese-Americans
were interred during World War II seems totally detached. One might argue,
of course, that starkness itself may be impressive:

   The relocation centers resembled minimum-security prisons where
the bare necessities of life were provided. At each center hundreds of
wood-frame tar-paper barracks housed the evacuees. Divided into four
20 x 25 foot rooms, each barrack housed four families or thirty people.
Community mess halls and latrines met basic physical needs, and
schools and hospitals were added later. Barbed-wire fences surrounded
each center, and military police patrolled the perimeter. Within each
center the evacuees were permitted some self-government. Several barracks had a block leader and an elected block council responsible to a
WRA [War Relocation Authority] administrator. They maintained records, kept count of evacuees, planned cultural events, and carried
grievances to the WRA. Buddhist and Christian churches flourished at
each camp, but because of its emperor worship Shinto was suppressed.
Camp authorities permitted inmates to publish newspapers in both
English and Japanese.

The Ethnic Dimension in American History, pp. 340–41

Similar descriptive austerity may be found even in works in which the authors are clearly sympathetic with their subjects. The following unembellished description appears in a book that is highly sensitive to the problems of aging. Perhaps in this instance the unadorned details speak forcefully for themselves:

> The second woman to be considered here suffers from many seriously disabling conditions. An inveterate smoker and a diabetic, she has had one leg amputated and is confined to a wheelchair. She has a chronic heart condition and kidney and bladder trouble. Bad circulation indicates that she may soon lose her second leg to surgery. Not too long ago, she underwent major surgeries on her gall bladder, rectum, reproductive system, and varicose veins. In addition, she is legally blind and her hearing is deteriorating.
>
> ERIK H. ERIKSON, JOAN M. ERIKSON, and HELEN Q. KIVNICK, *Vital Involvement in Old Age*, p. 192

It is in the language of the sciences, however, that we have come to expect the most consistent conservatism in regard to descriptive language. Scientific writing avoids impressions and relies heavily on professional terminology:

> In the true mosses, the gametophyte is leafy and usually upright, not dorsiventrally flattened as it is in the leafy liverworts. It grows from an apical initial cell that is similar to that of the leafy liverworts, that is, like an inverted pyramid with three sides. Although three ranks of leaves are produced initially, subsequent twisting of the axis results in displacement of these ranks and the appearance of a spiral leaf arrangement. In some genera (*Fontinalis*, a genus of aquatic mosses, for example) the three-ranked condition of the leaves is obvious in the mature gametophytes.
>
> The gametophytes of mosses range from a few millimeters to 5 decimeters or more in length, and they exhibit varying degrees of differentiation and complexity. All have multicellular rhizoids, and the leaves are normally only one cell layer thick except at the midrib (which is lacking in some genera). In some mosses, such as the common *Polytrichum*, there is often a central strand of elongate cells in the stem which may function in conduction . . . , but many other genera lack such specialized tissues.
>
> PETER H. RAVEN, RAY F. EVERT, and HELENA CURTIS, *Biology of Plants*, p. 291

In context, the mention of the pyramid seems more like a geometric reference than a simile. In any case, the passage is clearly more objective in its description than Kieran's account of natural activity in April or Shimer's view of the Painted Desert; and in contrast to Ordish's description of furniture beetles, it creates the sense of objectivity through botanical **jargon** alone.

USING DESCRIPTION

In accordance with what you are hoping to communicate, including your thesis, decide whether your description is to be objective or impressionistic. You may wish to use both types either alternately or in combination, according to your essay's requirements.

Generally, and especially in impressionistic writing, be sure that your descriptions do not call excessive attention to themselves but remain means to achieving your larger purpose. Many would regard the paragraph describing the dark and stormy night at the beginning of this chapter as overwritten—perhaps even if its intentions were made clear.

You may escape such a trap by controlling the number of descriptive words and by choosing those you use carefully. Similarly, avoid "showcasing" **figurative language.** If it is to vivify and clarify your points without becoming a distraction, you need to make such language part of an integral, seamless whole. When possible, follow the axiom "Show, don't tell," and let active verbs bear much of the descriptive burden.

As a rule, your descriptions should be so organized that the reader can clearly see the verbal picture as it evolves. The description of the property boundaries on pages 69–70 takes the reader around the perimeter of the parcel of land as it proceeds. The contrasting real-estate ad (p. 72) also has its order, beginning with the house, then expanding to the grounds and then to the community, radiating outward. It might also have been written in reverse:

> Picture a location close to schools, shopping, and major highways. Picture a community of warm, friendly people. Picture an expansive front lawn covered with prizewinning roses. Envision a freshly painted 4 bdr. gem! A must-see at 1 arm and 1 leg!

This approach is perhaps familiar to you from films and TV. It takes a wide shot and then zooms in on its object of principal focus. What either approach does for the reader is establish a literal point of view. And the techniques apply whether it is a scene, an object, or a person being described—although when describing people there may be psychological as well as physical features to be considered.

A physical description of a person might, as the revised real-estate ad does, move from the perimeter to significant details:

> Albert is of slender build, carrying no more than 145 pounds on his five-foot, nine-inch frame. Perhaps to give the illusion of greater bulk, he prefers loose-fitting clothing, full-cut or baggy trousers or sweats, oversized shirts or sweaters, usually in pale earth tones. He wears little jewelry beyond a ring and a gold chain.

Albert is an outgoing sort, greeting strangers with a broad smile and a welcoming look in his large, widely spaced eyes that breaks down any possible barriers. His friendliness and easy manner have made him a favorite of the children at the Community Service Center where he volunteers three days a week. It has also helped him move from clerk to assistant manager at Worthington's, where he works part time while attending the university as a marketing major.

His extracurricular activities include membership in African-Americans United and playing on a three-man intramural basketball team. He has an active social life centered on music, movies, and Audrey, whom he has dated since freshman year. Albert calls home once a week to speak with his parents and sisters and visits regularly—without laundry.

Here we move from the shallows of physical appearance to somewhat greater depth in activities and character.

Kamo No Chōmei

(Japan; 1155–1216)

A courtier until the age of twenty-one, Chōmei left the imperial palace after the deaths of his father and patron to follow the arts. He excelled as poet, critic, essayist, and lutenist. Chōmei traveled widely but gradually began to lead a retired life, a pattern accelerated after he took Buddhist orders in 1204.

In addition to his poetry, Chōmei is remembered for three prose works. Mumyōshō (The Nameless Treatise), a tract on the art of poetry, is a valuable tool for those attempting to understand the poetic techniques of Chōmei's time. Hossinshū is accurately described by its translated title, A Collection of Religious Awakenings—on Buddhist themes. Finally, Hōjōki (An Account of My Hut), from which "The Hut Ten Feet Square" is taken, is a miscellany of ideas and observations of the type represented elsewhere in this text by selections from Sei Shōnagon (p. 34) and Yoshida Kenkō (p. 354). Indebted to an earlier work in Chinese by Yoshishige Yasutane, Chōmei's collection is unified by its recurrent spiritual themes. The account of the hut is, in fact, an account of life in the hut—in which Chōmei spent his last seven or eight years; it also examines the meaning of his life and of life in general. The reading that follows, therefore, has implications beyond mere physical description.

The Hut Ten Feet Square

NOW THAT I have reached the age of sixty, and my life seems about to evaporate like the dew, I have fashioned a lodging for the last leaves of my years. It is a hut where, perhaps, a traveler might spend a single night; it is like the cocoon spun by an aged silkworm. This hut is not even a hundredth the size of the cottage where I spent my middle years.

Before I was aware, I had become heavy with years, and with each remove my dwelling grew smaller. The present hut is of no ordinary appearance. It is a bare ten feet square and less than seven feet high. I did not choose this particular spot rather than another, and I built my house without consulting any diviners.[1] I laid a foundation and roughly thatched a roof. I fastened hinges to the joints of the beams, the easier to move elsewhere should anything displease me. What difficulty would there be in changing my dwelling? A bare two carts would suffice to carry off the whole house, and except for the carter's fee there would be no expenses at all.

Since first I hid my traces here in the heart of Mount Hino, I have added a lean-to on the south and a porch of bamboo. On the west I have built a shelf

---

[1]Normally the site of a house was selected after consulting *yin-yang* diviners, but for a Buddhist priest one place was as good as another. [Tr.]

for holy water, and inside the hut, along the west wall, I have installed an image of Amida. The light of the setting sun shines between its eyebrows.[2] On the doors of the reliquary I have hung pictures of Fugen and Fudō.[3] Above the sliding door that faces north I have built a little shelf on which I keep three or four black leather baskets that contain books of poetry and music and extracts from the sacred writings. Beside them stand a folding koto and a lute.

Along the east wall I have spread long fern fronds and mats of straw which serve as my bed for the night. I have cut open a window in the eastern wall, and beneath it have made a desk. Near my pillow is a square brazier in which I burn brushwood. To the north of the hut I have staked out a small plot of land which I have enclosed with a rough fence and made into a garden. I grow many species of herbs there.

This is what my temporary hut is like. I shall now attempt to describe its surroundings. To the south there is a bamboo pipe which empties water into the rock pool I have laid. The woods come close to my house, and it is thus a simple matter for me to gather brushwood. The mountain is named Toyama. Creeping vines block the trails and the valleys are overgrown, but to the west is a clearing, and my surroundings thus do not leave me without spiritual comfort.[4] In the spring I see waves of wistaria like purple clouds, bright in the west. In the summer I hear the cuckoo call, promising to guide me on the road of death. In the autumn the voice of the evening insects fills my ears with a sound of lamentation for this cracked husk of a world. In winter I look with deep emotion on the snow, piling up and melting away like sins and hindrances to salvation.

When I do not feel like reciting the *nembutsu*[5] and cannot put my heart into reading the Sutras, no one will keep me from resting or being lazy, and there is no friend who will feel ashamed of me. Even though I make no special attempt to observe the discipline of silence, living alone automatically makes me refrain from the sins of speech; and though I do not necessarily try to obey the Commandments, here where there are no temptations what should induce me to break them?

On mornings when I feel myself short-lived as the white wake behind a boat,[6] I go to the banks of the river and, gazing at the boats plying to and fro, compose verses in the style of the Priest Mansei. Or if of an evening the wind in the maples rustles the leaves, I recall the river at Jinyo, and play the lute in the manner of Minamoto no Tsunenobu.[7] If still my mood does not desert

---

[2]The Buddha was said to have emitted light between his eyebrows. [Tr.]   [3]Fugen (Sanskrit, Samantabhadra) is the highest of the bodhisattvas [spiritually enlightened ones]. Fudō Myōō (Sanskrit, Acalanātha) is the chief of the Guardian Kings. [Tr.]   [4]The west is the direction of Paradise and it was thus auspicious that it should have been clear in that direction. The purple cloud is the one on which Amida Buddha descends to guide the believer to the Western Paradise. [Tr.]   [5]the invocation to Amida Buddha practiced particularly by believers in Jōdo Buddhism. [Tr.]   [6]from a poem by the priest Mansei.... [Tr.]   [7]reference to the famous "Lute Song" (P'i-p'a Chi) by Po Chü-i. Minamoto no Tsunenobu (1016–1097) was a famous musician and poet. [Tr.]

me, I often tune my lute to the echoes in the pines, and play the "Song of the Autumn Wind," or pluck the notes of the "Melody of the Flowing Stream," modulating the pitch to the sound of the water. I am but an indifferent performer, but I do not play to please others. Alone I play, alone I sing, and this brings joy to my heart.

At the foot of this mountain is a rough-hewn cottage where the guardian of the mountain lives. He has a son who sometimes comes to visit me. When I am bored with whatever I am doing, I often go for a walk with him as my companion. He is sixteen and I sixty: though our ages greatly differ we take pleasure in each other's company.

Sometimes I pick flowering reeds or the wild pear, or fill my basket with berries and cress. Sometimes I go to the rice fields at the foot of the mountain and weave wreaths of the fallen ears. Or, when the weather is fine, I climb the peak and look out toward Kyoto, my old home, far, far away. The view has no owner and nothing can interfere with my enjoyment.

When I feel energetic and ready for an ambitious journey, I follow along   10
the peaks to worship at the Iwama or Ishiyama Temple. Or I push through the fields of Awazu to pay my respects to the remains of Semimaru's hut, and cross the Tanagami River to visit the tomb of Sarumaru.[8] On the way back, according to the season, I admire the cherry blossoms or the autumn leaves, pick fern-shoots or fruit, both to offer to the Buddha and to use in my house.

If the evening is still, in the moonlight that fills the window I long for old friends or wet my sleeve with tears at the cries of the monkeys. Fireflies in the grass thickets might be mistaken for fishing-lights off the island of Maki; the dawn rains sound like autumn storms blowing through the leaves. And when I hear the pheasants' cries, I wonder if they call their father or their mother; when the wild deer of the mountain approach me unafraid, I realize how far I am from the world. And when sometimes, as is the wont of old age, I waken in the middle of the night, I stir up the buried embers and make them companions in solitude.

It is not an awesome mountain, but its scenery gives me endless pleasure regardless of the season, even when I listen in wonder to the hooting of the owls.[9] How much more even would the sights mean to someone of deeper thought and knowledge!

When I first began to live here I thought it would be for just a little while, but five years have already passed. My temporary retreat has become rather old as such houses go: withered leaves lie deep by the eaves and moss has spread over the floor. When, as chance has had it, news has come to me from

[8]Semimaru was a poet of the Heian period [794–1185] who lived in a hut near the Barrier of Ausakayama. . . . Sarumaru-dayū was an early Heian poet, but nothing is known about him. . . . [Tr.] [9]from a poem by Saigyō: "The mountain is remote; I do not hear the voices of the birds I love, but only the eerie cries of the owl." [Tr.]

the capital, I have learned how many of the great and mighty have died since I withdrew to this mountain. And how to reckon the numbers of lesser folk? How many houses have been destroyed by the numerous conflagrations? Only in a hut built for the moment can one live without fears. It is very small, but it holds a bed where I may lie at night and a seat for me in the day; it lacks nothing as a place for me to dwell. The hermit crab chooses to live in little shells because it well knows the size of its body. The osprey stays on deserted shores because it fears human beings. I am like them. Knowing myself and the world, I have no ambitions and do not mix in the world. I seek only tranquillity; I rejoice in the absence of grief.

Most people do not build houses for their own sake. Some build for their families or their relatives; some for their friends and acquaintances. Some build for their masters or teachers, and some even to hold their possessions or beasts. I have built for myself and not for others. This is because in times like these, being in the position I am, I have no companion and no servant to help me. Supposing that I had built a spacious house, whom should I have lodged? Whom should I have had live there?

A man's friends esteem him for his wealth and show the greatest affection 15 for those who do them favors. They do not necessarily have love for persons who bear them warm friendship or who are of an honest disposition. It is better to have as friends music and the sights of nature. A man's servants crave liberal presents and are deferential to those who treat them generously. But however great the care and affection bestowed on them, they do not care the slightest for their master's place and happiness. It is best to be one's own servant.

If there is something which must be done, I naturally do it myself. I do sometimes weary of work, but I find it simpler to work than to employ a servant and look after him. If some errand requires walking, I do the walking myself. It is disagreeable at times, but it is preferable to worrying about horse-trappings or an oxcart. I divide my body and make two uses of it: my hands are my servants, my feet my vehicle, and they suit me well. When my mind or body is tired, I know it at once and I rest. I employ my servants when they are strong. I say "employ," but I do not often overwork them. If I do not feel like working, it does not upset me. And is it not true that to be thus always walking and working is good for the body? What would be the point in idly doing nothing? It is a sin to cause physical or mental pain: how can we borrow the labor of others?

My clothing and food are as simple as my lodgings. I cover my nakedness with whatever clothes woven of wistaria fiber and quilts of hempen cloth come to hand, and I eke out my life with berries of the fields and nuts from the trees on the peaks. I need not feel ashamed of my appearance, for I do not mix in society and the very scantiness of the food gives it additional savor, simple though it is.

I do not prescribe my way of life to men enjoying happiness and wealth, but have related my experiences merely to show the differences between my former and present life. Ever since I fled the world and became a priest, I have known neither hatred nor fear. I leave my span of days for Heaven to determine, neither clinging to life nor begrudging its end. My body is like a drifting cloud—I ask for nothing, I want nothing. My greatest joy is a quiet nap; my only desire for this life is to see the beauties of the seasons.

The Three Worlds are joined by one mind.[10] If the mind is not at peace, neither beasts of burden nor possessions are of service, neither palaces nor pavilions bring any cheer. This lonely house is but a tiny hut, but I somehow love it. I naturally feel ashamed when I go to the capital and must beg, but when I return and sit here I feel pity for those still attached to the world of dust. Should anyone doubt the truth of my words, let him look to the fishes and the birds. Fish do not weary of the water, but unless one is a fish one does not know why. Birds long for the woods, but unless one is a bird one does not know why. The joys of solitude are similar. Who could understand them without having lived here?

Now the moon of my life sinks in the sky and is close to the edge of the   20
mountain. Soon I must head into the darkness of the Three Ways:[11] why should I thus drone on about myself? The essence of the Buddha's teaching to man is that we must not have attachment for any object. It is a sin for me now to love my little hut, and my attachment to its solitude may also be a hindrance to salvation. Why should I waste more precious time in relating such trifling pleasures?

One calm dawning, as I thought over the reasons for this weakness of mine, I told myself that I had fled the world to live in a mountain forest in order to discipline my mind and practice the Way. "And yet, in spite of your monk's appearance, your heart is stained with impurity. Your hut may take after Jōmyō's,[12] but you preserve the Law even worse than Handoku. If your low estate is a retribution for the sins of a previous existence, is it right that you afflict yourself over it? Or should you permit delusion to come and disturb you?" To these questions my mind could offer no reply. All I could do was to use my tongue to recite two or three times the *nembutsu*, however unacceptable from a defiled heart.

It is now the end of the third moon of 1212, and I am writing this at the hut on Toyama.

Translated by Donald Keene

---

[10] . . . The Three Worlds may be interpreted as the past, the present, and the future. [Tr.]   [11] the three paths in the afterworld leading to different types of hells. [Tr.]   [12] Jōmyō (Vimalakirti) was a priest of Sakyamuni's [the Buddha's] time who built himself a stone hut much like Chōmei's. Handoku (Panthaka) was the most foolish of Sakyamuni's disciples. [Tr.]

THESIS AND THOUGHT

1. Describe, in your own words, Chōmei's hut and its environs.
2. With what activities does Chōmei occupy himself?
3. Why has Chōmei chosen to build such a hut and to live as he does?

STRUCTURE

1. What is the overall impression created by Chōmei's account? How is it achieved? Cite specific techniques and passages.
2. To what extent is the description here objective? Examine, for instance, paragraphs 2–5.
3. In what sense does the account progress from the local and physical to the cosmic and spiritual? See the first sentence of paragraph 5 for one of Chōmei's transitions.

STYLE

1. How do Chōmei's references to his age (paras. 1 and 20), solitude (paras. 5, 7, and 11), and the temporary nature of his dwelling (paras. 1, 5, and 13) shape the **tone** of the reading?
2. Chōmei uses similes throughout the piece. Identify several of them and assess their contribution to the whole.
3. Explain Chōmei's reservations in paragraphs 20–21 about his having written this account. Explain whether these paragraphs detract from the reading or are consistent with it. Do they in any sense present a **paradox**?

CONSIDERATIONS

1. What, if anything, might induce you to lead the kind of life Chōmei describes? Note that in paragraph 18 he writes, "I do not prescribe my way of life to men enjoying happiness and wealth. . . ."
2. In paragraph 8 Chōmei introduces the son of "the guardian of the mountain" as his sometime companion: "He is sixteen and I sixty: though our ages greatly differ we take pleasure in each other's company." Apart from relatives, what sorts of personal relationships do you have with people who are forty or fifty years older than you? Write a paragraph describing one of these relationships or, if you have none, a paragraph explaining why you think that is the case.
3. In *Out of My Later Years*, Albert Einstein writes a sentence that might have been written by Chōmei: "I live in that solitude which is so painful in youth

but delicious in years of maturity." Write an essay in which you comment either on the joy or pain of solitude—whether in youth or age.

4. Chōmei's religious retirement is a phenomenon hardly restricted to Buddhism alone—witness, for example, the monasteries and convents of Christianity. Granting the possible spiritual benefits of such a life and its use in promoting a particular faith, consider what value it has for society. Should a standard of contributing to the public good be applied to any occupation or mode of existence? Write a brief essay in which you compare the effects a recluse might have on society with those of one of the following professions:

munitions manufacturer	bellhop
stripper	sculptor
professional athlete	garbage collector
fashion model	chauffeur, maid, or butler
public defender	hit man

—— Views of the Galapagos Islands ——

Herman Melville
(United States; 1819–1891)

Although born into a prominent and prosperous family, Melville faced poverty and failure most of his life. His grandfathers had been high-ranking officers in the Revolutionary War; one of them had participated in the Boston Tea Party. On his mother's side he was connected to the wealthy descendants of the original Dutch settlers in New York's Hudson valley.

But his father's bankruptcy and early death left the teenage Melville psychologically and financially devastated. At twenty, he went to sea to seek his fortune, but found instead the realities of the sailor's life and material for several novels, including the masterpiece Moby-Dick (1851).

His earliest novels, Typee (1846) and Omoo (1847), were widely popular. Those that followed were less well received, as darker, philosophical qualities, influenced by the writings and friendship of Nathaniel Hawthorne, began to appear in his work. The popular and critical failure of Moby-Dick sent Melville into deep depression.

Unable to support his family, Melville survived with the help of loans and gifts. In 1866, however, he found work as a customs inspector on the New York waterfront, a job he held until his retirement in 1885. Although he continued to write during this interval, he published poetry almost exclusively. But after his death, the short novel Billy Budd, completed just months before, was found among his papers.

Public notice of Melville's death consisted of a brief obituary in the New York Tribune, which mentioned only the two earliest novels. Not until after World

War I was Melville's work rediscovered and his reputation restored, but on grounds other than those which underlay his early popularity.

This selection is taken from The Encantadas *(1854), a collection of sketches about the Galapagos Islands. It is based on Melville's experiences as a seaman on the whaler* Acushnet, *which had stopped at the islands in 1841–42.*

As you read, observe the mood Melville creates and how he creates it.

The Isles at Large

TAKE FIVE-AND-TWENTY HEAPS of cinders dumped here and there in an outside city lot; imagine some of them magnified into mountains, and the vacant lot the sea; and you will have a fit idea of the general aspect of the Encantadas, or Enchanted Isles. A group rather of extinct volcanoes than of isles; looking much as the world at large might, after a penal conflagration.

It is to be doubted whether any spot of earth can, in desolateness, furnish a parallel to this group. Abandoned cemeteries of long ago, old cities by piecemeal tumbling to their ruin, these are melancholy enough; but, like all else which has but once been associated with humanity, they still awaken in us some thoughts of sympathy, however sad. Hence, even the Dead Sea, along with whatever other emotions it may at times inspire, does not fail to touch in the pilgrim some of his less unpleasurable feelings.

And as for solitariness; the great forests of the north, the expanses of unnavigated waters, the Greenland ice-fields, are the profoundest of solitudes to a human observer; still the magic of their changeable tides and seasons mitigates their terror; because, though unvisited by men, those forests are visited by the May; the remotest seas reflect familiar stars even as Lake Erie does; and in the clear air of a fine Polar day, the irradiated, azure ice shows beautifully as malachite.

But the special curse, as one may call it, of the Encantadas, that which exalts them in desolation above Idumea and the Pole, is, that to them change never comes; neither the change of seasons nor of sorrows. Cut by the Equator, they know not autumn, and they know not spring; while already reduced to the lees of fire, ruin itself can work little more upon them. The showers refresh the deserts; but in these isles rain never falls. Like split Syrian gourds left withering in the sun, they are cracked by an everlasting drought beneath a torrid sky. "Have mercy upon me," the wailing spirit of the Encantadas seems to cry, "and send Lazarus that he may dip the tip of his finger in water and cool my tongue, for I am tormented in this flame."

Another feature in these isles is their emphatic uninhabitableness. It is   5
deemed a fit type of all-forsaken overthrow, that the jackal should den in the wastes of weedy Babylon; but the Encantadas refuse to harbour even the

outcasts of the beasts. Man and wolf alike disown them. Little but reptile life is here found: tortoises, lizards, immense spiders, snakes, and that strangest anomaly of outlandish nature, the *aguano*. No voice, no low, no howl is heard; the chief sound of life here is a hiss.

On most of the isles where vegetation is found at all, it is more ungrateful than the blankness of Aracama. Tangled thickets of wiry bushes, without fruit and without a name, springing up among deep fissures of calcined rock, and treacherously masking them; or a parched growth of distorted cactus trees.

In many places the coast is rock-bound, or, more properly, clinker-bound; tumbled masses of blackish or greenish stuff like the dross of an iron-furnace, forming dark clefts and caves here and there, into which a ceaseless sea pours a fury of foam; overhanging them with a swirl of gray, haggard mist, amidst which sail screaming flights of unearthly birds heightening the dismal din. However calm the sea without, there is no rest for those swells and those rocks; they lash and are lashed, even when the outer ocean is most at peace with itself. On the oppressive, clouded days, such as are peculiar to this part of the watery Equator, the dark, vitrified masses, many of which raise themselves among white whirlpools and breakers in detached and perilous places off the shore, present a most Plutonian sight. In no world but a fallen one could such lands exist.

Those parts of the strand free from the marks of fire stretch away in wide level beaches of multitudinous dead shells, with here and there decayed bits of sugarcane, bamboos, and cocoa-nuts, washed upon this other and darker world from the charming palm isles to the westward and southward; all the way from Paradise to Tarturus; while mixed with the relics of distant beauty you will sometimes see fragments of charred wood and mouldering ribs of wrecks. Neither will anyone be surprised at meeting these last, after observing the conflicting currents which eddy throughout nearly all the wide channels of the entire group. The capriciousness of the tides of air sympathises with those of the sea. Nowhere is the wind so light, baffling, and every way unreliable, and so given to perplexing calms, as at the Encantadas. Nigh a month has been spent by a ship going from one isle to another, though but ninety miles between; for owing to the force of the current, the boats employed to tow barely suffice to keep the craft from sweeping upon the cliffs, but do nothing toward accelerating her voyage. Sometimes it is impossible for a vessel from afar to fetch up with the group itself, unless large allowances for prospective leeway have been made ere its coming in sight. And yet, at other times, there is a mysterious indraft, which irresistibly draws a passing vessel among the isles, though not bound to them.

True, at one period, as to some extent at the present day, large fleets of whalemen cruised for spermaceti upon what some seamen call the Enchanted Ground. But this, as in due place will be described, was off the great outer isle of Albemarle, away from the intricacies of the smaller isles, where there is plenty of sea-room; and hence, to that vicinity, the above remarks do not altogether apply; though even there the current runs at times with singular force, shifting, too, with as singular a caprice.

Indeed, there are seasons when currents quite unaccountable prevail for a great distance round about the total group, and are so strong and irregular as to change a vessel's course against the helm, though sailing at the rate of four or five miles the hour. The difference in the reckonings of navigators, produced by these causes, along with the light and variable winds, long nourished a persuasion, that there existed two distinct clusters of isles in the parallel of the Encantadas, about a hundred leagues apart. Such was the idea of their earlier visitors, the Bucaniers; and as late as 1750, the charts of that part of the Pacific accorded with the strange delusion. And this apparent fleetingness and unreality of the locality of the isles was most probably one reason for the Spaniards calling them the Encantada, or Enchanted Group.

But not uninfluenced by their character, as they now confessedly exist, the modern voyager will be inclined to fancy that the bestowal of this name might have in part originated in that air of spell-bound desertness which so significantly invests the isles. Nothing can better suggest the aspect of once living things malignly crumbled from ruddiness into ashes. Apples of Sodom, after touching, seem these isles.

However wavering their place may seem by reason of the currents, they themselves, at least to one upon the shore, appear invariably the same; fixed, cast, glued into the very body of cadaverous death.

Nor would the appellation, enchanted, seem misapplied in still another sense. For concerning the peculiar reptile inhabitant of these wilds—whose presence gives the group its second Spanish name, Gallipagos—concerning the tortoises found here, most mariners have long cherished a superstition, not more frightful than grotesque. They earnestly believe that all wicked sea-officers, more especially commodores and captains, are at death (and, in some cases, before death) transformed into tortoises; thenceforth dwelling upon these hot aridities, sole solitary lords of Asphaltum.

Doubtless, so quaintly dolorous a thought was originally inspired by the woebegone landscape itself; but more particularly, perhaps, by the tortoises. For, apart from their strictly physical features, there is something strangely self-condemned in the appearance of these creatures. Lasting sorrow and penal hopelessness are in no animal form so supplicantly expressed as in theirs; while the thought of their wonderful longevity does not fail to enhance the impression.

Nor even at the risk of meriting the charge of absurdly believing in enchantments, can I restrain the admission that sometimes, even now, when leaving the crowded city to wander out July and August among the Adirondack Mountains, far from the influences of towns and proportionally nigh to the mysterious ones of nature; when at such times I sit me down in the mossy head of some deep-wooded gorge, surrounded by prostrate trunks of blasted pines, and recall, as in a dream, my other and far-distant rovings in the baked heart of the charmed isles; and remember the sudden glimpses of dusky shells, and long languid necks protruded from the leafless thickets; and again have beheld the vitreous inland rocks worn down and grooved into deep ruts by ages and ages of the slow draggings of tortoises in quest of pools of scanty water; I can hardly resist the feeling that in my time I have indeed slept upon evilly enchanted ground.

Nay, such is the vividness of my memory, or the magic of my fancy, that I know not whether I am not the occasional victim of optical delusion concerning the Gallipagos. For, often in scenes of social merriment, and especially at revels held by candle-light in old-fashioned mansions, so that shadows are thrown into the further recesses of an angular and spacious room, making them put on a look of haunted undergrowth of lonely woods, I have drawn the attention of my comrades by my fixed gaze and sudden change of air, as I have seemed to see, slowly emerging from those imagined solitudes, and heavily crawling along the floor, the ghost of a gigantic tortoise, with "Memento * * * * * " burning in live letters upon his back.

Charles Darwin

(England; 1809–1882)

Darwin was born into privileged circumstances, which precluded any need for employment apart from his scientific studies. His father was a prominent physician; one grandfather, Erasmus Darwin, a renowned physician and man of science; the other, Josiah Wedgwood, founder of a ceramics industry that still prospers today.

Darwin, however, came to his intellectual life as a student at Cambridge. It was his mentor, John Stevens Henslow, who recommended him for the unpaid post of naturalist aboard the HMS Beagle, then undertaking a scientific expedition to the South American coasts. The five-year journey changed Darwin's life and history forever.

During the voyage, Darwin made copious notes on the geology and biology of the regions explored. In particular, variations among separate but related species on the Galapagos Islands stimulated and reinforced his thinking about evolution and natural selection. Upon his return, he spent nearly a quarter century accumulating further evidence and refining his ideas. But when in 1858 Darwin received a letter from Alfred Russel Wallace outlining his own version of the theory, Darwin's hand was forced. Later that year, he and Wallace presented their work jointly before the Linnaean Society of London. A year later, Darwin published The Origin of Species, *exposing his ideas to public scrutiny.*

Many in the scientific and religious communities objected strenuously, but by century's end, Darwinian thinking had largely won the day. In the social

sphere, Darwin's theory of natural selection was modified (or distorted)
through the thought of Herbert Spencer, coiner of the phrase "survival of the
fittest." Some Spencerians, in emphasizing competitive individualism, applied
the idea to justify—as a consequence of nature's "law"— what later would be
seen as abuses committed by the powerful against the underprivileged.

Darwin's aims, however, were purely scientific. For the remainder of his life
he published works that supplemented or complemented Origin, the best
known of which is The Descent of Man (1871). He also wrote on a number
of highly specialized topics ranging from barnacles to carnivorous plants.

As you read the extracts from Darwin's accounts of the Galapagos, compare
their tone with Melville's in "The Isles at Large." Specifically, what are the
differences in purpose and methods for achieving it?

The Galapagos

From The Beagle Diary

September 16th [1835]. We landed for an hour on the N.W. end of
Chatham Isd. These islands at a distance have a sloping uniform outline,
excepting where broken by sundry paps & hillocks; the whole black Lava,
completely covered by small leafless brushwood & low trees. The fragments of
Lava where most porous, are reddish like cinders; the stunted trees show little
signs of life. The black rocks heated by the rays of the Vertical sun, like a
stove, give to the air a close & sultry feeling. The plants also smell unpleas-
antly. The country was compared to what we might imagine the cultivated
parts of the Infernal regions to be.

This day, we now being only 40 miles from the Equator, has been the first
warm one; up to this time all on board have worn cloth clothese, & although
no one would complain of cold, still less would they of too much warmth. The
case would be very different if we were cruizing on the Atlantic side of the
Continent.

September 17th. The *Beagle* was moved into St. Stephen's harbor. We
found there an American Whaler & we previously had seen two at Hoods
Island. The Bay swarmed with animals; Fish, Shark & Turtles were popping
their heads up in all parts. Fishing lines were soon put overboard & great
numbers of fine fish 2 & even 3 feet long were caught. This sport makes all
hands very merry; loud laughter & the heavy flapping of the fish are heard on
every side. After dinner a party went on shore to try to catch Tortoises, but
were unsuccessful. These islands appear paradises for the whole family of
Reptiles. Besides three kinds of Turtles, the Tortoise is so abundant that [a]
single Ship's company here caught 500–800 in a short time. The black Lava
rocks on the beach are frequented by large (2–3 ft.) most disgusting, clumsy

Lizards. They are as black as the porous rocks over which they crawl & seek their prey from the Sea. Somebody calls them "imps of darkness." They assuredly well become the land they inhabit. When on shore I proceeded to botanize & obtained 10 different flowers; but such insignificant, ugly little flowers, as would better become an Arctic than a Tropical country. The birds are Strangers to Man & think him as innocent as their countrymen the huge Tortoises. Little birds, within 3 or 4 feet, quietly hopped about the Bushes & were not frightened by stones being thrown at them. Mr. King killed one with his hat & I pushed off a branch with the end of my gun a large Hawk.

From *The Geology of the HMS Beagle*

GALAPAGOS ARCHIPELAGO

This archipelago is situated under the Equator, at a distance of between five and six hundred miles from the west coast of South America. It consists of five principal islands, and of several small ones, which together are equal in area, but not in extent of land, to Sicily conjointly with the Ionian islands. They are all volcanic: on two, craters have been seen in eruption, and on several of the other islands, streams of lava have a recent appearance. The larger islands are chiefly composed of solid rock, and they rise with a tame outline, to a height of between one and four thousand feet. They are sometimes, but not generally, surmounted by one principal orifice. The craters vary in size from mere spiracles to huge caldrons, several miles in circumference; they are extraordinarily numerous, so that I should think, if enumerated, they would be found to exceed two thousand; they are formed either of scoriae and lava, or of a brown coloured tuff; and these latter craters are in several respects remarkable. The whole group was surveyed by the officers of the *Beagle*. I visited myself four of the principal islands, and received specimens from all the others. Under the head of the different islands, I will describe only that which appears to me deserving of attention.

CHATHAM ISLAND

Craters composed of a singular kind of tuff. Towards the eastern end of this island, there occur two craters, composed of two kinds of tuff; one kind being friable, like slightly consolidated ashes; and the other compact, and of a different nature from any thing, which I have met with described. This latter substance, where it is best characterized, is of a yellowish-brown colour, translucent, and with a lustre somewhat resembling resin; it is brittle, with an angular, rough, and very irregular fracture, sometimes, however, being slightly granular, and even obscurely crystalline: it can readily be scratched with a knife, yet some points are hard enough just to mark common glass; it fuses with ease into a blackish-green glass. The mass contains numerous broken crystals of olivine and augite, and small particles of black and brown scoriae: it is often traversed by thin seams of calcareous matter. It generally affects a nodular or concretionary structure. In a hand specimen, this substance would certainly be mistaken for a pale and peculiar variety of pitchstone; but when seen in mass, its stratification, and the numerous layers of fragments of basalt, both angular and rounded, at once render its subaqueous origin evident. An examination of a series of specimens, shows that this resin-like substance, results from a chemical change on small particles of pale and dark-coloured, scoriaceous rocks; and this change could be distinctly traced in different stages, round the edges of event the same particle. The position near the coast, of all the craters composed of this kind of tuff or peperino, and their breached condition, renders it probable that they were all formed, when standing immersed in the sea. . . .

Small basaltic craters. A bare, undulating tract, at the eastern end of Chatham Island, is remarkable from the number, proximity, and form of the small basaltic craters with which it is studded. They consist, either of a mere conical pile, or, but less commonly, of a circle, of black and red, glossy scoriae, partially cemented together. They vary in diameter from 30 to 150 yards, and rise from about 50 to 100 feet above the level of the surrounding plain. From one small eminence, I counted sixty of these craters, all of which were within a third of a mile from each other, and many were much closer. I measured the distance between two very small craters, and found that it was only thirty yards from the summit-rim of one, to the rim of the other. Small streams of black, basaltic lava, containing olivine and much glassy feldspar, have flowed from many, but not from all of these craters. The surfaces of the more recent streams were exceedingly rugged, and were crossed by great fissures; the older streams were only a little less rugged; and they were all blended and mingled together in complete confusion. The different growth, however, of the trees on the streams, often plainly marked their different ages. Had it not been for this latter character, the streams could in few cases have been distinguished; and consequently, this wide undulatory tract might have (as probably many tracts have), been erroneously considered as formed by one great deluge of lava, instead of by a multitude of small streams, erupted from many small orifices.

In several parts of this tract, and especially at the base of the small craters, there are circular pits, with perpendicular sides, from twenty to forty feet deep. At the foot of one small crater, there were three of these pits. They have probably been formed, by the falling in of the roofs of small caverns. In other parts, there are mammiform hillocks, which resemble great bubbles of lava, with their summits fissured by irregular cracks, which appeared, upon entering them, to be very deep; lava has not flowed from these hillocks. There are, also, other very regular, mammiform hillocks, composed of stratified lava, and surmounted by circular, steep-sided hollows, which, I suppose have been formed by a body of gas, first, arching the strata into one of the bubble-like hillocks, and then, blowing off its summit. These several kinds of hillocks and pits, as well as the numerous, small scoriaceous craters, all show that this tract has been penetrated, almost like a sieve, by the passage of heated vapours. The more regular hillocks could only have been heaved up, whilst the lava was in a softened state.

ALBEMARLE ISLAND

This island consists of five, great, flat-topped craters, which, together with the one on the adjoining island of Narborough, singularly resemble each other, in form and height. The southern one is 4700 feet high, two others are 3720 feet, a third only 50 feet higher, and the remaining ones apparently of nearly the same height. Three of these are situated on one line, and their craters appear elongated in nearly the same direction. The northern crater, which is not the largest, was found by the triangulation to measure externally, no less than three miles and one-eighth of a mile, in diameter. Over the lips of these great, broad caldrons, and from little orifices near their summits, deluges of black lava have flowed down their naked sides. . . .

Craters of tuff. About a mile southward of Banks' Cove, there is a fine elliptic crater, about 500 feet in depth, and three quarters of a mile in diameter. Its bottom is occupied by a lake of brine, out of which some little crateriform hills of tuff rise. The lower beds are formed of compact tuff, appearing like subaqueous deposit; whilst the upper beds, round the entire circumference, consist of a harsh, friable tuff, of little specific gravity, but often containing fragments of rock in layers. This upper tuff contains numerous pisolitic balls, about the size of small bullets, which differ from the surrounding matter only in being slightly harder and finer grained. The beds dip away very regularly on all sides, at angles varying, as I found by measurement, from 25 to 30 degrees. The external surface of the crater slopes at a nearly similar inclination; and is formed by slightly convex ribs, like those on the shell of a pecten or scallop, which become broader as they extend from the mouth of the crater to its base. These ribs are generally from eight to twenty feet in breadth, but sometimes they are as much as forty feet broad; and they resemble old, plastered, much flattened vaults, with the plaster scaling off in plates: they are separated from each other by gullies, deepened by alluvial action. At their upper and narrow ends, near the mouth of the crater, these ribs often consist of real hollow passages, like, but rather smaller than, those often formed by the cooling of the crust of a lavastream, whilst the inner parts flowed onward—of which structure I saw many examples at Chatham Island. There can be no doubt, but that these hollow ribs or vaults have been formed in a similar manner, namely, by the setting or hardening of a superficial crust on streams of mud, which have flowed down from the upper part of the crater. In another part of this same crater, I saw open concave gutters, between one and two feet wide, which appeared to have been formed by the hardening of the lower surface of a mud-stream, instead of, as in the former case, of the upper surface. From these facts, I think it is certain, that the tuff must have flowed as mud. This mud may have been formed either within the crater, or from ashes deposited on its upper parts, and afterwards washed down by torrents of rain. The former method, in most of the cases, appears the more probable one; at James Island, however, some beds of the friable kind of tuff, extend so continuously over an uneven surface, that probably they were formed by the falling of showers of ashes. . . .

Directions of the fissures of eruption. The volcanic orifices in this group, cannot be considered as indiscriminately scattered. Three great craters on Albemarle Island form a well marked line, extending N.W. by N. and S.E. by S. Narborough Island, and the great crater on the rectangular projection of Albemarle Island, form a second parallel line. To the east, Hood's Island, and the islands and rocks between it and James Island, form another, nearly parallel line, which, when prolonged, includes Culpepper and Wenman Islands, lying seventy miles to the north. The other islands lying further eastward, form a less regular fourth line. Several of these islands, and the vents on Albemarle Island, are so placed, that they likewise fall on a set of rudely parallel lines, intersecting the former lines at right angles; so that the principal craters appear to lie on the points, where two sets of fissures cross each other. The islands themselves, with the exception of Albemarle Island, are not elongated in the same direction with the lines on which they stand. The direction of these islands, is nearly the same with that, which prevails in so remarkable a manner, in the numerous archipelagos of the great Pacific Ocean. Finally, I may remark, that amongst the Galapagos islands, there is no one dominant vent, much higher than all the others, as may be observed in many volcanic archipelagos: the highest is the great mound on the south-western extremity of Albemarle Island, which exceeds by barely a thousand feet, several other neighbouring craters.

THESIS AND THOUGHT

1. According to Melville, what are the essential characteristics of the Encantadas?
2. What is the significance of the inscription on the tortoise's back in Melville's final paragraph?
3. What lasting effects have the isles had on the narrator?
4. To what extent does Darwin share Melville's perceptions? Be specific.
5. What is the subject of the second extract from Darwin? How does Darwin's purpose here differ from that of the *Beagle* diary or from Melville's?

STRUCTURE

1. Apart from imagery, what methods does Melville employ in organizing his description? Consider both rhetorical structures and his survey of the physical environment.

2. Why might Darwin's diary entries be regarded as narrative?

3. Does the apparent design of the excerpted geology chapter seem more familiar to you than Melville's or that of the diary? Explain.

STYLE

1. How do Melville's allusions to Pluto (para. 7), Tartarus (para. 8), "Apples of Sodom" (para. 11), and "lords of Asphaltum" (para. 13)—among others— contribute to the idea of the narrator's having "slept upon evilly enchanted ground" (para. 15)? What other language reinforces the idea?

2. Find several instances of impressionistic language in Darwin's diary entries, particularly those that overlap Melville's. Explain why, even when they are close to some of Melville's, they fail to establish the intensity of the dominant impression found in "The Isles at Large."

3. Examine the following sentence from paragraph 2 of the extract from the geological study: "The mass contains numerous broken crystals of olivine and augite, and small particles of black and brown scoriae: it is often traversed by thin seams of calcareous matter." How is the language here characteristic of the selection as a whole? How does it differ from that of both the diary and the reading from Melville?

4. Identify the figure of speech used in the following quotation: " 'Have mercy upon me,' the wailing spirit of the Encantadas seems to cry, 'and send Lazarus that he may dip the tip of his finger in water and cool my tongue, for I am tormented in this flame.' " What figures of speech are more prevalent in "The Isles at Large"? Comment on the function and effectiveness of two or three examples.

CONSIDERATIONS

1. Do natural environments possess the kinds of moral qualities that Melville describes in *The Isles at Large?* If the Galapagos are a kind of hell (as even Darwin agrees), what is your idea of a natural paradise? Write a paragraph in which you outline its features.

2. Write several paragraphs or a brief essay in which you present an impression of a specific environment and its influence on you.

3. Without censoring any impressions, keep a daily journal devoted to a particular activity. After a week, write both a summary objective report based on your entries and a brief impressionistic essay that presents your reaction to the recorded events.

Margaret Mead

(United States; 1901–1978)

Renowned anthropologist Margaret Mead was born into a family of social scientists. Her father was a professor of economics, her mother a sociologist, and her paternal grandmother an early child psychologist. Mead, however, was more interested in art and literature until she came under the influence of anthropologists Franz Boas and Ruth Benedict while attending Barnard College.

For most of her career, Mead was a curator for the American Museum of Natural History in New York. She published her first book, Coming of Age in Samoa *(1928), two years after beginning work at the museum and a year before receiving her doctorate from Columbia University.*

Much of Mead's work in social anthropology was done in the South Pacific. In addition to Samoans, she studied groups in New Guinea, the Admiralty Islands, and Bali. Growing Up in New Guinea *(1930) and* Sex and Temperament in Three Primitive Societies *(1935) are the results of these investigations.*

Building on such research, her later career centered on broader topics. In Male and Female *(1949) she explored the issue of sexual behavior and role formation. A cultural determinist, Mead believed that our sexual roles and expression are essentially controlled by the society in which we live. Decades later she joined essayist-novelist James Baldwin in writing* A Rap on Race *(1971). Throughout her life, Mead was identified with feminist causes and, besides race, such issues as overpopulation and hunger.*

In recent years, Mead's objectivity and therefore the results of her investigations have sometimes been called into question. The tone of the present selection is undoubtedly more poetic than conventionally scientific, but here, at least, Mead is frankly creating an impression.

A Day in Samoa

THE LIFE OF THE DAY begins at dawn, or if the moon has shown until daylight, the shouts of the young men may be heard before dawn from the hillside. Uneasy in the night, populous with ghosts, they shout lustily to one another as they hasten with their work. As the dawn begins to fall among the soft brown roofs and the slender palm trees stand out against a colourless, gleaming sea, lovers slip home from trysts beneath the palm trees or in the shadow of beached canoes, that the light may find each sleeper in his appointed place. Cocks crow, negligently, and a shrill-voiced bird cries from the breadfruit trees. The insistent roar of the reef seems muted to an undertone for the sounds of a waking village. Babies cry, a few short wails before sleepy mothers give them the breast. Restless little children roll out of their sheets and wander drowsily down to the beach to freshen their faces in the sea. Boys, bent upon an early fishing, start collecting their tackle and go to rouse their more laggard companions. Fires are lit, here and there, the white smoke hardly visible against the paleness of the dawn. The whole village, sheeted and frowsy, stirs, rubs its eyes, and stumbles towards the beach. "Talofa!" "Talofa!" "Will the journey start to-day?" "Is it bonito fishing our lordship is going?" Girls stop to giggle over some young ne'er-do-well who escaped during the night from an angry father's pursuit and to venture a shrewd guess that the daughter knew more about his presence than she told. The boy who is taunted by another, who has succeeded him in his sweetheart's favour, grapples with his rival, his foot slipping in the wet sand. From the other end of the village comes a long drawn-out, piercing wail. A messenger has just brought word of the death of some relative in another village. Half-clad, unhurried women, with babies at their breasts, or astride their hips, pause in their tale of Losa's outraged departure from her father's house to the greater kindness in the home of her uncle, to wonder who is dead. Poor relatives whisper their requests to rich relatives, men make plans to set a fish trap together, a woman begs a bit of yellow dye from a kinswoman, and through the village sounds the rhythmic tattoo which calls the young men together. They gather from all parts of the village, digging sticks in hand, ready to start inland to the plantation. The older men set off upon their more lonely occupations, and each household, reassembled under its peaked roof, settles down to the routine of the morning. Little children, too hungry to wait for the late breakfast, beg lumps of cold taro which they munch greedily. Women carry piles of washing to the sea or to the spring at the far end of the village, or set off inland after weaving materials. The older girls go fishing on the reef, or perhaps set themselves to weaving a new set of Venetian blinds.

In the houses, where the pebbly floors have been swept bare with a stiff long-handled broom, the women great with child and the nursing mothers, sit and gossip with one another. Old men sit apart, unceasingly twisting palm husk on their bare thighs and muttering old tales under their breath. The carpenters begin work on the new house, while the owner bustles about trying to keep them in a good humour. Families who will cook today are hard at work; the taro, yams and bananas have already been brought from inland; the children are scuttling back and forth, fetching sea water, or leaves to stuff the pig. As the sun rises higher in the sky, the shadows deepen under the thatched roofs, the sand is burning to the touch, the hibiscus flowers wilt on the hedges, and little children bid the smaller ones, "Come out of the sun." Those whose excursions have been short return to the village, the women with strings of crimson jelly fish, or baskets of shell fish, the men with cocoanuts, carried in baskets slung on a shoulder pole. The women and children eat their breakfasts, just hot from the oven, if this is cook day, and the young men work swiftly in the midday heat, preparing the noon feast for their elders.

It is high noon. The sand burns the feet of the little children, who leave their palm leaf balls and their pin-wheels of frangipani blossoms to wither in the sun, as they creep into the shade of the houses. The women who must go abroad carry great banana leaves as sun-shades or wind wet cloths about their heads. Lowering a few blinds against the slanting sun, all who are left in the village wrap their heads in sheets and go to sleep. Only a few adventurous children may slip away for a swim in the shadow of a high rock, some industrious woman continue with her weaving, or a close little group of women bend anxiously over a woman in labour. The village is dazzling and dead; any sound seems oddly loud and out of place. Words have to cut through the solid heat slowly. And then the sun gradually sinks over the sea.

A second time, the sleeping people stir, roused perhaps by the cry of "a boat," resounding through the village. The fishermen beach their canoes, weary and spent from the heat, in spite of the slaked lime on their heads, with which they have sought to cool their brains and redden their hair. The brightly coloured fishes are spread out on the floor, or piled in front of the houses until the women pour water over them to free them from taboo. Regretfully, the young fishermen separate out the "Taboo fish," which must be sent to the chief, or proudly they pack the little palm leaf baskets with offerings of fish to take to their sweethearts. Men come home from the bush, grimy and heavy laden, shouting as they come, greeted in a sonorous rising cadence by those who have remained at home. They gather in the guest house for their evening kava drinking. The soft clapping of hands, the high-pitched intoning of the talking chief who serves the kava echoes through the village, Girls gather flowers to weave into necklaces; children, lusty from their naps and bound to no particular task, play circular games in the half shade of the late afternoon. Finally the sun sets, in a flame which stretches from the mountain behind to the horizon on the sea, the last bather comes up from the beach, children straggle home, dark little figures etched against the sky; lights shine in the houses, and each household gathers for its evening meal. The suitor humbly presents his offering, the children have been summoned from their noisy play, perhaps there is an honoured guest who must be served first, after the soft, barbaric singing of Christian hymns and the brief and graceful evening prayer. In front of a house at the end of the village, a father cries out the birth of a son. In some family circles a face is missing, in others little runaways have found a haven! Again quiet settles upon the village, as first the head of the household, then the women and children, and last of all the patient boys, eat their supper.

After supper the old people and the little children are bundled off to bed. 5 If the young people have guests the front of the house is yielded to them. For day is the time for the councils of old men and the labours of youth, and night is the time for lighter things. Two kinsmen, or a chief and his councillor, sit and gossip over the day's events or make plans for the morrow. Outside a crier goes through the village announcing that the communal breadfruit pit will be opened in the morning, or that the village will make a great fish trap. If it is moonlight, groups of young men, women by twos and threes, wander through the village, and crowds of children hunt for land crabs or chase each other among the breadfruit trees. Half the village may go fishing by torchlight and the curving reef will gleam with wavering lights and echo with shouts of triumph or disappointment, teasing words or smothered cries of outraged modesty. Or a group of youths may dance for the pleasure of some visiting maiden. Many of those who have retired to sleep, drawn by the merry music, will wrap their sheets about them and set out to find the dancing. A white-clad, ghostly throng will gather in a circle about the gaily lit house, a circle from which every now and then a few will detach themselves and wander away among he trees. Sometimes sleep will not descend upon the village until long past midnight; then at last there is only the mellow thunder of the reef and the whisper of lovers, as the village rests until dawn.

Thesis and Thought

1. Does this selection have a thesis? If so, state it. If not, what is Mead's purpose in writing the description?
2. What do we learn about Samoan culture from this account? Consider such topics as occupations and division of labor, parent-child relationships, recreation, and so on.

Structure

1. What simple structural device does Mead use to organize her description and provide **unity** to the whole?
2. Considering Mead's structural and thematic purposes, why is it appropriate for the essay to begin and end with dawn?

Style

1. Find three instances of Mead's auditory imagery in paragraph 1 and comment on their effectiveness. Do the same for the tactile images in paragraphs 2 and 3.
2. Mead writes: "The whole village, sheeted and frowsy, stirs, rubs its eyes, and stumbles towards the beach" (para. 1). Is she using personification here?

Explain whether your answer would be the same if instead of *its* and *stumbles* she had written *their* and *stumble*.

3. Is the line in paragraph 3, "The village is dazzling and dead," in any sense paradoxical?

4. In paragraph 4 Mead refers to "the soft, barbaric singing of Christian hymns." Is the term *barbaric* pejorative or derogatory? Look up the word in a standard dictionary to discover its origin.

5. It is usually a good idea to vary the patterns of your sentences. Mead's, however, vary only slightly. How are her relatively monotonous sentences useful in this case?

CONSIDERATIONS

1. Basing your response on this reading alone, explain why you would or would not care to live in Samoa.

2. Using only the reading as your source, write a brief *objective* description of one aspect of Samoan life presented here. See question 2 under "Thesis and Thought" for some suggestions.

3. With "A Day in Samoa" as a model, write an *impressionistic* description of a day in a place with which you are familiar. Like Mead, try to reveal the nature of life there rather than particular events.

Dylan Thomas
(Wales; 1914–1953)

Dylan Thomas was among the most romantic literary figures of the twentieth century, in great part through his own mythmaking. Although married for seventeen years before his death, he projected the public image of the great lover. Never in good health, he envisioned an early death, which his excessive drinking helped promote. His income, derived principally from scriptwriting, reading for the BBC, and occasional acting, was never great, but mismanagement as well as poverty sent him into debt. He attempted to extricate himself by giving public readings in the United States, where he was extremely popular. It was during his last tour that he died in New York City in consequence of an alcohol overdose.

Thomas's formal education ended at the Swansea grammar school where his father taught. However, he steeped himself in poetry and by his early twenties published work that brought him to public prominence, although he had already earned some reputation as a poet through his radio broadcasts.

Many of Thomas's poems deal with childhood and lost innocence ("Fern Hill"), creative energy ("The force that through the green fuse drives the flower" and "In my Craft or Sullen Art"), and death ("Do not go gentle into that good night" and "A Refusal to Mourn the Death, by Fire, of a Child in London"). They are characterized by their vivid imagery and astounding musicality in original rhythms and other creative uses of sound. Thomas published his Collected Poems in 1952.

Among his prose works are a series of autobiographical sketches, such as the one presented here, and Under Milk Wood, "a play for voices," which has been performed on radio and in staged productions. The play has many affinities with "Quite Early One Morning" in regard to setting, imagery, and even specific characters—most notably Mrs. Ogmore-Pritchard.

"Quite Early One Morning" should be read with ears as well as eyes.

Quite Early One Morning

QUITE EARLY ONE MORNING in the winter in Wales, by the sea that was lying down still and green as grass after a night of tar-black howling and rolling, I went out of the house, where I had come to stay for a cold unseasonable holiday, to see if it was raining still, if the outhouse had been blown away, potatoes, shears, rat-killer, shrimpnets, and tins of rusty nails aloft on the wind, and if all the cliffs were left. It had been such a ferocious night that someone in the smoky ship-pictured bar had said he could feel his tombstone shaking even though he was not dead or, at least, was moving; but the morning shone as clear and calm as one always imagines tomorrow will shine.

The sun lit the sea-town, not as a whole—from topmost down—zinc-roofed chapel to empty but for rats and whispers grey warehouse on the harbour, but in separate bright pieces. There, the quay shouldering out, nobody on it now but the gulls and the capstans like small men in tubular trousers. Here, the roof of the police station, black as a helmet, dry as a summons, sober as Sunday. There, the splashed church, with a cloud in the shape of a bell poised above it, ready to drift and ring. Here, the chimneys of the pink-washed pub, the pub that was waiting for Saturday night as an overjolly girl waits for sailors.

The town was not yet awake. The milkman lay still, lost in the clangour and music of his Welsh-spoken dreams, the wish-fulfilled tenor voices, more powerful than Caruso's, sweeter than Ben Davies's, thrilling past Cloth Hall and Manchester House up to the frosty hills.

The town was not yet awake. Babies in upper bedrooms of salt-white houses dangling over water, or of bow-windowed villas squatting prim in neatly treed but unsteady hill-streets, worried the light with their half-in-sleep cries. Miscellaneous retired sea-captains emerged for a second from deeper waves than ever tossed their boats, then drowned again, going down, down into a perhaps Mediterranean-blue cabin of sleep, rocked to the sea-beat of their years. Landladies, shawled and bloused and aproned with sleep in the curtained, bombasined-black of their once spare rooms, remembered their loves, their bills, their visitors dead, decamped, or buried in English deserts till the trumpet of next expensive August roused them again to the world of holiday rain, dismal cliff and sand seen through the weeping windows of front parlours, tasselled tablecloths, stuffed pheasants, ferns in pots, fading photographs of the bearded and censorious dead, autograph albums with a look of limp and colourless beribboned hair, lolling out between the thick black boards.

The town was not yet awake. Birds sang in eaves, bushes, trees, on   5
telegraph wires, rails, fences, spars and wet masts, not for love or joy, but to keep other birds away. The landlords in feathers disputed the right of even the flying light to descend and perch.

The town was not yet awake, and I walked through the streets like a stranger come out of the sea, shrugging off weed and wave and darkness with each step, or like an inquisitive shadow, determined to miss nothing: not the preliminary tremor in the throat of the dawn-saying cock or the first whirring nudge of arranged time in the belly of the alarm clock on the trinketed chest of drawers under the knitted text and the done-by-hand water colours of Porthcawl or Trinidad.

I walked past the small sea-spying windows, behind whose trim curtains lay mild-mannered men and women not yet awake and, for all I could know, terrible and violent in their dreams. In the head of Miss Hughes "The Cosy" clashed the cymbals of an Eastern court. Eunuchs struck gongs the size of Bethesda Chapel. Sultans with voices fiercer than visiting preachers demanded a most un-Welsh dance. Everywhere there glowed and rayed the colours of the small, slate-grey woman's dreams: purple, magenta, ruby, sapphire, emerald, vermilion, honey. But I could not believe it. She knitted in her tidy sleep-world a beige woollen shroud with "Thou Shalt Not" on the bosom.

I could not imagine Cadwallader Davies the grocer, in his near-to-waking dream, riding on horseback, two-gunned and Cody-bold, through the cactused prairies. He added, he subtracted, he receipted, he filed a prodigious account with a candle dipped in dried egg.

What big seas of dreams ran in the Captain's sleep? Over what blue-whaled waves did he sail through a rainbow-hail of flying fishes to the music of Circe's swinish island? Do not let him be dreaming of dividends and bottled beer and onions.

Someone was snoring in one house, I counted ten savagely indignant   10
grunts-and-groans like those of a pig in a model and mudless farm, which ended with a window-rattler, a washbasin-shaker, a trembler of tooth glasses,

a waker of dormice. It thundered with me up to the chapel railings, then brassily vanished.

The chapel stood grim and grey, telling the day there was to be no nonsense. The chapel was not asleep; it never cat-napped nor nodded nor closed its long cold eye. I left it telling the morning off and a seagull hung, rebuked, above it.

And climbing down again, and up out of the town, I heard the cocks crow from hidden farmyards, from old roosts above waves, where fabulous seabirds might sit and cry, "Neptune!" And a faraway clock struck from another church, in another village, in another universe, though the wind blew the time away. And I walked in a timeless morning past a row of white cottages, almost expecting that an ancient man with a great beard and an hourglass and a scythe under his nightdressed arm might lean from a window and ask *me* the time. I would have told him: "Arise, old counter of the heartbeats of albatrosses, and wake the cavernous sleepers of the town to a dazzling new morning." I would have told him: "You unbelievable father of Eva and Dai Adam, come out, old chicken, and stir up the winter morning with your spoon of a scythe." I would have told him—I would have scampered like a scalded ghost, over the cliffs and down into the bilingual sea.

Who lived in those cottages? I was a stranger to the sea-town, fresh or stale from the city where I worked for my bread and butter, wishing it were laver-bread and country salty butter yoke-yellow. Fishermen, certainly; no painters but of boats, no man-dressed women with shooting-sticks and sketchbooks and voices like macaws, to paint the reluctant heads of critical and sturdy natives who posed by the pint, against the chapel-dark sea which would be made more blue than the Bay of Naples, though shallower.

I walked on to the cliff path again, the town behind and below waking up now so very slowly; I stopped, and turned, and looked. Smoke from one chimney. The cobbler's, I thought, but from that distance it may have been the chimney of the retired male-nurse who had come to live in Wales after many years successful wrestling with the mad rich of southern England. He was not liked. He measured you for a strait jacket, carefully, with his eye. He saw you bounce from rubber walls like a sorbo ball. No behaviour surprised him. Many people of the town found it hard to resist leering at him suddenly around the corner, or convulsively dancing, or pointing with laughter and devilish good humour to invisible dogfights, merely to prove to him that they were "normal."

Smoke from another chimney now: they were burning their last night's dreams: up from a chimney came a long-haired wraith, like an old politician: somebody had been dreaming of the Liberal party. But no, the smoky figure wove, attenuated into a refined and precise grey comma: someone had been dreaming of reading Charles Morgan.

Oh! the town was waking now and I heard distinctly, insistent over the slow-speaking sea, the voices of the town blown up to me. And some of the voices said:

15

I am Miss May Hughes "The Cosy," a lonely lady,
    waiting in her house by the nasty sea,
    waiting for her husband and pretty baby
      to come home at last from wherever they may
      be.

I am Captain Tiny Evans, my ship was the *Kidwelly,*
    and Mrs. Tiny Evans has been dead for many a
    year.
    Poor Captain Tiny all alone, the neighbours whisper,
    but I like it all alone and I hated her.

Clara Tawe Jenkins, "Madame" they call me,
    an old contralto with her dressing gown on.
    And I sit at the window and I sing to the sea,
    for the sea doesn't notice that my voice has gone.

Parchedig Thomas Evans making morning tea,   20
    very weak tea, too, you mustn't waste a leaf.
    Every morning making tea in my house by the sea,
    I am troubled by one thing only, and that's—
    Belief.

Open the curtains, light the fire, what are servants
    for?
    I am Mrs. Ogmore-Pritchard and I want another
    snooze.
    Dust the china, feed the canary, sweep the drawing-
    room floor.
    And before you let the sun in, mind he wipes his
    shoes.

I am only Mr. Griffiths, very shortsighted, B.A., Aber.
    As soon as I finish my egg I must shuffle off to
    school.
    Oh, patron saint of teachers, teach me to keep order,
    and *forget* those words on the blackboard—
    "Griffiths Bat is a fool."

Do you hear that whistling?—It's me, I am Phoebe,
    the maid at the King's Head, and I am whistling
    like a bird.
    Someone spilt a tin of pepper in the tea.
    There's twenty for breakfast, and I'm not going
    to say a word.

    Thus some of the voices of a cliff-perched town at the far end of
Wales moved out of sleep and darkness into the newborn, ancient and
ageless morning, moved and were lost.

THESIS AND THOUGHT

1. Where is the town? What seem to be its physical features and principal activities? What do we learn about the inhabitants individually and collectively?

2. Who is the narrator? How does this identity or status affect his perceptions?

3. What does the narrator think or feel about the town? On what do you base your opinion?

STRUCTURE

1. To some extent, Thomas is describing at least one process as well as a place. Identify the process and indicate its stages.

2. In paragraphs 7–9 the narrator presents imagined dreams of the sleepers. How does his vision of their inner lives compare with the statements of the residents themselves in paragraphs 17–23? Note that only Miss Hughes and, possibly, the Captain specifically appear in both sections.

3. Do the speeches of the residents in paragraphs 17–23 fundamentally alter the essay's point of view?

STYLE

1. What is the effect of the repeated opening line of paragraphs 3–6?

2. Find evidence of Thomas's humor and explain its function in creating the overall tone.

3. As a poet foremost, Thomas tends to use figurative language extensively, even in prose. Similes, metaphors, personifications, strong verbs, and strings of descriptive words abound here. Choose three descriptive passages that you find especially attractive (or overdone) and explain their effectiveness (or failure).

4. Rewrite paragraph 4 or 7, attempting to eliminate all descriptive language. Assess what you have learned about both versions for having done the exercise.

CONSIDERATIONS

1. Explain how each of the speakers at the end of the essay might have perceived the town. How (and why) might their perceptions differ from the narrator's or Thomas's? Choose one of the figures and write a description of the town through his or her eyes.

2. Walk through a familiar part of town at a quiet time of day and write an impressionistic essay in which you describe the neighborhood and imagine the lives of its unseen inhabitants.

3. Ride a bus or train for at least half an hour, studying your fellow passengers. Create and write brief, imaginary biographical sketches for three or four of them. Choose one of these and explain what suggested the "information" you include.

Khushwant Singh
(India; b. 1915)

Born in the portion of India that is now Pakistan, Singh attended universities in both India and England. Upon receiving his law degree from London's Inner Temple, he returned home to practice law for seven years before entering politics. He has served as a press attaché, staff member for UNESCO, and member of parliament.

Primarily a journalist, Singh has broadcast for Air India, the BBC, and the CBC and written for various newspapers and magazines, including the Observer (London) and the New York Times. *At home, he has edited several publications, among them the* Illustrated Weekly of India, *the* National Herald, *and the* Hindustan Times.

Singh's best-known fiction is Train to Pakistan *(1956), a novel rooted in the chaos and strife that accompanied the partition of India and Pakistan in 1947. He has, in addition, written short stories and done a number of translations from Indian languages into English.*

Much of Singh's nonfiction has been devoted to the history and religion of the Sikhs, a group of which he himself is a member. Most prominent are A History of the Sikhs: 1469–1964 *(1963–1966) and* The Sikhs Today, *third edition (1985).*

"The Haunted Simla Road," originally published in the Observer, *appeared in the collection of short pieces called* Singh's India: A Mirror for Its Monsters and Monstrosities *(1969). In what way the road is haunted and whether it is monstrous are two questions you might ask yourself as you read.*

The Haunted Simla Road

MANY YEARS AGO the bells of St. Crispin woke up the people of Mashobra on Sunday mornings. We threw open our windows and let the chimes flood into the room along with the sunlight. We watched the English folk coming from the hotels and houses for service. It was the only day in the week they were up before the local inhabitants. All morning, visitors continued to pour in from Simla in rickshaws, on horseback and on foot. At evensong when the religious were at prayer once more, the road to Simla echoed with songs and laughter of people returning to the city.

The bells of St. Crispin do not toll any more. The lychgate is padlocked and there is mildew on the golden letters of the church notice board. The haunts of the English holiday-makers, "Wild Flower Hall" and "Gables," have not had their shutters down since they were put up in the autumn of 1947. The only white people about are a couple of elderly missionary ladies who walk about briskly, stopping occasionally to inspect a wild flower, inhale the crisp mountain air holding their arms stiff on their sides with beatific expressions on their upturned faces. There is a young English writer in khaki shorts and sandals getting the feel of the country liquor shop. Sometimes Italian priests from the monastery of San Damiano stray into the bazar to buy provisions.

Apart from the people little else has changed. There is the deckle-edged snow-line beyond the peaks of Shali in the north, and vast plains of Hindustan towards the south; one can see the Sutlej winding its silvery serpentine course through the orange haze. There are the dense forests of deodar, fir and mountain hemlocks. There are the terraced fields with clusters of villages in their midst—and flat roofs with corn drying on them. All day long the lammergeiers circle in the deep blue of the sky or sit on crags amongst the rhododendrons sunning themselves with their wings stretched out. Barbets call in the valleys and the cicadas drown the distant roar of the stream with their chirpings. Convoys of mules bell their way endlessly into the Himalayas with the muleteer's plaintive flute receding in the distance. A hill-woman's song rises above all other sounds and for one ecstatic minute fills the hills and valleys with its long melodious monotone. It ends abruptly and there again are the barbet, cicada, mule bells, the flute and the roar of the stream.

There are things that make you pause and wonder whether the British have really left. Houses which look like English country homes are still unoccupied and give the impression that they await their departed masters. Local inhabitants never tire of gassing about Mem Sahibs who did their shopping in the bazar. Even now the Bania will slip into quoting price for the pound instead of the seer or kilogram. An asthmatic old Singhalese who made jams and pickles for hotel residents still refers wheezily to England as home and presses his syrupy rhubarb wines on his listeners with a toothless "doch and dorres." One comes across names and pierced hearts on trunks of trees that tell tales of romance which lichen and moss have not obliterated. Then there is the cuckoo—the English cuckoo with its two distinct notes which people say was imported by an Englishman in a fit of nostalgia.

In the evening when the mules are tethered and muleteers sip tea or smoke their hookahs they tell of the many foreigners who had lived in and around Mashobra. The eccentric American missionary who converted the whole of the apple-growing valley of Kotgarh to Christianity and then converted them back to Hinduism; of an ayah who still haunts the house in which she was murdered by her master's wife; of the people who had simply abandoned homes they had built and lived in for many years because they could not be bothered to come back from England; of phantom rickshaws and phantom ladies riding side-saddle on phantom horses.

It is a long walk back from Mashrobra to Simla. The road is deserted after sunset and only the lights of the city scattered in profusion on Jacko Hill keep your spirits up. On the right is the Koti Valley with its stream glistening like quick-silver and the soft glow of oil lamps that come on unnoticed in distant farmsteads. There is something which makes you keep looking back over your shoulder. You hear the stamp of rickshaw pullers' feet and whiffs of perfume and cigar-smell steal mysteriously across the moon-flecked road—and your heart is too full for words.

THESIS AND THOUGHT

1. By what is the road "haunted"?
2. What evidence of the British presence in Mashobra remains? Include—but go beyond—physical artifacts.
3. Explain the last line of the essay.

STRUCTURE

1. Is Singh's description generally objective or impressionistic? To what purpose? Compare the degree of objectivity and impression in paragraphs 2 and 3.
2. The first two paragraphs, even in their initial sentences, are an obvious contrast. What more general comparison do they reflect?

STYLE

1. Which of Singh's words are uncommon or unknown in American English? Which of these are British terms? Which indigenous to India? Use an unabridged dictionary or the *Oxford English Dictionary* if necessary.
2. Comment on the effect or effectiveness of each of the following:
   a. the use of *bell* as a verb in "Convoys of mules bell their way endlessly into the Himalayas. . . . " (para. 3)
   b. the sounds and rhythm of "A hill-woman's song rises above all other sounds and for one ecstatic minute fills the hills and valleys with its long melodious monotone." (para. 3)

c.   the use of *gassing* in "Local inhabitants never tire of gassing about Mem Sahibs who did their shopping in the bazar." (para. 4)

3.   Singh seems to write in various grammatical persons, using first-person plural ("we") at the start of paragraph 1, third person generally throughout, and second person ("you") at the opening of paragraph 4 and at the very end of the essay. Are these apparent shifts at all functional? Consistently so?

CONSIDERATIONS

1.   Examine the essay in light of the following stanzas from a short poem by Tennyson. Might its sentiments explain the essay's nostalgia? If not, what do you think does?

>   Tears, idle tears, I know not what they mean,
> Tears from the depth of some divine despair
> Rise in the heart, and gather to the eyes,
> In looking on the happy autumn-fields,
> And thinking of the days that are no more.
>   ....
>   Dear as remember'd kisses after death,
> And sweet as those by hopeless fancy feign'd
> On lips that are for others; deep as love,
> Deep as first love, and wild with all regret;
> O Death in Life, the days that are no more!

2.   It has been said that few things are so boring as the nostalgia of others. Does the essay avoid this "nostalgia trap"? If so, how? If not, why does it fail?

3.   Do you suppose that after the American Revolution, citizens at all "missed" the British presence? That Europeans outside of France "missed" the Napoleonic presence after 1815? That the subject peoples "missed" the Romans after the empire's decay and collapse? How and to what extent might the presence of an occupying power become essential to the vitality of a native population?

4.   Using contrast between present and past as background, write an essay in which you express your nostalgia for a particular time or place and keep the active interest of your readers.

Doris Lessing

(England; b. 1919)

Although Doris Lessing has resided in England since 1949, she was born in Iran, where her father served in the British army, and in the quarter century between 1924 and 1949 lived in the former Rhodesia. There she attended a convent school until she was fourte, worked as an au pair, was a secretary for the Rhodesian government, married twice, had three children, and became involved with Marxist politics. Her efforts to achieve racial justice, stemming from both her childhood perceptions and political awareness, eventually made her persona non grata in southern Africa. Not surprisingly, African settings—from her first novel, The Grass Is Singing (1950), to collections such as The Sun Between Their Feet (1973), whose title story appears here— are prominent in her work.

In addition to individual novels or story collections, the prolific Lessing has written two series of books, one set in southern Africa and published collectively as Children of Violence (1964–1965) and the five-part Canopus in Argos: Archives (1974–1983). The last is characteristic of the later phase of her work, in which she turns frequently to fantasy and science fiction.

Among other prominent themes or features of her writing are her feminism and left-wing political views, which have been somewhat moderated over time. The Good Terrorist (1985), for example, focuses on a group of revolutionaries living in London but in part questions their zealous idealism. In addition to fiction, Lessing has also written plays.

Observe, as you read, the persistence of both the narrator and the subjects of her observation.

The Sun Between Their Feet

THE ROAD FROM THE BACK of the station went to the Roman Catholic Mission, which was a dead-end, being in the middle of a Native Reserve. It was a poor mission, with only one lorry, so the road was always deserted, a track of sand between long or short grasses. The station itself was busy with trains and people, and the good country in front was settled thick with white farmers, but all the country behind the station was unused because it was granite boulders, outcrops, and sand. The scrub cattle from the Reserve strayed there. There were no human beings. From the track it seemed the hills of boulders were so steep and laced with vines and weed there would be no place to go between them. But you could force your way in, and there it became clear that in the past people had made use of this wilderness. For one thing there were the remains of earth and rock defences built by the Mashona against the Matabele when they came raiding after cattle and women before Rhodes put an end to all that.[1] For another, the under-surfaces of the great boulders were covered with Bushmen paintings. After a hundred yards or so of clambering and squeezing there came a flattish sandy stretch before the boulders erupted again. In this space, at the time of the raiding, the women

[1]Since writing this I have understood that this version of history is not necessarily the true one. Some Mashona authorities dispute it. [Au.]

and the cattle would have been kept while the men held the surrounding defences. From this space, at the time of the Bushmen, small hunting-men took coloured clays, and earths, and plant juices for their pictures.

It had rained last night and the low grass was still wet around my ankles and the early sun had not dried the sand. There was a sharp upjut of rock in the middle of the space. The rock was damp, and I could feel the wet heat being dragged up past my bare legs.

Sitting low here, the encircling piles of boulders seemed like mountains, heightening the sky on tall horizons. The rocks were dark grey, but stained with lichens. The trees between the boulders were meagre, and several were lightning-struck, no more than black skeletons. This was hungry country, growing sand and thin grass and rocks and heat. The sun came down hard between heat-conserving rocks. After an hour of sun the sand between the grasses showed a clean, dry glistening surface, and a dark wet underneath.

The Reserve cattle must have moved here since the rains last night, for there were a score of fresh cow pats laid on the grass. Big blue flies swore and tumbled over them, breaking the crust the sun had baked. The air was heavy and sweet. The buzzing of the flies, the tiny sucking sound of the heat, the cooing of the pigeons, made a morning silence.

Hot, and silent; and save for the flies, no movement anywhere, for what winds there were blew outside this sheltered space.   5

But soon there was new movement. Where the flies had broken the crust of the nearest dung-clot, two beetles were at work. They were small, dusty, black, round-bodied beetles. One had set his back legs over a bit of dung and was heaving and levering at it. The other, with a fast rolling movement, the same that a hen makes settling roused feathers over eggs, was using his body to form the ball even before it was heaved clear of the main lump of matter. As soon as the piece was freed, both beetles assaulted it with legs and bodies, modelling fast, frantic with creation, seizing it between their back legs, spinning it, rolling it under them, both tugging and pushing it through the thick encumbering grass stems that rose over them like forest trees until at last the ball rolled away from them into a plain, or glade, or inch-wide space of sand. The two beetles scuttled about among the steins, looking for their property. They were on the point of starting again on the mother-pile of muck, when one of them saw the ball lying free in the open, and both ran after it.

All over the grassy space around the cow pats, dung-beetles were at work, the blowflies hustled and buzzed, and by night all the new cow-stomach-worked grass would be lifted away, rolled away, to feed flies, beetles and new earth. That is, unless it rained hard again, when everything would be scattered by rods of rain.

But there was no sign of rain yet. The sky was the clear slow blue of African mornings after night-storms. My two beetles had the sky on their side. They had all day.

The book says that dung-beetles form a ball of dung, lay their eggs in it, search for a gentle slope, roll the ball up it, and then allow it to roll down again so that in the process of rolling 'the pellet becomes compacted'.

Why must the pellet be compacted? Presumably so that the blows of sun   10 and rain do not belt it to fragments. Why this complicated business of rolling up and rolling down?

Well, it is not for us to criticize the processes of nature; so I sat on top of the jutting rock, and watched the beetles rolling the ball towards it. In a few minutes of work they had reached it, and had hurled themselves and the dung-ball at its foot. Their momentum took them a few inches up the slope, then they slipped, and ball and beetles rolled back to the flat again.

I got down off the rock, and sat in the grass behind them to view the ascent through their eyes.

The rock was about four feet long and three feet high. It was a jutting slab of granite, wooded and lichened, its edges blunted by rain and by wind. The beetles, hugging their ball between legs and bellies, looked up to a savage mountain, whose first slopes were an easy foot-assisting invitation. They rolled their ball, which was now crusted with dirt, to a small ridge under the foothills, and began, this time with slow care, to hitch it up from ridge to ridge, from one crust of lichen to the next. One beetle above, one below, they cherished their ball upwards. Soon they met the obstruction that had defeated them before: a sudden upswelling in the mountain wall. This time, one remained below the ball, holding its weight on its back legs, while the other scouted off sideways to find an easier path. It returned, gripped the ball with its legs, and the two beetles resumed their difficult, sideways scrambling progress, up around the swell in the rock into a small valley which led, or so it seemed, into the second great stage of the ascent. But this valley was a snare, for there was a crevasse across it. The mountain was riven. Heat and cold had split it to its base, and the narrow crack sloped down to a mountain lake full of warm fresh water over a bed of wind-gathered leaves and grass. The dung-ball slipped over the edge of the crevasse into the gulf, and rolled gently into the lake where it was supported at its edge by a small fringe of lichen. The beetles flung themselves after it. One, straddling desperate legs from a raft of reed to the shore, held the ball from plunging into the depths of the lake. The other, gripping fast with its front legs to a thick bed of weed on shore, grappled the ball with its black legs, and together they heaved and shoved that precious dung out of the water and back into the ravine. But now the mountain walls rose high on either side, and the ball lay between them. The beetles remained still a moment. The dirt had been washed from the dung, and it was smooth and slippery.

They consulted. Again one remained on guard while the other scouted, returning to report that if they rolled the ball clear along the bottom of the ravine, this would in due course narrow, and they could, by use of legs and shoulders and backs, lift the ball up the crack to a new height on the mountain and, by crossing another dangerous shoulder, attain a gentle weed-roughed slope that led to the summit. This they tried. But on the dangerous shoulder there was a disaster. The lake-slippery ball left their grasp and plunged down the mountain-side to the ground, to the point they had started from half an hour before. The two beetles flung themselves after it, and again they began their slow difficult climb. Again their dung-ball fell into the crevasse, rolled down into the lake, and again they rescued it, at the cost of infinite resource and patience, again they pushed and pulled it up the ravine, again they manoeuvred it up the crack, again they tried to roll it around the mountain's sharp shoulder, and again it fell back to the foot of the mountains, and they plunged after it.

"The dung-beetle, *Scarabaeus* or *Aleuchus sacer,* lays its eggs in a ball of   15
dung, then chooses a gentle slope, and compacts the pellet by pushing it uphill backwards with its hind legs and allowing it to roll down, eventually reaching its place of deposit."

I continued to sit in the low, hot grass, feeling the sun first on my back, then hard down on my shoulders, and then direct from above on my head. The air was dry now, all the moisture from the night had gone up into the air. Clouds were packing the lower skies. Even the small pool in the rock was evaporating. Above it the air quivered with steam. When, for the third time, the beetles lost their ball in the mountain lake, it was no lake, but a spongy marsh, and getting it out involved no danger or difficulty. Now the ball was sticky, had lost its shape, and was crusted with bits of leaf and grass.

At the fourth attempt, when the ball rolled down to the starting point and the beetles bundled after it, it was past midday, my head ached with heat, and I took a large leaf, slipped it under the ball of dung and the beetles, and lifted this unit away to one side, away from the impossible and destructive mountain.

But when I slid the leaf from under them, they rested a moment in the new patch of territory, scouted this way and that among the grass-stems, found their position, and at once rolled their ball back to the foot of the mountain where they prepared another ascent.

Meanwhile, the cow pats on the grass had been dismantled by flies and other dung-beetles. Nothing remained but small grassy fragments, or dusty brown stains on the lifting stems. The buzzing of the flies was silenced. The pigeons were stilled by the heat. Far away thunder rolled, and sometimes there was the shriek of a train at the station or the puffing and clanging of shunting engines.

The beetles again got the ball up into the ravine, and this time it rolled   20
down, not into a marsh, but into a damp bed of leaves. There they rested awhile in a steam of heat.

Sacred beetles, these, the sacred beetles of the Egyptians, holding the symbol of the sun between their busy stupid feet. Busy, silly beetles, mothering their ball of dung again and again up a mountain when a few minutes march to one side would take them clear of it.

Again I lifted them, dung and beetles, away from the precipice, to a clear place where they had the choice of a dozen suitable gentle slopes, but they rolled their ball patiently back to the mountain's foot.

"The slope is chosen," says the book, "by a beautiful instinct, so that the ball of dung comes to rest in a spot suitable for the hatching of the new generation of sacred insect."

The sun had now rolled past midday position and was shining on to my face. Sweat scattered off me. The air snapped with heat. The sky where the sun would go down was banked high with darkening cloud. Those beetles would have to hurry not to get drowned.

They continued to roll the dung up the mountain, rescue it from the   25
dried bed of the mountain lake, and force it up to the exposed dry shoulder. It rolled down and they plunged after it. Again and again and again, while the ball became a ragged drying structure of fragmented grass clotted with dung. The afternoon passed. The sun was low in my eyes. I could hardly see the beetles or the dung because of the glare from a black pack of clouds which were red-rimmed from the lowering sun behind. The red streaming rays came down and the black beetles and their dung-ball on the mountain side seemed dissolved in sizzling light.

It was raining away on the far hills. The drumming of the rain and the drumming of the thunder came closer. I could see the skirmishing side-lances of an army of rain pass half a mile away beyond the rocks. A few great shining drops fell here, and hissed on burning sand and on the burning mountain-side. The beetles laboured on.

The sun dropped behind the piled boulders and now this glade rested in a cool, spent light, the black trees and black boulders standing around it, waiting for the rain and for the night. The beetles were again on the mountain. They had the ball tight between their legs, they clung on to the lichens, they clung on to rock-wall and their treasure with the desperation of stupidity.

Now the hard red glare was gone it was possible to see them clearly. It was difficult to imagine the perfect shining globe the ball had been—it was now nothing more than a bit of refuse. There was a clang of thunder. The grasses hissed and swung as a bolt of wind come fast from the sky. The wind hit the ball of dung, it fell apart into a small puff of dusty grass, and the beetles ran scurrying over the surface of the rock looking for it.

Now the rain came marching towards us, it reached the boulders in a grey envelopment of wet. The big shining drops, outrunners of the rain-army, reached the beetles' mountain and one, two! the drops hit the beetles smack, and they fell off the rock into the already seething wet grasses at its foot.

I ran out of the glade with the rain sniping at my heels and my shoulders,   30
thinking of the beetles lying under the precipice up which, tomorrow, after the rain had stopped, and the cattle had come grazing, and the sun had come out, they would again labour and heave a fresh ball of dung.

Thesis and Thought

1. Account for the narrator's interest in the beetles.

2. Why is the ball of dung "the symbol of the sun" (para. 21)?

3. Why does the narrator interfere and to what effect? Why do the beetles fail to take advantage of the opportunities she presents them?

4. The narrator's story is about the beetles. Is Lessing's story in any way about the narrator? Thematically speaking, about anything else?

Structure

1. We are introduced to the beetles in paragraph 6. What is accomplished in the first five paragraphs? What, particularly, is the purpose of the opening paragraph?

2. There are two processes at work here: the passage of time and the activity of the beetles. How do these affect the condition of the ball of dung? How is its condition significant? To what inevitabilities are the two processes bound?

3. In paragraphs 9, 15, and 23 the narrator cites passages in a book that describes the behavior of dung beetles. How do these relate to what the narrator herself sees and describes? Is their presence in any way ironic?

Style

1. Examine paragraphs 3, 16, and 26, and explain how Lessing achieves her effects in describing environmental conditions.

2. Lessing periodically coins a word (*upjut*, para. 2) or fuses two or more to create an original term (*mother-pile*, para. 6). Find one or two other novel constructions and discuss whether these are effective.

3. In paragraph 12, the narrator decides "to view the ascent" through the beetles' eyes. To what extent does paragraph 13 illustrate this approach? Does the narrator maintain it consistently thereafter? Among other things, consider the use of personification—for example, in "they consulted" (para. 14)—and the attitude toward the beetles in paragraphs 21 and 27.

4. In *The Insect Comedy*, an early twentieth-century play by Karel and Josef Čapek, a pair of dung beetles are depicted as symbols of greed, accumulating an ever larger ball—their "precious pile"—only to bitterly lament its loss when it is stolen. Again, in a chapter in *Walden*, Henry David Thoreau presents an allegorical battle between two "armies" of ants fighting over minuscule territory, by which means he ridicules human warfare. Are Lessing's insects at all symbolic?

CONSIDERATIONS

1. Humans sometimes behave as if they were dung beetles in running (to change species) an endless "rat race," walking "the treadmill to oblivion," or banging their heads against stone walls (or mountains). Write an essay about such persistent unproductive or counterproductive human behavior, perhaps using people you know.

2. Observe the activity of insects, spiders, or small wild animals (squirrels, chipmunks, and so on) and write either a clinical or impressionistic description of their behavior.

3. How, generally, do people in the United States react to the presence of insects or spiders? Why? Does the response vary with the species or with the stage of development (e.g., caterpillars as opposed to butterflies)? Do people in other countries or cultures react differently? Explain. Write a humorous essay on the topic "Maggots: Man's Best Friend," "The Care and Feeding of Roaches," or one of your own devising. If you find little amusing in these creatures, write a paper in which you describe your feelings and reactions to them—for example, "Crickets Make Me Cringe." If you are familiar with reactions to insects in a non-Western culture, write an essay in which you describe and perhaps account for those reactions.

────────── **Cityscapes** ──────────

Dennis Brutus
(South Africa; b. 1924)

Although born in Rhodesia (now Zimbabwe) and long resident in the United States, where he teaches at Northwestern University, Brutus was inevitably shaped by his South African experience, which extended from childhood through early middle age. His formal education was erratic, but he was regularly exposed to poetry read at home. After attending Fort Hare University College, he spent fourteen years teaching English and Afrikaans in the public high schools.

His work in the anti-apartheid movement, however, cost him his job and led to his arrest in 1963. Out on bail but continuing his open opposition, he left for Swaziland and then Mozambique. There he was detained, returned to the South African police (who shot him when he tried to escape), and sentenced to eighteen months in the Robben penal colony. Released in 1965 and forbidden to publish, Brutus went into exile.

In the United States, he continued to fight for the cause. He directed the World Campaign for the Release of South African Prisoners and was president of the South Africa Non-Racial Open Committee for Olympic Sports. In the latter capacity, he worked successfully to bar South Africa from Olympic competi-

tion. Brutus also struggled against United States government opposition to his resident status. Not until 1983 was he finally granted permission to remain as a political refugee.

Although he has written in various genres, Brutus is primarily known as a poet. His works include Letters to Martha and Other Poems from a South African Prison *(1969),* A Simple Lust *(1972),* China Poems *(1975), and* Stubborn Hope *(1978).*

Nightsong: City

Sleep well, my love, sleep well:
the harbour lights glaze over restless docks,
police cars cockroach through the tunnel streets;

from the shanties creaking iron-sheets
violence like a bug-infested rag is tossed   5
and fear is imminent as sound in the wind-swung bell;

the long day's anger pants from sand and rocks;
but for this breathing night at least;
my land, my love, sleep well.

William Wordsworth
(England; 1770–1850)

Along with Samuel Taylor Coleridge (author of "The Rime of the Ancient Mariner"), William Wordsworth launched the English romantic movement in poetry with the publication of Lyrical Ballads *in 1798. He had been born into an upper-middle-class family in the Lake District of northern England, and subsequently suffered the loss of both parents by the age of thirteen and the guardianship of uncles whose views on finances and education were at odds with his own.*

Although he took a degree at Cambridge, it was at grammar school that he was thoroughly grounded in poetry and allowed to explore the natural world around him—a world that would become a source and vehicle for his own poetic inspiration.

The outstanding features of his personal life were the spiritual union he shared with his sister Dorothy and Coleridge and his romantic alliance with Annette Vallon. Wordsworth met Vallon during a 1791 visit to France and soon fathered a child (Caroline) by her. Out of funds, he left for England before his daughter's birth. War between France and England prevented his return until shortly before his marriage to Mary Hutchinson in 1802. Wordsworth, however, henceforth kept a discreet distance, although he made some financial provision for Caroline upon her marriage.

At first strongly republican in his political views, Wordsworth was later condemned by some—including Robert Browning—for betraying freedom's cause. His new conservatism earned him a place in the good graces of the British government and appointment as poet laureate in 1843, decades after most of his best work had appeared.

Among his best-known works are The Prelude, an autobiographical poem of extraordinary length, and the far more accessible "Ode on the Intimations of Immortality," "Tintern Abbey," a group of lyrics known as the "Lucy" poems, and miscellaneous sonnets—of which the following lines are an example.

Composed upon Westminster Bridge

SEPTEMBER 3, 1802

Earth has not anything to show more fair:
Dull would he be of soul who could pass by
A sight so touching in its majesty:
This city now doth, like a garment, wear
The beauty of the morning; silent, bare,   5
Ships, towers, domes, theatres, and temples lie
Open unto the fields, and to the sky;
All bright and glittering in the smokeless air.
Never did sun more beautifully steep
In his first splendour, valley, rock, or hill;   10
Ne'er saw I, never felt, a calm so deep!
The river glideth at his own sweet will:
Dear God! the very houses seem asleep;
And all that mighty heart is lying still!

THESIS AND THOUGHT

1. Describe each poet's vision of the city central to his poem.
2. How does the time of day contribute to each poem's significance?
3. Compare the nature of the tranquility at the ends of the two poems.

STRUCTURE

1. Wordsworth's poem is an Italian sonnet, which is divided into an eight-line introduction (octave) with one rhyme pattern and a six-line conclusion (sestet) with another. How do the last six lines contrast with, comment on, or respond to the first eight?

2. Describe the pattern of "Nightsong: City." Does the arrangement of ideas parallel the stanzaic form? Where would you begin and end paragraphs if you were writing this as prose?

STYLE

1. Which key words and images create the dominant impression in Wordsworth's piece? Which in Brutus's?

2. Are Wordsworth's exclamations in the sestet necessary or useful?

3. What is unusual about the use of the word *cockroach* in line 3 of "Nightsong: City"? Explain the simile "fear is imminent as sound in the wind-swung bell" (l. 6). How do the rhythms and vowel sounds contribute to the meaning of line 7?

4. What in the vocabulary or sentence structure of "Composed upon Westminster Bridge" seems archaic? Does it affect your understanding or appreciation of the poem?

CONSIDERATIONS

1. Which of the two poems seems more applicable to your own city or town? Explain why.

2. Write an essay in which, as Brutus does, you express compassion for the troubles in your nation or community, or as Wordsworth does, express a feeling of awe in regard to its potential vigor.

Suggestions for Writing: Description

I. Write separate objective and impressionistic descriptions of one of the following:

—one of your professors

—a pet

—the scene from your window

—one of your possessions

—a shopkeeper, waiter, or clerk with whom you deal regularly

—a local landmark

II. Write an essay that features impressionistic description of one of the following:

—a favorite or despised food

—a contemporary political figure

—the ideal "significant other" or its opposite

—a visit to the doctor, dentist, hospital traffic court, jail, or cemetery

—a scene of childhood revisited

—an experience with a culture other than your own

III. Using any of the topics suggested above (or another of your choice), write an essay in which you achieve your effect through a governing image (metaphors or similes), personification, or hyperbole. (By definition, personification can be applied only to nonhuman subjects.)

IV. Using any combination of techniques, describe one of the human subjects suggested above (or another person of your choice) as if he or she were inanimate.

3

Example

An essay is a work of literary art which has a minimum of one anecdote and one universal idea.

CAROL BLY, *The Passionate, Accurate Story*

You are discussing the questionable fidelity of your latest love with a sympathetic friend when your companion suggests wryly, "Maybe you should get a dog instead. At least dogs are loyal."

You half-smile and snort sarcastically. Then, avoiding the painful topic for a moment and because you had only a pet rock yourself, you ask, "What makes you think dogs are so loyal?"

"Well," your friend replies, "they've been known to return to their masters after having been separated for years and by thousands of miles; they've helped rescue their owners and others from serious trouble; and sometimes they've even given up their lives. Greater love hath no human."

"Certainly not You-Know-Who," you respond, reality breaking in again.

Momentarily oblivious to the issue at hand, your friend continues: "Just a few weeks ago, an Irish setter, lost during a camping trip in the Rockies, made its way back to Sheboygan, Wisconsin, after four months. A couple of years ago, when a child fell into the shaft of an abandoned mine in Kentucky, her eight-month-old Labrador retriever practically dragged her parents to the site. And as for sacrifice, you only have to remember the attempted robbery at Snyder's last fall when that magnificent German shepherd forced the gun from the criminal's hand even after being shot."

"I don't know," you answer doubtfully. "Maybe you have a point. But the low-down, dirty dog I'm involved with is certainly no hero."

ABSTRACT GENERALIZATIONS AND CONCRETE DETAILS

We shall never know, alas, how the love problem was resolved (you are free to draw and write your own conclusions), for our interest here lies in the

127

digression—not in the topic of dogs per se, but in how the information about them is conveyed. The friend in the conversation above makes three separate statements about dogs. After the last, you are sufficiently convinced to concede the possibility of canine loyalty. Why? The answer is, roughly speaking, that the friend has moved from a broad generalization to particular instances, from an intangible abstraction to increasingly tangible concrete detail.

The first passage is most **abstract,** simply asserting the loyalty of dogs. The second is somewhat more **concrete** in presenting the kinds of behaviors that lead us to the general notion of loyalty. The third presents specific examples that demonstrate the behaviors. Once such examples have been presented, you are on your way to accepting the idea that dogs are loyal— though not quite there yet.

Specific examples and details are essential to effective writing. They clarify, vivify, and illustrate the points that you are attempting to make. In doing so, they both explain and support your ideas. This is true whether examples are the primary means for developing a piece of expository writing, as is the case in this chapter, or whether they are used in conjunction with other techniques.

REPRESENTATIVE AND SUFFICIENT EXAMPLES

At the end of the discussion above, the lovelorn speaker concedes that dogs generally might be loyal but does not fully subscribe to the idea. Putting aside any possible prejudice or hostility toward dogs and preoccupation with the traitorous "dog" in question, what more would have been needed to make the generalization wholly acceptable? Quite possibly a greater range of examples and more of them.

If they are presented fairly, examples must be representative of the idea they are intended to support or illustrate—not exceptions to rules. If dogs were, in fact, disloyal, showing rare instances of loyalty would present a distorted perspective because such examples would be atypical and would deny or ignore the overwhelming number of more usual instances. Insistence on the exceptional example may, in fact, be hazardous to your intellectual health since it could lead to stereotyping. For instance, it is unreasonable to use the play of NBA pros like Shaquille O'Neal, Larry Johnson, and Patrick Ewing as examples of the basketball skills prevalent among African-American men as a whole and therefore to assert that African Americans make great basketball players. Doing so ignores the performance level of the other 99.999 percent of the group. Again, to discuss the African-American community's response to affirmative action by citing only the opposition of people like Supreme Court Justice Clarence Thomas and political scientist Thomas Sowell would be similarly distorting.

In both instances, you must consider the whole group and choose examples accordingly. In the case of basketball, you will have to draw from performances at the local schoolyard or playground, the pickup game at the gym, the one-on-one competitions in the backyard; you will also need to consider those who don't play at all. In the case of political opinion, you would have to include supporters of affirmative action such as Jesse Jackson, Senator Carol Moseley-Braun of Illinois, and United Negro College Fund president William Gray, as well as people whose positions might lie between the extremes. The object is not to establish an arbitrary "balance" but to represent the subject as it is. In these two cases, the play of the professional athletes is certainly not representative and the opinions of the conservatives perhaps representative of proportionally few people only. Of course, if you were attempting to show that many (or most) of the NBA's finest players are African American or that some African Americans do not support affirmative action, the first set of examples would be appropriate.

Examples must be sufficient as well as relevant. That is, their number and variety should convince the reader that you are not dealing with isolated instances—although extended or typical examples may be exceptions. In the earlier discussion of dogs' loyalty, the examples of the setter, the retriever, and the shepherd are representative, but each provides only a single instance of the point it illustrates. Together they are enough to lead to the concession "You might have a point," but they do not convince. More examples are needed.

How many? There is no fixed number; as a writer you will have to establish for yourself the fine line between inadequacy and overkill. As a rough standard, two or three good examples will usually suffice—depending on how thoroughly they are developed and the complexity of the proposition that they are intended to support. At least until you get your "sea legs," it might be useful to think in terms of three. While there is nothing magical about this number, it often suggests completeness. Crudely put, the first gets the reader's attention, the second reduces doubt while maintaining interest, and the third clinches the point. However, you should not treat this as a formula. First, several sets of three examples will create monotony. Second, whatever number of examples you use, they need not be developed uniformly.

Let us see how this applies in the case of the opening scenario by following up one of the points raised but established only in part:

> Dogs have been known to return to their masters after having been separated for years and by thousands of miles. A few weeks ago, for example, an Irish setter, lost during a camping trip in the Rockies, made its way back to Sheboygan, Wisconsin, after four months. During some of the worst oppression in the former Soviet Union, several dogs, including a Samoyed named Nikki, trekked halfway across the country to find their owners imprisoned in Siberia. And in my own family, two

years after Dimples had been given away because of my uncle's allergy, the mutt showed up on his doorstep. There she was, dirty and bedraggled, with a torn ear and only three good legs. She had come all the way from Amarillo to Des Moines.

Although you might not be entirely persuaded by this paragraph, you are undoubtedly closer to being convinced than you were after the second sentence (the original material). The stories of Nikki and Dimples provide additional support. That the dogs are named make these two instances more concrete than that of the anonymous setter, and the final instance, a personal one presented in more graphic detail than the others, is perhaps (therefore) the most effective. In addition, the example of the Samoyed suggests that the behavior is not exclusive to dogs in the United States.

Someone especially nit-picking might object to the fact that these are all fairly recent examples. It is true that some historical perspective might be useful in attempting to show the nature of dogs, and in a more formal or argumentative paper you might want to find ancient occurrences. A passage in Homer's *Odyssey*, for example, suggests that the early Greeks recognized such canine virtue. Here, the human, Odysseus, having wandered far and wide, returns home to the faithful dog Argos, who lies decrepit and abandoned on a dung heap:

> Yet the instant Odysseus approached, the beast knew him. He thumped his tail and drooped his ears forward, but lacked power to drag himself ever so little towards his master. . . . Argos the dog went down into the blackness of death, that moment he saw Odysseus again after twenty years.
>
> *The Odyssey of Homer*, pp. 239–40 (T. E. Shaw, trans.)

But, given other solid, representative examples, such high drama is not essential. And, except for some documented research papers, your writing task will not require compilation of scrupulously thorough lists of data, but deft presentation of apt detail. The appropriate stroke is not that of a calculator key but of an artist's brush.

DETAIL AND DEVELOPMENT

Examples may be developed to varying degrees and may therefore differ in length. They may range from a brief specific instance or detail to a more elaborate anecdote to a full-blown extended account, which stands as the sole illustration of a point. In the passages concerning dogs, the examples of the setter and the Samoyed are brief instances; those concerning Dimples and Argos are more elaborate. None is an extended example, but one of them might have been chosen to typify canine behavior—provided more information had been supplied. The case of Dimples might have been a good choice, since the sympathetic speaker probably knows more about this dog than the others. What might have been added? The relationship between Dimples and her master, the trauma of separation, the uncle's reaction to the dog's return, and so on. Such an account would have enhanced both the intellectual and emotional appeal of the example and, presented well and thoroughly, could have eliminated the need for further illustration.

When a series of examples is presented (as in this example by Frank Wilczek and Betsy Devine), it sometimes is hardly more than a collection of details:

> The rainbow bridge between earth and sky is an ancient and powerful symbol. Norse gods climbed the rainbow from Earth to Asgard; to keep frost giants out, the band of red was filled with flames. The Greek goddess Iris, wearing an iridescent gown of water droplets, sped across the rainbow with messages from Olympus. Noah's God assured him that the rainbow would stand between them as a giant mnemonic [memory device]: ". . . when the bow shall be seen in the cloud . . . I will remember my covenant which is between me and you and every living creature of all flesh; and the waters shall no more become a flood to destroy all flesh."
>
> *Longing for the Harmonies: Themes and Variations from Modern Physics*, p. 3

Here the antiquity and power of the rainbow symbol are established by brief references to three mythologies, with just a single sentence of further explanation in regard to the Norse and Hebrew myths.

At times, as in the passage in which Dimples is first introduced, a single example in the series will receive greater emphasis than the others. The relationship here is roughly analogous to that between a lead singer and the back-ups or chorus. The lead carries the principal burden but is supported by the rest. The technique is apparent in the following passage by Edwin Emery et al.:

> Book and newspaper publishing were . . . closely identified in early United States history. . . . Benjamin Harris, who got out one issue of his *Publick Occurrences* in Boston in 1690, was a bookseller importing from London. Editors such as James and Benjamin Franklin had sizable libraries and reprinted literary material in their papers—including Daniel Defoe's *Robinson Crusoe*. The patriot journalist Isaiah Thomas was also an important book publisher; his shop at Worcester produced the first American novel, the first American dictionary, more than 400 technical books, and 100 children's books. Thomas was the first American to publish Blackstone's *Commentaries* [on English law], Bunyan's *Pilgrim's Progress*, and Defoe's *Robinson Crusoe* in book form. He himself wrote a two-volume history of American printing.
>
> *Introduction to Mass Communications*, 4th ed., p. 332

After presenting two very brief examples in Harris and the Franklins, the authors elaborate on Thomas, providing details about the variety of material published and three specific titles.

As noted previously, an extended example may serve as all the illustration a piece of writing provides, and may itself be the piece. This is especially likely to occur if the example is seen as typical and therefore representative of the subject under discussion. Jo Goodwin Parker's "What Is Poverty?" in chapter 8 is a case in point. The following passage, although not a full-length essay or article, suggests how an extended example might be developed. Here, Hawaii's solution to the problem of paying for public schools is presented by Gene Maeroff as a model for others to follow:

> The ultimate attempt to remove local disparities in school funding is found in Hawaii, where the entire state comprises a single school district. The state has assumed all of the cost of local education, spending approximately the same amount of money on each pupil whether he attends an urban school in bustling Honolulu or a rural school on the most remote island in the archipelago. The income from all of the state's taxable wealth flows into a general fund and then is doled out, school by school, to equalize spending. All of the teachers in the state are paid on a single salary scale, and no town, however affluent, may levy additional local taxes to enrich its schools beyond those in the rest of the state. Hawaii is the nation's showplace of tax equalization in education. . . .
>
> *Don't Blame the Kids*, p. 198

In your own writing you are free to choose any of these approaches or any combination of them, taking care to maintain reader interest. As a means of illustrating how such diversity may be created in a brief essay, let us persist, doggedly, in the discussion of canine loyalty with which the chapter began:

> Perhaps more than any other creatures, dogs are famous for their loyalty. They've been known to return to their masters after having been separated for years and by thousands of miles; they have helped rescue their owners and others from serious trouble; and they've even sacrificed their lives in protecting human beings.
>
> Stories of dogs finding their masters over great distances and long stretches of time are legion. A few weeks ago, for example, an Irish setter lost during a camping trip in the Rockies made its way back to Sheboygan, Wisconsin, after four months. With less happy results, during the most severe period of Soviet oppression of its citizens, several dogs, including a Samoyed named Nikki, trekked halfway across the country to find their owners imprisoned in Siberia. In my own family, two years after Dimples had been given away because of my uncle's allergy, the mutt showed up on his doorstep. There she was, dirty and bedraggled, with a torn ear and only three good legs. She had come all the way to Amarillo from Des Moines.
>
> Stories of rescue are even more common. There was the case two years ago of a Labrador retriever in Kentucky practically dragging the

parents of a four-year-old child to the site of an abandoned mine shaft, into which she had fallen. Not long afterward, a stray mongrel paddled out into the Nile to drag ashore a frail twelve-year-old whose boat had capsized. The child had sometimes fed it scraps. Though not the only breed, the Saint Bernard, even without a brandy keg attached, has earned its reputation for saving people from both the treachery of Alpine snows and their own carelessness. And let's not forget the dogs of whatever stripe (or spot) whose barks and growls regularly discourage unwelcome visitors.

Sometimes, sad to say, dogs pay for their devotion with their lives. The attempted robbery at Snyder's Emporium last fall, when Darth, the manager's German shepherd, forced the gun from the criminal's hand after being shot fatally himself, is one recent, local example. Similarly, there have been periodic reports from India and Africa of dogs attacking poisonous snakes threatening their masters and falling victim to the lethal venom themselves. But for canine self-sacrifice, the story of Rosie is hard to beat. According to survivors of the Harvey massacre, Rosie, an old, arthritic Newfoundland, was lying next to the cradle in which the Harvey baby was asleep, when a crazed intruder burst into the Maine farmhouse shooting wildly. Unfortunately, her barking did not wake the family, five of whom were shot, two fatally. But before the gunman entered the room in which she lay, Rosie pulled herself up and stretched her body across the cradle. She growled as the door was flung open, and took the bullet that might otherwise have struck the infant—who miraculously (and luckily) slept through it all.

Such behavior has earned dogs a respected place in human myth and legend. Whether it is Argos waiting twenty years for Odysseus to return or Yukon King, the canine companion of radio and TV's Sergeant Preston, or some generic "Fido"—a name derived from the Latin word for *loyalty*—the special bond between dogs and people endures, despite the fact that as pets in the United States dogs are now outnumbered by (horrors!) cats.

In addition to what has already been said about the first two paragraphs of this material, we may add that the third paragraph presents four examples, none more developed than the others. The first two are quite specific, the last two more general but still concrete. This is acceptable because the main idea of the paragraph is to demonstrate how pervasive the dog's protective behavior is.

In the fourth paragraph we have two brief examples—one specific, one general—but the focus here is on the extended example of Rosie. While Rosie's behavior might not be typical, it illustrates in its extremity one ideal of canine behavior.

Rosie's tale (correct spelling) leads nicely to the conclusion in which three idealized dogs (two specific, one generic) are mentioned briefly. The final statement suggests that the historic loyalty will persist.

The conclusion, however, raises one stylistic question. To maintain the casual tone and light touch, the writer has added the final reference to cats, which may be viewed by some readers as tangential or even irrelevant. On the other hand, ending with *endures*, although it leaves the conclusion squarely on topic, seems to suggest a greater earnestness than is appropriate here. You might consider which of the two options you prefer and why, as well as other possible endings.

EXAMPLE IN ACADEMIC WRITING

Regardless of the discipline or topic, academic writing (like most other types) requires specifics. No historian, for example, would explain the "greatness" of Alexander the Great by simply repeating his title. Readers would want to know what exactly Alexander did to deserve his appellation. As Herbert J. Muller shows, it turns out that Alexander was not so honored for his military prowess alone:

> Soon learning that the Persians he had conquered were not the "barbarians" or the slaves "by nature" that his master Aristotle was wont to assume of all men who were not Hellenes [Greeks], he began to employ them as high officials, while adding other Asiatics to his army. He himself married a daughter of the Persian Emperor Darius, and encouraged his officers likewise to take foreign wives. . . . For Alexander had conceived the idea of making partners of his subjects, to build an empire that would be a genuine commonwealth. At a great banquet, during which Macedonians, Greeks, and Asiatics drank from a common mixing bowl, he offered a prayer for *homonoia*, "a union of hearts." He was the first known ruler to have this vision of brotherhood, centuries before Christ. . . .
>
> *Freedom in the Ancient World*, p. 223

In this passage, the author at least lends credence to the idea of Alexander's greatness by listing those actions through which Alexander's goal of unity is made evident—provided, of course, we accept the goal as worthy.

Sound examples are useful and essential in other disciplines in the humanities as well. Suppose you have been reading Chinua Achebe's novel *Things Fall Apart* and comment that Okonkwo, its central character, is a macho traditionalist. In order to persuade others that such is the case you will have to cite specific instances in support of your contention:

> Okonkwo's machismo is apparent from the start in his rejection of Unoka, his weak father. It is also seen in his becoming the local wrestling champion, his striving to achieve various honorific titles, and his participating—against sound advice—in the tribal execution of Ikemefuna, who had become like a son to him. Finally, it is clear in his

effectively choosing to die rather than succumb to British rule. His death, his participation in the execution of Ikemefuna, and his pursuit of titles also indicate the strength of his commitment to tradition—as does his obedient acceptance of exile as punishment for the accidental killing of a fellow tribesman.

Though other observers may disagree with some of these contentions, at least they will understand—through your examples—what it is you meant by the initial offhand remark.

In the social sciences, the case study, although ultimately an analytic tool, is also often an extended example. Anthropologist Oscar Lewis, for instance, has written several popular books, beginning with *Five Families* (1959), which illustrate not only the lives of their subjects in their own words but suggest ways in which they typify the culture and class of which they are part. Within more traditional longer works, of course, social scientists, like other effective writers, must illustrate the various subordinate points they wish to make.

As part of a chapter called "The Origins of Language" (Richard E. Leakey and Roger Lewin), the following passage illustrates specifically, if paradoxically, some ideas about generalization. (The chimps mentioned in the text have been taught Ameslan—American Sign Language.)

> Generalizing is something we do all the time. Chairs, for instance, come in all shapes and sizes, and yet we can instantly recognize and name such structures as basically the same thing. We have a concept of a chair in our heads, and we can slot tubular chrome creations, solid oak carvers, and plush velvet easy chairs into the same mental pigeonhole. Generalizing to concepts like this is cognitively economical, and it is essential for language. Chimps can do it. For instance, Lucy calls a watermelon a *drink fruit*; Washoe refers to ducks as *water birds*, and she invented the name *rock berry* for a brazil [sic] nut when she first encountered one; Lana calls a cucumber a *banana which is green* and she refers to Fanta orange drink as *Coke which is orange*. . . .
>
> *People of the Lake: Mankind and Its Beginnings*, pp. 202–203

What is true of example in other disciplines is true for the arts and sciences as well. The excerpt below from a well-known history of art by Helen Gardner depends heavily on exemplification:

> Polynesian artists excelled in carving figural sculptures in wood, stone, and ivory in sizes ranging from the gigantic fabled stone images of Easter Island to tiny ivory Marquesan ear plugs an inch long. . . . Polynesians were also adept in making decorative bark cloth called *tapa*, and the art of tattoo was highly developed.
>
> Polynesian carving at its most dramatic is represented by the Hawaiian figure of the war god Kukailimoku. . . . Huge wooden images of this deity were erected on stone temple platforms that, in varied forms,

were part of the apparatus of all Polynesian state religions. Although relatively small, [one such figure in the British Museum] is majestic in scale and forcefully carved to convey . . . the ferocity attributed to the deity. Flexed limb and faceted, conventionalized muscles combine with the aggressive, flaring mouth and serrated headdress to achieve a tense dynamism seldom rivaled in any art.

Gardner's Art through the Ages, 7th ed., p. 443

Both paragraphs depend on specific details but present them in different ways. The first lists the materials and the arts other than carving. It also illustrates the range of sculpture by referring briefly to contrasting types in two specified places. Returning to the major topic, carving, the second paragraph is more elaborate. It uses a single developed example to demonstrate the dramatic quality of Polynesian sculpture. The descriptive details permit us to visualize the piece even without benefit of the illustration that appears in the original text.

Similarly, the passage that follows uses example to both illustrate and explain the phenomenon of surface tension:

> Surface tension is an interesting property of liquids. . . . The reader has probably observed insects walking on the surface of water, apparently defying the laws of gravity. Similarly, a steel needle will float if carefully placed on the surface of water. However, if the needle breaks through the surface, it promptly sinks, and insects will sink and drown if pushed into the liquid. Apparently, the surface of the liquid acts as a skin.
>
> The theory explains this phenomenon as follows: Within the body of the liquid the molecules are attracted by the neighboring molecules from all directions. However, the molecules at the surface are attracted only on one side—namely, from the molecules within the liquid. . . . This produces an extra compression in the first few layers and the surface acts as a skin. Thus, unlike a crowd of people, liquids have sharp surfaces. The forces at the surface are called "surface tension." They explain, for example, why small drops of liquid always tend to assume a spherical form.

T. A. Ashford, *The Physical Sciences: From Atoms to Stars,* 2nd ed., p. 222

USING EXAMPLE

Appropriate Examples

Be sure that the examples you use are appropriate to the points they are intended to illustrate. If you were attempting to show that some of our presidents have been inept, you might exempt Washington, Lincoln, and the Roosevelts, among others; but you might include such presidents as Grant and Harding. What about Rutherford B. Hayes, Chester A. Arthur, and Benjamin Harrison? You would have to learn something about their perform-ance to see if it measured up to your idea of incompetence. A well-defined thesis often points the way to its own support.

Representative and Sufficient Examples

Your examples should be representative of your topic and sufficient (and sufficiently strong) to establish your points. Grant and Harding alone, for instance, will probably not suffice to persuade the reader that "some of our presidents have been inept," although they might serve to show that "very few of our presidents have been inept." The word *some* suggests the need for greater breadth; perhaps you can add others. Perhaps also you can modify your thesis: "Several of our presidents have been inept to varying degrees." Now you can use Grant and Harding as extreme instances, cite another pair or trio as moderately inept, and point to several who have failed miserably from time to time.

Developing Examples

Decide to what extent each of your examples should be developed. It is conceivable that for the thesis presented at the end of the previous paragraph, the examples of Grant and Harding would be given rather full treatment, as might the examples of those presidents labeled "moderately inept." But in presenting those who were occasionally inadequate, you might not go beyond listing one significant shortcoming of each president named.

Remember also that brief and extended examples may be combined, and that in some circumstances, particularly if it is typical of its kind, a single extended example might suffice. It is possible, for instance, that after two or three examples of "moderately inept" presidents you might focus the bulk of your discussion on complex figures such as Lyndon Johnson, who was fre-quently seen as performing disastrously in regard to Vietnam but well on domestic social problems such as civil rights; or Richard Nixon, who was perceived as being effective in foreign policy (Vietnam aside)—especially with regard to China—but who was caught up in the Watergate scandal at home.

Presenting Examples

Vary the manner in which you present examples. The constant repetition of the phrase "for example" creates boredom in the reader. Many of the examples in this chapter have used "for instance" or "in the case of" or some other equivalent to create variety. At times, such transitions are unnecessary. If you examine the full sample essay about the loyalty of dogs, you will find "for example" and its synonyms used only once.

I. L. Peretz

(Poland; 1852–1915)

Along with Mendele Mocher S'forim and Shalom Aleichem (whose stories are the basis of Fiddler on the Roof*), Isaac Leib Peretz was one of the three figures responsible for the creation and flowering of Yiddish literature in the nineteenth century. Born in Lublin and educated in Jewish religious schools, Peretz eventually studied for the Russian bar (part of present-day Poland was then under Russian rule) and became a successful attorney in Warsaw. He spent the remainder of his life in the capital, practicing law, acting as a representative of the Jewish community, and writing.*

At first, Peretz wrote in Hebrew, which was then being revived as a secular language. He switched, however, to Yiddish, the language spoken nearly universally by Jews of Eastern Europe, in order to reach the masses. His efforts to create a Yiddish literature (together with those of Mendele and Shalom Aleichem) succeeded in both Eastern Europe and the United States well into the twentieth century, ending with the Holocaust and with the adoption of English by most American Jews after the great period of immigration. The tradition, however, has been preserved by several prominent writers, most notably Nobel laureate Isaac Bashevis Singer (1904–1991).

Peretz was primarily a writer of short stories (several translated collections are currently available) but also wrote poetry. It was in the midst of writing a poem that he died at his desk. The lines he had written were put to music, and the piece served as a memorial. The one hundred thousand people in Peretz's funeral procession testify to his popularity with his original audience.

Bontsha the Silent

HERE ON EARTH the death of Bontsha the Silent made no impression at all. Ask anyone: Who was Bontsha, how did he live, and how did he die? Did his strength slowly fade, did his heart slowly give out—or did the very marrow of his bones melt under the weight of his burdens? Who knows? Perhaps he just died from not eating—starvation, it's called.

If a horse, dragging a cart through the streets, should fall, people would run from blocks around to stare, newspapers would write about this fascinating event, a monument would be put up to mark the very spot where the horse had fallen. Had the horse belonged to a race as numerous as that of human beings, he wouldn't have been paid this honor. How many horses are there, after all? But human beings—there must be a thousand million of them!

Bontsha was a human being; he lived unknown, in silence, and in silence he died. He passed through our world like a shadow. When Bontsha was born no one took a drink of wine; there was no sound of glasses clinking. When he was confirmed, he made no speech of celebration. He existed like a grain of sand at the rim of a vast ocean, amid millions of other grains of sand exactly similar, and when the wind at last lifted him up and carried him across to the other shore of that ocean, no one noticed, no one at all.

During his lifetime his feet left no mark upon the dust of the streets; after his death the wind blew away the board that marked his grave. The wife of the gravedigger came upon that bit of wood, lying far off from the grave, and she picked it up and used it to make a fire under the potatoes she was cooking; it was just right. Three days after Bontsha's death no one knew where he lay, neither the gravedigger nor anyone else. If Bontsha had had a headstone, someone, even after a hundred years, might have come across it, might still have been able to read the carved words, and his name, Bontsha the Silent, might not have vanished from this earth.

His likeness remained in no one's memory, in no one's heart. A shadow! 5
Nothing! Finished!

In loneliness he lived, and in loneliness he died. Had it not been for the infernal human racket someone or other might have heard the sound of Bontsha's bones cracking under the weight of his burdens; someone might have glanced around and seen that Bontsha was also a human being, that he had two frightened eyes and a silent trembling mouth; someone might have noticed how, even when he bore no actual load upon his back, he still walked with his head bowed down to earth, as though while living he was already searching for his grave.

When Bontsha was brought to the hospital ten people were waiting for him to die and leave them his narrow little cot; when he was brought from the hospital to the morgue twenty were waiting to occupy his pall; when he was taken out of the morgue forty were waiting to lie where he would lie forever. Who knows how many are now waiting to snatch from him that bit of earth?

In silence he was born, in silence he lived, in silence he died—and in an even vaster silence he was put into the ground.

Ah, but in the other world it was not so! No! In paradise the death of Bontsha was an overwhelming event. The great trumpet of the Messiah announced through the seven heavens: Bontsha the Silent is dead! The most exalted angels, with the most imposing wings, hurried, flew, to tell one another, "Do you know who has died? Bontsha! Bontsha the Silent!"

And the new, the young little angels with brilliant eyes, with golden 10
wings and silver shoes, ran to greet Bontsha, laughing in their joy. The sound of their wings, the sound of their silver shoes, as they ran to meet him, and the bubbling of their laughter, filled all paradise with jubilation, and God Himself knew that Bontsha the Silent was at last here.

In the great gateway to heaven Abraham our Father stretched out his arms in welcome and benediction: "Peace be with you!" And on his old face a deep sweet smile appeared.

What, exactly, was going on up there in paradise?

There, in paradise, two angels came bearing a golden throne for Bontsha to sit upon, and for his head a golden crown with glittering jewels.

"But why the throne, the crown, already?" two important saints asked. "He hasn't even been tried before the heavenly court of justice to which each new arrival must submit." Their voices were touched with envy. "What's going on here, anyway?"

And the angels answered the two important saints that, yes, Bontsha's   15
trial hadn't started yet, but it would only be a formality, even the prosecutor wouldn't dare open his mouth. Why, the whole thing would take five minutes!

"What's the matter with you?" the angels asked. "Don't you know whom you're dealing with? You're dealing with Bontsha, Bontsha the Silent!"

When the young, the singing angels encircled Bontsha in love, when Abraham our Father embraced him again and again, as a very old friend, when Bontsha heard that a throne waited for him, and for his head a crown, and that when he would stand trial in the court of heaven no one would say a word against him—when he heard all this, Bontsha, exactly as in the other world, was silent. He was silent with fear. His heart shook, in his veins ran ice, and he knew this must all be a dream or simply a mistake.

He was used to both, to dreams and mistakes. How often, in that other world, had he not dreamed that he was wildly shoveling up money from the street, that whole fortunes lay there on the street beneath his hands—and then he would wake and find himself a beggar again, more miserable than before the dream.

How often in that other world had someone smiled at him, said a pleasant word—and then, passing and turning back for another look, had seen his mistake and spat at Bontsha.

Wouldn't that be just my luck, he thought now, and he was afraid to lift   20
his eyes, lest the dream end, lest he awake and find himself again on earth, lying somewhere in a pit of snakes and loathsome vipers, and he was afraid to make the smallest sound, to move so much as an eyelash; he trembled and he could not hear the paeans of the angels; he could not see them as they danced in stately celebration about him; he could not answer the loving greeting of Abraham our Father, "Peace be with you!" And when at last he was led into the great court of justice in paradise he couldn't even say "Good morning." He was paralyzed with fear.

And when his shrinking eyes beheld the floor of the courtroom of justice, his fear, if possible, increased. The floor was of purest alabaster, embedded with glittering diamonds. On such a floor stand my feet, thought Bontsha. My feet! He was beside himself with fear. Who knows, he thought, for what very rich man, or great learned rabbi, or even saint, this whole thing's meant? The rich man will arrive, and then it will all be over. He lowered his eyes; he closed them.

In his fear he did not hear when his name was called out in the pure angelic voice: "Bontsha the Silent!" Through the ringing in his ears he could make out no words, only the sound of that voice like the sound of music, of a violin.

Yet did he, perhaps, after all, catch the sound of his own name, "Bontsha the Silent?" And then the voice added, "To him that name is as becoming as a frock coat to a rich man."

What's that? What's he saying? Bontsha wondered, and then he heard an impatient voice interrupting the speech of his defending angel. "Rich man! Frock coat! No metaphors, please! And no sarcasm!"

"He never," began the defending angel again, "complained, not against   25
God, not against man; his eye never grew red with hatred, he never raised a protest against heaven."

Bontsha couldn't understand a word, and the harsh voice of the prosecuting angel broke in once more. "Never mind the rhetoric, please!"

"His sufferings were unspeakable. Here, look upon a man who was more tormented than Job!"

Who? Bontsha wondered. Who is this man?

"Facts! Facts! Never mind the flowery business and stick to the facts, please!" the judge called out.

"When he was eight days old he was circumcised—"   30
"Such realistic details are unnecessary—"
"The knife slipped, and he did not even try to staunch the flow of blood—"
"—are distasteful. Simply give us the important facts."

"Even then, an infant, he was silent, he did not cry out his pain," Bontsha's defender continued. "He kept his silence, even when his mother died, and he was handed over, a boy of thirteen, to a snake, a viper—a stepmother!"

Hm, Bontsha thought, could they mean me?   35

"She begrudged him every bite of food, even the moldy rotten bread and the gristle of meat that she threw at him, while she herself drank coffee with cream."

"Irrelevant and immaterial," said the judge.

"For all that, she didn't begrudge him her pointed nails in his flesh—flesh that showed black and blue through the rags he wore. In winter, in the bitterest cold, she made him chop wood in the yard, barefoot! More than once were his feet frozen, and his hands, that were too young, too tender, to lift the heavy logs and chop them. But he was always silent, he never complained, not even to his father—"

"Complain! To that drunkard!" The voice of the prosecuting angel rose derisively, and Bontsha's body grew cold with the memory of fear.

"He never complained," the defender continued, "and he was always   40
lonely. He never had a friend, never was sent to school, never was given a new suit of clothes, never knew one moment of freedom."

"Objection! Objection!" the prosecutor cried out angrily. "He's only trying to appeal to the emotions with these flights of rhetoric!"

"He was silent even when his father, raving drunk, dragged him out of the house by the hair and flung him into the winter night, into the snowy, frozen night. He picked himself up quietly from the snow and wandered into the distance where his eyes led him.

"During his wanderings he was always silent; during his agony of hunger he begged only with his eyes. And at last, on a damp spring night, he drifted to a great city, drifted there like a leaf before the wind, and on his very first night, scarcely seen, scarcely heard, he was thrown into jail. He remained silent, he never protested, he never asked, Why, what for? The doors of the jail were opened again, and, free, he looked for the most lowly filthy work, and still he remained silent.

"More terrible even than the work itself was the search for work. Tormented and ground down by pain, by the cramp of pain in an empty stomach, he never protested, he always kept silent.

"Soiled by the filth of a strange city, spat upon by unknown mouths,   45
driven from the streets into the roadway, where, a human beast of burden, he pursued his work, a porter, carrying the heaviest loads upon his back, scurrying between carriages, carts, and horses, staring death in the eyes every moment, he still kept silent.

"He never reckoned up how many pounds he must haul to earn a penny; how many times, with each step, he stumbled and fell for that penny. He never reckoned up how many times he almost vomited out his very soul, begging for his earnings. He never reckoned up his bad luck, the other's good luck. No, never. He remained silent. He never even demanded his own earnings; like a beggar, he waited at the door for what was rightfully his, and only in the depths of his eyes was there an unspoken longing. 'Come back later!' they'd order him; and, like a shadow, he would vanish, his eyes begging, imploring, for what was his. He remained silent even when they cheated him, keeping back, with one excuse or another, most of his earnings, or giving him bad money. Yes, he never protested, he always remained silent.

"Once," the defending angel went on, "Bontsha crossed the roadway to the fountain for a drink, and in that moment his whole life was miraculously changed. What miracle happened to change his whole life? A splendid coach, with tires of rubber, plunged past, dragged by runaway horses; the coachman, fallen, lay in the street, his head split open. From the mouths of the frightened horses spilled foam, and in their wild eyes sparks struck like fire in a dark night, and inside the carriage sat a man, half alive, half dead, and Bontsha caught at the reins and held the horses. The man who sat inside and whose life was saved, a Jew, a philanthropist, never forgot what Bontsha had done for him. He handed him the whip of the dead driver, and Bontsha, then and there, became a coachman—no longer a common porter! And what's more, his great benefactor married him off, and what's still more, this great philanthropist himself provided a child for Bontsha to look after.

"And still Bontsha never said a word, never protested."

They mean me, I really do believe they mean me. Bontsha encouraged himself, but still he didn't have the gall to open his eyes, to look up at his judge.

"He never protested. He remained silent even when that great philanthropist shortly thereafter went into bankruptcy without ever having paid Bontsha one cent of his wages.

"He was silent even when his wife ran off and left him with her helpless infant. He was silent when, fifteen years later, that same helpless infant had grown up and become strong enough to throw Bontsha out of the house."

They mean me, Bontsha rejoiced, they really mean me.

"He even remained silent," continued the defending angel, "when the same benefactor and philanthropist went out of bankruptcy, as suddenly as he'd gone into it, and still didn't pay Bontsha one cent of what he owed him. No, more than that. This person, as befits a fine gentleman who has gone through bankruptcy, again went driving the great coach with the tires of rubber, and now, now he had a new coachman, and Bontsha, again a porter in the roadway, was run over by the coachman, carriage, horses. And still, in his agony, Bontsha did not cry out; he remained silent. He did not even tell the police who had done this to him. Even in the hospital, where everyone is allowed to scream, he remained silent. He lay in utter loneliness on his cot, abandoned by the doctor, by the nurse; he had not the few pennies to pay them—and he made no murmur. He was silent in that awful moment just before he was about to die, and he was silent in that very moment when he did die. And never one murmur of protest against man, never one murmur of protest against God!"

Now Bontsha begins to tremble again. He senses that after his defender has finished, his prosecutor will rise to state the case against him. Who knows of what he will be accused? Bontsha, in that other world on earth, forgot each present moment as it slipped behind him to become the past. Now the defending angel has brought everything back to his mind again—but who knows what forgotten sins the prosecutor will bring to mind?

The prosecutor rises. "Gentlemen!" he begins in a harsh and bitter voice, and then he stops. "Gentlemen—" he begins again, and now his voice is less harsh, and again he stops. And finally, in a very soft voice, that same prosecutor says, "Gentlemen, he was always silent—and now I too will be silent."

The great court of justice grows very still, and at last from the judge's chair a new voice rises, loving, tender. "Bontsha my child, Bontsha"—the voice swells like a great harp—"my heart's child . . ."

Within Bontsha his very soul begins to weep. He would like to open his eyes, to raise them, but they are darkened with tears. It is so sweet to cry. Never until now has it been sweet to cry.

"My child, my Bontsha . . ."

Not since his mother died has he heard such words, and spoken in such a voice.

"My child," the judge begins again, "you have always suffered, and you have always kept silent. There isn't one secret place in your body without its bleeding wound; there isn't one secret place in your soul without its wound and blood. And you never protested. You always were silent.

"There, in that other world, no one understood you. You never understood yourself. You never understood that you need not have been silent, that you could have cried out and that your outcries would have brought down the world itself and ended it. You never understood your sleeping strength. There in that other world, that world of lies, your silence was never rewarded, but here in paradise is the world of truth, here in paradise you will be rewarded. You, the judge can neither condemn nor pass sentence upon. For you there is not only one little portion of paradise, one little share. No, for you there is everything! Whatever you want! Everything is yours!"

Now for the first time Bontsha lifts his eyes. He is blinded by light. The splendor of light lies everywhere, upon the walls, upon the vast ceiling, the angels blaze with light, the judge. He drops his weary eyes.

"Really?" he asks, doubtful, and a little embarrassed.

"Really!" the judge answers. "Really! I tell you, everything is yours. Everything in paradise is yours. Choose! Take! Whatever you want! You will only take what is yours!"

"Really?" Bontsha asks again, and now his voice is stronger, more assured.

And the judge and all the heavenly host answer, "Really! Really! Really!"

"Well then"—and Bontsha smiles for the first time—"well then, what I would like, Your Excellency, is to have, every morning for breakfast, a hot roll with fresh butter."

A silence falls upon the great hall, and it is more terrible than Bontsha's has ever been, and slowly the judge and the angels bend their heads in shame at this unending meekness they have created on earth.

Then the silence is shattered. The prosecutor laughs aloud, a bitter laugh.

Translated by Hilde Abel

THESIS AND THOUGHT

1. Explain the reasons for Bontsha's silence both in the court and on earth.
2. To what extent does the story uphold silence as a virtue? Consider the defender's speeches, the judge's comments in paragraph 61, and Bontsha's request and the response to it in paragraphs 67–68.
3. Explain the prosecutor's laugh in the final paragraph.

STRUCTURE

1. Of what is Bontsha an example?
2. How does Peretz illustrate the pervasiveness of Bontsha's silence?
3. Peretz contrasts Bontsha's treatment on earth with the treatment he receives in the other world. Is Bontsha's response to the latter in proportion to the contrast? Explain why.
4. What use does Peretz make of anticlimax?
5. Is the story in any sense an argument?

STYLE

1. Some of Peretz's examples of Bontsha's silence strain belief—such as his not crying out at his circumcision. What is Peretz's purpose in exaggerating? Is the story in any sense a satire?
2. What effect does the repetition of *silent* and its variants produce? Examine the repetitive parallel structure in paragraphs 6–8. Find several other instances of this in the story and discuss whether its effect reinforces that created by the repetition of *silent*.

CONSIDERATIONS

1. Had you been in Bontsha's place, what might you have asked for? Why? How might your request have been greeted by the court?
2. Part of Peretz's point is to attack that aspect of religious thought which upholds meekness as a virtue. The Bible, for example, asserts that the meek "shall inherit the earth." Write an essay in which you either discuss the value of submissiveness or argue against some other precept such as "Thou shalt love thy neighbor as thyself."
3. What might Bontsha have accomplished had he not kept silent? Write an essay on the effectiveness of protest.
4. Peretz wrote the original of this story in Yiddish for an Eastern European Jewish audience. Explain whether these facts alter or enhance your interpretation. In what ways does the story transcend its (or Peretz's) time and place?

Marianne Moore

(United States; 1887–1972)

A native of St. Louis, Moore went east to attend Bryn Mawr College. She later taught at the Carlisle Indian School and eventually moved to Brooklyn. In New York during the 1920s, Moore worked at the public library and later edited the Dial, *a leading literary magazine of the day.*

Devoted to baseball as well as to poetry and criticism, Moore was an avid Brooklyn Dodger fan who often attended games. Sports sometimes find their way into her work either as subject or allusion. (Note her eye for the "athletic" skills of some of the animals in the present selection.) If you love poetry less than Moore did baseball, you might be momentarily surprised by the opening of her poem "Poetry," which begins "I too dislike it." Of course, she vindicates her art by poem's end.

In her day, Moore's work earned the praise of such leading poets As T. S. Eliot, Ezra Pound, and William Carlos Williams (see p. 37). Her Collected Poems *(1951) led to three major literary awards.*

What There Is to See at the Zoo

THE PEACOCK SPREADS HIS TAIL, and the nearly circular eyes at regular intervals in the fan are a sight at which to marvel—forming a lacework of white on more delicate white if the peacock is a white one; of indigo, lighter blue, emerald and fawn if the peacock is blue and green.

Look at a tiger. The light and dark of his stripes and the black edge encircling the white patch on his ear help him to look like the jungle with flecks of sun on it. In the way of color, we rarely see a blacker black than tiger stripes, unless it is the black body down of the blue bird of paradise.

Tiger stripes have a merely comparative symmetry beside the almost exact symmetry of a Grevy's zebra. The small lines on one side of the zebra's face precisely match those on the other side, and the small sock stripes on one front leg are an exact duplicate of those on the other front leg.

Although a young giraffe is also an example of "marking," it is even more impressive as a study in harmony and of similarities that are not monotony— of sycamore-tree white, beside amber and topaz yellow fading into cream. The giraffe's tongue is violet; his eyes are a glossy cider brown. No wonder Thomas Bewick (pronounced Buick, like the car), whose woodcuts of birds and animals are among the best we have, said, "If I were a painter, I would go to nature for all my patterns."

146

Such colors and contrasts educate the eye and stir the imagination. They 5
also demonstrate something of man's and the animals' power of adaptation to
environment, since differing surroundings result in differences of appearance
and behavior.

The giraffe grows to the height of certain trees that it may reach its leafy
food. David Fleay, an authority on Australian wild life, tells us that the
lyrebird "has a very large eye that it may see [grubs] in the dim light of the
tree-fern gullies in which it lives." Certain chameleons have an eye that
revolves in its socket, as some searchlights turn on a revolving swivel, in order
to look forward and back.

The bodies of sea lions, frogs, and eels are streamlined so that they can
slip through the water with the least possible effort. Living almost entirely in
the water, an alligator is shaped like a boat and propels itself by its tail as if it
were feathering a sculling oar.

The elephant has an inconsequential tail, but its long nose, or trunk, has
the uses of a hand as well as the power of a battering-ram. It can pull down
branches for food or push flat the trees that block its progress through the
jungle. Helen Fischer, in her photo series "The Educated Elephants of Thai-
land," shows how "up and onto the waiting trunk, an elephant maneuvers a
heavy log as easily as we would a piece of kindling." Then "after work, it
wades and splashes in a cool stream."

An elephant can use its trunk to draw up water and shower its back or to
hose an intruder. With the finger at the end of its trunk, the elephant can
pluck grass that has overgrown a paved walk, leaving a line as even as if
sheared by man. It can pick up a coin and reach it up to the rider on its
back—its mahout ("mahowt," as he is called in India). What prettier sight is
there than the parabola described by an elephant's trunk as it spirals a banana
into its mouth?

A certain gorilla at the Central Park Zoo in New York sometimes takes 10
a standing leap to her broad trapeze. She sits there, swinging violently for
a time, and then suddenly drops without a jar—indeed, descends as lightly as
a feather might float to the ground. Walking through the monkey house at
the Bronx Zoo, we stop before the cage of an orangutan as he jumps to his
leadpipe trapeze with half an orange in one hand and a handful of straw in the
other. He tucks the wisp of hay under his neck and, lying on his back as
contentedly as if at rest in a hammock, sucks at the orange from time to
time—an exhibition of equilibrium that is difficult to account for.

The gorilla's master feat—the standing leap to a swing the height of her
head—is matched by the pigeon when it flies at full speed, stops short, pauses
and without a detour flies back in the direction from which it came. At dusk,
four or five impalas will timidly emerge from their shelter, then bound
through the air, in a succession of twenty-four leaps, to the end of their
runway. Perhaps Clement Moore had seen or heard of impalas and was

thinking of them when, in *A Visit from St. Nicholas*, he wrote of Santa Claus' reindeer skimming the housetops.

The swimmer has a valuable lesson in muscular control as he watches a sea lion round the curve of its pool, corkscrewing in a spiral as it changes from the usual position to swim upside down. Hardening-up exercises in military training, with obstacles to surmount and ditches to clear, involve skills neatly mastered by animals. In the wilds, bands of gibbons swing from tree to tree as army trainees swing by ropes or work along the bars of a jungle-gym.

Animals are "propelled by muscles that move their bones as levers, up and down or from side to side." The ways in which the movements of their muscles vary provide an ever fascinating sight. The motions of animals are so rapid that we really need the aid of an expert such as James Gray to analyze them for us. In his book *The Motions of Animals*, Mr. Gray says that the bear—a browser, not a runner—rests on the entire foot when walking. The horse and the deer—built for speed—rest on tiptoes (the hoof); the hock never touches the ground.

An essential rule of safe living is well illustrated by animals: work when you work, play when you play, and rest when you rest. Watch two young bears wrestling, rolling, pushing and attacking. One tires, climbs to a broad rock and stretches out full length on its paws. The other stands up, strains forward till it can reach with its mouth the ear of the bear on the rock and keeps tugging at the ear as though dragging a hassock forward by the ear. The rester gets up, comes down and once more both are tumbling, capsized and capsizing.

There is nothing more concentrated than the perseverance with which   15
a duck preens its feathers or a cat washes its fur. The duck spreads oil on its feathers with its beak from a small sac above the tail. The feathers then lie smooth and waterproof, reminding us that we too must take time for our bodies and equipment. For as much as fifteen minutes at a time, a leopard will, without digressing to another area, wash a small patch of fur that is not sleek enough to satisfy it. It may then leap to its shelf, a board suspended by rods from the ceiling of the cage. Dangling a foreleg and a hindleg on either side of the shelf, its tail hanging motionless, the leopard will close its eyes and rest.

Patience on the part of animals is self-evident. In studying, photographing or rearing young animals, human beings also need patience. We have in Helen Martini a thrilling example of what may be done for young animals by a human being. Mrs. Martini has reared two sets of tiger cubs, a lion cub and various other baby animals for the Bronx Zoo.

The zoo shows us that privacy is a fundamental need of all animals. For considerable periods, animals in the zoo will remain out of sight in the quiet of their dens or houses. Glass, recently installed in certain parts of the snake house at the Bronx Zoo, makes it possible to see in from the outside, but not out from the inside.

We are the guests of science when we enter a zoo; and, in accepting privileges, we incur obligations. Animals are masters of earth, air and water, brought from their natural surroundings to benefit us. It is short-sighted, as well as ungrateful, to frighten them or to feed them if we are told that feeding will harm them. If we stop to think, we will always respect chains, gates, wires or barriers of any kind that are installed to protect the animals and to keep the zoo a museum of living marvels for our pleasure and instruction.

Thesis and Thought

1. According to Moore, what is there to see at the zoo? (You will have to go well beyond simply listing the animals.) What verb other than *see* might she have chosen?

2. What is Moore's governing idea? Where does she imply or state it?

3. In several places (paras. 4, 6, 8, 13, and 16), Moore cites or refers to various authorities. Explain how these citations and references help establish her points. How might their omission have altered the essay?

Structure

1. Aside from the animals themselves, might the references and citations in question 3 above be considered examples? If so, of what?

2. Describe the differences in how Moore presents her examples in paragraphs 6, 8–9, and 15, and explain how each approach is appropriate for the passage in which it is used.

3. Moore also varies the arrangement of her examples. Consider the following groups of paragraphs: 1–5, 5–9, 10–11, 12–13 (or possibly 10–13). At which point in each of these clusters do we learn what the examples are supposed to illustrate? Which sentence or phrase indicates each example's significance? Explain why paragraph 5 is included in both the first and second cluster.

Style

1. Explain why Moore's descriptions in the first four paragraphs (note, for example, the giraffe, whose coloring is "sycamore-tree white, beside amber and topaz yellow fading into cream") are more intense than they are in the remainder of the essay.

2. Since Moore is essentially a poet, it is hardly surprising that the essay employs figures of speech—metaphor and simile in particular. Identify two or three of these, explain how they are designed to work in the passage in which they occur, and decide whether (and why) you find them effective.

3. In dealing with animals, we sometimes attribute human characteristics to the creatures with which we are involved. The essay on the loyalty of dogs at the beginning of the chapter is an example of this. Does Moore indulge in such practices? On the other hand, is her attitude scientific and detached? Write a sentence or two in which you characterize the tone of the essay.

CONSIDERATIONS

1. Since this essay was written (1955) some of our attitudes toward zoos have changed. In 1993, the London Zoo was closed for financial reasons related, in part, to poor attendance. But ecological concerns and, to a lesser extent, the question of whether humans have the right to hold animals in captivity had also been raised. Similarly, the Bronx Zoo, to which Moore refers, now calls itself (not without some ridicule) an International Wildlife Conservation Park, a name designed to suggest the new nature and function of zoos in our time. Considering such ecological matters as endangered species, ethical issues such as the purported "rights" of animals, and the proliferation of mass-media materials dealing with animal life, do you think zoos are as useful and necessary today as they seemed to Moore four decades ago? Write an essay in which you explain your position. Be sure to use examples.

2. The sympathy toward animals expressed by both Moore and the writer of the piece about dogs (earlier in this chapter) may be expressions of culture as well as individual experience. The Kenyan whose village and crops are being trampled by an elephant, for instance, would hardly be so admiring as Moore. We might be upset about clubbing infant harp seals to death, but to Norwegian fur traders this is a means of survival. Nor do the Japanese seem to share the somewhat more general Western concern about the welfare of dolphins and whales. You might want to do one or more of the following:

   a. Read about how particular species or animals collectively are treated within a culture other than your own.

   b. Rent and watch an old film called *Mondo Cane* (*A Dog's World*), which takes a sometimes sardonic view of how dogs (and other creatures) are treated throughout the world.

   c. Make a short list of animals you won't eat but which you know others do (e.g., muskrat, squid, grasshoppers, lizard, pig, cow, camel, dog) and write a brief essay in which you explain your refusal or disgust. Alternatively, do the same with parts of animals (e.g., tails, feet, brains, intestines, tongues). If you are vegetarian to whatever degree, explain your vegetarianism—although more in terms of opposing beef than defending beans.

W. H. Auden

(England and United States; 1907–1973)

Poet, playwright, opera librettist, critic, professor, and schoolmaster, Auden had a varied career. Although raised in a conservative Anglican household, he came to prominence with the publication of Poems *(1930), work that expressed pronounced leftist views. Later in the decade, he served briefly as a medic during the Spanish civil war. A year earlier (1936) he had married Erika, daughter of German novelist Thomas Mann, simply to enable her to obtain a British passport and leave Nazi Germany. They had never before met.*

With the outbreak of World War II and thereafter, Auden returned to his religious roots. The renewal is apparent in the collections For the Time Being *(1944) and* The Age of Anxiety *(1947); the latter earned Auden a Pulitzer Prize. His other honors include a Bollingen Prize for poetry (1953) and a National Book Award (1956).*

Although Auden became a U.S. citizen in 1946, he regularly divided his time between the United States and Europe. From 1956 to 1961 he was professor of poetry at Oxford and in 1972 was poet in residence there.

As you read (and reread) "Musée des Beaux Arts," consider whether the poem is a piece of social criticism or a more detached observation on the human condition.

Musée des Beaux Arts

About suffering they were never wrong,
The Old Masters: how well they understood
Its human position; how it takes place
While someone else is eating or opening a window or just walking
    dully along;
How, when the aged are reverently, passionately waiting   5
For the miraculous birth, there always must be
Children who did not specially want it to happen, skating
On a pond at the edge of the wood:
They never forgot
That even the dreadful martyrdom must run its course   10
Anyhow in a corner, some untidy spot
Where the dogs go on with their doggy life and the torturer's horse
Scratches its innocent behind on a tree.

In Brueghel's *Icarus*, for instance: how everything turns away
Quite leisurely from the disaster; the ploughman may   15
Have heard the splash, the foresaken cry,
But for him it was not an important failure; the sun shone
As it had to on the white legs disappearing into the green
Water; and the expensive delicate ship that might have seen
Something amazing, a boy falling out of the sky,   20
Had somewhere to get to and sailed calmly on.

THESIS AND THOUGHT

1. State Auden's main idea in a sentence or two.
2. As Auden sees it, what is the relationship between the usual and the extraordinary? How do adults involved with their own pursuits and agenda respond to unusual events? Why? How do the animals (and children) respond? Do these reactions suggest that events such as "the miraculous birth," "the dreadful martyrdom," and the fall of Icarus are fairly insignificant in the totality of human experience? Why or why not?

STRUCTURE

1. The example of Icarus (ll. 14–21) is the most fully developed in the poem. Explain its relevance to Auden's purpose.
2. Identify two earlier examples, both derived from other Brueghel paintings, and describe their probable subjects.
3. Together, the three examples illustrate that the old master Brueghel "understood [the] human position" in regard to suffering. But what justifies Auden's use of the plural in line 2?
4. Explain how contrasts between events and responses help shape the poem.

STYLE

1. Auden's language is often quite casual—in line 4, for instance, or in phrases like "doggy life" and "innocent behind." How do word choices such as these serve his purposes?
2. Describe in what way "Musée des Beaux Arts" meets or fails to meet your expectations of poetry. If there are discrepancies, do you think the difficulties lie with the poem, your expectations, or both? Explain.
3. Although "Musée des Beaux Arts" was the name of the museum at which Auden saw the paintings described in the poem, he did not have to choose

the name for his title. What overtones are present in the French and how do they relate to the earthy perspective and language of the poem? Is there any difference between using this title for a poem in English and using "*pommes frites*" for French fries on a diner menu?

CONSIDERATIONS

1. Test the validity of Auden's contention in your own experience. How do you react to extraordinary events? Take the first night of the Gulf war, for example. Ask some older relatives or friends what they did upon learning that Pearl Harbor had been bombed, or that President Kennedy or Martin Luther King had been assassinated.

2. Go to your local "musée des beaux arts" and find some other idea that the old masters were right (or wrong) about. Write a brief essay in which you explain your discovery by using works of art as examples.

3. Consult a work such as the *Larousse Encyclopedia of Mythology* to find a more complete version of the story of Icarus.

Jean Latham
(England; b. 1910)

Born in London, Jean Latham attended the Westminster and Chelsea schools of art. According to her daughter, she has "had a lifelong interest in antiques and their social and historical significance." This interest is reflected in Latham's work as both popular historian and collector. One of her historical accounts is The Pleasure of Your Company: A History of Manners and Meals *(1972), from which "Royal Feasts" is taken. In a similar vein, she has also written* Happy Families: Growing Up in the Eighteenth and Nineteenth Centuries *(1974). Latham has published two books about antiques,* Victoriana *(1971) and* Collecting Miniature Antiques *(1972).*

Royal Feasts

THE BY-WAYS OF HISTORY are so to speak paved with stories of the rich gourmandizing. As Pepys so wisely remarked, "Strange to see how a good dinner and feasting reconciles everybody." Dryden had the same thought when he wrote how much he had enjoyed an evening party, calling it "a very merry, dancing, drinking, laughing, quaffing and unthinking time."

William the Conqueror's court, in spite of cutting down the meals relished by the Anglo-Saxons from four a day to only two, still knew how to
enjoy themselves and indeed brought with them better manners. The Normans frowned upon such behaviour as banging about the womenfolk or being
drunk from dawn to midnight. Occasionally the King and his courtiers feasted
on delicacies from as far away as Phoenicia and Syria, Tripoli, Babylon and
Constantinople. The price of these luxuries was of secondary importance.
Probably our conquered compatriots were paying so that their King might
impress foreign ambassadors. William sent his purveyors great distances to
procure rare and unusual food for his banquets.

That very energetic Plantaganet King Henry II was forever in the saddle
riding about his kingdom and settling disputes. His domains were considerable in France as well as England, as he had married Eleanor of Aquitaine, his
senior by eight years. After many hours on horseback he would sit down at
table and hastily consume three courses and then jump up immediately and
start on his next project. Everybody else was prostrated with fatigue, but
Henry's vitality was unflagging. No wonder the food was rather unpalatable
then. The poor courtiers must have suffered from chronic dyspepsia. By
contrast Thomas à Becket, his first Minister of State, kept a table renowned
for its excellent food and wine, holding court in a magnificently princely style
that was unrivalled in the kingdom. By the time he became Archbishop of
Canterbury and had cut down on his extravagant ostentation, he was peril-
ously near his martyrdom.

Edward I, a high-spirited and exhuberant King, ordered for his Coronation Feast in Westminster, "380 oxen, 450 porkers, 430 sheep, 278 bacon hogs
and 22,600 hens and capons." This gargantuan meal lasted for two weeks
non-stop, and yet historians assure us that his Court was not considered to be
an especially lavish one. In those days the Court travelled from place to place
in great luxury, carrying the king's own tent and during one year the king's
Butler managed to spend the astronomical sum of £6,934 6s 4$\frac{1}{2}$ d, on wine
alone.

Richard II, son of the Black Prince, had a Court of ten thousand retain-   5
ers. One Christmastide these hungry mouths were filled with a daily quota of
28 oxen, 300 sheep besides an unlisted number of poultry.[1] Richard has the
reputation of being one of our first kingly gourmets.

Edward IV, who was equally fond of his meals, had a partiality for simple
jests, of the kind which most of us now would consider as both boring and
crude. Since laughter is believed to stimulate the digestive juices, court jesters
were always on hand to keep everyone's juices flowing freely. The Lord
Mayors of London expected jesters at their banquets to jump into a huge
tureen of custard, which always caused enormous merriment. Custard-pie
humour must be as old as man.

---

[1] *Chronicles* of Holinshed. [Au.]

In Tudor days the wonder is that anyone survived the unhygienic preparation of food. The master-cooks kept their scullions unclothed or dressed in
unusually dirty garments, and then let them lie all night long by the kitchen
fire, leaving the used dishes to be washed up by the dogs.

Wolsey drew up an order for Henry VIII's household, in an effort to
reform this state of affairs. He had to put up with his royal master's favourite
jester called Will Sommers, whose practical jokes amused Henry inordinately
and Wolsey not at all.

We know all about Henry VIII's capacity for food. Here is a sample of
what he expected to see on his table. Bread and soup, beef, venison, mutton
and veal were there in quantity and a swan, capons, rabbits and fish were all
included in the first course. This was followed by the inevitable custard
though the jester is not reported to have had to jump into this, and eight or
nine other dishes made up the second course. Nobody minded in what order
they ate the food then. Next came the jelly and cream of almonds, pheasants,
herons, shoveller ducks, partridges, cocks, quails, plovers and gulls, pigeons
and larks and chickens and many, many other delicacies besides. This was
accompanied by as much ale and wine as the company was able to manage.
Then at supper in the evening the whole operation started all over again,
with the addition probably of a few teal, godwits, sparrows, quinces, bread and
butter, eggs and "blank mange."

Now and again there were awful days of famine when only fish was
permitted to be eaten. Then the fasting king was offered bread, soup, lam-
preys, pike, salmon and haddock, whiting, bream, trout, lobsters, crab, tar-
tlets, fruit, fritters—and yes, of course, the custard. For the second course he
could fill up with another soup, tench, crayfish, eels, perch, a little more
salmon, sturgeon and more tart, fruit, eggs and butter ending up with a nice
baked pippin with a few oranges.

The Lord Chamberlain and those seated at his table did not do so badly
either. They had a first course of ten dishes and six dishes for the second course. The next table in the scale of importance was that of the Gentlemen of the Privy Chamber and they were offered at dinner only seven
dishes for their first course, four for the second course and the same for their
supper. Going down lower in the social scale we find the physicians receiving
only one course in all, comprising nine dishes for their dinner and six for
supper. They could always get their own back, of course, when they prescribed
those dreadful medicines. As for the servants and the maids, they just had
two meat dishes for dinner and two more for their supper. The left-overs
were handed out to the poor at the gates, whom one imagines must have
done quite well. Even Tudor noblemen's stomachs cannot have been quite
bottomless.

Perquisites in the kitchen were such delectable tit-bits as pig's heads,
ox-skins and salmon tails. Poultry feathers went to the grooms, who no doubt
found good use for them, and yeomen had to make do with just the down from

10

the Queen's swans and "the garbage of poultry," whatever that was. It doesn't sound much of a "perk," but it appears that everybody was satisfied.

One of the hazards of court life in the sixteenth century must been the rather over-powering sense of fun that animated the leisured classes. In 1528 *A Book of the Courtier* was first published in Italy. It reached our shores in 1561. The author strongly objected to horseplay and besides condemning such gay little jokes as pushing people down the stairs, throwing bricks at them or riding men on horseback into ditches, he also took exception to those who threw "potage, sauce, jellies and whatever cometh to hand" into people's faces. His votes on certain forms of behaviour give us a startling picture of what might happen to an unwary guest in those good old days.

Many books before this and after it were written on matters of etiquette and behaviour. Our ancestors' mealtime manners must have been extremely displeasing. Filling up the mouth with food so that the lips cannot close over it is described in one book as "a foul sight and loathsome." Diners are also advised strongly against continually calling upon others to drink toasts. As late as 1671, when people were learning to drink tea and coffee, to wear nightgowns and stockings, to read newspapers and to use forks, books on correct manners still recommended readers to "gnaw not bones, nor handle Dogs, nor sprawl upon the floor. Drink not with your mouth full nor unwiped." Let us hope some of these admonishments did not fall upon deaf ears.

A king who was endowed with an extraordinary appetite was Louis XIV   15
of France, the Sun King. His sister-in-law, the Princess Palatine, wrote that she had seen him eat four full plates of different soups, followed by a whole pheasant, a partridge, a large plateful of salad, two big slices of beef, some mutton laced with gravy and garlic, an ample plateful of *pâtisserie*, some fruit and a few hard-boiled eggs to top it all up. Apparently this was no solitary feat; he partook every day of similar vast collations. He would regularly eat up some *hors d'oeuvres*, followed by four plates of cold meat, a couple of salads and four *entremets*, some jam, some fruit and those hard-boiled eggs he liked so much. This, admittedly, was taken at 6 o'clock in the evening after a long day's hunting. Yet, at 10 o'clock, four hours later, he was able to do justice to a good supper. . . .

THESIS AND THOUGHT

1. Which statement provokes the series of examples here and unifies the selection?

2. Since the period between the Norman Conquest (1066) and the reign of Louis XIV (1643–1715) touches upon three major epochs in European his-

tory—the Middle Ages, the Renaissance, and the Enlightenment—you should not assume that any consistencies you find in Latham imply general uniformity during that span. Remember that she has a particular focus and chooses her examples accordingly. That said, beyond the details of diet themselves, what do you learn from the selection about life during these centuries? Based on the reading, write a brief paragraph describing court life during this time.

STRUCTURE

1. What determines the order in which Latham presents her examples? Is the order effective? Can you suggest an alternative arrangement?
2. Compare the examples in paragraphs 2 and 3 with those in paragraphs 4 and 5. What is a significant difference between them?
3. Does Latham succeed in preventing her series of examples from degenerating into a mere list? If so, how? If not, why not?

STYLE

1. What do statements and phrases such as these contribute to the tone of the writing? "The Normans frowned upon such behaviour as banging about the womenfolk . . ." (para. 2), "Custard-pie humour must be as old as man" (para. 6), "leaving the used dishes to be washed up by the dogs" (para. 7), and "Now and again there were awful days of famine," which is followed by a long list of foods (para. 10).
2. What evidence of British authorship do the spelling, vocabulary, and phrasing provide?

CONSIDERATIONS

1. Based on the reading alone, would you have liked to have been a member of the royal households described? Which features of these households do you find attractive? Which repellent?
2. Write a substantial paragraph in which you fantasize about a feast of your own.
3. Appearances here to the contrary notwithstanding, during the period described in the essay gluttony was taken seriously, at least by the Church, as one of the seven deadly sins. Is there a distinction between gluttony and "gourmandizing"? Can you conceive of any reason why people in the times Latham describes might have had appreciably greater caloric requirements than we do today?

Alexander Calandra

(United States; b. 1911)

Scientist and science educator, Alexander Calandra earned his bachelor's degree at Brooklyn College and his doctorate in statistics at New York University. He has taught at the University of Chicago, Webster College, and Washington University, where he was professor of physics. His work in science education includes consulting for the American Council on Education, research into the statistical techniques of tests and measurements, and the creation of integrated courses in basic science and mathematics. He has also served as science advisor and editor for programs on both public and commercial television.

"Angels on a Pin" was written during the late fifties, partly as a comment on the push for scientific education in the United States after the Soviets launched the first space satellite, Sputnik. It is also a comment on the nature of creativity.

Angels on a Pin

SOME TIME AGO, I received a call from a colleague who asked if I would be the referee on the grading of an examination question. He was about to give a student a zero for his answer to a physics question, while the student claimed he should receive a perfect score and would if the system were not set up against the student. The instructor and the student agreed to submit this to an impartial arbiter, and I was selected.

I went to my colleague's office and read the examination question: "Show how it is possible to determine the height of a tall building with the aid of a barometer."

The student had answered: "Take the barometer to the top of the building, attach a long rope to it, lower the barometer to the street, and then bring it up, measuring the length of the rope. The length of the rope is the height of the building."

I pointed out that the student really had a strong case for full credit, since he had answered the question completely and correctly. On the other hand, if full credit were given, it could well contribute to a high grade for the student in his physics course. A high grade is supposed to certify competence in physics, but the answer did not confirm this. I suggested that the student have another try at answering the question. I was not surprised that my colleague agreed, but I was surprised that the student did.

I gave the student six minutes to answer the question, with the warning   5
that his answer should show some knowledge of physics. At the end of five
minutes, he had not written anything. I asked if he wished to give up, but he
said no. He had many answers to this problem; he was just thinking of the
best one. I excused myself for interrupting him, and asked him to please go
on. In the next minute, he dashed off his answer, which read:

"Take the barometer to the top of the building and lean over the edge of
the roof. Drop the barometer, timing its fall with a stopwatch. Then, using
the formula $S = \frac{1}{2}at^2$, calculate the height of the building."

At this point, I asked my colleague if *he* would give up. He conceded, and
I gave the student almost full credit.

In leaving my colleague's office, I recalled that the student had said he
had other answers to the problem, so I asked him what they were. "Oh, yes,"
said the student. "There are many ways of getting the height of a tall building
with the aid of a barometer. For example, you could take the barometer out
on a sunny day and measure the height of the barometer, the length of its
shadow, and the length of the shadow of the building, and by the use of a
simple proportion, determine the height of the building."

"Fine," I said. "And the others?"

"Yes," said the student. "There is a very basic measurement method that   10
you will like. In this method, you take the barometer and begin to walk up
the stairs. As you climb up the stairs, you mark off the length of the barometer
along the wall. You then count the number of marks, and this will give you
the height of the building in barometer units. A very direct method.

"Of course, if you want a more sophisticated method, you can tie the
barometer to the end of a string, swing it as a pendulum, and determine the
value of 'g' at the street level and the top of the building. From the difference
between the two values of 'g,' the height of the building can, in principle, be
calculated."

Finally he concluded, there are many other ways of solving the problem.
"Probably the best," he said, "is to take the barometer to the basement and
knock on the superintendent's door. When the superintendent answers, you
speak to him as follows: 'Mr. Superintendent, here I have a fine barometer. If
you will tell me the height of this building, I will give you this barometer.' "

At this point, I asked the student if he really did not know the conventional answer to this question. He admitted that he did, but said that he was
fed up with high school and college instructors trying to teach him how to
think, to use the "scientific method," and to explore the deep inner logic of
the subject in a pedantic way, as is often done in the new mathematics,
rather than teaching him the structure of the subject. With this in mind, he
decided to revive scholasticism as an academic lark to challenge the Sputnik-
panicked classrooms of America.

Thesis and Thought

1. Why does the student refuse to give the "conventional answer" to the physics question?

2. From his refusal, the answers he supplies instead, and the manner in which he presents them, what do we learn about the student's personality and mode of thinking?

3. State the theme of the essay, and explain how the conflict between the student and his professor reveals it.

Structure

1. What does the essay as a whole exemplify? How do the student's individual responses contribute to this total effect?

2. How does the narrative framework contribute to the essay's overall effectiveness?

3. Granting that the events are reported in the sequence in which they occurred, explain why the examples in paragraphs 3 and 12, looked at structurally, seem particularly well placed.

Style

1. Identify any humorous elements. What is the basis of their humor?

2. Rewrite the original question in paragraph 2 so that a response other than the conventional one would have been impossible.

3. Examine the student's speech in paragraph 10 and in the address to the superintendent in paragraph 13. What is the effect of such simple and repetitive diction? How does the language here differ from that in paragraphs 6 and 8? Account for the stylistic discrepancy in terms of the student's attitudes and motives in each instance. Describe the effect of such variation on the essay's narrative and thematic conflicts.

Considerations

1. Why do you think Calandra gave the response in paragraph 6 "*almost* full credit"? [emphasis added] Why does he not explain the formula in paragraph 6, "the value of 'g'" in paragraph 11, or, indeed, tell us what answer the professor expected? What, by the way, is that answer?

2. Explain the distinction drawn in paragraph 13 between "the deep inner logic of the subject" and "the structure of the subject." Apply the distinction to the manner of instruction in several courses that you have taken or are taking currently. Which approach do you prefer, and why?

3. As Calandra indicates in paragraph 13, the sudden interest in science education in the late fifties—and its consequent abuses—was the result of panic produced by the sudden appearance of a potential threat. The search for preventives and cures for AIDS goes on with analogous urgency today. Write an essay in which through copious examples you explain how to deal with an unanticipated threat to public or personal health or safety.

Desmond M. Tutu
(South Africa; b. 1931)

A former caddy, peanut vendor, and classroom teacher, Bishop Desmond M. Tutu has long been one of the leading spiritual leaders in South Africa. Born to Christian parents who worked in mission schools, he came to the church early. As an adolescent, he was attracted particularly to the leadership and faith of Trevor Huddleston, a white Anglican priest staunchly opposed to apartheid.

Ordained himself in 1961, Tutu studied and served in both England and his homeland, rising to dean of Johannesburg in 1975 and bishop of Lesotho a year later. As first black head of the multiracial South African Council of Churches, Tutu continued to press for social justice. For his various verbal and written protests, and especially for advocating economic sanctions against the white-ruled government, he twice had his passport revoked.

Because of his efforts on behalf of the oppressed majority and his appeal for essentially nonviolent means of achieving reform, Tutu was awarded the Nobel Peace Prize in 1984. Since then, he has continued in his cause. The fruits of his and others' efforts may be seen in the economic boycott of South Africa, the release of African National Congress president Nelson Mandela in 1990, revocation of apartheid regulations, the open elections of 1994, and the ongoing process of a political solution to racial hostility and unrest.

In examining the excerpt from Tutu's Nobel Prize acceptance speech, consider whether the examples he uses are particularly chosen for an audience of listeners rather than readers.

The Evils of Apartheid

YOUR MAJESTY, members of the Royal Family, Mr. Chairman, Ladies and Gentlemen:

Before I left South Africa, a land I love passionately, we had an emergency meeting of the Executive Committee of the South African Council of Churches with the leaders of our member churches. We called the meeting because of the deepening crisis in our land, which has claimed nearly 200 lives this year alone. We visited some of the trouble spots on the Witwatersrand. I went with others to the East Rand. We visited the home of an old lady. She told us that she looked after her grandson and the children of neighbors while their parents were at work. One day the police chased some pupils who had been boycotting classes, but they disappeared between the township houses. The police drove down the old lady's street. She was sitting at the back of the house in her kitchen, whilst her charges were playing in the front of the house in the yard. Her daughter rushed into the house, calling out to her to come quickly. The old lady dashed out of the kitchen into the living room. Her grandson had fallen just inside the door, dead. He had been shot in the back by the police. He was six years old. A few weeks later, a white mother, trying to register her black servant for work, drove through a black township. Black rioters stoned her car and killed her baby of a few months old, the first white casualty of the current unrest in South Africa. Such deaths are two too many. These are part of the high cost of apartheid.

Every day in a squatter camp near Cape Town, called K.T.O., the authorities have been demolishing flimsy plastic shelters which black mothers have erected because they were taking their marriage vows seriously. They have been reduced to sitting on soaking mattresses, with their household effects strewn round their feet, and whimpering babies on their laps, in the cold Cape winter rain. Every day the authorities have carried out these callous demolitions. What heinous crime have these women committed, to be hounded like criminals in this manner? All they wanted is to be with their husbands, the fathers of their children. Everywhere else in the world they would be highly commended, but in South Africa, a land which claims to be Christian, and which boasts a public holiday called Family Day, these gallant women are treated so inhumanely, and yet all they want is to have a decent and stable family life. Unfortunately, in the land of their birth, it is a criminal offence for them to live happily with their husbands and the fathers of their children. Black family life is thus being undermined, not accidentally, but by deliberate Government policy. It is part of the price human beings, God's children, are called to pay for apartheid. An unacceptable price.

I come from a beautiful land, richly endowed by God with wonderful natural resources, wide expanses, rolling mountains, singing birds, bright shining stars out of blue skies, with radiant sunshine, golden sunshine. There is enough of the good things that come from God's bounty, there is enough for everyone, but apartheid has confirmed some in their selfishness, causing them to grasp greedily a disproportionate share, the lion's share, because of their power. They have taken 87 percent of the land, though being only about 20 percent of our population. The rest have had to make do with the remaining 13 percent. Apartheid has decreed the politics of exclusion. Seventy-three percent of the population is excluded from any meaningful participation in the political decision-making processes of the land of their birth. The new constitution, making provision for three chambers, for whites, coloureds, and Indians, mentions blacks only once, and thereafter ignores them completely. Thus this new constitution, lauded in parts of the West as a step in the right direction, entrenches racism and ethnicity. The constitutional committees are composed in the ratio of four whites to two coloureds and one Indian. Zero black. Two plus one can never equal, let alone be more than, four. Hence this constitution perpetuates by law and entrenches white minority rule. Blacks are expected to exercise their political ambitions in unviable, poverty-striken, arid, bantustan homelands, ghettoes of misery, inexhaustible reservoirs of cheap black labor, bantustans into which South Africa is being balkanized. Blacks are systematically being stripped of their South African citizenship and being turned into aliens in the land of their birth. This is apartheid's final solution, just as Nazism had its final solution for the Jews in Hitler's Aryan madness. The South African Government is smart. Aliens can claim but very few rights, least of all political rights.

In pursuance of apartheid's ideological racist dream, over 3,000,000 of   5
God's children have been uprooted from their homes, which have been demolished, whilst they have then been dumped in the bantustan homeland resettlement camps. I say dumped advisedly; only things or rubbish is dumped, not human beings. Apartheid has, however, ensured that God's children, just because they are black, should be treated as if they were things, and not as of infinite value as being created in the image of God. These dumping grounds are far from where work and food can be procured easily. Children starve, suffer from the often irreversible consequences of malnutrition—this happens to them not accidentally, but by deliberate Government policy. They starve in a land that could be the bread basket of Africa, a land that normally is a net exporter of food.

The father leaves his family in the bantustan homeland, there eking out a miserable existence, whilst he, if he is lucky, goes to the so-called white man's town as a migrant, to live an unnatural life in a single sex hostel for 11 months of the year, being prey there to prostitution, drunkenness, and worse. This migratory labor policy is declared Government policy, and has been condemned, even by the white D.R.C. [Dutch Reformed Church], not noted for being quick to criticise the Government, as a cancer in our society. This cancer, eating away at the vitals of black family life, is deliberate Government policy. It is part of the cost of apartheid, exorbitant in terms of human suffering.

Apartheid has spawned discriminatory education, such as Bantu Education, education for serfdom, ensuring that the Government spends only about one tenth on one black child per annum for education what it spends on a white child. It is education that is decidedly separate and unequal. It is to be wantonly wasteful of human resources, because so many of God's children are prevented, by deliberate Government policy, from attaining to their fullest potential. South Africa is paying a heavy price already for this iniquitous policy because there is a desperate shortage of skilled manpower, a direct result of the short-sighted schemes of the racist regime. It is a moral universe that we inhabit, and good and right and equity matter in the universe of the God we worship. And so, in this matter, the South African Government and its supporters are being properly hoisted with their own petard.

Apartheid is upheld by a phalanx of iniquitous laws, such as the Population Registration Act, which decrees that all South Africans must be classified ethnically, and duly registered according to these race categories. Many times, in the same family one child has been classified white whilst another, with a slightly darker hue, has been classified coloured, with all the horrible consequences for the latter of being shut out from membership of a greatly privileged caste. There have, as a result, been several child suicides. This is too high a price to pay for racial purity, for it is doubtful whether any end, however desirable, can justify such a means. There are laws, such as the Prohibition of Mixed Marriages Act, which regard marriages between a white and a person of another race as illegal. Race becomes an impediment to a valid marriage. Two persons who have fallen in love are prevented by race from consummating their love in the marriage bond. Something beautiful is made to be sordid and ugly. The Immorality Act decrees that fornication and adultery are illegal if they happen between a white and one of another race. The police are reduced to the level of peeping Toms to catch couples red-handed. Many whites have committed suicide rather than face the disastrous consequences that follow in the train of even just being charged under the law. The cost is too great and intolerable.

Such an evil system, totally indefensible by normally acceptable methods, relies on a whole phalanx of draconian laws such as the security legislation which is almost peculiar to South Africa. There are the laws which permit the indefinite detention of persons whom the Minister of Law and Order has decided are a threat to the security of the State. They are detained at his pleasure, in solitary confinement, without access to their family, their own doctor, or a lawyer. That is severe punishment when the evidence apparently available to the Minister has not been tested in an open court—perhaps it could stand up to such rigorous scrutiny, perhaps not; we are never to know. It is a far too convenient device for a repressive regime, and the minister would have to be extra special not to succumb to the temptation to circumvent the awkward process of testing his evidence in an open court, and thus he lets his power under the law to be open to the abuse where he is both judge and prosecutor. Many, too many, have died mysteriously in detention. All this is too costly in terms of human lives. The minister is able, too, to place people under banning orders without being subjected to the annoyance of the checks and balances of due process. A banned person for three or five years becomes a nonperson, who cannot be quoted during the period of her banning order. She cannot attend a gathering, which means more than one other person. Two persons together talking to a banned person are a gathering! She cannot attend the wedding or funeral of even her own child without special permission. She must be at home from 6:00 P.M. of one day to 6:00 A.M. of the next and on all public holidays, and from 6:00 P.M. on Fridays until 6:00 A.M. on Mondays for three years. She cannot go on holiday outside the magisterial area to which she has been confined. She cannot go to the cinema, nor to a picnic. That is severe punishment, inflicted without the evidence allegedly justifying it being made available to the banned person, nor having it scrutinized in a court of law. It is a serious erosion and violation of basic human rights, of which blacks have precious few in the land of their birth. They do not enjoy the rights of freedom of movement and association. They do not enjoy freedom of security of tenure, the right to participate in the making of decisions that affect their lives. In short, this land, richly endowed in so many ways, is sadly lacking in justice.

Once a Zambian and a South African, it is said, were talking. The   10
Zambian then boasted about their Minister of Naval Affairs. The South African asked, "But you have no navy, no access to the sea. How then can you have a Minister of Naval Affairs?" The Zambian retorted, "Well, in South Africa you have a Minister of Justice, don't you?"

It is against this system that our people have sought to protest peacefully since 1912 at least, with the founding of the African National Congress. They have used the conventional methods of peaceful protest—petitions, demonstrations, deputations, and even a passive resistance campaign. A tribute to our people's commitment to peaceful change is the fact that the only South Africans to win the Nobel Peace Prize are both black. Our people are peace-loving to a fault. The response of the authorities has been an escalating intransigence and violence, the violence of police dogs, tear gas, detention without trial, exile, and even death. Our people protested peacefully against the Pass Laws in 1960, and 69 of them were killed on March 21, 1960, at Sharpeville, many shot in the back running away. Our children protested against inferior education, singing songs and displaying placards and marching peacefully. Many in 1976, on June 16th and subsequent times, were killed or imprisoned. Over 500 people died in that uprising. Many children went into exile. The whereabouts of many are unknown to their parents. At present, to protest that self-same discriminatory education, and the exclusion of blacks from the new constitutional dispensation, the sham local black government, rising unemployment, increased rents and General Sales Tax, our people have boycotted and demonstrated. They have staged a successful two-day stay away. Over 150 people have been killed. It is far too high a price to pay. There has been little revulsion or outrage at this wanton destruction of human life in the West. In parenthesis, can somebody please explain to me something that has always puzzled me. When a priest goes missing and is subsequently found dead, the media in the West carry his story in very extensive coverage. I am glad that the death of one person can cause so much concern. But in the self-same week when this priest is found dead, the South

African Police kill 24 blacks who had been participating in the protest, and 6,000 blacks are sacked for being similarly involved, and you are lucky to get that much coverage. Are we being told something I do not want to believe, that we blacks are expendable and that blood is thicker than water, that when it comes to the crunch, you cannot trust whites, that they will club together against us? I don't want to believe that is the message being conveyed to us.

Be that as it may, we see before us a land bereft of much justice, and therefore without peace and security. Unrest is endemic, and will remain an unchanging feature of the South African scene until apartheid, the root cause of it all, is finally dismantled. At this time, the Army is being quartered on the civilian population. There is a civil war being waged. South Africans are on either side. When the ANC [African National Congress] and the PAC [Pan-Africanist Congress] were banned in 1960, they declared that they had no option but to carry out the armed struggle. We in the SACC [South African Council of Churches] have said we are opposed to all forms of violence—that of a repressive and unjust system, and that of those who seek to overthrow that system. However, we have added that we understand those who say they have had to adopt what is a last resort for them. Violence is not being introduced into the South African situation de novo from outside by those who are called terrorists or freedom fighters, depending on whether you are an oppressed or an oppressor. The South African situation is violent already, and the primary violence is that of apartheid, the violence of forced population removals, of inferior education, of detention without trial, of the migratory labor systems, etc.

There is war on the border of our country. South African faces fellow South African. South African soldiers are fighting against Namibians who oppose the illegal occupation of their country by South Africa, which has sought to extend its repressive systems of apartheid, unjust and exploitative.

There is no peace in Southern Africa. There is no peace because there is no justice. There can be no real peace and security until there be first justice enjoyed by all the inhabitants of that beautiful land. The Bible knows nothing about peace without justice, for that would be crying "peace, peace, where there is no peace." God's Shalom, peace, involves inevitably righteousness, justice, wholeness, fullness of life, participation in decision making, goodness, laughter, joy, compassion, sharing and reconciliation. . . .

THESIS AND THOUGHT

1. Identify Tutu's purposes in this address.
2. According to Tutu, in which areas of personal and public life is apartheid especially devastating? By what specific means does the government maintain its oppressive control?
3. Summarize Tutu's position on violence as expressed in the speech.

STRUCTURE

1. Explain how the anecdotal examples in paragraphs 2 and 10 serve Tutu's purposes—with particular regard to their tone and to where in the speech they occur.

2. Many of Tutu's details involve numbers (see paras. 2, 4, 5, 7, 9). Assess their impact and explain how Tutu prevents his figures from becoming dehumanized data.

3. Compare the manner in which the examples in paragraphs 8 and 9 are developed.

4. Why are "the father" (para. 6) and especially "she" (para. 9) "typical" examples?

5. Explain why you agree or disagree with the following statement: Tension between the realities of South Africa and its possibilities is central to the design of Tutu's speech.

STYLE

1. What is characteristic of the sentence patterns in paragraph 2? What effect does it create? Compare the sentence structure of the second paragraph with that of paragraph 3.

2. Can you account for the sudden change in style? What is its impact on the reader (listener) and essay?

3. Examine the sentence fragments in paragraphs 3 ("An unacceptable price") and 4 ("Zero black"), and discuss whether they are effective or should have been parts of whole sentences.

4. What special meaning does the word *coloureds* (para. 4) have in South Africa's racial system? How does it differ (spelling aside) from *colored* as it might be used as a racial term in the United States? Explain whether *colored* and "people of color" have the same meanings, in terms both of **denotation** and **connotation.**

5. How certain is Tutu that his listeners will understand the Hebrew word *shalom* (para. 14)? Was it familiar to you before you read the selection? If so, and if you do not speak or read Hebrew, explain how you came to know it. Is *shalom* as American as pizza pie? Can you think of other words that English has borrowed from other languages?

6. In paragraph 12 how does Tutu distinguish terrorists from freedom fighters? Explain why you agree or disagree with his distinction.

CONSIDERATIONS

1. What value will Tutu's speech have once the issues of apartheid and majority rule are fully resolved?

2. Explain how it is or is not possible to be "peace-loving to a fault" (para. 11).

3. In paragraph 7 Tutu says, "It is a moral universe that we inhabit." Write a brief essay in which you comment on this statement.

4. We are told in paragraph 9 that the Minister of Law and Order may detain people indefinitely for "the security of the state." While detention of this sort rarely occurs in the United States, government officials are sometimes suspected of refusing to release, on grounds of "national security," information or documents that might jeopardize their careers or expose them to criminal charges. Discuss the confusion of political or personal motives with the public good by writing an essay based on Samuel Johnson's remark that "patriotism is the last refuge of a scoundrel."

5. You might like to read more about life in South Africa under apartheid. *The Anti-Apartheid Reader* (edited by David Mermelstein) is a good place to start. Some others are Alan Paton's novel *Cry, the Beloved Country*, Mark Mathabane's autobiography *Kaffir Boy*, almost any of the plays by Athol Fugard, and numerous essays, poems, and fiction by such writers as Doris Lessing, Es'kia Mphahlele, and Richard Rive.

Sam Gill
(United States; b. 1943)

Sam Gill is a leading authority on Native American religions. In breaking new scholarly ground with this subject, he has stated two goals: "to introduce an academically and humanistically useful way of trying to appreciate and understand the complexity and diversity of Native American religions" and "to help establish Native American religions as a significant field within religious studies."

Gill did his graduate study at the University of Chicago and later taught at Arizona State University. He is currently professor of religion at the University of Colorado. Among Gill's publications are Native American Religions: An Introduction *(1982),* Native American Traditions: Sources and Interpretations *(1983), and* Native American Religion: A Performance Approach to Religion *(1987).*

Although Gill's particular expertise is apparent in the essay that follows, you will immediately observe that he is familiar with religions in various cultures and with how the phenomenon he describes functions crossculturally. As you read, be certain that you understand what disenchantment *means.*

Disenchantment

FOR MODERN MAN in his complex secular world, religion has faded as an integral element of everyday life. Removed to the fringes of life, religion is allowed to play a central role only in time of crisis—a grave illness or death. But throughout history, religion has celebrated the tasks of a working day, the seasonal unfolding of the year, and the plateaus of personal development. When it marks these day-to-day experiences, religion pervades life and gives it meaning, but when the mundane events of human existence are no longer celebrated through regular and formal ritual, much of the power of religion is lost.

A vital religious life commonly begins with a formal rite of initiation. This rite is crucial, for it awakens in the individual the special character of religious life and spurs him to involvement in activities which nurture continual religious development. Rituals of initiation generally follow a pattern of symbolic death and rebirth, as Arnold van Gennep and Mircea Eliade have shown. Childhood and all its associations die for the initiate, and he is reborn into his adulthood having to accept both the privileges and responsibilities of this new life. In these rites the initiate is transformed into a new person— from a child into an adult, from a novice into an adept. Moreover, Eliade has demonstrated that the fundamental purpose of the religious initiation—the revelation of the sacred—is accomplished through this initiatic pattern. The special knowledge of the sacred is what distinguishes the initiated.

But occasionally these rites, which should germinate relationships with the holy, focus upon the intentional destruction or defamation of sacred objects in the presence of the initiates. It would seem in these cases that the symbolic blow of death is dealt to the gods or the sacred rather than to the initiates. How can an initiation be meaningful if its ritual process desecrates or defames the objects that reveal the sacred? The enigma is darkened by the fact that the adepts of the society often go to great lengths to deceive the initiates, to set them up for the disillusionment they will suffer. Occasionally these acts of chicanery are carried out with such hilarity that the success of the deception is threatened. The whole business of religious initiation, when conducted in this way, takes on the appearance of little more than a cruel joke, a miserable hoax. Such patent deception seems to negate the essential task of the rite: instead of revealing to the initiate a compelling sacred reality, the revered objects are defamed in his presence. Since the dire religious implications of such a conclusion are abhorrent to me, I am faced with the task of uncovering what must be going on beneath this perplexing surface. Upon examining several examples of this process, from widely diverse regions of the world, we may be able to see something of how these rude surface phenomena play an essential and profound role in initiation.

A striking example of the defamation of sacred objects in the initiatory process occurs in the rites of initiation into one of the healing cults of the Ndembu of Africa. As we would expect, the revelation of the nature of *Kavula*, the spirit of the healing cult, is an essential part of the initiation. But the process by which the initiates learn of *Kavula* is startling. The adepts prepare a frame made of sticks covered with a white blanket to represent the divinity. It is called *isoli*. One of the initiated hides beneath the blanket to play the part of *Kavula*. The initiates are chased by the adepts, caught, interrogated with unanswerable questions, taunted for being unable to supply appropriate answers, and eventually led to the *isoli*. The initiates are in-structed regarding the formal procedure of greeting *Kavula*. When they ad-dress the spirit in the *isoli*, its voice returns their greeting. The initiates approach the structure, and when instructed to kill *Kavula*, they beat the object with the butts of their rattles. With each blow, "*Kavula*" shakes con-vulsively, as if dying. The initiates are then led back to the village. When they enter it an adept takes a firebrand, strikes it violently on the ground and cries out, "He is dead!" And after a brief closing oration the initiation is concluded.

Victor Turner, who reported these events, elicited comment on the "killing of *Kavula*" from the Ndembu people. Muchona, a very knowledgeable old man, said, "*Kavula* is killed to frighten the candidate. For he believes he is really killing *Kavula*. He has been instructed by the adepts that 'If you see the spirit of *Kavula*, you must consider this is a spirit which helps people....' The adepts are just deceiving the candidates at *isoli*." One of the female initiates told Turner that it was "*Kavula's* back that we saw in *isoli*. When *Kavula* was killed the spirit flew away into the sky, not to *Nzambi* (the High God), but 'into the wind.' It could come again."

In this initiation rite, the adepts use techniques of deception to build an illusion, a fictitious conception of reality, for the initiates. Bringing the initiates into *Kavula's* sacred presence, they confuse them with unanswerable questions, tell them to kill the very spirit that is to be revealed to them, and assure them at the conclusion of the rite that "he is dead." Once the rites are over, the initiates are even shown the construction of the *isoli*. The illusion is disclosed; the enchantment with *isoli* broken. *Kavula*, as presented to them, is shown to be nothing but a blanket-covered framework of sticks. Remark-ably, however, the initiate demonstrates in her comments on the event that she discovered in it something of the mysterious nature of *Kavula*. She has come to realize that *Kavula* is not limited to his appearance in the *isoli* but is something more. Somehow in the process she gained the knowledge that *Kavula* is a spirit that flew "into the wind" and can come back, or perhaps as Muchona told Turner, "*Kavula* takes all powers." It is through the creation of an illusion that is subsequently shattered by a dramatic and powerful act of disenchantment that the revelation of the spiritual nature of the sacred is effected.

In a comparable fashion, Hopi children are initiated into the *kachina* cult which signals the start of their formal participation in religious activities. Prior to the age of initiation, the children are very carefully protected from seeing *kachina* figures without their masks or seeing the masks when not being worn. The children are led to believe that the *kachinas* visit the village at certain intervals through the year, and they come to expect gifts from them. During the *kachina* cult initiation rites the children are frightened by the ogre *kachinas*; they are entertained by numerous *kachina* dances; they come into close contact with a great many *kachinas*; they may even be whipped by the *kachinas*; and they are told secret stories about the origin of the *kachinas*. But the most lasting impression comes during the last night of the ceremony. The children are taken into a *kiva* to await a *kachina* dance—a now familiar event. They hear the *kachinas* calling as they approach the *kiva*. They witness the invitation extended from within the *kiva* for the dancing gods to enter. But to the children's amazement, the *kachinas* enter without masks, and for the first time in their lives, the initiates discover that the *kachinas* are actually members of their own village impersonating the gods.

Dorothy Eggan found that this revelation distresses the children and that most Hopi recall it as a traumatic and disorienting experience. She selected the following comment as representative:

> I cried and cried into my sheepskin that night, feeling I had been made a fool of. How could I ever watch the Kachinas dance again? I hated my parents and thought I could never believe the old folks again, wondering if Gods had ever danced for the Hopi as they said and if people really lived after death. I hated to see the other children fooled and felt mad when they said I was a big girl now and should act like one. But I was afraid to tell the others the truth for they might whip me to death. I know now it was best and the only way to teach the children, but it took me a long time to know that.

The Hopi children, unlike the Ndembu initiates, are not a party to a ritual killing of the gods, but the effect is much the same. For observing the unmasked *kachinas* produces within the children the sense that the *kachinas*, as they had so fondly known them, are dead. Once disenchanted with the masked figures, the children can never feel he same about the *kachina* figures or the things they had been taught about them. Yet it is clear there is more to the initiation than revealing to the children that "the *kachinas* are not real gods, but merely masked impersonations of them," as the rite has commonly been interpreted, for Eggan's informant indicated that she realized the value of the technique in teaching children, and surely she means more than simply disclosing the masked nature of the *kachinas*.

This initiatory process begins with the careful nurturing of a naively realistic perspective in the children. They are encouraged to be enchanted by surface appearances. They are led to believe that the *kachinas* are nothing more or less than what they appear in material form to be. This "education" into a simplistic, one-dimensional world view sets them up for the shock of disenchantment which is experienced at the conclusion of the rites. It culti-vates their childish outlook into a ripe fruit ready for plucking.

With the unmasking of the *kachinas* the naiveté of the children is shat-tered all at once and forever. The existence of the *kachinas*, the nature of one's own destiny, the trust in parents and elders, and the very shape of reality itself are all, in a flash, brought into radical question. The children can either accept the world as bereft of meaning, with Hopi religion a sham, or find some deeper sense in the ceremonies and objects which had come to mean so much to them. Necessarily, they begin their religious life in a state of serious reflection and in quest of an understanding of the sacred profound enough to sustain their new life. There is tremendous incentive for the children to listen even more carefully to the stories of the old people and to participate in the ceremonies with a new seriousness.

Once again the process of disenchantment can be seen at work in the initiation rites of the Wiradthuri tribes of Australia. The occasion is the initiation of boys into manhood. The rites are loaded with chicanery. The boys are frequently commanded to walk with their eyes fixed on their feet so that they may not observe the staging of the trickery. A principal focus of the several rites rests upon the revelation of the nature of the spirit *Dhuramoolan*. Frequently the boys are told that *Dhuramoolan* is coming near and are advised to listen for his approaching voice. They hear a whirring noise that grows louder and louder, but they do not know that the sound is being made by men whirling bullroarers. At a critical juncture in the rites, the boys are covered with blankets and told that *Dhuramoolan* is coming and that he may eat them. With bullroarers roaring close by, the elders reach under each blanket and with hammer and chisel they knock out an incisor tooth of each boy. The boys think the spirit is taking their teeth, while sparing their lives.

Again an illusion of the nature of the sacred is prepared, and it is fully accepted by the initiates. And once again the initiation culminates in disen-chantment. On the last day the boys are covered with blankets and a crack-ling fire is built. The bullroarers are whirled nearby, and the boys are told that *Dhuramoolan* is going to burn them. When the boys appear sufficiently fright-ened, the blankets are removed from their heads, and they see for the first time the men whirling the bullroarers and learn that this artificial noisemak-ing is what they've taken to be the voice of *Dhuramoolan*. Pointing to these men, the head man says, "There he is! That is *Dhuramoolan*," and he explains to the boys how the noise is made by whirling flat pieces of wood on strings. Then the boys are given the bullroarer to examine; they may even try whirling them. They are forbidden to tell the uninitiated about them or ever to make a bullroarer except during the initiation rites. Then the adepts destroy the bullroarers by splitting them into pieces and driving them into the ground, or sometimes by burning them. There is little information about how the boys respond to this revelation, but clearly they can never be terrified as they once were by the voice of the bullroarers. Nor can they retain the naive knowledge of *Dhuramoolan's* nature engendered in them during the initiation rites. They too have learned that the sacred is more than it appears to be, that it can never be identified wholly with one mode of revelation. The medium of epiphany is shown to be something trivial and powerless in itself.

In these examples, the whole process of initiation builds to a climax in the shock of disenchantment. The sacred objects are destroyed in the eyes of the initiates. But despite this, the initiations evidently succeed, although the revelation of the sacred occurs more as a result of the initiatic process than as a part of it.

When the dynamic of disenchantment is the driving power in an initia-   15
tion rite, the first and essential ingredient is encouraging identification of the sacred with the cult object. The uninitiated must come to believe that the objects and the sacred are exactly identical. The white blanket in the framework of sticks *is Kavula;* the masked dancers *are* Hopi gods; and the roar of the noisemakers *is Dhuramoolan* shouting. Ingenious techniques of secrecy and deception have been devised to nurture a perspective of naive realism, and the effectiveness of the initiation depends on how firmly this viewpoint is established.

The whole initiatic process reinforces this sense that the fullness of the sacred is invested in the cult objects. Then in the concluding moments, upon the threshold of a new life, the illusion is dissolved and the shock of disenchantment shatters all that went before. The experience makes a return to the previous state of life impossible. The naive realism of the uninitiated perspective has been exploded. The rites have demonstrated irreversibly that things are not simply what they appear to be, that one-dimensional literalism is a childish faith that one has to grow beyond or else despair of a life rich in meaning and worth. Surely, being thus forced to abandon one's ingrained notion of reality is to experience a true death of the former self. And this loss of self constitutes the concrete transformation signified by the symbolic dying experienced in the rites.

The purpose of initiation—revealing the nature of the sacred reality—is, of course, one with the nature of religion itself. For religion springs from the unique human capacity to grasp a reality which is infinite and "wholly other," to use Rudolf Otto's phrase. This is possible only because of our gift for symbolization, in which, as Goethe said, "the particular represents the general, not as a dream or a shadow, but as a living and momentous revelation of the inexplorable." It is through the dynamics of symbolization that the sacred is manifest in ordinary, mundane objects. In religion, symbols mediate the infinite through the finite, the general through the the particular. The challenge of initiation is to begin with the cult object, which is finite and particular, and to reveal in it the infinite fullness of the sacred. The rites of initiation have to show that the symbols are only a form or a representation of the sacred; and at the same time, they must demonstrate that the transcendent is really embodied in them. The initiate must be simultaneously convinced that the divinity is independent of its finite manifestation and that the contingent symbols are vital to the revelation of the sacred.

Through initiation culminating in disenchantment, the novice enters religious life in a state of crisis, disappointment, or perplexity about the nature of the sacred. The only thing he knows is that he has been fooled and his sense of what is real and what is not is confounded. His options seem clear. He may see the sacred objects as meaningless—childhood toys to be put away with the onset of maturity—in which case a life centered in these symbols is likewise pointless and empty. Or he may undertake a quest for a fuller, adult understanding of the higher reality that has been revealed and regard the symbols as pointers to an encompassing mystery that is inexhaustible. The newly initiated are invited and expected to participate in the religious activities. Through such participation, they begin gradually to grasp the full scope of the higher reality revealed in the symbols. With this expanding awareness, meaning is conferred on the sacred objects in an enhanced and maturing way. For it is only when the fullness of religious meaning is grasped that the symbols genuinely mediate the sacred.

The profound wisdom of the method of initiation by disenchantment lies in its capacity to bring the initiate through succeeding stages of perception to an encounter with the full reality of the sacred. The rites necessarily must end on the threshold of revelation, for it is only through the living of the religious way that the sacred becomes fully known.

Victor Turner has discerned a similarity between the symbolic structures 20 of the "killing of *Kavula*" and the Gospel story of the Empty Tomb. The death and resurrection motif also involves the enchantment-disenchantment process at work in the initiation of the first Christians as a religious tradition.

The Gospels recount the life and teachings of Jesus as the story of the incarnate revelation of God. The episode of the Empty Tomb concludes the books of Matthew, Mark, and Luke, and in John only one chapter follows it. It comes directly after the account of the Crucifixion, and for those destined to be members of the first Christian community, this death caused fear, despondency, and consternation. This is especially clear in the conclusion of the last chapter in Mark:

> And very early in the morning the first day of the week, they came unto the sepulchre at the rising of the sun. And they said among themselves, Who shall roll us away the stone from the door of the sepulchre? And when they looked, they saw that the stone was rolled away: for it was very great. And entering into the sepulchre, they saw a young man sitting on the right side, clothed in a long white garment; and they were affrighted. And he saith unto them, Be not affrighted: Ye seek Jesus of Nazareth, which was crucified: he is risen; he is not here: behold the place where they laid him. But go your way, tell his disciples

and Peter that he goeth before you into Galilee: there shall ye see him, as he said unto you. And they went out quickly, and fled from the sepulchre; for they trembled and were amazed: neither said they any thing to any man; for they were afraid.

Considering this as the concluding event in the initiation of the first Christians, several elements are remarkably similar to the rites of initiation described above. As the Ndembu experienced the death of *Kavula*, the Hopi the unmasking of the *kachina* figures, the Wiradthuri the destruction of the bullroarers, so the followers of Jesus were forced to witness his death. They had come to know him well and had accepted him as their Lord. Yet, they saw him captured, tortured, and crucified. They saw that he was a man who felt pain, suffered, and died. He, like any man, was placed in a tomb. The followers of Jesus had embraced a naive view of his reality—that Jesus the man and Jesus the Christ were simply identical. But going to the tomb, they found that he was not there. The Ndembu who examined the *isoli* found only a framework of sticks—*Kavula* was not there. The Hopi found only their own relatives under the masks—the *Kachina* gods were not there. The Wiradthuri coming from under their blankets found only old men whirling bullroarers—*Dhuramoolan* was not there.

The story of the Empty Tomb in Christianity follows a pattern akin to the process of disenchantment. Christianity as a religion begins with the Empty Tomb which is received not with joy and comfort, but with trembling, astonishment, and fear. That which had appeared to be so real, the man Jesus, had ceased to be and not even his body remained as an object to care for and reverence. It has been in the face of the fear and astonishment at the loss of Jesus, the man, that Christians throughout the Christian era have been led to grasp the reality of Jesus, the Christ, who was resurrected from the tomb, and hence the reality of God Himself. It must follow that only with that revelation could it be clearly recognized that it is the life and teachings of Jesus that are the "living and the momentous revelation of the inexplorable" God.

An event occurring at the initiation of a Zen monk into his order is again comparable to what has been discussed. A statue of the Buddha is placed before the initiate, whereupon it is broken and cast aside. The initiate is told, "We are throwing the Buddha to the dogs." It is, of course, the object of Zen to come to know the wisdom of the Buddha directly and not through doctrine or teachings, and this act of disenchantment with the image of the Buddha serves to shock the initiate into grasping the higher reality of the Buddha-nature. Zen methods are well known for their use of shock and illusion to lead the followers toward the experience of *satori*—the grasping of and union with the higher reality. The initiatory process of disillusionment is uniquely reflected in an ancient Zen saying, "To begin with, everyone sees mountains as mountains and trees as trees; then when one seeks to come to terms with them, mountains no longer appear as mountains, nor trees as trees; but finally when enlightenment is attained, mountains are again seen as mountains and trees as trees."

In these few examples from a broad spectrum of religious contexts, there   25
appears the common structure of a technique of disenchantment used to initiate the mature religious perspective and to promote authentic apprehension of the sacred. The apparent effect of disenchantment is itself illusory. Acts which seem to spell the end of religion have been found to be techniques that thrust the initiate into the arena of adult religious life with incentive to plumb its full depths. They lay bare the limitations of naive views of reality so that through deepened participation in a religious community and celebration of the day-to-day events of life in religious ritual, the individual may increasingly experience the mysterious fullness of the sacred, sustaining realm. And a mature sense emerges that the sacred symbols can reveal the sacred without ever exhausting its reality.

THESIS AND THOUGHT

1. Define *disenchantment* as it is used in the essay.
2. According to Gill, what is the function of disenchantment in each of the cultures he discusses? In the cultures collectively?
3. Where is Gill's most explicit statement of his thesis? Compare that statement with those that appear at the ends of paragraphs 3, 6, 11, and 13 and in paragraph 14. What purposes do these less elaborate versions serve in their specific contexts, and how do they collectively contribute to our understanding of the essay as a whole?

STRUCTURE

1. Except for Zen Buddhism, the examples here are presented with almost uniform elaboration. How does this relative uniformity contribute to your understanding of the article? Does this uniformity imply anything about instances of disenchantment that lie beyond the essay itself? Explain.
2. The five examples of disenchantment here seem to be grouped in an initial cluster of three—involving the Ndembu, the Hopi, and Wiradthuri—and a second cluster of two—the examples of Christianity and Zen Buddhism. They are, in fact, physically separated by paragraphs 14–19, which analyze disenchantment as it appears in the first cluster. Do you see any thematic or

structural purpose in the separation? What effects, if any, might have resulted from discussing the five examples in succession and leaving the intervening analytic passage to the end?

3. Gill employs two principal techniques other than exemplification. They are process analysis (see chapter 4) and comparison (see chapter 5).

   a. Examine one of the initiation rites described in paragraphs 4, 7, or 12–13. By what means has Gill merged the various steps into a unified whole? What other means might have been used?

   b. Consider such sentences as these: "The Hopi children, unlike the Ndembu initiates, are not party to a ritual killing of the gods, but the effect is much the same" (para. 9); "Again an illusion of the nature of the sacred is prepared, and it is fully accepted by the initiates. And once again the initiation culminates in disenchantment" (para. 13); or "The story of the Empty Tomb in Christianity follows a pattern akin to the process of disenchantment" (para. 23). How essential are comparisons such as these to establishing Gill's thesis?

STYLE

1. Gill uses a great number of non-English words, such as *isoli, kiva,* and *satori.* By what means and to what extent does he explain them? Are there any whose meaning is still unclear once the discussion is over?

2. Frequently, scholars such as Gill write in the jargon peculiar to their academic discipline. How prevalent here is language that seems special to Gill's field of study? Cite specific instances, if any. Given the extent of jargon present, draw a conclusion about the nature of Gill's intended audience.

3. In the main, Gill's attitude toward his topic is objective and detached, that is, appropriately scholarly. Explain, then, this sentence from paragraph 3: "Since the dire religious implications of such a conclusion [the defamation of deities or sacred objects] are abhorrent to me, I am faced with the task of uncovering what must be going on beneath this perplexing surface."

   Is writing in first person (*I*) a breach of academic etiquette here? Of tone? Or is it justifiable or even useful? When, generally, do you think writing in first person is acceptable? When is third person preferable?

CONSIDERATIONS

1. If you have a commitment to Christianity or to any of the religions discussed, what is your reaction to its being compared (objectively) with the others? If you identify with some faith not included by Gill, how might you have responded had he used yours as an example? If you have no particular religious

convictions, does the essay stimulate your intellectual interest in the subject? In all cases, explain.

2. Comparative religion is a field of study that burgeoned in the nineteenth century and has persisted to our own day. You might find it interesting to explore one of the pioneering works in the field, Sir James Frazer's *The Golden Bough*. You might also look into Joseph Campbell's *The Hero with a Thousand Faces*, a more recent, complex, and challenging work.

3. Write an essay comparing (and perhaps contrasting) two rites of a similar type (e.g., initiation) in two cultures with which you are familiar. Focus especially on their purposes.

4. Write an essay describing your reaction to discovering that Santa Claus or the tooth fairy does not exist—or discovering that a particular hero (an object of metaphorical idol worship) had feet of clay.

5. Religious contexts aside, as a matter of either ethics or emotional health, do you believe that it is acceptable for people to be deceived for their own good?

Suggestions for Writing: Example

I. Write an essay in which you illustrate the truth or falsity of one of the following adages or quotations. Use the statement you choose as a springboard, but formulate your own thesis.

—A fool and his money are soon parted.

—Necessity is the mother of invention.

—"There is no life but [i.e., without] pain."—John Keats

—Absence makes the heart grow fonder.

—"He who can, does. He who can't, teaches."—George Bernard Shaw

—People are judged by the color of their skin, not by the "content of their character." (adapted from Martin Luther King)

—An adage or quotation of your choice

II. Generate a thesis about one of the following subjects; then use it as the basis for an essay that you develop primarily through examples. Avoid categorizing and stereotyping. (For example, if the subject were restaurants, you would not write primarily about various kinds of restaurants—e.g., fast food, family, and fine—but about a particular characteristic. "Good restaurant service is increasingly hard to find" would be acceptable, as would "Most fast-food restaurants are grease city.")

—magazines

—politicians

—conformists or nonconformists

—diets

—advertisements

—mentors

—heroes

4

Process Analysis

"Let the jury consider their verdict," the King said, for about
the twentieth time that day.

"No, No!" said the Queen. "Sentence first—verdict afterwards."

LEWIS CARROLL, *Alice's Adventures in Wonderland*

Alone in the kitchen for the first time, stomach growling, you reach for
the book that will save you from starvation, *Easy Recipes for the Novice Cook.*
Opening it at random, you find the following:

1ST WITCH Round about the cauldron go;
In the poisoned entrails throw.
Toad, that under cold stone
Days and nights has thirty-one
Swelt'red venom, sleeping got,
Boil thou first i' th' charmed pot.

ALL Double, double, toil and trouble,
Fire burn and cauldron bubble.

2ND WITCH Fillet of a fenny snake,
In the cauldron boil and bake;
Eye of newt, and toe of frog,
Wool of bat, and tongue of dog,
Adder's fork,[1] and blindworm's sting,
Lizard's leg, and howlet's wing
For a charm of pow'rful trouble
Like a hell-broth boil and bubble.

ALL Double, double, toil and trouble,
Fire burn and cauldron bubble.

---

[1]**Adder's fork:** forked tongue. [All notes are the editor's.]

3RD WITCH Scale of dragon, tooth of wolf,
Witch's mummy, maw and gulf[2]
Of the ravined salt-sea shark,
Root of hemlock digged i' th' dark,
Liver of blaspheming Jew,
Gall of goat, and slips of yew
Slivered in the moon's eclipse,
Nose of Turk, and Tartar's lips,
Finger of birth-strangled babe
Ditch-delivered by a drab[3]
Make the gruel thick and slab.[4]
Add thereto a tiger's chaudron[5]
For the ingredience of our cauldron.

ALL Double, double, toil and trouble,
Fire burn and cauldron bubble.

2ND WITCH Cool it with a baboon's blood,
Then the charm is firm and good.

Yuck! Examining the cover, you realize that you have mistakenly grabbed a copy of *Macbeth*. Looking through the shelf more carefully this time, you find the cookbook and, turning to page one, discover this recipe:

Toast

Equipment: Toaster
Ingredients: Slice of bread

Take a slice of bread from the package and place it in the toaster. (Be sure that the toaster is plugged in.) Set the dial to the desired degree of doneness. Some dials will read "light" to "dark"; others will use a numbered range, 1–10, for example. When the dial has been set, depress the lever. This will simultaneously turn the toaster on and lower the bread into toasting position. In a matter of minutes the toaster will shut off automatically, popping the now toasted slice up to its original position. Remove and eat.

Well, this isn't exactly pheasant under glass, but unlike the witches' brew, it is ingestible. You follow the steps, succeed, and though mumbling something about "not by bread alone" as you wolf down the slice, you stave off hunger—for now.

INFORMATIONAL AND DIRECTIONAL PROCESSES

Everything in this whimsical, if exaggerated, scenario illustrates the idea of process—either explaining how to do something or explaining how some-

---

[2]**gulf:** gullet. [3]**drab:** whore. [4]**slab:** sticky. [5]**chaudron:** entrails.

thing is (or was) done. Had Shakespeare chosen to, he might have called the passage from *Macbeth*, "How to Concoct a Charm." Similarly and obviously, the second recipe could be titled, "How to Make Toast." Both of these, however, may be seen as part of yet another process that might be called, "How You Got Started in Your Culinary Career."

Recipes like those for the charm and toast are directional processes; that is, they present the reader with a set of directions, which, if followed, will reproduce the results described. Indeed, the reader usually studies such processes in order to reproduce them. Familiar sources of such processes, in addition to cookbooks, are auto-repair manuals, guides to writing research papers, instructions that accompany sewing patterns, tax forms, or toys that require assembly. Here, for example, are some instructions for interior painting:

> Fill your paint tray about two-thirds full, leaving empty space at the top of the sloping section so you can roll off excess after each dip. Make sure the roller cover is uniformly saturated to avoid dripping or splattering. When painting walls, make your first stroke with the fully loaded roller in an *upward* direction. On ceilings the first stroke should always be *away* from you. On both walls and ceilings, try to reach as close as possible into each corner. . . . It is usually best to start applying the paint to the wall with a series of angled strokes so that the pattern forms a large 'V' on the surface. . . . Then roll back and forth with parallel strokes to fill in the open spaces and eliminate ridges while spreading the paint uniformly. . . .
>
> BERNARD GLADSTONE, *The New York Times Guide to Simple Home Repairs*, pp. 17–18

The larger process in which the recipes for toast and the charm are embedded—the one that describes your first time in the kitchen—is informational, that is, a process that imparts knowledge without any expectation of action being based on it. In most cases, action would be impossible—you can't, for instance, repeat that first time in the kitchen. Similarly, you might learn how petroleum is refined or how marriages in India are traditionally arranged, but you do not build a refinery or wait patiently to be informed about your prospective spouse. Nor could you ever hope to duplicate the actions either of the animal or the molecules described by Maurice Burton in the following informational process:

> In 1945 an Alsatian dog used by the Cairo police was called to follow the track of a donkey that had walked across rocky ground four and a half days previously. The dog stopped barking only outside the house where the donkey was found.
>
> To appreciate the Alsatian's performance we can examine what happens each time we put a foot to the ground. Each time the bare foot touches the ground 0.000001 gramme of sweat, the odorous part of which is butyric acid, is deposited. Even when [we are] wearing a leather

or rubber shoe, billions of molecules pass through the material at each step. The composition of the sweat trace we leave soon begins to change, which is why a dog can tell the direction in which a person has walked after sniffing a trail. A gradient is formed, passing from the oldest to the newest, and a dog can pick up the direction after sniffing over a few metres of trail. Secondly, . . . not only is the composition of the sweat molecules changing, [but the molecules] are sinking into the material of the ground, most readily in loose soil, but rapidly also even in rock.

The Sixth Sense of Animals, p. 104

The grammatical "mood" in which they are written is another difference between informational and directional processes. Like most other writing, informational processes use the indicative mood, whereas directional ones use the imperative (command). For example, if you were to explain how an assembly-line worker mounts a car tire, you would write, "Once the tire is in place, the assembler *tightens* the nuts." But if you were directing someone to change a tire, you would write, "Once the tire is in place, *tighten* the nuts." Note that the subject of the one sentence is the third-person "assembler," whereas the subject of the other is the elusive second-person "you" (understood)—as it is in this very sentence.

Although the matters of action and mood distinguish directional from informational processes, the two have points in common. Each is a clear sequence of actions or events marked by such chronological transitions as *when, next, then, after, following,* or by ordinal numbers (*first, second, third,* and so on). In addition, each may offer a word of warning, caution, or advice regarding the consequences of actions taken or ignored. In the case of the toast, you were told to be sure that the toaster was plugged in. Similarly, in reading the charm you learned that "baboon's blood" will cool the potion and that the long list of ingredients preceding the last will make the gruel "thick and slab." Again, in the quotation above concerning painting, you were advised to saturate the roller cover uniformly in order "to avoid dripping or splattering." Even the informational account of your actions in the kitchen makes indirect note of the need to be careful about which book you reach for.

PROCESS ANALYSIS AND NARRATIVE

Because process analysis is based on chronology, the pattern has something in common with narrative. There are, however, several differences. First, in narrative the order in which events are presented is not necessarily crucial. Much detective fiction, for example, focuses on events prior to that of the ongoing action in hopes of discovering whodunit and why it was done. A work such as Homer's *Iliad* presents another instance of this flexibility. It begins in the last year of the ten-year war against Troy and only later catches up the readers (listeners, originally) with preceding events. In process analysis, however, one rarely flashes back or forward. Second, even when strict chronological order is present, narrative emphasizes *what* occurred, its significance, or who was responsible for its occurring; process is devoted more strictly to *how* something is, was, or might be done.

At times, for instance in the presentation of history, the distinctions might be less clear. In reading about World War II we might learn the mechanics of how Allied forces under British Field Marshal Montgomery defeated General Rommel at El Alamein, or of how the Russians stopped the German army at Stalingrad, but our focus is often far less concentrated on the processes themselves than on the human issues of greed, courage, hatred, foresight, sacrifice, and anguish—among others—that such events raise.

PROCESS IN ACADEMIC WRITING

Academic life will regularly involve you in both directional and informational processes. Experiments in the sciences or social sciences require that you explain your method or procedure. The professor who teaches you how to write a research paper is likely to tell you to find sources, then evaluate them, next take notes from them, and finally support your ideas from the notes. The physical and health education department might give instruction in CPR or the Heimlich maneuver, and its team trainers might instruct their charges in the techniques of warming up, weight training, and bodybuilding. Classes in acting or singing will offer instruction in how to breathe efficiently as in the following passage:

> Lie down on the floor on your back. Place one hand on your chest and the other on your belly. See if you can get into the frame of mind for sleep. Feel your hands rise and fall as your body expands and contracts naturally while it takes in and releases air.
>
> In order to feel the full expansion of your body as you continue lying on the floor, place your hands right above your waistline at your sides, enclosing the area between your thumb and the other fingers. Now push in forcibly against the diaphragm muscle as your body expands. Continue giving your body the resistance, and your ability to expand, maintain the expansion, and breathe fully will improve.
>
> Try singing a tone or a familiar melody as you breathe in this position. Listen for the difference in your voice between the way you usually sound and the way you sound now. . . .
>
> Working within these guidelines will help you develop your body expansion so that you have enough strength to sing long, full phrases. . . .
>
> SHELLEY KATSCH AND CAROL MERLE-FISHMAN, *The Music Within You*, pp. 148–49

If anything, informational process are more pervasive. You might discover how a deaf Beethoven composed his Ninth Symphony or how a visually impaired and ultimately blind Milton wrote *Paradise Lost*. How were the teachings of Islam spread? How, exactly, do the Japanese run their schools and factories? How were immigrants processed at Ellis Island? Writing in present tense to create an impression of immediacy, Oscar Handlin provides an answer to the last question:

> They are arranged in lines cut off from each other by wooden barriers, and they begin wearily to tread an incomprehensible maze. Officials in uniform survey them, look at the already large collection of papers, peer at eyes, down throats, thump chests, make notes on cards, and affix tags of various colors to the hesitant bodies that pass uneasily along before them. Now and again one of the fellow travellers is separated out from the rest—to go who knows where. . . .
>
> The handful of inspectors are too few to permit more than a perfunctory examination. They look for surface disabilities (trachoma, an infection of the eyelids, is one; favus, a skin disease, is another), for obvious deformities, and for signs of idiocy or insanity. . . . [T]he impatient officials . . . now and then single out for more than casual study a case from the long rows that move stolidly before them. The rest get by. They escape to the free American air and leave behind the luckless who must still face medical boards of review, hearings, and appeals, perhaps soon to be sent back from whence they came or to spend more months in the confinement rooms of the station while distant powers thumb through the dossiers that pile up on Washington desks.

The Uprooted, pp. 57–58

You might explore such questions as how life was lived in the original ghetto in Venice. In the Warsaw ghetto. How it is lived today in the modern American ghettos of Harlem or Watts, South African ones like Soweto, or the "favelas" of Rio de Janeiro. How were the hanging gardens of Babylon built? The Brooklyn Bridge? Stonehenge? The following passage describes the construction of the Egyptian pyramids.

> In the absence of the pulley—a device which does not seem to have been known in Egypt before Roman times—only one method of raising heavy weights was open to the ancient Egyptians, namely by means of ramps composed of brick and earth which sloped upwards from the level of the ground to whatever height was desired. If, for instance, a short wall were to be built, the stones for each course after the lowest would be taken to the required level on a ramp constructed against the wall for the whole of its length and projecting outwards at right angles to the line of the wall. With the addition of each successive course of masonry, the ramp would be raised and also extended so that the gradient remained unchanged. Finally, when the wall had been built to its full

height, the ramp would be dismantled and the outer faces of the stones, which had not previously been made smooth, dressed course by course downwards as the level of the ramp was reduced. . . .

I. E. S. EDWARDS, *The Pyramids of Egypt*, p. 205

You might learn how the women's, ecology, or labor movement originated, evolved, expanded—whether at home or abroad:

> Until the last years of the nineteenth century, almost all labor organizations in Chile were mutual aid societies (*socorros mutuos*) formed by artisans and skilled workers. They provided members with sickness or accident pay, a "dignified" burial, death benefits paid to dependents, and, in some cases, retirement payments. Other activities of the mutual aid societies included the establishment of savings plans, night classes for workers and their families, cultural and social events, and consumer cooperatives. The first mutualist groups were established in Santiago during the 1840s, but it was not until the formation of the printers' societies in Santiago and Valparaíso in 1853 and 1855 that a working class organization achieved any institutional stability. Other skilled or semiskilled workers, such as tailors, carpenters, bricklayers, bakers, and railway workers, also organized mutual aid societies. While many were established along purely craft lines, other *socorros mutuos* admitted workers of several industries, served all the employees of a single establishment, or included only female or Catholic workers.

PETER DE SHAZO, *Urban Workers and Labor in Chile: 1902–1927*, p. 89

In all of these, you might also discover the "why" as well as the "how," but that is a story for another chapter—chapter 7, to be precise.

USING PROCESS ANALYSIS

Neither the recipe for toast nor that for the witches' charm has a clearly stated thesis. But each of them has an implicit one: "You can make a good piece of toast/charm if you follow these directions." Almost any directional process has an analogous central idea. In some cases, however, you might want a more elaborate and focused statement: "Preparing an Indonesian feast is not easy, but it is well worth the effort." Or, "Model ships don't grow in bottles. They are built and placed there through skill, concentration, patience, and love." Such theses tend to humanize the process and to engage the reader.

Informational processes almost invariably require a thesis statement, at least one that may be deduced from the material presented. A good thesis for this kind of writing will allow the reader to see the sequence presented from the writer's perspective; that is, it will offer a rationale by which the chronology may be interpreted or understood.

Consider the following: "Becoming a nun is paradoxical, at once self-sacrificing and self-fulfilling." Or, "The British managed to survive World War II largely by accepting Winston Churchill's offer of 'blood, sweat, toil, and tears.' " Or, "The building of Angkor Wat was fraught with peril." In the first instance, the reader expects to learn how one becomes a nun, but also to see the steps in light of the terms the thesis proposes—sacrifice and fulfillment. In the second, one anticipates that events will be associated with the four items named. In the last, the reader rightly presupposes danger at every step in the construction of the Cambodian temple.

Regardless of whether the process is directional or informational, of whether the thesis is stated or implied, be sure to include clear chronological transitions, some of which are mentioned on page 184. If you need to describe concurrent events or actions, use words such as *meanwhile, simultaneously,* or *during*.

Although it is briefer than papers that you are likely to write, the following self-contained process, describing the reproductive cycle of the water flea (*Daphnia*), suggests how such a paper might be developed:

> *Daphnia* is . . . abundant in lakes around the world. And almost all of these *Daphnia* . . . are females.
>
> In the spring, as warmer days melt the last thin panes of ice covering the lake, female *Daphnia* hatch out from hard-shelled eggs buried in the muddy bottom. Nibbling at the burgeoning algae . . . , those females grow rapidly and reproduce rapidly—asexually. They need no male to fertilize their eggs, for these eggs can develop without sperm. Only a few days apart in age, their daughters, granddaughters, and great-granddaughters are all clones, continuing to reproduce asexually during the bountiful . . . months of summer.
>
> As the year wears on, the lake becomes exhausted of some of the nutrients needed by the water fleas. Essential chemicals become scarce. Finally, the impoverished environment throws a biological switch in the *Daphnia,* who respond . . . by producing sons as well as daughters. . . .
>
> Ten generations of female *Daphnia* producing identical daughters are ideal for life in a nu[r]turant and warm environment, but the hardships and uncertainties of the coming winter demand new gene combinations. Only sexual mating can provide that. Indeed, the mating of female and male water fleas results in a special kind of daughter: an egg wrapped in a particularly thick shell and imbued with the ability to suspend development, to stop its metabolism and rest until the winter passes and spring comes again. Only eggs produced by a sexual union survive to hatch in the warming, welcoming lake and start the asexual cycle again.
>
> EVELYN SHAW AND JOAN DARLING, *Female Strategies*, p. 22

Although the passage might not have an explicit thesis, it clearly emphasizes the predominantly female character of the species. You may also observe that the stages of the cycle described are well defined.

Shen Kua

(China; 1031–1095)

Shen Kua was a public official of the early Sung dynasty. He was at various times chancellor of a college, director of flood-control projects, and a military leader. Banished to the provinces after a crushing defeat at the hands of the Tartars, he wrote sketches and notes describing both his rural environment and the technological advances of the day. Clearly, he was contemporary with the invention detailed in the selection.

Shen is known chiefly by the miscellaneous collection Jottings of the Brook of Dreams *(Meng-hsi pi t'an) from which "The Invention of Movable Type" is taken.*

The Invention of Movable Type

During the Ch'ing-li period (1041–1048) a commoner named Pi Sheng first invented . . . movable type. Each [piece of] type was made of moistened clay upon which was carved one Chinese character. The portion that formed the character was as thin as the edge of a small coin. The type was then hardened by fire and thus made permanent.

To proceed with the process of printing, a printer smeared an iron plate with a mixture of turpentine, resin, wax, and burned paper ash. Pieces of movable type were then placed on the plate [close] together and were arranged in such a way as to reflect[1] the text of a book to be printed. They were confined . . . by an iron fence fastened tightly to the plate.

The iron plate was then placed on a gentle fire in order to melt the mixture previously described. A wooden board with smooth surface was pressed upon the type so that the heads of all pieces would appear on the same level. The plate was then ready for printing.

The cost would be very high if the printer intended to print only two or three copies of a book. If, on the other hand, hundreds or thousands of copies were to be printed, the amount of time required to print each copy would be reduced to a minimum. Usually two plates were used when a book was printed. While one plate was in the process of printing, pieces of movable type were arranged and set on the other. . . . When the required number of copies had been printed by the first plate, the second plate was ready. Thus the two . . . changed their role alternately.

[1] **to reflect:** that is, to create a reverse image [Ed.]

For each Chinese character there were several pieces of type. The num-   5
ber reached twenty or more for each of such commonly used characters as *chih*
and *yeh*. The availability of a large number of the same piece of type was
necessitated by the repeated occurrences of the same Chinese character on
the page of a book to be printed. When pieces of type were not in use, they
were covered with paper for . . . protection, were grouped together according
to rhymes, and were stored away in wooden frames. Occasionally there were
uncommon Chinese characters that had not been prepared in advance. In
such cases the printer had to carve them on the spot, harden them by fire,
and make them fit for printing in a minimum amount of time. . . .

Moistened clay, instead of wood, was used as the material to make
movable type . . . because wood was subject to change and tended to distort
the Chinese character carved on it. When exposed to moisture, the surface
of a piece of wooden type became uneven, and the type itself became thus
unusable. Moreover, after it had been glued to the plate by the mixture
previously described, it was extremely difficult to detach it when this particular piece of type had to be used somewhere else. The movable type made of
clay, on the other hand, encountered no such difficulties. When exposed to
a gentle fire which melted the mixture that glued it to the plate, it required
only a gentle push by . . . hand before it easily came loose. . . .

Translated by Dun J. Li

THESIS AND THOUGHT

1. Identify the two processes described in the selection. Does the title apply to
   both? How? Create a title that you think is more clearly inclusive.

2. Prior to the invention of movable type, books were produced by block printing. This process involved carving a text in reverse relief upon blocks of
   wood, inking the surface, then pressing one side of a sheet of paper against it
   to produce a print. How was the invention of movable type an improvement
   on this method? Base your response both the selection and your general
   knowledge.

3. Clarify the relationship between price and time implicit in the first two
   sentences of paragraph 4. Rewrite the sentences so that the relationship
   becomes explicit.

STRUCTURE

1. Suggest a change in paragraph sequence that might make the essay more
   unified and coherent.

2. The essay uses the transitions *then* and *when* repeatedly. Does the author avoid
   monotony? If so, how?

STYLE

1. Paragraph 5 includes the following sentence: "When pieces of type were not in use, they were covered with paper for . . . protection, were grouped together according to rhymes, and were stored away in wooden frames." If you were to eliminate the word *were* in its third and fourth uses would the phrasing still be parallel? Explain. Which version of the sentence do you prefer? Why?

2. Find another instance of **parallelism** in paragraph 5.

CONSIDERATIONS

1. Traditional Chinese writing is based on ideograms, depictions in which the symbols (characters) represent concepts instead of sounds. That there are tens of thousands of such characters perhaps explains why they were stored in groups ("according to rhymes").

   In what ways might the twenty-six letters of the English alphabet be stored and to what purpose? How are they "stored" on conventional keyboards? Is there a more efficient system?

2. Movable type was "invented" in the West almost four hundred years after Pi Sheng invented it; the German printer Johannes Gutenberg (ca. 1397–1468) is usually credited with the achievement. What were the effects of Gutenberg's invention on the development of Western culture?

3. Is movable type still essential to modern printing processes? How is most printing done today? You might need to consult a current encyclopedia.

4. What do you foresee as the future of the printed word—or of writing itself, for that matter? Write a brief essay outlining and justifying your prediction. (Note that modern means of communication include not only the telephone, radio, and television but also the copier, the fax machine, and the electronic printer.)

Stephen Crane
(United States; 1871–1900)

In his brief and tumultuous life, Stephen Crane made his literary mark as poet, journalist, novelist, and writer of short stories. He is perhaps best known for The Red Badge of Courage, *a novel set in the Civil War. It presents the story of Henry Fleming, an adolescent infantryman, who evolves and matures through confronting his inner conflicts as well as the combat itself. The novel's psychological realism influenced many American writers in the decades immediately following Crane's death—most notably Ernest Hemingway.*

Also influential was his first major work, Maggie, A Girl of the Streets, *which records the decline and destruction of a girl in the Bowery slums of New*

*York, an area that Crane knew well as a free-lance journalist. Its content was
so shocking for its time that Crane published the work under a pseudonym.*

*Among Crane's most memorable shorter pieces are "The Bride Comes to
Yellow Sky," "George's Mother," "The Open Boat," and "The Blue Hotel."*

*Late in his abbreviated career, Crane covered the Greco-Turkish War (1897)
and the Spanish-American War (1898) as a reporter. Having lived recklessly
with regard to both his finances and his health, Crane died of tuberculosis at
age twenty-eight.*

The Upturned Face

"WHAT WILL WE DO NOW?" said the adjutant, troubled and excited.

"Bury him," said Timothy Lean.

The two officers looked down close to their toes where lay the body of
their comrade. The face was chalk-blue; gleaming eyes stared at the sky. Over
the two upright figures was a windy sound of bullets, and on the top of the
hill Lean's prostrate company of Spitzbergen infantry was firing measured
volleys.

"Don't you think it would be better—" began the adjutant. "We might
leave him until to-morrow."

"No," said Lean. "I can't hold that post an hour longer. I've got to fall   5
back, and we've got to bury old Bill."

"Of course," said the adjutant, at once. "Your men got entrenching
tools?"

Lean shouted back to his little line, and two men came slowly, one with
a pick, one with a shovel. They started in the direction of the Rostina
sharpshooters. Bullets cracked near their ears. "Dig here," said Lean gruffly.
The men, thus caused to lower their glances to the turf, became hurried and
frightened, merely because they could not look to see whence the bullets
came. The dull beat of the pick striking the earth sounded amid the swift snap
of close bullets. Presently the other private began to shovel.

"I suppose," said the adjutant, slowly, "we'd better search his clothes
for—things."

Lean nodded. Together in curious abstraction they looked at the body.
Then Lean stirred his shoulders suddenly, arousing himself.

"Yes," he said, "we'd better see what he's got." He dropped to his knees,   10
and his hands approached the body of the dead officer. But his hands wavered
over the button of the tunic. The first button was brick-red with drying blood,
and he did not seem to dare touch it.

"Go on," said the adjutant, hoarsely.

Lean stretched his wooden hand, and his fingers fumbled the blood-stained buttons. At last he rose with ghastly face. He had gathered a watch, a whistle, a pipe, a tobacco-pouch, a handkerchief, a little case of cards and papers. He looked at the adjutant. There was a silence. The adjutant was feeling that he had been a coward to make Lean do all the grisly business.

"Well," said Lean, "that's all, I think. You have his sword and revolver?"

"Yes," said the adjutant, his face working, and then he burst out in a sudden strange fury at the two privates. "Why don't you hurry up with that grave? What are you doing, anyhow? Hurry, do you hear? I never saw such stupid—"

Even as he cried out in his passion the two men were labouring for their   15
lives. Ever overhead the bullets were spitting.

The grave was finished. It was not a masterpiece—a poor little shallow thing. Lean and the adjutant again looked at each other in a curious silent communication.

Suddenly the adjutant croaked out a weird laugh. It was a terrible laugh, which had its origin in that part of the mind which is first moved by the singing of the nerves. "Well," he said humorously to Lean, "I suppose we had best tumble him in."

"Yes," said Lean. The two privates stood waiting, bent over their implements. "I suppose," said Lean, "it would be better if we laid him in ourselves."

"Yes," said the adjutant. Then, apparently remembering that he had made Lean search the body, he stooped with great fortitude and took hold of the dead officer's clothing. Lean joined him. Both were particular that their fingers should not feel the corpse. They tugged away, the corpse lifted, heaved, toppled, flopped into the grave, and the two officers, straightening, looked again at each other—they were always looking at each other. They sighed with relief.

The adjutant said, "I suppose we should—we should say something. Do   20
you know the service, Tim?"

"They don't read the service until the grave is filled in," said Lean, pressing his lips to an academic expression.

"Don't they?" said the adjutant, shocked that he had made the mistake. "Oh, well," he cried, suddenly, "let us—let us say something—while he can hear us."

"All right," said Lean. "Do you know the service?"

"I can't remember a line of it," said the adjutant.

Lean was extremely dubious. "I can repeat two lines, but—"   25

"Well, do it," said the adjutant. "Go as far as you can. That's better than nothing. And the beasts have got our range exactly."

Lean looked at his two men. "Attention," he barked. The privates came to attention with a click, looking much aggrieved. The adjutant lowered his helmet to his knee. Lean, bareheaded, stood over the grave. The Rostina sharpshooters fired briskly.

"O Father, our friend has sunk in the deep waters of death, but his spirit has leaped toward Thee as the bubble arises from the lips of the drowning. Perceive, we beseech, O Father, the little flying bubble, and—"

Lean, although husky and ashamed, had suffered no hesitation up to this point, but he stopped with a hopeless feeling and looked at the corpse.

The adjutant moved uneasily, "And from Thy superb heights—" he 30 began, and then he too came to an end.

"And from Thy superb heights," said Lean.

The adjutant suddenly remembered a phrase in the back of the Spitzbergen burial service, and he exploited it with the triumphant manner of a man who has recalled everything, and can go on.

"O God, have mercy—"

"O God, have mercy—" said Lean.

"Mercy," repeated the adjutant, in quick failure. 35

"Mercy," said Lean. And then he was moved by some violence of feeling, for he turned upon his two men and tigerishly said, "Throw the dirt in."

The fire of the Rostina sharpshooters was accurate and continuous.

One of the aggrieved privates came forward with his shovel. He lifted his first shovel-load of earth, and for a moment of inexplicable hesitation it was held poised above this corpse, which from its chalk-blue face looked keenly out from the grave. Then the soldier emptied his shovel on—on the feet.

Timothy Lean felt as if tons had been swiftly lifted from off his forehead. He had felt that perhaps the private might empty the shovel on—on the face. It had been emptied on the feet. There was a great point gained there—ha, ha!—the first shovelful had been emptied on the feet. How satisfactory!

The adjutant began to babble. "Well, of course—a man we've messed 40 with all these years—impossible—you can't, you know, leave your intimate friends rotting on the field. Go on, for God's sake, and shovel, you."

The man with the shovel suddenly ducked, grabbed his left arm with his right hand, and looked at his officer for orders. Lean picked the shovel from the ground. "Go to the rear," be said to the wounded man. He also addressed the other private. "You get under cover, too: I'll finish this business."

The wounded man scrambled hard still for the top of the ridge without devoting any glances to the direction from whence the bullets came, and the other man followed at an equal pace; but he was different, in that he looked back anxiously three times.

This is merely the way—often—of the hit and unhit.

Timothy Lean filled the shovel, hesitated, and then, in a movement which was like a gesture of abhorrence, he flung the dirt into the grave, and as it landed it made a sound—plop. Lean suddenly stopped and mopped his brow—a tired labourer.

"Perhaps we have been wrong," said the adjutant. His glance wavered 45
stupidly. "It might have been better if we hadn't buried him just at this time.
Of course, if we advance tomorrow the body would have been—"

"Damn you," said Lean, "shut your mouth." He was not the senior officer.

He again filled the shovel and flung the earth. Always the earth made
that sound—plop. For a space Lean worked frantically, like a man digging
himself out of danger.

Soon there was nothing to be seen but the chalk-blue face. Lean filled
the shovel. "Good God," he cried to the adjutant. "Why didn't you turn him
somehow when you put him in? This—" Then Lean began to stutter.

The adjutant understood. He was pale to the lips. "Go on, man," he
cried, beseechingly, almost in a shout.

Lean swung back the shovel. It went forward in a pendulum curve. When 50
the earth landed it made a sound—plop.

Thesis and Thought

1. Both burial and warfare have their rituals. To what extent are the rites of
   burial properly observed in "The Upturned Face"? The rites of war and
   military discipline?

2. Identify the moments of hesitancy and doubt that the adjutant and Lean both
   display. How do you account for them? What do the officers' reservations say
   about them as "officer material"? As human beings? Can you argue that the
   responses of the two officers are more significant than the actual examination, interment, and burial of the corpse? Make your case.

3. What is the significance of the title and of the face as it appears in the text?

4. Explain why the adjutant speaks "humorously" in paragraph 17 and begins "to
   babble" in paragraph 40.

Structure

1. If "The Upturned Face" were an essay instead of a short story, would "How a
   Burial Was Botched" be an accurate title? Explain.

2. Here is a summary of the central action (process) described in the story:

   > Their fellow officer dead, the adjutant and Timothy Lean de-
   > cide to bury him. They set two privates to dig a shallow grave while
   > Lean hesitantly removes and gathers the dead man's effects. When
   > the grave is finished, the officers "tumble" the corpse in by tugging
   > at its clothing. Once the body is in place, Lean and the adjutant say

as much of the burial service over it as they can remember. One of the privates begins to fill the grave, but when he is wounded (enemy fire having persisted all the while), he and his companion are sent to the rear. After damning the adjutant for his doubts about whether the burial should have been attempted at this time, Lean sets to completing the task.

In what ways is this summary unacceptable?

3. Rewrite the summary presented in question 2 so that it more nearly reflects both the central action as Crane presents it and your responses to questions 1 and 2 in "Thesis and Thought."

4. Conflict lies at the heart of most dramatic or narrative action. What kinds of conflict are present in the story? Explain how the rituals of war and burial are involved in any of the conflict.

STYLE

1. Is Crane's depiction realistic? If not, what other adjectives would you use to describe the style here? In either case, why do you think so?

2. What is the difference between referring to the deceased as "old Bill" (para. 5) and describing the body as in paragraph 3: "The face was chalk-blue; gleaming eyes stared at the sky"? Find as many examples of each type of description as you can. Which predominates? To what effect?

3. Crane twice (paras. 27 and 38) calls the privates "aggrieved." Look up the word if it is unfamiliar to you. Why are the men aggrieved?

4. An unusual adverb, *tigerishly*, appears in paragraph 36. Explain why you think it is or is not effective.

5. What is the meaning of *messed* in paragraph 40?

6. In paragraphs 44, 47, and 50, Crane uses *plop* to describe the sound of the shoveled earth falling into the grave. What is the effect of this sound on Lean? Of its repetition on the reader? Crane does not include the sound when the private shovels the dirt in paragraph 38. Why not?

CONSIDERATIONS

1. What view of war do you come away with after reading "The Upturned Face"? Is the story in any sense a protest?

2. Consider the rituals of a large group (such as a religious denomination), a smaller group (such as a fraternity or family), and individuals. What seem to be the purposes of rituals in each case? How are participants affected when rituals are altered or abandoned? Why?

3. Write a short biographical or autobiographical essay in which you describe a process (ritual or otherwise) performed under adverse conditions.

Rachel Carson

(United States; 1907–1964)

An aquatic biologist for most of her working life, Carson was a pioneer of modern ecology. Her book Silent Spring *(1962), documenting the dangers of uncontrolled use of pesticides, including DDT, provided impetus for stricter pesticide regulation and the ultimate prohibition of DDT in the United States.*

Her other books are studies of the sea. Most prominent among them is The Sea Around Us *(the source of the present selection), winner of a National Book Award for 1951.*

Carson studied at the Pennsylvania College for Women (now Chatham College) and Johns Hopkins University, taking degrees at both, and did postgraduate work at the Woods Hole Marine Biological Laboratory. She joined the U.S. Bureau of Fisheries as a biologist and was later editor-in-chief for U.S. Fish and Wildlife Service publications. After the success of The Sea Around Us, *Carson left government service to devote herself to writing, which had in fact been her first love.*

The Gray Beginnings

And the earth was without form, and void; and darkness was upon the face of the deep.

GENESIS

BEGINNINGS ARE APT to be shadowy, and so it is with the beginnings of that great mother of life, the sea. Many people have debated how and when the earth got its ocean, and it is not surprising that their explanations do not always agree. For the plain and inescapable truth is that no one was there to see, and in the absence of eyewitness accounts there is bound to be a certain amount of disagreement. So if I tell here the story of how the young planet Earth acquired an ocean, it must be a story pieced together from many sources and containing whole chapters the details of which we can only imagine. The story is founded on the testimony of the earth's most ancient rocks, which were young when the earth was young; on other evidence written on the face of the earth's satellite, the moon; and on hints contained in the history of the sun and the whole universe of star-filled space. For although no man was there to witness this cosmic birth, the stars and the moon and the rocks were there, and, indeed, had much to do with the fact that there is an ocean.

The events of which I write must have occurred somewhat more than 2 billion years ago. As nearly as science can tell, that is the approximate age of the earth, and the ocean must be very nearly as old. It is possible now to

197

discover the age of the rocks that compose the crust of the earth by measuring the rate of decay of the radioactive materials they contain. The oldest rocks found anywhere on earth—in Manitoba—are about 2.3 billion years old. Allowing 100 million years or so for the cooling of the earth's materials to form a rocky crust, we arrive at the supposition that the tempestuous and violent events connected with our planet's birth occurred nearly $2\frac{1}{2}$ billion years ago. But this is only a minimum estimate, for rocks indicating an even greater age may be found at any time.

The new earth, freshly torn from its parent sun, was a ball of whirling gases, intensely hot, rushing through the black spaces of the universe on a path and at a speed controlled by immense forces. Gradually the ball of flaming gases cooled. The gases began to liquefy, and Earth became a molten mass. The materials of this mass eventually became sorted out in a definite pattern: the heaviest in the center, the less heavy surrounding them, and the least heavy forming the outer rim. This is the pattern which persists today—a central sphere of molten iron, very nearly as hot as it was 2 billion years ago, an intermediate sphere of semiplastic basalt, and a hard outer shell, relatively quite thin and composed of solid basalt and granite.

The outer shell of the young earth must have been a good many millions of years changing from the liquid to the solid state, and it is believed that, before this change was completed, an event of the greatest importance took place—the formation of the moon. The next time you stand on a beach at night, watching the moon's bright path across the water, and conscious of the moon-drawn tides, remember that the moon itself may have been born of a great tidal wave of earthly substance, torn off into space. And remember that if the moon was formed in this fashion, the event may have had much to do with shaping the ocean basins and the continents as we know them.

There were tides in the new earth, long before there was an ocean. In response to the pull of the sun the molten liquids of the earth's whole surface rose in tides that rolled unhindered around the globe and only gradually slackened and diminished as the earthly shell cooled, congealed, and hardened. Those who believe that the moon is a child of Earth say that during an early stage of the earth's development something happened that caused this rolling, viscid tide to gather speed and momentum and to rise to unimaginable heights. Apparently the force that created these greatest tides the earth has ever known was the force of resonance, for at this time the period of the solar tides had come to approach, then equal, the period of the free oscillation of the liquid earth. And so every sun tide was given increased momentum by the push of the earth's oscillation, and each of the twice-daily tides was larger than the one before it. Physicists have calculated that, after 500 years of such monstrous, steadily increasing tides, those on the side toward the sun became too high for stability, and a great wave was torn away and hurled into space. But immediately, of course, the newly created satellite became subject to

5

physical laws that sent it spinning in an orbit of its own about the earth. This is what we call the moon.

There are reasons for believing that this event took place after the earth's crust had become slightly hardened, instead of during its partly liquid state. There is to this day a great scar on the surface of the globe. This scar or depression holds the Pacific Ocean. According to some geophysicists, the floor of the Pacific is composed of basalt, the substance of the earth's middle layer, while all other oceans are floored with a thin layer of granite, which makes up most of the earth's outer layer. We immediately wonder what became of the Pacific's granite covering and the most convenient assumption is that it was torn away when the moon was formed. There is supporting evidence. The mean density of the moon is much less than that of the earth (3.3 compared with 5.5), suggesting that the moon took away none of the earth's heavy iron core, but that it is composed only of the granite and some of the basalt of the outer layers.

The birth of the moon probably helped shape other regions of the world ocean besides the Pacific. When part of the crust was torn away, strains must have been set up in the remaining granite envelope. Perhaps the granite mass cracked open on the side opposite the moon scar. Perhaps, as the earth spun on its axis and rushed on its orbit through space, the cracks widened and the masses of granite began to drift apart, moving over a tarry, slowly hardening layer of basalt. Gradually the outer portions of the basalt layer became solid and the wandering continents came to rest, frozen into place with oceans between them. In spite of theories to the contrary, the weight of geologic evidence seems to be that the locations of the major ocean basins and the major continental land masses are today much the same as they have been since a very early period of the earth's history.

But this is to anticipate the story, for when the moon was born there was no ocean. The gradually cooling earth was enveloped in heavy layers of cloud, which contained much of the water of the new planet. For a long time its surface was so hot that no moisture could fall without immediately being reconverted to steam. This dense, perpetually renewed cloud covering must have been thick enough that no rays of sunlight could penetrate it. And so the rough outlines of the continents and the empty ocean basins were sculptured out of the surface of the earth in darkness, in a Stygian world of heated rock and swirling clouds and gloom.

As soon as the earth's crust cooled enough, the rains began to fall. Never have there been such rains since that time. They fell continuously, day and night, days passing into months, into years, into centuries. They poured into the waiting ocean basins, or, falling upon the continental masses, drained away to become sea.

That primeval ocean, growing in bulk as the rains slowly filled its basins,   10
must have been only faintly salt. But the falling rains were the symbol of the dissolution of the continents. From the moment the rains began to fall, the

lands began to be worn away and carried to the sea. It is an endless, inexorable process that has never stopped—the dissolving of the rocks, the leaching out of their contained minerals, the carrying of the rock fragments and dissolved minerals to the ocean. And over the eons of time, the sea has grown ever more bitter with the salt of the continents.

In what manner the sea produced the mysterious and wonderful stuff called protoplasm we cannot say. In its warm, dimly lit waters the unknown conditions of temperature and pressure and saltiness must have been the critical ones for the creation of life from non-life. At any rate they produced the result that neither the alchemists with their crucibles not modern scientists in their laboratories have been able to achieve.

Before the first living cell was created, there may have been many trials and failures. It seems probable that, within the warm saltiness of the primeval sea, certain organic substances were fashioned from carbon dioxide, sulphur, nitrogen, phosphorus, potassium, and calcium. Perhaps these were transition steps from which the complex molecules of protoplasm arose—molecules that somehow acquired the ability to reproduce themselves and begin the endless stream of life. But at present no one is wise enough to be sure.

Those first living things may have been simple microorganisms rather like some of the bacteria we know today—mysterious borderline forms that were not quite plants, not quite animals, barely over the intangible line that separates the non-living from the living. It is doubtful that this first life possessed the substance chlorophyll, with which plants in sunlight transform lifeless chemicals into the living stuff of their tissues. Little sunshine could enter their dim world, penetrating the cloud banks from which fell the endless rains. Probably the sea's first children lived on the organic substances then present in the ocean water, or, like the iron and sulphur bacteria that exist today, lived directly on inorganic food.

All the while the cloud cover was thinning, the darkness of the nights alternated with palely illumined days, and finally the sun for the first time shone through upon the sea. By this time some of the living things that floated in the sea must have developed the magic of chlorophyll. Now they were able to take the carbon dioxide of the air and the water of the sea and of these elements, in sunlight, build the organic substances they needed. So the first true plants came into being.

Another group of organisms, lacking the chlorophyll but needing organic food, found they could make a way of life for themselves by devouring the plants. So the first animals arose, and from that day to this, every animal in the world has followed the habit it learned in the ancient seas and depends, directly or through complex food chains, on the plants for food and life.   15

As the years passed, and the centuries, and the millions of years, the stream of life grew more and more complex. From simple, one-celled creatures, others that were aggregations of specialized cells arose, and then creatures with organs for feeding, digesting, breathing, reproducing. Sponges grew on the rocky bottom of the sea's edge and coral animals built their habitations in warm, clear waters. Jellyfish swam and drifted in the sea. Worms evolved, and starfish, and hard-shelled creatures with many jointed legs, the arthropods. The plants, too, progressed, from the microscopic algae to branched and curiously fruiting seaweeds that swayed with the tides and were plucked from the coastal rocks by the surf and cast adrift.

During all this time the continents had no life. There was little to induce living things to come ashore, forsaking their all-providing, all-embracing mother sea. The lands must have been bleak and hostile beyond the power of words to describe. Imagine a whole continent of naked rock, across which no covering mantle of green had been drawn—a continent without soil, for there were no land plants to aid in its formation and bind it to the rocks with their roots. Imagine a land of stone, a silent land, except for the sound of the rains and winds that swept across it. For there was no living voice, and no living thing moved over the surface of the rocks.

Meanwhile, the gradual cooling of the planet, which had first given the earth its hard granite crust, was progressing into its deeper layers; and as the interior slowly cooled and contracted, it drew away from the outer shell. This shell, accommodating itself to the shrinking sphere within it, fell into folds and wrinkles—the earth's first mountain ranges.

Geologists tell us that there must have been at least two periods of mountain building (often called "revolutions") in that dim period, so long ago that the rocks have no record of it, so long ago that the mountains themselves have long since been worn away. Then there came a third great period of upheaval and readjustment of the earth's crust, about a billion years ago, but of all its majestic mountains the only reminders today are the Laurentian hills of eastern Canada, and a great shield of granite over the flat country around Hudson Bay.

The epochs of mountain building only served to speed up the processes of erosion by which the continents were worn down and their crumbling rock and contained minerals returned to the sea. The uplifted masses of the mountains were prey to the bitter cold of the upper atmosphere and under the attacks of frost and snow and ice the rocks cracked and crumbled away. The rains beat with greater violence upon the slopes of the hills and carried away the substance of the mountains in torrential streams. There was still no plant covering to modify and resist the power of the rains.

And in the sea, life continued to evolve. The earliest forms have left no fossils by which we can identify them. Probably they were soft-bodied, with no hard parts that could be preserved. Then, too, the rock layers formed in those early days have since been so altered by enormous heat and pressure, under the foldings of the earth's crust, that any fossils they might have contained would have been destroyed.

For the past 500 million years, however, the rocks have preserved the fossil record. By the dawn of the Cambrian period, when the history of living things was first inscribed on rock pages, life in the sea had progressed so far that all the main groups of backboneless or invertebrate animals had been developed. But there were no animals with backbones, no insects or spiders, and still no plant or animal had been evolved that was capable of venturing onto the forbidding land. So for more than three-fourths of geologic time the continents were desolate and uninhabited, while the sea prepared the life that was later to invade them and make them habitable. Meanwhile, with violent tremblings of the earth and with the fire and smoke of roaring volcanoes, mountains rose and wore away, glaciers moved to and fro over the earth, and the sea crept over the continents and again receded.

It was not until Silurian time, some 350 million years ago, that the first pioneer of land life crept out on the shore. It was an arthropod, one of the great tribe that later produced crabs and lobsters and insects. It must have been something like a modern scorpion, but, unlike some of its descendants, it never wholly severed the ties that united it to the sea. It lived a strange life, half-terrestrial, half-aquatic, something like that of the ghost crabs that speed along the beaches today, now and then dashing into the surf to moisten their gills.

Fish, tapered of body and stream-molded by the press of running waters, were evolving in Silurian rivers. In times of droughts in the drying pools and lagoons, the shortage of oxygen forced them to develop swim bladders for the storage of air. One form that possessed an air-breathing lung was able to survive the dry periods by burying itself in mud, leaving a passage to the surface through which it breathed.

It is very doubtful that the animals alone would have succeeded in colonizing the land, for only the plants had the power to bring about the first amelioration of its harsh conditions. They helped make soil of the crumbling rocks, they held back the soil from the rains that would have swept it away, and little by little they softened and subdued the bare rock, the lifeless desert. We know very little about the first land plants, but they must have been closely related to some of the larger seaweeds that had learned to live in the coastal shallows, developing strengthened stems and grasping, rootlike hold-fasts to resist the drag and pull of the waves. Perhaps it was in some coastal lowlands, periodically drained and flooded, that some such plants found it possible to survive, though separated from the sea. This also seems to have taken place in the Silurian period.

The mountains that had been thrown up by the Laurentian revolution gradually wore away, and as the sediments were washed from their summits and deposited on the lowlands, great areas of the continents sank under the load. The seas crept out of their basins and spread over the lands. Life fared well and was exceedingly abundant in those shallow, sunlit seas. But with the later retreat of the ocean water into the deeper basins, many creatures must have been left stranded in shallow, landlocked bays. Some of these animals found means to survive on land. The lakes, the shores of the rivers, and the coastal swamps of those days were the testing grounds in which plants and animals either became adapted to the new conditions or perished.

As the lands rose and the seas receded, a strange fishlike creature emerged on the land, and over the thousands of years its fins became legs, and instead of gills it developed lungs. In the Devonian sandstone this first amphibian left its footprint.

On land and sea the stream of life poured on. New forms evolved; some old ones declined and disappeared. On land the mosses and the ferns and the seed plants developed. The reptiles for a time dominated the earth, gigantic, grotesque, and terrifying. Birds learned to live and move in the ocean of air. The first small mammals lurked inconspicuously in hidden crannies of the earth as though in fear of the reptiles.

When they went ashore the animals that took up a land life carried with them a part of the sea in their bodies, a heritage which they passed on to their children and which even today links each land animal with its origin in the ancient sea. Fish, amphibian, and reptile, warm-blooded bird and mammal— each of us carries in our veins a salty stream in which the elements sodium, potassium, and calcium are combined in almost the same proportions as in sea water. This is our inheritance from the day, untold millions of years ago, when a remote ancestor, having progressed from the one-celled to the many-celled stage, first developed a circulatory system in which the fluid was merely the water of the sea. In the same way, our lime-hardened skeletons are a heritage from the calcium-rich ocean of Cambrian time. Even the protoplasm that streams within each cell of our bodies has the chemical structure impressed upon all living matter when the first simple creatures were brought forth in the ancient sea. And as life itself began in the sea, so each of us begins his individual life in a miniature ocean within his mother's womb, and in the stages of his embryonic development repeats the steps by which his race evolved, from gill-breathing inhabitants of a water world to creatures able to live on land.

Some of the land animals later returned to the ocean. After perhaps 50 million years of land life, a number of reptiles entered the sea about 170 million years ago, in the Triassic period. They were huge and formidable creatures. Some had oarlike limbs by which they rowed through the water; some were web-footed, with long, serpentine necks. These grotesque monsters disappeared millions of years ago, but we remember them when we come upon a large sea turtle swimming many miles at sea, its barnacle-encrusted shell eloquent of its marine life. Much later, perhaps no more than 50 million years ago, some of the mammals, too, abandoned a land life for the ocean. Their descendants are the sea lion, seals, sea elephants, and whales of today.

Among the land mammals there was a race of creatures that took to an arboreal existence. Their hands underwent remarkable development, becoming skilled in manipulating and examining objects, and along with this skill came a superior brain power that compensated for what these comparatively

30

small mammals lacked in strength. At last, perhaps somewhere in the vast interior of Asia, they descended from the trees and became again terrestrial. The past million years have seen their transformation into beings with the body and brain and spirit of man.

Eventually man, too, found his way back to the sea. Standing on its shores, he must have looked out upon it with wonder and curiosity, compounded with an unconscious recognition of his lineage. He could not physically re-enter the ocean as the seals and whales had done. But over the centuries, with all the skill and ingenuity and reasoning powers of his mind, he has sought to explore and investigate even its most remote parts, so that he might re-enter it mentally and imaginatively.

He built boats to venture out on its surface. Later he found ways to descend to the shallow parts of its floor, carrying with him the air that, as a land mammal long unaccustomed to aquatic life, he needed to breathe. Moving in fascination over the deep sea he could not enter, he found ways to probe its depths, he let down nets to capture its life, he invented mechanical eyes and ears that could re-create for his senses a world long lost, but a world that, in the deepest part of his subconscious mind, he had never wholly forgotten.

And yet he has returned to his mother sea only on her own terms. He cannot control or change the ocean as, in his brief tenancy of earth, he has subdued and plundered the continents. In the artificial world of his cities and towns, he often forgets the true nature of his planet and the long vistas of its history, in which the existence of the race of men has occupied a mere moment of time. The sense of all these things comes to him most clearly in the course of a long ocean voyage, when he watches day after day the receding rim of the horizon, ridged and furrowed by waves; when at night he becomes aware of the earth's rotation as the stars pass overhead; or when, alone in this world of water and sky, he feels the loneliness of his earth in space. And then, as never on land, be knows the truth that his world is a water world, a planet dominated by its covering mantle of ocean, in which the continents are but transient intrusions of land above the surface of the all-encircling sea.

Thesis and Thought

1. Define Carson's purposes in writing this selection.
2. Explain the appropriateness of the epigraph from Genesis.
3. In Carson's view, what is the relationship between sea and land?
4. According to Carson, in what ways is the sea significant to the life of the planet? To human beings in particular?

STRUCTURE

1. Carson's informational process is filled with transitional words and phrases: for example, "eventually" (para. 3), "As the years passed" (para. 16), and "It was not until Silurian time" (para. 23). Find other instances of such expressions both between and within paragraphs and describe their role in developing the process.

2. Identify the transitions in paragraphs 14, 18, and 22 that Carson uses when she must deal with events that occur simultaneously.

3. How significant are Carson's descriptions in shaping the essay? Choose a particularly attractive passage, define its appeal, and explain how it helps achieve her purposes. Rewrite the passage, omitting as much description as possible. Is what you have produced less suitable to Carson's purposes than the original? Explain why.

STYLE

1. Carson often uses evocative (charged) language. Consider for example the following passages:

   > And so the rough outlines of the continents and the empty ocean basins were sculptured out of the surface of the earth in darkness, in a Stygian world of heated rock and swirling clouds and gloom. (para. 8)

   > The plants, too, progressed, from the microscopic algae to branched and curiously fruiting seaweeds that swayed with the tides and were plucked from the coastal rocks by the surf and cast adrift. (para. 16)

   > They [plants] helped make soil of the crumbling rocks, they held back the soil from the rains that would have swept it away, and little by little they softened and subdued the bare rock, the lifeless desert. (para. 25)

   Identify the elements in these descriptions that are impressionistic. Do the same for one or two other passages of your own choosing.

2. Evaluate the following statement: In Carson's prose, one must attend to the various repetitions of clausal patterns (parallel structure) and of sound (**alliteration**) together with the long, rolling, powerful sweep of sentences in their entirety, which suggests the endurance and recurrence of the sea itself, as a force shaping our planet's destiny. Base your opposition or defense on three or four specific passages.

3. Explain in detail whether you find the closing passage (beginning "The sense of all these things") typical of Carson's style here.

4. Given your responses to the previous questions, what overall impressions is Carson attempting to create?

CONSIDERATIONS

1. Carson is apparently comfortable in using a biblical quotation in conjunction with a scientific work that is rooted in evolutionary theory. Some religious denominations, insisting on a literal reading of Genesis, would dispute Carson's account. Do you (or does your faith) find the Bible and evolutionary science compatible? Why? If your tradition uses other scriptures, does the same issue of conflict or reconciliation apply?

2. In this rather lyrical essay, what evidence is there of Rachel Carson the scientist? Consider both the information provided and appropriate caution or skepticism.

3. Are people as universally curious about the sea or as attracted to it as Carson believes? Explain in a brief essay why you agree or disagree.

Theodore Roethke
(United States; 1908–1963)

Born in Saginaw, Michigan, Roethke was educated at the University of Michigan and Harvard. He taught at various institutions, most notably at the University of Washington from 1947 until his death.

During his moderately brief career, Roethke won the Pulitzer and Bollingen prizes and the National Book Award for poetry. His work is often marked by its nature imagery and the depth of its psychological perception. Along with "My Papa's Waltz," "Dolor," "Elegy for Jane," and "I knew a woman lovely in her bones" are among his best-known poems.

My Papa's Waltz

The whiskey on your breath
Could make a small boy dizzy;
But I hung on like death:
Such waltzing was not easy.

We romped until the pans   5
Slid from the kitchen shelf;
My mother's countenance
Could not unfrown itself.

The hand that held my wrist
Was battered on one knuckle;   10
At every step you missed
My right ear scraped a buckle.

You beat time on my head
With a palm caked hard by dirt,
Then waltzed me off to bed   15
Still clinging to your shirt.

THESIS AND THOUGHT

1. So far as you can tell, how do the boy and his father relate to each other? Is the relationship ambiguous? ambivalent? What is the mother's view of the dance? Does this extend to the father-son relationship?

2. Is there any suggestion that the behavior described is habitual? Explain.

STRUCTURE

1. Write a prose paragraph outlining the progress of the dance. Note that Roethke provides clear transitions twice—in lines 5 and 15. Use others as well in your version.

2. Do the stanzas represent stages of the dance or do they, with the clear exception of the last, simply record action without regard to time? Elaborate.

STYLE

1. Roethke records several instances of limited violence or minor injury. How are these balanced or countered? What effect does the presence of both kinds of detail create?

2. Keep time as you or a partner reads the poem aloud. How does Roethke's rhythm reinforce and help create the poem's mood, meaning, and movement?

3. Does the poet comment on the action or merely describe it? How does this help establish his tone?

CONSIDERATIONS

1. Is the child being abused? Why do you think so?

2. Does the dance have metaphorical or symbolic significance? Justify your response.

3. If you have engaged in an activity with one parent (or similar figure) of which
    the other disapproved, write a paragraph or two describing the activity and
    the reaction.

Primo Levi
(Italy; 1919–1987)

*Working as a chemist both before and after World War II, Levi wrote poetry,
memoirs, and fiction. However, his ten-month internment in Auschwitz, a
Nazi concentration camp, was the central fact of Levi's personal and literary
life. Most of his postwar works either record his experiences in the camp, are
based on them, or deal with issues—such as human suffering—that his
confinement necessarily raised. In addition to* Survival in Auschwitz (Se
questo e un uomo), *from which the chapter below is taken, his other
autobiographical volumes include* The Reawakening (La tregua) *and* The
Periodic Table (Il sistema periodico).

*With Mussolini's death and the fall of the Fascist government in 1943, Levi
joined a guerilla band intent on resisting the occupying Germans and their
Italian collaborators. When the band was betrayed, he identified himself as an
"Italian citizen of Jewish race" and was turned over to the Nazis.*

*Levi managed to survive Auschwitz because of his mental and physical fitness
(he had been a trained mountain climber), his indoor work in a camp
chemistry laboratory, extra rations supplied surreptitiously by a civilian brick-
layer named Lorenzo, and the "good fortune" of being left to die of scarlet
fever when the Nazis abandoned the camp before the onrushing Soviet army.
Thousands of other "healthy" victims were marched to their wintry deaths.*

*Levi's literary success, including two Italian awards, the Strega and Campiello
prizes, did not entirely release him from inner torment. In the spring of 1987,
suffering bouts of depression, compounded by concerns for his own health and
that of his aged mother, Levi committed suicide.*

October 1944

WE FOUGHT with all our strength to prevent the arrival of winter. We
clung to all the warm hours, at every dusk we tried to keep the sun in the sky
for a little longer, but it was all in vain. Yesterday evening the sun went down
irrevocably behind a confusion of dirty clouds, chimney stacks and wires, and
today it is winter.

We know what it means because we were here last winter; and the others
will soon learn. It means that in the course of these months, from October

till April, seven out of ten of us will die. Whoever does not die will suffer minute by minute, all day, every day: from the morning before dawn until the distribution of the evening soup we will have to keep our muscles continually tensed, dance from foot to foot, beat our arms under our shoulders against the cold. We will have to spend bread to acquire gloves, and lose hours of sleep to repair them when they become unstitched. As it will no longer be possible to eat in the open, we will have to eat our meals in the hut, on our feet, everyone will be assigned an area of floor as large as a hand, as it is forbidden to rest against the bunks. Wounds will open on everyone's hands, and to be given a bandage will mean waiting every evening for hours on one's feet in the snow and wind.

Just as our hunger is not that feeling of missing a meal, so our way of being cold has need of a new word. We say "hunger," we say "tiredness," "fear," "pain," we say "winter" and they are different things. They are free words, created and used by free men who lived in comfort and suffering in their homes. If the Lagers had lasted longer a new, harsh language would have been born; and only this language could express what it means to toil the whole day in the wind, with the temperature below freezing, wearing only a shirt, underpants, cloth jacket and trousers, and in one's body nothing but weakness, hunger and knowledge of the end drawing nearer.

In the same way in which one sees a hope end, winter arrived this morning. We realized it when we left the hut to go and wash: there were no stars, the dark cold air had the smell of snow. In roll-call square, in the grey of dawn, when we assembled for work, no one spoke. When we saw the first flakes of snow, we thought that if at the same time last year they had told us that we would have seen another winter in Lager, we would have gone and touched the electric wire-fence; and that even now we would go if we were logical, were it not for this last senseless crazy residue of unavoidable hope.

Because "winter" means yet another thing. 5

Last spring the Germans had constructed two huge tents in an open space in the Lager. For the whole of the good season each of them had catered for over a thousand men: now the tents had been taken down, and an excess two thousand guests crowded our huts. We old prisoners knew that the Germans did not like these irregularities and that something would soon happen to reduce our number.

One feels the selections arriving. "*Selekcja*": the hybrid Latin and Polish word is heard once, twice, many times, interpolated in foreign conversations; at first we cannot distinguish it, then it forces itself on our attention, and in the end it persecutes us.

This morning the Poles had said "*Selekcja*." The Poles are the first to find out the news, and they generally try not to let it spread around, because to know something which the others still do not know can always be useful. By the time that everyone realizes that a selection is imminent, the few possibilities of evading it (corrupting some doctor or some prominent with bread or tobacco; leaving the hut for Ka-Be or vice-versa at the right moment so as to cross with the commission) are already their monopoly.

In the days which follow, the atmosphere of the Lager and the yard is filled with "*Selekcja*": nobody knows anything definite, but all speak about it, even the Polish, Italian, French civilian workers whom we secretly see in the yard. Yet the result is hardly a wave of despondency: our collective morale is too inarticulate and flat to be unstable. The fight against hunger, cold and work leave little margin for thought, even for this thought. Everybody reacts in his own way, but hardly anyone with those attitudes which would seem the most plausible as the most realistic, that is with resignation or despair.

All those able to find a way out, try to take it; but they are the minority   10 because it is very difficult to escape from a selection. The Germans apply themselves to these things with great skill and diligence.

Whoever is unable to prepare for it materially, seeks defence elsewhere. In the latrines, in the washroom, we show each other our chests, our buttocks, our thighs, and our comrades reassure us: "You are all right, it will certainly not be your turn this time. . . . *du bist kein Muselmann* . . . more probably mine . . ." and they undo their braces in turn and pull up their shirts.

Nobody refuses this charity to another; nobody is so sure of his own lot to be able to condemn others. I brazenly lied to old Wertheimer; I told him that if they questioned him, he should reply that he was forty-five, and he should not forget to have a shave the evening before, even if it cost him a quarter-ration of bread; apart from that he need have no fears, and in any case it was by no means certain that it was a selection for the gas chamber; had he not heard the *Blockältester* say that those chosen would go to Jaworszno to a convalescent camp?

It is absurd of Wertheimer to hope: he looks sixty, he has enormous varicose veins, he hardly even notices the hunger any more. But he lies down on his bed, serene and quiet, and replies to someone who asks him with my own words; they are the command-words in the camp these days: I myself reported them just as—apart from details—Chajim told them to me, Chajim, who has been in Lager for three years, and being strong and robust is wonderfully sure of himself; and I believed them.

On this slender basis I also lived through the great selection of October 1944 with inconceivable tranquillity. I was tranquil because I managed to lie to myself sufficiently. The fact that I was not selected depended above all on chance and does not prove that my faith was well-founded.

Monsieur Pinkert is also, a priori, condemned: it is enough to look at his   15 eyes. He calls me over with a sign, and with a confidential air tells me that he has been informed—he cannot tell me the source of information—that this time there is really something new: the Holy See, by means of the International Red Cross . . . in short, he personally guarantees both for himself and for me, in the most absolute manner, that every danger is ruled out; as a civilian he was, as is well known, attaché to the Belgian embassy at Warsaw.

Thus in various ways, even those days of vigil, which in the telling seem as if they ought to have passed every limit of human torment, went by not very differently from other days.

The discipline in both the Lager and Buna is in no way relaxed: the work, cold and hunger are sufficient to fill up every thinking moment.

Today is working Sunday, *Arbeitssonntag:* we work until one p.m., then we return to camp for the shower, shave and general control for skin diseases and lice. And in the yards, everyone knew mysteriously that the selection would be today.

The news arrived, as always, surrounded by a halo of contradictory or suspect details: selection in the infirmary took place this morning; the percentage was seven per cent of the whole camp, thirty, fifty per cent of the patients. At Birkenau, the crematorium chimney has been smoking for ten days. Room has to be made for an enormous convoy arriving from the Poznan ghetto. The young tell the young that all the old ones will be chosen. The healthy tell the healthy that only the ill will be chosen. Specialists will be excluded. German Jews will be excluded. Low Numbers will be excluded. You will be chosen. I will be excluded.

At one p.m. exactly the yard empties in orderly fashion, and for two   20
hours the grey unending army files past the two control stations where, as on every day, we are counted and recounted, and past the military band which for two hours without interruption plays, as on every day, those marches to which we must synchronize our steps at our entrance and our exit.

It seems like every day, the kitchen chimney smokes as usual, the distribution of the soup is already beginning. But then the bell is heard, and at that moment we realize that we have arrived.

Because this bell always sounds at dawn, when it means the reveille; but if it sounds during the day, it means "*Blocksperre*," enclosure in huts, and this happens when there is a selection to prevent anyone avoiding it, or when those selected leave for the gas, to prevent anyone seeing them leave.

Our *Blockältester* knows his business. He has made sure that we have all entered, he has had the door locked, he has given everyone his card with his number, name, profession, age and nationality and he has ordered everyone to undress completely, except for shoes. We wait like this, naked, with the card in our hands, for the commission to reach our hut. We are hut 48, but one can never tell if they are going to begin at hut 1 or hut 60. At any rate, we can rest quietly at least for an hour, and there is no reason why we should not get under the blankets on the bunk and keep warm.

Many are already drowsing when a barrage of orders, oaths and blows proclaim the imminent arrival of the commission. The *Blockältester* and his helpers, starting at the end of the dormitory, drive the crowd of frightened, naked people in front of them and cram them in the *Tagesraum* which is the Quartermaster's office. The *Tagesraum* is a room seven yards by four: when the drive is over, a warm and compact human mass is jammed into the *Tagesraum*, perfectly filling all the corners, exercising such a pressure on the wooden walls as to make them creak.

Now we are all in the *Tagesraum*, and besides there being no time, there   25 is not even any room in which to be afraid. The feeling of the warm flesh pressing all around is unusual and not unpleasant. One has to take care to hold up one's nose so as to breathe, and not to crumple or lose the card in one's hand.

The *Blockältester* has closed the connecting-door and has opened the other two which lead from the dormitory and the *Tagesraum* outside. Here, in front of the two doors, stands the arbiter of our fate, an SS sub-altern. On his right is the *Blockältester*, on his left, the quartermaster of the hut. Each one of us, as he comes naked out of the *Tagesraum* into the cold October air, has to run the few steps between the two doors, give the card to the SS man and enter the dormitory door. The SS man, in the fraction of a second between two successive crossings, with a glance at one's back and front, judges everyone's fate, and in turn gives the card to the man on his right or his left, and this is the life or death of each of us. In three or four minutes a hut of two hundred men is "done," as is the whole camp of twelve thousand men in the course of the afternoon.

Jammed in the charnel-house of the *Tagesraum*, I gradually felt the human pressure around me slacken, and in a short time it was my turn. Like everyone, I passed by with a brisk and elastic step, trying to hold my head high, my chest forward and my muscles contracted and conspicuous. With the corner of my eye I tried to look behind my shoulders, and my card seemed to end on the right.

As we gradually come back into the dormitory we are allowed to dress ourselves. Nobody yet knows with certainty his own fate, it has first of all to be established whether the condemned cards were those on the right or on the left. By now there is no longer any point in sparing each other's feelings with superstitious scruples. Everybody crowds around the oldest, the most wasted-away, the most "muselmann"; if their cards went to the left, the left is certainly the side of the condemned.

Even before the selection is over, everybody knows that the left was effectively the "*schlechte Seite*," the bad side. There have naturally been some irregularities; René, for example, so young and robust, ended on the left; perhaps it was because he has glasses, perhaps because he walks a little stooped like a myope, but more probably because of a simple mistake: René passed the commission immediately in front of me and there could have been a mistake with our cards. I think about it, discuss it with Alberto, and we agree that the hypothesis is probable; I do not know what I will think tomorrow and later; today I feel no distinct emotion.

It must equally have been a mistake about Sattler, a huge Transylvanian 30 peasant who was still at home only twenty days ago; Sattler does not understand German, he has understood nothing of what has taken place, and stands in a corner mending his shirt. Must I go and tell him that his shirt will be of no more use?

There is nothing surprising about these mistakes: the examination is too quick and summary, and in any case, the important thing for the Lager is not that the most useless prisoners be eliminated, but that free posts be quickly created, according to a certain percentage previously fixed.

The selection is now over in our hut, but it continues in the others, so that we are still locked in. But as the soup-pots have arrived in the meantime, the *Blockältester* decides to proceed with the distribution at once. A double ration will be given to those selected. I have never discovered if this was a ridiculously charitable initiative of the *Blockältester*, or an explicit disposition of the SS, but in fact, in the interval of two or three days (sometimes even much longer) between the selection and the departure, the victims at Monowitz-Auschwitz enjoyed this privilege.

Ziegler holds out his bowl, collects his normal ration and then waits there expectantly. "What do you want?" asks the *Blockältester*: according to him, Ziegler is entitled to no supplement, and he drives him away, but Ziegler returns and humbly persists. He was on the left, everybody saw it, let the *Blockältester* check the cards; he has the right to a double ration. When he is given it, he goes quietly to his bunk to eat.

Now everyone is busy scraping the bottom of his bowl with his spoon so as not to waste the last drops of the soup, a confused, metallic clatter, signifying the end of the day. Silence slowly prevails and then, from my bunk on the top row, I see and hear old Kuhn praying aloud, with his beret on his head, swaying backwards and forwards violently. Kuhn is thanking God because he has not been chosen.

Kuhn is out of his senses. Does he not see Beppo the Greek in the bunk 35 next to him, Beppo who is twenty years old and is going to the gas chamber the day after tomorrow and knows it and lies there looking fixedly at the light without saying anything and without even thinking any more? Can Kuhn fail to realize that next time it will be his turn? Does Kuhn not understand that what has happened today is an abomination, which no propitiatory prayer, no pardon, no expiation by the guilty, which nothing at all in the power of man can ever clean again.

If I was God, I would spit at Kuhn's prayer.

THESIS AND THOUGHT

1. In part because this is a portion from a longer work, "October 1944" has no explicit thesis. Compose two or three possible thesis statements for the chapter. Be sure that they apply to the piece in its entirety.

2. By what means do the inmates of Auschwitz cope with the prospect and actuality of the "selection"? With other aspects of their existence?

3. What impressions of the Germans do you derive from Levi's account? Support your response with reference to specific passages.

4. Explain the behavior of the SS and Ziegler in paragraphs 32–33.

5. Why, if he were God, would Levi spit at Kuhn's prayer (para. 36)?

STRUCTURE

1. Since only about half of "October 1944" is an account of the "selection" process proper, how does Levi establish **unity** and **coherence** for the chapter as a whole?

2. Of what larger, ongoing process is the "selection" a part? Consult your answer to question 1 in "Thesis and Thought."

3. Looked at another way, the chapter may be said to have a three-part structure—of which the actual "selection" is the second. The others may be called "anticipation" and "aftermath." Where do these begin and end? How well do the paragraphs preceding the "anticipation" serve as an introduction?

STYLE

1. After the "selection" has taken place, Levi writes: "today I feel no distinct emotion" (para. 29). Determine to what degree this lack of feeling describes the tone of the writing. (Tone, you will recall, is the author's attitude toward a subject as evidenced by word choice and phrasing.) How does the tone affect your response to Levi's account? The *Times Literary Supplement* (London) called Levi's presentation "undramatized and therefore all the more moving." Judging from the chapter at hand, do you agree with this assessment? Why?

2. Why does Levi use German words and phrases even when he presents English (originally Italian) equivalents, for example, "Today is working Sunday, *Arbeitssontag*" (para. 18)?

3. Levi sometimes paints forceful verbal pictures. For example, consider the final sentence of paragraph 1: "Yesterday evening the sun went down irrevocably behind a confusion of dirty clouds, chimney stacks and wires, and today it is winter." Find other instances of such graphic language.

4. Occasionally, Levi offers an unexpected phrase or observation. See, for instance, the "residue of unavoidable hope" at the end of paragraph 4, or, in the

midst of the "selection" (para. 25), "the feeling of the warm flesh pressing all around is unusual and not unpleasant." What other phrases or comments do you find unconventional, given the circumstance being described? How does this originality affect your response to the chapter's content?

CONSIDERATIONS

1. In paragraph 3, Levi says that the language of free people is inadequate to express the experiences of those in the camps. More generally, how adequate is language to express experience at all? Does language propose to reproduce experience or to report it? What other means of conveying experience, if any, are available to us? Write a paragraph describing an important event in your life and your feelings at the time. Then write another in which you evaluate how well your first paragraph captured the episode.

2. Levi adds in paragraph 3 that had the camps "lasted longer" a new, more adequate language would have necessarily evolved. Examine the probability of such an assertion by investigating vocabulary used for events or phenomena that had not occurred or did not exist extensively before you were born—for example, language concerning computers. For instance, look up a word such as *interface* in current and earlier editions of several dictionaries and determine (approximately) when the word came into general use or acquired a specialized meaning. Why did *interface* and such words as *mouse, bit, byte, and hard drive* either come to exist or gain new meanings?

3. To what extent have the inmates of hut 48 managed to preserve their humanity amidst deliberately dehumanizing conditions? To what extent, so far as you can tell, might preservation be a function of the length of incarceration? Levi, for example, had been in the camp for about ten months.

4. What do you know about the Nazi death camps, and particularly, the genocidal destruction of the Jews usually referred to as the Holocaust? To what extent is the present chapter informative or enlightening in this regard? If you know little, read a reputable history of Germany or European Jewry that focuses on the period 1933–1945.

5. Although the Holocaust is the sole recorded instance of the attempted destruction of an entire people purely because of hatred (bolstered by allegations of moral, spiritual, and physical inferiority), there have been other instances of attempted annihilation for political or economic reasons. Surviving Native Americans, for example, assert that their peoples have been victims of European and American genocide since the coming of Columbus. Likewise, beginning in the late sixties, more than a million Cambodians—many of Vietnamese ancestry—were killed by the Marxist Khmer Rouge, who were attempting to achieve dominance. More recent examples include Saddam Hussein's gassing of the Kurds in Iraq and Serbia's attempted "ethnic cleansing" (a phrase strongly reminiscent of Nazism) of Muslims in Bosnia. If you are appalled by such needless, unjustifiable, and horrific destruction, what can you do to prevent another occurrence? Will you do it? If you are not appalled, why not?

Camara Laye

(Guinea; 1928–1980)

Writing in French, Camara Laye produced four books, of which The Dark
Child (L'enfant noir), *excerpted here, is the first. In its entirety, the autobiographical work is a record of the author's evolution, beginning with his rural
origins in Guinea and ending with his university experience in Paris. The
conflict or contrast between Laye's two cultures is present throughout.*

Laye's most highly acclaimed work, The Radiance of the King (Le regarde
du roi), *embraces a similar theme. In this novel, however, Laye describes the
attempt of a white European to survive in an alien African civilization.*

Laye was forced to flee Guinea in 1966 when the political criticism in A
Dream of Africa (Dramouss) *offended Guinea's president Sékou Touré.
During his ensuing exile in Senegal, he wrote* The Guardian of the Word
(Le maître de la parole), *a novel of West African life in the thirteenth
century.*

*In addition to writing, Laye worked as an auto mechanic, an engineer,
and—both before and after Guinea became independent of France—a diplomat.*

The Wonders of Working in Gold

OF ALL THE DIFFERENT KINDS of work my father engaged in, none fascinated
me so much as his skill with gold. No other occupation was so noble, no other
needed such a delicate touch. And then, every time he worked in gold it was
like a festival—indeed it *was* a festival—that broke the monotony of ordinary
working days.

So, if a woman, accompanied by a go-between, crossed the threshold of
the workshop, I followed her in at once. I knew what she wanted: she had
brought some gold, and had come to ask my father to transform it into a
trinket. She had collected it in the placers of Siguiri where, crouching over
the river for months on end, she had patiently extracted grains of gold from
the mud.

These women never came alone. They knew my father had other things
to do than make trinkets. And even when he had the time, they knew they
were not the first to ask a favor of him, and that, consequently, they would
not be served before others.

Generally they required the trinket for a certain date, for the festival of
Ramadan or the Tabaski or some other family ceremony or dance.

Therefore, to enhance their chances of being served quickly and to more
easily persuade my father to interrupt the work before him, they used to

5

request the services of an official praise-singer, a go-between, arranging in advance the fee they were to pay him for his good offices.

The go-between installed himself in the workshop, tuned up his *cora*, which is our harp, and began to sing my father's praises. This was always a great event for me. I heard recalled the lofty deeds of my father's ancestors and their names from the earliest times. As the couplets were reeled off it was like watching the growth of a great genealogical tree that spread its branches far and wide and flourished its boughs and twigs before my mind's eye. The harp played an accompaniment to this vast utterance of names, expanding it with notes that were now soft, now shrill.

I could sense my father's vanity being inflamed, and I already knew that after having sipped this milk-and-honey he would lend a favorable ear to the woman's request. But I was not alone in my knowledge. The woman also had seen my father's eyes gleaming with contented pride. She held out her grains of gold as if the whole matter were settled. My father took up his scales and weighed the gold.

"What sort of trinket do you want?" he would ask.

"I want. . . . "

And then the woman would not know any longer exactly what she   10 wanted because desire kept making her change her mind, and because she would have liked all the trinkets at once. But it would have taken a pile of gold much larger than she had brought to satisfy her whim, and from then on her chief purpose in life was to get hold of it as soon as she could.

"When do you want it?"

Always the answer was that the trinket was needed for an occasion in the near future.

"So! You are in that much of a hurry? Where do you think I shall find the time?"

"I am in a great hurry, I assure you."

"I have never seen a woman eager to deck herself out who wasn't in a   15 great hurry! Good! I shall arrange my time to suit you. Are you satisfied?"

He would take the clay pot that was kept specially for smelting gold, and would pour the grains into it. He would then cover the gold with powdered charcoal, a charcoal he prepared by using plant juices of exceptional purity. Finally, he would place a large lump of the same kind of charcoal over the pot.

As soon as she saw that the work had been duly undertaken, the woman, now quite satisfied, would return to her household tasks, leaving her go-between to carry on with the praise-singing which had already proved so advantageous.

At a sign from my father the apprentices began working two sheepskin bellows. The skins were on the floor, on opposite sides of the forge, connected to it by earthen pipes. While the work was in progress the apprentices sat in front of the bellows with crossed legs. That is, the younger of the two sat, for the elder was sometimes allowed to assist. But the younger—this time it was

Sidafa—was only permitted to work the bellows and watch while waiting his turn for promotion to less rudimentary tasks. First one and then the other worked hard at the bellows: the flame in the forge rose higher and became a living thing, a genie implacable and full of life.

Then my father lifted the clay pot with his long tongs and placed it on the flame.

Immediately all activity in the workshop almost came to a halt. During   20
the whole time that the gold was being smelted, neither copper nor aluminum could be worked nearby, lest some particle of these base metals fall into the container which held the gold. Only steel could be worked on such occasions, but the men, whose task that was, hurried to finish what they were doing, or left it abruptly to join the apprentices gathered around the forge. There were so many, and they crowded so around my father, that I, the smallest person present, had to come near the forge in order not to lose track of what was going on.

If he felt he had inadequate working space, my father had the apprentices stand well away from him. He merely raised his hand in a simple gesture: at that particular moment he never uttered a word, and no one else would: no one was allowed to utter a word. Even the go-between's voice was no longer raised in song. The silence was broken only by the panting of the bellows and the faint hissing of the gold. But if my father never actually spoke, I know that he was forming words in his mind. I could tell from his lips, which kept moving, while, bending over the pot, he stirred the gold and charcoal with a bit of wood that kept bursting into flame and had constantly to be replaced by a fresh one.

What words did my father utter? I do not know. At least I am not certain what they were. No one ever told me. But could they have been anything but incantations? On these occasions was he not invoking the genies of fire and gold, of fire and wind, of wind blown by the blast-pipes of the forge, of fire born of wind, of gold married to fire? Was it not their assistance, their friendship, their espousal that he besought? Yes. Almost certainly he was invoking these genies, all of whom are equally indispensable for smelting gold.

The operation going on before my eyes was certainly the smelting of gold, yet something more than that: a magical operation that the guiding spirits could regard with favor or disfavor. That is why, all around my father, there was absolute silence and anxious expectancy. Though only a child, I knew there could be no craft greater than the goldsmith's. I expected a ceremony; I had come to be present at a ceremony; and it actually was one, though very protracted. I was still too young to understand why, but I had an inkling as I watched the almost religious concentration of those who followed the mixing process in the clay pot.

When finally the gold began to melt I could have shouted aloud—and perhaps we all would have if we had not been forbidden to make a sound. I trembled, and so did everyone else watching my father stir the mixture—it was still a heavy paste—in which the charcoal was gradually consumed. The next stage followed swiftly. The gold now had the fluidity of water. The genies had smiled on the operation!

"Bring me the brick!" my father would order, thus lifting the ban that   25
until then had silenced us.

The brick, which an apprentice would place beside the fire, was hollowed out, generously greased with Galam butter. My father would take the pot off the fire and tilt it carefully, while I would watch the gold flow into the brick, flow like liquid fire. True, it was only a very sparse trickle of fire, but how vivid, how brilliant! As the gold flowed into the brick, the grease sputtered and flamed and emitted a thick smoke that caught in the throat and stung the eyes, leaving us all weeping and coughing.

But there were times when it seemed to me that my father ought to turn this task over to one of his assistants. They were experienced, had assisted him hundreds of times, and could certainly have performed the work well. But my father's lips moved and those inaudible, secret words, those incantations he addressed to one we could not see or hear, was the essential part. Calling on the genies of fire, of wind, of gold and exorcising the evil spirits—this was a knowledge he alone possessed.

By now the gold had been cooled in the hollow of the brick, and my father began to hammer and stretch it. This was the moment when his work as a goldsmith really began. I noticed that before embarking on it he never failed to stroke the little snake stealthily as it lay coiled up under the sheepskin. I can only assume that this was his way of gathering strength for what remained to be done, the most trying part of his task.

But was it not extraordinary and miraculous that on these occasions the little black snake was always coiled under the sheepskin? He was not always there. He did not visit my father every day. But he was always present whenever there was gold to be worked. His presence was no surprise to *me*. After that evening when my father had spoken of the guiding spirit of his race I was no longer astonished. The snake was there intentionally. He knew what the future held. Did he tell my father? I think that he most certainly did. Did he tell him everything? I have another reason for believing firmly that he did.

The craftsman who works in gold must first of all purify himself. That is,   30
he must wash himself all over and, of course, abstain from all sexual commerce during the whole time. Great respecter of ceremony as he was, it would have been impossible for my father to ignore these rules. Now, I never saw him make these preparations. I saw him address himself to his work without any apparent preliminaries. From that moment it was obvious that, forewarned in a dream by his black guiding spirit of the task which awaited him in the morning, my father must have prepared for it as soon as he arose, entering his workshop in a state of purity, his body smeared with the secret potions hidden in his numerous pots of magical substances; or perhaps he

always came into his workshop in a state of ritual purity. I am not trying to make him out a better man than he was—he was a man and had his share of human frailties—but he was always uncompromising in his respect for ritual observance.

The woman for whom the trinket was being made, and who had come often to see how the work was progressing, would arrive for the final time, not wanting to miss a moment of this spectacle—as marvelous to her as to us—when the gold wire, which my father had succeeded in drawing out from the mass of molten gold and charcoal, was transformed into a trinket.

There she would be. Her eyes would devour the fragile gold wire, following it in its tranquil and regular spiral around the little slab of metal which supported it. My father would catch a glimpse of her and I would see him slowly beginning to smile. Her avid attention delighted him.

"Are you trembling?" he would ask.

"Am I trembling?"

And we would all burst out laughing at her. For she would be trembling!   35
She would be trembling with covetousness for the spiral pyramid in which my father would be inserting, among the convolutions, tiny grains of gold. When he had finally finished by crowning the pyramid with a heavier grain, she would dance in delight.

No one—no one at all—would be more enchanted than she as my father slowly turned the trinket back and forth between his fingers to display its perfection. Not even the praise-singer whose business it was to register excitement would be more excited than she. Throughout this metamorphosis he did not stop speaking faster and ever faster, increasing his tempo, accelerating his praises and flatteries as the trinket took shape, shouting to the skies my father's skill.

For the praise-singer took a curious part—I should say rather that it was direct and effective—in the work. He was drunk with the joy of creation. He shouted aloud in joy. He plucked his *cora* like a man inspired. He sweated as if he were the trinket-maker, as if he were my father, as if the trinket were his creation. He was no longer a hired censer-bearer, a man whose services anyone could rent. He was a man who created his song out of some deep inner necessity. And when my father, after having soldered the large grain of gold that crowned the summit, held out his work to be admired, the praise-singer would no longer be able to contain himself. He would begin to intone the *douga*, the great chant which is sung only for celebrated men and which is danced for them alone.

But the *douga* is a formidable chant, a provocative chant, a chant which the praise-singer dared not sing, and which the man for whom it is sung dared not dance before certain precautions had been taken. My father had taken them as soon as he woke, since he had been warned in a dream. The praise-singer had taken them when he concluded his arrangements with the woman. Like my father he had smeared his body with magic substances and had made himself invulnerable to the evil genies whom the *douga* inevitably set free; these potions made him invulnerable also to rival praise-singers, perhaps jealous of him, who awaited only this song and the exaltation and loss of control which attended it, in order to begin casting their spells.

At the first notes of the *douga* my father would arise and emit a cry in which happiness and triumph were equally mingled; and brandishing in his right hand the hammer that was the symbol of his profession and in his left a ram's horn filled with magic substances, he would dance the glorious dance.

No sooner had he finished, than workmen and apprentices, friends and   40
customers in their turn, not forgetting the woman for whom the trinket had been created, would flock around him, congratulating him, showering praises on him and complimenting the praise-singer at the same time. The latter found himself laden with gifts—almost his only means of support, for the praise-singer leads a wandering life after the fashion of the troubadours of old. Aglow with dancing and the praises he had received, my father would offer everyone cola nuts, that small change of Guinean courtesy.

Now all that remained to be done was to redden the trinket in a little water to which chlorine and sea salt had been added. I was at liberty to leave. The festival was over! But often as I came out of the workshop my mother would be in the court, pounding millet or rice, and she would call to me:

"Where have you been?" although she knew perfectly well where I had been.

"In the workshop."

"Of course. Your father was smelting gold. Gold! Always gold!"

And she would beat the millet or rice furiously with her pestle.   45

"Your father is ruining his health!"

"He danced the *douga*."

"The *douga*! The *douga* won't keep him from ruining his eyes. As for you, you would be better off playing in the courtyard instead of breathing dust and smoke in the workshop."

My mother did not like my father to work in gold. She knew how dangerous it was: a trinket-maker empties his lungs blowing on the blow-pipe and his eyes suffer from the fire. Perhaps they suffer even more from the microscopic precision which the work requires. And even if there had been no such objections involved, my mother would scarcely have relished this work. She was suspicious of it, for gold can not be smelted without the use of other metals, and my mother thought it was not entirely honest to put aside for one's own use the gold which the alloy had displaced. However, this was a custom generally known, and one which she herself had accepted when she took cotton to be woven and received back only a piece of cotton cloth half the weight of the original bundle.

Thesis and Thought

1. The first paragraph and especially the final sentence may be said to be the thesis of this selection. Show how its elements—Laye's fascination, the nobility of the work, and, especially, the idea of festivity—are developed throughout the piece.

2. In what spirit or attitude does Laye's father approach his work? What connection is there between the actual process of working the gold and the goldsmith's "uncompromising . . . respect for ritual observance" (para. 30)? What is Laye's view of his father's work? You should be able to justify your response by referring to specific passages in the text.

3. In what sense is the making of the trinket a social and communal activity?

4. Describe and explain how Laye's mother reacts to the process.

Structure

1. Identify processes at work here other than the physical manufacture of the trinket. At which points and by what methods does Laye fuse or blend these various elements?

2. Explain how paragraph 16 is a process in miniature.

3. Do the passages concerning the snake in paragraphs 28–29 seem to interrupt the various processes or are they integral to them? Does your response change if you learn that chapter 1 of *The Dark Child* contains a substantial account of the snake and its spiritual importance?

4. Why doesn't the chapter end with "The festival was over!" (para. 41)? What effect do Laye's conversation with his mother and the concluding paragraph have on the selection as a whole? Notice that the transition to Laye's encounter with his mother ("But often as I came out . . .") is incorporated with the triumphant exclamation in paragraph 41. Is this more effective than having it begin paragraph 42? Explain.

5. The account here is presented from Laye's point of view. Is he simply an adult looking back, or is he attempting to recreate the experiences and feelings of childhood? Justify your response with specific references to the text. You may wish to compare Laye's approach with that of Anand in chapter 1.

Style

1. What does Laye's sporadic dialogue (paras. 11–15, 25, 33–34, 42–48) contribute to the presentation of the processes? How does it affect the reader?

2. Laye occasionally repeats words as part of a pattern, for example, "But the *douga* is a formidable chant, a provocative chant, a chant which the praise-

singer dared not sing . . ." (para. 38). What is the effect of such repetition here and in the other examples you find?

3. Observe the series of parallel sentences in paragraph 37 beginning with "He was drunk with the joy of creation." Explain how they are appropriate to both the context established at the end of paragraph 36 and as an introduction to the *douga*.

CONSIDERATIONS

1. The text suggests a clear division of labor and status according to gender. By contemporary Western standards is this—or is anything else in the selection—explicitly sexist? Explain.

2. If not part of the same structure, Laye's residence and the workshop are at least in close proximity. Since the industrial revolution, this has been progressively less true in Western life—witness the morning and evening rush hours during which multitudes move between suburban home and city job. What are the advantages or disadvantages in Laye's arrangement for both individuals and the larger community?

3. Have you observed your parents at work? How often? Do you react to the experience as Laye does? Write a brief essay describing a process one of your parents performs at work and your reaction to it.

4. From what you can gather of its general content, write a "praise-song" in prose for someone you know well. Include as many generations of his or her family as you can.

5. In the context, does the snake seem to be more a lucky charm or a guardian angel? If touching the snake seems superstitious to you, consider all those athletes you've seen cross themselves before stepping to the plate or attempting a foul shot. Does their behavior seem acceptable because it is familiar or part of your own customs or tradition? Is superstition simply any spiritual belief (as well as an act based on it) that you happen not to share? See how several dictionaries (including dictionaries of theological terms) define *superstition*. Write a brief essay in which you either distinguish superstition from its opposite (perhaps knowledge or truth), or explain why it is impossible to do so.

W. S. Merwin

(United States; b.1927)

W. S. Merwin is a prizewinning poet and translator who has worked from Latin and Russian originals as well as from Portuguese, Spanish, and French. The Poem of the Cid and The Song of Roland are, respectively, among his productions from the last two languages. Merwin's Selected Translations earned him the PEN Translation Prize for 1968.

*Prolific as a poet in his own right, Merwin has published ten volumes of
poetry. Among them is* The Carrier of Ladders *(1970), for which he won
the Pulitzer Prize. Merwin received the Bollingen Prize for poetry in 1979.*

"Unchopping a Tree" is from The Miner's Pale Children *(1970), the first
of his three volumes of prose.*

Unchopping a Tree

START WITH THE LEAVES, the small twigs, and the nests that have been
shaken, ripped, or broken off by the fall; these must be gathered and attached
once again to their respective places. It is not arduous work, unless major
limbs have been smashed or mutilated. If the fall was carefully and correctly
planned, the chances of anything of the kind happening will have been
reduced. Again, much depends upon the size, age, shape, and species of the
tree. Still, you will be lucky if you can get through this stage without having
to use machinery. Even in the best of circumstances it is a labor that will make
you wish often that you had won the favor of the universe of ants, the empire
of mice, or at least a local tribe of squirrels, and could enlist their labors and
their talents. But no, they leave you to it. They have learned, with time. This
is men's work. It goes without saying that if the tree was hollow in whole or
in part, and contained old nests of bird or mammal or insect, or hoards of nuts
or such structures as wasps or bees build for their survival, the contents will
have to be repaired where necessary, and reassembled, insofar as possible, in
their original order, including the shells of nuts already opened. With spiders'
webs you must simply do the best you can. We do not have the spider's
weaving equipment, nor any substitute for the leaf's living bond with its point
of attachment and nourishment. It is even harder to simulate the latter when
the leaves have once become dry—as they are bound to do, for this is not the
labor of a moment. Also it hardly needs saying that this is the time for
repairing any neighboring trees or bushes or other growth that may have been
damaged by the fall. The same rules apply. Where neighboring trees were of
the same species it is difficult not to waste time conveying a detached leaf
back to the wrong tree. Practice, practice. Put your hope in that.

Now the tackle must be put into place, or the scaffolding, depending on
the surroundings and the dimensions of the tree. It is ticklish work. Almost
always it involves, in itself, further damage to the area, which will have to be
corrected later. But as you've heard, it can't be helped. And care now is likely
to save you considerable trouble later. Be careful to grind nothing into the
ground.

At last the time comes for the erecting of the trunk. By now it will
scarcely be necessary to remind you of the delicacy of this huge skeleton.

Every motion of the tackle, every slight upward heave of the trunk, the branches, their elaborately re-assembled panoply of leaves (now dead) will draw from you an involuntary gasp. You will watch for a leaf or a twig to be snapped off yet again. You will listen for the nuts to shift in the hollow limb and you will hear whether they are indeed falling into place or are spilling in disorder—in which case, or in the event of anything else of the kind—operations will have to cease, of course, while you correct the matter. The raising itself is no small enterprise, from the moment when the chains tighten around the old bandages until the bole hangs vertical above the stump, splinter above splinter. Now the final straightening of the splinters themselves can take place (the preliminary work is best done while the wood is still green and soft, but at times when the splinters are not badly twisted most of the straightening is left until now, when the torn ends are face to face with each other.) When the splinters are perfectly complementary the appropriate fixative is applied. Again we have no duplicate of the original substance. Ours is extremely strong, but it is rigid. It is limited to surfaces, and there is no play in it. However the core is not the part of the trunk that conducted life from the roots up into the branches and back again. It was relatively inert. The fixative for this part is not the same as the one for the outer layers and the bark, and if either of these is involved in the splintered section they must receive applications of the appropriate adhesives. Apart from being incorrect and probably ineffective, the core fixative would leave a scar on the bark.

When all is ready the splintered trunk is lowered onto the splinters of the stump. This, one might say, is only the skeleton of the resurrection. Now the chips must be gathered, and the sawdust, and returned to their former positions. The fixative for the wood layers will be applied to chips and sawdust consisting only of wood. Chips and sawdust consisting of several substances will receive applications of the correct adhesives. It is as well, where possible, to shelter the materials from the elements while working. Weathering makes it harder to identify the smaller fragments. Bark sawdust in particular the earth lays claim to very quickly. You must find your own ways of coping with this problem. There is certain beauty, you will notice at moments, in the pattern of the chips as they are fitted back into place. You will wonder to what extent it should be described as natural, to what extent man-made. It will lead you on to speculations about the parentage of beauty itself, to which you will return.

The adhesive for the chips is translucent, and not so rigid as that for the   5
splinters. That for the bark and its subcutaneous layers is transparent and runs into the fibers on either side, partially dissolving them into each other. It does not set the sap flowing again but it does pay a kind of tribute to the preoccupations of the ancient thoroughfares. You could not roll an egg over the joints but some of the mine-shafts would still be passable, no doubt. For the first exploring insect who raises its head in the tight echoless passages. The day comes when it is all restored, even to the moss (now dead) over the wound.

You will sleep badly, thinking of the removal of the scaffolding that must begin the next morning. How you will hope for sun and a still day!

The removal of the scaffolding or tackle is not so dangerous, perhaps, to the surroundings, as its installation, but it presents problems. It should be taken from the spot piece by piece as it is detached, and stored at a distance. You have come to accept it there, around the tree. The sky begins to look naked as the chains and struts one by one vacate their positions. Finally the moment arrives when the last sustaining piece is removed and the tree stands again on its own. It is as though its weight for a moment stood on your heart. You listen for a thud of settlement, a warning creak deep in the intricate joinery. You cannot believe it will hold. How like something dreamed it is, standing there all by itself. How long will it stand there now? The first breeze that touches its dead leaves all seems to flow into your mouth. You are afraid the motion of the clouds will be enough to push it over. What more can you do? What more can you do?

But there is nothing more you can do.

Others are waiting.

Everything is going to have to be put back.

Thesis and Thought

1. Merwin provides a set of directions, formally (and superficially) similar to the recipe for toast at the beginning of this chapter. But whereas bread can be toasted, a tree cannot be "unchopped." Show how this fact is crucial to Merwin's purposes here.

2. The essay might be read, at one level, as a commentary on the relationship between humans and their environment. Describe the nature of this relationship as Merwin sees it. How, according to the essay, are people affected by both the chopping and the "unchopping"?

3. Especially according to the last four paragraphs, how successful is the enterprise? Why?

4. Does the tree represent issues or conditions beyond those of ecology? Elaborate.

Structure

1. Identify the transitions both between and within paragraphs that are typical of process writing.

2. The essay also includes a substantial number of qualifications and conditions, ostensibly as guides or cautions to the reader. For instance: "The fixative for this part is not the same as the one for the outer layers and the bark, and if

either of these is involved in the splintered section they must receive applications of the appropriate adhesives" (para. 3). Find several other examples of these warnings throughout the selection.

3. The two questions above and question 1 in "Thesis and Thought" suggest that the essay, structurally, is an excellent example of directional process. But why does Merwin insist on this rhetorical pattern if his purpose is not to teach the reader how to perform the action named—or perhaps any other? To what extent is his use of the pattern paradoxical?

STYLE

1. As the headnote indicates, Merwin is a prizewinning poet. What features of this prose piece, if any, remind you of poetry?

2. In paragraph 3, Merwin mentions a "panoply of leaves (now dead)" and in paragraph 5, "the moss (now dead)." What other references or allusions to death are present? What is their collective effect?

3. Why is the question at the end of paragraph 6 repeated? Similarly, what impact do paragraphs 7–9 have as single sentences as compared with the impact they might have in one combined paragraph?

4. Consider the following from paragraph 5: "That [the adhesive] for the bark and its subcutaneous layers is transparent and runs into the fibers on either side. . . ." Its tone is unemotional, objective, scientific perhaps. Find other instances of such phrasing. How does this stylistic *detachment* relate to Merwin's theme? Does he seem to be doing the same thing with language as with structure? Explain.

CONSIDERATIONS

1. Following Merwin's suggestion at the end of paragraph 4, speculate on "the parentage of beauty." Are humans ever its parents? If so, what sorts of parents do they make? Elaborate.

2. Is your answer to the question "What more can you do?" (para. 6) the same as Merwin's? Why?

3. Write a short essay that explains how to undo some event or action—for instance, "uncutting" your hair, "uncomposing" a piece of music, or "unwriting" an essay. Be sure to clarify your purpose before you begin.

Suggestions for Writing: Process Analysis

I. Using directional process, write an essay on one of the topics that follow. In most cases, the essay should be governed by an overriding idea or prevalent attitude.

    —how to adjust to college life

    —how to communicate with parents

    —how to solve a specific problem in your community or on campus

    —how to spend Saturday night alone

    —how to impress a date, a professor, or a prospective employer

    —how to assemble a wardrobe

    —Teach someone an activity that you perform well.

    —Dale Carnegie once wrote a popular book called *How to Win Friends and Influence People*. Use either half of the title.

    —the negative of any of the topics above

II. Doing informal research as necessary, write an informational process on one of the topics below. Follow your instructor's directions in regard to any required documentation.

    —how a specific product is manufactured or marketed

    —how a treatment, prevention, or cure for a particular disease was achieved and implemented (You might, for instance, look into smallpox vaccination or any of the many activities of Louis Pasteur.)

    —how a specific battle was fought, won, or lost

    —how a religious service or rite is conducted (Either investigate one in a religion other than your own or choose one from your own faith and attempt to explain it to a novice.)

    —how fish are farmed

    —how children acquire speech

    —how a government agency like the Federal Reserve Bank or the Securities Exchange Commission operates—either ideally or in fact

    —how a political- and social-action organization, for example, the NAACP, was created and evolved

    —how an illegal drug makes its way from its original source to the street

    —how a particular item or style of dress either gained or lost acceptance (You might consider—among many other possibilities—jeans, neckties, bustles, tuxedos, panty hose, poodle skirts, and knickers.)

5

Comparison-Contrast
and Analogy

If you pick up a starving dog and make him prosperous, he will
not bite you. This is the principal difference between a dog and
a man.

MARK TWAIN, *Pudd'nhead Wilson*

Scenario 1: While planning next semester's schedule, you realize that
there are two sections of the elementary German course you want to take.
One meets at 8:00 A.M. Monday and Wednesday, the other at 2:00 P.M.
Tuesday and Thursday. Professor Hauptmann teaches the first section, Dr.
Ziegler the second. The thought of an eight o'clock class, especially on
Monday morning, makes you groan. If you take it, you'll certainly have to
return to campus early on those weekends away. But if you can manage to end
your classes before two o'clock each day, you'll have an easy time scheduling
work-study. Rumor also has it that Hauptmann is an "easy A."

The afternoon section will allow you to stretch the weekend for a few
hours at least (unless you schedule some other early class) and not compel
you to be up before seven o'clock twice a week. But getting out of class
at three-thirty or so, assuming it's the last class of the day, might make
work-study somewhat more difficult to arrange. Ziegler, you have heard, is
demanding, but his class is the one to take if you really want to learn the
language.

You poise your pen above the registration card and then withdraw it half
a dozen times.

Scenario 2: You and "a guest" have been invited to your cousin's formal
wedding reception. Since you haven't been dating anyone special lately, you
go over your list of possible candidates and narrow it down to Pat and Terry.

Pat looks great dressed up, while Terry is usually a wrinkled mess. Pat, though, is a bit of a klutz, but Terry is an awesome dancer. Pleasant and conservative, Pat blends easily into most environments. Brash and outspoken, Terry is occasionally embarrassing. Although a good listener, Pat is sometimes a little short of conversation—a possible problem over a six-hour haul. Not so with Terry, who can discuss everything from soap operas to submarines—the ship and the sandwich.

Opening your phone book, you leaf back and forth between their numbers.

Scenario 3:   You are back on the used-car lot for the third time in three days. The '82 red Mustang two-door is still there; so is the '87 brown Cavalier four-door sedan. The Mustang, you already know, has ninety-six thousand miles on it, an eight-cylinder, 120-horsepower engine, air conditioning, AM/FM radio, power windows and locks, and a price tag of $4,700. The Cavalier has fifty-eight thousand miles, a four-cylinder 90-horsepower engine, air conditioning, AM/FM with cassette, and manual windows and locks, and is priced at $3,400.

The Mustang will cost you all the money you've saved for nearly two years and the $2,500 your parents have generously offered. It uses a lot of gas, and, at ninety-six thousand miles, it might not see you through the next three years of college. If you buy the Cavalier you will still have more than half the money currently in your account. In addition, this car is easier on fuel and might hold up through graduation.

No doubt the Cavalier is decent transportation. But the Mustang is a set of wheels.

After fifteen minutes of staring alternately at each, you leave, resolving only to return on day four.

All three of the scenarios above are based on comparison—the examination of similarities or differences (or both) between members of the same class of beings or objects, in relation to one or more standards. In scenario 1, for example, the two course sections are clearly members of the class of elementary German offerings. The hours, the days, and the professors are the standards or bases for comparison. In scenario 2, Pat and Terry are both potential dates that are compared in regard to appearance, personality, physical grace, and social skills. Similarly, scenario 3 presents two automobiles and considers them in relation to price, durability, and image, among other things.

The words *compare* and *comparison* are used in two senses: narrowly, to apply only to similarities, and broadly, to include differences as well. Often, the word *contrast* (both as verb and as noun) is used exclusively to describe differences or their examination. Comparison, therefore, could include contrast—but not vice versa.

PATTERNS OF COMPARISON

Generally, comparison takes either of two patterns—by wholes and point by point—or combines them. Comparison by wholes presents all information about the first subject, followed by *parallel* information about the second. In scenario 1, for example, you are presented with the time, days, problems, and professors first for one section and then for the other. An outline of the key paragraphs would look like this:

I. First Section
    A. Time (8:00 A.M.) and (in)convenience
    B. Days (Monday and Wednesday) and (in)convenience
    C. Ease in scheduling work-study
    D. Professor Hauptmann—easy

II. Second Section
    A. Time (2:00 P.M.) and convenience
    B. Days (Tuesday and Thursday) and convenience
    C. Difficulty in scheduling work-study
    D. Dr. Ziegler—demanding.

Such an approach is most useful in brief comparisons. Making the points of the divisions parallel (i.e., presenting them in identical order) aids in establishing clarity and in allowing the reader to recall in the second half what was said about a particular point in the first. But with a complex subject and a great many points discussed over more than a few pages, readers will not be able to maintain focus on the comparison being attempted—even if their memories are jogged. For example, "As laid-back as Professor Hauptmann is, Dr. Ziegler is intense," would work well here but not in a ten-page paper.

For longer or more intricate pieces, then, we have the point-by-point approach. The advantage of this technique is that the members of the comparison and one basis for comparing them can always be seen in conjunction. Scenario 2 (despite its simplicity) is arranged in point-by-point fashion. Its outline looks like this:

I. Appearance in Formal Clothes
    A. Pat
    B. Terry

II. Physical Grace
    A. Pat
    B. Terry

And so on for sociability (III) and conversation (IV). The chief difference between point-by-point comparison and comparison by wholes is whether the bases of comparison or the items compared are central to the structure. Comparison by wholes organizes according to the items; point by point emphasizes the standards by which they are compared.

As suggested above, one can use both techniques in a piece of writing. Scenario 3 does this. It begins by comparing wholes:

I.   Mustang

    A. Miles
    B. Equipment
    C. Price

II.   Cavalier

    A. Miles
    B. Equipment
    C. Price

The middle paragraphs discuss the advantages and disadvantages of buying each car. Viewed one way, this is a point-by-point approach. But formally, the considerations for each car are dealt with separately:

III. Advantages and Disadvantages—Mustang

    A. Financial Resources
    B. Fuel Economy
    C. Durability

IV.   Advantages and Disadvantages—Cavalier

    A. Financial Resources
    B. Fuel Economy
    C. Durability

However, there is no doubt that the final comments about the car are purely point by point:

V.   Image

    A. Cavalier (transportation)
    B. Mustang (wheels)

THESIS AND EMPHASIS

Usually, the order in which the members of the comparison are discussed is preserved throughout. So in scenario 3, sections I and III deal with the

Mustang, II and IV with the Cavalier. Although (and possibly because) section V breaks the pattern, the order within it is reversed. Placing the Mustang last also emphasizes its image.

Such emphasis, however, is largely absent from the three scenarios, and the issues within them remain unresolved because the significance of the various qualities is never clarified. In scenario 3, is economy more important to you than appearance? In scenario 2, is the risk of Terry's embarrassing you greater than the potential dullness of an evening with Pat? In scenario 1, do you want the "easy A" (assuming the rumor is true) or do you want to learn German (assuming the professor's reputation is deserved)? In these scenarios, as in any comparison you write, what you emphasize and decide (in short, what will form your thesis) will depend on what you value more or most.

Let us rewrite the first of these scenarios with a purpose clearly in mind:

> You want to take German I next semester and notice that there are two sections being offered.
>
> The first meets at 8:00 A.M. Monday and Wednesday and is taught by Professor Hauptmann who, you hear, is an "easy A." The time, however, is not entirely convenient. You are a late riser, and in order to meet Monday's class you'll have to cut off-campus weekends short. True, if you work out an early-morning roster, your work-study will be easy to schedule. As for the professor, although no one turns down an A, you would like to learn some German as well.
>
> The second section meets at 2:00 P.M. on Tuesday and Thursday. With this class, you won't have to be up at seven, and unless you choose some other early course on Monday and Wednesday, you can return from weekends well past midnight on Monday morning. Yes, your work-study time might be less flexible with a midday or afternoon schedule, but you can probably arrange it. Dr. Ziegler might be more demanding than Professor Hauptmann, so maybe you'll learn more German even if you get (gulp!) a B.
>
> You can deal with the work-study problem, but not the early Monday class. And if necessary, you can handle Ziegler's B, if you learn the language. The choice is clear. Two o'clock Tuesday and Thursday it is.

This is but one possibility of several. You could have chosen the early class because of the potential A (your GPA needs one desperately) and/or because, despite the inconvenience of the hour and day, the work-study scheduling is easy—perhaps enabling you to hold an off-campus job as well (since you're broke—possibly because you bought the Mustang of scenario 3). What is crucial, however, is that your preferences are now revealed. You have not merely gauged the situation by a set of criteria but interpreted the results. Underlying the objective measurement were a set of personal values, negatively—a dislike of shortened weekends and getting up early—and, affirmatively—a preference for acquiring knowledge over simply acquiring a high grade.

How you organize your comparison is often crucial to establishing your ideas and the reader's comprehension. As a rule of thumb (and thumbs do vary), if your purpose is to emphasize similarities, present and dispose of the less essential differences at the start:

> It is difficult to imagine two men more different than the late Vladimir Horowitz and Itzhak Perlman. The pianist was aloof, narcissistic, reclusive; the violinist is affable, gregarious, and very much a public figure. Horowitz appeared on television, for example, almost exclusively as a performer, rarely as the subject of an interview. Perlman, however, has also appeared with Johnny Carson, the Muppets, and the Frugal Gourmet. Nevertheless, despite their vast differences in personality, the two soloists have made enduring contributions to our musical heritage.

If you propose to stress differences, on the other hand, simply the reverse the order:

> Isadora Duncan and Alvin Ailey were two of the leading twentieth-century proponents of modern dance. Duncan essentially led an assault against the classical aesthetic. But for Ailey, who came later, issues of race and culture were perhaps more significant.

More often than not, issues are not so clear-cut. The strengths and weaknesses, virtues and vices, attractions and repellents of many pairs subject to comparison are likely to be overlapping and mixed. This is true of all three scenarios above and explains why the decisions are so difficult. You'd like the A in German, but you hate getting up early. Pat dresses well and is well mannered but not the best dancer or conversationalist. Terry is somewhat sloppy and potentially embarrassing but knows how to dance and converse. Comparisons, like life, are not always rose gardens—and even these have thorns.

As a final illustration of all the issues raised so far, let's look at a version of scenario 3 written as a first-person essay.

Car-isma

For the fourth time in a week, I was back on the lot at Hugh's Hughniversity Motors. The cars were there too—an '87 brown Cavalier four-door sedan and an '82 red Mustang. I'd been trying to decide between them for days and the moment of truth was now.

Though it was a "family" sedan (and brown, at that), the Cavalier seemed the better deal. It had only fifty-eight thousand miles on it, compared with the Mustang's ninety-six thousand. The sound system included a cassette player, a feature the Mustang lacked. And at $3,400, the Cavalier's price was $1,300 less than the Mustang's.

Of course, the Mustang (red two-door as it was) had power windows and locks and at eight cylinders to the Cavalier's four was far more powerful. A hundred twenty horses could get me onto highways and past slow-moving traffic a lot more effectively than ninety.

But not without cost. The Mustang's engine (I could hear it roar) would use far more gas per mile than the Cavalier's. I knew I could not easily afford the added expense, since if I bought the Mustang in the first place—with my parents' generous assistance—my bank account would be close to zero. And with ninety-six thousand miles on it, there was the possibility that the Mustang would not last me through senior year as the Cavalier was likely to do.

No doubt the Cavalier was the logical, practical choice. But I bought the Mustang. Although the (brown) Cavalier was fine transportation, my red Mustang is a set of truly excellent wheels.

The first paragraph here simply presents the items to be compared and the narrator's dilemma. It does not state the thesis explicitly. In this case, the thesis evolves, and its evolution—reserving both the choice and its basis until the close—creates suspense and interest.

Through point-by-point comparison, the second paragraph shows the advantages of the Cavalier. The third paragraph, again using point by point, shows the advantages of the Mustang. Although within the paragraphs differences are clearly established, each paragraph as a whole asserts the virtue of one vehicle over the other. The reader remains uncertain about which way the decision will go.

The fourth paragraph, again presenting a point-by-point comparison, seems to tip the decision in favor of the Cavalier, as does the first sentence of the fifth paragraph. But suddenly the direction of the essay is thrown into reverse. Despite all that precedes it, the ultimate difference, transportation versus wheels, is one that favors the Mustang.

Even so, the surprise should not be total. The parenthetical comments in previous paragraphs and their partial repetition in the final sentence provide clues to the narrator's attitude. In fact, there is a second and possibly more central comparison at work here, one involving the conflict between rational and emotional choices.

ANALOGY

You might have heard that you can't compare apples and oranges. But, as the song says, "It ain't necessarily so." If you see them as belonging to the same general class of fruit, you can surely compare them on the bases of size, color, taste, nutritive value, where they can be grown, and so on.

It is true that you can't compare a Macintosh apple with a navel orange. In this case, "apple" and "orange" are seen as distinct classes in themselves. Therefore, you are limited to comparing kinds of apples or kinds of oranges—

the Macintosh with a Winesap or a Granny Smith, for example, the navel orange with a Jaffa or Valencia.

It is also true that you can't compare apples with aardvarks and oranges with orangutans. Beyond the accident of spelling and the fact that members of both pairs are living things, the pairs have nothing in common.

"But," you might object, "my mother often compares my room to a sty," or, waving your most recent Valentine, "It says here that my smile is as radiant as the sun." You (and possibly Mom and your admirer as well) have a point—but *only* a point. Your room and the sty belong to fundamentally *different* classes. They are made of different materials, for different purposes, and are meant to be inhabited by different species. They are alike only in their slovenliness (and there are farmers and pigs who might deny that). Again, your smile might be bright, but probably not sufficiently brilliant to support life on Earth and not the product of nuclear reactions that create temperatures up to fourteen million degrees Kelvin.

What we have in both these instances is not comparison but **analogy,** the discovery of limited commonality between entities that are essentially *unlike*. To illustrate further, let us consider how two subjects, lions and tigers, might be treated comparatively and analogically. In a simple comparison, we might find standard attributes or conditions applicable to both species—sociability, hunting patterns, habitat, endangerment, for example, and upon examining the animals in relation to these standards reach a conclusion about both kinds: "Although more truly the king of beasts than the lion, the tiger is in greater danger of extinction."

But an analogical treatment of lions or tigers involves focusing on a particular characteristic and applying it beyond the classes to which the creatures are usually assigned. For instance, Emperor Haile Selassie of Ethiopia was known as the "Lion of Judah" and Richard I of England was called "the lionhearted." Both titles suggest that the men were bold, fierce, powerful—qualities commonly attributed to the lion. But neither emperor nor king lived in a pride, ate raw meat killed with fang and claw, nor weighed five hundred pounds. It is not the actual lion, but its perceived characteristics that are essential to the analogy. Any fan of *The Wizard of Oz* knows that what the Cowardly Lion (an oxymoron) seeks is courage, the very essence of metaphorical lionhood.

The tiger has also been the focus of analogies, implying ferocity. One boxing champion, for example, appropriated the animal's name and reputation for his own. Dick Tiger was born Richard Ihetu and there were no tigers in his native Nigeria. But his opponents would face a "tiger"—and all that the word implied—when they entered the ring against him. Similarly, French premier Georges Clemenceau was called "the tiger" because of his vigorous political attacks. Unlike the rather rare cowardly lion, there have been many "paper" tigers, those whose ferocity proved bogus when put to the test.

Much of the imagery that underlies most poetry depends upon analogy. While you might have learned (in chapter 2 and elsewhere) that both simile and metaphor involve comparisons, the one using *like* or *as*, the other not, they are more accurately perceived as analogical. In the *Iliad*, for example, Homer often uses the phrase (in one translation) "rosy-fingered dawn" to describe the sunrise. What he means to show us is that the early rays of light look as if they were rosy fingers. But he does not press beyond general shape and color to establish a series of relationships between the rays of light and the fingers, as he would have done if, in fact, the two different kinds of things were comparable. There are no well-chewed cuticles, no acrylic nails, no guitar-string-induced calluses on dawn's "fingers." The phrase is descriptive, suggestive, implicit—an appeal to the psyche, not to reason.

Similarly, when two and a half millennia later the Scots poet Robert Burns declares, "O, my love is like a red, red rose/That's newly sprung in June" he means to say nothing about stems, thorns, or possible infestation by Japanese beetles. He means only to suggest (again) the intensity of his feeling by alluding to the depth of the color ("red, red") and depending on his reader's probable association (another psychological appeal) to the flower's overpowering fragrance.

Even when the image is extended, as in the metaphor in the following poem by Emily Dickinson, the elements of the analogy (unlike those in comparison) are fundamentally different. The abstraction "hope" is not *literally* like a bird at all; it is *figuratively* (i.e., analogically) like a bird, intangibly aperch in an intangible soul, singing wordless comfort and asking nothing in return. We have no concern here with birdbaths, feeders, cuttlebone, or even speciation.

> Hope is the thing with feathers
> That perches in the soul,
> And sings the tune without the words
> And never stops at all,
>
> And sweetest in the gale is heard;
> And sore must be the storm
> That could abash the little bird
> That kept so many warm.
>
> I've heard it in the chillest land,
> And on the strangest sea;
> Yet, never, in extremity,
> It asked a crumb of me.

Although less elaborate in prose, analogy is nevertheless useful there for illustrating a writer's ideas or attitudes. Here is a sentence from Ronald W. Clark's biography of Albert Einstein:

> Einstein saw Rathenau's murder as symbolic of a rising tide of anti-Semitism which would soon be lapping round his own feet.
>
> *Einstein: The Life and Times,* p. 292

"Rising tide" itself is a nearly dead metaphor. (Do we still picture the sea when we read it?) However, "lapping" does provide some vitality. Consider this version without the (analogous) image: "Einstein saw Rathenau's murder as a sign that anti-Semitism was increasing and would soon affect him." While the meaning is clear, this sentence seems less forceful than the original.

Again, in his fictitious, mildly salacious, and by current standards chauvinistic letter to a young man, Benjamin Franklin begins by advocating marriage:

> A single man has not nearly the value he would have in the state of union. . . . He resembles the odd half of a pair of scissors.

That is to say, without marriage a man is useless. But the analogy of the original puts the case vigorously. Remember, though, except for the desirability of their working together, husbands and wives and halves of scissors have nothing at all in common.

In a final example, Antarctic explorer Admiral Richard E. Byrd draws a more extensive analogy between an emperor penguin (note the name) and an aristocrat:

> We sighted our first penguins today. First, a lone Emperor Penguin, which was nearly four feet tall. In attitude and action, he more than lived up to his reputation as the aristocrat among his kind. This most primitive of birds, which alone of all animals survived the glaciation of the once tropical or semi-tropical Antarctic, was standing erect, when we caught sight of him, and his attitude plainly implied a lordly proprietorship over the wastes he surveyed. His resemblance to a man in formal dress was so close as to be positively embarrassing. To see him standing so, dignified, unafraid—did I not also detect scorn?—gave one the feeling that one should address him in carefully chosen speech. Alas, he paid scant attention to us. A scant bow, beak touching the breast, not at all the ceremonial bow for which he is distinguished, then off he went.

Little America, p. 73

There is, of course, a great deal of anthropomorphism in this passage, that is, the attribution of human traits and behavior to another species. But Byrd is attempting to convey to his readers something of the penguin's demeanor; he is not attempting a zoological analysis. But again, a human aristocrat and a penguin (emperor or otherwise) have nothing intrinsically in common. What we have here is simply the admiral's projection of the characteristics of "his lordship" onto the appearance and movements of the bird—a psychological sleight of hand (another analogy), which humans often perform with regard to other creatures.

How common is analogy as a descriptive or illustrative technique in prose? The citations above were all found in books within arm's reach, chosen randomly and leafed through for a few minutes each. The examples here, however, even the one from Byrd, are rather brief. It is possible and often effective to structure an extensive piece of writing upon analogy.

COMPARISON-CONTRAST IN ACADEMIC WRITING

The importance of comparison as a technique for attaining knowledge is often apparent in college catalogs. Many institutions have departments, programs or courses embracing such subjects as comparative anatomy, literature, religion, or anthropology. But whether studies are labeled "comparative" or not, comparison is likely to have a prominent place in the way issues are raised, papers assigned, and examination questions asked.

In a world civ or social science course, for example, we might want to compare the origins, histories, religions, and structures of the various societies, or, more concretely, how they deal with the elderly, sexual expression, or strangers. Topics are legion:

1. Considering issues of wealth, social status, intellectual independence, and psychological stress, compare the life of the Bedouin nomad of the Middle East with that of a European or North American industrial worker of the late nineteenth century.

2. Discuss three ways in which tribal societies differ from those of nation-states. Illustrate your answer by referring to several tribes and nations.

3. Consider two eight-year-olds of the same gender—one from a "barrio" in the American Southwest, the other from a village in rural India. What are the similarities and differences in their societies' expectations of them in regard to education or occupation, social mobility, sex and marriage?

Such topics command the attention of professionals as well. Professor David Elkind, for example, in exploring the premature rush to adulthood among contemporary adolescents, contrasts features of today's behavior—in this case dress—with those of an earlier day:

> Only a few decades ago children dressed differently from teenagers. I recall that when I was growing up I had to wear knickers. At that time boys were not allowed to wear long pants until they reached the teen years. And I really wanted long pants. . . . At that time, too, girls were not allowed to wear long stockings, high heels, or makeup until they reached the teen years. Wearing long pants or long stockings was a sign that young people had reached a new stage of life.

Today, even infants wear designer diaper covers and by the age of two or three many children are dressed like miniature versions of their parents. Similarly, girls of six and seven now often have expensive makeup kits and feel undressed if they go out of doors without their mascara and eye shadow. By the time girls are in their teen years, they are so adultlike in appearance that it is hard even to guess their age. Teenage boys, too, are indistinguishable in their dress from school-age boys and young men. The ubiquity of blue jeans for all ages and all sexes has just about eliminated clothing as a marker of anything other than affluence and image consciousness.

All Grown Up and No Place to Go: Teenagers in Crisis, p. 95

In a very different context, political scientist Robert G. Neumann compares two kinds of federal government created, respectively, by what he calls centripetal and centrifugal social forces:

Each of the two classic types of federalism, the United States and Switzerland, began as a federation of independent states and eventually turned into a federal union. To them, therefore, federalism denotes a trend toward a more centralized authority. Thus it is not accidental that in the early days of American history the Federalist party stood for a stronger national government. But the contrary development is also in evidence; where unity is endangered by diversity, a combination of the two is necessary in order to avoid serious difficulties and possible disintegration. An extreme case in point is the (British) Commonwealth, in which centrifugal tendencies had to be accommodated increasingly over the years until the present structure was reached, which can no longer be called federalist in any sense but is rather a league of independent states. Likewise the Soviet Union and the Federal People's Republic of Yugoslavia, although not truly federal within the scope of the above definition, were persuaded to adopt the federal form in order to make ostensible concessions to the various nations and races which inhabit those countries. Federal forms of government may thus be the result of both centrifugal and centripetal developments.

European and Comparative Government, 3rd ed., p. 680

Although Neumann could not have predicted the demise of either the Soviet Union or Yugoslavia at the time he wrote, his comparison nevertheless reveals some of the forces responsible for their collapse.

What's the point of such comparisons? In fact, there are several: to clarify our understanding of the cultures in question; to increase our appreciation and acceptance of human diversity; and to understand how we and our culture fit and function in a larger global one. As a result, we—collectively and individually—are likely to attain a richer, more complete knowledge of ourselves.

When we learn that, while his wife is giving birth, the Gabbra tribesman of Kenya removes his belt in order to ease the delivery of their child, we might examine the role of males in our own birth practices in light of such symbolic sympathy. When we discover that, among traditional Jews, boys brought to study for the first time experience the "sweetness" of learning by tasting the honey with which sacred texts have been daubed, we might reflect on the attitudes we attempt to instill in our own young scholars. If we chance to come upon a passage in the modern Chinese writer, Lu Xun, that describes children in his native village as building "snow Buddhas," then we might find in that creative impulse a common human thread in the political, social, economic, and theological patchwork of the species.

In those fields that involve experimentation, test subjects will be compared with controls and the effects of variables will be compared with each other. For example, in conditioning dogs to salivate at the sound of a bell, the Russian physiologist Ivan Pavlov and his successors found that the conditioned reflex is established far more effectively if, during conditioning, the bell precedes the presentation of food rather than following it. More important, other experimenters attempting to verify this finding could repeat previous experiments and compare results.

Such verifiability is crucial to all scientific investigation. As recently as 1989, two physicists claimed that they had created cold fusion in their laboratory, that is, that they had combined (as opposed to split) atomic nuclei without significant expenditure of energy. This would have been a major advance in nuclear physics with enormous industrial and ecological implications. But, when other researchers following their procedures could not duplicate the results, the "discovery" was rejected as spurious.

Science, however, depends on observation as well as experimentation. And observation may well lead to the discovery of parallels among the phenomena observed. Ethologist Konrad Lorenz, for instance, in discussing demonstrative behavior often seen in courtship, finds that both the Greylag gander and the human male engage in displays that feature the "expenditure of energy" far exceeding requirements for specific tasks or actions:

> [T]he bird sticks out its chest and holds itself upright. . . . The normal side-to-side rotation of the body in walking is exaggerated so that it virtually looks as if the bird finds walking more laborious than normal. Whereas Greylag geese otherwise make little use of their wings and only fly off in face of actual danger, the "demonstrative" gander makes use of every opportunity to demonstrate the strength of his wings. . . . In particular, he will fly headlong towards any actual or apparent opponent and then, after chasing off the intruder, fly back with just as much expenditure of energy to the female he is impressing. He subsequently lands by her with his wings raised and uttering a loud triumph-call. . . .
>
> [Similarly], under circumstances involving physical activity (for example when skiing or ice-skating), [men] become considerably more vigorous and dashing when the number of spectators is increased by one

attractive girl. In primitive or not quite grown-up men, this is often accompanied—as in the gander described—by attacking or . . . molesting weaker pseudo-opponents. The most remarkable fact . . . , however, is that many men perform the dissipation of energy characteristic of demonstrative behaviour with a *machine*. . . . I have repeatedly observed that motor cyclists . . . increase the noise-level and energy consumption of their machines by revving and simultaneously adjusting the ignition, without greatly increasing their speed. Sharp braking and much too rapid acceleration of motor vehicles can often be explained in the same way.

Studies in Animal and Human Behaviour, vol. 1, p. 190

Comparison will also be central to courses in the arts and humanities. If you study Sophocles' *Medea* in your classical literature class, you might also read the *Medea* of Euripedes to examine their respective styles, characterization, language (allowing for translation), and themes. Which playwright, for example, is more sympathetic to Medea in her abandonment by Jason? Which tends more to justify her murder of her sons?

If your course includes epic poetry, you might investigate what roles the gods play in Homer's *Iliad* and in the *Ramayana* of India. As for fiction, perhaps you will study two African-American characters—Joe Christmas in William Faulkner's *Light in August* and the titular hero of Ralph Ellison's *Invisible Man*. How do these outcast figures differ? Do such differences depend upon the racial perspectives of their creators?

Of course, the judgments you will make have their counterparts in the writings of scholars and critics. Here, for example, Alfred Kazin contrasts the life experience and consequent literary achievement of two American novelists:

> The fortunes of literature can reverse the fortunes of life. The luxury that nourished Edith Wharton and gave her the opportunities of a gentlewoman cheated her as a novelist. It kept her from what was crucial to the world in which she lived; seeking its manners, she missed its passion. Theodore Dreiser had no such handicap to overcome. From the first he was so oppressed by suffering, by the spectacle of men struggling aimlessly and alone in society, that he was prepared to understand the very society that rejected him. The cruelty and squalor of the life to which he was born suggested the theme of existence; the pattern of American life was identified as the figure of destiny. . . .
>
> *On Native Grounds*, pp. 61–62

While the author, title, and subjects in this quotation are, so to speak, homegrown, the following observations by Polish critic Jan Kott concern an English poet and his Italian counterpart. (Michelangelo may be better known to you as a sculptor and painter.)

Shakespeare's Sonnets have often been compared with the poems of Michelangelo, which are also centred around two persons: a youth and a woman. The drama of choice was a similar one. But the tone of Michelangelo's poems is a darker one, and the transitions from pure animality to mysticism, from exaltation over the youth's beauty—compared with the sun in whose brightness the Divine beauty is reflected—to absolute asceticism and resignation are more violent. . . . Feelings inspired by the youth are free from the original sin; there is in them a longing for lost purity. . . .

Shakespeare was far more down to earth, but the choice between angelic and diabolic, between the sphere of light and the sphere of shadow is the same for him as for Michelangelo. . . .

Shakespeare Our Contemporary, p. 300

Like the study of literature, the study of art relies on the ability to discern differences while acknowledging similarities. What distinguishes a portrait by Bronzino from one by Velázquez? Consider line, color, arrangement, expression. How does a Donatello sculpture differ from one by Bernini? Examine materials, scale, technique. And if your art history course goes beyond the West, you might want to compare the methods and aesthetic of the Italian sculptors with their counterparts in, for example, India or the ancient African kingdom of Benin. In the passage that follows, art historian Frank Willett compares the sculpture of two Nigerian peoples:

A comparison of Nok and Ife sculptures . . . leaves one with little doubt that there is a cultural and an artistic connection between them, though the precise nature of the link remains obscure. These are the only two artistic traditions we know in the whole of Africa which have attempted human figure sculpture on a scale approaching life-size. The fragments of trunk and limbs are very similar indeed in their simplification, despite the great naturalism of Ife faces. In both styles the sculptures are sometimes set on a globular base; the hair is occasionally represented as rings, and similar pendant locks are represented. The figures are usually heavily beaded: not only are large numbers of anklets and bracelets worn, but the arrangement of beads on the chest is very similar in many cases in both traditions—a heavy rope of beads overlies many strings of smaller beads which cover the whole chest. This, of course, is a cultural rather than an artistic similarity, though the style of representation of the beads is often close in both. . . .

African Art: An Introduction, p. 73

Perhaps through comparisons like these we can approach discovering what is beautiful, useful, and true—and why we think so.

Such issues, of course, are philosophical ones, and while their discussion often seems speculative, people have regularly attempted to incorporate the views of philosophers into their collective and personal lives. What sort of government, for example, is best? One ruled by Plato's philosopher-kings, Machiavelli's skillful despot, or, as John Locke and his followers (Jefferson among them) would have it, ourselves? Is our morality dependent on divinely established precepts as the Church fathers maintained, or on an essentially secular code of obligations and duties as Confucius and his disciples held? As for self-knowledge, should we affirm with René Descartes, "I think; therefore, I am?" Should we, like Freud, wonder whether we are ego, id, or superego—conscious or unconscious? Or should we assert with the Bushman Nxou in Laurens van der Post's *The Lost World of the Kalahari* that "there is a dream dreaming us"? Answers to any of these questions depend in part upon our understanding what philosophy is and does. Elmer Sprague provides some direction and definition through this comparison:

> The difference between philosophy and religion, at least as Jews, Christians, and Muslims understand it . . . , is in the contrast between method in philosophy and revelation in religion. To the Philosopher the ultimate nature of reality is discoverable through the use of human powers by anyone who has the intellect, energy, and perseverance to seek. But for the religious person, God, who is the ultimate reality, may be sought by anyone, but he is found only when he chooses to reveal himself. God's grace, not human persistence, explains the success of any religious quest. In contrast with religion then, philosophy is squarely for the use of human powers to know what can be known. There is nothing hidden to be noticed only when it chooses to reveal itself. Whatever is, is discoverable; and nothing else is. . . .
>
> *What Is Philosophy?*, p. 10

One task facing the modern student is to integrate, so far as possible, the various information and insights received through many disciplines. In painting Pope Innocent X, for example, does Velázquez depict the inner (unconscious) or outer (conscious) man? Would Velázquez have agreed with Machiavelli's political theories? Would his subject? Are there similarities between the paintings of Velázquez and the plays of his near contemporary Lope de Vega? In what ways does Velázquez's painting reflect Spanish or European civilization of the seventeenth century? And finally, what in Velázquez and his age is useful or instructive today? One way of approaching responses to such questions is to compare and contrast.

Using Comparison-Contrast and Analogy

When comparing or contrasting be sure that the subjects you examine are, in fact, comparable and that you have at least one clear basis (standard) by which to evaluate them. Most of the time you will have several. Having decided on what to compare and how, establish a thesis to govern your comparison.

Decide whether comparing by wholes or point by point would establish your thesis more effectively. Remember that comparisons of more than a few pages are usually more effective if presented point by point. In using either approach, arrange your subtopics in the most effective and emphatic order, that is, the order that best supports your thesis.

Remember that, unlike comparison-contrast, analogy depends on one or two points in common between entities that are essentially dissimilar. As the following passage demonstrates, its purpose is primarily illustrative:

> The way in which the cerebral hemisphere is organized reminds one of the traditional government of Japan. The primary receptive area is like the emperor; he is the primary one, the acknowledged head of the government. The secondary or parasensory area is like the shogun; he is the minister and is therefore only secondary. Although the emperor was the most important man in Japan, he had no power to transact any business whatsoever. All business and all political affairs, all communication with ambassadors from other countries had to be performed by the shogun. In the brain, all communication is carried out by the secondary areas. Each primary receptive area merely receives. It then passes on messages to its secondary area; and the secondary areas pass messages among themselves and communicate with association areas.

PETER NATHAN, *The Nervous System*, pp. 225–26

John Donne

(England; 1572–1631)

*Born into a staunch Catholic family related to Sir Thomas More, Donne
wrestled long and hard with the religious controversies of his day. With firm
conviction but also with an awareness of the possibilities of personal advancement, he converted to Anglicanism, was ordained in 1615, and rose to the
deanship of Saint Paul's Church (London). Famous as a preacher, he delivered what was essentially his own funeral sermon some months before his
death.*

*Donne's early expectations of a career at court were shattered when, after he
eloped with Ann More, his reluctant father-in-law intervened against him.
The elopement, however, illustrates Donne's secular passion. He is among the
foremost poets of love and seduction in the language, often using intellectual
arguments and highly unconventional imagery in his creations. The secular
and sacred aspects of Donne's work, however, are often commingled: he uses
the language of faith in his most profane pieces, and that of romantic ardor in
his Holy Sonnets.*

"Sleep and Death" (editor's title) is taken from Devotions upon Emergent
Occasions *(1621), in which Donne traces the progress of his illness and
recovery through twenty-three physical and spiritual stages. The present selection is the meditative portion of the fifteenth, originally called "I sleep not day
nor night."*

Sleep and Death

NATURAL MEN have conceived a twofold use of sleep; that it is a refreshing
of the body in this life; that it is a preparing of the soul for the next; that it
is a feast, and it is the grace at that feast; that it is our recreation and cheers
us, and it is our catechism and instructs us; we lie down in a hope that we
shall rise the stronger, and we lie down in a knowledge that we may rise no
more. Sleep is an opiate which gives us rest, but such an opiate, as perchance,
being under it, we shall wake no more.

But though natural men, who have induced secondary and figurative
considerations, have found out this second, this emblematical use of sleep,
that it should be a representation of death, God, who wrought and perfected
his work before nature began (for nature was but his apprentice, to learn in
the first seven days, and now is his foreman, and works next under him), God,
I say, intended sleep only for the refreshing of man by bodily rest, and not for
a figure of death, for he intended not death itself then. But man having
induced death upon himself, God hath taken man's creature, death, into his

246

hand, and mended it; and whereas it hath in itself a fearful form and aspect, so that man is afraid of his own creature, God presents it to him in a familiar, in an assiduous, in an agreeable and acceptable form, in sleep; that so when he awakes from sleep, and says to himself, "Shall I be no otherwise when I am dead, than I was even now when I was asleep?" he may be ashamed of his waking dreams, and of his melancholy fancying out a horrid and an affrightful figure of that death which is so like sleep.

As then we need sleep to live out our threescore and ten years, so we need death to live that life which we cannot outlive. And as death being our enemy, God allows us to defend ourselves against it (for we victual ourselves against death twice every day), as often as we eat, so God having so sweetened death unto us as he hath in sleep, we put ourselves into our enemy's hands once every day, so far as sleep is death; and sleep is as much death as meat is life. This then is the misery of my sickness, that death, as it is produced from me and is mine own creature, is now before mine eyes, but in that form in which God hath mollified it to us, and made it acceptable, in sleep I cannot see it.

How many prisoners, who have even hollowed themselves their graves upon that earth on which they have lain long under heavy fetters, yet at this hour are asleep, though they be yet working upon their own graves by their own weight? He that hath seen his friend die today, or knows he shall see it tomorrow, yet will sink into a sleep between. I cannot, and oh, if I be entering now into eternity, where there shall be no more distinction of hours, why is it all my business now to tell clocks? Why is none of the heaviness of my heart dispensed into mine eyelids, that they might fall as my heart doth? And why, since I have lost my delight in all objects, cannot I discontinue the faculty of seeing them by closing mine eyes in sleep? But why rather, being entering into that presence where I shall wake continually and never sleep more, do I not interpret my continual waking here, to be a parasceve[1] and a preparation to that?

THESIS AND THOUGHT

1. Summarize the relationship(s) between sleep and death presented by Donne.
2. Explain what Donne means by saying God "intended not death itself then" and that man "induced death upon himself" (para. 2).
3. What is "that life which we cannot outlive" (para. 3)?
4. What is Donne's attitude toward death? Taking this into account, explain why you think the selection is either optimistic or pessimistic.

[1]**parasceve:** preparation for the Jewish sabbath and the Friday evening on which it begins; here an allusion to Good Friday, which anticipates resurrection. [Ed.]

STRUCTURE

1. Outline the similarities and differences between sleep and death. You might find your answer to "Thesis and Thought" question 1 helpful.

2. The selection contains several comparative elements aside from those directly shared by sleep and death. Identify them and explain how they help establish unity.

3. Based on the discussion at the beginning of this chapter, your responses to the questions above, and your own considered judgment, explain whether "Sleep and Death" is an analogy or a simple comparison.

STYLE

1. Since the selection was written nearly four hundred years ago, it is not surprising that some of its language is archaic. Identify four or five archaic words or constructions. Then rewrite (in modern idiom) the passages in which they appear. Do you think your versions are more effective? Do they detract from or enhance the rest of the piece?

2. Donne often writes balanced or antithetical sentences, such as "As then we need sleep to live out our threescore and ten years, so we need death to live that life which we cannot outlive" (para. 3). Find several other examples of this or similar constructions.

3. What is the effect of the series of questions with which the selection ends? In what sense might the final question be read as apart from the series rather than as part of it?

4. Explain the allusions implicit in "the first seven days" (para. 2) and "threescore and ten years" (para. 3).

CONSIDERATIONS

1. What are your views of death? Of an afterlife? Compare them with Donne's.

2. In paragraph 2, Donne refers to the "emblematical use of sleep." Suggest and list emblematic or metaphorical applications for three or four other bodily processes or conditions.

3. Ostensibly, if not in actuality, Donne composed this meditation during a sleepless night. What do you do when you can't fall asleep? Is your activity productive? Write an essay on the topic "Meditations on a Sleepless Night."

4. Filling in the blanks with topics of your choice, write a long paragraph or brief essay on "Sleep and ———" or "——— and Death."

Chief Seattle

(Duwamish, ca. 1790–1866)

Seattle (also spelled "Seathl") was chief of the Duwamish and a number of other small tribes along Puget Sound. His friendship toward white settlers even during a major period of armed hostility and his late conversion to Catholicism suggest his westernization. However, he continued to wear native dress and insisted on speaking in Duwamish. Moreover, the speech below, delivered in 1854 upon Seattle's acceptance of the terms of the Port Elliott Treaty (1855), underscores the chief's clear perception of differences between the two populations.

One source reports that Seattle initially resisted the settlers' proposal to name their city after him, believing that he would be disturbed after death by people calling his name. He relented when the settlers agreed to pay him during his lifetime for the anticipated inconvenience.

Seattle's speech was addressed to Governor Isaac I. Stevens with Dr. Henry A. Smith serving as translator. In the opinion of one commentator, although the authenticity of the language may be called into question, the underlying sentiments may be ascribed to the chief.

The Red Man and the White

"YONDER SKY that has wept tears of compassion upon my people for centuries untold, and which to us appears changeless and eternal, may change. Today is fair. Tomorrow it may be overcast with clouds. My words are like the stars that never change. Whatever Seattle says the great chief at Washington can rely upon with as much certainty as he can upon the return of the sun or the seasons. The White Chief says that Big Chief at Washington sends us greetings of friendship and good will. This is kind of him for we know he has little need of our friendship in return. His people are many. They are like the grass that covers vast prairies. My people are few. They resemble the scattering trees of a storm-swept plain. The Great—and I presume—good White Chief sends us word that he wishes to buy our lands but is willing to allow us enough to live comfortably. This indeed appears just, even generous, for the Red Man no longer has rights that he need respect, and the offer may be wise also, as we are no longer in need of an extensive country.

"There was a time when our people covered the land as the waves of a wind-ruffled sea cover its shell-paved floor, but that time long since passed away with the greatness of tribes that are now but a mournful memory. I will not dwell on, nor mourn over, our untimely decay, nor reproach my pale face brothers with hastening it as we too may have been somewhat to blame.

249

"Youth is impulsive. When our young men grow angry at some real or imaginary wrong, and disfigure their faces with black paint, it denotes that their hearts are black—and then they are often cruel and relentless, and our old men and old women are unable to restrain them. Thus it has ever been. Thus it was when the white man first began to push our forefathers westward. But let us hope that the hostilities between us may never return. We would have everything to lose and nothing to gain. Revenge by young braves is considered gain, even at the cost of their own lives, but old men who stay at home in times of war, and mothers who have sons to lose, know better.

"Our good father at Washington—for I presume he is now our father as well as yours, since King George has moved his boundaries further north—our great and good father, I say, sends us word that if we do as he desires he will protect us. His brave warriors will be to us a bristling wall of strength, and his wonderful ships of war will fill our harbors so that our ancient enemies far to the northward—the Hidas and Timpsions, will cease to frighten our women, children and old men. Then in reality will he be our father and we his children. But can that ever be? Your God is not our God! Your God loves your people and hates mine. He folds his strong protecting arms lovingly about the pale face and leads him by the hand as a father leads his infant son—but He has forsaken His red children—if they are really His. Our God, the Great Spirit, seems also to have forsaken us. Your God makes your people wax strong every day. Soon they will fill all the land. Our people are ebbing away like a rapidly receding tide that will never return. The white man's God can not love our people or He would protect them. They seem to be orphans who can look nowhere for help. How then can we be brothers? How can your God become our God and renew our prosperity and awaken in us dreams of returning greatness. If we have a common Heavenly Father He must be partial—for He came to His pale-face children. We never saw Him. He gave you laws but had no word for His red children whose teeming multitudes once filled this vast continent as stars fill the firmament. No. We are two distinct races with separate origins and separate destinies. There is little in common between us.

"To us the ashes of our ancestors are sacred and their resting place is   5
hallowed ground. You wander far from the graves of your ancestors and seemingly without regret. Your religion was written on tables of stone by the iron finger of your God so that you could not forget. The Red Man could never comprehend nor remember it. Our religion is the traditions of our ancestors—the dreams of our old men, given them in the solemn hours of night by the Great Spirit; and the visions of our sachems, and is written in the hearts of our people.

"Your dead cease to love you and the land of their nativity as soon as they pass the portals of the tomb and wander away beyond the stars. They are soon forgotten and never return. Our dead never forget the beautiful world that gave them being. They still love its verdant valleys, its murmuring rivers, its magnificent mountains, sequestered vales and verdant-lined lakes and bays, and ever yearn in tender, fond affection over the lonely hearted living, and often return from the Happy Hunting Ground to visit, guide, console and comfort them.

"Day and night can not dwell together. The Red Man has ever fled the approach of the White Man as the morning mist flees before the rising sun.

"However, your proposition seems fair, and I think that my folks will accept it and will retire to the reservation you offer them. Then we will dwell apart in peace for the words of the Great White Chief seem to be the voice of Nature speaking to my people out of dense darkness.

"It matters little where we pass the remnant of our days. They will not be many. The Indian's night promises to be dark. Not a single star of hope hovers above his horizon. Sad-voiced winds moan in the distance. Grim Nemesis seems to be on the Red Man's trail, and wherever he goes he will hear the approaching footsteps of his fell destroyer and prepare to stolidly meet his doom, as does the wounded doe that hears the approaching footsteps of the hunter.

"A few more moons. A few more winters—and not one of the descen- 10 dants of the mighty hosts that once moved over this broad land or lived in happy homes, protected by the Great Spirit, will remain to mourn over the graves of a people—once more powerful and hopeful than yours. But why should I mourn at the untimely fate of my people? Tribe follows tribe, and nation follows nation, like the waves of the sea. It is the order of nature, and regret is useless. Your time of decay may be distant—but it will surely come, for even the White Man whose God walked and talked with him as friend with friend, can not be exempt from the common destiny. We may be brothers after all. We will see.

"We will ponder your proposition and when we decide we will let you know. But should we accept it, I here and now make this condition—that we will not be denied the privilege without molestation, of visiting at any time the tombs of our ancestors, friends and children. Every part of this soil is sacred, in the estimation of my people. Every hillside, every valley, every plain and grove, has been hallowed by some sad or happy event in days long vanished. Even the rocks, which seem to be dumb and dead as they swelter in the sun along the silent shore thrill with memories of stirring events connected with the lives of my people, and the very dust upon which you now stand responds more lovingly to their footsteps than to yours, because it is rich with the dust of our ancestors and our bare feet are conscious of the sympathetic touch. Our departed braves, fond mothers, glad, happy-hearted maidens, and even the little children who lived here and rejoiced here for a brief season, still love these sombre solitudes and at eventide they grow shadowy of returning spirits. And when the last Red Man shall have perished, and the memory of my tribe shall have become a myth among the white man, these shores will swarm with the invisible dead of my tribe, and when your children's children think themselves alone in the field, the store, the shop, upon the highway, or in the silence of the pathless woods, they will not be alone. In all the earth there is no place dedicated to solitude. At night when the streets of your cities and villages are silent and you think them deserted, they will throng with the returning hosts that once filled them and still love this beautiful land. The White Man will never be alone.

Let him be just and deal kindly with my people, for the dead are not powerless. Dead—I say? There is no death. Only a change of worlds.

THESIS AND THOUGHT

1. To what extent is Seattle's oration a response to the proposed treaty? Identify the paragraphs that deal specifically with the proposal.

2. To what subject other than the treaty is the speech devoted? How are the two topics interrelated?

3. According to Seattle, what is the nature of the relationship between the two peoples? Is the relationship complex? paradoxical? Explain.

STRUCTURE

1. The central comparison here is developed in paragraphs 4–7 and 10–11. On what bases are the two peoples compared? Which set of paragraphs focuses on differences? Which on similarities? Is there significance in the sequence of the two sets?

2. What comparisons does Seattle make other than those between whites and Native Americans? How do these contribute to the overall design of the speech?

3. To what degree is the movement from topic to topic the result of psychological suggestion or association rather than logical necessity?

STYLE

1. Seattle speaks in a variety of tones. He is by turns sorrowful, resigned, ironic, and optimistic. Identify specific passages in which these attitudes are apparent. List and illustrate any other tonal qualities as well.

2. Possibly as the result of overuse or distortion by mass media, some phrases, such as "pale-face children" (para. 4), seem almost **clichéd** or stereotypic. Find other words or phrases that have a similar quality. Explain whether they diminish the impact of the whole.

3. Seattle's speech is rife with imagery. Choose three examples and discuss their effectiveness. Try rewriting the passages without the images. What do you notice?

4. Examine the alternation of short and long sentences in paragraph 3 or 11. What is its effect? To what extent is this alternation characteristic of the style throughout the speech?

CONSIDERATIONS

1. Judging solely from the speech, does Seattle seem heroic or otherwise larger than life? Explain.

2. What implications for current Native American–U.S. relations do you see in the statement, "The White Man will never be alone" (para. 11)?

3. Investigate whether the United States has generally lived up to its treaty obligations to Native Americans. Report the results of your investigation in a brief but specific essay.

Robinson Jeffers
(United States; 1887–1962)

Learning Greek, Latin, and Hebrew during childhood, Jeffers received a bachelor's degree from Occidental College at eighteen, then continued study in forestry, medicine, and biology in California and Switzerland. Throughout most of his life, he had sufficient means to devote himself to writing exclusively and, ultimately, to live in isolation near Carmel, California.

Jeffers's poetry is distinguished by the theme of power, whether in the admirable forces of nature or in violence perpetrated by human beings. But at best, Jeffers regards rape, incest, and murder (prominent in his long poems) as inevitable because the human race is inferior and degenerate. Such misanthropic views led Jeffers to withdraw from society, scorn social reforms such as Franklin Roosevelt's New Deal, and mock the struggles culminating in World War II.

Despite his extreme positions, Jeffers is connected to literary and cultural tradition in at least two ways. First, he shares the general Western disillusion that characterized the period after World War I. Second, he loosely follows the poetic style of Whitman.

Among Jeffers's significant narrative poems are Tamar *(1924) and* Roan Stallion *(1925). His version of Euripedes'* Medea *(1946) was both a literary and dramatic success. "Hurt Hawks" and "The Bloody Sire" are among his powerful shorter poems.*

The Deer Lay Down Their Bones

I followed the narrow cliffside trail half way up the
   mountain
Above the deep river-canyon. There was a little cataract
   crossed the path, flinging itself
Over tree roots and rocks, shaking the jeweled fern-
   fronds, bright bubbling water
Pure from the mountain, but a bad smell came up.
   Wondering at it I clambered down the steep stream
Some forty feet, and found in the midst of bush-oak and   5
   laurel,
Hung like a bird's nest on the precipice brink a small
   hidden clearing,
Grass and a shallow pool. But all about there were bones
   lying in the grass, clean bones and stinking bones,
Antlers and bones: I understood that the place was a
   refuge for wounded deer; there are so many
Hurt ones escape the hunters and limp away to lie hidden;
   here they have water for the awful thirst
And peace to die in; dense green laurel and grim cliff   10
Make sanctuary, and a sweet wind blows upward from
   the deep gorge.—I wish my bones were with theirs.
But that's a foolish thing to confess, and a little
   cowardly. We know that life
Is on the whole quite equally good and bad, mostly gray
   neutral, and can be endured
To the dim end, no matter what magic of grass, water
   and precipice, and pain of wounds,
 Makes death look dear. We have been given life and have   15
   used it—not a great gift perhaps—but in honesty
Should use it all. Mine's empty since my love died—
   Empty? The flame-haired grandchild with great blue eyes
That look like hers?—What can I do for the child? I gaze
   at her and wonder what sort of man
In the fall of the world . . . I am growing old, that is the
   trouble. My children and little grandchildren
Will find their way, and why should I wait ten years yet,
   having lived sixty-seven, ten years more or less,
Before I crawl out on a ledge of rock and die snapping,   20
   like a wolf
Who has lost his mate?—I am bound by my own thirty-
   year-old decision: who drinks the wine

Should take the dregs; even in the bitter lees and
  sediment
New discovery may lie. The deer in that beautiful place
  lay down their bones: I must wear mine.

Thesis and Thought

1. Summarize the speaker's view of human life. How does it differ from the life of the deer, or implicitly, all other nonhuman life?
2. What do we learn about the narrator that might help explain his attitude?
3. Complete the interrupted thought in lines 17–18.
4. Explain why the narrator must continue to "wear" his bones.

Structure

1. On balance, is the comparison here by wholes or point by point? Where does Jeffers deviate from this pattern? To what purpose?
2. How do lines 11 and 23 reinforce the essential contrast?

Style

1. How dependent is this poem on imagery? Do all the descriptions in lines 1–11 qualify as images?
2. Jeffers uses exceptionally long lines here. Are they essentially different from lines of prose? Why? Rewrite one of the following passages as a prose paragraph: lines 1–7, 7–11, 12–16, 18–23. What differences are there between your paragraph and the original?

Considerations

1. In what sense may the speaker's attitude be called stoic? Is it at all optimistic?
2. Consider the statement, "I am bound by my own thirty-year-old decision." How does it inhibit our viewing the speaker merely as an unhappy old man?
3. Address one of the following:
   a. Imagine you are "the flame-haired grandchild." Write your grandfather a letter in which you either support his views or convince him that life is better than he thinks.
   b. Imagine that you have met the narrator in the clearing. Capture your encounter in a brief dialogue that reveals both his and your character or attitudes.

Dorothy Parker

(United States; 1893–1967)

Wit, critic, novelist, and poet, Dorothy Parker was among the leading figures of literary New York in the period between the world wars. She was an early contributor to the New Yorker *magazine and one of the founders of the Round Table group of writers, which met regularly at the Algonquin Hotel to talk shop and scandal.*

Although she wrote for the screen, contributed lyrics to Leonard Bernstein's Candide, *and won the 1929 O. Henry Memorial Award for her short story "Big Blonde," her pithy and barbed one-liners established her reputation as both critic and wit. She said of one author, for example, that "the only 'ism' she believes in is plagiarism" and of actress Katharine Hepburn that "she runs the gamut of emotions from A to B."*

For most of her life she was associated with liberal political causes. During the Spanish civil war (1936–39), for instance, she headed the Joint Anti-Fascist Refugee Committee. Parker was among the hundreds of artists and writers called before the House Un-American Activities Committee during the anti-Communist hysteria following World War II. Upon her death, she bequeathed the bulk of her modest estate to Martin Luther King, whom she had never met, thus perpetuating her interest in civil liberties.

The Waltz

WHY, *Thank you so much. I'd adore to.*

I don't want to dance with him. I don't want to dance with anybody. And even if I did, it wouldn't be him. He'd be well down among the last ten. I've seen the way he dances; it looks like something you do on Saint Walpurgis Night. Just think, not a quarter of an hour ago, here I was sitting, feeling so sorry for the poor girl he was dancing with. And now *I'm* going to be the poor girl. Well, well. Isn't it a small world?

And a peach of a world, too. A true little corker. Its events are so fascinatingly unpredictable, are not they? Here I was, minding my own business, not doing a stitch of harm to any living soul. And then he comes into my life, all smiles and city manners, to sue me for the favor of one memorable mazurka. Why, he scarcely knows by name, let alone what it stands for. It stands for Despair, Bewilderment, Futility, Degradation, and Premeditated Murder, but little does he wot. I don't wot his name, either; I haven't any idea what it is. Jukes would be my guess from the look in his eyes. How do you do, Mr. Jukes? And how is that dear little brother of yours, with the two heads?

Ah, now why did he have to come around me, with his low requests? Why can't he let me lead my own life? I ask so little—just to be left alone in my quiet corner of the table, to do my evening brooding over all my sorrows. And he must come, with his bows and his scrapes and his may-I-have-this-ones. And I had to go and tell him that I'd adore to dance with him. I cannot understand why I wasn't struck right down dead. Yes, and being struck dead would look like a day in the country, compared to struggling out a dance with this boy. But what could I do? Everyone else at the table had got up to dance, except him and me. There was I, trapped. Trapped like a trap in a trap.

What can you say, when a man asks you to dance with him? I most   5
certainly will *not* dance with you; I'll see you in hell first. Why, thank you, I'd like to awfully, but I'm having labor pains. Oh, yes, *do* let's dance together— it's so nice to meet a man who isn't a scaredy-cat about catching my beri-beri. No. There was nothing for me to do, but say I'd adore to. Well, we might as well get it over with. All right, Cannonball, let's run out on the field. You won the toss; you can lead.

Why, I think it's more of a waltz, really. Isn't it? We might just listen to the music a second. Oh, yes, it's a waltz. Mind? Why, I'm simply thrilled. I'd love to waltz with you.

I'd love to waltz with you. I'd love to waltz with you. I'd love to have my tonsils out, I'd love to be in a midnight fire at sea. Well, it's too late now. We're getting under way. *Oh.* Oh, dear. Oh, dear, dear, dear. Oh, this is even worse than I thought it was going to be. Oh, if I had any real grasp of what this dance would be like, I'd have held out for sitting it out. Well, it will probably amount to the same thing in the end. We'll be sitting it out on the floor in a minute, if he keeps this up.

I'm so glad I brought it to his attention that this is a waltz they're playing. Heaven knows what might have happened, if he had thought it was something fast; we'd have blown the sides right out of the building. Why does he always want to be somewhere that he isn't? Why can't we stay in one place just long enough to get acclimated? It's this constant rush, rush, rush, that's the curse of American life. That's the reason we're all of us so—*Ow!* For God's sake, don't *kick,* you idiot; this is only second down. Oh, my shin. My poor, poor shin, that I've had ever since I was a little girl!

Oh, no, no, no. Goodness, no. It didn't hurt the least little bit. And anyway it was my fault. Really it was. Truly. Well, you're just being sweet, to say that. It really was all my fault.

I wonder what I'd better do—kill him this instant, with my naked hands,   10
or wait and let him drop in his traces. Maybe it's best not to make a scene. I guess I'll just lie low, and watch the pace get him. He can't keep this up indefinitely—he's only flesh and blood. Die he must, and die he shall, for what he did to me. I don't want to be of the over-sensitive type, but you can't tell me that kick was unpremeditated. Freud says there are no accidents. I've led no cloistered life, I've known dancing partners who have spoiled my

slippers and torn my dress; but when it comes to kicking, I am Outraged Womanhood. When you kick me in the shin, *smile*.

Maybe he didn't do it maliciously. Maybe it's just his way of showing his high spirits. I suppose I ought to be glad that one of us is having such a good time. I suppose I ought to think myself lucky if he brings me back alive. Maybe it's captious to demand of a practically strange man that he leave your shins as he found them. After all, the poor boy's doing the best he can. Probably he grew up in the hill country, and never had no larnin'. I bet they had to throw him on his back to get shoes on him.

Yes, it's lovely, isn't it? It's simply lovely. It's the loveliest waltz. Isn't it? Oh, I think it's lovely, too.

Why, I'm getting positively drawn to the Triple Threat here. He's my hero. He has the heart of a lion, and the sinews of a buffalo. Look at him—never a thought of the consequences, never afraid of his face, hurling himself into every scrimmage, eyes shining, cheeks ablaze. And shall it be said that I hung back? No, a thousand times no. What's it to me if I have to spend the next couple of years in a plaster cast? Come on, Butch, right through them! Who wants to live forever?

Oh. Oh, dear. Oh, he's all right, thank goodness. For a while I thought they'd have to carry him off the field. Ah, I couldn't bear to have anything happen to him. I love him. I love him better than anybody else in the world. Look at the spirit he gets into a dreary, commonplace waltz; how effete the other dancers seem, beside him. He is youth and vigor and courage; he is strength and gaiety and—*Ow!* Get off my instep, you hulking peasant! What do you think I am, anyway—a gangplank? *Ow!*

No, of course it didn't hurt. Why, it didn't a bit. Honestly. And it was all my 15 *fault. You see, that little step of yours—well, it's perfectly lovely, but it's just a tiny bit tricky to follow at first. Oh, did you work it up yourself? You really did? Well, aren't you amazing! Oh, now I think I've got it. Oh I think it's lovely. I was watching you do it when you were dancing before. It's awfully effective when you look at it.*

It's awfully effective when you look at it. I bet I'm awfully effective when you look at me. My hair is hanging along my cheeks, my skirt is swaddling about me, I can feel the cold damp of my brow. I must look like something out of the "Fall of the House of Usher." This sort of thing takes a fearful toll of a woman my age. And he worked up his little step himself, he with his degenerate cunning. And it was just a tiny bit tricky at first, but now I think I've got it. Two stumbles, slip and a twenty-yard dash; yes. I've got it. I've got several other things, too, including a split shin and a bitter heart. I hate this creature I'm chained to. I hated him the moment I saw his leering, bestial face. And here I've been locked in his noxious embrace for the thirty-five years this waltz has lasted. Is that orchestra never going to stop playing? Or must this obscene travesty of a dance go on until hell burns out?

Oh, they're going to play another encore. Oh, goody. Oh, that's lovely. Tired? I should say I'm not tired. I'd like to go on like this forever.

I should say I'm not tired. I'm dead, that's all I am. Dead, and in what a cause! And the music is never going to stop playing, and we're going on like this, Double-Time Charlie and I, throughout eternity. I suppose I won't care any more, after the first hundred thousand years. I suppose nothing will matter then, not heat nor pain nor broken heart nor cruel, aching weariness. Well. It can't come too soon for me.

I wonder why I didn't tell him I was tired. I wonder why I didn't suggest going back to the table. I could have said let's just listen to the music. Yes, and if he would, that would be the first bit of attention he has given it all evening. George Jean Nathan said that the lovely rhythms of the waltz should be listened to in stillness and not be accompanied by strange gyrations of the human body. I think that's what he said. I think it was George Jean Nathan. Anyhow, whatever he said and whoever he was and whatever he's doing now, he's better off than I am. That's safe. Anybody who isn't waltzing with this Mrs. O'Leary's cow I've got here is having a good time.

Still if we were back at the table, I'd probably have to talk to him. Look at him—what could you say to a thing like that! Did you go to the circus this year, what's your favorite kind of ice cream, how do you spell cat? I guess I'm as well off here. As well off as if I were in a cement mixer in full action. 20

I'm past all feeling now. The only way I can tell when he steps on me is that I can hear the splintering of bones. And all the events of my life are passing before my eyes. There was the time I was in a hurricane in the West Indies, there was the day I got my head cut open in the taxi smash, there was the night the drunken lady threw a bronze ash-tray at her own true love and got me instead, there was that summer that the sailboat kept capsizing. Ah, what an easy, peaceful time was mine, until I fell in with Swifty, here. I didn't know what trouble was, before I got drawn into this *danse macabre*. I think my mind is beginning to wander. It almost seems to me as if the orchestra were stopping. It couldn't be, of course; it could never, never be. And yet in my ears there is a silence like the sound of angel voices . . .

Oh, they've stopped, the mean things. They're not going to play any more. Oh, darn. Oh, do you think they would? Do you really think so, if you gave them twenty dollars? Oh, that would be lovely. And look, do tell them to play this same thing. I'd simply adore to go on waltzing.

THESIS AND THOUGHT

1. Using only what the narrator *thinks*, briefly describe her character. What modifications, if any, do you need to make in your description if you consider what she *says* as well?

2. Explain why the narrator continues to dance and why she does not say what she thinks.

3. Is there a point here beyond the comic discrepancy between thought and speech? Is the story purely entertainment or is it also commentary? If commentary, identify its subject and thesis.

STRUCTURE

1. The antagonism between speech and thought is fundamental to the design of "The Waltz." How is this formal contrast reinforced by contrasts in characterization?

2. What are the advantages of the first-person narration used here? Are there disadvantages? Consider, for example, what we know of the narrator's dance partner and how we know it.

3. At story's end, the dance is about to be repeated and the last sentence echoes the second sentence of paragraph 1. What does such repetition imply?

STYLE

1. From paragraph 5 on, the story is governed, in part, by an evolving metaphor. Identify the metaphor, illustrate its evolution, and define its purpose.

2. In reviewing a Broadway show, Parker once wrote, "*The House Beautiful* is the play lousy." She uses wordplay of various sorts in "The Waltz" as well. Find instances of it in paragraphs 3, 10, 11, 12, and 13.

3. Parker frequently exaggerates—for instance, "the thirty-five years this waltz has lasted" (para. 16). List several other instances of the technique and evaluate its effectiveness.

4. Do you find anything satirical in Parker's methods? If so, what is the object of her satire?

5. Beyond the waltz itself, what elements tend to date the story?

CONSIDERATIONS

1. Do you think that a contemporary woman might behave as the narrator does? Why?

2. Learn a dance done in your parents' generation or earlier—perhaps a waltz—or one common in a culture other than your own.

3. Using a college dance or party, write an updated version of "The Waltz"—possibly from a male point of view.

4. Like most arts, popular or otherwise, the waltz is reflective of its time and place, not the 1930s when Parker wrote the story, but of Europe—principally Vienna—before World War I. Write an essay comparing how the dances you do and those done by a previous generation reflect the eras of which they are a part.

Santha Rama Rau

(India; b. 1923)

*Born in India into a prominent Brahmin family, Rau was educated in England
and the United States, where she attended Wellesley College. Her father was
a diplomat while India was still under British rule and after independence
(1947) served as India's first ambassador to Japan. Her mother was active in
India's family-planning movement.*

*Rau's writing includes fiction and nonfiction dealing with travel. Among the
latter, in addition to* Home to India *(1944) excerpted below, are* East of
Home *(1950),* This Is India *(1954), and* My Russian Journey *(1959).
Her books about India helped educate Americans, especially, about that
nation and its diverse cultures, bridging East and West for them as she has in
her own life.*

On Learning to Be an Indian

MY GRANDMOTHER cannot speak English. I have never discovered
whether this is from principle or simply because she has never tried, but
she understands it perfectly. In England Mother had kept Premila and me
familiar with Hindustani by speaking it to us sometimes when we were
home for vacations, and by teaching us Indian songs. So during our first few
weeks in Bombay we could both understand the language though we were still
too out of practice to try speaking it. Consequently my grandmother and I
spoke different languages to each other. But we got along very easily in spite
of it.

I found after a few days that in her own indirect way she was trying to
instill in me something of the traditional Hindu girl's attitude to the household, the rest of the family, and living in general. The servants were the first
problem that came up. Whenever the telephone rang, one of the servants
would run to answer it. They were unanimously terrified of the instrument
and would hold the receiver well away from the ear and scream "Allo?"

Naturally unless the caller and the name of the person who was being
called were both very familiar to the servant, nothing was understood or
accomplished. After watching this procedure for some time, I began to sprint
for the telephone, too, whenever it rang. As long as I won it was all right, but
occasionally I would reach it at the same time as the house boy. The first time
this happened he grasped the receiver and ignored my outstretched hand. I
asked him please to let me answer the phone in future if I were in the
house—this in very polite if halting Hindustani. I used the formal form of
"you" as I would have to any stranger.

Afterwards my grandmother called me into her room. In her own mysterious way she had overheard the conversation and wanted now to warn me against treating the servants in such a way again.

"They are not your equals, so do not treat them as such. It is not enough   5
for the servants to be frightened of you; that fear must be founded on respect.
This pandering to them is some unreasonable sentimentality you have picked
up in the West. It embarrasses them as much as it irritates me. . . ."

She went on to explain that one could retain a feeling of equality (tinged
all the same with condescension) for the cook, because he, after all, had to
be a Brahmin—one of our own caste—as he handled the food. By all means
we should give the servants medicines if they were sick, see that their children
were well treated, visit their quarters and make sure that their rooms were
kept clean, even give their children an education—which they would never
get if it were left to their families—but we should always keep our social
distance.

Then there was the matter of prayers in the mornings. My grandmother
was always up by five o'clock and said her prayers, decorated the images in
her shrine, and sang the hymns of the day at that time. She would light a little
ceremonial fire, throw spices and something that smelt like incense on it;
when the fire died she rubbed her fingers in the ash and smeared it on her
forehead. This provided the white part of her caste mark for the rest of the
day. The other women of the house were expected to join her, though there
was no expressed compulsion. After a few days of this I decided that if I
expected to be able to stay awake after nine at night I must stop keeping these
hours.

One afternoon I told my grandmother that the prayers were meaningless
to me except as a curiosity, that I could make no sense of the hymns, which
were sung in Sanskrit (I'm pretty certain they were incomprehensible to her
also), and that I felt I was too old to be converted to Hinduism now.

She assured me briskly that even if I wanted to, I could not be reconverted to Hinduism, and that no such expectation had prompted her to
suggest that I come to prayers with her. I had been born a Hindu, but since I
had crossed water, eaten beef, neglected to wear my caste mark, and committed innumerable other offenses, I had lost my right to both my religion and
my caste.

"But don't assume from that that you may marry anyone outside the   10
Brahmin caste!" The real reason, it turned out, for this religious indoctrination had been to show me something of the values by which Indians live.

"Do you realize that you know nothing of a factor which is vital to the
lives of most of your countrymen? Do you always want to see India through
the eyes of a visitor? The real Indians are the villagers, the peasants. Poverty
and the work on the land is so much a part of their daily living that they must
have a tremendous, inclusive faith to make such living possible. If you want
to understand these people, you must also understand something of Hindu-

ism. It is the most rigid of beliefs, the most realistic of philosophies, and it determines for them everything from their food to their morals.

"We have been called pacifists," she continued, showing for the only time that I can remember a consciousness of the existence of contemporary politics, "but it is not ignorance that makes us so. We could be the most highly educated country in the world. We have all the prerequisites for intelligent 'political consciousness'—*if that were an end*. But I, for one, can only hope that the religion and philosophy of our people will secure them against civilization, and what you call 'progress'. Bless you, my child, progress is a convenient term for describing our journey from the great age of India."

If I had at the time been less scared of my grandmother, I would have argued with her about her attitude toward conditions in India, which I thought hopelessly reactionary. Concepts which had always seemed to me self-evident she ignored or nullified with her strange, kindly, patronizing attitude toward "those Indians less fortunate than ourselves." Equality of opportunity? Absurd!

"But I can see that you do not even know what I am talking about. Because we let politics pass us by, because we have evolved no way of writing down our music, because we do not preserve in a concrete form our art and our stories, the West considers that we have lost our culture. But it is in the oral traditions of the villages that the arts of India are really alive. The brief Western immortality of museums is pointless to people who have seen eternity in their earth. In comparison with this the people of the West are short-sighted, are they not?"

"I suppose so."   15

"And we are long-sighted—which is not the same as being far-sighted," she added.

I was growing impatient because I had invited a friend to tea, it was dangerously near tea time, and I had yet to change.

"Is it all right," I asked my grandmother casually, "if I have a friend to tea?" It was a very informal meal and Asha frequently had girls from her school to it, so I didn't think there would be any objections.

"Perfectly all right, my child, if she is a suitable friend."

"Well, it's a he. I should think he's suitable. He traveled over from South   20 Africa with us. Mother liked him."

I have never seen anyone look as shocked as my grandmother did then.

"The more I see of you girls the more amazed I am at your mother for the extraordinary education she has given you, and above all for allowing such outrageous behavior from any girl in our family!"

"I don't think this concerns her at all," I said, surprised. "Because, she could scarcely have kept us in a vacuum during all those years in England— particularly when she was away so much of the time!"

"That is exactly what I told her. You should never have been taken to England. You should have been left here in our care."

"But we wanted—"   25

"Don't argue with me, my dear child. I will discuss this with your mother."

I turned to leave the room. "Well, shall I call him up and tell him not to come?"

"Of course, you cannot do that. If you have invited him already, we are obliged to extend hospitality to him. But while I am the head of this house it will not happen again."

Upstairs I asked Mother what to do. I told her that my grandmother had not yet heard the whole story. I had promised John that I would have dinner with him. Mother looked at me despairingly. "Was it for this that I learned to be a diplomat's wife?"

"I don't see that I've done anything so awful."   30

"I suppose it never occurred to you that your grandmother never receives Englishmen in her house?"

"Why *would* it occur to me?" I asked.

"For obvious reasons. The situation being what it is in India, in her own inimitable way your grandmother makes a personal—or rather a social—issue of it."

"I thought she was supposed to be so detached from politics."

Then Mother began to think that the whole situation was funny. "But   35
the really appalling thing is your dinner engagement with him! If you go out alone with him, and the family knows about it, you're as good as married to him."

"You mean I'm not supposed to be alone with any man until I decide I want to marry him?"

"I'm afraid that's right, as long as we stay in your grandmother's house."

"But *Mother*, doesn't that seem to you a little absurd?"

"Darling, I was never alone with your father until I was married to him."

"But *Mother*—"   40

"I know, I know, times are changing, *everybody* does it, but I'm sorry, dear, you'll have to break the dinner appointment."

"But *Mother*—"

"Let's not discuss it, further, shall we?"

When John came we had tea in icy solitude on the front veranda. His first remark was, "You look pale. Do you feel all right?"

"I feel fine. I'm not allowed to wear make-up around here." I had had a   45
brief argument with Mother about that, too.

"Never thought it would make so much difference."

"My grandmother doesn't approve of it."

"Damn right. Now you won't get lipstick all over the cups and the napkins."

As Mother came out to join us the curtains to the living room swung behind her, and I saw that the family was gathered there. I don't know how anything immoral could have gone on with the gardeners as an audience and on an open veranda, but I suppose they just wanted to make sure. I was thankful that John was facing out toward the garden.

He asked Mother where the family, of whom he had heard so much, were.   50
"Oh, they went out."

"*All* of them?"

"Of course," Mother said, as if it were the most natural thing.

"Oh."

"They went to the tennis tournament." When Mother says something in   55
that carefully explanatory way, as if it were absurd that anyone shouldn't know, nobody can say, "What tournament?"

I took John out into the garden to tell him I couldn't dine with him that evening. I thought it would be best to tell him the whole story. I don't think he had the least idea what it all meant, for he just looked very hunted and said, "But you *don't* want to marry me, do you?"

The incident, when I looked back on it, brought into sharp contrast for me the astonishing changes that have taken place within fifty years in the ordinary girl's life in India. My grandmother was married when she was nine years old. When I heard that, I was profoundly shocked. Child marriage in books was one thing, but such a barbarous thing in my own family was quite another. Apparently I too had been influenced by the sensational inaccuracies that have been put out about India in books like Katherine Mayo's *Mother India.*

When my grandmother says that she was married when she was nine, she means that a betrothal ceremony was performed between her and my grandfather. Perhaps "betrothal" indicates too weak a link, for she could not then have married any other man—even if my grandfather were to have died before the actual wedding ceremony. Her "husband's" family would have been obliged to clothe her and shelter her just as they would the widow of one of their sons. As soon as the betrothal was completed she went to live in her mother-in-law's home. She stayed there until her mother-in-law died and she, as the oldest woman in the house, became the head of the family.

Between the time when she first came to live at the house and the time that the real marriage ceremony took place, about seven years later, she was carefully chaperoned by some member of her "husband's" family on all occasions when she had to appear socially or in the presence of any men. This, Mother assures me, is the traditional method, at least in our caste. She took her place at once in the daily life of the home. A Hindu girl's duties in her mother-in-law's home are specific and exacting. Their purpose is to train the girl to be, as nearly as possible, the perfect wife and mother.

It is practically a tradition among Hindu women that their mother-in-   60
law is always a monster of efficiency and demands equal competence from them. She insists that the young bride must give no order to a servant which

she cannot perfectly carry out herself. Consequently the bride must learn to cook, sew, clean, bring up children (and there are always several in the house on whom she can practice), run the family life, advise those younger than herself, keep the accounts of the household and keep a careful check on the finances of each individual member of the family. I'm sure every Hindu wife of that generation can tell stories about having had to cook meals for twenty-five people single-handed, or of having had to rip out a seam fifteen times because it was not sewn finely enough.

In those days, half a century ago, the joint-family system still dominated the social life of Hindus. My grandmother's mother-in-law, for instance, presided over her family, with her husband as a sort of consort. All their sons lived in the house with them, and as the boys married brought their wives to live in the family home. The daughters lived there until they were married and then they, like my grandmother, went to live in the homes of their mothers-in-law. The children of the sons were educated in the house by tutors until they were old enough to go abroad to college. My grandmother learned to read and write along with her nieces and nephews after she was married, but that was the limit of her education. Besides these close members of the family, various cousins, and great-uncles left over from another generation, lived in the same house. It was a joint family of the most conservative type.

Originally this social unit had grown out of the fact that India was almost entirely an agricultural country, and wealth was measured only in land. The sons of any land-owning family, therefore, were compelled to live together for economic reasons, and because the laws for property division were so sketchy. As the system took root and grew, somehow the women seem to have taken charge. Their province—and this is true to a wide extent even today—was the home and there they were dictators. The wife of the oldest man in the house held and dispensed all the money in the household. Anything that any member earned was given to her and she drew from each according to his capacity and gave to each according to his need. So although she had no legal rights, she could, if she wanted, have absolute control over the members of her own family.

By the time my grandmother, as the wife of the oldest son, came to be head of the household, the system was already breaking down. Our family moved from the south, which is our home, to Bombay. My grandmother found that her sons showed a regrettable tendency to wander off to what she considered the less civilized parts of the world. One of them, Shivan, even married a Viennese girl, beautiful—but a foreigner. Grandmother found that she had no control either over whom her sons married or over the education of her grandchildren. But to look at her and the way in which she lived you would never suspect that the conditions which made her standards valid were vanishing from India.

One of the minor forms which my grandmother's continued autocracy took was the examination of the mail received by anybody living in the house. Asha told me that she used to censor, and sometimes entirely remove, letters from people of whom she did not approve. She did not know the people who wrote to me, and still had not gathered in her own way their respective life histories, so she would just question me closely about all my mail. From whom were the letters? Any of them from men? Where had I met them? Did my mother know their families? If the questions were not satisfactorily answered, she would say, "In my opinion you should not reply to that letter," or, "Surely a brief note will be sufficient answer."

To me even Mother's education—which seemed to her so progressive and   65
enlightened—appeared incredibly narrow. Certainly she was not married at an appallingly early age—although her sisters were; she was given, on her own insistence and on the arguments of one of her brothers who was at an English university, a formal education at school and college. She had wanted to be a doctor and after endless arguments with her mother she was allowed to go to medical school in Madras. But unfortunately her mother heard that she was the only girl in her class and that every morning she would find notes on her desk from the men students—some expressing their view of women who broke the fine conventions of Indian womanhood by leaving their homes and entering a world of men, and some exclaiming poetically, "If I were Dante, you would be my Beatrice. . . ." She was taken out of the school immediately and continued, instead, more ladylike work in English literature in a women's college.

All the same, Mother defied two of the most rigid social conventions of the time before she was twenty-five. She earned a living by lecturing in English literature in a Madras college; and at twenty-five she was the first Kashmiri girl to marry outside her community. When we went back to Kashmir—more than twenty years after Mother's marriage—I met women who still would not receive Mother, and could scarcely be civil to her if they met her at somebody else's house, because of the shocking way in which she had broken their social rules when she was a girl. For at that time in India there was a prejudice not only against inter-caste marriages but against inter-community ones too. If your family or your ancestors came from Kashmir, your husband should come from there too.

Because Mother had to fight against the old standards and because she was brought up to believe in them, she has an emotional understanding of them which my sister and I will never have. Brought up in Europe and educated in preparatory and public schools in England, we felt that the conventions were not only retrogressive and socially crippling to the country, but also a little ridiculous. We thought at the time that one needed the perspective of travel to see these things. But we were only flattering ourselves, for later we found many young Indians who had lived at home all their lives and had a far clearer picture of India's social problems and, moreover, were doing a great deal more toward solving them than we ever thought of doing.

Thesis and Thought

1. Although there is no explicit thesis in this selection, its dominant idea is apparent. State it in a sentence or two.
2. How well does Rau get along with her grandmother? Justify your response.
3. Rau makes several references to "caste." Explain the term, doing some elementary research if necessary. You might want to read "What Is Caste?" in chapter 8.
4. Explain what Rau means in paragraph 3 by "I used the formal form of 'you' as I would have to any stranger."

Structure

1. Like the rest of the book from which it is taken, the selection is essentially narrative. What, then, justifies its being placed in a chapter dealing with comparison?
2. Identify the principal issues of contrast or conflict between Rau and her grandmother. To what degree are the differences cultural? To what degree generational?
3. Compared with the elaborate description of her grandmother's views, Rau's are presented minimally or indirectly. Why does this apparent imbalance not diminish the contrast or conflict? What expectations does Rau have of her audience in this regard?
4. Rau compares the roles and expectations for women in her grandmother's day, her mother's, and implicitly, her own. Write a brief outline of these differences among the three generations.

Style

1. Much of the selection is developed through dialogue. Comment on the effectiveness of this method in establishing the themes of the chapter and in creating and maintaining reader interest. Is the use of dialogue in any sense dramatic?
2. Beginning with paragraph 57, the tone and technique of the selection seem to change. Is the unity of the chapter affected by these alterations?

Considerations

1. Investigate either the current status of women or caste restriction in contemporary India. What changes seem to have occurred in the half century since Rau's return?

2. Consider the conflict over religion between Rau and her grandmother. Can you conceive of an analogous controversy between generations in your own faith? In a paragraph or two, describe one with which you are familiar.

3. Similarly, examine paragraphs 36–43. Do the exchanges here have a contemporary ring? Explain.

4. One conflict perhaps underlying the others here is that of Rau's own cultural identity. If you perceive yourself as bicultural, write a paper explaining how you reconcile (or fail to reconcile) the two cultures. If you perceive yourself as monocultural, write a paper describing how people you know deal with their cultural diversity.

Susan Sontag
(United States; b. 1933)

Although she has written screenplays and fiction, including The Volcano Lover: A Romance *(1992), Sontag is best known for her nonfiction. Critic, philosopher, and social historian, she has written on topics ranging from politics to popular culture, from photography to fascism. Her best-known work includes* Against Interpretation and Other Essays *(1966),* Styles of Radical Will *(1969),* On Photography *(1977),* Illness as Metaphor *(1978), and* AIDS as Metaphor *(1988).*

Sontag completed her B.A. in philosophy in two years at the University of Chicago and took master's degrees in English literature and philosophy at Harvard. She is a member of the American Academy and Institute of Arts and Letters and has been president of the United States chapter of PEN, an international association of writers. Her humanitarian and artistic concerns prompted her spending parts of 1993 and 1994 in Sarajevo, in an effort to maintain the cultural life of that beseiged city. An intellectual whose ideas are diverse and evolving, Sontag is generally included among the original and influential thinkers of our day.

"TB and Cancer As Metaphor" (editor's title) is section 2 of Illness as Metaphor, *a work rooted in Sontag's own experience with breast cancer. Her interest in TB may also have a biographical basis, since her father died of the disease early in her childhood.*

TB and Cancer as Metaphor

THROUGHOUT MOST OF THEIR HISTORY, the metaphoric uses of TB and cancer crisscross and overlap. The *Oxford English Dictionary* records "consumption" in use as a synonym for pulmonary tuberculosis as early as 1398.[1] (John of Trevisa: "Whan the blode is made thynne, soo folowyth consump-cyon and wastyng.") But the pre-modern understanding of cancer also in-vokes the notion of consumption. The OED gives as the early figurative definition of cancer: "Anything that frets, corrodes, corrupts, or consumers slowly and secretly." (Thomas Paynell in 1528: "A canker is a melancolye impostume, eatynge partes of the bodye.") The earliest literal definition of cancer is a growth, lump, or protuberance, and the disease's name—from the Greek *karkínos* and the Latin *cancer*, both meaning crab—was inspired, ac-cording to Galen,[2] by the resemblance of an external tumor's swollen veins to a crab's legs; not, as many people think, because a metastatic disease crawls or creeps like a crab. But etymology indicates that tuberculosis was also once considered a type of abnormal extrusion: the word tuberculosis—from the Latin *tūberculum*, the diminutive of *tūber*, bump, swelling—means a morbid swelling, protuberance, projection, or growth.[3] Rudolf Virchow, who founded the science of cellular pathology in the 1850s, thought of the tubercle as a tumor.

Thus, from late antiquity until quite recently, tuberculosis was—ty-pologically—cancer. And cancer was described, like TB, as a process in which the body was consumed. The modern conceptions of the two diseases could not be set until the advent of cellular pathology. Only with the microscope was it possible to grasp the distinctiveness of cancer, as a type of cellular activity, and to understand that the disease did not always take the form of an external or even palpable tumor. (Before the mid-nineteenth century, nobody could have identified leukemia as a form of cancer.) And it was not possible definitively to separate cancer from TB until after 1882, when tuber-culosis was discovered to be a bacterial infection. Such advances in medical thinking enabled the leading metaphors of the two diseases to become truly distinct and, for the most part, contrasting. The modern fantasy about cancer could then begin to take shape—a fantasy which from the 1920s on would inherit most of the problems dramatized by the fantasies about TB, but with the two diseases and their symptoms conceived in quite different, almost opposing, ways.

* * *

[1]Godefroy's *Dictionnaire de l'ancienne langue française* cites Bernard de Gordon's *Pratiqum* (1495): "Tisis, c'est ung ulcere du polmon qui consume tout le corp." [Au.]   [2]**Galen:** Greek physician (129–ca. 199) considered authoritative for more than a thousand years after his death.   [3]The same etymology is given in the standard French dictionaries. "*La tubercule*" was introduced in the sixteenth century by Ambroise Paré from the Latin *tūberculum*, meaning "*petite bosse*" (little lump). In Diderot's *Encyclopédie*, the entry on tuberculosis (1765) cites the definition given by the English physician Richard Morton in his *Phthisiologia* (1689): "*des petits tumeurs qui paraisent sur la surface du corps.*" In French, all tiny surface tumors were once called "*tubercules*"; the word became limited to what we identify as TB only after Koch's discovery of the tubercle bacillus. [Au.]

TB is understood as a disease of one organ, the lungs, while cancer is understood as a disease that can turn up in any organ and whose outreach is the whole body.

TB is understood as a disease of extreme contrasts: white pallor and red flush, hyperactivity alternating with languidness. The spasmodic course of the disease is illustrated by what is thought of as the prototypical TB symptom, coughing. The sufferer is wracked by coughs, then sinks back, recovers breath, breathes normally; then coughs again. Cancer is a disease of growth (sometimes visible; more characteristically, inside), of abnormal, ultimately lethal growth that is measured, incessant, steady. Although there may be periods in which tumor growth is arrested (remissions), cancer produces no contrasts like the oxymorons of behavior—febrile activity, passionate resignation—thought to be typical of TB. The tubercular is pallid some of the time; the pallor of the cancer patient is unchanging.

TB makes the body transparent. The X-rays which are the standard   5
diagnostic tool permit one, often for the first time, to see one's insides—to become transparent to oneself. While TB is understood to be, from early on, rich in visible symptoms (progressive emaciation, coughing, languidness, fever), and can be suddenly and dramatically revealed (the blood on the handkerchief), in cancer the main symptoms are thought to be, characteristically, invisible—until the last stage, when it is too late. The disease, often discovered by chance or through a routine medical checkup, can be far advanced without exhibiting any appreciable symptoms. One has an opaque body that must be taken to a specialist to find out if it contains cancer. What the patient cannot perceive, the specialist will determine by analyzing tissues taken from the body. TB patients may see their X-rays or even possess them: the patients at the sanatorium in *The Magic Mountain*[4] carry theirs around in their breast pockets. Cancer patients don't look at their biopsies.

TB was—still is—thought to produce spells of euphoria, increased appetite, exacerbated sexual desire. Part of the regime for patients in *The Magic Mountain* is a second breakfast, eaten with gusto. Cancer is thought to cripple vitality, make eating an ordeal, deaden desire. Having TB was imagined to be an aphrodisiac, and to confer extraordinary powers of seduction. Cancer is considered to be de-sexualizing. But it is characteristic of TB that many of its symptoms are deceptive—liveliness that comes from enervation, rosy cheeks that look like a sign of health but come from fever—and an upsurge of vitality may be sign of approaching death. (Such gushes of energy will generally be self-destructive, and may be destructive of others: recall the Old West legend of Doc Holliday, the tubercular gunfighter released from moral restraints by the ravages of his disease.) Cancer has only true symptoms.

TB is disintegration, febrilization, dematerialization; it is a disease of liquids—the body turning to phlegm and mucus and sputum, and, finally,

[4]*The Magic Mountain:* German novel written by Thomas Mann (1875–1955). [Ed.]

blood—and of air, of the need for better air. Cancer is degeneration, the body tissues turning to something hard. Alice James,[5] writing in her journal a year before she died from cancer in 1892, speaks of "this unholy granite substance in my breast." But this lump is alive, a fetus with its own will. Novalis,[6] in an entry written around 1798 for his encyclopedia project, defines cancer, along with gangrene, as "full-fledged *parasites*—they grow, are engendered, engender, have their structure, secrete, eat." Cancer is a demonic pregnancy. St. Jerome must have been thinking of a cancer when he wrote: "The one there with his swollen belly is pregnant with his own death" ("*Alius tumenti aqualiculo mortem parturit*"). Though the course of both diseases is emaciating, losing weight from TB is understood very differently from losing weight from cancer. In TB, the person is "consumed," burned up. In cancer, the patient is "invaded" by alien cells, which multiply, causing an atrophy or blockage of bodily functions. The cancer patient "shrivels" (Alice James's word) or "shrinks" (Wilhelm Reich's[7] word).

TB is a disease of time; it speeds up life, highlights it, spiritualizes it. In both English and French, consumption "gallops." Cancer has stages rather than gaits; it is (eventually) "terminal." Cancer works slowly, insidiously: the standard euphemism in obituaries is that someone has "died after a long illness." Every characterization of cancer describes it as slow, and so it was first used metaphorically. "The word of hem crepith as a kankir," Wyclif[8] wrote in 1382 (translating a phrase in II Timothy 2:17); and among the earliest figurative uses of cancer are as a metaphor for "idleness" and "sloth."[9] Metaphorically, cancer is not so much a disease of time as a disease or pathology of space. Its principal metaphors refer to topography (cancer "spreads" or "proliferates" or is "diffused"; tumors are surgically "excised"), and its most dreaded consequence, short of death, is the mutilation or amputation of part of the body.

TB is often imagined as a disease of poverty and deprivation—of thin garments, thin bodies, unheated rooms, poor hygiene, inadequate food. The poverty may not be as literal as Mimi's garret in *La Bohème*;[10] the tubercular Marguerite Gautier in *La Dame aux camélias*[11] lives in luxury, but inside she

---

[5]**Alice James** (1848–1892): sister of novelist Henry James and philosopher-psychologist William James; her letters and diary reveal the plight of a woman whose life was constricted by the social structure and conventions of her day; James welcomed her death from breast cancer. [Ed.]
[6]**Novalis** [pseudonym of Friedrich Leopold, Baron von Hardenberg]: German poet (1772–1801) whose work influenced the Romantic movement in literature. [Ed.]   [7]**Wilhelm Reich:** German psychoanalyst (1897–1957) chiefly known for his orgone therapy, which assumes that sexual potency (orgasm) is a sign of the biological vigor that underlies emotional health. [Ed.]
[8]**Wyclif:** John Wycliffe (ca. 1330–1384); incipient Protestant and early translator of the Bible into English. [Ed.]   [9]As cited in the OED, which gives as an early figurative use of "canker": "that pestilent and most infectious canker, idlenesse"—T. Palfreyman, 1564. And of "cancer" (which replaced "canker" around 1700): "Sloth is a Cancer, eating up that Time Princes should cultivate for Things sublime"—Edmund Ken, 1711. [Au.]   [10]*La Bohème:* opera by Giacomo Puccini (1858–1924). [Ed.]   [11]*La Dame aux camélias:* novel, known in English as *Camille*, by the younger Alexandre Dumas (1824–1895). [Ed.]

is a waif. In contrast, cancer is a disease of middle-class life, a disease associated with affluence, with excess. Rich countries have the highest cancer rates, and the rising incidence of the disease is seen as resulting, in part, from a diet rich in fat and proteins and from the toxic effluvia of the industrial economy that creates affluence. The treatment of TB is identified with the stimulation of appetite, cancer treatment with nausea and the loss of appetite. The undernourished nourishing themselves—alas, to no avail. The overnourished, unable to eat.

The TB patient was thought to be helped, even cured, by a change in   10
environment. There was a notion that TB was a wet disease, a disease of humid and dank cities. The inside of the body became damp ("moisture in the lungs" was a favored location) and had to be dried out. Doctors advised travel to high, dry places—the mountains, the desert. But no change of surroundings is thought to help the cancer patient. The fight is all inside one's own body. It may be, is increasingly thought to be, something in the environment that has caused the cancer. But once cancer is present, it cannot be reversed or diminished by a move to a better (that is, less carcinogenic) environment.

TB is thought to be relatively painless. Cancer is thought to be, invariably, excruciatingly painful. TB is thought to provide an easy death, while cancer is the spectacularly wretched one. For over a hundred years TB remained the preferred way of giving death a meaning—an edifying, refined disease. Nineteenth-century literature is stocked with descriptions of almost symptomless, unfrightened, beatific deaths from TB, particularly of young people, such as Little Eva in *Uncle Tom's Cabin* and Dombey's son Paul in *Dombey and Son* and Smike in *Nicholas Nickleby*, where Dickens described TB as the "dread disease" which "refines" death

> of its grosser aspect . . . in which the struggle between soul and body is so gradual, quiet, and solemn, and the result so sure, that day by day, and grain by grain, the mortal part wastes and withers away, so that the spirit grows light and sanguine with its lightening load. . . . [12]

Contrast these enobling, placid TB deaths with the ignoble, agonizing cancer deaths of Eugene Gant's father in Thomas Wolfe's *Of Time and the River* and of the sister in Bergman's[13] film *Cries and Whispers*. The dying tubercular is pictured as made more beautiful and soulful; the person dying of

[12]Nearly a century later, in his edition of Katherine Mansfield's posthumously published *Journal*, John Middleton Murry uses similar language to describe Mansfield on the last day of her life. "I have never seen, nor shall I ever see, any one so beautiful as she was on that day; it was as though the exquisite perfection which was always hers had taken possession of her completely. To use her own words, the last grain of 'sediment,' the last 'traces of earthly degradation,' were departed for ever. But she had lost her life to save it." [Au.]   [13]**Bergman:** Ingmar Bergman (b. 1918); contemporary Swedish film director whose works include *The Seventh Seal* and *Scenes from a Marriage*. [Ed.]

cancer is portrayed as robbed of all capacities of self-transcendence, humili-
ated by fear and agony.

These are contrasts drawn from the popular mythology of both diseases.
Of course, many tuberculars died in terrible pain, and some people die of
cancer feeling little or no pain to the end; the poor and the rich both get TB
and cancer; and not everyone who has TB coughs. But the mythology persists.
It is not just because pulmonary tuberculosis is the most common form of TB
that most people think of TB, in contrast to cancer, as a disease of one organ.
It is because the myths about TB do not fit the brain, larynx, kidneys, long
bones, and other sites where the tubercle bacillus can also settle, but do have
a close fit with the traditional imagery (breath, life) associated with the lungs.
   While TB takes on qualities assigned to the lungs, which are part of the
upper, spiritualized body, cancer is notorious for attacking parts of the body
(colon, bladder, rectum, breast, cervix, prostate, testicles) that are embarrassing to acknowledge. Having a tumor generally arouses some feelings of shame,
but in the hierarchy of the body's organs, lung cancer is felt to be less shameful
than rectal cancer. And one non-tumor form of cancer now turns up in
commercial fiction in the role once monopolized by TB, as the romantic
disease which cuts off a young life. (The heroine of Erich Segal's *Love Story*
dies of leukemia—the "white" or TB-like form of the disease, for which no
mutilating surgery can be proposed—not of stomach or breast cancer.) A
disease of the lungs is, metaphorically, a disease of the soul.[14] Cancer, as a
disease that can strike anywhere, is a disease of the body. Far from revealing
anything spiritual, it reveals that the body is, all too woefully, just the body.
   Such fantasies flourish because TB and cancer are thought to be much
more than diseases that usually are (or were) fatal. They are identified with
death itself. In *Nicholas Nickleby*, Dickens apostrophized TB as the

> disease in which death and life are so strangely blended that death takes
> the glow and hue of life, and life the gaunt and grisly form of death; a
> disease which medicine never cured, wealth never warded off, or pov-
> erty could boast exemption from. . . .

And Kafka[15] wrote to Max Brod in October 1917 that he had "come to
think that tuberculosis . . . is no special disease, or not a disease that deserves

---

[14]The Goncourt brothers, in their novel *Madame Gervaisais* (1869), called TB "this illness of the
lofty and noble parts of the human being," contrasting it with "the diseases of the crude, base
organs of the body, which clog and soil the patient's mind. . . ." In Mann's early story "Tristan,"
the young wife has tuberculosis of the trachea: ". . . the trachea, and not the lungs, thank God!
But it is a question whether, if it had been the lungs, the new patient could have looked any more
pure and ethereal, any remoter from the concerns of this world, than she did now as she leaned
back pale and weary in her chaste white-enamelled arm-chair, beside her robust husband, and
listened to the conversation." [Au.]   [15]**Kafka:** Franz Kafka (1883–1924); existential novelist
born in Prague; author of *The Trial*. Max Brod was his friend and literary executor. [Ed.]

a special name, but only the germ of death itself, intensified. . . ." Cancer inspires similar speculations. Georg Groddeck, whose remarkable views on cancer in *The Book of the It* (1923) anticipate those of Wilhelm Reich, wrote:

> Of all the theories put forward in connection with cancer, only one has in my opinion survived the passage of time, namely, that cancer leads through definite stages to death. I mean by that that what is not fatal is not cancer. From that you may conclude that I hold out no hope of a new method of curing cancer . . . [only] the many cases of so-called cancer. . . .

For all the progress in treating cancer, many people still subscribe to Groddeck's equation: cancer = death. But the metaphors surrounding TB and cancer reveal much about the idea of the morbid, and how it has evolved from the nineteenth century (when TB was the most common cause of death) to our time (when cancer is the most dreaded disease). The Romantics moral-ized death in a new way with the TB death, which dissolved the gross body, etherealized the personality, expanded consciousness. It was equally possible, through fantasies about TB, to aestheticize death. Thoreau, who had TB, wrote in 1852: "Death and disease are often beautiful, like . . . the hectic glow of consumption." Nobody conceives of cancer the way TB was thought of—as a decorative, often lyrical death. Cancer is a rare and still scandalous subject for poetry; and it seems unimaginable to aestheticize the disease.

THESIS AND THOUGHT

1. Explain why it is inaccurate to say that the topic of this reading is "TB and Cancer."
2. Write several sentences tracing the evolution of the two metaphors. Does what you've written constitute a thesis statement? Explain.
3. According to Sontag, what effect did scientific discovery have on the meta-phoric function of the two diseases?
4. Write a brief paragraph summarizing Sontag's view of the aesthetics of TB compared with those of cancer. (See especially paras. 12–14.)

STRUCTURE

1. Sontag divides the chapter into three sections (paras. 1–2, 3–11, 12–14). Describe the content of each section (you might want to write subheadings) and explain how together they form a coherent whole.
2. Which paragraphs deal essentially with similarities? Which with differences? How do their proportion and sequence suggest the author's emphasis?

3. Sontag consistently uses point-by-point comparison. For each of the fourteen paragraphs, list the standard by which the two diseases are compared.

STYLE

1. What does Sontag's liberal use of etymology, scientific discovery, literary allusion, and annotation suggest about her perceived audience?

2. What is characteristic of the concluding sentences in paragraphs 4, 5, 6, and 9? Explain their effect.

3. Do you find Sontag's vocabulary excessively technical or academic? If so, give examples. If not, explain and illustrate how she avoids such excesses.

4. What characteristics of paragraph 11 are typical of Sontag's writing here? Consider sentence structure and length, the use of descriptions, punctuation, juxtapositions, and illustrations. For each point you make, find two examples elsewhere in the reading.

CONSIDERATIONS

1. Once nearly eradicated in the West, TB is again on the rise. Investigate the proposed causes for its resurgence and prospects for controlling it.

2. What effect, if any, would you expect the current increase in TB incidence to have on its mythology and importance as a metaphor? Write a paragraph explaining your views.

3. What other diseases either have or have had the general metaphorical significance Sontag ascribes to TB and cancer? (Note: Sontag published *AIDS as Metaphor* in 1988.)

4. Generally, why is our society so heavily invested, metaphorically speaking, in these two diseases? Might other societies make other investments? Explain. If you find that specific metaphors may be culture bound, is the tendency to create metaphors universal?

S. Robert Ramsey
(United States; b. 1941)

A native of Tennessee, Ramsey earned three degrees in linguistics from Yale and has since been engaged in scholarship and teaching. He is an authority on East Asian languages and currently is on the faculty of the University of Maryland. He has also taught at Columbia University and the University of Pennsylvania. In addition to his work on Chinese, represented by the selection reprinted here from The Languages of China *(1987), Ramsey has done specialized studies of both Japanese and Korean.*

China, North and South

TODAY, in the last decades of the twentieth century, Chinese is spoken by about one billion people. No other language is remotely comparable. English, the next most widely spoken language, has fewer than half that many speakers.

Almost all of the Chinese people live in the densely populated eastern half of China, an area geographically about the size of the United States east of the Mississippi. Relatively few live outside this region. In modern times the Chinese have begun to colonize more intensively the immense territories in the western half of their country. Manchuria and Inner Mongolia to the north, areas forbidden to most Chinese as long as the Manchus were in power, have also begun to feel the pressures of intense immigration. But all of China's territorial possessions, both in the North and in the West, are as yet relatively sparsely settled. More than 95 per cent of the Chinese still live in Inner China, the part of the country east of the Tibetan Plateau and south of the Great Wall.

Inner China, the traditional homeland of the Chinese people, is divided naturally into two parts, the North and the South. . . . North China is a treeless expanse of plain and plateau that extends south from the Great Wall over the area drained by the Yellow River and its tributaries. South China is the Yangtze River valley and the well-watered hills and valleys and rice-growing areas that lie to its south. These two regions, each of which is dominated by a great river, together form the geographical setting for Chinese civilization and history.

North China belongs climatically and geographically to the interior of the Asian continent. The entire western half of the region is a dry and dusty highland known as the Loess Plateau. Here, for 100,000 square miles, the hills and mountains are covered with a powdery yellow dust, called loess, that in places is as much as 300 feet thick. Loess is believed to have blown down from the deserts of Inner Asia into the western half of North China during the last Ice Age, when the north winds were unimaginably fiercer than anything known today. It erodes easily. The modern continental winds may be mild by comparison with those that blew in prehistoric times, but during the winter they are still powerful enough to raise great dust storms and fill the air with grit all the way to the Yellow Sea. Sometimes the air-borne yellow powder is carried far enough east to sting eyes and faces in Korea and dust windows and gardens in Japan. To the east of the Loess Plateau lies the Yellow Plain. Its yellow soils, too, come from the Asian interior. This broad, flat flood plain of the Yellow River consists entirely of thick deposits of loess silt that have been built up over the ages. Where the Yellow River flows down from the mountains of the Loess Plateau, it is colored bright yellow by the soil that it and its tributaries have picked up in cutting through several hundred miles of loess deposits. At this point, the solids held in suspension sometimes make up almost half of the flow of the Yellow River by weight. As the river enters the flat Yellow Plain, it slows down abruptly and the silt begins to settle, building up the flood plain at a rate exceeded by no other major river system in the world. This river is with justice called "China's Sorrow." The Chinese have tried for millennia to keep the Yellow River within its banks by building elaborate systems of dikes. But as the silt in the water settles, the bed of the river rises higher and higher, and the dikes must also be built up higher to keep pace. Some dikes are forty or more feet above the surrounding land. Eventually the river must break through these restraining walls, and then it deposits thick layers of sediment over many miles of the surrounding countryside. In this way the yellow substance from the deserts of Inner Asia is spread over North China all the way to the sea.

The loess soils of the Loess Plateau and the Yellow Plain are fertile but   5
relatively dry. In good years when rainfall is adequate, fine stands of wheat, millet, and other crops that require less water than rice can be and are grown. The traditional staples of the region are therefore noodles, breads, and other foods made from these grains. But water is too scarce or unpredictable to sustain the intensive irrigation that rice requires, and the bowls of this grain that are eaten in Peking must usually be shipped from South China.

The climate of South China is more oceanic. The colors are not brown and yellow, but green. Most of the region is protected from the northern continental winds by the Qinling Mountains, the range that forms the watershed between the Yellow and the Yangtze rivers, and the loess deposits of North China stop at this mountain barrier. The rivers and streams that flow from its southern slopes therefore do not pick up the characteristic yellow silt that is found in northern rivers. Here the prevailing winds are generally from the south—the so-called summer monsoons—and they bring with them moisture and warm air from the ocean. Summers in South China are hot and steamy; clothes and books mold and mildew. Winters are cooler and drier than summers, but in many areas they are still mild enough for crops to grow. South China is a region of rice fields and terraces, lakes, rivers, and canals; hilly or mountainous areas not under cultivation are often covered with trees and thick vegetation, which in the southwestern part of the country turn into the jungles of Southeast Asia.

The South has China's best farmland. Rainfall makes it a richer place than North China; population densities are higher, and the people are generally better nourished. In contrast with the North, with its harsh climatic extremes, the fresh and verdant lands of the South are almost ideal for the growing of rice. Around Canton, for example, two good rice crops are regularly grown each year. The region is also well suited to the cultivation of a variety of other warm-weather crops as well, including teas, cotton, tangerines and other fruits, and mulberry bushes for silk production.

The Chinese language, like China itself, is geographically divided into the North and the South. . . . The Northern varieties of the language, usually known in English as the "Mandarin dialects," are spread across the Yellow Plain and the Loess Plateau. This dialect area also creeps south to the Yangtze River and a long arm bends down to the extreme Southwest, extending across the provinces of Sichuan and Yunnan all the way to the Thai border. This southwestern branch is for the most part recently settled territory, as are Manchuria, Inner Mongolia, and the far Northwest, where Mandarin is the only kind of Chinese spoken. As a result of the accretions, the Mandarin area now covers more than three-fourths of the country. The Southern varieties of the language—the so-called "non-Mandarin dialects"—are confined to the wedge of land formed in the Southeast by the lower course of the Yangtze River and the South China Sea.

There is a qualitative difference between these two areas. The Mandarin area, on the one hand, is unusually uniform; virtually all of the dialects spoken there are mutually intelligible—or very nearly so. A native of Harbin, in the extreme northeastern corner of the Mandarin range, has little trouble conversing with someone from Chungking, a city in the extreme Southwest over 1,600 miles away. Mandarin has no more variety than French, say, or German. But the non-Mandarin area is extremely varied, and within it sharply divergent forms of speech are often separated by only a few miles. The Amoy dialect, for example, which is spoken on the southeastern coast opposite Taiwan, is completely unintelligible to anyone living much farther away than a hundred miles in any direction. The variety of the language in the South is so great that the dialects there can be classified into at least six groups, each of which is as varied as the entire Mandarin area.

This remarkable linguistic difference between a unified North and a   10
fragmented South is a measure of how much life and society have been affected by geography. It is not surprising, of course, that the newly settled Mandarin territories are uniform; that is only to be expected. It usually takes time for regional differences to grow up—as we can see in recently populated areas of North America and Australia, where only the subtlest differences in speech can be detected across thousands of miles of land. What is unusual about Chinese is the difference in homogeneity between the North and the South of Inner China; both of these regions have long been inhabited by the Chinese people, and for much of that time the country has been culturally and even politically united. The correlation between the dichotomy in the language and the climatic and geographical division of the country is therefore all the more striking. The physical character of the land on which the Chinese live has apparently affected the ability to communicate.

One way the Chinese describe the contrast between the North and the South is with the catchword *Nán chuán běi mă*—in the South the boat, in the North the horse. In traditional times the horse was the best way to travel in North China. Mounted, one could generally move at will over the dry open terrain without encountering serious obstacles. Even the great Yellow River itself was in most places so shallow it could be forded. But in the South the horseman had to dismount. The lakes, rivers, and canals in the flat low-lying areas on the flood plains of the Yangtze and its tributaries could be crossed only by ferry. Still farther to the south, beyond the Yangtze Plain, the rugged hills and mountains with their high terraced rice fields and dense vegetation were difficult to cross even on foot, and on horseback virtually impossible. From the Yangtze on south, there were few roads of the kind that stretched across the North; in this southern half of China the highways were the rivers, streams, and canals that connected rice-growing area to market, town to town. The only efficient means of transportation in the South was by boat.

In the North there was much more freedom of movement. Water is an efficient medium of transport for bulk shipments of grain or freight, but it is less convenient for personal travel, because waterways and currents do not necessarily flow in the direction one wants to go. In the open spaces of the North, communication and transportation were quicker and easier than in the South, a region finely crosshatched with natural barriers.

The linguistic homogeneity of North China shows what a difference this has made. Mandarin has dialects, of course, especially in the hillier parts of the Loess Plateau. But there is nothing in the North to compare with the complex variety of the Southern dialects. The open terrain made possible linguistic cohesion.

South China, by contrast, has an abundance of the linguistic variety we expect to find where there are many barriers to communication and where people have stayed put for relatively long periods of time. Over much of the South the speech of each community—commonly a group of farming villages served by the same market—has tended to diverge from that of other, neighboring communities. The amount of divergence depends largely on the degree to which it is isolated from its neighbors. In general, the greater the barriers to travel and communication, the greater will be the differences in speech. Wuzhou and Taishan, for example, are both towns in the Far South that are served by Canton, the capital of Guangdong Province, as a commercial and cultural center. Wuzhou is a fairly new town that lies 120 miles directly upstream from Canton on the West River, a major shipping artery into the provincial capital. It was largely settled from Canton and still maintains close contacts with that city. Taishan, on the other hand, is only about 60 miles southwest of Canton, but several rivers must be crossed to get there. Thus in spite of the fact that Taishan is actually twice as close as Wuzhou to the provincial capital, it is much less accessible, and the dialect has diverged far more. A considerable number of linguistic changes separate Taishan from the cosmopolitan variety of Cantonese. An even sharper example of the effects of isolation can be drawn when the city of Swatow is brought into the picture. Although Swatow is located in Guangdong Province, it is separated from Canton by rows of rugged mountains. It was therefore settled from the north along the coastline and is still culturally and commercially independent of Canton. As a result, the dialect spoken there is totally unintelligible to a speaker of Cantonese.

Complicating this regional stratification, especially in the Far South, are   15 the linguistic layers left by successive waves of immigrants. The modern city of Hong Kong with its hodgepodge of people from all over China is in any case exceptional; but commercial centers along the South China coast have long been places where different linguistic groups have lived side by side for extended periods of time. Also, to a slightly lesser degree, various groups have been able to coexist fairly close to each other in the geographically fragmented hill country farther inland. The physical isolation imposed by geography has helped to keep these groups from being assimilated. . . .

THESIS AND THOUGHT

1. Identify the two major comparisons made in the selection. What connection does Ramsey draw between them? Where in the writing does he do so?

2. Having answered the previous question, state Ramsey's thesis.

3. What are the linguistic implications of the "catchword" Ramsey mentions in paragraph 11: "in the South the boat, in the North the horse"?

STRUCTURE

1. Ramsey uses both point-by-point comparison and comparison by wholes. Find instances of each type and discuss whether his choices are effective.

2. The author supports his comparisons with numerous examples and details. Choose a particularly well-illustrated paragraph and explain how the specifics it contains support the **topic sentence.**

3. Do you find any of the detail excessive? Why? Are there places that you feel require additional illustration? Explain.

4. Comment on the appropriateness of the opening paragraph to the material presented here. Since it is not the thesis paragraph, what is its purpose?

Style

1. "China, North and South," is an excerpt from a serious academic study. What, if anything, in the vocabulary or sentence patterns suggests this? If you think that Ramsey has avoided a pedantic or excessively formal tone, explain how he has done so.

2. Paragraphs 4 and 14 are far longer than most you are likely to write in this course. Would you divide them into further paragraphs? If so, where and why? If not, why not?

Considerations

1. Consult a recent map of China and locate the regions and cities mentioned in the text. To what extent, if any, does your knowledge of Chinese geography augment or limit your comprehension of the selection?

2. On occasion (as in paras. 9 and 10) Ramsey mentions the relative homogeneity of language in various Western countries, including (implicitly) our own. Do you think this relative lack of difference (as compared with South China) is at all attributable to geography? Identify other causes as well. Did the same degree of difference exist in earlier times? The same causes? Explain.

3. Write a paragraph detailing differences in vocabulary or grammar among speakers of English in the United States, to the extent that you are familiar with them. Do these differences inhibit communication either intellectually or psychologically?

4. Write a paragraph outlining the problems that the linguistic diversity in South China might create. Write another in which you describe how the diversity may be beneficial.

5. Language has often been a focal point of cultural and political conflict, as in Ireland, Canada, Belgium, the Philippines, and India. Choose one of these conflicts, or another of which you are aware, and investigate its history and current status.

6. Largely in response to new immigration, the past decade or so has seen the growth of a movement dedicated to making English the official language of the United States. Write an essay in which you either explain the possible motives, merits, and liabilities of such action or argue for or against the plan's adoption.

Suggestions for Writing:
Comparison-Contrast and Analogy

I. Write a comparison-contrast paper on one of the topics below. Be sure that the purpose of your comparison, its standards, and the conclusions you draw (your thesis) are clear.

—the personalities of two people you know well

—the music of two performers (or groups) that you enjoy or dislike

—the manner in which two families or ethnic groups celebrate the same holiday

—your past foolishness and present wisdom (or the reverse) with regard to either dates, jobs, or studies

—the means by which two people you judge successful achieved their success, or the means by which two who failed attained their failure

—two candidates currently running for the same public office

—two recent movies you've seen or books you've read, or a book you've read and the film based on it

—two works by the same artist or two by different artists using similar subjects

—two styles of dress on campus

II. The following comparison-contrast topics might require some research. Provide documentation as your instructor requires.

—two generals from the same war (perhaps directing the same battle) as military tacticians

—an early symphony of Beethoven and a later one (You may substitute another appropriate composer.)

—the messages of rap lyrics and those of American folk songs from the 1930s to the 1960s

—the folktales or legends of two traditions (at least one of them non-Western) as reflections of the civilizations from which they emerge

—the experiences of two immigrant groups in the United States

—two television news programs or newspapers that you watch or read for a week (You may choose either local or national publications or programs, and you are not restricted to mainstream broadcasters or press.)

—rituals surrounding birth, marriage, puberty, or death in two cultures other than your own

—the origins, purposes, and influence of two religious orders within Roman Catholicism

—the nature of the relationships between the United States and two Third World countries (Consider such topics as degrees of diplomatic contact, trade, political affiliation or philosophy, and prior history.)

III.   Use analogy to develop one of the topics below.

—Write an essay in which you attempt to model an ideal society on the life and behavior of one species of animal. (Exclude creatures such as ants and bees to avoid the obvious.) Alternatively write a similar paper using a species of plant. (Do not fear the ludicrous. Rutabagas are okay.)

—Choose a colloquial or conventional expression that contains an analogy (usually in the form of a metaphor or simile) and write an essay in which you elaborate the image literally. Some examples and possible suggestions: "She's a rock," "He's a saint," "The company is drowning in red ink," "The kid is hell on wheels."

—Reflecting on the death of his queen, Macbeth defines life as follows:

Life's but a walking shadow, a poor player
That struts and frets his hour upon the stage
And then is heard no more. It is a tale
Told by an idiot, full of sound and fury,
Signifying nothing.

Elaborate on one of these images or create your own, completing the formula "Life is . . ." with either a noun or noun phrase.

6

Division-Classification
and Analysis

I hold it equally impossible to know the parts without knowing
the whole and to know the whole without knowing the parts in
detail.

BLAISE PASCAL, *Pensées*

Samuel Johnson, eighteenth-century man of letters and compiler of the
first useful dictionary in English, once described our species as the animal that
classifies. People not only are capable of perceiving or creating orderly arrangements in the world around them, but need to do so in order to understand and explain the world. Classifying, dividing, and analyzing are three
related methods for achieving this comprehension and communication in
both daily life and in writing.

Consider a pile of clean laundry sitting on your bed. You need to put it
away (so that you can sleep comfortably, if for no other reason), so you gather
it up in both arms and toss it into the closet. Of course, in the morning, late
for class as you already are, you will find it difficult to locate a matched pair
of socks, your favorite jeans (the ones with holes in both knees), and the
camouflage T-shirt (now more than cleverly concealed) that you had planned
on wearing.

But there is an alternative. Instead of tossing the pile into the closet, you
might sort it—socks in one smaller pile, jeans in another, shirts in a third, and
so on. You might go further and match the socks, separate "good" jeans from
those you wouldn't be caught dead wearing in public or T-shirts from shirts
with collars. You might go further still and place each of these groups of
clothes into designated bureau drawers or hang them in a particular place in
the closet. Doing all of this will certainly help you dress more efficiently (and
stylishly) the next hurried day.

Division and classification will have helped you make your fashion statement. You will have *divided* the laundry according to types of clothes and *classified* each item as it came to hand, assigning it to its proper type. Sorting completed, you will have classified once again in putting the various clothes into their designated (divided) bureau drawers.

Is it easier just to shove the unsorted mess into the closet? Perhaps. But such indiscriminate dumping certainly impedes your achieving that "look"—just as chaotic writing and thinking prevent rather than promote communication.

As another instance of the practical consequences of division and classification, let's take a typical supermarket. Here, food and nonfood items are distinguished from each other. Foods are further separated by type—fresh produce, dairy, soft drinks, and so forth; and nonfood items may be categorized as (among other things) paper goods, kitchen gadgets, and household cleansers. Although any two markets might not be arranged identically (the chopped dates, for example, may be in the produce section or the baking-needs aisle), average consumers unfamiliar with a particular store are likely to find most items easily because they quickly catch on to the division-classification system.

Of course, other systems are possible. Why not arrange the market alphabetically? In this model, burritos would be found between the butter and the bug spray; at the other end of the store, one might encounter waffles, walnuts, and wart remover. Or perhaps the products could be divided and classified by color. Here you'll find blueberries beside the Windex, tofu next to loose-leaf paper, and spring water near the plastic wrap.

Such arrangements are novel but not helpful—that is, they do not further the purpose either of the store (to sell as much to as many people as possible) or of the shopper (to make purchases efficiently and conveniently). In your writing, the ideal system of dividing and classifying is the one that furthers your purpose: to produce and develop your thesis clearly and forcefully.

AVOIDING CLASSIFICATION CLICHÉS

This is not to say that you should avoid an original—perhaps unique—system of division-classification when you write. In fact, some of the best such writing succeeds in great part because of a novel approach—one that avoids the prefabricated, familiar (and dull) categories. For example, suppose you were given the sadistically boring topic "Kinds of Cars." It might be poetic justice to deal with the topic in a similarly deadly fashion by noting gravely at the start, "There are three kinds of cars: sports cars, sedans, and station wagons." There is not much thought here, and the paper is likely to be stuck in neutral. On the other hand, an enterprising writer might take the challenge of the topic and come up with this: "There are cars that excite, cars that must be tolerated, and cars that should never be driven." This, at least, has promise. The categories are not retreads, and the mental gears are engaged.

Looked at in one way, division-classification is a method for imposing order on chaos. And imposition it is, for principles of arranging material are not necessarily self-evident or written in stone. Suppose a researcher wants to know whether skin color correlates with incidence of skin cancer. She divides her population by race—white and black (to oversimplify)—and discovers that the incidence is vastly greater for whites. She follows up by dividing whites alone, according to skin tone gradations, and ultimately concludes that skin cancer (all other considerations being equal) increases with pallor. However, the same group of people might be divided in many other ways—by age, income, educational level achieved, marital status, dietary habits, *ad infinitum*, depending on the purpose of the study.

Such potential flexibility in classification has been realized in contemporary approaches to gender. As we have learned over the past several decades, inherent differences between the sexes are less numerous and significant than was previously believed. Partly as a consequence of such discoveries, and partly as a result of social and political movements, we have observed the changed and changing attitudes, expectations, behavior, and roles of both men and women—in short, the extensive modification of classes previously established and thought to be permanently fixed.

The work of Swedish botanist and taxonomist Carolus Linnaeus (1707–1778) and his successors provides another graphic instance of how classification systems may be subject to change. For Linnaeus, as for his predecessors, the world of living things was divided between animals and plants. But Linnaeus and his disciples further classified the members of these kingdoms on the basis of gross structural similarities determined through systematic observation. The technique was somewhat arbitrary since one set of common traits—the number of stamens in flowers of two different species, for example—does not assure other, more general similarity. In like fashion, Plato once assigned humans and birds to the same class because both walk on two legs; he felt obliged, however, to create subclasses according to the presence or absence of feathers.

Whatever its defects and need for refinement, Linnaeus's systematic movement from species through increasingly broad categories of genus, family, order, class, phylum, and kingdom was a marked improvement on Aristotle's method two thousand years before. The Greek philosopher had divided living things according to habitat—air, land, water—a useful division for hunters and fishers perhaps or for the most casual amateur nature study. But science has known for barely two centuries that a whale, for instance, has less in common with a halibut than with a hamster.

Even without challenges later posed by evolutionary theory and discoveries in genetics, the Linnaean system was frequently in need of internal refinement or qualification. Early in the twentieth century, for example, rabbits and hares were removed from the order of rodents (Rodentia) and assigned one (Lagomorpha) to themselves. The similarity between rodents and lagomorphs, that members of both groups gnaw food with incisors that continue to grow throughout the animals' lives, seemed superficial in light of differences in jaw movement, use of forelimbs, and blood composition, especially in the absence of any evolutionary connection. In 1991, scientists proposed a similar reassignment of guinea pigs and porcupines.

Changing biological classification, then, depends on changes in criteria. Having a fixed idea of what a mammal was, for example, many scientists were so puzzled by the discovery of the egg-laying, duck-billed platypus that they believed it was a hoax. Everyone "knew" that mammals bore live young. Ultimately, the definition of "mammal" was altered so that members of the class were identified by the presence of milk glands, sweat glands, and hair. Since it met this standard, the platypus (along with the echidna) was recognized as mammalian and placed in the subclass Protheria, for mammals with reptilian characteristics, including the laying of eggs.

But the greatest challenge to the Linnaean system was, in fact, evolution and genetics. At bottom, these sciences refocused taxonomists' attention from physical structure to biochemical substructures and historical relationships. One consequence was calling into question not whether a rabbit is a rodent or a platypus a mammal, but whether a particular organism is an animal or plant. As far back as the nineteenth century, Ernst Haeckel proposed establishing a third kingdom, Protista, for one-celled organisms that seemed to be intermediary between animals and plants. Later scholars suggested a fourth kingdom, Monera, which would include bacteria and blue-green algae (organisms whose cells, unlike those of other creatures, have no nuclear membrane). Finally in 1969, R. H. Whittaker formulated a model with fungi as the fifth kingdom. Fungi, because they do not perform photosynthesis, were separated from the plants. Moreover, since fungi have a nuclear membrane, they could not be Monera; nor, having more than one cell, could they be Protista—at least according to those that in part define Protista as single-celled.

These staggering choices of two-, three-, four-, and five-kingdom systems appear perplexing. But if we ask what our purpose is in subscribing to or adopting any of them, perhaps our anxiety might be eased. If we are in search of an abstract and cosmic truth about the nature and interrelationship of living things, then we are likely to be involved with Whittaker's formulation or some version of it. If we are curious about whether pandas are related to bears, we might not have to go much beyond an updated Linnaean classification (which Whittaker, in fact, incorporates). If we wish only to know where we are most likely to find trout, perhaps Aristotle is as useful a source as any.

The Single Standard

The examples of the platypus and the rabbit illustrate another fundamental principle: Classification may be made according to only one standard at a time.

Suppose you were a college-housing officer given the thankless task of dorm assignments. You have four criteria to work with: whether students smoke, whether they are neat, whether they stay up past midnight, and what their musical preferences are. Correctly done, division-classification of the potential residents would take place in separate stages, with one criterion used at a time, *not* all four simultaneously. You might first separate smokers from nonsmokers (one criterion), then divide smokers between the neat and the slovenly (a second), next distinguish between the neat smokers who are up late and those who go to bed early (the third), and finally sort the neat, smoking stay-up-lates who like heavy metal from the neat, smoking night owls who listen to fifties pop.

Then, of course, you would have to repeat several of these steps for those smokers who are sloppy, and so on. The entire process must be repeated for the nonsmokers. It is confusing and laborious enough working with one standard at a time. Imagine the difficulty and overlap if you attempted to deal with all four at once!

How is it, then, that so many two-pack-a-day, neat-freak, late-night, Connie Francis groupies get to room with nonsmoking slobs who go to bed at nine listening to Guns N' Roses? A likely answer is faulty division-classification by the housing officers.

Analysis

Like division, analysis deals with a whole and its components. Here, however, we do not have established categories (a drawer for socks, another for pajamas, etc.) but individual parts—pupil, iris, cornea, retina, lens, for example. Our focus, however, is not so much on the parts themselves but on how each contributes to the functioning of that organ we call an eye. Analysis is less a matter of knowing the whole by its separate parts (which is often the case in division-classification) than of recognizing it as the sum of its parts. Although in some scientific investigations, perhaps, analysis might emphasize isolating or identifying a specific component (a blood factor, for instance, or a chemical isotope), its purpose more generally is to enable us to reintegrate the elements and thereby understand the whole more completely.

In literature, for example, we might understand a work through examining its parts: plot, theme, character, and style (to be most basic). Dickens's *Great Expectations* is not just a narrative of Pip's maturation, or the unraveling of the mystery of his benefactor, or the development of his relationship with

Estella; nor is it simply a matter of love—whether filial, romantic, or warped, as in the life and vision of the jilted Miss Havisham, sitting for years in her bridal gown amidst decay; nor is it exclusively the sensibility of Pip, the simplicity of Joe, the pomposity of Pumblechook, the monomania of Jaggers and the legal world in which he moves; nor is it only the comic thrust of some of the names or of their bearers' trademark characteristics—Wemmick's mouth opening and closing like a post office, for instance.

Even if you have not read *Great Expectations*, the preliminary and woefully incomplete analysis just presented must at least indicate the richness of the book as a whole.

Analysis, then, enables us to penetrate surfaces and plumb a subject's depths, to go beyond its obvious, external, and single dimensionality to discover its complexities and their interrelationships. For instance, a casual, nonanalytic description of American painter Georgia O'Keeffe's *Red Poppy* (often reproduced in books or as posters) might simply be the title itself. But only a slightly more careful observation is needed for most viewers to recognize that this is not the sort of innocuous floral painting often hung in hotel rooms or sold at K Mart. The sensitive (and analytic) eye perceives the intensity of the color and the sinuous curve of the petals; feels itself drawn to the dark center—as if the painting were three-dimensional; observes that the flower nearly fills the frame—as if it were asserting its own significance. Ultimately, the viewer understands what has perhaps already been felt: the painting's fundamental sensuality. Such a viewer can no longer describe the piece as simply a "red poppy," for analysis has now become part of the new visual experience.

Although analysis of a novel, a work of art, or an idea might seem to diminish the enthusiastic spontaneity with which these first were met, it enriches, in fact, subsequent experiences with both them and others. And the sense of wonder might as easily be enhanced as inhibited.

None of this should be altogether unfamiliar; we regularly employ and apply analysis in making decisions in our own lives. Choosing a college or buying a house, for example, depends on analytic thinking, at least in part. In choosing a college, we might want to know the institution's academic reputation, the size and diversity of the student body, its costs, the distance from home, and its special programs. In buying a house, its size and arrangement, the quality of the neighborhood, its distance from work, tax rates—and, if children are involved, the quality of the school system and whether potential playmates are available—would all be crucial elements in our deliberation. In both instances, the objective is to discover whether the collective components will work for us either as students or as homeowners.

Some types of formal analysis are rather specific. Chapter 4 of this text, for example, deals with process analysis whereas chapter 7 is concerned with analysis of causes and effects. Analysis itself, it seems, is not exempt from division and classification.

DIVISION-CLASSIFICATION IN ACADEMIC WRITING

The Linnaean system, mentioned earlier in the chapter, is hardly the only example of division-classification in scholarly pursuits. Division-classification pervades writing (and thinking) not only in the sciences but in other disciplines as well.

The organization of the periodic table of elements is another instance in the sciences that comes almost immediately to mind, particularly since it demonstrates the importance of having a clear, accurate basis for classifying. Having observed that the properties of apparently related elements recur as functions of their atomic weights, Dmitri Ivanovich Mendeleev published in 1869 a table of elements arranged by these weights, and presumably classifying (grouping) elements according to their properties. Recognizing that not all elements were known, Mendeleev left gaps in the table for elements yet to be discovered but whose positions were predictable —gallium, for example.

Although Mendeleev's predictions were remarkably accurate, his system, like that of Linnaeus, had a platypus or two in its midst. For example, cobalt and nickel had the same atomic weight but vastly different characteristics. In addition, the positions of iodine and tellurium had to be reversed (and the arrangement of weight ignored) in order for them to be grouped with elements whose properties they shared. A similar situation arose involving argon and potassium. The difficulty was resolved early in the twentieth century when atomic number (i.e., the number of charged particles in the nucleus of an atom) rather than atomic weight was found to be the true determinant of the regular recurrence of similar chemical properties known as periodicity. Looked at in terms of our purposes here, the basis of classification was revised and improved.

The evolution of the Linnaean system or the periodic table is less important to our discussion than the mode of thinking these examples illustrate. Dividing and classifying are central to our perception of the natural world. The following passage, titled "Classification of the Rocks," is typical:

> The rocks of the earth's surface may be classified according to their mode of formation. It is believed that below the earth's outer solid crust, rock material exists at immensely high temperatures, but under enormous pressure. When the pressure is relieved locally, this rock material becomes fluid, rising through lines of weakness towards the surface. . . . The *igneous rocks* have been formed by solidification in various ways of this molten rock material, known as *magma,* so comprising a group of "heat-formed" rocks which constitute about 95 percent of the outer 16 km (10 miles) of the earth. The *sedimentary rocks* consist for the most part of the remains of previously existing rocks, reassembled and consolidated in various forms; they are sometimes known as *derived rocks.* They also include a number of rocks formed of the organic remains of

plants and animals, and others formed chemically by the precipitation of substances from solution. The *metamorphic rocks* are those in which pre-existing rocks, both igneous and sedimentary, have undergone chemical or physical changes, either by heat or by pressure, to cause degrees of alteration and modification.

F. J. MONKHOUSE, *Principles of Physical Geography*, pp. 2–3

Not surprisingly, the text goes on to examine each type in turn.

But division-classification and analysis need not be written according to formula. Azaria Alon's presentation of the flora of Israel is less schematic than the passage from Monkhouse:

> For many of the [plant] species, Israel represents the limit of their distribution. This is the eastern limit for many Mediterranean varieties, the western boundary of some steppeland species, the northern extent of African plant life and the southern limit of the few Euro-Siberian plants to be found. It is not surprising therefore that, in a small country where the variations of climate can accommodate such a wide variety of species, it is possible to find such a wide range of types concentrated in a small area.

> *The Natural History of the Land of the Bible*, pp. 36–37

Disciplines other than those in the sciences use analogous classification systems. In literature and history, for example, we divide the wholes of writing and time by chronological periods, sometimes using significant dates or terms to describe them (e.g., the colonial period in American history). Sometimes we identify eras by their essential characteristics as in the Renaissance or the Age of Reason. At still other times, we identify the era by a dominant figure (the Elizabethan age) or group (the Han, Tang, or Ming dynasty of China). And even within such periods, further classification is likely to be found. Czeslaw Milosz, for example, introduces a section in his *History* as follows:

> Seventeenth-century Polish prose is composed of diaries, journals and memoirs, and of a multitude of political writings which today would rank as journalism.

> *History of Polish Literature*, p. 145

More elaborately, Henri Peyre presents an analysis of existentialism as part of his discussion of the post–World War II French novel:

> The first notion stressed by existentialism is that of nothingness. . . . Why do I exist? Why does anything exist? Why is there not just nothingness? If the idea of nothingness does not lend itself to analysis, it can at least be experienced in fear and trembling . . . [which] is the starting point of a personal philosophical reflection.

Man facing nothingness has the revelation of the absurd: thus the second tenet of existentialism is man's thirst for rationality, and he finds irrationality prevailing. . . . He would like a presence to watch over him and warn him of perils, but the heavens and their "eternal silence" fill him with dread. . . .

Atheism is the third postulate. . . . [M]an must fully assume his duties to himself and to others and set himself up in the place of an absent or silent God. He must create his own essence and accept his total freedom.

The fourth credo of the existentialists is the well-known assertion that existence precedes essence. Man was not created according to a pre-existing mold or pattern. . . . And the only essence that is conceivable for him is the one that he can progressively create himself, by living.

The Contemporary French Novel, pp. 221–22

But the mode of thinking (and writing) is hardly limited to literature either. Derek Hill and Oleg Grabar, for example, describe Islamic monumental architecture according to "five basic elements" of ornamentation:

The first category is the rarest. Human and animal features existed in medieval Islamic sculpture. . . . A few instances of sculpture of human beings and mostly of animals exist [currently] in Anatolia. . . .

A second decorative theme may be called architectural. . . . Such elements are columns . . . and mouldings recombined in a peculiarly unarchitectonic fashion . . . , or strange conglomerations of pilasters . . . , capitals, bases. . . . But the single most common architectonic element in decoration is the so-called *muqarnas,* stalactite or honeycomb, . . . whose origins are as unclear as its ubiquity is certain. . . .

A third theme of ornamentation was quite clearly geometry. . . .

The fourth theme of decoration was writing. . . . Koranic passages, eulogies to builders, or triumphal inscriptions served to explain the function of buildings or of parts of buildings and to perpetuate the pious memory of the founder. . . .

The last of the major decorative themes of this period consisted of vegetal elements . . . [,] mostly various modifications of the palmette. . . .

Islamic Architecture and Its Decoration: A.D. 800–1500, pp. 79–81

No less than other disciplines, the social sciences depend heavily on such analytic patterns. Psychologist Rollo May, for instance, outlines the personal and social functions of mythology:

The many contributions of myths to our lives can be listed under four headings. First, myths give us our *sense of personal identity,* answering the question, Who am I? When Oedipus cried, "I must find out who I am and where I came from!" and when Alex Haley searches for his *Roots,* they are both illustrating this function of myth.

Second, myths make possible our *sense of community*. The fact that we think mythically is shown in our loyalty to our town and nation and even our loyalty to our college and its various teams which produce such mythic phenomena as the Trojans and 49ers. These would be absurd except that they illustrate the important bonding of social interest and patriotism and other such deeply rooted attitudes towards one's society and nation.

Third, *myths undergird our moral values*. This is crucially important to members of our age, when morality has deteriorated and seems to have vanished altogether in some distraught places.

Fourth, mythology is our way of dealing with the inscrutable *mystery of creation*. This refers not only to the creation of our universe but creation in science, the mysterious "dawning" in art and poetry and other new ideas in our minds. "Myth is the garment of mystery," writes Thomas Mann insightfully in the preface to his great book on ancient myths, *Joseph and His Brothers*.

The Cry for Myth, pp. 30–31

The following introductory paragraph to a section of a college anthropology text maintains that classification has simplified scholars' tasks. But it also suggests something of the possible complexity of classification, a complexity that must often be presented, perhaps paradoxically, for the sake of clarity:

Political organization is the means through which a society maintains social order and reduces social disorder. It assumes a variety of forms among the peoples of the world, but scholars have simplified this complex subject by identifying four basic kinds of political systems: bands, tribes, chiefdoms, and states. The first two forms are uncentralized systems; the latter two are centralized.

WILLIAM A. HAVILAND, *Anthropology*, 5th ed., p. 482

Here the classes themselves have been classified.

Finally, after an opening that offers several possible approaches to classification or analysis, the passage that follows presents aspects of "sport socialization" typical of various scholastic levels. It also provides an example of a structural pattern commonly found in division-classification papers: unlike the excerpts from Peyre and May above, the divisions here are labeled rather than enumerated. In addition, involving a process and touching on causation as it does, the extract suggests the interdependence that often exists among rhetorical types. You might expect, however, that any complete account (including one of your own) would be more fully detailed.

The educational system in the United States . . . is an influential institution in the process of sport role socialization. Similar to other social systems, the role of the educational system varies—by sport, by roles within sports, by sex, and by stage in the life cycle. . . .

The public elementary school system seems to play a minor role in sport socialization. Rather, the family, neighborhood, peer group, and voluntary sport association play the major roles. This is not surprising considering that sport is not considered an important part of the curriculum in most elementary schools. . . .

In secondary schools, sport is an integral part of the youth subculture and is highly valued by students, parents, and teachers. Adolescents thus have both opportunity and impetus to participate in sport. . . . Many Olympic athletes report that they attended high schools where the students and teachers considered their particular sports to be among the most important extracurricular activities. . . .

At the college or university level, a socialization process operates in sports such as football and basketball to prepare elite athletes for careers in sport. . . . This period of socialization involves learning and repeated testing against other elite athletes.

Similar to secondary schools, universities encourage students to become sport consumers, especially to become consumers of football and basketball. The adults most likely to consume professional football regularly are those who have attended college. Of these, football fans are more likely to have graduated from a college where attending football games was an integral part of the social scene. . . .

BARRY D. MCPHERSON, JAMES E. CURTIS, AND JOHN W. LOY, *The Social Significance of Sport*, pp. 66–68

As the examples presented in this chapter attest, topics subject to division-classification or analysis are many and diverse. Numerous others might leap instantly to mind: the atom, the types of classical Greek column, the periods of geologic time (Why *Jurassic* Park and not Pliocene or Devonian?), and so on. Dr. Johnson's definition of our species as the animal that classifies seems to be accurate.

USING DIVISION-CLASSIFICATION AND ANALYSIS

Using division-classification as a dominant rhetorical pattern is appropriate for answering questions that ask you to deal with kinds or types. Similarly, analysis is best suited for writing that requires examining parts of wholes or the relationship of parts to wholes.

So far as possible, divide and classify according to only one consistent principle. In general, shun the ready-made classification or division, and almost always avoid such easy (and often meaningless) triads as *good, bad,* and *indifferent,* or *high, medium,* and *low.*

Remember that the division or classification in itself is not necessarily the thesis. The sentence "Numbering more than a thousand, the languages of Africa consist of four major groups" might be adequate for a paper whose purpose is merely to list and describe the languages. But a paper with the thesis "The variety that is Africa can be seen clearly in its wealth of languages" is far more promising and lively. Here, the emphasis is not on the types themselves but on their *wealth* and, especially, how their kinds and number illustrate the *variety* of the continent. Throughout this paper the reader will (justifiably) expect the writer to emphasize the scope, breadth, similarities, and differences among or between language groups and individual languages. With a thousand or so languages possibly to be considered, the illustrations, of course, must be highly selective.

Similarly, analysis might often move beyond examining technique itself. For instance, a piece discussing certain Persian miniature paintings could concern itself with such topics as color, range, composition, subject matter, multiple points of view (as opposed to single visual perspective), and the blending of textual and graphic elements. Such an approach might do very well for some kinds of art criticism. However, for art courses with a more historical approach, as well as others in the humanities and social sciences, a paper that discusses the painting's fusion of indigenous, Islamic, and Chinese-Mongol elements might be more appropriate and rewarding because it looks at the work as a product of the cultures that produced it.

As in all your writing, be specific. Provide examples or illustrations of the classes you propose to discuss. For instance, if you were writing about the kind of shopper who buys only items that carry "designer" labels you might include a passage like this:

> Through the tightly woven fabric of her Pierre Cardin luggage, she can almost hear her Liz Claiborne tank top clashing with her Anne Klein shorts.
> "And I thought that they went so well together," she mumbles aloud, absently touching the back pocket of her jeans.
> Guess again.

If you are involved with something less frivolous, such as the languages of Africa, you might point out not only that many of them have initial consonant clusters that are unusual elsewhere, but that these clusters are, specifically, *mb* and *nd*.

Many of the illustrations used in this chapter have three or four components—numbers that are often convenient to deal with in a short paper. Ideally, any piece of writing should be of sufficient length to develop its thesis satisfactorily, and a particular topic might easily yield many more than three or four divisions. If, however, you are working within an imposed word limit, select your categories or analytic components accordingly. One caution: Be careful of dividing in two since this will tend to result in a simple comparison, which is a rhetorical horse of a somewhat different color.

Thucydides

(Greece; ca. 455–ca. 403 B.C.)

Principally known as the "father" of Western historical study and writing (a title he shares with Herodotus), Thucydides was a well-born, well-educated Athenian with family connections to prominent political and military figures. Little is known of his personal life, but the central event from the standpoint of posterity is that as an Athenian commander in the Peloponnesian War (431–404 B.C.) he was exiled from Athens for nearly twenty years after failing to prevent the fall of Amphipolis to Spartan forces.

The event enabled Thucydides to devote himself after 422 B.C. to his History of the Peloponnesian War, *a work he had already begun. Although the history is incomplete, stopping abruptly in 411 B.C., it is nevertheless a valuable document. In addition to a detailed account of the war that effectively brought the golden age of Athens to a close, it includes significant material concerning the city's growth and development. Among the history's novel features are that it is based on research (including interviews of participants with conflicting views), contains interpretation and analysis rather than the mere recording of events or beliefs (which is often characteristic of Herodotus's writing), and includes speeches by major participants. These speeches are largely reconstructions by Thucydides, who attempts to preserve the sense of what was (or might have been) said.*

The selection below is from one such speech, the funeral oration of Pericles, delivered for his fallen troops toward the close of the first year of the war. Pericles was the principal leader of democratic Athens during the fifth century B.C.

Ask, as you read, to what extent Pericles' (or Thucydides') view of Athenian democracy parallels your (or America's) own.

The Glory of Athens

(Pericles' Funeral Oration)

"THAT PART OF OUR HISTORY which tells of the military achievements which gave us our several possessions, or of the ready valour with which either we or our fathers stemmed the tide of Hellenic or foreign aggression, is a theme too familiar to my hearers for me to dilate on, and I shall therefore pass it by. But what was the road by which we reached our position, what the form of government under which our greatness grew, what the national habits out of which it sprang; these are questions which I may try to solve before I proceed to my panegyric upon these men; since I think this to be a subject upon which on the present occasion a speaker may properly dwell, and to which the whole assemblage, whether citizens or foreigners, may listen with advantage.

"Our constitution does not copy the laws of neighbouring states; we are rather a pattern to others than imitators ourselves. Its administration favours the many instead of the few; this is why it is called a democracy. If we look to the laws, they afford equal justice to all in their private differences; if no social standing, advancement in public life falls to reputation for capacity, class considerations not being allowed to interfere with merit; nor again does poverty bar the way, if a man is able to serve the state, he is not hindered by the obscurity of his condition. The freedom which we enjoy in our government extends also to our ordinary life. There, far from exercising a jealous surveillance over each other, we do not feel called upon to be angry with our neighbour for doing what he likes, or even to indulge in those injurious looks which cannot fail to be offensive, although they inflict no positive penalty. But all this ease in our private relations does not make us lawless as citizens. Against this fear is our chief safeguard, teaching us to obey the magistrates and the laws, particularly such as regard the protection of the injured, whether they are actually on the statute book, or belong to that code which, although unwritten, yet cannot be broken without acknowledged disgrace.

"Further, we provide plenty of means for the mind to refresh itself from business. We celebrate games and sacrifices all the year round, and the elegance of our private establishments forms a daily source of pleasure and helps to banish the spleen; while the magnitude of our city draws the produce of the world into our harbour, so that to the Athenian the fruits of other countries are as familiar a luxury as those of his own.

"If we turn to our military policy, there also we differ from our antagonists. We throw open our city to the world, and never by alien acts exclude foreigners from any opportunity of learning or observing, although the eyes of an enemy may occasionally profit by our liberality; trusting less in system and policy than to the native spirit of our citizens; while in education, where our rivals from their very cradles by a painful discipline seek after manliness, at Athens we live exactly as we please, and yet are just as ready to encounter every legitimate danger. In proof of this it may be noticed that the Lacedaemonians do not invade our country alone, but bring with them all their confederates; while we Athenians advance unsupported into the territory of a neighbour, and fighting upon a foreign soil usually vanquish with ease men who are defending their homes. Our united force was never yet encountered by any enemy, because we have at once to attend to our marine and to dispatch our citizens by land upon a hundred different services; so that, wherever they engage with some such fraction of our strength, a success against a detachment is magnified into a victory over the nation, and a defeat into a reverse suffered at the hands of our entire people. And yet if with habits not of labour but of ease, and courage not of art but of nature, we are still willing to encounter danger, we have the double advantage of escaping the experience of hardships in anticipation and of facing them in the hour of need as fearlessly as those who are never free from them.

"Nor are these the only points in which our city is worthy of admiration.   5 We cultivate refinement without extravagance and knowledge without effeminacy; wealth we employ more for use than for show, and place the real disgrace of poverty not in owning to the fact but in declining the struggle against it. Our public men have, besides politics, their private affairs to attend to, and our ordinary citizens, though occupied with the pursuits of industry, are still fair judges of public matters; for, unlike any other nation, regarding him who takes no part in these duties not as unambitious but as useless, we Athenians are able to judge at all events if we cannot originate, and instead of looking on discussion as a stumbling-block in the way of action, we think it an indispensable preliminary to any wise action at all. Again, in our enterprises we present the singular spectacle of daring and deliberation, each carried to its highest point, and both united in the same persons; although usually decision is the fruit of ignorance, hesitation of reflection. But the palm of courage will surely be adjudged most justly to those, who best know the difference between hardship and pleasure and yet are never tempted to shrink from danger. In generosity we are equally singular, acquiring our friends by conferring, not by receiving, favours. Yet, of course, the doer of the favour is the firmer friend of the two, in order by continued kindness to keep the recipient in his debt; while the debtor feels less keenly from the very consciousness that the return he makes will be a payment, not a free gift. And it is only the Athenians who, fearless of consequences, confer their benefits not from calculations of expediency, but in the confidence of liberality.

"In short, I say that as a city we are the school of Hellas; while I doubt if the world can produce a man, who where he has only himself to depend upon, is equal to so many emergencies, and graced by so happy a versatility, as the Athenian. And that this is no mere boast thrown out for the occasion, but plain matter of fact, the power of the state acquired by these habits proves. For Athens alone of her contemporaries is found when tested to be greater than her reputation, and alone gives no occasion to her assailants to blush at the antagonist by whom they have been worsted, or to her subjects to question her title by merit to rule. Rather, the admiration of the present and succeeding ages will be ours, since we have not left our power without witness, but have shown it by mighty proofs; and far from needing a Homer for our panegyrist, or other of his craft whose verses might charm for the moment only for the impression which they gave to melt at the touch of fact, we have forced every sea and land to be the highway of our daring, and everywhere, whether for evil or for good, have left imperishable monuments behind us. Such is the Athens for which these men, in the assertion of their resolve not to lose her, nobly fought and died; and well may every one of their survivors be ready to suffer in her cause. . . ."

Thesis and Thought

1. According to Thucydides, what are the virtues of Athens that distinguish it from her neighbors?
2. Describe the relationship between Athenian public and private life as Thucydides presents it.
3. How is the Athenian citizen a "complete" person?

Structure

1. Explain how the opening paragraph provides a basis for the analysis that follows.
2. Examine the **transitions** in this selection and discuss whether they move the speech effectively from point to point.
3. With the possible exception of the reference to the Spartans (Lacedaemonians) in paragraph 4, the speech is void of examples. What justification, if any, is there for Pericles' lack of precision? What sorts of illustrations might you have preferred to see?

Style

1. What in the choice of topics, the manner in which they are introduced, and even the lack of specifics mentioned above, suggests that Pericles might have been an effective politician and military leader?
2. An image such as "we are the school of Hellas" (para. 6) is rare in this piece; the diction, though elaborate, usually lacks color. Antithesis, however, such as in "We cultivate refinement without extravagance and knowledge without effeminacy" (para. 5) occurs with some frequency. Find other examples and explain what such contrasts help achieve for the selection as a whole.
3. Written for a similar occasion, specifically for the dedication of a national cemetery, Lincoln's Gettysburg address is printed below. In what ways, particularly stylistic ones, does it parallel or differ from Pericles'?

> Fourscore and seven years ago our fathers brought forth on this continent a new nation, conceived in liberty, and dedicated to the proposition that all men are created equal.
>
> Now we are engaged in a great civil war, testing whether that nation, or any nation so conceived and so dedicated, can long endure. We are met on a great battlefield of that war. We have come to dedicate a portion of that field as a final resting place for those who here gave their lives that that nation might live. It is altogether fitting and proper that we should do this.

But in a larger sense, we cannot dedicate—we cannot consecrate—we cannot hallow—this ground. The brave men, living and dead, who struggled here, have consecrated it far above our poor power to add or detract. The world will little note nor long remember what we say here, but it can never forget what they did here. It is for us, the living, rather, to be dedicated here to the unfinished work which they who fought here have thus far so nobly advanced. It is rather for us to be here dedicated to the great task remaining before us—that from these honored dead we take increased devotion to that cause for which they gave the last full measure of devotion; that we here highly resolve that these dead shall not have died in vain; that this nation, under God, shall have a new birth of freedom, and that government of the people, by the people, for the people, shall not perish from the earth.

CONSIDERATIONS

1. How much of what Pericles says about Athens and Athenian democracy applies to the United States? Consider, among other things, the matters of wealth and class and application of the unwritten code mentioned in paragraph 2.

2. According to Pericles' view of liberality (paras. 4–5), should the United States permit the export of its technology? Erect or eliminate trade barriers? Do your answers depend at all on whether you see Athens and the United States operating from positions of strength? Explain.

3. Choose any of America's wars or episodes of mass internal violence, or that of another people whose heritage you share, and write a funeral oration for those who died in its cause. You may wish to challenge yourself by writing one from the standpoint of the enemy—for example, the Japanese after Hiroshima and Nagasaki or the British after Yorktown.

Sir Francis Bacon
(England; 1561–1626)

A man of great intellect (he was admitted to Cambridge at age twelve), Bacon was born into a politically prominent family. He was trained in the law and after much struggle—despite his connections—obtained a series of legal positions under both Elizabeth I and her successor James I. As Lord Chancellor from 1618 to 1621, Bacon was at the height of his success, having previously been knighted and made Viscount St. Alban. But, convicted of accepting bribes, he was forced from office.

Although posterity does not admire his political maneuvering (which, in fact, was fairly typical of the age) or subscribe to his belief in the divine right of kings, it does recognize his philosophical and literary achievements. In such works as The Advancement of Learning (1605), Instauratio Magna (Grand Instauration, 1620) and the Novum Organon (New Method, 1620) Bacon helped establish the theoretical framework for the age of scientific investigation that lay just beyond him in the time of Newton. His two most significant ideas were to separate science from theological dogma and, consequently, to propose the reinvestigation of the natural world according to empirical, inductive principles free of preconceptions.

Bacon's literary achievement lies chiefly in his Essays or Counsels, Civil and Moral, first published in 1597 and augmented and refined in 1612 and 1625. Although based on the form developed by Michel de Montaigne in the sixteenth century, Bacon's pieces are far more compact, terse, and aphoristic.

You need to exercise particular care in reading "Of Studies," perhaps less because of the unfamiliar vocabulary and style than because every word counts so heavily. The spelling here has been updated, but current British usage, as in humour, has been retained.

Of Studies

STUDIES SERVE FOR DELIGHT, for ornament, and for ability. Their chief use for delight is in privateness, and retiring; for ornament, is in discourse; and for ability, is in the judgment and disposition of business; for, expert men can execute, and perhaps judge of particulars, one by one; but the general counsels, and the plots and marshaling of affairs, come best from those that are learned. To spend too much time in studies, is sloth; to use them too much for ornament, is affectation; to make judgment wholly by their rules, is the humour of a scholar; they perfect nature, and are perfected by experience—for natural abilities are like natural plants, that need pruning by study; and studies themselves do give forth directions too much at large, except they be bounded in by experience. Crafty men contemn studies, simple men admire them, and wise men use them, for they teach not their own use; but that is a wisdom without them, and above them, won by observation. Read not to contradict and confute nor to believe and take for granted, nor to find talk and discourse, but to weigh and consider. Some books are to be tasted, others to be swallowed, and some few to be chewed and digested; that is, some books are to be read only in parts; others to be read, but not curiously;[1] and some few to be read wholly, and with diligence and attention. Some books also may be read by deputy, and extracts made of them by others; but that would be only in the less important arguments, and the meaner sort of books; else distilled books are, like common distilled waters, flashy things. Reading

---

[1]**curiously:** attentively. [All notes are by the editor.]

maketh a full man, conference a ready man, and writing an exact man; and, therefore, if a man write little, he had need have a great memory; if he confer little, he had need have a present wit; and if he read little, he had need have much cunning, to seem to know that[2] he doth not. Histories make men wise; poets witty; the mathematics subtle; natural philosophy deep; moral, grave; logic and rhetoric, able to contend: "abeunt studia in mores"[3]—nay, there is not stond[4] or impediment in the wit, but may be wrought out by fit studies, like as diseases of the body may have appropriate exercises—bowling is good for the stone and reins,[5] shooting for the lungs and breast, gentle walking for the stomach, riding for the head, and the like; so, if a man's wits be wandering, let him study the mathematics, for in demonstrations, if his wit be called away never so little, he must begin again; if his wit be not apt to distinguish or find differences, let him study the schoolmen,[6] for they are "cymini sectores,"[7] if he be not apt to beat over matters, and to call upon one thing to prove and illustrate another, let him study the lawyers' cases—so every defect of the mind may have a special receipt.

THESIS AND THOUGHT

1. Because of its prominent position, the opening sentence of the essay appears to be the thesis. Is it? Why?

2. Summarize, in one sentence, if you can, Bacon's view(s) of education. Is your summary a more suitable thesis statement than Bacon's opening sentence?

3. According to Bacon, what is the purpose of reading? To judge from the essay, what might Bacon's attitude toward the stereotypic bookworm have been?

4. What might Bacon say about a *Reader's Digest* version of *War and Peace* (or some other fiction "classic")? *Jane Fonda's New Workout and Weight-Loss Program? The Autobiography of Malcolm X?* This text? Some other books with which you are familiar?

5. Bacon's thought in general, and his ideas concerning education in particular, have been said to contain strong pragmatic elements. What evidence for such pragmatism does this essay provide?

STRUCTURE

1. There are no paragraph divisions in the version of "Of Studies" printed here. Supply them by marking the text appropriately. Then, reread the essay. Do your paragraph divisions improve comprehension? Why?

---

[2]**that:** that which.   [3]**"abeunt . . . mores":** "Studies affect manners."   [4]**stond:** obstacle.
[5]**reins:** kidneys.   [6]**schoolmen:** medieval scholars or philosophers.   [7]**"cymini sectores":** hair-splitters; literally, splitters of cumin (seed).

2. Clearly, the dominant rhetorical pattern here is division-classification. List (or mark in the text) all the instances in which Bacon establishes categories. With what frequency does a threefold division occur?

3. Except for the discussion of physical and mental exercises, there is little in the essay that is **concrete.** Is the absence of detail a flaw? Explain.

4. The first published version of the essay (1597) appears below. After reading it, explain how Bacon revised and developed the piece for the 1625 edition. Are the alterations improvements? Compare the paragraphing of this version with that in your response to question 1.

> Studies serve for pastimes, for ornaments and for abilities. Their chief use for pastime is in privateness and retiring; for ornament is in discourse, and for ability is in judgment. For expert men can execute, but learned men are fittest to judge or censure.
>
> To spend too much time in them is sloth, to use them too much for ornament is affectation: to make judgment wholly by their rules, is the humour of a scholar.
>
> They perfect nature, and are perfected by experience.
>
> Crafty men [contemn] them, simple men admire them, wise men use them: For they teach not their own use, but that is a wisdom without them: and above them won by observation.
>
> Read not to contradict, nor to believe, but to weigh and consider.
>
> Some books are to be tasted, others to be swallowed, and some few to be chewed and digested: That is, some books are to be read only in part; others to be read, but cursorily, and some few to be read wholly and with diligence and attention.
>
> Reading maketh a full man, conference a ready man, and writing an exact man. And therefore if a man write little, he had need have a great memory, if he confer little, he had need have a present wit, and if he read little, he had need have much cunning, to seem to know that he doth not.
>
> Histories make men wise, poets witty: the mathematics subtle, natural philosophy deep: moral [philosophy], grave, logic and rhetoric able to contend.

5. Given your responses to "Thesis and Thought" questions 1 and 2, do you find the conclusion satisfactory? Why?

STYLE

1. Explain how the structural pattern of division-classification here is also a stylistic device.

2. Bacon twice uses similes. Identify them. Are they useful in establishing his meaning? Why?

3. Although written in modern English, the essay contains vocabulary and constructions that are far less familiar today than they were to Bacon's original readers. Assume that you are bringing out a contemporary edition of

the essay. Write a version that would be more easily understood by contemporary educated readers. What kinds of changes did you make? What do they say about changes in the language over the past 375 years? About your expectations of the contemporary audience? Your own verbal skills?

CONSIDERATIONS

1. What have you studied for "delight"? For "ornament"? For "ability"? Of the three, which motivation seems the most prevalent today? The least? Does the fact that, unlike Bacon, you might not move in aristocratic circles affect your answers? Are there people or groups today whose responses might differ from yours? Explain.

2. Compile short lists of books that you feel should be tasted, swallowed, or chewed and digested. What were your bases of classification?

3. Has what you have studied so far shaped the manner of your thought? If so, how? If not, what effect, if any, have your studies had? Write an essay in which you trace and account for your intellectual development.

4. Examine Bacon's prescriptions for intellectual deficits. Do you agree that they might be effective? Justify your response to one of them in a substantial paragraph.

William Shakespeare
(England; 1564–1616)

Shakespeare should hardly need introducing to students using this text. As playwright and poet, he is, of course, among the world's major literary figures.

Born into a middle-class family in Stratford-on-Avon, Shakespeare was probably educated at the local grammar school. He was likely in London by his mid-twenties, leaving behind his wife, Anne Hathaway (to whom he would curiously will his "second best bed"), and his children. As playwright and sometime actor, he was soon actively engaged in the life of the theater. He is most closely associated with the Lord Chamberlain's Company, later the King's company at the Globe.

Like most poets of his time, Shakespeare was caught up in the sonnet craze of the 1590s (154 of them were published surreptitiously long after the fad had passed). It is his plays, however, that are the principal basis for his enduring fame. He wrote thirty-seven in all, including tragedies (e.g., Hamlet, King Lear, Othello), romantic and dark comedies (e.g., As You Like It, A Midsummer Night's Dream, The Tempest), and histories (e.g., Henry IV, in two parts, and Richard III). His work has been so pervasive that even those unfamiliar with the plays themselves are often aware of titles and characters, some of which have become archetypes or touchstones in the language. Many of us have known a Lady Macbeth or a Romeo, a puckish fellow, a person of Falstaffian proportions, or perhaps a shylock.

"The Seven Ages of Man" is taken from As You Like It, one of the romantic comedies. Rather a set speech of the melancholy Jaques than in any way essential to the plot, it is, nevertheless, among the best-known passages in Shakespeare, offering as it does a sobering view of the nature of human existence.

The Seven Ages of Man

All the world's a stage,
And all the men and women, merely players;
They have their exits and their entrances,
And one man in his time plays many parts,
His Acts being seven ages. At first the infant,   5
Mewling, and puking in the nurse's arms:
Then, the whining school-boy with his satchel
And shining morning face, creeping like a snail
Unwillingly to school. And then the lover,
Sighing like furnace, with a woeful ballad   10
Made to his mistress' eyebrow. Then, a soldier,
Full of strange oaths, and bearded like the pard,[1]
Jealous in honour, sudden and quick in quarrel,
Seeking the bubble reputation
Even in the cannon's mouth: and then, the justice,   15
In fair round belly, with good capon lin'd,
With eyes severe, and beard of formal cut,
Full of wise saws, and modern instances,
And so he plays his part. The sixth age shifts
Into the lean and slipper'd pantaloon,   20
With spectacles on nose, and pouch on side,
His youthful hose well sav'd, a world too wide
For his shrunk shank, and his big manly voice,
Turning again toward childish treble, pipes
And whistles in his sound. Last scene of all,   25
That ends this strange eventful history,
Is second childishness, and mere oblivion,
Sans[2] teeth, sans eyes, sans taste, sans everything.

[1]**pard:** leopard. [Ed.]   [2]**Sans:** "without" (French). [Ed.]

THESIS AND THOUGHT

1. In *As You Like It,* this speech is delivered by the "melancholy" (i.e., despondent, depressed) Jaques (pronounced jay' kweez). What is Jaques' view of the human condition? How might his mind-set have affected that view?

STRUCTURE

1. Although the structure here is clearly analytical, with a life broken down into component parts, the analysis is inseparable from the passage's governing extended metaphor. Identify the metaphor and explain how Shakespeare develops it.
2. Explain how the passage might also be considered a process.

STYLE

1. Do the details for each age describe an individual or a type? If there are types, to what extent are they caricatures? How is caricature related to the central metaphor?
2. What is Jaques' attitude toward each of the figures he describes? Which words indicate it? How do they collectively establish his (and the passage's) tone?
3. Identify techniques of poetry (other than metaphor) employed in the speech. Which, if any, might also be appropriate to prose? To what extent?

CONSIDERATIONS

1. Which of the types Jaques lists are not clearly recognizable today? Why not?
2. The speech begins with a reference to "all the men and women" but continues with male references exclusively. Why? (You need to go beyond the mere label of "sexism.")
3. Write an updated prose version of the speech. Regardless of your gender, you might find it interesting (and challenging) to write one using female types. You might also try to write a version that contains no gender reference. If you attempt more than one, which is the more (most) vivid? Why?

Maria Luisa Bombal

(Chile; 1910–1980)

Although Bombal was born and died in Chile, she spent many of her formative years and the period of her greatest creativity in a variety of other places. Living in Paris from 1920 to 1931 enabled her to take a degree in French literature at the Sorbonne and, more important, exposed her to avant-garde intellectual and artistic developments.

Back in South America, she was also associated with the great figures of the age, principally (in Buenos Aires) Pablo Neruda, and produced her first novel La ultima niebla (House of Mist, 1934). *The book introduced to Latin American literature both the new philosophical and psychological concepts concerning the nature of reality—including surrealism—and raised questions about the status of women in Latin American culture. Such questions reappear in Bombal's subsequent work as well, for example in another novel,* La amortajada (The Shrouded Woman, 1938) *and in several short stories, such as* "Braids." *A prominent element in Bombal's writing is her exploration of women's spirituality.*

Despite her considerable influence on Latin American literature, Bombal's output was small. To the titles mentioned above one might add a posthumous collection in English translation New Islands and Other Stories *(1984) and the novella* La historia de Maria Griselda (The Story of Maria Griselda, 1976), *for which Bombal received the prize of the Chilean Academy of Arts and Letters.*

Bombal's personal life was often painful, marked by divorce, a suicide attempt, alcoholism, and final poverty. During the latter half of her life, much of it spent in New York, Bombal published little.

"Sky, Sea and Earth" will pose problems if you approach it literally. Its reality is at least as internal as external—an interior landscape of the narrator's psyche whose edges are blurred and whose features may be ambiguous.

Sky, Sea and Earth

I KNOW ABOUT MANY THINGS of which no one knows. I am familiar with an infinite number of tiny and magical secrets from the sea and from the earth.

I know, for example, that in the ocean depths, much lower than the fathomless and dense zone of darkness, the ocean illuminates itself again and that a golden and motionless light sprouts from gigantic sponges as radiant and as yellow as suns. All types of plants and frozen beings live there submerged in that light of glacial, eternal summer: green and red sea anemones crowd themselves in broad live meadows to which transparent jellyfish that have not yet broken their ties intertwine themselves before embarking on an errant destiny through the seas; hard white coral becomes entangled in enchanted thickets where slithering fish of shadowy velvet softly open and close themselves like flowers; there are sea horses whose manes of algae scatter round them in a sluggish halo when they silently gallop, and if one lifts certain grey shells of insignificant shape, one is frequently sure to find below a little mermaid crying.

I know about an underwater volcano in constant eruption; its crater boils indefatigably day and night and it blows thick bubbles of silvery lava toward the surface of the waters.

I know that during the low-tide, painted beds of delicate anemones remain uncovered on the reefs, and I commiserate with the one who smells that ardent carpet that devours.

I know about gulfs replete with eternal foam where the west winds slowly 5 drag their innumerable rainbow tails.

There is a pure white and nude drowned woman that all of the fishermen of the coast vainly try to catch in their nets . . . but perhaps she is nothing more than an enraptured sea gull that the Pacific currents drag back and forth.

I am familiar with hidden roads, terrestrial channels where the ocean filters the tides, in order to climb up to the pupils of certain women who suddenly look at us with deeply green eyes.

I know that the ships that have fallen down the ladder of a whirlwind continue travelling centuries below in between submerged reefs; that their masts entangle infuriated octopi and that their holds harbor starfish.

All this I know about the sea.

I know from the earth, that whoever removes the bark from certain trees 10 will find sleeping and adhering to the trunk, extraordinary dusty butterflies that the first ray of light pierces and destroys like an implacable, irreverent pin.

I remember and I see an autumn park. In its wide avenues the leaves pile up and decay, and below them palpitate timid moss colored frogs that wear a golden crown on their heads. No one knows it, but the truth is that all frogs are princes.

I fear "la gallina ciega"[1] with the immeasurable fright of a child. "La gallina ciega" is smoke colored, and she lives cast below the thickets, like a miserable pile of ashes. She doesn't have legs to walk, nor eyes to see; but she usually flies away on certain nights with short and thick wings. No one knows

---

[1]La gallina ciega is more commonly identified with the childhood game of "blind man's bluff." Here, Bombal creates a legend about the figure of an actual blind hen and refers to her in mysterious and somewhat macabre terms. [Tr.]

where she goes, no one knows from where she returns, at dawn, stained in blood that isn't her own.

I am familiar with a distant southern jungle in whose muddy ground opens a hole narrow and so deep that if you lie face downwards upon the earth and you look, you will encounter as far as the eye can see, something like a cloud of golden dust that vertiginously turns.

But nothing is more unforseen than the birth of wine. Because it isn't true that wine is born under the sky and within the dark grape of water and sun. The birth of wine is tenebrous and slow; I know a lot about that furtive assassin's growth. Only after the doors of the cold wine cellar are closed and after the spiders have spread out their first curtains, is when the wine decides to grow in the depths of the large, hermetically closed barrels. Like the tides, wine suffers from the taciturn influence of the moon that now incites it to retreat, now helps it to flow back. And this is how it is born and grows in the darkness and the silence of its winter.

I can tell something more about the earth. I know about a deserted region   15
where a village has remained buried in the dunes, the only thing emerging is the peak of the tower of the church. During stormy nights every lightning rod moves recklessly over the solitary arrow, erect in the middle of the plain, coiling around her, whistling, in order to later sink into the sand. And they say that then, the missing tower shakes from top to bottom and a subterranean toll of bells is heard resonating.

The sky, on the other hand, does not have even one small and tender secret. Implacable, it completely unfurls its terrifying map above us.

I would like to believe that I have my star, the one that I see break through first and shine an instant only for me everyday at dusk, and that in that star not only my steps but also my laughter and my voice have an echo. But, alas, I know too well that there cannot be life of any kind there where the atoms change their form millions of times per second and where no pair of atoms can remain united.

It even makes me afraid to name the sun. It is so powerful! If they were to cut us off from its radiation, the course of the rivers would immediately stop.

I barely dare to speak about a condor that the winds pushed beyond the terrestrial atmosphere and that, still alive, has been falling in infinite space for an uncountable number of years.

Perhaps the sudden fall of shooting stars responds to a foreseen call from   20
eternity that hurls them in order to form particular geometric figures, made of glittering stars inlaid in a remote corner of the sky. Perhaps.

No, I don't want, I don't want to talk about the sky any more, because I fear it, and I fear the dreams with which it frequently enters into my nights. Then, it extends a sidereal ladder to me through which I climb toward the shining dome. The moon stops being a pallid disk stuck in the firmament in order to become a scarlet ball that rolls through space in solitude. The stars grow larger in a blinking of rays, the milky way approaches and pours out its wave of fire. And, second by second, I am closer to the edge of that burning precipice.

No, I prefer to imagine a diurnal sky with roaming castles of clouds in whose floating rooms flutter the dry leaves of a terrestrial autumn and the kites that the sons of men lost, playing.

Translated by Celeste Kostopulos-Cooperman

THESIS AND THOUGHT

1. Is Bombal's actual subject what the title seems to indicate? If so, to what extent? If not, how would you define her actual topic?

2. What does the narrator claim to know? To fear? Evaluate the knowledge and explain why she is fearful. Is the passage from knowledge to fear at all progressive?

STRUCTURE

1. Are the distinctions among Bombal's divisions merely geographical? Explain. Which seems at greatest variance with the other two? Why? (Notice, for example, the exclusion of "sky" in para. 1).

2. Do you find the order in which the three locales are presented particularly significant? Explain. (You might have observed that the sequence sea, earth, sky is at variance with that of the title. This is true of the original Spanish text as well, in which the title is arranged as sea, sky, and earth.)

3. Are sky, sea, and earth, either separately or collectively, symbolic? If so, of what? If not, explain why you consider them simply literal.

STYLE

1. Paragraph 2 is a seamless fusion of (ostensible) fact—the presence of various sea creatures, for example—and fantasy—the mermaid, among other things. To what extent is this typical of the story as a whole? What does this fusion suggest about the narrator's state of mind or, perhaps, of its development?

2. The vocabulary here is often sophisticated: *indefatigably* (para. 3), *vertiginously* (para. 13), *tenebrous* (para. 14), *implacable* (para. 16), *sidereal* (para. 21), *diurnal* (para. 22). At times the sentences are elaborate—as in much of paragraph 2, the sentence that is paragraph 4, the opening sentence of

paragraph 17. Many other sentences, however, are quite simple, as in paragraphs 1 and 9 and the beginnings of paragraphs 11, 15, and 18. Informalities, as in contractions and such expressions as "a lot" (para. 14) and the colloquial and dramatic "No I don't want, I don't want to talk about the sky any more . . . " (para. 21), are also present. What is the effect of such variety—particularly in regard to shaping Bombal's theme and tone? See, for example, the juxtapositions in paragraphs 11, 14, and 20.

3. Identify examples of Bombal's figurative language—simile, metaphor, and especially personification—and explain its importance for the story as a whole.

CONSIDERATIONS

1. Write an essay in which you express your own secret "knowledge" of the world around you.

2. Using first a child's, then an adult's perspective and style, write an essay in which you present a childhood impression of a person or place and contrast it with your mature perception.

3. Discuss whether it is possible to distinguish what we know from what we believe we know. Write a paragraph or brief essay in which you explain the effect of your having had a belief exposed as erroneous.

4. Write a letter to yourself in which you discuss a fear with which you are usually reluctant to deal.

Desmond Morris

(England; b. 1928)

Desmond Morris has had a varied career, principally as a prolific popular writer on scientific and anthropological topics. In addition, as an Oxford-trained zoologist and ethologist, he has been a scholar and curator of mammals for the London Zoo. He has also hosted the BBC television show Zootime. *A painter who exhibits his work, Morris has written about art as well.*

Morris's first major literary success was The Naked Ape *(1967), which was followed in short order by* The Human Zoo *(1969). In both these books, as well as in several subsequent ones, he applies the principles of zoology and ethology to humans in an attempt to study the species with the same detachment he would any other.* Manwatching: A Field Guide to Human Behaviour *(1977), from which "Territorial Behaviour" is taken, is another in the series.* Gestures: Their Origins and Distributions *(1979) is rather more technical. More recently, with* Dogwatching *(1987),* Catwatching *(1987) and* Horsewatching *(1989), Morris has resumed studying species other than our own.*

Territorial Behaviour

A TERRITORY is a defended space. In the broadest sense, there are three kinds of human territory: tribal, family, and personal.

It is rare for people to be driven to physical fighting in defence of these "owned" spaces, but fight they will, if pushed to the limit. The invading army encroaching on national territory, the gang moving into a rival district, the trespasser climbing into an orchard, the burglar breaking into a house, the bully pushing to the front of a queue, the driver trying to steal a parking space, all of these intruders are liable to be met with resistance varying from the vigorous to the savagely violent. Even if the law is on the side of the intruder, the urge to protect a territory may be so strong that otherwise peaceful citizens abandon all their usual controls and inhibitions. Attempts to evict families from their homes, no matter how socially valid the reasons, can lead to siege conditions reminiscent of the defence of a medieval fortress.

The fact that these upheavals are so rare is a measure of the success of Territorial Signals as a system of dispute prevention. It is sometimes cynically stated that "all property is theft," but in reality it is the opposite. Property, as owned space which is *displayed* as owned space, is a special kind of sharing system which reduces fighting much more than it causes it. Man is a co-operative species, but he is also competitive, and his struggle for dominance has to be structured in some way if chaos is to be avoided. The establishment of territorial rights is one such structure. It limits dominance geographically. I am dominant in my territory and you are dominant in yours. In other words, dominance is shared out spatially, and we all have some. Even if I am weak and unintelligent and you can dominate me when we meet on neutral ground, I can still enjoy a thoroughly dominant role as soon as I retreat to my private base. Be it ever so humble, there is no place like a home territory.

Of course, I can still be intimidated by a particularly dominant individual who enters my home base, but his encroachment will be dangerous for him and he will think twice about it, because he will know that here my urge to resist will be dramatically magnified and my usual subservience banished. Insulted at the heart of my own territory, I may easily explode into battle— either symbolic or real—with a result that may be damaging to both of us.

In order for this to work, each territory has to be plainly advertised as such. Just as a dog cocks its leg to deposit its personal scent on the trees in its locality, so the human animal cocks its leg symbolically all over his home base. But because we are predominantly visual animals we employ mostly visual signals, and it is worth asking how we do this at three levels: tribal, family and personal.

First: the Tribal Territory. We evolved as tribal animals, living in comparatively small groups, probably of less than a hundred, and we existed like that for millions of years. It is our basic social unit, a group in which everyone knows everyone else. Essentially, the tribal territory consisted of a home base surrounded by extended hunting grounds. Any neighbouring tribe intruding on our social space would be repelled and driven away. As these early tribes swelled into agricultural super-tribes, and eventually into industrial nations, their territorial defence systems became increasingly elaborate. The tiny, ancient home base of the hunting tribe became the great capital city, the primitive war-paint became the flags, emblems, uniforms and regalia of the specialized military, and the war-chants became national anthems, marching songs and bugle calls. Territorial boundary-lines hardened into fixed borders, often conspicuously patrolled and punctuated with defensive structures—forts and lookout posts, checkpoints and great walls, and, today, customs barriers.

Today each nation flies its own flag, a symbolic embodiment of its territorial status. But patriotism is not enough. The ancient tribal hunter lurking inside each citizen finds himself unsatisfied by membership of such a vast conglomeration of individuals, most of whom are totally unknown to him personally. He does his best to feel that he shares a common territorial defence with them all, but the scale of the operation has become inhuman. It is hard to feel a sense of belonging with a tribe of fifty million or more. His answer is to form sub-groups, nearer to his ancient pattern, smaller and more personally known to him—the local club, the teenage gang, the union, the specialist society, the sports association, the political party, the college fraternity, the social clique, the protest group, and the rest. Rare indeed is the individual who does not belong to at least one of these splinter groups, and take from it a sense of tribal allegiance and brotherhood. Typical of all these groups is the development of Territorial Signals—badges, costumes, headquarters, banners, slogans, and all the other displays of group identity. This is where the action is, in terms of tribal territorialism, and only when a major war breaks out does the emphasis shift upwards to the higher group level of the nation.

Each of these modern pseudo-tribes sets up its own special kind of home base. In extreme cases non-members are totally excluded, in others they are allowed in as visitors with limited rights and under a control system of special rules. In many ways they are like miniature nations, with their own flags and emblems and their own border guards. The exclusive club has its own "customs barrier": the doorman who checks your "passport" (your membership card) and prevents strangers from passing in unchallenged. There is a government: the club committee; and often special displays of the tribal elders: the photographs or portraits of previous officials on the walls. At the heart of the specialized territories there is a powerful feeling of security and importance, a sense of shared defence against the outside world. Much of the club chatter, both serious and joking, directs itself against the rottenness of everything outside the club boundaries—in that "other world" beyond the protected portals.

In social organizations which embody a strong class system, such as military units and large business concerns, there are many territorial rules, often unspoken, which interfere with the official hierarchy. High-status individuals, such as officers or managers, could in theory enter any of the regions occupied by the lower levels in the peck order, but they limit this power in a striking way. An officer seldom enters a sergeant's mess or a barrack room unless it is for a formal inspection. He respects those regions as alien territories even though he has the power to go there by virtue of his dominant role. And in businesses, part of the appeal of unions, over and above their obvious functions, is that with their officials, headquarters and meetings they add a sense of territorial power for the staff workers. It is almost as if each military organization and business concern consists of two warring tribes: the officers versus the other ranks, and the management versus the workers. Each has its special home base within the system, and the territorial defence pattern thrusts itself into what, on the surface, is a pure social hierarchy. Negotiations between managements and unions are tribal battles fought out over the neutral ground of a boardroom table, and are as much concerned with territorial display as they are with resolving problems of wages and conditions. Indeed, if one side gives in too quickly and accepts the other's demands, the victors feel strangely cheated and deeply suspicious that it may be a trick. What they are missing is the protracted sequence of ritual and counter-ritual that keeps alive their group territorial identity.

Likewise, many of the hostile displays of sports fans and teenage gangs   10
are primarily concerned with displaying their group image to rival fan-clubs and gangs. Except in rare cases, they do not attack one another's headquarters, drive out the occupants, and reduce them to a submissive, subordinate condition. It is enough to have scuffles on the borderlands between the two rival territories. This is particularly clear at football matches, where the fan-club becomes temporarily shifted from the club-house to a section of the stands, and where minor fighting breaks out at the unofficial boundary line between the massed groups of rival supporters. Newspaper reports play up the few accidents and injuries which do occur on such occasions, but when these are studied in relation to the total numbers of displaying fans involved it is clear that the serious incidents represent only a tiny fraction of the overall group behaviour. For every actual punch or kick there are a thousand war-cries, war-dances, chants and gestures.

Second: the Family Territory. Essentially, the family is a breeding unit and the family territory is a breeding ground. At the centre of this space, there is the nest—the bedroom—where, tucked up in bed, we feel at our most territorially secure. In a typical house the bedroom is upstairs, where a safe nest should be. This puts it farther away from the entrance hall, the area where contact is made, intermittently, with the outside world. The less private reception rooms, where intruders are allowed access, are the next line of defence. Beyond them, outside the walls of the building, there is often a symbolic remnant of the ancient feeding grounds—a garden. Its symbolism often extends to the plants and animals it contains, which cease to be nutritional and become merely decorative—flowers and pets. But like a true territorial space it has a conspicuously displayed boundary-line, the garden fence, wall or railings. Often no more than a token barrier, this is the outer territorial demarcation, separating the private world of the family from the public world beyond. To cross it puts any visitor or intruder at an immediate disadvantage. As he crosses the threshold, his dominance wanes, slightly but unmistakably. He is entering an area where he senses that he must ask permission to do simple things that he would consider a right elsewhere. Without lifting a finger, the territorial owners exert their dominance. This is done by all the hundreds of small ownership "markers" they have deposited on their family territory: the ornaments, the "possessed" objects positioned in the rooms and on the walls; the furnishings, the furniture, the colours, the patterns, all owner-chosen and all making this particular home base unique to them.

It is one of the tragedies of modern architecture that there has been a standardization of these vital territorial living-units. One of the most important aspects of a home is that it should be similar to other homes only in a general way, and that in detail it should have many differences, making it a particular home. Unfortunately, it is cheaper to build a row of houses, or a block of flats, so that all the family living-units are identical, but the territorial urge rebels against this trend and house-owners struggle as best they can to make their mark on their mass-produced properties. They do this with garden-design, with front-door colours, with curtain patterns, with wallpaper and all the other decorative elements that together create a unique and different family environment. Only when they have completed this nest-building do they feel truly "at home" and secure.

When they venture forth as a family unit they repeat the process in a minor way. On a day-trip to the seaside, they load the car with personal belongings and it becomes their temporary, portable territory. Arriving at the beach they stake out a small territorial claim, marking it with rugs, towels, baskets and other belongings to which they can return from their seaboard wanderings. Even if they all leave it at once to bathe, it retains a characteristic territorial quality and other family groups arriving will recognize this by setting up their own "home" bases at a respectful distance. Only when the whole beach has filled up with these marked spaces will newcomers start to position themselves in such a way that the inter-base distance becomes reduced. Forced to pitch between several existing beach territories they will feel a momentary sensation of intrusion, and the established "owners" will feel a similar sensation of invasion, even though they are not being directly inconvenienced.

The same territorial scene is being played out in parks and fields and on riverbanks, wherever family groups gather in their clustered units. But if rivalry for spaces creates mild feelings of hostility, it is true to say that, without the territorial system of sharing and space-limited dominance, there would be chaotic disorder.

Third: the Personal Space. If a man enters a waiting-room and sits at one end of a long row of empty chairs, it is possible to predict where the next man to enter will seat himself. He will not sit next to the first man, nor will he sit at the far end, right away from him. He will choose a position about halfway between these two points. The next man to enter will take the largest gap left, and sit roughly in the middle of that, and so on, until eventually the latest newcomer will be forced to select a seat that places him right next to one of the already seated men. Similar patterns can be observed in cinemas, public urinals, aeroplanes, trains and buses. This is a reflection of the fact that we all carry with us, everywhere we go, a portable territory called a Personal Space. If people move inside this space, we feel threatened. If they keep too far outside it, we feel rejected. The result is a subtle series of spatial adjustments, usually operating quite unconsciously and producing ideal compromises as far as this is possible. If a situation becomes too crowded, then we adjust our reactions accordingly and allow our personal space to shrink. Jammed into an elevator, a rush-hour compartment, or a packed room, we give up altogether and allow body-to-body contact, but when we relinquish our Personal Space in this way, we adopt certain special techniques. In essence, what we do is to convert these other bodies into "nonpersons." We studiously ignore them, and they us. We try not to face them if we can possibly avoid it. We wipe all expressiveness from our faces, letting them go blank. We may look up at the ceiling or down at the floor, and we reduce body movements to a minimum. Packed together like sardines in a tin, we stand dumbly still, sending out as few social signals as possible.

Even if the crowding is less severe, we still tend to cut down our social interactions in the presence of large numbers. Careful observations of children in play groups revealed that if they are high density groupings there is less social interaction between the individual children, even though there is theoretically more opportunity for such contacts. At the same time, the high-density groups show a higher frequency of aggressive and destructive behaviour patterns in their play. Personal Space—"elbow room"—is a vital commodity for the human animal, and one that cannot be ignored without risking serious trouble.

Of course, we all enjoy the excitement of being in a crowd, and this reaction cannot be ignored. But there are crowds and crowds. It is pleasant enough to be in a "spectator crowd," but not so appealing to find yourself in the middle of a rush-hour crush. The difference between the two is that the spectator crowd is all facing in the same direction and concentrating on a distant point of interest. Attending the theatre, there are twinges of rising hostility towards the stranger who sits next to you. The shared armrest can become a polite, but distinct, territorial boundary-dispute region. However, as soon as the show begins, these invasions of Personal Space are forgotten and the attention is focused beyond the small space where the crowding is taking place. Now, each member of the audience feels himself spatially related, not to his cramped neighbours, but to the actor on the stage, and this distance is, if anything, too great. In the rush-hour crowd, by contrast, each member of the pushing throng is competing with his neighbours all the time. There is no escape to a spatial relation with a distant actor, only the pushing, shoving bodies all around.

Those of us who have to spend a great deal of time in crowded conditions become gradually better able to adjust, but no one can ever become completely immune to invasions of Personal Space. This is because they remain forever associated with either powerful hostile or equally powerful loving feelings. All through our childhood we will have been held to be loved and held to be hurt, and anyone who invades our Personal Space when we are adults is, in effect, threatening to extend his behaviour into one of these two highly charged areas of human interaction. Even if his motives are clearly neither hostile nor sexual, we still find it hard to suppress our reactions to his close approach. Unfortunately, different countries have different ideas about exactly how close is close. It is easy enough to test your own "space reaction": when you are talking to someone in the street or in any open space, reach out with your arm and see where the nearest point on his body comes. If you hail from western Europe, you will find that he is at roughly fingertip distance from you. In other words, as you reach out, your fingertips will just about make contact with his shoulder. If you come from eastern Europe you will find you are standing at "wrist distance." If you come from the Mediterranean region you will find that you are much closer to your companion, at little more than "elbow distance."

Trouble begins when a member of one of these cultures meets and talks to one from another. Say a British diplomat meets an Italian or an Arab diplomat at an embassy function. They start talking in a friendly way, but soon the fingertips man begins to feel uneasy. Without knowing quite why, he starts to back away gently from his companion. The companion edges forward again. Each tries in this way to set up a Personal Space relationship that suits his own background. But it is impossible to do. Every time the Mediterranean diplomat advances to a distance that feels comfortable for him, the British diplomat feels threatened. Every time the Briton moves back, the other feels rejected. Attempts to adjust this situation often lead to a talking pair shifting slowly across a room, and many an embassy reception is dotted with western-European fingertip-distance men pinned against walls by eager elbow-distance men. Until such differences are fully understood, and allowances made, these minor differences in "body territories" will continue to act as an alienation factor which may interfere in a subtle way with diplomatic harmony and other forms of international transaction.

If there are distance problems when engaged in conversation, then there   20
are clearly going to be even bigger difficulties where people must work
privately in a shared space. Close proximity of others, pressing against the
invisible boundaries of our personal body-territory, makes it difficult to con-
centrate on non-social matters. Flatmates, students sharing a study, sailors in
the cramped quarters of a ship, and office staff in crowded workplaces, all
have to face this problem. They solve it by "cocooning." They use a variety
of devices to shut themselves off from the others present. The best possible
cocoon, of course, is a small private room—a den, a private office, a study or
a studio—which physically obscures the presence of other nearby territory-
owners. This is the ideal situation for non-social work, but the space-sharers
cannot enjoy this luxury. Their cocooning must be symbolic. They may, in
certain cases, be able to erect small physical barriers, such as screens or
partitions, which give substance to their invisible Personal Space boundaries,
but when this cannot be done, other means must be sought. One of these is
the "favoured object." Each space-sharer develops a preference, repeatedly
expressed until it becomes a fixed pattern, for a particular chair, or table, or
alcove. Others come to respect this, and friction is reduced. This system is
often formally arranged (this is my desk, that is yours), but even where it is
not, favoured places soon develop. Professor Smith has a favourite chair in
the library. It is not formally his, but he always uses it and others avoid it.
Seats around a mess-room table, or a boardroom table, become almost personal property for specific individuals. Even in the home, father has his
favourite chair for reading the newspaper or watching television. Another
device is the blinkers-posture. Just as a horse that over-reacts to other horses
and the distractions of the noisy race-course is given a pair of blinkers to
shield its eyes, so people studying privately in a public place put on pseudo-
blinkers in the form of shielding hands. Resting their elbows on the table,
they sit with their hands screening their eyes from the scene on either side.

A third method of reinforcing the body-territory is to use personal markers. Books, papers and other personal belongings are scattered around the
favoured site to render it more privately owned in the eyes of companions.
Spreading out one's belongings is a well-known trick in public-transport
situations, where a traveller tries to give the impression that seats next to him
are taken. In many contexts carefully arranged personal markers can act as an
effective territorial display, even in the absence of the territory owner. Experiments in a library revealed that placing a pile of magazines on the table in
one seating position successfully reserved that place for an average of 77
minutes. If a sports-jacket was added, draped over the chair, then the "reservation effect" lasted for over two hours.

In these ways, we strengthen the defences of our Personal Spaces, keeping out intruders with the minimum of open hostility. As with all territorial
behaviour, the object is to defend space with signals rather than with fists and
at all three levels—the tribal, the family and the personal—it is a remarkably

efficient system of space-sharing. It does not always seem so, because newspapers and newscasts inevitably magnify the exceptions and dwell on those cases where the signals have failed and wars have broken out, gangs have fought, neighbouring families have feuded, or colleagues have clashed, but for every territorial signal that has failed, there are millions of others that have not. They do not rate a mention in the news, but they nevertheless constitute a dominant feature of human society—the society of a remarkably territorial animal.

THESIS AND THOUGHT

1. According to Morris, what is the purpose of our territorial behavior and how successful is that behavior in achieving it?
2. How does Morris explain the need for subgroups?
3. Why is most human territorial marking visual? Does this differ from marking in other species? Explain.
4. Discuss some of the ways you might maintain or mark personal space in a crowded environment. In addition to elevators, consider movie theaters, pep or political rallies, or department stores or malls during the holiday rush.

STRUCTURE

1. Where does Morris first introduce his threefold division? Explain how it determines the development of the remainder of the essay.
2. Examine paragraphs 18 and 20–21 and explain how division occurs within smaller units of the essay as well. Can you find other instances?
3. Examine Morris's transitions within each division, for example, at the end of paragraph 12 and the beginning of paragraph 13. Then compare them with those that introduce new divisions. What difference do you observe? Is it fair to say that the latter are themselves verbal territorial markers?
4. Morris frequently employs rhetorical techniques other than division-classification. Discuss the effectiveness of several of his examples and find instances of process analysis, comparison, and definition.

STYLE

1. Giving specific instances, explain whether the language and tone of "Territorial Behaviour" are what you might have expected from a trained zoologist.

2. Observe the juxtaposition of terse, simple sentences with longer, complex ones in paragraph 20:

> This is the ideal situation for non-social work, but space-sharers cannot enjoy this luxury. Their cocooning must be symbolic. They may, in certain cases, be able to erect small physical barriers, such as screens or partitions, which give substance to their invisible Personal Space boundaries, but when this cannot be done, other means must be sought. One of these is the "favoured object."

Find other instances of the technique and describe to what extent it is characteristic of the writing as a whole.

3. Do you find any humor here? If so, assess its significance or effect. If not, explain whether the essay escapes being written in deadly earnest.

CONSIDERATIONS

1. How do you respond to Morris's observing human beings as he would any other creature? Consider the description of marking behavior in dogs and humans in paragraph 5 and the definitions of family and "family territory" in paragraph 11. How might Morris's detachment be advantageous to his purpose? To the reader?

2. Observe the arrangement of your own family "nest." Does it differ significantly from Morris's description in paragraphs 11–12? Explain in a paragraph or two how any differences affect your or your family's territorial behavior.

3. Define yourself as a member of various "tribes." How strong is your loyalty to each of them? What are their territorial markers? Write a brief essay on this topic.

4. Examine your own behavior or that of others in crowded places such as those Morris describes in paragraphs 15–17 and 20–21. Does it differ materially from those in the text? Explain. Write an essay in which you define personal space on some basis other than physical proximity.

John S. Mbiti
(Kenya; b. 1931)

Primarily a theologian, Mbiti is also a linguist, folklorist, and poet. He was educated at Makerere College (now University) in Uganda, Barrington College in the United States, and Cambridge University, at which he took a bachelor's degree and doctorate in theology. He has been professor of theology and comparative religion at Makerere University and has also taught at the University of Hamburg, the University of Bern, and the Union Theological

Seminary in New York. For seven years he directed the Ecumenical Institute in Switzerland, where he currently resides.

Mbiti's scholarly writings include the source of the present selection, African Religions and Philosophy (1969), Concepts of God in Africa (1970), An Introduction to African Religion (1974), and African and Asian Contributions to Contemporary Theology (1977). His poetry, which he writes in both his native Kikamba and English, has appeared in several collections and in the independent volume Poems of Nature and Faith (1969). He has also translated stories from Kikamba in Akamba Stories (1966).

Following Mbiti's contrasts between Africa and the West will be especially useful to your understanding "The African Concept of Time."

The African Concept of Time

I PROPOSE TO DISCUSS the African concept of time as the key to our understanding of the basic religious and philosophical concepts. The concept of time may help to explain beliefs, attitudes, practices and general way of life of African peoples not only in the traditional set up but also in the modern situation (whether political, economic, educational or Church life). On this subject there is, unfortunately, no literature, and this is no more than a pioneer attempt which calls for further research and discussion.

A. Potential Time and Actual Time

The question of time is of little or no academic concern to African peoples in their traditional life. For them, time is simply a composition of events which have occurred, those which are taking place now and those which are immediately to occur. What has not taken place or what has no likelihood of an immediate occurrence falls in the category of "No-time." What is certain to occur, or what falls within the rhythm of natural phenomena, is in the category of inevitable or *potential time*.

The most significant consequence of this is that, according to traditional concepts, time is a two-dimensional phenomenon, with a long *past*, a *present* and virtually *no future*. The linear concept of time in western thought, with an indefinite past, present and infinite future, is practically foreign to African thinking. The future is virtually absent because events which lie in it have not taken place, they have not been realized and cannot, therefore, constitute time. If, however, future events are certain to occur, or if they fall within the inevitable rhythm of nature, they at best constitute only *potential time*, not *actual time*. What is taking place now no doubt unfolds the future, but once an event has taken place, it is no longer in the future but in the present and the past. *Actual time* is therefore what is present and what is past. It moves "backward" rather than "forward"; and people set their minds not on future things, but chiefly on what has taken place.

This time orientation, governed as it is by the two main dimensions of the present and the past, dominates African understanding of the individual, the community and the universe. . . . Time has to be experienced in order to make sense or to become real. A person experiences time partly in his own individual life, and partly through the society which goes back many generations before his own birth. Since what is in the future has not been experienced, it does not make sense; it cannot, therefore, constitute part of time, and people do not know how to think about it—unless, of course, it is something which falls within the rhythm of natural phenomena.

In the east African languages in which I have carried out research and tested my findings, there are no concrete words or expressions to convey the idea of a distant future. We shall illustrate this point by considering the main verb tenses in the Kikamba and Gikuyu languages. (See table.)

The three verb tenses which refer to the future (numbers 1–3), cover the period of about six months, or not beyond two years at most. Coming events have to fall within the range of these verb tenses, otherwise such events lie beyond the horizon of what constitutes actual time. At most we can say that this short future is only an extension of the present. People have little or no active interest in events that lie in the future beyond, at most, two years from now; and the languages concerned lack words by which such events can be conceived or expressed.

B. Time Reckoning and Chronology

When Africans reckon time, it is for a concrete and specific purpose, in connection with events but not just for the sake of mathematics. Since time is a composition of events, people cannot and do not reckon it in vacuum. Numerical calendars, with one or two possible exceptions, do not exist in African traditional societies as far as I know. If such calendars exist, they are likely to be of a short duration, stretching back perhaps a few decades, but certainly not into the realms of centuries.

Instead of numerical calendars there are what one would call *phenomenon calendars,* in which the events or phenomena which constitute time are reckoned or considered in their relation with one another and as they take place, i.e. as they constitute time. For example, an expectant mother counts the lunar months of her pregnancy; a traveller counts the number of days it takes him to walk (in former years) from one part of the country to another. The day, the month, the year, one's life time or human history, are all divided up or reckoned according to their specific events, for it is these that make them meaningful.

Analysis of African Concept of Time, as Illustrated by a Consideration of Verb Tenses among the Akamba and Gikuyu of Kenya

	TENSE	KIKAMBA	GIKUYU	ENGLISH	APPROXIMATE TIME
	1. Far Future or Remote Future	Ningauka	Ningoka	I will come	About 2 to 6 months from now
	2. Immediate or Near Future	Ninguka	Ninguka	I will come	Within the next short while
	3. Indefinite Future or Indefinite Near Future	Ngooka (ngauka)	Ningoka	I will come	Within a foreseeable while, after such and such an event
Sasa	4. Present or Present Progressive	Ninukite	Nindiroka	I am coming	In the process of action, now
	5. Immediate Past or Immediate Perfect	Ninauka (ninooka)	Nindoka	I came (I have just come)	In the last hour or so
	6. Today's Past	Ninukie	Ninjukire	I came	From the time of rising up to about two hours ago
Zamani	7. Recent Past or Yesterday's Past	Nininaukie (nininookie)	Nindirokire	I came	Yesterday
	8. Far Past or Remote Past	Ninookie (ninaukie)	Nindokire	I came	Any day before yesterday
	9. Unspecified Tene (Zamani)	Tene ninookie (Nookie tene)	Nindookire tene	I came	No specific time in the "past"

324

For example, the rising of the sun is an event which is recognized by the whole community. It does not matter, therefore, whether the sun rises at 5 A.M. or 7 A.M., so long as it rises. When a person says that he will meet another at sunrise, it does not matter whether the meeting takes place at 5 A.M. or 7 A.M., so long as it is during the general period of sunrise. Likewise, it does not matter whether people go to bed at 9 P.M. or at 12 midnight; the important thing is the event of going to bed, and it is immaterial whether in one night this takes place at 10 P.M. while in another it is at midnight. For the people concerned, time is meaningful at the point of the event and not at the mathematical moment.

In western or technological society, time is a commodity which must   10 be utilized, sold and bought; but in traditional African life, time has to be created or produced. Man is not a slave of time; instead, he "makes" as much time as he wants. When foreigners, especially from Europe and America, come to Africa and see people sitting down somewhere without, evidently, doing anything, they often remark, "These Africans waste their time by just sitting down idle!" Another common cry is, "Oh, Africans are always late!" It is easy to jump to such judgments, but they are judgments based on ignorance of what time means to African peoples. Those who are seen sitting down, are actually *not wasting* time, but either waiting for time or in the process of "producing" time. One does not want to belabour this small point, but certainly the basic concept of time underlies and influences the life and attitudes of African peoples in the villages, and to a great extent those who work or live in the cities as well. Among other things, the economic life of the people is deeply bound to their concept of time; and as we shall attempt to indicate, many of their religious concepts and practices are intimately connected with this fundamental concept of time.

The day in traditional life, is reckoned according to its significant events. For example, among the Ankore of Uganda, cattle are at the heart of the people. Therefore the day is reckoned in reference to events pertaining to cattle. Thus approximately:

6 A.M. is milking time (*akasbesbe*).

12 noon is time for cattle and people to take rest (*bari omubirago*), since, after milking the cattle, the herdsmen drive them out to the pasture grounds and by noon when the sun is hot, both herdsmen and cattle need some rest.

1 P.M. is the time to draw water (*baaza ahamaziba*), from the wells or the rivers, before cattle are driven there to drink (when they would pollute it, or would be a hindrance to those drawing and carrying the water).

2 P.M. is the time for cattle to drink (*amasyo niganywa*), and the herdsmen drive them to the watering places.

3 P.M. is the time when cattle leave their watering places and start grazing again (*amasyo nigakuka*).

5 P.M. is the time when the cattle return home (*ente niitaha*), being driven by the herdsmen.

6 P.M. is the time when the cattle enter their kraals or sleeping places (*ente zaataha*).

7 P.M. is milking time again, before the cattle sleep; and this really closes the day.

The month. Lunar rather than numerical months are recognized, because of the event of the moon's changes. In the life of the people, certain events are associated with particular months, so that the months are named according to either the most important events or the prevailing weather conditions. For example, there is the "hot" month, the month of the first rains, the weeding month, the beans harvest month, the hunting month, etc. It does not matter whether the "hunting month" lasts 25 or 35 days: the event of hunting is what matters much more than the mathematical length of the month. We shall take an example from the Latuka people, to show how the events govern the approximate reckoning of months:

October is called "The Sun," because the sun is very hot at that time.

December is called "Give your uncle water," because water is very scarce and people become thirsty readily.

February is called "Let them dig!" because it is at this time that people begin to prepare their fields for planting, since the rains are about to return.

May is known as "Grain in the ear," for at that time grain begins to bear.

June is called "Dirty mouth," because children can now begin to eat the new grain, and in so doing get their mouths dirty.

July is known as "Drying grass," because the rains stop, the ground becomes dry and the grass begins to wither.

August is "Sweet grain," when people eat and harvest "sweet grain."

September is known as "Sausage Tree," because at this time the sausage tree (*kigalia africana*) begins to bear fruit.[1] (The fruit looks like a huge sausage, hence the name.)

And so the cycle is complete; the natural phenomena begin to repeat themselves once more and the year is over.

The year is likewise composed of events, but of a wider scale than those which compose either the day or the month. Where the community is agricultural, it is the seasonal activities that compose an agricultural year.

---

[1]Cf. L. F. Naider, ed., *A Tribal Survey of Mongalla Province* (1937), p. 11f., from which this has been adapted. [Au.]

Near the equator, for example, people would recognize two rain seasons and two dry seasons. When the number of season-periods is completed, then the year is also completed, since it is these four major seasons that make up an entire year. The actual number of days is irrelevant, since a year is not reckoned in terms of mathematical days but in terms of events. Therefore one year might have 350 days while another year has 390 days. The years may, and often do, differ in their length according to days, but not in their seasons and other regular events.

Since the years differ in mathematical length, numerical calendars are both impossible and meaningless in traditional life. Outside the reckoning of the year, African time concept is silent and indifferent. People expect the years to come and go, in an endless rhythm like that of day and night, and like the waning and waxing of the moon. They expect the events of the rain season, planting, harvesting, dry season, rain season again, planting again, and so on to continue for ever. Each year comes and goes, adding to the time dimension of the past. Endlessness or "eternity" for them is something that lies only in the region of the past, i.e. something in tense number 9 of our chart multiplied endless times. (When Christians speak of eternity in Kikamba or Gikuyu, they say "tene na tene," i.e. "tene and tene," or the period or state of tense number 9 multiplied by itself. This means that what is "eternal" lies beyond the horizon of events making up human experience or history.)

C. The Concept of Past, Present and Future

We must discuss further time dimensions and their relationship with African ontology.[2] Beyond a few months from now, as we have seen, African concept of time is silent and indifferent. This means that the future is virtually non-existent as *actual* time, apart from the relatively short projection of the present up to two years hence. To avoid the thought associations of the English words past, present and future, I propose to use two Swahili words, "Sasa" and "Zamani."

In our chart of the verb tenses, Sasa covers the "now-period" of tenses 1 to 7. Sasa has the sense of immediacy, nearness, and "now-ness"; and is the period of immediate concern for the people, since that is "where" or "when" they exist. What would be "future" is extremely brief. This has to be so because any meaningful event in the future must be so immediate and certain that people have almost experienced it. Therefore, if the event is remote, say beyond two years from now (tense number 4), then it cannot be conceived, it cannot be spoken of and the languages themselves have no verb tenses to cover that distant "future" dimension of time. When an event is far in the future, its reality is completely beyond or outside the horizon of the Sasa

15

[2] **ontology**: the nature of existence or being; the branch of philosophical study that deals with this subject. [Ed.]

period. Therefore, in African thought, the Sasa "swallows" up what in western or linear concept of time would be considered as the future. Events (which compose time) in the Sasa dimension must be either about to occur, or in the process of realization, or recently experienced. Sasa is the most meaningful period for the individual, because he has a personal recollection of the events or phenomena of this period, or he is about to experience them. Sasa is really an experiential extension of the Now-moment (tense number 4) stretched into the short future and into the unlimited past (or Zamani). Sasa is not mathematically or numerically constant. The older a person is, the longer is his Sasa period. The community also has its own Sasa, which is greater than that of the individual. But for both the community and the individual, the most vivid moment is the NOW point, the event of tense number 4. Sasa is the time region in which people are conscious of their existence, and within which they project themselves both into the short future and mainly into the past (Zamani). Sasa is in itself a complete or full time dimension, with its own short future, a dynamic present, and an experienced past. We might call it the *Micro-Time* (Little-Time). The Micro-Time is meaningful to the individual or the community only through their participating in it or experiencing it.

Zamani is not limited to what in English is called the past. It also has its own "past," "present" and "future," but on a wider scale. We might call it the *Macro-Time* (Big Time). Zamani overlaps with Sasa and the two are not separable. Sasa feeds or disappears into Zamani. But before events become incorporated into the Zamani, they have to become realized or actualized within the Sasa dimension. When this has taken place, then the events "move" backwards from the Sasa into the Zamani. So Zamani becomes the period beyond which nothing can go. Zamani is the graveyard of time, the period of termination, the dimension in which everything finds its halting point. It is the final storehouse for all phenomena and events, the ocean of time in which everything becomes absorbed into a reality that is neither after nor before.

Both Sasa and Zamani have quality and quantity. People speak of them as big, small, little, short, long, etc., in relation to a particular event or phenomenon. Sasa generally binds individuals and their immediate environment together. It is the period of conscious living. On the other hand, Zamani is the period of the myth, giving a sense of foundation or "security" to the Sasa period, and binding together all created things, so that all things are embraced within the Macro-Time.

D. The Concept of History and Pre-history

Each African people has its own history. This history moves "backward" from the Sasa period to the Zamani, from the moment of intense experience to the period beyond which nothing can go. In traditional African thought, there is no concept of history moving "forward" towards a future climax, or towards an end of the world. Since the future does not exist beyond a few months, the future cannot be expected to usher in a golden age, or a radically different state of affairs from what is in the Sasa and the Zamani. The notion of a messianic hope, or a final destruction of the world, has no place in [the] traditional concept of history. So African peoples have no "belief in progress," the idea that the development of human activities and achievements move from a low to a higher degree. The people neither plan for the distant future nor "build castles in the air." The centre of gravity for human thought and activities is the Zamani period, towards which the Sasa moves. People set their eyes on the Zamani, since for them there is no "World to Come," such as is found in Judaism and Christianity.

Both history and pre-history are dominated by the myth. There are   20 innumerable myths all over the continent of Africa explaining items like the creation of the universe, the first man, the apparent withdrawal of God from the world of mankind, the origin of the tribe and its arrival in its present country, and so on. People constantly look towards the Zamani, for Zamani has foundations on which the Sasa rests and by which it is explainable or should be understood. Zamani is not extinct, but a period full of activities and happenings. It is by looking towards the Zamani that people give or find an explanation about the creation of the world, the coming of death, the evolution of their language and customs, the emergence of their wisdom, and so on. The "golden age" lies in the Zamani, and not in the otherwise very short or non-existent future.

Such history and pre-history tend to be telescoped into a very compact, oral tradition and handed down from generation to generation. If we attempt to fit such traditions into a mathematical time-scale, they would appear to cover only a few centuries whereas in reality they stretch much further back; and some of them, being in the form of myths, defy any attempt to describe them on a mathematical time-scale. In any case, oral history has no dates to be remembered. Man looks back from whence he came, and man is certain that nothing will bring this world to a conclusion. According to this interpretation of African view of history, there are innumerable myths about Zamani, but no myths about any end of the world, since time has no end.[3] African peoples expect human history to continue forever, in the rhythm of moving from the Sasa to the Zamani and there is nothing to suggest that this

---

[3] The only possible exception to this statement comes from the Sonjo of Tanzania who think that the world will one day shrink to an end. This is not, however, something that dominates their life, and they go on living as though the idea did not exist. It could be that at one point in their history, their volcanic mountain (known in Maasai as Oldonyo Lengai: Mountain of God) erupted and caused an "end of the world" in their small country. This event may have been retained in the form of a myth which has been transferred to the unknown future, as a warning about possible future eruptions. See R. F. Gray *The Sonjo of Tanganyika* (1963) who, however, does not offer an explanation of this myth. [Au.]

rhythm shall ever come to an end: the days, months, seasons and years have no end, just as there is no end to the rhythm of birth, marriage, procreation and death.

E. The Concept of Human Life in Relation to Time

Human life has another rhythm of nature which nothing can destroy. On the level of the individual, this rhythm includes birth, puberty, initiation, marriage, procreation, old age, death, entry into the community of the departed and finally entry into the company of the spirits. It is an ontological rhythm, and these are the key moments in the life of the individual. On the community or national level, there is the cycle of the seasons with their different activities like sowing, cultivating, harvesting and hunting. The key events or moments are given more attention than others, and may often be marked by religious rites and ceremonies. Unusual events or others which do not fit into this rhythm, such as an eclipse, drought, the birth of twins and the like, are generally thought to be bad omens, or to be events requiring special attention from the community, and this may take the form of a religious activity. The abnormal or unusual is an invasion of the ontological harmony. . . .

G. Space and Time

Space and time are closely linked, and often the same word is used for both. As with time, it is the content which defines space. What matters most to the people is what is geographically near, just as Sasa embraces the life that people experience. For this reason, Africans are particularly tied to the land, because it is the concrete expression of both their Zamani and their Sasa. The land provides them with the roots of existence, as well as binding them mystically to their departed. People walk on the graves of their forefathers, and it is feared that anything separating them from these ties will bring disaster to family and community life. To remove Africans by force from their land is an act of such great injustice that no foreigner can fathom it. Even when people voluntarily leave their homes in the countryside and go to live or work in the cities, there is a fundamental severing of ties which cannot be repaired and which often creates psychological problems with which urban life cannot as yet cope.

H. Discovering or Extending the Future Dimension of Time

Partly because of Christian missionary teaching, partly because of western-type education, together with the invasion of modern technology with all it involves, African peoples are discovering the future dimensions of time. On the secular level this leads to national planning for economic growth, political independence, extension of educational facilities and so on. But the change from the structure built around the traditional concept of time, to one which should accommodate this new discovery of the future dimension, is not a smooth one and may well be at the root of, among other things, the political instability of our nations. In church life this discovery seems to create a strong expectation of the millennium. This makes many Christians escape from facing the challenges of this life into the state of merely hoping and waiting for the life of paradise. This strong millennial expectation often leads to the creation of many small independent churches centred around individuals who symbolize, and more or less fulfil, this messianic expectation.

The discovery and extension of the future dimension of time poses great 25 potentialities and promises for the shaping of the entire life of African peoples. If these are harnessed and channelled into creative and productive use, they will no doubt become beneficial; but they can get out of control and precipitate both tragedy and disillusionment.

The traditional concept of time is intimately bound up with the entire life of the people, and our understanding of it may help to pave the way for understanding the thinking, attitude and actions of the people.

THESIS AND THOUGHT

1. Describe the African concept of time as Mbiti presents it. In what specific ways does it differ from the western concept?

2. Explain how the African concept of time is integral to African culture as Mbiti describes it.

3. How is the African concept of time related to the traditional African connection to the land?

4. What philosophical and practical problems arise when Western views of time are introduced into African cultures—particularly through Christianity?

STRUCTURE

1. Beginning with the subheads, identify the various divisions or classifications of topics that are central to the essay. Explain their role in establishing Mbiti's analysis.

2. Mbiti employs several rhetorical techniques in addition to the dominant analysis. Examine his comparisons in paragraphs 3, 8, 10, and elsewhere and evaluate their contribution to the essay's effectiveness. Do the same for examples in paragraphs 8, 9, 11, 12, and 13. Do you find any of them excessive? Explain.

STYLE

1. Aside from those included in the chart, Mbiti uses words of African origin in paragraphs 11 and 15ff. Do you find them necessary or useful to understanding Mbiti's ideas? Equally so?

2. The opening sentence of the selection is an "announcement." Is it essential to the reading as we have it here? Rewrite the paragraph in which it appears so that it suggests Mbiti's purposes more fully and smoothly.

3. The word *people* appears twice in the sentence that comprises paragraph 26. Rewrite the sentence to eliminate one of them. Which version do you prefer? Why?

CONSIDERATIONS

1. In what ways do Westerners deal with the future beyond the two-year outside limit Mbiti attributes to Africans?

2. By Western standards, Africans pay too little attention to the future. Do we pay sufficient attention to our past or *Zamani*? Write a substantial paragraph in which you explain how your being a college student is consistent with the concept of time to which you (and your culture) subscribe.

3. Of what importance is the cycle of natural events to Western culture? To your life personally? Write an essay in which you compare living according to the calendar with living according to natural cycles.

Raymond Chang
(China and United States; b. 1939)

Margaret Scrogin Chang
(United States; b. 1941)

Born in Hong Kong, Raymond Chang spent his childhood there, in Shanghai, and finally in Hong Kong once more, as his family fled first the Japanese occupation of China and then the Maoist revolution. In England by seventeen, he eventually earned a degree in chemistry from the University of London. Chang later took his master's and doctorate at Yale and today is professor of chemistry at Williams College. He has written several textbooks and is a specialist in physical chemistry.

For some years at Williams, Chang taught an intersession course in introductory Chinese. Finding no suitable lay text for Chinese language and culture, he conceived the idea for Speaking of Chinese *(1978), which he wrote with his wife, Margaret. "Four Treasures of the Study" is a selection from this text.*

Margaret Scrogin Chang took her B.A. at Scripps College and master's degrees from Simmons College and Rutgers University. A writer, particularly of literature for children, she teaches children's literature at North Adams State College. Among her major publications is In the Eye of War *(1991), a juvenile novel, which she wrote jointly with her husband.*

Four Treasures of the Study

THE Oriental calligrapher has four basic tools, called "Four Treasures of the Study." They are brush, ink, inkstone, and paper. The first three have certainly been used since the Shang dynasty (ca. 1766–ca. 1122 B.C.), most likely even earlier.

In the Han dynasty (202 B.C.–220 A.D.), the glorious age that gave its name to the Chinese people, the quartet of scholarly treasures became complete with the invention of paper. The most formal styles of calligraphy are taken from inscriptions on stone and bronze made during the earlier Chou (ca. 1122–249 B.C.) and Ch'in (221–207 B.C.) dynasties, yet because the brush moves more freely over paper than any other writing surface in use before the Han dynasty, Chinese characters had reached a form modern readers of Chinese would recognize, and basic calligraphic styles had been established, to be practiced with infinite variations by generations of calligraphers to come.

The oldest and most distinctively Chinese of the Four Treasures is the writing brush, or *brush-pen,* as it is sometimes called. The Chinese brush . . . is perfectly round, unlike the flat lettering brushes of Western sign painters. It consists of three basic parts: holder, hair, and sheath. The holder, or handle, is a length of bamboo tube or a hollow wooden rod. The hair, or brush, is constructed in layers. A central bunch of deer or rabbit hair is surrounded by an outer circle of softer hairs taken from goats or wolves. This bundle of hair is tied firmly with silk or hemp string; the tied end is then dipped in lacquer or glue and inserted into the holder. Fine brushes are then covered with a sheath or cap to protect the delicate hairs.

Brushes come in all different sizes. The biggest, large enough to paint a house, is used for billboard-sized characters. The tiniest, the size of a single grain of rice, is used for the most delicate lines. With a brush, the writer can alter the width and strength of strokes because a brush can absorb different quantities of ink and respond to rapid changes in pressure against the paper. With a brush, the writer can create a pleasing symmetry of strokes within each character, and can imbue his writing with the dynamic life of natural forms: rivers, waterfalls, mountains, and leaves. Good brushes may last a lifetime; calligraphers can and do spend fortunes on them, especially when their handles are made of ivory, jade, or gold. An excellent brush is a writer's beloved friend, and calligraphers who outlive their brushes have been known to bury the worn-out tool with great ceremony.

The Chinese brush is almost certainly as old as the language itself.   5
Pottery five thousand years old, excavated from various sites around northern China, bears decorations of black slip, skillfully applied with a brush. This Neolithic brush is the direct ancestor of all the ones used today. Oracle bone inscriptions were written first with a brush, then incised by a craftsman skilled enough to push his sharp instrument along the wendings of every brushstroke.

Meng T'ien, a Ch'in dynasty general who supervised construction of the Great Wall, gets traditional credit for inventing the brush, even though all he really did was make it better. As court historian for Shih Huang-ti, the Tiger of Ch'in, his constant use of brushes must have inspired plenty of ideas for improved construction. Brushes in his day were about a foot long and made of bamboo. One of Meng's ideas may have been to substitute a smooth wooden rod for the more awkward bamboo holder.

A brush must be dipped in ink, though Chinese brushes never sink into bottles. Chinese ink is stored and carried as a solid black bar, sometimes incised with decorations and characters traced in gold. This bar, or ink stick . . . is prepared by jelling crushed soot with glue. When ready to write, the calligrapher grinds the bar with a few drops of water on an inkstone until he has achieved his desired consistency.

The stick form allows a writer to vary the ink solution according to his needs, from blackest black to palest gray. Bottled liquid ink may be more convenient, but it does not allow this flexibility. In the days of the emperors, a scholar kept a young boy called a "scholar-kid" in his household. This little person would fetch and carry, do odd jobs, and grind the scholar's ink. Then as now, an ink stick just six inches long and one inch wide used daily by a calligrapher would last at least a year.

The Chinese have always been master inkmakers. Western artists, who appreciated its quality, have used Chinese ink for centuries, although they call it "India ink." Ink in solid form was probably always used in China. Soot, available wherever fire burns, is obviously good for making black marks. Very early on, controlled burning of tung oil, petroleum, or pine wood was found to produce a fine-grade soot called lampblack, which was then mixed with glue extracted from fish skins or leather by-products. Red ink made from cinnabar was used in the Shang dynasty, particularly for the most important official documents, but its use fell off in later eras, except as an ink for seals.

The invention of ink is traditionally attributed to a calligrapher and   10
inkmaker named Wei Tan, who lived during the late Han dynasty, around the third century A.D. In those days, it was common for the emperor to present favored courtiers with ink. Wei Tan refused the present, preferring to make his own ink, which was said to be most intensely black. Wei Tan's contribution to inkmaking amounted to improvement only, for we know ink was used

before the Han dynasty. A recipe handed down since the fifth century A.D., possibly Wei Tan's own, goes as follows:

> Fine and pure soot is to be pounded and strained in a jar through a sieve of thin silk. This process is to free the soot of any adhering vegetable substance so that it becomes like fine sand or dust. It is very light in weight, and great care should be taken to prevent it from being scattered around by not exposing it to the air after straining. To make one catty of ink, five ounces of the best glue must be dissolved in the juice of the bark of the *ch'in* tree which is called *fan-chi* wood in the southern part of the Yangtze valley. The juice of this bark is green in color; it dissolves the glue and improves the color of the ink.
>
> Add five egg whites, one ounce of cinnabar, and the same amount of musk, after they have been separately treated and well strained. All these ingredients are mixed in an iron mortar; a paste, preferably dry rather than damp, is obtained after pounding thirty thousand times, or pounding more for a better quality.
>
> The best time for mixing ink is before the second and after the ninth month in a year. It will decay and produce a bad odor if the weather is too warm, or will be hard to dry and melt if too cold, which causes breakage when exposed to air. The weight of each piece of ink cake should not exceed two to three ounces. The secret of an ink is as described; to keep the pieces small rather than large.[1]

The inkstone . . . is the companion of the ink stick. Its most basic form, easily found these days at Chinese stationeries and ordinary art supply stores, is a rectangular black stone with a shallow tray carved in the top. The tray dips down to a trough at one end. The dry ink stick is ground against the flat surface of the tray and mixed with water brushed up from the trough. A good inkstone should be slightly rough and absorbent, for a perfectly smooth inkstone would be unfit for grinding, while an overly porous one would take in all the ink. Since ink was probably solid from the earliest days, it is safe to assume that there was some kind of palette to grind it on, although the oldest known inkstone dates from the Han dynasty. Early calligraphers used ink-stones made of earthen bricks, and later generations prized the fine brick tiles from a palace called Bronze Bird, built by Ts'ao Ts'ao in 210 A.D., as well as the smooth stones from Tuan-chi Quarry in Kwangtung Province. Inkstones may be had in many shapes and sizes. Some are elaborately carved and decorated, with handsome fittings of wood or lacquer.

Finally, a calligrapher needs paper, the fourth treasure of his retreat. The best paper is handmade, even today, with a coarse texture that will absorb and spread the ink. This rough paper is perfect for a calligraphic style marked by irregularity, asymmetry, and individual eccentricities. The ink-laden brush

---

[1]**Fine . . . large:** Tsien Tsien-hsuin, *Written on Bamboo and Silk* (Chicago: University of Chicago Press, 1962), 166–67.

traveling across its textured surface leaves a line richer for being absorbed and spread; the nearly dry brush skimming its little hills and valleys leaves a strong, roughly broken line. . . .

Oriental paper is entirely unsuited to pen writing, as many a casual customer of a Chinese stationer discovers when he puts fountain pen to letter paper from Japan or Taiwan. The pen skips and clogs, making a dreadful mess on a surface intended as a vehicle for the brush.

Orientals cherish good paper. In Japan, where paper is still made by hand, master papermakers, as holders of "intangible cultural properties," i.e., the techniques of papermaking, are designated "Living National Treasures" by a national cultural committee and the Ministry of Education. Japanese paper is tough, slightly stretchy, absorbent, and long-lasting. Natural dyes added during the manufacturing process create a rainbow of muted colors. Because one of its ingredients is mashed fiber from the paper mulberry tree, Japanese paper, or *washi,* is correctly termed "mulberry paper."

The basic steps in making paper are as follows. First, cellulose fibers from   15
trees, grasses, or rags are macerated until every single fiber is separate. These individual fibers are then mixed with water, and lifted from the water in a thin sheet spread over a *mold,* or large, flat screen. Water drains through the screen, and the matted fibers left to dry on the screen's surface become paper. This process, one of China's contributions to world technology, is still the foundation of the most sophisticated machine manufacturing techniques.

The invention of paper in China is accurately recorded as 105 A.D. Before then, characters had been brushed on bamboo, silk, and a kind of quasi-paper produced from silk scraps by a method akin to feltmaking.

Now a woman steps onto the scene, one of those women we meet now and then in Chinese history whose brains and strong will repudiate our traditional image of the silent, submissive Oriental female. She was the emperor's consort, Madam Teng, crowned empress in 102 A.D. A lover of literature, she scorned the rare and precious gifts she received from other countries on the occasion of her coronation. All she wanted was quasi-paper and ink.

Into this court, where literature and calligraphy were the royal fashion, came Ts'ai Lun, a eunuch placed at the head of an imperial manufacturing office. Unlike Meng T'ien and Wei Tan, to whom Chinese tradition gives totally undeserved credit for inventing brush and ink, Ts'ai Lun may actually have invented paper. Although he probably did not spend his nights fiddling around with wet rags, shredded grass, and a mold, he supervised workers who did. He could well have been the person who looked at a pile of silk scraps, discarded fishing nets, hemp, and tree bark, and thought, "There's paper in there."

True paper has been found that may predate Ts'ai Lun, but scholars do not agree on its authenticity, and until more certain evidence is found, the world must, like old-fashioned Chinese papermakers who burned incense before his portrait, honor Ts'ai Lun as the inventor of paper.

The History of the Later Han Dynasty tells us that in 105 A.D. Ts'ai Lun   20
reported the manufacture of paper to the emperor, and that the emperor was pleased enough to ennoble Ts'ai Lun. History does not report Empress Teng's reaction, but she must have prized the new material and may have been one of the first to try her calligraphy on it. Ts'ai Lun's product was called *zhǐ*, written with the radical for *silk*, ever after the word for *paper* in Chinese. (The English word *paper* is rooted in the Latin *papyrus*, a writing material used by the ancient Egyptians which is not true paper.)

Ts'ai Lun did not live to be an old man, basking in the glory of his creation. Years after he first made paper, he was caught in the middle of a court intrigue and had to poison himself, but his invention was a landmark in the history of world communication. Buddhist monks carried the paper-making process to Korea and Japan in the fourth and fifth centuries A.D. Merchants and bureaucrats moved it slowly westward, and Chinese paper-makers captured by Moslem troops in a battle fought in Turkestan (extreme western China) in 751 A.D. taught the craft to their captors. The Moslems began manufacturing paper in Samarkand, where bounteous fields of flax and hemp and plenty of pure water encouraged the production of superior paper.

By 1300, when Italy stood on the threshold of the Renaissance, the technique had reached Fabriano, Italy, still an important center of Italian papermaking. In another hundred years, paper was manufactured in Nurem-berg, Germany, and half a century later it was found to be the best surface for receiving ink off newly discovered movable type. From then on, history would never be the same. . . .

THESIS AND THOUGHT

1. What insights into Chinese civilization and history does the account of the four treasures provide?

2. What influence have some of the treasures had on other civilizations?

3. According to the Changs, how are the four treasures suited to each other and their common purpose?

STRUCTURE

1. Assess the significance of process analysis and narration here within the broader arrangement by types. Consider especially paragraphs 2, 7, 10, 15, and 17–22.

2. What function do the opening sentences of paragraphs 3, 7, 11, and 12 have in common? Is movement within each of the essay's major divisions as immediately apparent? Need it be? Explain.

3. The phrase "four treasures" appears in the opening paragraph, "treasures" in paragraph 2, and "the fourth treasure" in paragraph 12. Explain how the word and its variants might have been used more frequently and effectively as a structural (and stylistic) device.

STYLE

1. In paragraph 8 the Changs translate a Chinese word as "scholar-kid." In paragraph 18 they doubt that Ts'ai Lun spent "his nights fiddling around with wet rags." How characteristic of their style is such **colloquialism?** Describe the audience for which the writing seems generally intended.

2. Explain the meanings of *slip* in paragraph 5 and *retreat* in paragraph 12.

3. Of late, the word *Oriental* (paras. 14 and 17) has come under attack in some quarters, its opponents preferring *Asian* instead. What distinction, particularly in connotation, is there between the two words? Why might people to whom it refers find the difference significant? Check a current standard dictionary for definitions and etymologies. Do you see any parallel between the proposed shift from *Oriental* to *Asian* and that from *Negro* to *black* in the 1960s and the preference of some for *African American* currently? Who decides which terms to use?

CONSIDERATIONS

1. In paragraph 4 the authors report the ceremonial burial of brushes among the Chinese and in paragraph 14 the honor paid to "master papermakers" in Japan. Is there any similar reverence for a useful object or occupation in either Western civilization or in any other culture with which you may be familiar? If so, write a paragraph describing it and another defining its purpose. Alternatively, write a paragraph proposing such a ritual and another explaining its necessity.

2. In Chinese tradition, calligraphy is considered an art form. See, for example, paragraph 4: "With a brush, the writer can create a pleasing symmetry of strokes within each character, and can imbue his writing with the dynamic life of natural forms: rivers, waterfalls, mountains, and leaves." Is there a similar aesthetic view of writing in Western culture? If not, what status does it have? Write a paragraph in which you compare the Chinese and Western attitudes.

3. Write an essay in which you explain and describe the variety of tools used to perform a specific task or activity at which you excel. Emphasize types rather than processes.

Suggestions for Writing:
Division-Classification and Analysis

I. Write a division-classification essay based on one of the following undifferentiated groups. Avoid both ready-made categories and stereotypes. Be sure to clarify your purpose.

—physicians, plumbers, lawyers, clergy, athletes, salesclerks, or members of some other profession, trade, or occupation

—horror films

—poets, painters, dancers, musicians, actors, or other artists

—customs

—vices or virtues

—heroes and heroines

—folk or ethnic music

—campus characters

—fads or fashions

—television shows for children

—nonverbal communication

II. Write an analysis of one of the topics below. Keep the points of the analysis firmly in your mind and the reader's as you develop the essay.

—a character in a play, film, or work of fiction

—a painting, piece of music, or poem

—a current problem on campus or in your community

—a rite (or rites) of passage in a culture other than your own (Consider birth, naming, coming of age, marriage, or death.)

—the personality of someone you know well

—gender roles in the 1990s

—a scientific theory, philosophical system, or religious practice with which you are familiar

—the teaching technique of one of your professors

—contemporary etiquette

—a business, civic, or other organization with which you are familiar

—an event of either personal or historic significance

7

Cause and Effect

Cause and effect, means and ends, seed and fruit, cannot be
severed; for the effect already blooms in the cause, the end
preexists in the means, the fruit in the seed.

RALPH WALDO EMERSON, *Compensation*

Overanxious Parent: It's cold out. Better wear your coat or you'll catch
pneumonia.

Indestructible Offspring: I'll be warm enough. And you don't get pneumonia from being cold. You get it from a bacillus—bacteria.

Overanxious Parent: I know what a bacillus is. And if you're cold, your
resistance is lowered. And the lower your resistance, the more likely you
are to get sick.

Indestructible Offspring: Okay. Okay. I'll put on a sweater or something.
(*exits*)

Overanxious Parent: (*calling after*) And a pair of gloves. (*door slams*) Or
you'll get frostbite.

The true issues of this perhaps-familiar exchange are power and independence. But they are played out in the context of a debate about the causes of
pneumonia and the possible effects of not dressing warmly. Typical of ordinary
conversation, the dialogue treats cause and effect casually. Writing, however,
often demands that causal connections be established with considerable care.

DEFINING CAUSES AND EFFECTS:
THE POST HOC FALLACY

Causes are those actions or circumstances which can be (reasonably)
shown to help produce, wholly or in part, other, consequent events or conditions. Conversely, effects are those events or conditions that demonstrably

341

(or arguably) occur, wholly or in part, as a result of prior actions or circum-stances. The qualifications in the two preceding sentences are not "weasel words." They are used because exact correspondence between causes and effects is extremely difficult to establish: any isolated effect is likely to be the product of multiple causes of varying significance, just as any isolated cause is likely to produce many effects of differing importance and intensity, and the sequence of events or circumstances alone is insufficient to confirm connec-tions among them.

Although causes obviously precede effects and effects necessarily follow causes, mere chronology does not determine causation. The singing of the legendary tenor Enrico Caruso, for example, had no perceptible effect on the vocalizations of Axl Rose, although it preceded them by several decades. "But," you say, "you are talking about two very different types of music. No one would expect Caruso to have affected Rose. Rose might never have even heard Caruso sing." Two valid points.

It is not simply a matter of Caruso's having sung prior to Rose. It is, at least, also a matter of Rose's exposure. The principle that simple chronology does not determine causation applies, however, even within rock music itself. The raucous aggressiveness that typifies Rose's style might also describe ele-ments in Elvis Presley, or Little Richard. But Rose's style might not derive from these two, even if he was exposed to their music. Perhaps he didn't care for it much.

Perhaps, instead, he was fascinated by live performances of Disintegrat-ing Gallstones—a group that never recorded but was hot for six months in Birmingham about 1980. Suppose that after every show he'd go home to imitate the sound and gestures of its lead singer, Howland Yawp. Perhaps, since the foregoing account is entirely fictitious (sorry), he was enthralled in childhood with the sounds he produced by beating on pots and pans—or on his playmates. All of these might have *preceded* the emergence of his style. None of them *necessarily* contributed to it. The strongest model for causation, however, is presented here by the imaginary instance of the Gallstones. It is plausible precisely because it offers evidence of *interaction* and *interdepen-dence*. Moral: cause and effect do not live by chronology alone.

Of course, causation—influence, really—in music, art, or literature is often elusive at best. But the idea that precedence is insufficient to establish causal connections may be seen clearly in the context of more ordinary experience. Consider, for example, the old joke about the homeowner who, thousands of miles from either India or Siberia, has hung an exotic and reputedly powerful charm above the door:

Curious Visitor: Why is that charm up there?

Homeowner: Protects the house from tigers.

Curious Visitor: Does it work?

Homeowner: Haven't seen one yet.

Like the joke, superstitions of all sorts depend on faulty ideas of causation, particularly in regard to chronology. The supposed ill consequences of walking under ladders, stepping on cracks, and breaking mirrors all make irrational connections between actions and succeeding events based solely on their sequence. Ancient rhetoricians labeled such reasoning **post hoc**, *ergo propter hoc* ("after this, therefore because of this") and recognized it as fallacious. We still do.

What then constitutes legitimate causal analysis? Clearly a relationship between conditions or events that goes beyond simple chronology. Partly this is a matter of experience—whether experts' or your own.

For example, little more than a century ago, researchers such as Louis Pasteur showed, through both observation and experiment, that various diseases (effects) were associated with the presence of various microbes (causes). To oversimplify, if the microbes were present in sufficient numbers, illness would almost invariably occur. Other discoveries revealed the specific mechanisms (causes and effects) by which the diseases were produced and could be cured or prevented—including pasteurization. Although the germ theory of disease is a truth by which all Overanxious Parents and Indestructible Offspring now live, it was regarded skeptically until almost the end of the nineteenth century—until the causal connections between the microorganisms and specific illnesses were satisfactorily *demonstrated*.

Claims of causal connection are, in fact, only as strong as they are verifiable and demonstrable. It is true, however, that in other matters—social or historical rather than scientific—such hard evidence is difficult to come by. This difficulty alone suggests that assertions concerning cause be expressed in ways that imply something less than absolute certainty. We are wiser to think in terms of suspected "probable cause" or effect than to proclaim that our proposed causes or effects are valid "beyond a reasonable doubt." Especially in dealing with human behavior, such doubt is likely to be common.

THE CAUSAL CHAIN

Although chronology does not determine causes and effects, once a series of causal connections is established, it may be seen as a set of links in a sequential chain—or better still, a chain segment. Hypothetically, at least, causal chains may well be infinite, but even if they are finite, their end points and many intermediate links may be so far removed from our central concerns that their existence becomes insignificant. One might, like the medieval churchman and philosopher Saint Thomas Aquinas, trace all effects back to a single or original cause, namely, God. (Or, if one is of a scientific bent, back to the original all-creating "big bang.") But there is rarely a need to do either.

For instance, in the debate at the beginning of this chapter, the Over-anxious Parent begins with the fact that it is cold but ignores the movement of the jet stream, pressure systems, the tilt of the earth in relation to the sun—all of which might be contributing causes of the low temperature. Similarly, the Indestructible Offspring wisely disregards the evolutionary history of *Diplococcus pneumoniae*.

Had the Indestructible Offspring not left, perhaps the debate might have continued a bit further in exploring effects. The OP might have conjured up consequences of the dread pneumonia: missed classes, poor grades, lost financial aid, economic hardship, more time spent earning money, grades suffering further because of this, and—skipping a few hundred links—a mediocre job at mediocre pay in a mediocre career at the center of a mediocre existence, all because of not wearing a coat on a cold day. Taking another tack, the OP might have produced visions of medical bills, economic disaster, bankruptcy, and—ignoring current legal reality—debtor's prison. Perhaps our parents might also have foreseen permanently damaged lungs, chronic disability, and premature death.

As eavesdroppers, we might find some of these projected effects plausible—the bills, the missed classes—but we probably laugh at the idea of total ruin as a highly improbable (though remotely possible) consequence of not dressing appropriately. The point is that explorations of causes and effects are almost always limited to those that are essential to the topic at hand. As the topics themselves are necessarily limited, so must the discussion of causes and effects be restricted to the significant segments of possible causal chains.

Given such restrictions, we tend to treat these segments as chains in themselves, with the first and last links regarded as initial causes and ultimate effects, respectively. Any intermediate link may be seen as both cause and effect, depending upon our perspective. Take, for example, the following improbable system. It consists of the rising sun shining through a window, a sleeping cat, a mouse, a ramp, a bucket of water, and a trip device atop a platform, and beneath the platform, a sleeper whose head is approximately in line with the bucket. The sunlight awakens the cat, which, seeing the mouse, chases it up the ramp, where the rodent releases the mechanism, thus tilting the bucket—whose spill splashes and awakens the sleeper.

In this poor substitute for an alarm clock, we have the rising sun as the first cause and the sleeper's awakening as the ultimate effect (never mind why the sun rose or whether the sleeper caught pneumonia because of the dousing). These first and last links are connected only to one other; however, the intermediate links are joined to two others and therefore represent the consequences of preceding causes and the causes of a succeeding effects. For instance, because the cat chases it, the mouse runs (effect), but the running (cause) results in the release of the trip device (effect). Similarly, the tripping is responsible (cause) for the water spill (effect), and so on.

The designation of initial and final links in this or any other causal chain segment is purposeful and selective, not arbitrary. The issue is focus. If we are concerned with awakening the sleeper, once that is accomplished we need not continue. Nor do we have to include the rotation of the earth on its axis as a cause setting the "clock" in motion. But had we been interested in the sleeper's fate, we might have begun, not with the sunrise, but with the spilled water, and continued through the slip on the wet floor, the back injury, the canceled vacation, the short-term depression, and so on. Or, if we were interested in the mouse, we might have begun with the chase, omitted the tipped bucket and aroused sleeper altogether, and concentrated on what befell the creature apparently stranded on a platform with a cat in hot pursuit.

DEGREES OF CAUSATION

Notwithstanding what you have just read, it is necessary, particularly in dealing with a complex subject, to go beyond the most apparent and immediate causes or effects and examine more distant ones, which often are of greater significance. Generally, the degrees of causation may be described as immediate or precipitating, intermediate, and ultimate, underlying, or fundamental.

A precipitating cause is often a triggering event—the straw that breaks the camel's back. But the camel has to be carrying a considerable load prior to the addition of that straw. This already large burden might be seen as an intermediate cause. Underlying causes might include the camel's physical condition, the carelessness of its driver, the greed of the straw merchant.

By way of illustration, let's examine some of the causes in one possible assessment of the Persian Gulf War.

> In response to Iraq's August 1990 invasion and occupation of Kuwait and recognizing that further attempts at negotiation were likely to be futile, the United Nations issued an ultimatum demanding that Saddam Hussein withdraw his troops by January 15, 1991. When Hussein failed to comply, UN forces, led by the United States, felt free to take military action against him. The war began with allied air and missile attacks against Baghdad on the night of January 16.
>
> Iraq had attempted to justify its invasion on two grounds. One was a simple territorial claim that Kuwait was in fact an Iraqi province. More plausibly, Iraq charged that Kuwait had been siphoning its oil through wells along the border. In addition, Hussein apparently misread (perhaps deliberately) the position of the United States, taking the message in a diplomatic exchange prior to the invasion as a sign of American indifference to the forthcoming action. Perhaps, too, Hussein believed that the United States, although not an ally, would be a passive sup-

porter. After all, it had kept Iraqi forces heavily armed and well supplied during the Iran-Iraq war of the 1980s.

Underlying all of this, of course, are the usual motives of economic and political power. Hussein's move might easily be read as an attempt to extend his political influence and prestige in the Arab world (and the Third World generally). As part of the process, he would control significantly more of the vast Middle Eastern oil supply and perhaps position himself to acquire more still. On the other hand, the oil-dependent West believed it must protect that supply by keeping it in hands friendlier than Hussein's.

It takes only a little effort to see that the precipitating causes here, and perhaps some of the intermediate ones as well, were merely means for achieving more intrinsically significant ends.

The principle of looking beyond the immediate or obvious applies also to effects. In discussing the consequences of the collapse of the British Empire, we might begin with the lowering of the Union Jack and the raising of new national flags in the former Asian, African, and Caribbean colonies. Although of great symbolic importance, these acts had little practical significance (except to flag makers—but that's another chain). On the other hand, if we were to look at the economic and political impact on Great Britain, we might be able to judge if in the long run the loss of colonies relieved or contributed to its financial burdens, and delayed or accelerated its decline as a world power. Either of these distant effects is of far greater magnitude than the exchange of cloths atop a pole.

MULTIPLE CAUSES AND EFFECTS

All the examples presented so far deal with a single segment of one causal chain. But such a perspective oversimplifies and therefore falsifies reality. In fact, an effect (if we can isolate just one) is most often the result of diverse and multiple causes just as one cause may be said to create many and varied consequences. In truth, multiple causes simultaneously operate to produce multiple effects. Most causal analyses, however, will not attempt to be exhaustive. Just as you must qualify assertions of causal connection, you must also recognize the limited focus of whatever causation you suggest.

For example, conditions after World War II, including the loss of empire, created more than just economic and political consequences for Britain. There were social effects as well. Encouraged to emigrate because of British labor shortages, people arrived from the colonies in great numbers. They continued to do so, however, even when the needs of the work force had been met, for despite independence and increasing restrictions after 1962, former colonials were often free to enter Great Britain as subjects of the crown. Many did. This increased the pressures of immigration, including cultural and racial conflicts. But the end of the empire also produced varied effects in the newly independent nations themselves.

> British withdrawal made way for diverse political development in the former colonies—the tumultuous democracy of India, the overthrow of the king of Uganda and the alternating despotism of Milton Obote and Idi Amin, single-party African socialism in Tanganyika (now Tanzania) under Julius Nyerere. Much as in the recent case of the Soviet Union's collapse, the absence of externally imposed power also allowed ancient hostilities and rivalries to surface after long suppression. The civil war in Nigeria (1967–70), for example, would have been most unlikely to have occurred had Nigeria remained under British control. Birth pangs and problems aside, however, British withdrawal meant that the destinies of these new states were more firmly in the hands of local populations, a condition that was at once the immediate effect of achieved nationhood and the ultimate goal of the movements for independence.

Another way of looking at the multiplicity of causes and effects is to consider each link as a point through which an infinite number of chains may pass. For instance, the Overanxious Parent projects a chain of consequences for the ill-clad offspring that includes, en route to a life of mediocrity, economic hardship. But such hardship could well be a part of other chains. Financial problems might lead to stress, leading to loss of appetite, poor nutrition, and weight loss, ending in physical degeneration and chronic disease. Alternatively and simultaneously, the hardship could lead to the weight loss, which prompts purchase of new clothes, thus increasing the financial burden and the stress, driving the distraught and coatless offspring to the psychiatrist's couch, creating another expense to compound the original problem, which in turn . . .

What webs we mortals weave! Similarly, in the "alarm clock" the beleaguered mouse trips the mechanism that spills the water, but it cannot be seen as merely frozen at the switch. It continues to flee, falls off the platform onto the bed vacated by the roused sleeper where, startled and disoriented, it becomes the breakfast (mouselix, perhaps?) of the pursuing cat. In addition, the mouse might be part of yet another chain that includes the failure of the sleeper to patch a hole in the foundation.

CAUSE AND EFFECT IN ACADEMIC WRITING

Causal analysis has many academic applications. As already noted, it appears, somewhat weakly, as influence studies in the arts. But connections here are almost always suggestive and imprecise, and you need to be careful of assuming that similarity even implies influence. One might notice, for example, elongation of figures in the paintings of the modern artist Modigliani, the nineteenth-century impressionist Pissarro, and the seventeenth-century master El Greco, but that alone is not sufficient for claiming that Modigliani was at all affected by his predecessors. (The *post hoc* fallacy would apply here.)

There are times, however, when testimony, history, and product coincide. We can hear the influence of African music in the recent work of Paul Simon, that of Indian music in the later instrumentation of the Beatles. But we know that both Simon and some of the Beatles studied these other styles of music. Similarly, if we know the condition of Japanese civilization before the massive importation of Chinese culture in the sixth to eighth centuries, we can assess the influence of China in the aftermath—again, provided we look beyond the dates alone. Here is a portion of one such assessment:

> [M]ost far-reaching in their influence on the future were the writers and scribes. A religion as developed and as philosophical as [the newly embraced] Buddhism depended to a much greater degree than the native Shinto upon the written word for its transmission and propagation. The first scribes were foreigners, but soon the Japanese themselves were copying out the sutras destined for the libraries in the new temples. Before long, even the aristocrats were toiling over the difficult script, for it became a social hallmark at court to be able to read and write Chinese. At once the value of a written script became evident in fields other than the religious. The new possibility of keeping accurate and permanent records, particularly tax records, led in turn to an increase of power and of centralization in the government.
>
> W. SCOTT MORTON, *Japan: Its History and Culture*, pp. 22–23

Pending further substantiation, the passage suggests a range of literary, social, and political causes and effects involving writing that go well beyond the original religious motivation. In addition, the author conservatively uses the word *influence* rather than *effect* even in regard to the adoption of the writing system, for which a causal connection between Chinese and Japanese culture has been firmly established.

Historical studies generally go beyond establishing facts and chronological sequences to focus on reasons and results. Long before you got to college you were exposed to exam questions that asked you for the causes of the American Revolution or the Civil War, or the effects of the Louisiana Purchase or the invention of the steam engine.

Historical topics, however, may also have sociological, psychological, anthropological, and economic dimensions, many of which also involve examination of causes and effects. Social scientists might ask questions such as these: What in the American culture and psyche permitted the forced internment of Japanese-Americans during World War II? What explains the incidence of alcoholism and unemployment among Native Americans living on reservations? What caused the stock-market crash of 1929? What were the economic and social consequences of introducing cassava into the agriculture of eastern Nigeria? In a popular work blending elements of sociology, social history, and anthropology, feminist social critic Susan Brownmiller accounts causally for aspects of female grooming and dress that most of us perhaps take for granted:

> Leg hair was not a problem to American women before the 1920s because the legs of most women were never on public view. When a change in attitude toward recreation, fashion, and female emancipation during the prosperous post-war Jazz Age made it socially acceptable for women of all ages and classes to expose their limbs, modesty regarding the propriety of showing legs was transformed with astonishing rapidity into a dainty self-consciousness regarding "unsightly" hair. As depilatory advertisements reminded their audience in the women's magazines, the classic Greek ideal of feminine beauty appeared hairless in sculptured white marble. More to the point, perhaps, the showgirl's smooth, leggy glamour, the sleek, hairless models in the fashion illustrations, and the changing rules of etiquette at the beach had upped the ante of feminine competition. . . .
>
> With the unprecedented exposure given the feminine leg, the stocking trade went through a revolution of its own. At the turn of the century, when skirts touched the floor, 88 percent of women's hosiery had been woven of durable cotton, typically embellished with clock-work, embroidery, lace insets and colorful patterns. . . . But with the vogue for short skirts and the popularization of bare legs at the beach, the stocking of choice in the Twenties was silk, flesh-colored, and as sheer as the looms could make it, to give the illusion of nudity in an impeccable, luxurious casing.

Femininity, pp. 245–46

At times, the interplay of history and the social sciences seems more limited. Whether violence on TV provokes violent behavior in the audience or whether pornography promotes sexual stereotyping and abuse are questions far more relevant to the social scientist than to the historian. So too are the causes and consequences related to such phenomena as drug abuse, teenage pregnancy, white-collar crime, or illiteracy and its implications. Priscilla L. Vail suggests, for example, that missing breakfast diminishes the chances of academic success:

> It is virtually impossible for a hungry child to rouse himself to a symbolic task. This has always been true, but the number of children who come to school without breakfast is increasing to include many from affluent and middle-class families.

As the number of women in the work force increases, the number of traditional breakfast makers decreases. Independence is the mealtime theme, particularly in the morning, when family members rush to keep to their various timetables. The child is often expected to prepare his own dish of cereal, muffin, or whatever [, and] . . . the schoolchild's breakfast habits may be overlooked. . . .

A child who goes to school hungry may be all right for the first period or even the first hour and a half, but the two periods before lunch are worthless. When physical energy wanes, psychological availability wilts.

Smart Kids with School Problems, pp. 137–38

Causal analysis is at least as crucial in the sciences. In biology, you might conduct an ecological experiment in which you observe the effects of soil acidity, temperature, light, or moisture on germination of seeds. In a basic physics course, you and a classmate might learn an elementary principle of mechanics by riding a seesaw to discover how weight and distance from a fulcrum affect leverage.

Elsewhere on campus, researchers might be attempting to identify effects of the damaged ozone layer or of eating irradiated tomatoes. Off doing fieldwork, a group of professors and graduate students investigates reasons for the sudden drop in the world's frog population—a decline that may be significant for the survival of other species, including our own. Obviously, a vast number of causal analyses concerning natural phenomena have already been performed and validated. Here, for instance, Victor F. Weisskopf briefly examines the effects of proliferating plant life one or two billion years ago:

Before the spread of plant life, it was most useful for a living unit to contain chlorophyll because the unit then could produce its own sugar. Sugar, since it was produced most inefficiently by ultraviolet radiation, was very scarce on Earth. After the spread . . . , however, sugar was plentifully available in the plants. The same is true to an even higher degree with respect to amino acids. . . .

Consequently . . . , living units could exist that were unable to produce their own sugar or amino acid. They could develop easily and multiply by "feeding" on the supply of these substances in plants. . . .This is why, after the plant cover, new kinds of living species developed; we call them animals. Freed from the necessity of producing fundamental chemicals, such as amino acids and chlorophyll, these new units developed their nucleic master plan in new directions. Multicellular units originated where the different cells had other functions too, such as locomotion and sensitivity to light and sound. They could move, see, and hear.

Knowledge and Wonder: The Natural World as Man Knows It, 2nd ed., pp. 260–62

Clearly, scientists and scientific historians are committed to questions of causation—as you are likely to be, in the sciences or elsewhere, throughout your academic career.

USING CAUSE AND EFFECT

Limiting the Discussion

Since causation is often complex and your analyses must be selective, make your readers aware of how your discussion will be limited. This includes letting them know whether your essay will emphasize causes or effects or, in longer papers, both. For example, you might begin a paper about the effects of homelessness as follows:

> In recent years, homelessness in America has strained welfare and police services, added significantly to the financial burdens of munici-palities, and contributed to the spread of AIDS and tuberculosis. But one moral consequence has usually been overlooked. Each time we step around someone sleeping on a steam grate, ignore a request for money or food, avert our eyes from the cardboard carton used for shelter, we become increasingly desensitized to the human misery surrounding us.

Here you have not only indicated your awareness of the acknowledged effects of homelessness, but you have also directed the reader's particular attention to an effect less well known.

Moderating the Language

Since causation is difficult to establish absolutely, moderate the language you use to describe or assert it. Avoid writing "Reaganomics is responsible for the huge debt the United States faces today." Prefer:

> Vast increases in spending for defense, a reduction in tax revenue, and relaxation of banking regulations that led to failures and subsequent bailouts all contributed to quadrupling the national debt during the Reagan and Bush administrations.

Far more specific, the second version is also more moderate in its causal claims, allowing opportunity to explore even those causes responsible for whatever debt President Reagan inherited.

Avoiding Post Hoc Reasoning

To say that the football team had an undefeated season because they sang the fight song backwards before each game, regularly burned the enemy mascot in effigy, or wore their lucky unwashed underwear defies not only principles of musicianship, ecology, and personal hygiene but logic as well.

But such reasoning is fallacious even if charms and rituals are not involved. Consider the following argument:

> Prior to the banning of prayer in the public schools the levels of crime, drug abuse, and teenage pregnancy were far lower than they are today. Let us return prayer to the schools and so restore the nation to its former condition of social health.

Ignoring altogether such issues as freedom of religion and the principle of separation of church and state, we should recognize that the statement assumes—without evidence—direct correlation between the absence or presence of school prayer and the subsequent rise or decline in social problems. Although it is true that the Supreme Court decision of 1962 preceded the increases in crime, drug abuse, and teenage pregnancy, simple chronology is insufficient to establish that the decision caused current difficulties. Nor is there a rational expectation that restored prayer will lead automatically to their abatement. Such post hoc reasoning also disregards other, more demonstrable causes, such as changes in familial structure and influence, economic pressures, the "sexual revolution," and the proliferation of weapons, to name a few.

Interrelationship of Causes and Effects

It is useful to regard the sequence of causes and effects as links in a chain. Remember that except for the end links in a chain segment, all may be perceived as both an effect of a preceding cause and a cause of a succeeding effect. This idea may be illustrated by nuclear fission, a reaction that has the added complexity of occurring as multiplying series of chains. The event begins with the splitting of single nuclei, whose released energy renews the fission process in adjoining atoms until the fuel is spent—the final nucleus in each chain releasing energy but finding no other to act upon. Again, all intermediate atoms are affected by those already split and produce further fission in others.

The popular amusement of arranging thousands of dominoes to fall in a precise order and pattern provides an analogous illustration. Quite often the dominoes do not simply collapse in single file. Rather, at strategic points, one domino will take down two others or more, each beginning a new sequence of falling pieces until the number of available dominoes is exhausted.

Degrees of Causation

Bear in mind the distinctions among degrees of causation (precipitating, intermediate, and underlying causes or effects). No doubt John Brown's raid on Harper's Ferry helped initiate the American Civil War. But was it more significant than the Dred Scott decision and the various nineteenth-century legislative compromises concerning the expansion of slavery? And were these more fundamental than the existence of slavery itself and the other vast differences in the cultures and economies of the North and South?

Although somewhat more abstract, the question of what conditions are necessary and sufficient to produce an effect should be considered as well. In the matter of the camel's back, for example, one straw is sufficient to cause the fracture but only in the presence of the necessary (but not sufficient) pre-existing burden. An example of greater human concern can be found in disorders produced by the pairing of recessive genes, such as sickle-cell anemia. It is necessary that both parents *carry* the troublesome gene; but only *inheriting* the recessive genes from both parents is sufficient to produce the disorder in the offspring.

Such instances illustrate the idea of causes acting in concert. Although the scope of your analyses will be limited, you still must avoid oversimplification, at the very least by acknowledging essential complexities.

Yoshida Kenkō

(Japan; ca. 1283–ca. 1352)

Upon the death of his patron, Emperor Go-Uda, Yoshida Kaneyoshi took Buddhist orders, assumed the title Kenkō (monk), and began a retired rural life in the region outside Kyoto, then capital of Japan. It is likely that the work for which he is remembered (and from which "On Drinking" is taken) was written during his retirement, although its date is uncertain.

Kenkō's Tsurezuregusa (Essays in Idleness) is representative of a Japanese literary tradition known as zuihitsu, an informal collection of writings on miscellaneous subjects. Kenkō's miscellany consists of 243 passages, none lengthy, some only a few sentences long. Its range of topics, however, is vast: love, women's hair, moonlight, ritual, longing for the past, sexual desire, pride, and carp are but a few of them.

Kenkō's collection has remained popular in Japan from its own day to the present. It has also been influential in shaping Japanese aesthetics. In emphasizing the transitory nature of all things, Kenkō treats all stages of development and decline as beautiful, especially as they express this impermanence. A rose just past its peak, therefore, might be more appealing than one at its height of color and form.

In regard to drinking, Kenkō seems to be of two minds. As you read, think about whether they need to be reconciled and whether the essay is a unified whole.

On Drinking

THERE ARE MANY THINGS in the world I cannot understand. I cannot imagine why people find it so enjoyable to press liquor on you the first thing, on every occasion, and force you to drink it. The drinker's face grimaces as if with unbearable distress, and he looks for a chance to get rid of the drink and escape unobserved, only to be stopped and senselessly forced to drink more. As a result, even dignified men suddenly turn into lunatics and behave idiotically, and men in the prime of health act like patients afflicted with grave illnesses and collapse unconscious before one's eyes. What a scandalous way to spend a day of celebration! The victim's head aches even the following day, and he lies abed, groaning, unable to eat, unable to recall what happened the day before, as if everything had taken place in a previous incarnation. He neglects important duties, both public and private, and the result is disaster. It is cruel and a breach of courtesy to oblige a man to undergo such experiences. Moreover, will not the man who has been put through this ordeal feel bitter and resentful towards his tormentors? If it were reported that such a custom, unknown among ourselves, existed in some foreign country, we should certainly find it peculiar and even incredible.

I find this practice distressing to observe even in strangers. A man whose thoughtful manner had seemed attractive laughs and shouts uncontrollably; he chatters interminably, his court cap askew, the cords of his cloak undone, the skirts of his kimono rolled up to his shins, presenting so disreputable a picture that he is unrecognizable as his usual self. A woman will brush the hair away from her forehead and brazenly lift up her face with a roar of laughter. She clings to a man's hand as he holds a saké cup, and if badly bred she will push appetizers into the mouth of her companion, or her own, a disgraceful sight. Some men shout at the top of their lungs, singing and dancing, each to his own tune. Sometimes an old priest, invited at the behest of a distinguished guest, strips to the waist, revealing grimy, sallow skin, and twists his body in a manner so revolting that even those watching with amusement are nauseated. Some drone on about their achievements, boring their listeners; others weep drunkenly. People of the lower classes swear at one another and quarrel in a shocking and frightening manner; after various shameful and wretched antics they end up by grabbing things they have been refused, or falling from the verandah (or from a horse or a carriage) and injuring themselves. Or, if they are not sufficiently important to ride, they stagger along the main thoroughfares and perform various unmentionable acts before earthen walls or at people's gates. It is most upsetting to see an old priest in his shawl leaning on the shoulder of a boy and staggering along, mumbling something incomprehensible.

If such behavior were of benefit either in this world or the next, there might be some excuse. It is, however, the source of numerous calamities in this world, destroying fortunes and inviting sickness. They call liquor the chief of all medicines, but it is, in fact, the origin of all sicknesses. Liquor makes you forget your unhappiness, we are told, but when a man is drunk he may remember even his past griefs and weep over them. As for the future life, liquor deprives a man of his wisdom and consumes his good actions like fire; he therefore increases the burden of sin, violates many commandments and, in the end, drops into hell. Buddha taught that a man who takes liquor and forces another to drink will be reborn five hundred times without hands.

Though liquor is as loathsome as I have described it, there naturally are some occasions when it is hard to dispense with. On a moonlit night, a morning after a snowfall, or under the cherry blossoms, it adds to our pleasure if, while chatting at our ease, we bring forth the wine cups. Liquor is cheering on days when we are bored, or when a friend pays an unexpected visit. It is exceedingly agreeable too when you are offered cakes and wine most elegantly from behind a screen of state by a person of quality you do not know especially well. In winter it is delightful to sit opposite an intimate friend in a small room, toasting something to eat over the fire, and to drink deeply together. It is pleasant also when stopping briefly on a journey, or picnicking in the countryside, to sit drinking on the grass, saying all the while, "I wish we had something to eat with this saké." It is amusing when a man who hates liquor has been made to drink a little. How pleasing it is, again, when some distinguished man deigns to say, "Have another. Your cup looks a little empty." I am happy when some man I have wanted to make my friend is fond of liquor, and we are soon on intimate terms.

Despite all I have said, a drinker is amusing, and his offense is pardonable. It happens sometimes that a guest who has slept late in the morning is awakened by his host flinging open the sliding doors. The startled guest, his face still dazed by sleep, pokes out his head with its thin topknot and, not stopping to put on his clothes, carries them off in his arms, trailing some behind as he flees. It is an amusing and appropriate finale to the drinking party to catch a glimpse of the skinny, hairy shanks he reveals from behind as he lifts his skirts in flight.

THESIS AND THOUGHT

1. Since paragraphs 4–5 seem to express an attitude toward drinking very different from the one expressed by paragraphs 1–3, does this selection have a governing idea? If so, state it. If not, explain why the two sets of paragraphs are irreconcilable.

2. Apart from drinking habits, what information (explicit or implied) does Kenkō's essay provide about the Japan of his day?

3. What evidence is there in the essay of Kenkō the Buddhist priest? Of Kenkō the urbane courtier?

STRUCTURE

1. Note Kenkō's transitions from paragraph to paragraph. Do they help unify the writing? You may want to re-examine your response to "Thesis and Thought" question 1.

2. Kenkō depends heavily on example to illustrate the effects he describes. Examples are present in all paragraphs but the third. How extensively are they developed in paragraphs 1 and 5? Paragraphs 2 and 4? Are the examples more vivid in paragraphs 1 and 5 or 2 and 4? Explain. Suggest reasons for the diminished dynamism of the other set.

STYLE

1. Precise, active verbs (*strut* or *shuffle*, for example, instead of *walk*) are often crucial to vigorous writing. Identify such verbs in paragraph 2 and explain what they contribute to its effectiveness.

2. What is the mood that Kenkō establishes in paragraph 4? Explain how descriptive words (adjectives and adverbs) in the paragraph collectively create this mood.

3. Noting Kenkō's shifting tone, justify the assertion that he is "a moralist with a sense of humor."

CONSIDERATIONS

1. How contemporary does this essay seem nearly seven centuries after it was written?

2. Is alcohol use or abuse a problem on your campus? If so, what do you suggest be done about it? If not, explain how or why your school has avoided the problem.

3. Write a brief critique of "On Drinking" from the perspective of the president of the local MADD chapter, a counselor for Alcoholics Anonymous, the head of Animal House, or one of your parents.

Frederick Douglass
(United States; ca. 1817–1895)

Frederick Douglass, born a slave in Maryland, escaped to the North in 1838 where he assumed the name by which he is known. Beginning in 1841, he lectured on behalf of the abolitionist cause and in 1845 published an autobiography, The Narrative of the Life of Frederick Douglass, *a work that further exposed the harsh realities of slavery. Its publication, however, put Douglass in danger of recapture. He left for England, and returned only after his friends had obtained his legal emancipation.*

Upon his return, Douglass established the North Star, *an abolitionist newspaper, in Rochester, New York, and thus became the first African-American printer-publisher. In addition, his home was the local headquarters for the underground railroad.*

Becoming more activist in his political thinking, Douglass broke with William Lloyd Garrison to join with more radical abolitionists. He was, for example, a close friend of John Brown. Although Douglass did not support Brown's raid on Harper's Ferry, he fled briefly to Canada for fear of being implicated in the plot.

During the Civil War, Douglass actively recruited black soldiers, including his two sons. He also met with Lincoln twice, at least in part to spur the president toward emancipation. After the war, he was involved in Republican politics and in protecting the interests of newly freed African Americans. His political activity earned him posts in three administrations, most notably that of minister to Haiti.

Douglass was a staunch supporter of women's rights as well. He attended the first women's rights convention at Seneca Falls, New York, in 1848. And on the day he died, nearly fifty years later, he delivered a speech at a women's rights meeting in Washington.

Douglass wrote two additional autobiographical works: My Bondage and My Freedom (1855) *and* Life and Times of Frederick Douglass (1881). *The reading that follows is from the 1845* Narrative.

Learning to Read

MY NEW MISTRESS proved to be all she appeared when I first met her at the door,—a woman of the kindest heart and finest feelings. She had never had a slave under her control previously to myself, and prior to her marriage she had been dependent upon her own industry for a living. She was by trade a weaver; and by constant application to her business, she had been in a good degree preserved from the blighting and dehumanizing effects of slavery. I was utterly astonished at her goodness. I scarcely knew how to behave towards her. She was entirely unlike any other white woman I had ever seen. I could not approach her as I was accustomed to approach other white ladies. My early instruction was all out of place. The crouching servility, usually so acceptable a quality in slave, did not answer when manifested toward her. Her favor was not gained by it; she seemed to be disturbed by it. She did not deem it impudent or unmannerly for a slave to look her in the face. The meanest slave was put fully at ease in her presence, and none left without feeling better for having seen her. Her face was made of heavenly smiles, and her voice of tranquil music.

But, alas! this kind heart had but a short time to remain such. The fatal poison of irresponsible power was already in her hands, and soon commenced its infernal work. That cheerful eye, under the influence of slavery, soon became red with rage; that voice, made all of sweet accord, changed to one of harsh and horrid discord; and that angelic face gave place to that of a demon.

Very soon after I went to live with Mr. and Mrs. Auld, she very kindly commenced to teach me the A, B, C. After I had learned this, she assisted me in learning to spell words of three or four letters. Just at this point of my progress, Mr. Auld found out what was going on, and at once forbade Mrs. Auld to instruct me further, telling her, among other things, that it was unlawful, as well as unsafe, to teach a slave to read. To use his own words, further, he said, "If you give a nigger an inch, he will take an ell. A nigger should know nothing but to obey his master—to do as he is told to do. Learning would *spoil* the best nigger in the world. Now," said he, "if you teach that nigger (speaking of myself) how to read, there would be no keeping him. It would forever unfit him to be a slave. He would at once become unmanageable, and of no value to his master. As to himself, it could do him no good, but a great deal of harm. It would make him discontented and unhappy." These words sank deep into my heart, stirred up sentiments within that lay slumbering, and called into existence an entirely new train of thought. It was a new and special revelation, explaining dark and mysterious things, with which my youthful understanding had struggled, but struggled in vain. I now understood what had been to me a most perplexing difficulty—to wit, the white man's power to enslave the black man. It was a grand achievement, and I prized it highly. From that moment, I understood the pathway from slavery to freedom. It was just what I wanted, and I got it at a time when I the least expected it. Whilst I was saddened by the thought of losing the aid of my kind mistress, I was gladdened by the invaluable instruction which, by the merest accident, I had gained from my master. Though conscious of the difficulty of learning without a teacher, I set out with high hope, and a fixed purpose, at whatever cost of trouble, to learn how to read. The very decided manner with which he spoke, and strove to impress his wife with the evil consequences of giving me instruction, served to convince me that he was deeply sensible of the truths he was uttering. It gave me the best assurance that I might rely with the utmost confidence on the results which, he said, would flow from teaching me to read. What he most dreaded, that I most desired. What he most loved, that I most hated. That which to him was a great evil, to be carefully shunned, was to me a great good, to be diligently sought; and the argument which he so warmly urged, against my learning to read, only served to inspire me with a desire and determination to learn. In learning to read, I owe almost as much to the bitter opposition of my master, as to the kindly aid of my mistress. I acknowledge the benefit of both. . . .

I lived in Master Hugh's family about seven years. During this time, I succeeded in learning to read and write. In accomplishing this, I was compelled to resort to various stratagems. I had no regular teacher. My mistress, who had kindly commenced to instruct me, had, in compliance with the advice and direction of her husband, not only ceased to instruct, but had set her face against my being instructed by any one else. It is due, however, to my mistress to say of her, that she did not adopt this course of treatment immediately. She at first lacked the depravity indispensable to shutting me up in mental darkness. It was at least necessary for her to have some training in the exercise of irresponsible power, to make her equal to the task of treating me as though I were a brute.

My mistress was, as I have said, a kind and tender-hearted woman; and   5
in the simplicity of her soul she commenced, when I first went to live with her, to treat me as she supposed one human being ought to treat another. In entering upon the duties of a slaveholder, she did not seem to perceive that I sustained to her the relation of a mere chattel, and that for her to treat me as a human being was not only wrong, but dangerously so. Slavery proved as injurious to her as it did to me. When I went there, she was a pious, warm,

and tender-hearted woman. There was no sorrow or suffering for which she had not a tear. She had bread for the hungry, clothes for the naked, and comfort for every mourner that came within her reach. Slavery soon proved its ability to divest her of these heavenly qualities. Under its influence, the tender heart became stone, and the lamblike disposition gave way to one of tiger-like fierceness. The first step in her downward course was in her ceasing to instruct me. She now commenced to practise her husband's precepts. She finally became even more violent in her opposition than her husband himself. She was not satisfied with simply doing as well as he had commanded; she seemed anxious to do better. Nothing seemed to make her more angry than to see me with a newspaper. She seemed to think that here lay the danger. I have had her rush at me with a face made all up of fury, and snatch from me a newspaper, in a manner that fully revealed her apprehension. She was an apt woman; and a little experience soon demonstrated, to her satisfaction, that education and slavery were incompatible with each other.

From this time I was most narrowly watched. If I was in a separate room any considerable length of time, I was sure to be suspected of having a book, and was at once called to give an account of myself. All this, however, was too late. The first step had been taken. Mistress, in teaching me the alphabet, had given me the *inch*, and no precaution could prevent me from taking the *ell*.

The plan which I adopted, and the one by which I was most successful, was that of making friends of all the little white boys whom I met in the street. As many of these as I could, I converted into teachers. With their kindly aid, obtained at different times and in different places, I finally succeeded in learning to read. When I was sent of errands, I always took my book with me, and by going one part of my errand quickly, I found time to get a lesson before my return. I used also to carry bread with me, enough of which was always in the house, and to which I was always welcome; for I was much better off in this regard than many of the poor white children in our neighborhood. This bread I used to bestow upon the hungry little urchins, who, in return, would give me that more valuable bread of knowledge. I am strongly tempted to give the names of two or three of those little boys, as a testimonial of the gratitude and affection I bear them; but prudence forbids;—not that it would injure me, but it might embarrass them; for it is almost an unpardonable offence to teach slaves to read in this Christian country. . . .

I was now about twelve years old, and the thought of being *a slave for life* began to bear heavily upon my heart. Just about this time, I got hold of a book entitled "The Columbian Orator." Every opportunity I got, I used to read this book. Among much of other interesting matter, I found in it a dialogue between a master and his slave. The slave was represented as having run away from his master three times. The dialogue represented the conversation which took place between them, when the slave was retaken the third time. In this dialogue, the whole argument in behalf of slavery was brought forward by the master, all of which was disposed of by the slave. The slave was made to say some very smart as well as impressive things in reply to his master— things which had the desired though unexpected effect; for the conversation resulted in the voluntary emancipation of the slave on the part of the master.

In the same book, I met with one of Sheridan's mighty speeches on and in behalf of Catholic emancipation. These were choice documents to me. I read them over and over again with unabated interest. They gave tongue to interesting thoughts of my own soul, which had frequently flashed through my mind, and died away for want of utterance. The moral which I gained from the dialogue was the power of truth over the conscience of even a slaveholder. What I got from Sheridan was a bold denunciation of slavery, and a powerful vindication of human rights. The reading of these documents enabled me to utter my thoughts, and to meet the arguments brought forward to sustain slavery; but while they relieved me of one difficulty, they brought on another even more painful than the one of which I was relieved. The more I read, the more I was led to abhor and detest my enslavers. I could regard them in no other light than a band of successful robbers, who had left their homes, and gone to Africa, and stolen us from our homes, and in a strange land reduced us to slavery. I loathed them as being the meanest as well as the most wicked of men. As I read and contemplated the subject, behold! that very discontent- ment which Master Hugh had predicted would follow my learning to read had already come, to torment and sting my soul to unutterable anguish. As I writhed under it, I would at times feel that learning to read had been a curse rather than a blessing. It had given me a view of my wretched condition, without the remedy. It opened my eyes to the horrible pit, but to no ladder upon which to get out. In moments of agony, I envied my fellow-slaves for their stupidity. I have often wished myself a beast. I preferred the condition of the meanest reptile to my own. Any thing, no matter what, to get rid of thinking! It was this everlasting thinking of my condition that tormented me. There was no getting rid of it. It was pressed upon me by every object within sight or hearing, animate or inanimate. The silver trump of freedom had roused my soul to eternal wakefulness. Freedom now appeared, to disappear no more forever. It was heard in every sound, and seen in every thing. It was ever present to torment me with a sense of my wretched condition. I saw nothing without seeing it, I heard nothing without hearing it, and felt nothing without feeling it. It looked from every star, it smiled in every calm, breathed in every wind, and moved in every storm.

I often found myself regretting my own existence, and wishing my-   10
self dead; and but for the hope of being free, I have no doubt but that I should have killed myself, or done something for which I should have been killed. . . . I looked forward to a time at which it would be safe for me to escape. I was too young to think of doing so immediately; besides, I wished to learn how to write, as I might have occasion to write my own pass. I consoled myself with the hope that I should one day find a good chance.

THESIS AND THOUGHT

1. What is the "invaluable instruction" to which Douglass refers in paragraph 3? How is it related to the matter of literacy?

2. Why was teaching slaves to read forbidden? According to the example of Douglass and from the point of view of the slaveholders, how valid was the prohibition?

3. What evidence is there in the selection of Douglass's resourcefulness?

STRUCTURE

1. What are the intellectual and emotional effects of Douglass's learning to read? Consider the process as well as the ultimate acquisition of the skill.

2. A secondary causal chain is present here in the transformation of Mrs. Auld (paras. 1–2, 4–5). Account for the change and explain why "she finally became even more violent in her opposition than her husband himself" (para. 5).

3. What is the role of narrative here in relation to that of causal analysis?

STYLE

1. Mr. Auld says in paragraph 3, "If you give a nigger an inch, he will take an ell." Douglass writes in paragraph 6, "Mistress, in teaching me the alphabet, had given me the *inch*, and no precaution could prevent me from taking the *ell*." What is an ell? What is a more modern means of completing the formula "Give people an inch and they'll take _____"?

2. Using paragraph 1 as a model, discuss elements of Douglass's diction that might lead you to describe his style as formal, old-fashioned, or both.

3. What is the tone of the final sentence of paragraph 3? Of paragraph 7? Explain their use and whether either is typical of the selection.

4. What stylistic elements do the following passages have in common? What variations do you find?

> "That cheerful eye, under the influence of slavery, soon became red with rage; that voice, made all of sweet accord, changed to one of harsh and horrid discord; and that angelic face gave place to that of a demon." (para. 2)

> "What he most dreaded, that I most desired. What he most loved, that I most hated. That which to him was a great evil, to be carefully shunned, was to me a great good, to be diligently sought; and the argument which he so warmly urged, against my learning to

read, only served to inspire me with a desire and determination to learn." (para. 3)

"I saw nothing without seeing it, I heard nothing without hearing it, and felt nothing without feeling it. It looked from every star, it smiled in every calm, breathed in every wind, and moved in every storm." (para. 9)

CONSIDERATIONS

1. Can you think of other instances in which the United States or other ruling powers have exercised control over their populations (minority or not) by limiting or denying access to education? How successful have they been in each case?

2. Painfully aware of both his situation and his inability to alter it at the time, Douglass writes in paragraph 9, "Any thing, no matter what, to get rid of thinking! It was this everlasting thinking of my condition that tormented me." The matter of physical enslavement aside, discuss to what extent such sentiments may be common to all serious thinkers.

3. Write an essay in which you either explore the effects of reading (or of learning to read) in your own life or in which you examine an illuminating moment in your own experience that is analogous to Douglass's in paragraph 3.

4. Bearing the Mrs. Aulds of the world in mind, write an essay based on the adage "Power corrupts; absolute power corrupts absolutely."

Emily Dickinson
(United States; 1830–1886)

Emily Dickinson wrote 1,775 poems, almost none of which appeared before her death. Such public silence reflects the reclusiveness of much of her adult life. Although her father was a prominent public figure, Dickinson herself left Amherst, Massachusetts, only four times—apart from attending, briefly, Mount Holyoke Female Seminary in South Hadley. As Dickinson matured, she seemed to the outer world increasingly withdrawn and eccentric. After thirty, for example, she wore only white.

Never quite isolated (she lived with her sister Lavinia, had her brother and sister-in-law for neighbors, and for twenty years corresponded with Atlantic Monthly *editor Thomas Wentworth Higginson), she dwelt essentially within herself, using such domestic activities as gardening as stimuli and sources for her poetry.*

Not surprisingly, Dickinson's major themes center on her internal emotional and intellectual life. Her work includes such topics as the natural world, faith, death, and immortality. She is not without humor, referring, for example, to a snake that ultimately chills her to the bone as "*a narrow fellow in the grass.*"

Friends and family discovered Dickinson's poems upon her death and published a limited, severely altered selection shortly afterward. Complete, authentic versions did not appear until 1955, but even in edited form her poetry had already captured the attention of poets and critics. Today she is generally placed among the foremost poets in the language.

The poem that follows is obviously concerned with the effects of pain. In what ways does Dickinson describe the "formal feeling" introduced in the first line?

After Great Pain, a Formal Feeling Comes

After great pain, a formal feeling comes—
The Nerves sit ceremonious, like Tombs—
The stiff Heart questions was it He, that bore,
And Yesterday, or Centuries before?

The Feet, mechanical, go round—   5
Of Ground, or Air, or Ought—
A Wooden way
Regardless grown,
A Quartz contentment, like a stone—

This is the Hour of Lead—   10
Remembered, if outlived,
As Freezing persons, recollect the Snow—
First—Chill—then Stupor—then the letting go—

THESIS AND THOUGHT

1. Indicate your comprehension by rewriting as prose the question in lines 3–4 and the statement in lines 5–8.

2. How is the idea of "formal feeling" in line 1 expanded in the rest of the poem?

3. What, in the final line, is let go? Remember that the language of poetry often suggests multiple possibilities.

STRUCTURE

1. List the specific effects through which the "formal feeling" is manifested.
2. What reason or advantage might there be for dividing the lines into three verse paragraphs instead of arranging them as a single unbroken one?

STYLE

1. Eccentric punctuation is often present in Dickinson's poetry. What purpose, if any, does it serve here—particularly in the final line? Dickinson's capitalization is also original. Can you see any purpose or pattern in it?
2. The rhymes here are also typically Dickinsonian. Lines 3–4, 8–9, 12–13 are clearly exact rhymes. Do the others contain partial rhymes? Explain, citing specific pairs. What are the effects of this mixture of rhyme techniques?
3. What major images does Dickinson employ? What elements of subject matter or language unify them?

CONSIDERATIONS

1. What sorts of pain do you think Dickinson is writing about? Of what psychological use or benefit is the "formal feeling" she describes?
2. Write a prose piece in which you describe a "great pain" of your own and your reaction to it.
3. Write an experimental paragraph or essay on a topic of your choice in which your punctuation helps create the impact of your content.

Sadeq Hedayat
(Iran; 1903–1951)

Descended from a prominent Persian family, Hedayat spent his early years amid the political turmoil of the day and received a somewhat irregular European education. He went to Belgium in 1926 to study dentistry but four years later returned, apparently having spent most of his time writing; between 1930 and 1933 he published three collections of short stories.

Generally, Hedayat's fiction is introspective, brooding, pessimistic, and frequently tinged by violence. Although he was not an especially political figure, many of his stories reveal his opposition to the status of women in

Iranian society. His writings also reflect his religious skepticism in regard to Islam.

Hedayat's best-known work is the novel buf-e kur *(The Blind Owl, 1937). Seventeen of his short stories are available in English in* Sadeq Hedayat: An Anthology *(1979). He also wrote plays and satirical sketches, edited the poetry of Omar Khayyam, and stimulated interest in Iranian folklore.*

According to Professor Ehsan Yarshater, from whom much of the information presented above has been gathered, Hedayat's fame and influence in Iran perhaps reached their peak during the two decades following his suicide in Paris. He adds that, influenced by Western writers, Hedayat brought to Iranian literature a contemporary, idiomatic style—in contrast to conventional, formal elegance—and an objective, often naturalistic literary point of view.

Davud the Hunchback

"No, NO! I will never again have anything to do with such things. The only thing is to give up hope altogether. What gives pleasure to others brings me nothing but trouble and torment. Never, never . . ." As Davud spoke these words to himself, he repeatedly stabbed the ground with the short yellow stick which he held in his hand. He walked along with difficulty, as if he had trouble keeping his balance. His large head hung down between his lean shoulders, falling onto a protruding chest. Close up he looked spiritless and repulsive: his thin lips were pressed together, his eyebrows narrow and arched, his drooping eyelashes and prominent bony cheeks were set against a sallow complexion. But looked at from a distance, a silk jacket on his humped back, his incongruously long arms, the large hat stuck on his head, and especially his air of seriousness and the determination with which he thrust his stick to the ground, rendered him a rather comic spectacle.

He had turned off from Pahlavi Avenue into a street leading out of the city and was walking toward the Daulat Gate. It was near sunset and rather hot. On his left, plaster walls and brick pillars silently faced the sky, intercepting the last feeble rays of sunset. Here and there, on the right, alongside a ditch which had recently been filled in, stood some half-finished brick houses. It was comparatively secluded: only an occasional automobile or horse-drawn cart passed by to raise a little cloud of dust, although the road had been sprinkled with water. On both sides of the street saplings had been newly planted along the water conduits.

Davud walked on, absorbed in thought. From childhood on he had always been an object of ridicule or pity. He remembered when during a history lesson the teacher had said that the Spartans used to kill deformed or deficient children. All the pupils had turned around and looked at him—how lonely and outcast he had felt. But now he wished that this law had been enforced all over the world, or least that it had been forbidden for the deformed to marry. He knew that all his defects came from his father; his sallow face, bony cheeks, the lower part of his eyes sunken and dark, his half-opened mouth; the image of his father as he had seen him on his deathbed appeared before him. His father had been old and syphilitic when he married a young woman; all their children had been born blind or crippled. One of his brothers had been dumb and imbecile until he died two years ago. Perhaps they were the lucky ones.

But he had survived, sick of himself and of the world, and shunned by the rest of humanity. To some extent he had grown accustomed to living a life apart. At school he had never been able to take part in physical exercise, joking around, running races, playing ball, leapfrog, and all the other games which brought happiness to his contemporaries. At recess he would retreat into a corner of the school compound and put a book up to his face as he furtively watched the children playing. Sometimes he worked exceptionally hard at his studies so that at least he would come out better than the others. He would work day and night. For this reason, one or two of his lazier classmates tried to strike up a friendship with him so they could copy his answers to sums and exercises. But, of course, he knew that their friendship was put on for the sake of what they could get out of it. He envied Hasan Khan, who was handsome and always well turned out; most of the children tried to become his friends. Only one or two of the teachers displayed any compassion toward him, not on account of his work, but rather out of sympathy. In the end, despite all his agonies and exertions, he did not finish his studies.

Now he was reduced to indigence. Everyone avoided him; his old 5 companions were ashamed to walk with him. He heard the women remark, "Look at the hunchback." This upset him more than anything else. Some years ago he had twice tried to take a wife, but on both occasions he had been made fun of. As it happened one of them, called Zibandeh, lived in this very neighborhood of Fisherabad. They had seen one another several times; she had even talked to him. Some evenings, on his way back from school, he used to come here to see her. The one thing he remembered most vividly about her was the mole she had on the edge of her lip. Later, when he had sent his aunt to solicit this girl's hand on his behalf, she had mocked him, saying, "Is there such a shortage of men that I should marry a hunchback?" Although her father and mother had beaten her, she had never accepted, but had kept saying, "Is there then a shortage of men?" But Davud still loved her and cherished this as the best memory of his youth.

Now, whether knowingly or not, he often wandered around here, reliving old memories. Fed up with everything, he usually went out for walks alone, trying to avoid the crowds. Whenever people laughed or whispered to one another, he thought they were making fun of him. With the look of a sheep before its slaughterer, in abject misery, he would turn his head and shoulders, a contemptuous look in his eye, and pass on. As he walked, his senses focused on the passers-by. The muscles of his face tensed as he imagined what other people thought of him.

Davud walked slowly beside a water conduit, breaking the surface of the water with the tip of his stick. His thoughts were confused and frenzied. He saw a white dog with long hair, which raised its head at the sound of his stick striking a stone, and looked at him. Like a thing diseased and at the point of death, it was unable to move, and its head fell back to the ground.

Davud bent down painfully, and in the moonlight the dog's eyes met his. It was as though this was the first simple and honest look he had ever received. There they were, both spurned by fortune, rejected as so much rubbish, and banished from the society of human beings, for no fault of their own. He wanted to sit down and embrace this dog which had dragged its miseries here to the outskirts of the city to hide them from the sight of men; he pressed its head to his protuberant chest.

The thought then occurred to him that if anyone were to pass by and see him, people would mock him all the more. It was just sunset as he passed through the Yousufabad Gate. He looked at the radiant circle of the moon which, demure and lovely, had come up over the edge of the sky. He surveyed the halfbuilt houses, the untidy piles of bricks, the drowsy vista of the city with its trees and roofs, and the purple mountain. Blurred, gray curtains passed in front of his eyes; there was not a soul to be seen, near or far. The distant, stifled sound of someone singing was audible from the other side of the ditch.

Davud could hardly keep his head up. He was so tired, so overflowing   10
with pain and grief. His eyes were smarting; his head seemed to weigh his body down. He planted his stick on the edge of the conduit and crossed to the other side. Without thinking, he walked over the stones and sat down beside the road. Suddenly, he became aware that a veiled woman was sitting nearby. His heartbeat quickened.

Without introduction the woman turned her face towards him and smiling, said, "Hoshang! Where have you been till now?"

Davud was amazed at the ordinary tone of her voice. How was it that she had seen him and had not shied away? He felt the world had been laid at his feet—she wanted to talk with him. But what was she doing here at this time of night? Perhaps she was a loose woman? Perhaps she was seeking a lover? At any rate, he summoned up all his courage and said to himself, "Come what may, at least I have found somebody to talk to. Perhaps she will give me some comfort."

Impulsively, he said, "Are you lonely, miss? I too am lonely. I am always lonely. My whole life long I have been lonely."

He had hardly finished speaking when the woman turned and looked at him through her dark glasses. "Who are you, then? I thought you were Hoshang. Whenever he comes to see me here, he likes to play jokes."

Davud did not hear much of this last sentence nor did he understand   15
what the woman meant. He had never expected to understand anyway. It had been so long since any woman had spoken to him. He noticed that she was pretty; cold sweat ran down his body.

He struggled to say, "No, miss. I am not Hoshang. My name is Davud."

The woman smiled and answered, "I can't see you very well—my eyes are hurting me! Aha! Davud! Davud the hunch—." (He bit his lip.) "I thought I recognized the voice. I am Zibandeh. Do you recognize me?"

She shook the plaits of hair which had covered one side of her face. Davud saw the mole on the edge of her lip. A stinging twinge of pain shot through his chest to his throat; drops of sweat ran down from his forehead. He looked around him. No one was there. The voice of the singer drew nearer. His heart was thumping—beating so fast that he could hardly breathe. Without uttering a word he got up, shaking from head to foot, choking with tears. He picked up his stick and with heavy and faltering steps retraced the way he had come.

In a frayed voice he murmured, "So it was Zibandeh! She couldn't see me. Perhaps Hoshang is her fiancé or her husband. Who knows? No—never again. I must give it all up! No—I can't ever again . . ."

He picked his way back to the dog and sat down, pressing its head against   20
his chest. The dog was dead.

Translated by H. S. G. Darke

Thesis and Thought

1. As he takes his walk, what is Davud's state of mind? How is it affected by his experiences with Zibandeh? With the dog?

2. What, generally, has been the nature and basis of Davud's relationships?

3. What is the significance of the dog's death?

Structure

1. Recreate the causal chain or chains that have brought Davud to his present condition. Does he (according to the story) have control of his destiny?

2. Paragraph 1 offers a choice of ways in which Davud may be viewed: "Close up he looked spiritless and repulsive," whereas "looked at from a distance" he seemed "a rather comic spectacle." How do these perspectives affect the course of the narrative and the reader's perceptions?

3. About half the story is devoted to Davud's history (paras. 3–6), the rest to his current actions. Discuss whether this extensive background is essential to our comprehension of Davud's present behavior. If so, in what ways? If not, is the story structurally flawed?

STYLE

1. What is the significance of the conduit and ditch, Zibandeh's mole, the dog, and the approaching singer? Are any of these elements symbolic? Explain.

2. Writing of Davud's rejection by Zibandeh, Hedayat tells us that "Davud still loved her and cherished this [his suit] as the best memory of his youth" (para. 5). Explain why this is ironic and discuss whether the irony is heightened by his subsequent encounter with Zibandeh.

CONSIDERATIONS

1. In a subordinate clause in paragraph 5, Hedayat refers to Zibandeh's being beaten by her parents. Do you find the fact (and the reasons for it) shocking? What is your reaction to Hedayat's matter-of-fact presentation of the event? Is there artistic justification for it? Explain.

2. Consider diseases, disabilities, limitations, or deformities other than Davud's, and public reactions to them. Choose one and write an essay about how people with the condition are treated by others.

3. In paragraph 3 Davud proposes the destruction of deformed children or at least their elimination from the population by selective breeding (eugenics). Such policies have been proposed and defended from time to time, and, occasionally, as in Nazi Germany, actually implemented. Write a paper in which you argue the wisdom, justice, or morality of these and related policies, especially with regard to abortion, euthanasia, and sterilization.

4. In the story, Davud's destiny is determined by his deformity. Write an essay showing how a physical, psychological, or intellectual trait of someone you know has shaped the person's life and character. As a variant, considering *hunchback* as more a stigmatizing label than merely a descriptive term, write an essay explaining how someone's life was shaped by the emphasis placed by others on a particular physical, psychological, or intellectual trait.

Maurice Shadbolt

(New Zealand; b. 1932)

Born in Auckland, Shadbolt is known primarily as a short-story writer and novelist. The collection New Zealanders *(1959) was his first published work and* Strangers and Journeys *(1972) is among his most significant novels. A prominent figure in New Zealand literature, Shadbolt is also a journalist, playwright, and former documentary filmmaker.*

As you read the selection, observe how Shadbolt integrates his narration and causal analysis.

Who Killed the Bog Men of Denmark? And Why?

EVERY YEAR in the Danish town of Silkeborg, thousands of visitors file past the face of a murder victim. No one will ever know his name. It is enough to know that 2000 years ago he was as human as ourselves. That face has moved men and women to poetry, and to tears.

Last summer I journeyed to the lake-girt Danish town and, peering at that face behind glass in a modest museum, I felt awe—for his every wrinkle and whisker tell a vivid and terrible tale from Denmark's distant past. The rope which choked off the man's breath is still around his neck. Yet it is a perplexingly peaceful face, inscrutable, one to haunt the imagination.

This strangest of ancient murder mysteries began 27 years ago, on May 8, 1950, when two brothers, Emil and Viggo Højgaard, were digging peat in Tollund Fen, near Silkeborg. Their spring sowing finished, the brothers were storing up the umber-brown peat for their kitchen range, and for warmth in the winter to come. It was a peaceful task on a sunny morning. Snipe called from the aspens and firs fringing the dank bowl of the fen, where only heather and coarse grass grew. Then, at the depth of nine feet, their spades suddenly struck something.

They were gazing, with fright and fascination, at a face underfoot. The corpse was naked but for a skin cap, resting on its side as if asleep, arms and legs bent. The face was gentle, with eyes closed and lips lightly pursed. There was stubble on the chin. The bewildered brothers called the Silkeborg police.

Quick to the scene, the police did not recognize the man as anyone listed missing. Shrewdly guessing the brothers might have blundered into a black hole in Europe's past, the police called in archeologists.

Enter Professor Peter Glob, a distinguished scholar from nearby Aarhus University, who carefully dislodged a lump of peat from beside the dead man's head. A rope made of two twisted hide thongs encircled his neck. He had been strangled or hanged. But when, and by whom? Glob ordered a box to be built about the corpse and the peat in which it lay, so nothing might be disturbed.

Next day, the box, weighing nearly a ton, was manhandled out of the bog onto a horse-drawn cart, on its way for examination at Copenhagen's National Museum. One of Glob's helpers collapsed and died with the huge effort. It seemed a dark omen, as if some old god were claiming a modern man in place of a man from the past.

Bog bodies were nothing new—since records have been kept, Denmark's bogs have surrendered no fewer than 400—and the preservative qualities of the humic acid in peat have long been known. But not until the 19th century did scientists and historians begin to glimpse the finds and understand that the bodies belonged to remote, murky recesses of European prehistory. None survived long: the corpses were either buried again or crumbled quickly with exposure to light and air.

When peat-digging was revived during and after World War II, bodies were unearthed in abundance—first in 1942 at Store Arden, then in 1946, 1947 and 1948 at Borre Fen. Artifacts found beside them positively identified them as people of Denmark's Early Iron Age, from 400 B.C. to A.D. 400. None, then, was less than 1500 years old, and some were probably much older. The first of the Borre Fen finds—a full-grown male—was to prove especially significant: Borre Fen man, too, had died violently, with a noose about his neck, strangled or hanged. And his last meal had consisted of grain.

Peter Glob, alongside his artist father (a portraitist and distinguished amateur archeologist), had been digging into Denmark's dim past since he was a mere eight years old. For him, the Tollund man, who had by far the best-preserved head to survive from antiquity, was a supreme challenge. Since 1936, Glob had been living imaginatively with the pagan hunters and farmers of 2000 years ago, fossicking among their corroded artifacts, foraging among the foundations of their simple villages; he knew their habits, the rhythms of their lives. Suddenly, here was a man of that very time. "Majesty and gentleness," he recalls, "seemed to stamp his features as they did when he was alive." What was this enigmatic face trying to tell him?

Glob was intrigued by the fact that so many of the people found in bogs had died violently: strangled or hanged, throats slit, heads battered. Perhaps they had been travelers set upon by brigands, or executed criminals. But there might be a different explanation. These murder victims all belonged to the Danish Iron Age. If they were to be explained away as victims of robber bands, there should be a much greater spread in time—into other ages. Nor would executed criminals all have had so many common traits.

Glob considered the body with care. X rays of Tollund man's vertebrae, taken to determine whether he had been strangled or hanged, produced inconclusive results. The condition of the wisdom teeth suggested a man well over 20 years old. An autopsy revealed that the heart, lungs and liver were well preserved; most important, the alimentary canal was undisturbed, containing the dead man's last meal—a 2000-year-old gruel of hand-milled grains and seeds: barley, linseed, flaxseed, knotgrass, among others. Knowledge of prehistoric agriculture made it possible to determine that the man had lived in the first 200 years A.D. The mixture of grains and seeds suggested a meal prepared in winter or early spring.

Since Iron Age men were not vegetarians, why were there no traces of meat? Glob also marveled that the man's hands and feet were soft; he appeared to have done little or no heavy labor in his lifetime. Possibly, then, he was high-ranking in Iron Age society.

Then, on April 26, 1952, peat-digging villagers from Grauballe, 11 miles east of Tollund, turned up a second spectacularly well-preserved body, and again Glob was fast to the scene. Unmistakably another murder victim, this discovery was, unlike Tollund man, far from serene. The man's throat had been slashed savagely from ear to ear. His face was twisted with terror, and his lips were parted with a centuries-silenced cry of pain.

Glob swiftly removed the body—still imbedded in a great block of peat—   15
for preservation and study. Carbon-dating of body tissue proved Grauballe man to be about 1650 years old, a contemporary of Constantine the Great. Grauballe man was in extraordinary condition; his fingerprints and footprints came up clearly. Tallish and dark-haired, Grauballe man, like Tollund man, had never done any heavy manual work. He had been slain in his late 30s. Another similarity came to light when Grauballe man's last meal was analyzed: it had been eaten immediately before death and, like Tollund man's, like Borre Fen man's too, it was a gruel of grains and seeds, a meal of winter, or early spring. All three had perished in a similar season.

Who had killed these men of the bogs? Why in winter, or early spring? Why should they—apparently—have led privileged lives? And why the same kind of meals before their sudden ends?

The bodies had told Glob all they could. Now he turned to one of his favorite sources—the Roman historian Tacitus. Nearly 2000 years ago Tacitus recorded the oral traditions of Germanic tribes who inhabited northwest Europe. Tacitus' account of these wild, brave and generous blue-eyed people often shed light into dark corners of Denmark's past. Glob found these lines: "At a time laid down in the distant past, all peoples that are related by blood meet in a sacred wood. Here they celebrate their barbarous rites with a human sacrifice."

Elsewhere, Tacitus wrote: "These people are distinguished by a common worship of Nerthus, or Mother Earth. They believe that she interests herself in human affairs." Tacitus confirmed early spring as a time among the Germanic tribes for offerings and human sacrifice. They were asking the goddess to hasten the coming of spring, and the summer harvest. Men chosen for sacrifice might well have been given a symbolic meal, made up of plant seeds, before being consecrated through death to the goddess—thus explaining the absence of meat. The sacrificial men, with their delicate features, neat hands and feet, might have been persons of high rank chosen by lot for sacrifice, or priests, ritually married to Nerthus.

Tacitus supplied another essential clue: the symbol of Nerthus, he recorded, was a twisted metal "torque," or neck ring, worn by the living to honor the goddess. The leather nooses about the necks of Tollund man and the body from Borre Fen and some earlier bodies were replicas of those neck rings. Glob concluded that it was Nerthus—Mother Earth herself—who had preserved her victims perfectly in her peaty bosom long after those who had fed them into the bogs were dust.

Peter Glob was satisfied. He had found the killer and identified the   20
victims. The centuries-old mystery of Denmark's bog bodies was no more.

Thesis and Thought

1. By what means did the various bog men die? For what reason? How do we know?

2. Using information provided in the text as well as **inferences** drawn from it, write a paragraph describing the culture of the bog people in the period 400 B.C. to 400 A.D.

Structure

1. Using paragraph 16 as a basis for your response, and considering the means of execution and its motive as well, recreate in a brief paragraph the causal sequence that ended in the bog men's deaths.

2. Although the search for causes underlies the essay, it is embedded in narrative and process analysis. Why do you suspect Shadbolt takes this approach instead of engaging in a direct examination of causes? How might it have differed had Shadbolt been writing for a scholarly readership instead of for that of *Reader's Digest*?

Style

1. What mood or atmosphere does Shadbolt create in paragraphs 1, 2, and 7? For what purpose? Identify other language in the text that helps sustain the effect.

2. At the start of paragraph 3, Shadbolt describes the bog men's deaths as the "strangest of ancient murder mysteries." How does this description serve as a motif for the entire essay?

3. Comment on the effect or effectiveness of the following phrases:

"Enter Professor Peter Glob. . . ." (para. 6)

"fossicking among their corroded artifacts, foraging among the foundations of their simple villages" (para. 10)

"slashed savagely from ear to ear . . . twisted with terror . . . a centuries-silenced cry of pain" (para. 14)

"who had preserved her victims perfectly in her peaty bosom" (para. 19)

CONSIDERATIONS

1. Explain or speculate on why there seem to be no bog women.

2. Are there parallels among contemporary religions to the one apparently practiced in Iron-Age Denmark? Consider, among other things, the ideas of sacrifice and regeneration through death. In what ways, other than abstaining from human sacrifice, do modern religions differ from that described in the text?

3. Assume that you are one of those chosen for sacrifice and that it is now the day of the ritual. Write an essay, possibly in the form of a letter, in which you leave your thoughts on the occasion to posterity.

4. Writing of the bog man of Tollund Fen, Shadbolt claims that "2000 years ago he was as human as ourselves" (para. 1). Write an essay in which you support or attack this position.

Stanley Milgram

(United States; 1933–1984)

A son of immigrant parents, Milgram was raised in New York City, attended its public schools, and took his bachelor's degree at Queens College, a municipal institution. His graduate study at Harvard resulted in a doctoral dissertation on conformity in Norway and France. This was followed by the experiments in obedience Milgram conducted at Yale from 1960–63. The cornerstone of Milgram's reputation as a social psychologist, these studies led to the book Obedience to Authority: an Experimental View *(1974), the first chapter of which appears here. Although Milgram's experiment (described in the text) has sometimes been criticized on ethical grounds, his results and their implications for the individual and society have not been questioned seriously.*

In addition to his work on obedience, Milgram investigated the relationship between television viewing and violence, publishing Television and Antisocial Behavior: Field Experience *(1973). As an urban sociologist, he also explored the relationship between the overload of stimuli in city environments and the degree of involvement in the affairs of others. A consequence of this work was one of Milgram's several documentary films,* The City and the

Self, which won a silver medal at the Independent Film and Television Festival.

Milgram's academic honors include the sociopsychological prize, awarded for his obedience studies by the American Association for the Advancement of Science, and election to the American Academy of Arts and Science shortly before his death.

The Dilemma of Obedience

OBEDIENCE IS AS BASIC an element in the structure of social life as one can point to. Some system of authority is a requirement of all communal living, and it is only the man dwelling in isolation who is not forced to respond, through defiance or submission, to the commands of others. Obedience, as a determinant of behavior, is of particular relevance to our time. It has been reliably established that from 1933 to 1945 millions of innocent people were systematically slaughtered on command. Gas chambers were built, death camps were guarded, daily quotas of corpses were produced with the same efficiency as the manufacture of appliances. These inhumane policies may have originated in the mind of a single person, but they could only have been carried out on a massive scale if a very large number of people obeyed orders.

Obedience is the psychological mechanism that links individual action to political purpose. It is the dispositional cement that binds men to systems of authority. Facts of recent history and observation in daily life suggest that for many people obedience may be a deeply ingrained behavior tendency, indeed, a prepotent impulse overriding training in ethics, sympathy, and moral conduct. C. P. Snow (1961) points to its importance when he writes:

> When you think of the long and gloomy history of man, you will find more hideous crimes have been committed in the name of obedience than have ever been committed in the name of rebellion. If you doubt that, read William Shirer's "Rise and Fall of the Third Reich." The German Officer Corps were brought up in the most rigorous code of obedience . . . in the name of obedience they were party to, and assisted in, the most wicked large scale actions in the history of the world. (p. 24)

The Nazi extermination of European Jews is the most extreme instance of abhorrent immoral acts carried out by thousands of people in the name of obedience. Yet in lesser degree this type of thing is constantly recurring: ordinary citizens are ordered to destroy other people, and they do so because they consider it their duty to obey orders. Thus, obedience to authority, long praised as a virtue, takes on a new aspect when it serves a malevolent cause; far from appearing as a virtue, it is transformed into a heinous sin. Or is it?

The moral question of whether one should obey when commands conflict with conscience was argued by Plato, dramatized in *Antigone*, and treated to philosophic analysis in every historical epoch. Conservative philosophers argue that the very fabric of society is threatened by disobedience, and even when the act prescribed by an authority is an evil one, it is better to carry out the act than to wrench at the structure of authority. Hobbes stated further that an act so executed is in no sense the responsibility of the person who carries it out but only of the authority that orders it. But humanists argue for the primacy of individual conscience in such matters, insisting that the moral judgments of the individual must override authority when the two are in conflict.

The legal and philosophic aspects of obedience are of enormous import, but an empirically grounded scientist eventually comes to the point where he wishes to move from abstract discourse to the careful observation of concrete instances. In order to take a close look at the act of obeying, I set up a simple experiment at Yale University. Eventually, the experiment was to involve more than a thousand participants and would be repeated at several universities, but at the beginning, the conception was simple. A person comes to a psychological laboratory and is told to carry out a series of acts that come increasingly into conflict with conscience. The main question is how far the participant will comply with the experimenter's instructions before refusing to carry out the actions required of him.

But the reader needs to know a little more detail about the experiment. Two people come to a psychology laboratory to take part in a study of memory and learning. One of them is designated as a "teacher" and the other a "learner." The experimenter explains that the study is concerned with the effects of punishment on learning. The learner is conducted into a room, seated in a chair, his arms strapped to prevent excessive movement, and an electrode attached to his wrist. He is told that he is to learn a list of word pairs; whenever he makes an error, he will receive electric shocks of increasing intensity.

The real focus of the experiment is the teacher. After watching the learner being strapped into place, he is taken into the main experimental room and seated before an impressive shock generator. Its main feature is a horizontal line of thirty switches, ranging from 15 volts to 450 volts, in 15-volt increments. There are also verbal designations which range from SLIGHT SHOCK to DANGER—SEVERE SHOCK. The teacher is told that he is to administer the learning test to the man in the other room. When the learner responds correctly, the teacher moves on to the next item; when the other man gives an incorrect answer, the teacher is to give him an electric shock. He is to start at the lowest shock level (15 volts) and to increase the level each time the man makes an error, going through 30 volts, 45 volts, and so on.

The "teacher" is a genuinely naïve subject who has come to the laboratory to participate in an experiment. The learner, or victim, is an actor who actually receives no shock at all. The point of the experiment is to see how far a person will proceed in a concrete and measurable situation in which he is ordered to inflict increasing pain on a protesting victim. At what point will the subject refuse to obey the experimenter?

Conflict arises when the man receiving the shock begins to indicate that he is experiencing discomfort. At 75 volts, the "learner" grunts. At 120 volts he complains verbally; at 150 he demands to be released from the experiment. His protests continue as the shocks escalate, growing increasingly vehement and emotional. At 285 volts his response can only be described as an agonized scream.

Observers of the experiment agree that its gripping quality is some- 10
what obscured in print. For the subject, the situation is not a game; conflict is intense and obvious. On one hand, the manifest suffering of the learner presses him to quit. On the other, the experimenter, a legitimate authority to whom the subject feels some commitment, enjoins him to continue. Each time the subject hesitates to administer shock, the experimenter orders him to continue. To extricate himself from the situation, the subject must make a clear break with authority. The aim of this investigation was to find when and how people would defy authority in the face of a clear moral imperative.

There are, of course, enormous differences between carrying out the orders of a commanding officer during times of war and carrying out the orders of an experimenter. Yet the essence of certain relationships remain, for one may ask in a general way: How does a man behave when he is told by a legitimate authority to act against a third individual? If anything, we may expect the experimenter's power to be considerably less than that of the general, since he has no power to enforce his imperatives, and participation in a psychological experiment scarcely evokes the sense of urgency and dedication engendered by participation in war. Despite these limitations, I thought it worthwhile to start careful observation of obedience even in this modest situation, in the hope that it would stimulate insights and yield general propositions applicable to a variety of circumstances.

A reader's initial reaction to the experiment may be to wonder why anyone in his right mind would administer even the first shocks. Would he not simply refuse and walk out of the laboratory? But the fact is that no one ever does. Since the subject has come to the laboratory to aid the experimenter, he is quite willing to start off with the procedure. There is nothing very extraordinary in this, particularly since the person who is to receive the shocks seems initially cooperative, if somewhat apprehensive. What is surprising is how far ordinary individuals will go in complying with the experimenter's instructions. Indeed, the results of the experiment are both surpris-ing and dismaying. Despite the fact that many subjects experience stress, despite the fact that many protest to the experimenter, a substantial propor-tion continue to the last shock on the generator.

Many subjects will obey the experimenter no matter how vehement the pleading of the person being shocked, no matter how painful the shocks seem to be, and no matter how much the victim pleads to be let out. This was seen time and again in our studies and has been observed in several universities where the experiment was repeated. It is the extreme willingness of adults to go to almost any lengths on the command of an authority that constitutes the chief finding of the study and the fact most urgently demanding explanation.

A commonly offered explanation is that those who shocked the victim at the most severe level were monsters, the sadistic fringe of society. But if one considers that almost two-thirds of the participants fall into the category of "obedient" subjects, and that they represented ordinary people drawn from working, managerial, and professional classes, the argument becomes very shaky. Indeed, it is highly reminiscent of the issue that arose in connection with Hannah Arendt's 1963 book, *Eichmann in Jerusalem*. Arendt contended that the prosecution's effort to depict Eichmann as a sadistic monster was fundamentally wrong, that he came closer to being an uninspired bureaucrat who simply sat at his desk and did his job. For asserting these views, Arendt became the object of considerable scorn, even calumny. Somehow, it was felt that the monstrous deeds carried out by Eichmann required a brutal, twisted, and sadistic personality, evil incarnate. After witnessing hundreds of ordinary people submit to the authority in our own experiments, I must conclude that Arendt's conception of the *banality of evil* comes closer to the truth than one might dare imagine. The ordinary person who shocked the victim did so out of a sense of obligation—a conception of his duties as a subject—and not from any peculiarly aggressive tendencies.

This is, perhaps, the most fundamental lesson of our study: ordinary people, simply doing their jobs, and without any particular hostility on their part, can become agents in a terrible destructive process. Moreover, even when the destructive effects of their work become patently clear, and they are asked to carry out actions incompatible with fundamental standards of moral-ity, relatively few people have the resources needed to resist authority. A variety of inhibitions against disobeying authority come into play and suc-cessfully keep the person in his place.

Sitting back in one's armchair, it is easy to condemn the actions of the obedient subjects. But those who condemn the subjects measure them against the standard of their own ability to formulate high-minded moral prescrip-tions. That is hardly a fair standard. Many of the subjects, at the level of stated opinion, feel quite as strongly as any of us about the moral requirement of refraining from action against a helpless victim. They, too, in general terms know what ought to be done and can state their values when the occasion

15

arises. This has little, if anything, to do with their actual behavior under the pressure of circumstances.

If people are asked to render a moral judgment on what constitutes appropriate behavior in this situation, they unfailingly see disobedience as proper. But values are not the only forces at work in an actual, ongoing situation. They are but one narrow band of causes in the total spectrum of forces impinging on a person. Many people were unable to realize their values in action and found themselves continuing in the experiment even though they disagreed with what they were doing.

The force exerted by the moral sense of the individual is less effective than social myth would have us believe. Though such prescriptions as "Thou shalt not kill" occupy a pre-eminent place in the moral order, they do not occupy a correspondingly intractable position in human psychic structure. A few changes in newspaper headlines, a call from the draft board, orders from a man with epaulets, and men are led to kill with little difficulty. Even the forces mustered in a psychology experiment will go a long way toward removing the individual from moral controls. Moral factors can be shunted aside with relative ease by a calculated restructuring of the informational and social field.

What, then, keeps the person obeying the experimenter? First, there is a set of "binding factors" that lock the subject into the situation. They include such factors as politeness on his part, his desire to uphold his initial promise of aid to the experimenter, and the awkwardness of withdrawal. Second, a number of adjustments in the subject's thinking occur that undermine his resolve to break with the authority. The adjustments help the subject maintain his relationship with the experimenter, while at the same time reducing the strain brought about by the experimental conflict. They are typical of thinking that comes about in obedient persons when they are instructed by authority to act against helpless individuals.

One such mechanism is the tendency of the individual to become so   20
absorbed in the narrow technical aspects of the task that he loses sight of its broader consequences. The film *Dr. Strangelove* brilliantly satirized the absorption of a bomber crew in the exacting technical procedure of dropping nuclear weapons on a country. Similarly, in this experiment, subjects become immersed in the procedures, reading the word pairs with exquisite articulation and pressing the switches with great care. They want to put on a competent performance, but they show an accompanying narrowing of moral concern. The subject entrusts the broader tasks of setting goals and assessing morality to the experimental authority he is serving.

The most common adjustment of thought in the obedient subject is for him to see himself as not responsible for his own actions. He divests himself of responsibility by attributing all initiative to the experimenter, a legitimate authority. He sees himself not as a person acting in a morally accountable way but as the agent of external authority. In the postexperimental interview, when subjects were asked why they had gone on, a typical reply was: "I wouldn't have done it by myself. I was just doing what I was told." Unable to defy the authority of the experimenter, they attribute all responsibility to him. It is the old story of "just doing one's duty" that was heard time and time again in the defense statements of those accused at Nuremberg. But it would be wrong to think of it as a thin alibi concocted for the occasion. Rather, it is a fundamental mode of thinking for a great many people once they are locked into a subordinate position in a structure of authority. The disappearance of a sense of responsibility is the most far-reaching consequence of submission to authority.

Although a person acting under authority performs actions that seem to violate standards of conscience, it would not be true to say that he loses his moral sense. Instead, it acquires a radically different focus. He does not respond with a moral sentiment to the actions he performs. Rather, his moral concern now shifts to a consideration of how well he is living up to the expectations that the authority has of him. In wartime, a soldier does not ask whether it is good or bad to bomb a hamlet; he does not experience shame or guilt in the destruction of a village: rather he feels pride or shame depending on how well he has performed the mission assigned to him.

Another psychological force at work in this situation may be termed "counteranthropomorphism." For decades psychologists have discussed the primitive tendency among men to attribute to inanimate objects and forces the qualities of the human species. A countervailing tendency, however, is that of attributing an impersonal quality to forces that are essentially human in origin and maintenance. Some people treat systems of human origin as if they existed above and beyond any human agent, beyond the control of whim or human feeling. The human element behind agencies and institutions is denied. Thus, when the experimenter says, "The experiment *requires* that you continue," the subject feels this to be an imperative that goes beyond any merely human command. He does not ask the seemingly obvious question, "Whose experiment? Why should the designer be served while the victim suffers?" The wishes of a man—the designer of the experiment—have become part of a schema which exerts on the subject's mind a force that transcends the personal. "It's *got* to go on. It's *got* to go on," repeated one subject. He failed to realize that a man like himself wanted it to go on. For him the human agent had faded from the picture, and "The Experiment" had acquired an impersonal momentum of its own.

No action of itself has an unchangeable psychological quality. Its meaning can be altered by placing it in particular contexts. An American newspaper recently quoted a pilot who conceded that Americans were bombing Vietnamese men, women, and children but felt that the bombing was for a "noble cause" and thus was justified. Similarly, most subjects in the experiment see their behavior in a larger context that is benevolent and useful to society—the pursuit of scientific truth. The psychological laboratory has a strong claim to legitimacy and evokes trust and confidence in those who come to perform there. An action such as shocking a victim, which in isolation appears evil, acquires a totally different meaning when placed in this setting. But allowing an act to be dominated by its context, while neglecting its human consequences, can be dangerous in the extreme.

At least one essential feature of the situation in Germany was not studied   25 here—namely, the intense devaluation of the victim prior to action against him. For a decade and more, vehement anti-Jewish propaganda systematically prepared the German population to accept the destruction of the Jews. Step by step the Jews were excluded from the category of citizen and national, and finally were denied the status of human beings. Systematic devaluation of the victim provides a measure of psychological justification for brutal treatment of the victim and has been the constant accompaniment of massacres, pogroms, and wars. In all likelihood, our subjects would have experienced greater ease in shocking the victim had he been convincingly portrayed as a brutal criminal or a pervert.

Of considerable interest, however, is the fact that many subjects harshly devalue the victim *as a consequence* of acting against him. Such comments as, "He was so stupid and stubborn he deserved to get shocked," were common. Once having acted against the victim, these subjects found it necessary to view him as an unworthy individual, whose punishment was made inevitable by his own deficiencies of intellect and character.

Many of the people studied in the experiment were in some sense against what they did to the learner, and many protested even while they obeyed. But between thoughts, words, and the critical step of disobeying a malevolent authority lies another ingredient, the capacity for transforming beliefs and values into action. Some subjects were totally convinced of the wrongness of what they were doing but could not bring themselves to make an open break with authority. Some derived satisfaction from their thoughts and felt that— within themselves, at least—they had been on the side of the angels. What they failed to realize is that subjective feelings are largely irrelevant to the moral issue at hand so long as they are not transformed into action. Political control is effected through action. The attitudes of the guards at a concentration camp are of no consequence when in fact they are allowing the slaughter of innocent men to take place before them. Similarly, so-called "intellectual resistance" in occupied Europe—in which persons by a twist of thought felt that they had defied the invader—was merely indulgence in a consoling psychological mechanism. Tyrannies are perpetuated by diffident men who do not possess the courage to act out their beliefs. Time and again in the experiment people disvalued what they were doing but could not muster the inner resources to translate their values into action.

A variation of the basic experiment depicts a dilemma more common than the one outlined above; the subject was not ordered to push the trigger that shocked the victim, but merely to perform a subsidiary act (administering the word-pair test) before another subject actually delivered the shock. In this situation, 37 of 40 adults from the New Haven area continued to the highest shock level on the generator. Predictably, subjects excused their behavior by saying that the responsibility belonged to the man who actually pulled the switch. This may illustrate a dangerously typical situation in complex society: it is psychologically easy to ignore responsibility when one is only an intermediate link in a chain of evil action but is far from the final consequences of the action. Even Eichmann was sickened when he toured the concentration camps, but to participate in mass murder he had only to sit at a desk and shuffle papers. At the same time the man in the camp who actually dropped Cyclon-B into the gas chambers was able to justify *his* behavior on the grounds that he was only following orders from above. Thus there is a fragmentation of the total human act; no one man decides to carry out the evil act and is confronted with its consequences. The person who assumes full responsibility for the act has evaporated. Perhaps this is the most common characteristic of socially organized evil in modern society.

The problem of obedience, therefore, is not wholly psychological. The form and shape of society and the way it is developing have much to do with it. There was a time, perhaps, when men were able to give a fully human response to any situation because they were fully absorbed in it as human beings. But as soon as there was a division of labor among men, things changed. Beyond a certain point, the breaking up of society into people carrying out narrow and very special jobs takes away from the human quality of work and life. A person does not get to see the whole situation but only a small part of it, and is thus unable to act without some kind of over-all direction. He yields to authority but in doing so is alienated from his own actions.

George Orwell caught the essence of the situation when he wrote: 30

> As I write, highly civilized human beings are flying overhead, trying to kill me. They do not feel any enmity against me as an individual, nor I against them. They are only "doing their duty," as the saying goes. Most of them, I have no doubt, are kind-hearted law abiding men who would never dream of committing murder in private life. On the other hand, if one of them succeeds in blowing me to pieces with a well-placed bomb, he will never sleep any the worse for it.

THESIS AND THOUGHT

1. Describe Milgram's experiment and explain what it was designed to study or discover.
2. What were the results of Milgram's research?
3. What conclusions, particularly concerning authority and personal morality, does Milgram draw from these results?

STRUCTURE

1. The causal analysis begins in earnest at paragraph 14. How does Milgram prepare us for the analysis in the preceding paragraphs? You may wish to consider the following paragraphs as distinct groups: 1–5, 6–13—or 6–10, 11–13.

2. According to Milgram, what are the possible or probable causes of his subjects' behavior? What explanations does he reject? How do the subjects explain their own behavior? Are these explanations themselves in any sense effects of the action in which they are engaged?

3. Beginning with the opening paragraph, Milgram makes numerous references to the Nazi persecution of the Jews. Re-examine these and explain how Milgram uses them to develop his ideas.

STYLE

1. In paragraph 12, Milgram describes the results of the experiment as "surprising and dismaying." Might he have used such a phrase in writing up the actual experiment as opposed to writing about it as he is doing here?

2. Define or explain the following terms as used in context: *exquisite* (para. 20), and *counteranthropomorphism* and *schema* (para. 23); explain also Hannah Arendt's phrase, "the banality of evil" (para. 14).

3. Milgram makes reference to or quotes from physicist and social critic C. P. Snow (para. 2), Plato, the classical Greek play *Antigone*, seventeenth-century philosopher Thomas Hobbes (para. 4), political scientist and theorist Hannah Arendt (para. 14), the film *Dr. Strangelove* (para. 20), and author George Orwell (para. 30). What do these references tell us about Milgram and the audience he addresses?

CONSIDERATIONS

1. With your nation approaching war with Freedonia, you are attached to a detention camp in which civilian citizens of that country have been interned. Orders come down from headquarters to execute one of them chosen at random. You are a company clerk whose job is to process the order; an officer assigned to choose the prisoner; a sergeant assigned to assemble a firing squad; or a member of the firing squad. According to Milgram, how likely are you to carry out each of these orders? Explain why *you* think you are likely or unlikely to do so. Would your answers differ if all the tasks were yours? If the war had already begun? If the prisoners were soldiers? If you had (or lacked) the courage of your convictions? (You are free to consider other variables.)

2. To what events other than the Holocaust and Milgram's experiment do the conclusions reached here apply? Write an essay explaining such an occurrence in the light of Milgram's analysis.

3. The headnote to the selection mentions that the ethics of Milgram's experiment have been questioned. Write a piece in which you defend or criticize the experiment in regard to the ethical treatment of its subjects.

4. Milgram informs us that the subjects were residents of New Haven, Connecticut, who came from various economic classes. In a later chapter Milgram also tells us that the subjects varied in age (from twenty to fifty) and in the extent of their education. All were male. Speculate on the following:

   a. whether Milgram's results might have differed if the test had been conducted using women—either exclusively or as part of the pool

   b. whether the results might have differed if the subjects had come from New Delhi or New Guinea instead of New Haven—in short, whether Milgram's results are valid for other cultures and are as universal as he implies or assumes.

5. Write an essay in which you explain whether and when disobedience to authority is justifiable.

Beth L. Bailey

(United States; b. 1957)

Beth L. Bailey is director of American studies at Barnard College, where she was also an Ann Whitney Olin Junior Fellow. She received her doctorate in history from the University of Chicago and has taught at the University of Hawaii and the University of Kansas. In addition to writing From Front Porch to Back Seat: Courtship in Twentieth-Century America *(1988), the source of the present reading, Bailey has coauthored* The First Strange Place: The Alchemy of Race and Sex in World War II Hawaii *(1992).*

Calling Cards and Money

ONE DAY, the 1920s story goes, a young man asked a city girl if he might call on her. We know nothing else about the man or the girl—only that, when he arrived, she had her hat on. Not much of a story to us, but any American born before 1910 would have gotten the punch line. "She had her hat on": those five words were rich in meaning to early twentieth century Americans. The hat signaled that she expected to leave the house. He came on a "call," expecting to be received in her family's parlor, to talk, to meet her mother, perhaps to have some refreshments or to listen to her play the piano. She expected a "date," to be taken "out" somewhere and entertained. He ended up spending four weeks' savings fulfilling her expectations.

In the early twentieth century this new style of courtship, dating, had begun to supplant the old. Born primarily of the limits and opportunities of urban life, dating had almost completely replaced the old system of calling by the mid-1920s—and, in so doing, had transformed American courtship. Dating moved courtship into the public world, relocating it from family parlors and community events to restaurants, theaters, and dance halls. At the same time, it removed couples from the implied supervision of the private sphere—from the watchful eyes of family and local community—to the anonymity of the public sphere. Courtship among strangers offered couples new freedom. But access to the public world of the city required money. One had to buy entertainment, or even access to a place to sit and talk. Money—men's money—became the basis of the dating system and, thus, of courtship. This new dating system, as it shifted courtship from the private to the public sphere and increasingly centered around money, fundamentally altered the balance of power between men and women in courtship. . . .

By the late nineteenth century a new and relatively coherent social group had come to play an important role in the nation's cultural life. This new middle class, born with and through the rise of national systems of economy, transportation, and communication, was actively creating, controlling, and consuming a national system of culture. National magazines with booming subscription rates promulgated middle-class standards to the white, literate population at large. Women's magazines were especially important in the role of cultural evangelist.

These magazines carried clearly didactic messages to their readership. Unlike general-interest (men's) magazines, which were more likely to contain discussions of issues and events, women's magazines were highly prescriptive, giving advice on both the spiritual and the mundane. But while their advice on higher matters was usually vaguely inspirational, advice on how to look and how to act was extremely explicit.

The conventions of courtship, as set forth in these national magazines   5 and in popular books of etiquette, were an important part of the middle-class code of manners. Conventional courtship centered on "calling," a term that could describe a range of activities. The young man from the neighboring farm who spent the evening sitting on the front porch with the farmer's daughter was paying a call, and so was the "society" man who could judge his prospects by whether or not the card he presented at the front door found the lady of his choice "at home." The middle-class arbiters of culture, however, aped and elaborated the society version of the call. And, as it was promulgated by magazines such as the *Ladies' Home Journal,* with a circulation over one million by 1900, the modified society call was the model for an increasing number of young Americans.

Outside of courtship, this sort of calling was primarily a woman's activity, for women largely controlled social life. Women designated a day or days "at home" to receive callers; on other days they paid or returned calls. The caller would present her card to the maid (common even in moderate-income homes until the World War I era) who answered the door, and would be admitted or turned away with some excuse. The caller who regularly was "not received" quickly learned the limits of her family's social status, and the lady "at home" thus, in some measure, protected herself and her family from the social confusion and pressures engendered by the mobility and expansiveness of late nineteenth-century America. . . .

The call itself was a complicated event. A myriad of rules governed everything: the proper amount of time between invitation and visit (a fortnight or less); whether or not refreshments should be served (not if one belonged to a fashionable or semi-fashionable circle, but outside of "smart" groups in cities like New York and Boston, girls *might* serve iced drinks with little cakes or tiny cups of coffee or hot chocolate and sandwiches); chaperonage (the first call must be made on daughter and mother, but excessive chaperonage would indicate to the man that his attentions were unwelcome); appropriate topics of conversation (the man's interests, but never too personal); how leave should be taken (on no account should the woman "accompany [her caller] to the door nor stand talking while he struggles into his coat"). . . .

At the same time, however, the new system of dating was emerging. By the mid-1910s, the word *date* had entered the vocabulary of the middle-class public. In 1914, the *Ladies' Home Journal*, a bastion of middle-class respectability, used the term (safely enclosed in quotation marks but with no explanation of its meaning) several times. The word was always spoken by that exotica, the college sorority girl—a character marginal in her exoticness but nevertheless a solid product of the middle class. "One beautiful evening of the spring term," one such article begins, "when I was a college girl of eighteen, the boy whom, because of his popularity in every phase of college life, I had been proud gradually to allow the monopoly of my 'dates,' took me unexpectedly into his arms. As he kissed me impetuously I was glad, from the bottom of my heart, for the training of that mother who had taught me to hold myself aloof from all personal familiarities of boys and men."

Sugarcoated with a tribute to motherhood and virtue, the dates—and the kiss—were unmistakenly presented for a middle-class audience. By 1924, ten years later, when the story of the unfortunate young man who went to call on the city girl was current, dating had essentially replaced calling in middle-class culture. The knowing smiles of the story's listeners had probably started with the word *call*—and not every hearer would have been sympathetic to the man's plight. By 1924, he really should have known better.

Dating, that great American middle-class institution, was not at all a product of the middle class. Dating came to the middle class through the   10 upper classes—and from the lower. The first recorded uses of the word *date* in its modern meaning are from lower-class slang. George Ade, the Chicago author who wrote a column titled "Stories of the Streets and the Town" for the *Chicago Record* and published many slang-filled stories of working-class life, probably introduced the term to literature in 1896. Artie, Ade's street-smart protagonist, asks his unfaithful girlfriend, "I s'pose the other boy's fillin' all my dates?" And in 1899 Ade suggested the power of a girl's charms: "Her Date Book had to be kept on the Double Entry System." Other authors whose imaginations were captured by the city and the variety of its inhabitants—Frank Norris, Upton Sinclair, O. Henry—also were using the term by the first decade of the twentieth century.

The practice of dating was a response of the lower classes to the pressures and opportunities of urban-industrial America, just as calling was a response of the upper stratas. The strict conventions of calling enabled the middling and upper classes to protect themselves from some of the intrusions of urban life, to screen out some of the effects of social and geographical mobility in late nineteenth-century America. Those without the money and security to protect themselves from the pressures of urban life or to control the over-whelming opportunities it offered adapted to the new conditions much more directly.

Dating, which to the privileged and protected would seem a system of increased freedom and possibility, stemmed originally from the lack of oppor-tunities. Calling, or even just visiting, was not a practicable system for young people whose families lived crowded into one or two rooms. For even the more established or independent working-class girls, the parlor and the piano often simply didn't exist. The *Ladies' Home Journal* approvingly reported the case of six girls, workers in a box factory, who had formed a club and pooled part of their wages to pay the "janitress of a tenement house" to let them use her front room two evenings a week. It had a piano. One of the girls explained their system: "We ask the boys to come when they like and spend the evening. We haven't any place at home to see them, and I hate seeing them on the street."

Many other working girls, however, couldn't have done this even had they wanted to. They had no extra wages to pool, or they had no notions of middle-class respectability. Some, especially girls of ethnic families, were kept secluded—chaperoned according to the customs of the old country. But many others fled the squalor, drabness, and crowdedness of their homes to seek amusement and intimacy elsewhere. And a "good time" increasingly became identified with public places and commercial amusements, making young women whose wages would not even cover the necessities of life dependent on men's "treats." Still, many poor and working-class couples did not so much escape from the home as they were pushed from it.

These couples courted on the streets, sometimes at cheap dance halls or eventually at the movies. These were not respectable places, and women could enter them only so far as they, themselves, were not considered respectable. Respectable young women did, of course, enter the public world, but their excursions into the public were cushioned. Public courtship of middle-class and upper-class youth was at least *supposed* to be chaperoned; those with money and social position went to private dances with carefully controlled guest lists, to theater parties where they were a private group within the public. As rebels would soon complain, the supervision of society made the private parlor seem almost free by contrast. Women who were not respectable did have relative freedom of action—but the trade-off was not necessarily a happy one for them.

The negative factors were important, but dating rose equally from the   15 possibilities offered by urban life. Privileged youth, as Lewis Erenberg shows in his study of New York nightlife, came to see the possibility of privacy in the anonymous public, in the excitement and freedom the city offered. They looked to lower-class models of freedom—to those beyond the constraints of respectability. As a society girl informed the readers of the *Ladies' Home Journal* in 1914: "Nowadays it is considered 'smart' to go to the low order of dance halls, and not only be a looker-on, but also to dance among all sorts and conditions of men and women. . . . Nowadays when we enter a restaurant and dance place it is hard to know who is who." In 1907, the same magazine had warned unmarried women never to go alone to a "public restaurant" with any man, even a relative. . . .

The new freedom that led to dating came from other sources as well. Many more serious (and certainly respectable) young women were taking advantage of opportunities to enter the public world—going to college, taking jobs, entering and creating new urban professions. Women who belonged to the public world by day began to demand fuller access to the public world in general. City institutions gradually accommodated them. Though still considered risqué by some, dining out alone with a man or attending the theater with no chaperone did not threaten an unmarried woman's reputation by the start of the twentieth century. . . .

Between 1890 and 1925, dating—in practice and in name—had gradually, almost imperceptibly, become a universal custom in America. By the 1930s it had transcended its origins: Middle America associated dating with neither upper-class rebellion nor the urban lower classes. The rise of dating was usually explained, quite simply, by the invention of the automobile. Cars had given youth mobility and privacy, and so had brought about the system. This explanation—perhaps not consciously but definitely not coincidentally—revised history. The automobile certainly contributed to the rise of dating as a *national* practice, especially in rural and suburban areas, but it was simply accelerating and extending a process already well under way. Once its origins were located firmly in Middle America, however, and not in the extremes of urban upper- and lower-class life, dating had become an American institution.

Dating not only transformed the outward modes and conventions of American courtship, it also changed the distribution of control and power in courtship. One change was generational: the dating system lessened parental control and gave young men and women more freedom. The dating system also shifted power from women to men. Calling, either a simple visit or as the elaborate late nineteenth-century ritual, gave women a large portion of control. First of all, courtship took place within the girl's home—in women's "sphere," as it was called in the nineteenth century—or at entertainments largely devised and presided over by women. Dating moved courtship out of the home and into man's sphere—the world outside the home. Female controls and conventions lost much of their power outside women's sphere. And while many of the conventions of female propriety were restrictive and repressive, they had allowed women (young women and their mothers) a great deal of immediate control over courtship. The transfer of spheres thoroughly undercut that control.

Second, in the calling system, the woman took the initiative. Etiquette books and columns were adamant on that point: it was the "girl's privilege" to ask a young man to call. Furthermore, it was highly improper for the man to take the initiative. . . .

Contrast these strictures with advice on dating etiquette from the 1940s and 1950s: An advice book for men and women warns that "girls who [try] to usurp the right of boys to choose their own dates" will "ruin a good dating career. . . . Fair or not, it is the way of life. From the Stone Age, when men chased and captured their women, comes the yen of a boy to do the pursuing. You will control your impatience, therefore, and respect the time-honored custom of boys to take the first step." 20

One teen advice book from the 1950s told girls never to take the initiative with a boy, even under some pretext such as asking about homework: "Boys are jealous of their masculine prerogative of taking the initiative." Another said simply: *"Don't ask,"* and still another recounted an anecdote about a girl who asked a boy for a date to the Saturday-night dance. He cut her off in mid-sentence and walked away. . . .

This absolute reversal of roles almost necessarily accompanied courtship's move from woman's sphere to man's sphere. Although the convention-setters commended the custom of woman's initiative because it allowed greater exclusivity . . . , the custom was based on a broader principle of etiquette. The host or hostess issued any invitation; the guest did not invite himself or herself. An invitation to call was an invitation to visit in a woman's home.

An invitation to go out on a date, on the other hand, was an invitation into the man's world—not simply because dating took place in the public sphere (commonly defined as belonging to men), though that was part of it, but because dating moved courtship into the world of the economy. Money—men's money—was at the center of the dating system. Thus, on two counts, men became the hosts and assumed the control that came with that position. . . .

The centrality of money in dating had serious implications for courtship. Not only did money shift control and initiative to men by making them the "hosts," it led contemporaries to see dating as a system of exchange best understood through economic analogies or as an economic system pure and simple. Of course, people did recognize in marriage a similar economic dimension—the man undertakes to support his wife in exchange for filling various roles important to him—but marriage was a permanent relationship. Dating was situational, with no long-term commitments implied, and when a man, in a highly visible ritual, spent money on a woman in public, it seemed much more clearly an economic act.

In fact, the term *date* was associated with the direct economic exchange 25 of prostitution at an early time. A prostitute called "Maimie," in letters written to a middle-class benefactor/friend in the late nineteenth century, described how men made "dates" with her. And a former waitress turned prostitute described the process to the Illinois Senate Committee on Vice in this way: "You wait on a man and he smiles at you. You see a chance to get a tip and you smile back. Next day he returns and you try harder than ever to please him. Then right away he wants to make a date, and offer you money and presents if you'll be a good fellow and go out with him." These men, quite clearly, were buying sexual favors—but the occasion of the exchange was called a "date."

Courtship in America had always turned somewhat on money (or background). A poor clerk or stockyards worker would not have called upon the daughter of a well-off family, and men were expected to be economically secure before they married. But in the dating system money entered directly into the relationship between a man and a woman as the symbolic currency of exchange in even casual dating.

Dating, like prostitution, made access to women directly dependent on money. Quite a few men did not hesitate to complain about the going rate of exchange. In a 1925 *Collier's* article, "Why Men Won't Marry," a twenty-four-year-old university graduate exclaimed: "Get Married! Why, I can't even afford to go with any of the sorts of girls with whom I would like to associate." He explained: "When I was in college, getting an allowance from home, I used to know lots of nice girls. . . . Now that I am on my own I can't even afford to see them. . . . If I took a girl to the theatre she would have to sit in the gallery, and if we went to supper afterward, it would have to be a soda counter, and if we rode home it would have to be in the street cars." As he presents it, the problem is solely financial. The same girls who were glad to "go with" him when he had money would not "see" him when he lacked their price. And "nice girls" cost a lot. . . .

Yet another young man, the same year, publicly called a halt to such "promiscuous buying." Writing anonymously (for good reason) in *American Magazine,* the author declared a "one-man buyer's strike." This man estimated that, as a "buyer of feminine companionship" for the previous five years, he had "invested" about $20 a week—a grand total of over $5,000. Finally, he wrote, he had realized that "there is a point at which any commodity—even such a delightful commodity as feminine companionship—costs more than it is worth." The commodity he had bought with his $5,000 had been priced beyond its "real value" and he had had enough. This man said "enough" not out of principle, not because he rejected the implications of the economic model of courtship, but because he felt he wasn't receiving value for money.

In . . . these economic analyses, the men are complaining about the new dating system, lamenting the passing of the mythic good old days when "a man without a quarter in his pocket could call on a girl and not be embarrassed," the days before a woman had to be "bought." In recognizing so clearly the economic model on which dating operated, they also clearly saw that the model was a bad one—in purely economic terms. The exchange was not equitable; the commodity was overpriced. Men were operating at a loss.

Here, however, they didn't understand their model completely. True, the   30
equation (male companionship plus money equals female companionship) was imbalanced. But what men were buying in the dating system was not just female companionship, not just entertainment—but power. Money purchased obligation; money purchased inequality; money purchased control.

The conventions that grew up to govern dating codified women's inequality and ratified men's power. Men asked women out; women were condemned as "aggressive" if they expressed interest in a man too directly. Men paid for everything, but often with the implication that women "owed" sexual favors in return. The dating system required men always to assume control, and women to act as men's dependents.

Yet women were not without power in the system, and they were willing to contest men with their "feminine" power. Much of the public discourse on courtship in twentieth-century America was concerned with this contestation. Thousands of sources chronicled the struggles of, and between, men and women—struggles mediated by the "experts" and arbiters of convention—to create a balance of power, to gain or retain control of the dating system. These struggles, played out most clearly in the fields of sex, science, and etiquette, made ever more explicit the complicated relations between men and women in a changing society.

Thesis and Thought

1. What is Bailey's thesis? Where does she state it most explicitly?

2. According to Bailey, what forces or conditions contributed to the change from calling to dating?

3. In addition to any you might have mentioned in response to question 1, what were the consequences and implications of the change?

STRUCTURE

1. What evidence is there that Bailey is aware of the intricacies and complexities of causation? Comment especially on her appreciation of multiple causes or effects and their relative significance.

2. What is the purpose of the anecdote in the opening paragraph? How is it used later in the essay? Explain whether it is effective.

3. In the course of presenting her causal analysis, Bailey employs other rhetorical techniques, including process writing, exemplification, and comparison. Cite one or two instances of each of these and explain how they help achieve the author's purposes.

STYLE

1. Writing for an academic audience, Bailey uses a rather elevated vocabulary. Two words that you might not be familiar with are *fortnight* (para. 7) and *exotica* (para. 8). Look up these or any other words that are unfamiliar.

2. Does Bailey ever write **jargon** in either sense of the term? If you believe she does, identify two or three instances, comment on whether they impede communication, and suggest possible changes. If you think that the essay is free of jargon, choose two or three sentences that you find especially lucid and account for their effectiveness.

CONSIDERATIONS

1. In paragraph 25, Bailey associates the word and concept of *date* with prostitution and goes on to elaborate on dating as an economic process. In your own experience, how prevalent is the value-for-service attitude she delineates?

2. Although Bailey's work appeared in 1988, her last example, which shows dating in full flower, is from the 1950s. What changes in the dating system have occurred since then? Explain whether these have altered the economic and power structure Bailey describes.

3. The behavior Bailey presents is essentially that of white, middle-class heterosexuals. If one or more of these designations do not apply to you, explain how the dating behavior within your own racial, economic, or sexual sphere compares with that in the essay. If all of them apply, describe what differences in dating behavior you've observed in other racial, economic, and sexual groups. Allow for generational changes. See question 2 immediately above.

4. Write an essay in which you define an ideal system of courtship, explaining, of course, why it is ideal.

5. If you are curious about courtship in other societies, consult your library's subject listings for an appropriate title. (Keyword searching may be necessary.)

Suggestions for Writing: Cause and Effect

Using causal analysis write an essay on one of the topics listed below. Some of them might require informal investigation. Limit your topic appropriately.

—Speculate on the consequences of your never having been born.

—Examine changes in the United States that occurred as a result of the civil rights or women's movement over the last three or four decades.

—Assess your personality or character traits, and account for the people and forces that helped shape them.

—Discuss the impact of a new building, program, system, or leader at your college or university.

—Examine the changes in daily life wrought by the computer.

—Account for the popularity of a particular style of music or dress.

—Explain the effect an institution such as McDonald's or Disney has had either globally or on U.S. popular culture.

—Present reasons for the academic achievement (or underachievement) of someone you know.

—Assess the influence that an ethnic or racial minority has had on some aspect of American civilization.

—Discuss the social or political impact of AIDS in the United States.

—Choose a minor invention (the zipper or can opener as opposed to the telephone or automobile) and explain what benefits or problems its sudden removal might create.

—Discuss the causes of environmental pollution in your community or region.

—Account for the prevalence of homelessness, violence, or some other widespread phenomenon in the United States.

8

Definition

"What is truth?" said jesting Pilate, and would not stay for an answer.

Sir Francis Bacon, *Of Truth*

We have met the enemy, and he is us.

Pogo

In this chapter, the word *definition* applies to questions of what individual words mean and, particularly, how they convey (or even create) meaning. *Definition* also pertains to various techniques by which broader meanings of words, especially of abstractions, may be explained and made concrete. Such meanings, often indifferent to questions of common usage, may be social, philosophical, political, or even personal.

The paragraph above illustrates several of the points it raises. It presents the reader with the meanings of *definition* as it will be used here. It offers a simple analysis or distinction between the two meanings. Finally, as an introduction, it provides direction to a chapter whose purpose is to produce an extended definition of *definition* itself.

DENOTATION, CONNOTATION, AND EUPHEMISM

What is Niagara Falls?

Depending on the context and the experience of the person asked, we might find a great variety of answers. All of them, of course, will be definitions. If we question enough people, versions of two rather common responses are likely to recur:

a. a cascade 167 feet high, located in both western New York State and Ontario, Canada.

b. a honeymoon resort area in the vicinity of the great falls on the Niagara River, which forms part of the border between New York State and Ontario, Canada.

395

If we have asked the question merely to obtain information, these responses would do. They represent one of the essential kinds of definition
normally found in dictionaries: **denotative,** literal meanings, free of personal
reaction or interpretation. Each classifies its subject and distinguishes it from
other members of the class. The first definition places the term in the class
"cascade" and distinguishes it by its height and geography. The second definition places Niagara Falls in another category, "honeymoon resort," and
again distinguishes it geographically.

Here is another illustration. One collegiate dictionary defines *pouch* as "a
small drawstring bag carried on the person." *Pouch* belongs to the class of bags.
It is distinguished by its size, drawstring, and portability. Ideally, there is no
other bag that has this combination of features. For example, the popular
purse (already a different class, perhaps) worn fastened about the waist is
small and portable, but lacking a drawstring is not (according to one lexicographer) a pouch. The same dictionary says this about *poverty*: "the state of one
who lacks a usual or socially acceptable amount of money or material possessions." From this we know that poverty is a condition (state) that is determined (distinguished) by whether the quantity of one's material possessions
is usual or socially acceptable. However, although they give us a sense of what
the words mean, dictionary definitions do not go very far in explaining the
concepts that words represent.

Another type of definition is one that goes beyond a simple statement of
meaning to examine the etymology (origin and evolution) of a word as well
as its implications. An academic word such as *humanities,* for example, derives
from Latin *humanitas,* meaning "civility." Studying the humanities, therefore,
involves reading in those disciplines through which civility is promoted.
Today, the word is applied to such subjects as language, literature, history, and
philosophy because they were derived from the "civilizing" Latin and later,
Greek curricula of the earliest European universities.

In her essay "Four-Letter Words Can Harm You," Barbara Lawrence
presents etymological definitions to indicate their implicit violence and to
support her thesis that such words brutalize and denigrate women:

> The best known of the tabooed sexual verbs, for example, comes
> from the German *ficken,* meaning "to strike"; combined, according to
> Partridge's etymological dictionary *Origins,* with the Latin sexual verb
> *futuere;* associated in turn with the Latin *fustis,* "a staff or cudgel"; the
> Celtic *buc,* "a point, hence to pierce"; the Irish *bot,* "the male member";
> the Latin *battuere,* "to beat"; the Gaelic *batair,* "a cudgeller"; the Early
> Irish *bualaim,* "I strike"; and so forth. It is one of what etymologists
> sometimes call "the sadistic group of words for the man's part in copu-
> lation."
>
> The brutality of this word, then, and its equivalents ("screw,"
> "bang," etc.), is not an illusion of the middle class or a crotchet of
> Women's Liberation. In their origins and imagery these words carry

undeniably painful, if not sadistic, implications, the object of which is almost always female. Consider, for example what a "screw" actually does to the wood it penetrates; what a painful, even mutilating, activity this kind of analogy suggests. "Screw" is particularly interesting in this context, since the noun, according to Partridge, comes from words meaning "groove," "nut," "ditch," "breeding sow," "scrofula," and "swelling," while the verb, besides its explicit imagery, has antecedent associations to "write on," "scratch," "scarify," and so forth—a revealing fusion of a mechanical or painful action with an obviously denigrated object.

New York Times, 27 October 1973, 31:1

Although some of the etymology is conjectural and the conclusions depend upon interpretation, Lawrence's account is both informative and provocative. To be sure, few of us who employ or encounter the words are aware of their violent implications unless they are used as expletives. But language functions subconsciously as well. And we are aware that the words—as words—bear considerable force. Nevertheless, since the same collegiate dictionary cited above gives both "extreme force" and "sudden intense activity" for *violence*, perhaps we need additional etymological or other clarifications here.

But words do not simply mean what dictionaries say they do—or did originally or historically. One must also consider **connotative** meaning, meaning shaped by personal or cultural experiences, aesthetics, memories—in short, whole series of associations and emotional resonances ("vibes") words create. For example, if we again asked, "What is Niagara Falls?" we might come up with the following:

    c. It's a terrific place. I went there on my honeymoon. We stayed at the Bates Motel and had a fabulous time. The room came with a waterbed, a bottle of champagne, and continental breakfast. The waterfall was pretty good too.

    d. It's a combination of a gigantic strip mall and a sprawling flea market with hotel accommodations. If you like honky-tonk Americana, you'll love Niagara Falls.

    e. Significantly smaller than Bridal Veil Falls in Yosemite or Victoria Falls on the Zambezi, Niagara's commercial surroundings make it even less impressive.

    f. Cascading 167 feet, Niagara Falls is a breathtaking vision of nature's forces at work.

Fans of the Three Stooges who have read this far might have already recalled Moe and Larry's extreme personal reaction. Having lost their girlfriends in Niagara Falls, they have been so traumatized that the mere mention of the place produces a psychotic episode in which they relive the experience through a violent trance. Nyuk, nyuk? That depends on how you define *funny*.

The distinction between denotation and connotation is crucial to your choice of words generally. While several words may share a denotative meaning, their connotations—and hence the tone they create—may differ widely. Consider the following triads:

> student, scholar, sage
> call, shout, bellow
> overweight, fat, obese
> obnoxious, repulsive, vile
> casket, coffin, box

All of these are arranged in order of what many would agree is increasing emotional charge. Depending on their purposes, writers might choose any of the three words in a set. If, for instance, you are attempting to convey the stark reality of conventional burial, you might write "We pack the corpse in a box and then shove it into a hole in the ground" as opposed to, "We place our loved one in a casket, which is then lowered into a grave." If, however, we were to accompany our grieving Aunt Louise to the funeral director (or mortician or undertaker) to find something appropriate in which to bury Uncle Herman who has gone to his reward (or died or kicked the bucket), we might be less prone to say, "Auntie Lou, let's find a box for Uncle Herm," than "Auntie Lou, we need to choose a casket"—if we are specific at all. Perhaps we might say, "We have to go to Muller's"—using the name of the funeral home and leaving Aunt Louise to draw appropriate conclusions.

Often in the case of death and other unpleasant situations, word choice involves **euphemism**—a substitution that softens, removes, or reverses the anticipated impact of other words. Euphemism, therefore, is a means of controlling, limiting, or obscuring communication. It is frequently used to avoid pain or embarrassment. After all, since Aunt Louise is upset enough, why talk about a box?

We see euphemism at work in other potentially sensitive areas as well—including the subject of bodily functions. Do the "bathrooms" on campus, for example, contain baths? How about the "half bath" at home? Not many "rest rooms" have sofas and easy chairs. And how is it that full-grown adults excuse themselves to go to the "little boys' " or "little girls' " room? Seldom do we see public accommodations marked "toilet." Nor, for other reasons, do we see "john" or "can"—euphemisms of a more casual, colloquial, and perhaps vulgar sort.

But euphemism is potentially fraudulent and dangerous in contexts other than those involving common etiquette. When the president is said to "misspeak" instead of lie, or an official uses the term "police action" for war and "revenue enhancement" for tax increase, there is a deliberate attempt to distort and deceive. Citizen beware!

Even when intentions are less base, you should be alert to language used to promote a cause. The ongoing debate about abortion provides many examples. For instance, the pro*life* movement regularly refers to abortion as the *murder* of an unborn *child*. *Life* and *child* carry strong positive connotations, *murder* strong negative ones. Their juxtaposition reinforces the movement's basic position and is designed to persuade others to join the cause. The pro*choice* movement, on the other hand, speaks of *terminating* a pregnancy, expelling a *fetus*, removing the *products of conception*. Here, *choice* bears positive connotations, while the other italicized terms maintain clinical neutrality by avoiding both the idea of killing and any suggestion that the womb's contents constitute a life. At a more fundamental level, the whole of the (semantic) debate turns on the definition of *life* itself.

Choosing words for their particular connotations sometimes involves rejecting their denotative synonyms for the same reason. James Miller, Australian author of *Koori: A Will to Win*, explains his use of *Koori* in terms of such connotative options:

> In this book I will be using the word "Koori" to describe my people, instead of the more commonly used word "Aboriginal." The word Aboriginal is a Latin-derived English word . . . originally used to refer to any native people of any part of the world. The term Aboriginal did not give my people a separate identity. Furthermore, Aboriginal always has derogatory connotations. Nineteenth-century racial thinking portrayed my people as primitive, simple, savage, and barbaric. The word Aboriginal came to be associated with these pejorative terms. Twentieth-century racist school textbooks portrayed aborigines as poor simple-minded creatures who did not meet the standards of British civilisation, [causing] many Anglo-Australians to associate Aborigine with inferiority.
>
> The word Koori, however, is a generic term that was used by my ancestors and other peoples of the central coast of New South Wales to identify themselves. . . . The original inhabitants of the central east coast first felt the full impact of white settlement. By 1845 for instance, the Eora people of the Sydney Cove area had been eliminated, just 57 years after the British arrived in 1788. It is out of respect for the memories of the Eora, my ancestors, and other surrounding tribes that I will continue to use the word Koori.
>
> *Koori: A Will to Win*, p. vii

STIPULATIVE DEFINITION

At times, writers might find it necessary to tailor the meaning of a particular word to a specific context. In this case, they *stipulate* that the term in question will carry a specific meaning in the particular circumstances. This is analogous to marking a musical note with a sharp or flat sign in a given measure, thereby raising or lowering it a half tone, when in the rest of the piece the note maintains its normal (natural) tonal value. Algebra provides another analogy. For example, if $x = 3$ and $y = 4$, the value of xy is 12, because of the arbitrary assignment of values to x and y. We could as easily have let $x = 14$ and $y = 26$, or used any other numbers.

In order to follow your line of reasoning and understand your conclusions, readers need to know in what senses you are using particular words. This chapter's opening paragraph, for instance, stipulates the meaning of *definition*. Similarly, the definitions of *life* as used in debating the abortion issue are stipulative to the degree that assigning the quality to either birth or conception (or somewhere in between) is arbitrary. If one side were to accept the other's stipulation, in fact, the debate would end. **Stipulative definitions** will be of special use to you in preparing arguments.

If you will be using terms in limited, particular ways—especially unusual ones—it is best to let the reader know at once:

> *Conquistadores* in this paper applies only to those secular Spanish explorers who operated in North America.

Given this stipulative definition, readers will not anticipate finding much about priests, Pizarro, and Peru.

> By *imperialism,* I mean aggressive behavior of one nation toward another with intention to subjugate or control.

Here, readers might see discussion not only of Western European colonization or the recently disestablished Soviet hold on Eastern Europe, but perhaps also of Libyan aggression against Chad and the Chinese takeover of Tibet.

Stipulation (often in all its arbitrary splendor) is typical of legal definitions. In *The Peculiar Institution* (a title taken from the southern euphemism for *slavery*), Kenneth M. Stampp presents a series of statutory and judicial determinants of civil and racial status:

> In Virginia, according to the code of 1849, "Every person who has one-fourth part or more of negro blood shall be deemed a mulatto, and the word 'negro' . . . shall be construed to mean mulatto as well as negro." In Alabama a "mulatto" was "a person of mixed blood, descended, on the part of the mother or father, from negro ancestors, to the third generation inclusive, though one ancestor of each generation may have been a white person." In other southern states also the term *mulatto* was defined loosely, so as to include as a rule persons with one Negro grandparent (quadroon) or great grandparent (octoroon); such persons

were treated in law as Negroes. Only in South Carolina did the statutes refer to "negroes, mulattoes and persons of color" without defining these terms. The Court of Appeals, however, refused to infer from this that all persons "of any mixture of negro blood" were legally Negroes. Rather it ruled that there must be a "visible mixture" and that much depended upon a person's "reputation" among this neighbors.

Any person with Negro ancestors too remote to cause him to be classified as a mulatto was by law a white man. While such a person could be held as a slave, the burden of proof was placed upon the putative master.

The Peculiar Institution, pp. 195–96

Language is not necessarily liberating.

Although stipulative definitions may be arbitrary (as in "let $x = 3$"), in most situations writers will explain why they have chosen (or have been compelled) to define key words as they do. Radical feminist Mary Daly has coined the word *Gyn/Ecology* in deliberate contrast to "gynocidal" *gynecology*, a term that she expands beyond the idea of medical specialization to include all "patriarchal-ologies," which, she contends, collectively destroy women. As creator of the word, Daly both assigns it meaning and explains its cultural significance:

> The title *Gyn/Ecology* is a way of wrenching back some wordpower. The fact that most gynecologists are males . . . is a symptom and example of male control over women and over language, and a clue to the extent of this control. . . .
>
> Note that the *Oxford English Dictionary* defines *gynecology* as "that department of medical science which treats of the functions and diseases peculiar to women; also *loosely*, the science of womankind." I am using the term *Gyn/Ecology* very loosely, that is, freely, to describe the science, that is the process of know-ing, of "loose" women who choose to be subjects and not mere objects of enquiry. Gyn/Ecology is by and about women a-mazing all the male-authored "sciences of womankind," and weaving world tapestries *of our own kind*. That is, it is about dis-covering, de-veloping the complex web of living/loving relationships *of our own kind*. It is about women living, loving, creating our Selves, our cosmos. It *is* dispossessing our Selves, enspiriting our Selves, hearing the call of the wild, naming our wisdom, spinning and weaving world tapestries out of genesis and demise. In contrast to gynecology, which depends upon fixation and dismemberment, Gyn/Ecology affirms that everything is connected.

Gyn/Ecology: The Metaethics of Radical Feminism, pp. 9–11

While you need not accept Daly's views (or anyone else's), you must accept her definition of *Gyn/Ecology* if you are to understand them.

Extended Definition

You are likely to encounter writing situations in which presenting denotative, etymological, or stipulative definitions of key terms is useful or even necessary. As we have seen in the extract from Barbara Lawrence's essay, such definitions may well provide the basis of support for a thesis. But you might also have to define more extensively. In college writing assignments, you might devote several pages of a long paper to definition—or the whole of a briefer one. These will usually focus on abstractions: patriotism, pornography, power; faith, freedom, feminism. Such papers effectively answer the question, What is _____ ? or, What does it mean to be _____ ? The six abstractions just listed fit the first blank and, with minor alteration (What does it mean to be free? and so on), the second as well. But less lofty abstractions might also make suitable subjects. What is a dweeb, nerd, or wuss? What does it mean to be an Eagle, Jayhawk, Owl, Blue Hen, or Rubber Duckie? To be sure, even book-length works may essentially define. John Kenneth Galbraith's *The Affluent Society* and E. D. Hirsch, Jr.'s *Cultural Literacy* are but two examples of books that are essentially extended definitions. Regardless of length, however, the purpose of extended definitions is the same: to arrive at the essence of the object, situation, or abstraction under discussion.

Extended definition is arguably less a rhetorical pattern in its own right, however, than one dependent on or derived from others. We have already seen, for example, that the denotative definition of words involves classification. But the technique may be applied to the extended definition of abstractions as well. For instance, in "The Glory of Athens" (chapter 6), Thucydides explains what Athens is by enumerating its typical virtues. Similarly, in "The Seven Ages of Man" (chapter 6), each age (class) is defined by its own distinctive characteristics. Readings aside, you have probably observed that people often identify (define) themselves according to various groups—ethnic, racial, religious, political, and so on. "White Anglo-Saxon Protestant conservative," possibilities of stereotyping aside, is a shorthand definition arrived at through classification.

But extended definitions are as likely to employ, frequently in combination, narrative, illustration, process, comparison, and causal analysis—for we often can explain what something is by what it does, how it does it, why, and with what result. To the extent that it touches upon essential elements, Pliny's narrative of the eruption of Vesuvius (chapter 1) may be said to be *definitive*. Again, in "Calling Cards and Money" (chapter 7), Beth L. Bailey essentially defines one aspect of twentieth-century American courtship through tracing the evolution of social change (process), contrasting the evolved behavior with the original, and explaining the reasons (causes) for the change. Similarly, Sam Gill's essay in chapter 3 may be said to define *disenchantment* by providing several narrative examples that show how the process operates and to what effect.

Extended definitions are, in fact, often centered on processes and their effects. In definition, however, we are usually concerned less with procedures and their consequences than with their implications or meaning. We might, for instance, define "execution by lethal injection" by explaining how the condemned is strapped to the gurney, how the IV is inserted, how the tubing is arranged to allow for both the introduction of the fatal chemicals and the anonymity of the executioner, the course the substance follows once released, and how it operates on vital life systems. If our interest lies in the process itself, such an account might suffice. It would answer the question, How does lethal injection work? It would also answer, in a limited way, What is lethal injection? The latter formulation, however, establishes definition as the primary goal. A response beginning with "Lethal injection is a process of execution in which . . . ," followed by the outline of the procedure, would constitute a definition. But if the question were handled interpretively, the distinction between process in itself and process used to define might be more apparent:

> What is execution by lethal injection? It is a process that makes a mockery of medical science and technology and is no less inhumane than the other means of execution it was designed to replace. To begin, the victim is strapped to a gurney, a device usually used (paradoxically) to transport people on their way to having their illnesses cared for and lives saved. After a physician has perhaps inspected the veins for suitability, a medical technician inserts one or more IV needles into the arm of the condemned. Its tube or tubes (containing none of the usual life-sustaining fluids, you may be sure) run to a releasing device concealed behind a partition or in an adjoining room. There, at a signal from the warden or deputy, several people may operate a number of controls. Only one of them will actually allow the deadly solution to begin flowing. None of the operators knows which—a precaution against guilty dreams. Entering the bloodstream, the solution, usually containing a strong barbiturate, slows and stops the action of heart and lungs. Suffocation and cardiac arrest might not occur for several minutes. Then, all questions of bedside manner moot, the doctor approaches to pronounce the victim dead. The participants now depart and witnesses leave their vigil to resume . . . their lives.

This paragraph not only presents a process but uses it in support of a point of view, the definition presented in the second sentence. The language here is highly charged (*victim*, for example), and the author takes every opportunity to show that the process is a travesty of medical methods and technology. The definition is clearly more argumentative or persuasive than detached or neutral.

The essay that follows uses at least classification, example, and causal analysis in its attempt to define, at modest length, one aspect of comedy.

Whether it is the surprised response to an unanticipated physical or verbal action or the release of tension after heightened expectations have been met, comedy is often synonymous with cruelty.

Surprise and cruelty are most apparent in physical humor. Why is it that we laugh at someone slipping on a banana peel or taking a pie in the face? In part, the answer lies in deviation from established patterns. Someone walking along the street is supposed to continue walking, not slip and fall; and the pie's association with the face is via fork and mouth, not as an overall feature-obscuring ornament. But such actions may be too cliché for us to take the pain or embarrassment seriously.

On the other hand, television producer Chuck Barris has been quoted as saying that the ideal game show would involve a competition in which the lowest bidder would win the right to push someone down a flight of steps. Equally perverse is the student who recently proclaimed that the funniest thing in the world was an old lady in a wheelchair rolling down such a flight. This is clearly sadistic, but anyone who rents Mel Brooks's *Silent Movie* may see Paul Newman rolling along similarly out of control—and laugh. In this case, the "humor" is not simply that wheelchairs are not expected to move in this way. When the film was made, Newman was active as a race-car driver, so that the "vehicle" was also unexpected. The same film also has a character "dying" and "reviving" as his life support systems are switched off and on.

But the verbal barb is at least as powerful as slapstick. The material of stand-up comedian Henny Youngman is typical. His signature line, "Take my wife—please," runs counter to our expectation of *take* meaning "for example" but also denigrates the wife. In another Youngman joke a doctor tells a patient that he is going to die. The patient then calls for a second opinion. "Okay," the doctor replies. "You're ugly too." Again, in the old Smith and Dale vaudeville sketch, Dr. Kronkheit (the name means "illness"), discovering that his patient (Mr. Dubious) has no life insurance, asks what his wife will bury him with if he dies. The answer is, "With pleasure." And remarks like these lack the savagery of "insult" (or insulting) comedians such as Don Rickles or Andrew Dice Clay.

But even when we expect the peel to be stepped on or the pie to be thrown, or we anticipate a punch line (note the term), we still perceive the result as humorous. The victims' very innocence seems to intensify our appreciation of their misfortune (and our own intelligence). For years, when Milton Berle said the word *makeup* a fat man dressed in a baker's costume would run onstage to assault him with a sack of flour. For a time, celebrities vied to appear on one of Soupy Sales's shows, in order to be hit with a pie—though feigning innocence—much to the delight of the audience, who knew exactly what was coming. We also have an idea of what's coming when Curly makes a mistake. Our only doubt is whether Moe will use the eye-gouge or the nose-tweak. But this sort of humor is not restricted to low comedy. So distinguished a playwright as Eugène Ionesco uses the banana peel in the one-act monologue *Krapp's Last Tape,* in which the actor tosses the peel early on and only after several passes back and forth makes the obligatory slip—much to our amusement. Expectation fulfilled—and here the poor fool does himself in!

Sometimes, as in the case of Milton Berle and Soupy Sales, the cruel device is ritualized. We see this again in "Honeymooner" reruns—when Norton, sitting at the piano or about to sign a document, engages in elaborate and prolonged limbering up as Kramden does a slow burn and eventually pounds his "pal" while shouting in exasperation. We are conditioned to this type of comedic behavior rather early: Ernie's psychological torture of Bert and the predictable failure of Sherlock Hemlock to solve a case are regular occurrences even on "Sesame Street." And in the same vein, do we really expect Lucy to ever let Charlie Brown kick that football?

Perhaps it is the ritual that gives some of the cruelty "redeeming social value": it quite possibly provides an acceptable release for hostility, which might cause serious harm if expressed otherwise. Without this release, and without the psychological separation from actuality provided by the label "comedy," we might regularly be placing peels in the paths of our enemies and helping people downstairs without benefit of steps. Removed from reality, however, we can continue to take our perverse pleasures. After all, what's funnier than a guy slipping on a banana peel, tumbling down the stairs, and landing face first into a cream pie?

Two guys slipping. (Gotcha!)

DEFINITION IN ACADEMIC WRITING

In defining their terms, scholars (a word here stipulated to include students) ought to be as thorough and exact as possible if they wish to be understood clearly. In his introduction to *The Reformation of the Sixteenth Century,* for example, Roland H. Bainton writes this:

> The Reformation was above all else a revival of religion. So much is this the case that some have looked upon it as the last great flowering of the piety of the Middle Ages. . . . With justice they point out that the Reformation was intensely preoccupied with the world to come, viewed all life under the aspect of eternity, throbbed to the Church drama of redemption, subordinated even political alliances to the truth of God, was intolerant of dissent, credulous of superstition, addicted to belief in demonology and witchcraft, often millenarian [i.e., accepting the prophesied thousand-year reign of Christ on earth], and sometimes messianic.

The Reformation of the Sixteenth Century, pp. 3–4

Although Bainton goes on to qualify his definition, it is clear that he perceives the Reformation as a conservative movement; he elaborates on this view in the hundreds of pages that follow.

Similarly, attempting to write for a lay readership, mathematician and physicist Stephen Hawking offers a simplified, working definition of a "good theory":

> A theory is a good theory if it satisfies two requirements: It must accurately describe a large class of observations on the basis of a model that contains only a few arbitrary elements, and it must make definite predictions about the results of future observations. For example, Aristotle's theory that everything was made out of four elements, earth air, fire, and water, was simple enough to qualify, but it did not make any definite predictions. On the other hand, Newton's theory of gravity was based on an even simpler model, in which bodies attracted each other with a force that was proportional to a quantity called their mass and inversely proportional to the square of the distance between them. Yet it predicts the motions of the sun, the moon, and the planets to a high degree of accuracy.

A *Brief History of Time*, pp. 9–10

Here, Hawking offers a brief list of attributes and follows up with two illustrations to clarify the definition.

However, as indicated earlier in the chapter in the allusions to books by Galbraith and Hirsch, an extensive piece of writing—from a paper to a full-length book—may have definition as its overall aim. It is obviously impossible to reproduce book-length material here, but the following excerpts (together with the chapter readings) should indicate the variety of ways in which elaborate definitions may evolve. In literature and the arts, for example, terms descriptive of periods, styles, or techniques are often re-examined and redefined at length. What is *Renaissance, romantic, modern*—as applied to music, literature, or art? Here is part of music professor Douglas Moore's definition of *baroque*:

> The term "baroque" was originally used by historians of art to describe certain architectural and pictorial tendencies which developed at the end of the Renaissance, a sort of theatricalism which displayed itself in elaboration of design and proportions, effects of light and shade, a sought-after impressiveness of size and setting . . . [M]usic reflected the same tendencies apparent in the architecture and painting of this period, which extended from the latter part of the sixteenth century to the middle of the eighteenth. . . . In music it is characterized by a sudden break with polyphony [music that creates harmony by combining two independent melodies instead of chords] . . . and by the coming to the

fore of new dynamic and dramatic types, such as opera, oratorio, cantata, and various categories of instrumental music.

From Madrigal to Modern Music: A Guide to Musical Styles, p. 37

The rest of Moore's sixty-page chapter defines *baroque* chiefly by exploring examples of musical forms; the opening paragraph quoted above is part of a seven-page introduction to the general (defining) characteristics of the **style.**

The social sciences have their extended definitions as well. Classic texts such as Gordon Allport's *The Nature of Prejudice*, William Foote Whyte's *Street Corner Society*, and Ruth Benedict's *Patterns of Culture* attempt to define their key term, observed behavior, or both. Psychoanalyst and social critic Erich Fromm devoted one of his many books to defining: *The Sane Society*. Written in the context of the struggle against facism and nazism during World War II, this work analyzes the interaction of social and psychological processes. In the passage that follows, Fromm defines terms that are crucial for comprehending the broader meanings of the book as a whole:

> Firstly, from the standpoint of a functioning society, one can call a person normal or healthy if he is able to fulfill the social role he is to take in that given society. . . . Secondly, from the standpoint of the individual, we look upon health or normalcy as the optimum of growth and happiness of the individual. . . . [T]here is a discrepancy between the aims of the smooth functioning of society and of the full development of the individual [, which makes] it imperative to differentiate simply between the two concepts of health. The one is governed by social necessities, the other by values and norms concerning the aim of individual existence. . . .
>
> If we differentiate the two concepts of normal and neurotic, we come to the following conclusion: the person who is normal in terms of being well adapted is often less healthy than the neurotic person in terms of human values. Often he is well adapted only at the expense of having given up his self in order to become more or less the person he believes he is expected to be. All genuine individuality and spontaneity may have been lost. On the other hand, the neurotic person can be characterized as somebody who was not ready to surrender completely in the battle for himself. . . . [F]rom the standpoint of human values, he is less crippled than the kind of normal person who has lost his individuality altogether.

The Sane Society, pp. 138–39

Other fields bordering on or overlapping the social sciences offer their share of extended definitions as well. Journalist Charles Silberman defines *The Crisis in the Classroom*, and courses in women's studies might include such works as Betty Friedan's *The Feminine Mystique* and Simone de Beauvoir's *The Second Sex*.

Although the sciences make less frequent use of definition as it is understood in this chapter, precise terminology is essential to scientific thought. Citing "Report of the Subcommittee on Sediment Terminology," geologist F. J. Pettijohn records and then rejects its proposed definitions on grounds of imprecision and inconsistency:

> *Boulder* was defined as "a detached rock mass, somewhat rounded or otherwise modified by abrasion in transport, and larger than a 'cobble' with minimum size of 256 mm." . . . The term *block* was reserved for "a large angular fragment showing little or no modification by transporting agencies and similar in size to a boulder."
> A *cobble* is defined in the same manner as a boulder except that it is restricted in size from 64 to 256 mm. . . .
> A *pebble* is a "rock fragment larger than a coarse sand grain or granule and smaller than a cobble, which has been rounded or otherwise abraded by the action of water, wind, or glacial ice. It is therefore between 4 and 64 mm in diameter. . . ."
> The definitions as given above are defective in several respects. Several concepts other than size have been inadvertently introduced into definitions of what are supposed to be size or grade terms. The injection of roundness, the particular process of shape modification (abrasion), and the agents responsible (wind, water, or ice) is undesirable. Even granting the desirability of applying one term to the rounded fragments and another to the angular pieces, the Committee did not provide terms analogous to *block* for fragments of less than boulder size.
>
> *Sedimentary Rocks*, p. 20

The mathematical formula may do better in this regard. Not simply a shorthand, it is rooted, ideally, in a vocabulary in which meanings are exclusively denotative and universally understood. The propounding of theory, however, such as in the work of Darwin or Einstein, necessarily implies extended definition of concepts such as evolution and relativity.

USING DEFINITION

Defining Essential Terms

Be careful to define essential terms. Does "middle class," for example, refer to income level, aspirations, values, taste—some combination of these—or all? And you had better be certain that the words used to create the definition are themselves intelligible.

For example, in the following sentences "middle class" is understood essentially as descriptive of and inseparable from a system of values:

> When playwright George Bernard Shaw condemns "middle-class morality," he is not referring principally to the thousands that people earn or to their desire to earn thousands more. Instead, he means a value system generally adhered to by those at neither social nor economic extreme. This would include patriotism, marriage and family, the work ethic, and religious affiliation—respectable rather than ostentatious and more superficial than substantial. It would also mean a good deal of unintended and unperceived hypocrisy.

Denotation Versus Connotation

Distinguish carefully between denotative and connotative meanings. Choose words with connotations that best reflect (or create) your attitude toward your subject. In the first useful English dictionary, Samuel Johnson defined *lexicographer* as "a maker of dictionaries; a harmless drudge." The first half of the definition is straightforward denotation; the second, in which Johnson jokes about his labors, is clearly connotative. Similarly, in "The Death of the Hired Man," Robert Frost expresses a point of view in defining *home* as "the place where, when you have to go there, / They have to take you in."

Here are a group of words with definitions taken from the collegiate dictionary referred to earlier, paralleled by the connotative, comic, and eccentric definitions of American humorist Ambrose Bierce in his *Devil's Dictionary*:

cabbage:

> a leafy garden plant . . . of European origin that has a short stem and a dense globular head of usu[ally] green leaves and is used as a vegetable
>
> a familiar kitchen-garden vegetable about as large and wise as a man's head

history:

> a chronological record of significant events (as affecting a nation or institution) usu[ally] including an explanation of their causes
>
> an account mostly false, of events mostly unimportant, which are brought about by rulers mostly knaves, and soldiers mostly fools

jealous:

> disposed to suspect rivalry or unfaithfulness
>
> unduly concerned about the preservation of that which can be lost only if not worth keeping

litigation:

> [the act of carrying] on a legal contest by judicial process
>
> a machine which you go into as a pig and come out of as a sausage

saint:

> one eminent for piety or virtue
>
> a dead sinner revised and edited

Remember, too, that while denotative meaning has little flexibility, connotations may vary widely and in some cases (as in the Stooges' reaction to Niagara Falls) be entirely personal. Here are two passages offering physical descriptions of "Earl." Both use emotionally charged language, but the tone and nature differ greatly.

> Earl is a superb physical specimen, standing well over six feet tall and weighing a svelte 190 pounds. His face is clean shaven, its features large and well proportioned. His eyes, a rich brown, are deeply set in prominent sockets. His lips are full and sensuous, his chin square and strong. Beneath broad shoulders, his muscular chest is partly covered with rings of dark hair which end above his perfectly flat abdomen. Earl's waist is firm though not excessively slender. His buttocks are taut, his thighs and calves well muscled and sturdy. Silhouetted on the beach at sunset, he appears to be a demigod at least.

> Earl is a hunk—over six feet tall and a fat-free 190 pounds. His face is baby smooth and his features are perfect. His eyes, two pools of rich, dark chocolate, are deeply set. His lips were made for kissing, yet you could crack coconuts on his strong, square chin. Below his swimmer's shoulders, his heavenly chest is covered with curlicues of dark hair that end at his to-die-for flat tummy. His waist is arm-curl slender, his buns solid but not of steel. Like Earl himself, his thighs and calves are towers of strength. He looks good enough in his Speedo to star in one of those old beach-party flicks.

Both versions obviously approve of Earl's looks. But the language—and hence the tone—of the first is far more formal and reserved than that of the second. Perhaps the difference is between *admiration* and *enthrallment*. (Look them up.)

Using Rhetorical Methods to Define

For extended definitions you are likely to draw upon various rhetorical methods. You may define by presenting processes, causal analyses, descriptions, narratives, and comparisons. There are, however, two or three techniques that are special to extended definition, although not necessarily exclusive to it. One is negation, a version of comparison-contrast that operates by explaining what your subject is not. The earlier paragraph about middle-class morality uses this technique. The process of negation also may be seen in the familiar riddle, "It's not my sister; it's not my brother; yet it's the child of my father and mother." In a more serious vein, historian M. I. Finley defines the nature of Greek colonization in Italy during the eighth century B.C. by distinguishing it from more conventional kinds and by considering **etymology** as well:

> The Greek word we conventionally translate as "colony" is *apoikia*, which connotes "emigration." The point to be stressed is that each [settlement] was, from the outset and by intention, an independent Greek community, not a colony as that word is customarily understood. And since the movement was an answer to demographic and agrarian difficulties, the new communities were themselves agricultural settlements, not trading posts (in contrast to the Phoenician colonies in the west). Hence, numerous as were the "colonies" in southern Italy, there was none at the best harbour on the east coast, the site of Roman Brundisium (modern Brindisi). Hence, too, the aristocracy of the greatest of the new communities, Syracuse, were called *gamoroi*, which means "those who shared the land, landowners."

The Ancient Greeks, p. 23

Presenting Historical Context

Another technique you might find useful in writing extended definitions is to present historical context for the subject under discussion. You can help the reader know where your topic is headed by explaining where it has been. If you were to discuss the nature of the current authoritarian regime in China, for example, you would do well to go beyond the edicts of Marx, Lenin, and Chairman Mao to examine it in the light of thousands of years of philosophical and pragmatic authoritarianism that characterizes much of Chinese civilization. Similarly, if you were to explain the requirement of celibacy among Roman Catholic priests or the lack of female clergy in that church and others, examining the basis of current restrictions in church history and tradition might prove profitable. Questions of opposition or support entirely aside, you and your readers will be far better informed about the nature of the subject for your having done so.

The technique is apparent in Moore's elaboration on the word *baroque*:

> The moving spirit behind this tendency . . . was the Catholic Counter Reformation, which sought to oppose the Protestant movement and regain the lost provinces by overwhelming the world with a grandiose, emotional, and conquering church. The spirit of this movement found adequate expression in all the arts connected with the church. . . .

[However,] baroque music was ... handsomely subventioned [i.e., financially supported] by the nobility, which had now definitely supplanted the church as chief patron of the art. Not that the church was at all unappreciative, but secular music was more and more coming to the fore in social and artistic importance. All the various European courts employed bodies of musicians, whose performances were important features of the social life of the time. . . .

Even small [German] principalities often boasted of instrumental bands for civic occasions.

From Madrigal to Modern Music: A Guide to Musical Styles, pp. 37, 41

Combining Methods

In developing an effective extended definition, use whatever combination of methods you think best. Look at yourself as a sculptor, a plumber, a dentist. If you chisel here with comparison, you might have to file there with process. If you snake through a tangled topic by using several examples, you might, through description, have to seat them firmly into your text. To extract full meaning you may have to use a variety of analytic probes and burrs, then cement the whole with narrative.

The Role of Women: Two Ancient Views

Liu Hsiang

(China; 77 B.C.–6 B.C.)

Descended from the founder of the Han dynasty, Liu was a scholar and, like many other intellectuals in imperial China, was connected with the court of his day. He wrote poetry and political tracts and (sometimes in collaboration with his son, Liu Hsun) helped restore and compile ancient texts. Liu's Biographies of Eminent Women, *from which this selection is taken, is perhaps his most enduring work. Mencius (Meng-tzu, ca. 371 B.C.–ca. 289 B.C.) was the most prominent Confucian philosopher after Confucius himself.*

The Mother of Mencius

THE MOTHER of Mencius lived in Tsou in a house near a cemetery. When Mencius was a little boy he liked to play burial rituals in the cemetery, happily building tombs and grave mounds. His mother said to herself, "This is no place to bring up my son."

She moved near the marketplace in town. Mencius then played merchant games of buying and selling. His mother again said, "This is no place to bring up my son."

So once again she moved, this time next to a school house. Mencius then played games of ancestor sacrifices and practiced the common courtesies between students and teachers. His mother said, "At last, this is the right place for my son!" There they remained.

When Mencius grew up he studied the six arts of propriety, music, archery, charioteering, writing, and mathematics. Later he became a famous Confucian scholar. Superior men commented that Mencius' mother knew the right influences for her sons. The *Book of Poetry* says, "That admirable lady, what will she do for them!"

When Mencius was young, he came home from school one day and found   5
his mother was weaving at the loom. She asked him, "Is school out already?"

He replied, "I left because I felt like it."

His mother took her knife and cut the finished cloth on her loom. Mencius was startled and asked why. She replied, "Your neglecting your studies is very much like my cutting the cloth. The superior person studies to establish a reputation and gain wide knowledge. He is calm and poised and tries to do no wrong. If you do not study now, you will surely end up as a menial servant and will never be free from troubles. It would be just like a woman who supports herself by weaving to give it up. How long could such a person depend on her husband and son to stave off hunger? If a woman neglects her work or a man gives up the cultivation of his character, they may end up as common thieves if not slaves!"

Shaken, from then on Mencius studied hard from morning to night. He studied the philosophy of the Master and eventually became a famous Confucian scholar. Superior men observed that Mencius' mother understood the way of motherhood. The *Book of Poetry* says, "That admirable lady, what will she tell them!"

After Mencius was married, one day as he was going into his private quarters, he encountered his wife not fully dressed. Displeased, Mencius stopped going into his wife's room. She then went to his mother, begged to be sent home, and said, "I have heard that the etiquette between a man and a woman does not apply in their private room. But lately I have been too casual, and when my husband saw me improperly dressed, he was displeased. He is treating me like a stranger. It is not right for a woman to live as a guest; therefore, please send me back to my parents."

Mencius' mother called him to her and said, "It is polite to inquire before   10
you enter a room. You should make some loud noise to warn anyone inside, and as you enter, you should keep your eyes low so that you will not embarrass anyone. Now, you have not behaved properly, yet you are quick to blame others for their impropriety. Isn't that going a little too far?"

Mencius apologized and took back his wife. Superior men said that his mother understood the way to be a mother-in-law.

When Mencius was living in Ch'i, he was feeling very depressed. His mother saw this and asked him, "Why are you looking so low?"

"It's nothing," he replied.

On another occasion when Mencius was not working, he leaned against the door and sighed. His mother saw him and said, "The other day I saw that you were troubled, but you answered that it was nothing. But why are you leaning against the door sighing?"

Mencius answered, "I have heard that the superior man judges his capa-   15
bilities and then accepts a position. He neither seeks illicit gains nor covets glory or high salary. If the Dukes and Princes do not listen to his advice, then he does not talk to them. If they listen to him but do not use his ideas, then he no longer frequents their courts. Today my ideas are not being used in Ch'i, so I wish to go somewhere else. But I am worried because you are getting too old to travel about the country."

His mother answered, "A woman's duties are to cook the five grains, heat the wine, look after her parents-in-law, make clothes, and that is all! Therefore, she cultivates the skills required in the women's quarters and has no ambition to manage affairs outside of the house. The *Book of Changes* says, 'In her central place, she attends to the preparation of the food.' The *Book of Poetry* says, 'It will be theirs neither to do wrong nor to do good, / Only about the spirits and the food will they have to think.' This means that a woman's duty is not to control or to take charge. Instead she must follow the 'three submissions.' When she is young, she must submit to her parents. After her marriage, she must submit to her husband. When she is widowed, she must submit to her son. These are the rules of propriety. Now you are an adult and I am old; therefore, whether you go depends on what you consider right, whether I follow depends on the rules of propriety."

Superior men observed that Mencius' mother knew the proper course for women. The *Book of Poetry* says, "Serenely she looks and smiles, / Without any impatience she delivers her instructions."

Translated by Nancy Gibbs

A Virtuous Woman
(Proverbs 31:10–31)

Included in both the Jewish and Christian canons of sacred writings, Proverbs is a collection of ethical precepts and advice. Traditionally attributed to Solomon on the basis of his reputation for wisdom, the work was probably compiled from earlier collections in the second or third century B.C., seven or eight centuries after Solomon's reign. The literary form, however, might have flourished even earlier than the tenth century B.C.

Among traditional Jews, the selection presented here continues to be used as part of the home service for the Sabbath and, more widely, as a generic eulogy in funeral services for Jewish women.

Except for some modified punctuation, the text presented is that of the King James Version of the Bible.

Who can find a virtuous woman? For her price is far above rubies.

The heart of her husband doth safely trust in her, so that he shall have no need of spoil.

She will do him good and not evil all the days of her life.

She seeketh wool, and flax, and worketh willingly with her hands.

She is like the merchants' ships; she bringeth her food from afar. 5

She riseth also while it is yet night, and giveth meat to her household, and a portion to her maidens.

She considereth a field, and buyeth it; with the fruit of her hands she planteth a vineyard.

She girdeth her loins with strength, and strengtheneth her arms.

She perceiveth that her merchandise is good; her candle goeth not out by night.

She layeth her hands to the spindle, and her hands hold the distaff. 10

She stretcheth out her hand to the poor; yea, she reacheth forth her hands to the needy.

She is not afraid of the snow for her household: for all her household are clothed with scarlet.

She maketh herself coverings of tapestry; her clothing is silk and purple.

Her husband is known in the gates when he sitteth among the elders of the land.

She maketh fine linen, and selleth it; and delivereth girdles unto the merchant. 15

Strength and honor are her clothing; and she shall rejoice in time to come.

She openeth her mouth with wisdom; and in her tongue is the law of kindness.

She looketh well to the ways of her household, and eateth not the bread of idleness.

Her children arise up and call her blessed; her husband also, and he praiseth her.

Many daughters have done virtuously, but thou excellest them all. 20

Favor is deceitful, and beauty is vain. But a woman that feareth the Lord, she shall be praised.

Give her of the fruit of her hands; and let her own works praise her in the gates.

Thesis and Thought

1. Briefly state the ideal of womanhood represented by each selection. What do the two have in common? Where do they differ?

2. What implication does the selection from Proverbs make about the possibility of attaining the ideal? Do you find a similar, if less overt, implication in "The Mother of Mencius"? If not, does the text provide any basis for speculating on the possibility?

3. Judging solely from the readings, in which culture do women seem to have greater latitude or status? Be prepared to explain your response.

4. So far as you can tell, what roles do men in the two cultures have? What do the readings suggest about the relationships between the two genders?

Structure

1. Explain why both selections may be considered definitions.

2. What structural role do anecdote and comparison (in this case, between individual behavior and a set of precepts) play in "The Mother of Mencius"? How does directional process serve "A Virtuous Woman"?

STYLE

1. Comment on the effectiveness of the imagery in lines 5, 9, 11, 18, and 22 of "A Virtuous Woman."

2. "The Mother of Mencius" may be properly described as "stylized," that is, it contains repetitive formal elements that become characteristic of the writing. Identify several of these elements and explain their contribution to the biographical sketch.

CONSIDERATIONS

1. The views expressed in the two selections are more than two thousand years old. How prevalent are they in contemporary Western society? Have they been modified? Obliterated? Reduced in significance? If you are familiar with contemporary Chinese or Chinese-American culture, feel free to comment on that as well.

2. Write an essay in which you present an ideal member of society. You may choose to either consider or disregard gender.

3. Should a person's social, economic, or political functions be gender-based at all? Write an essay in support of your position.

Jacob Bronowski
(England; 1908–1974)

Perhaps best known to the public for narrating and writing the television series "The Ascent of Man," Bronowski was one of those increasingly rare people who achieved prominence in both the humanities and the sciences. Leaving his native Poland as a child, he eventually became a British subject and attended Cambridge on scholarship. At Cambridge, he excelled in both writing and mathematics, ultimately taking a doctorate in the latter. As a mathematician and scientist, Bronowski was an expert on fuels and research techniques, and during World War II, worked to improve the accuracy of bombing.

His postwar investigation of the bombing of Nagasaki led Bronowski to dissociate himself from further weapons research. Some of his reactions were recorded in Science and Human Values *(1958), one of several works on science written for a lay audience, and in a radio play,* Journey to Japan *(1948). In another radio play,* The Face of Violence *(1950), which won an Italia Prize for European drama, Bronowski explored violent behavior more generally. As a literary scholar and critic, Bronowski wrote* William Blake and the Age of Revolution *(1965) and articles on other figures, including John Donne.*

During the last ten years of his life, Bronowski was a fellow of the Salk Institutes of Biological Sciences. It was during the latter part of this period that "The Ascent of Man" (later available as a book) was developed and produced. These combined activities once more indicate the fusion of Bronowski's varied interests.

As you read "The Reach of Imagination," identify the characteristics that Bronowski finds crucial to imagination and the means by which he attempts to define his subject.

The Reach of Imagination

FOR THREE THOUSAND YEARS, poets have been enchanted and moved and perplexed by the power of their own imagination. In a short and summary essay I can hope at most to lift one small corner of that mystery; and yet it is a critical corner. I shall ask, What goes on in the mind when we imagine? You will hear from me that one answer to this question is fairly specific: which is to say, that we can describe the working of the imagination. And when we describe it as I shall do, it becomes plain that imagination is a specifically *human* gift. To imagine is the characteristic act, not of the poet's mind, or the painter's, or the scientist's, but of the mind of man.

My stress here on the word *human* implies that there is a clear difference in this between the actions of men and those of other animals. Let me then start with a classical experiment with animals and children which Walter Hunter thought out in Chicago about 1910. That was the time when scientists were agog with the success of Ivan Pavlov in forming and changing the reflex actions of dogs, which Pavlov had first announced in 1903. Pavlov had been given a Nobel prize the next year, in 1904; although in fairness I should say that the award did not cite his work on the conditioned reflex, but on the digestive glands.

Hunter duly trained some dogs and other animals on Pavlov's lines. They were taught that when a light came on over one of three tunnels out of their cage, that tunnel would be open; they could escape down it, and were rewarded with food if they did. But once he had fixed that conditioned reflex, Hunter added to it a deeper idea: he gave the mechanical experiment a new dimension, literally—the dimension of time. Now he no longer let the dog go to the lighted tunnel at once; instead, he put out the light, and then kept the dog waiting a little while before he let him go. In this way Hunter timed how long an animal can remember where he has last seen the signal light to his escape route.

The results were and are staggering. A dog or a rat forgets which one of the three tunnels has been lit up within a matter of seconds—in Hunter's experiment, ten seconds at most. If you want such an animal to do much better than this, you must make the task much simpler: you must face him with only two tunnels to choose from. Even so, the best that Hunter could do was to have a dog remember for five minutes which one of two tunnels had been lit up.

I am not quoting these times as if they were exact and universal: they surely are not. Hunter's experiment, more than fifty years old now, had many faults of detail. For example, there were too few animals, they were oddly picked, and they did not all behave consistently. It may be unfair to test a dog for what he *saw,* when he commonly follows his nose rather than his eyes. It may be unfair to test any animal in the unnatural setting of a laboratory cage. And there are higher animals, such as chimpanzees and other primates, which certainly have longer memories than the animals that Hunter tried.

Yet when all these provisos have been made (and met, by more modern experiments) the facts are still startling and characteristic. An animal cannot recall a signal from the past for even a short fraction of the time that a man can—for even a short fraction of the time that a child can. Hunter made comparable tests with six-year-old children, and found, of course, that they were incomparably better than the best of his animals. There is a striking and basic difference between a man's ability to imagine something that he saw or experienced, and an animal's failure.

Animals make up for this by other and extraordinary gifts. The salmon and the carrier pigeon can find their way home as we cannot: they have, as it were, a practical memory that man cannot match. But their actions always depend on some form of habit: on instinct or on learning, which reproduce by rote a train of known responses. They do not depend, as human memory does, on calling to mind the recollection of absent things.

Where is it that the animal falls short? We get a clue to the answer, I think, when Hunter tells us how the animals in his experiment tried to fix their recollection. They most often pointed themselves at the light before it went out, as some gun dogs point rigidly at the game they scent—and get the name *pointer* from the posture. The animal makes ready to act by building the signal into its action. There is a primitive imagery in its stance, it seems to me; it is as if the animal were trying to fix the light in its mind by fixing it in its body. And indeed, how else can a dog mark and (as it were) name one of three tunnels, when he has no such words as *left* and *right,* and no such numbers as *one, two, three?* The directed gesture of attention and readiness is perhaps the only symbolic device that the dog commands to hold on to the past, and thereby to guide himself into the future.

I used the verb *to imagine* a moment ago, and now I have some ground for giving it a meaning. *To imagine* means to make images and to move them about inside one's head in new arrangements. When you and I recall the past, we imagine it in this direct and homely sense. The tool that puts the human mind ahead of the animal is imagery. For us, memory does not demand the preoccupation that it demands in animals, and it lasts immensely longer, because we fix it in images or other substitute symbols. With the same symbolic vocabulary we spell out the future—not one but many futures, which we weigh one against another.

I am using the word *image* in a wide meaning, which does not restrict it   10 to the mind's eye as a visual organ. An image in my usage is what Charles Pierce called a *sign*, without regard for its sensory quality. Pierce distinguished between different forms of signs, but there is no reason to make his distinction here, for the imagination works equally with them all, and that is why I call them all images.

Indeed, the most important images for human beings are simply words, which are abstract symbols. Animals do not have words, in our sense; there is no specific centre for language in the brain of any animal, as there is in the human brain. In this respect at least we know that the human imagination depends on a configuration in the brain that has only evolved in the last one or two million years. In the same period, evolution has greatly enlarged the front lobes in the human brain, which govern the sense of the past and the future; and it is a fair guess that they are probably the seat of our other images. (Part of the evidence for this guess is that damage to the front lobes in primates reduces them to the state of Hunter's animal.) If the guess turns out to be right, we shall know why man has come to look like a highbrow or an egg-head: because otherwise there would not be room in his head for his imagination.

The images play out for us events which are not present to our senses, and thereby guard the past and create the future—a future that does not yet exist, and may never come to exist in that form. By contrast, the lack of symbolic ideas, or their rudimentary poverty, cuts off an animal from the past and the future alike, and imprisons him in the present. Of all the distinctions between man and animal, the characteristic gift which makes us human is the power to work with symbolic images: the gift of imagination.

This is really a remarkable finding. When Philip Sidney in 1580 defended poets (and all unconventional thinkers) from the Puritan charge that they were liars, he said that a maker must imagine things that are not. Halfway between Sidney and us, William Blake said, "What is now proved was once only imagin'd." About the same time, in 1796, Samuel Taylor Coleridge for the first time distinguished between the passive fancy and the active imagination, "the living Power and prime Agent of all human Perception." Now we see that they were right, and precisely right: the human gift is the gift of imagination—and that is not just a literary phrase.

Nor is it just a literary gift; it is, I repeat, characteristically human. Almost everything that we do that is worth doing is done in the first place in the mind's eye. The richness of human life is that we have many lives; we live the events that do not happen (and some that cannot) as vividly as those that do: and if thereby we die a thousand deaths, that is the price we pay for living a thousand lives. (A cat, of course, has only nine.) Literature is alive to us because we live its images, but so is any play of the mind—so is chess: the lines of play that we foresee and try in our heads and dismiss are as much a part of the game as the moves that we make. John Keats said that the unheard melodies are sweeter, and all chess players sadly recall that the combinations that they planned and which never came to be played were the best.

I make this point to remind you, insistently, that imagination is the   15 manipulation of images in one's head; and that the rational manipulation belongs to that, as well as the literary and artistic manipulation. When a child begins to play games with things that stand for other things, with chairs or chessmen, he enters the gateway to reason and imagination together. For the human reason discovers new relations between things not by deduction, but by that unpredictable blend of speculation and insight that scientists call induction, which—like other forms or imagination—cannot be formalised. We see it at work when Walter Hunter inquires into a child's memory, as much as when Blake and Coleridge do. Only a restless and original mind would have asked Hunter's questions and could have conceived his experiments, in a science that was dominated by Pavlov's reflex arcs and was heading towards the behaviorism of John Watson.

Let me find a spectacular example for you from history. What is the most famous experiment that you had described to you as a child? I will hazard that it is the experiment that Galileo is said to have made in Sidney's age, in Pisa about 1590, by dropping two unequal balls from the Leaning Tower. There, we say, is a man in the modern mold, a man after our own hearts; he insisted on questioning the authority of Aristotle and St Thomas Aquinas, and seeing with his own eyes whether (as they said) the heavy ball would reach the ground before the light one. Seeing is believing.

Yet seeing is also imagining. Galileo did challenge the authority of Aristotle, and he did look hard at his mechanics. But the eye that Galileo used was the mind's eye. He did not drop balls from the Leaning Tower of Pisa—and if he had, he would have got a very doubtful answer. Instead, Galileo made an imaginary experiment in his head, which I will describe as he did years later in the book he wrote after the Holy Office silenced him: the *Discorsi . . . intorno à due nuove scienze*, which was smuggled out to be printed in the Netherlands in 1638.

Suppose, said Galileo, that you drop two unequal balls from the tower at the same time. And suppose that Aristotle is right—suppose that the heavy ball falls faster, so that it steadily gains on the light ball, and hits the ground first. Very well. Now imagine the same experiment done again, with only one difference: this time the two unequal balls are joined by a string between them. The heavy ball will again move ahead, but now the light ball holds it back and acts as a drag or brake. So the light ball will be speeded up and the heavy ball will be slowed down; they must reach the ground together because they are tied together, but they cannot reach the ground as quickly as the heavy ball alone. Yet the string between them has turned the two balls into a single mass which is heavier than either ball—and surely (according to Aristotle) this mass should therefore move faster than either ball? Galileo's imaginary experiment has uncovered a contradiction; he says trenchantly:

> You see how, from your assumption that a heavier body falls more rapidly than a lighter one, I infer that a (still) heavier body falls more slowly.

There is only one way out of the contradiction: the heavy ball and the light ball must fall at the same rate, so that they go on falling at the same rate when they are tied together.

This argument is not conclusive, for nature might be more subtle (when the two balls are joined) than Galileo has allowed. And yet it is something more important: it is suggestive, it is stimulating, it opens a new view—in a word, it is imaginative. It cannot be settled without an actual experiment, because nothing that we imagine can become knowledge until we have translated it into, and backed it by, real experience. The test of imagination is experience. But then, that is as true of literature and the arts as it is of science. In science, the imaginary experiment is tested by confronting it with physical experience; and in literature, the imaginative conception is tested by confronting it with human experience. The superficial speculation in science is dismissed because it is found to falsify nature: and the shallow work of art is discarded because it is found to be untrue to our own nature. So when Ella Wheeler Wilcox died in 1919, more people were reading her verses than Shakespeare's; yet in a few years her work was dead. It had been buried by its poverty of emotion and its trivialness of thought: which is to say that it had been proved to be as false to the nature of man as, say, Jean Baptiste Lamarck and Trofim Lysenko were false to the nature of inheritance. The strength of the imagination, its enriching power and excitement, lies in its interplay with reality—physical and emotional.

I doubt if there is much to choose here between science and the arts: 20
the imagination is not much more free, and not much less free, in one than in the other. All great scientists have used their imagination freely, and let it ride them to outrageous conclusions without crying "Halt!" Albert Einstein fiddled with imaginary experiments from boyhood, and was wonderfully ignorant of the facts that they were supposed to bear on. When he wrote the first of his beautiful papers on the random movement of atoms, he did not know that the Brownian motion which it predicted could be seen in any laboratory. He was sixteen when he invented the paradox that he resolved ten years later, in 1905, in the theory of relativity, and it bulked much larger

in his mind than the experiment of Albert Michelson and Edward Morley which had upset every other physicist since 1881. All his life Einstein loved to make up teasing puzzles like Galileo's, about falling lifts and the detection of gravity; and they carry the nub of the problems of general relativity on which he was working.

Indeed, it could not be otherwise. The power that man has over nature and himself, and that a dog lacks, lies in his command of imaginary experience. He alone has the symbols which fix the past and play with the future, possible and impossible. In the Renaissance, the symbolism of memory was thought to be mystical, and devices that were invented as mnemonics (by Giordano Bruno, for example, and by Robert Fludd) were interpreted as magic signs. The symbol is the tool which gives man his power, and it is the same tool whether the symbols are images or words, mathematical signs or mesons. And the symbols have a reach and a roundness that goes beyond their literal and practical meaning. They are the rich concepts under which the mind gathers many particulars into one name, and many instances into one general induction. When a man says *left* and *right*, he is outdistancing the dog not only in looking for a light; he is setting in train all the shifts of meaning, the overtones and the ambiguities, between *gauche* and *adroit* and *dexterous*, between *sinister* and the sense of right. When a man counts *one, two, three,* he is not only doing mathematics; he is on the path to the mysticism of numbers in Pythagoras and Vitruvius and Kepler, to the Trinity and the signs of the Zodiac.

I have described imagination as the ability to make images and to move them about inside one's head in new arrangements. This is the faculty that is specifically human, and it is the common root from which science and literature both spring and grow and flourish together. For they do flourish (and languish) together: the great ages of science are the great ages of all the arts, because in them powerful minds have taken fire from one another, breathless and higgledy-piggledy, without asking too nicely whether they ought to tie their imagination to falling balls or a haunted island. Galileo and Shakespeare, who were born in the same year, grew into greatness in the same age; when Galileo was looking through his telescope at the moon, Shakespeare was writing *The Tempest;* and all Europe was in ferment, from Johannes Kepler to Peter Paul Rubens, and from the first table of logarithms by John Napier to the Authorised Version of the Bible.

Let me end with a last and spirited example of the common inspiration of literature and science, because it is as much alive today as it was three hundred years ago. What I have in mind is man's ageless fantasy, to fly to the moon. I do not display this to you as a high scientific enterprise; on the contrary, I think we have more important discoveries to make here on earth than wait for us, beckoning, at the horned surface of the moon. Yet I cannot belittle the fascination which that little ice-blue journey has had for the imagination of men, long before it drew us to our television screens to watch the tumbling of astronauts. Plutarch and Lucian, Ariosto and Ben Jonson wrote about it, before the days of Jules Verne and H. G. Wells and science fiction. The seventeenth century was heady with new dreams and fables about voyages to the moon. Kepler wrote one full of deep scientific ideas, which (alas) simply got his mother accused of witchcraft. In England, Francis Godwin wrote a wild and splendid work, *The Man in the Moone,* and the astronomer John Wilkins wrote a wild and learned one, *The Discovery of a New World.* They did not draw a line between science and fancy; for example, they all tried to guess just where in the journey the earth's gravity would stop. Only Kepler understood that gravity has no boundary, and put a law to it—which happened to be the wrong law.

All this was a few years before Isaac Newton was born, and it was all in his head that day in 1666 when he sat in his mother's garden, a young man of twenty-three, and thought about the reach of gravity. This was how he came to conceive his brilliant image, that the moon is like a ball which has been thrown so hard that it falls exactly as fast as the horizon, all the way round the earth. The image will do for any satellite, and Newton modestly calculated how long therefore an astronaut would take to fall round the earth once. He made it ninety minutes, and we have all seen now that he was right; but Newton had no way to check that. Instead he went on to calculate how long in that case the distant moon would take to round the earth, if indeed it behaves like a thrown ball that falls in the earth's gravity, and if gravity obeyed a law of inverse squares. He found that the answer would be twenty-eight days.

In that telling figure, the imagination that day chimed with nature, and   25
made a harmony. We shall hear an echo of that harmony on the day when we land on the moon, because it will be not a technical but an imaginative triumph, that reaches back to the beginning of modern science and literature both. All great acts of imagination are like this, in the arts and in science, and convince us because they fill out reality with a deeper sense of rightness. We start with the simplest vocabulary of images, with *left* and *right* and *one,* *two, three,* and before we know how it happened the words and the numbers have conspired to make a match with nature: we catch in them the pattern of mind and matter as one.

THESIS AND THOUGHT

1. According to Bronowski, what is the defining attribute of human beings?
2. What evidence does Bronowski provide to show the universality of that attribute in humans and its absence in other species?
3. How does Bronowski define *imagination* and *image*?

STRUCTURE

1. Examine the definitions in paragraphs 9 and 10 and decide whether they are stipulative.

2. Explain how the comparisons in paragraphs 2–8 constitute definition by negation.

3. Bronowski uses several extended examples: Galileo (paras. 17–19), Einstein (para. 20), and Newton (paras. 24–25). Choose one and explain how it helps fulfill Bronowski's purpose.

4. What does Bronowski accomplish by discussing poetry and fiction as well as scientific thought and experimentation? See especially how he treats these topics in paragraphs 23–25.

STYLE

1. Explain whether you find Bronowski's use of first person an asset or a liability. How might third person have changed the tone of the essay?

2. Bronowski employs parenthetical expression with fair frequency. Examine paragraphs 6, 11, 13, 14, 18, 19, and 21, and show how the purposes of the parenthetical material vary. How might omission or direct incorporation of this material in the text have affected the essay?

3. Occasionally, Bronowski creates some unusual juxtapositions of ideas. For example, he writes in paragraph 14, "John Keats said that the unheard melodies are sweeter [than those heard], and all chess players sadly recall that the combinations that they planned and which never came to be played were the best." Similarly, he ends paragraph 22 with "all Europe was in ferment, from [astronomer] Johannes Kepler to [painter] Peter Paul Rubens and from the first table of logarithms by John Napier to the Authorised Version of the Bible." What do such pairings or groupings contribute to the essay as a whole and to the reader's comprehension?

4. In paragraph 21 Bronowski writes, "When a man says *left* and *right*, . . . he is setting in train all the shifts of meaning, the overtones and the ambiguities, between *gauche* and *adroit* and *dexterous*, between *sinister* and the sense of right." Explain this sentence after looking up the meanings and etymologies of the last four italicized words.

CONSIDERATIONS

1. How does Bronowski reveal his own "reach of imagination" in this essay? If you are feeling less imaginative than usual, you might use some of the questions above as guides.

2. Bronowski uses **allusion** quite liberally. He refers, for example, to Sidney, Blake, and Coleridge (para. 13); Keats (para. 14); Watson (para. 15); Aris-

totle and Aquinas (para. 16); Michelson and Morley (para. 20); Bruno, Fludd, Pythagoras, Vitruvius, and Kepler (para. 21); Rubens and Napier (para. 22); Plutarch, Lucian, Ariosto, Jonson, Verne, and Wells (para. 23). Choose two or three of these people, with whom you are unfamiliar, and discover what their imaginative contribution to humanity was (or is) by reading an encyclopedia article about them. You may choose to follow up with reading more detailed accounts or by examining the products of their imagination in literature, art, and science.

3. Although in his opening paragraph Bronowski asserts that imagination is a universal human characteristic, his many illustrations are derived from prominent figures in the arts and sciences. Validate or question Bronowski's thesis by writing an essay in which you use examples from your own experience to demonstrate the general presence or absence of imagination in the human species.

4. By what attribute would you set humanity apart from other species? Write an essay in which you do so.

Octavio Paz
(Mexico; b. 1914)

Paz comes by his insights into the words of his title quite honestly. He is the son of an attorney who supported the Mexican revolution of 1910 and represented its leader, Emiliano Zapata. Decades later, Paz himself was to support the Republican cause in the Spanish civil war.

However, his zest for revolutionary politics was diminished both through his experiences in Spain and as a result of the nonaggression pact between the Soviet Union and Nazi Germany just before the outbreak of World War II. Ultimately joining the Mexican diplomatic corps, Paz served as secretary to the embassy in Paris and later was appointed ambassador to India. Nevertheless, he resigned this post after six years to protest the violent suppression of student activists at the National University of Mexico in 1968.

Paz is generally regarded as embodying the literary life of modern Mexico. This cultural bond may be seen in tracts such as The Labyrinth of Solitude *(El laberinto de la soledad, 1950) and in much of his poetry, most broadly represented in English by two volumes called* Selected Poems *(1962, 1984). One of his best-known pieces is* Sunstone *(Piedra de sol), a poem based on the 584 lines of the Aztec calendar. Paz has also founded a number of avant-garde Mexican literary journals.*

A precocious child, Paz read extensively in his grandfather's library. He founded a literary review and published his first poems while still in his teens. More than half a century later, Paz became the first Mexican recipient of the Nobel Prize for literature.

Revolt, Revolution, Rebellion

THE WORD *revuelta* is not often used in Spanish. Most people prefer to use the words *revolución* and *rebelión*. On first reflection, the contrary would seem more natural: the word *revuelta* is more popular and more expressive. In the year 1611, Covarrubias defines this latter concept as follows: "*Rebolver es ir con chismerías de una parte a otra y causar enemistades y quistiones: y a éste llamamos rebolvedor y reboltoso, rebuelta la cuestión.*"[1] The meanings of the Spanish word *revuelta* are numerous, ranging from *return* to *confusion* to a *mixture* of one thing with another; all these meanings have to do with the idea of a recurrence of something accompanied by disorder and irregularity. None of these meanings is a positive one; none of them suggests that *revuelta* is a good thing. In a society such as that of seventeenth-century Spain, *revuelta* was regarded as the root of many evils: the confusion of classes, the return to primordial chaos, agitation, and disorder that threatens the very fabric of society. *Revuelta* was something that reduced distinctions to a form-less mass. For Bernardo de Balbuena (the sixteenth-century Spanish poet), the foundation of civilization is the establishment of hierarchies, thus creat-ing a necessary inequality between individuals; barbarism is a return to the state of nature, to equality. It is no easy task to determine when the word *revuelta* came to be used with the meaning of a spontaneous uprising of the people. The word *révolte* appears in French around 1500, in the sense of "a change of party," and does not take on the connotation of *rebellion* until a century later. Although the Littré dictionary indicates that *révolte* comes from the Italian *rivoltare* (to turn inside out or upside down), Corominas believes that it may come from the Catalan *revolt, temps de revolt*. Whatever its origin, most Spanish-speaking people now use the word *revolución*, both in conver-sation and in writing, to refer to public disturbances and uprisings. The word *revuelta* is reserved for riots or agitation with no clearly defined purpose. It is a plebeian word.

There are marked differences in Spanish between the *revoltoso*, the *rebelde*, and the *revolucionario*. The first is a dissatisfied individual who is fond of intrigue and sows confusion; the second is someone who refuses to submit to authority, a disobedient or unruly person; the third is a person who seeks to change institutions through the use of violence. (I use the definitions in our dictionaries even though they seem to be inspired by Police Headquar-ters.) Despite these differences, the three words are intimately related. This

---

[1]Joan Corominas: *Diccionario crítico-etimológico de la lengua castellana*. "*Rebolver* is to go about spreading gossip and causing enmity and quarrels: and we call such a person a *rebolvedor* and a *reboltoso*, and the action, *rebuelta*." [Au.]

relationship is a hierarchical one: *revuelta* lives in the subsoil of the language; *rebelión* is individualist; *revolución* is an intellectual word and refers more to the uprisings of entire peoples and the laws of history than to the deeds of a rebellious hero. *Rebelión* is a military term; it comes from the Latin *bellum* and evokes the image of civil war. Minorities are rebels; majorities, revolutionaries. Although the origin of *revolución* is the same as that of *revuelta* (as is that of the two English words *revolution* and *revolt*, i.e., Latin *volvere*, to revolve, to turn around, to unroll), and although both words connote a *return* or a *recurrence*, the origin of *revolución* is philosophical and astronomical: the return of the stars and the planets to their earlier position, rotation around an axis, the cycle of the seasons and historical eras. The connotations of *return* and *movement* in the word *revolución* suggest an underlying order; these same connotations in the word *revuelta* suggest disorder. Thus *revuelta* does not imply any cosmic or historical vision; it is the chaotic or tumultuous present. In order for revolt to cease to be a mere passing disturbance and take its place in history, it must be transformed into a revolution. The same is true of rebellion: the acts of the rebel, however daring they may be, are fruitless gestures if they are not based on a revolutionary doctrine. Ever since the end of the eighteenth century, the cardinal word of this triad has been revolution. Bathed in the light of the Idea, it is philosophy in action, criticism that has become an act, violence with a clear purpose. As popular as revolt and as generous as rebellion, it encompasses them and guides them. Revolt is the violence of an entire people; rebellion the unruliness of an individual or an uprising by a minority; both are spontaneous and blind. Revolution is both planned and spontaneous, a science and an art.

The discredit into which the word *revuelta* has fallen is due to a precise historical fact. It is a word that aptly expresses the unrest and the discontent of a people still under the sway of the idea that authority is sacred, even though it may rise up in arms against one specific injustice or another. Although it is egalitarian, revolt respects the divine right of the monarch: *de rey abajo, ninguno.*[2] Its violence is the breaking of the ocean wave against the rocky cliff; the wave bathes the cliff in foam and retreats. The modern meaning of *revolución* in Spain and Hispano-America was an importation by intellectuals. *Revuelta*, a popular, spontaneous word but one that pointed in no particular direction, was replaced by one that had philosophical prestige. The fact that the new word became a very fashionable one is indicative not so much of a historical revolt, a popular uprising, as of the appearance of a new power: philosophy. From the eighteenth century on, reason becomes a subversive political principle. The revolutionary is a philosopher, or at least an intellectual: a man of ideas. The word *revolution* calls up many names and

[2]**de . . . ninguno:** literally, "Below the king, (there is) no one." The idea is that, in light of the monarch's superiority, all others are insignificant. [Ed.]

many meanings: Kant, the Encyclopedia, the Jacobin Terror, and, most vividly of all, the destruction of the order of privileges and exceptions and the founding of an order based not on authority but on the free exercise of reason. The old virtues went by the names of faith, fealty, honor. All of them strengthened the social bond and each of them was related to a universally recognized value: faith in the Church as the incarnation of revealed truth; fealty to the sacred authority of the monarch; honor to the tradition based on blood ties. These virtues had their counterpart in the charity of the Church, the magnanimity of the king, and the loyalty of feudal subjects, whether villeins or great lords. Revolution is a word for the new virtue: justice. All the other new virtues—liberty, fraternity, equality—are based on it. It is a virtue that does not depend on revelation, power, or blood. As universal as reason, it admits of no exceptions and is equally far removed from arbitrariness and compassion. Revolution: a word belonging to the vocabulary of the just and the dealers of justice. A little later another word suddenly appears, one previously looked upon with horror: rebellion. From the very outset it was a romantic, bellicose, aristocratic word referring to outlaws. The rebel: the accursed hero, the solitary poet, lovers who trample social conventions underfoot, the plebe of genius who defies one and all, the dandy, the pirate. Rebellion also has religious connotations. It refers not to Heaven but to Hell: the towering pride of the prince of darkness, the blasphemy of the titan in chains. Rebellion: melancholy and irony. Art and love were rebels; politics and philosophy revolutionaries.

In the second half of the nineteenth century, another word appears: *reformista*. This word came not from France but from the English-speaking countries. The word was not a new one; what was new was its meaning and the aura surrounding it. An optimistic word and an austere one, an unusual combination of Protestantism and Positivism. This alliance of the old heresy and the new, of Lutheranism and science, aroused the enmity of both the purists and the conservatives. There were good reasons for their hatred; the word concealed revolutionary contraband beneath its respectable outward trappings. It was a "decent" word. The place where it was heard most often was not in the haunts of the *revoltosos* or in the catacombs of the rebels, but in academic lecture halls and among the editorial staff of periodicals. The revolutionary appealed to philosophy; the reformist to the sciences, commerce, and industry: he was a fanatical admirer of Spencer and the railroads. Ortega y Gasset very cleverly, though perhaps not accurately, points out a basic difference between the revolutionary and the reformist: the former tries to change customary uses; the latter, to correct abuses. If this were true, the reformist would be a rebel who had come to his senses, a Satan who is eager to collaborate with the powers that be. I say this because the rebel, unlike the revolutionary, does not attempt to undermine the social order as a whole. The rebel attacks the tyrant; the revolutionary attacks tyranny. I grant that there are rebels who regard all governments as tyrannical; nonetheless, it is abuses that they condemn, not power itself. Revolutionaries, on the other hand, are convinced that the evil does not lie in the excesses of the constituted order but in order itself. The difference, it seems to me, is considerable. As I see it, the similarities between the revolutionary and the reformist are greater than the differences that separate them. Both are intellectuals, both believe in progress, both reject myths: their faith in reason is unswerving. The reformist is a revolutionary who has chosen the path of evolution rather than violence. His methods are different, but not his goals: the reformist also wants to change institutions. The revolutionary is an advocate of a sudden great leap forward; the reformist of one step at a time. Both believe in history as a linear process and as progress. Both are the offspring of the bourgeoisie, both are modern.

Revolution is a word that implies the notion of cyclical time and there- 5
fore that of regular and recurrent change. But the modern meaning of the word does not refer to an eternal return, the circular movement of worlds and stars, but rather to a sudden and *definitive* change in direction of public affairs. Cyclical time is brought to an end and a new rectilinear time begins. The new meaning destroys the old: the past will not return, and the archetype of events is not what has been but what will be. In its original meaning, revolution is a word that affirms the primacy of the past: anything new is a return. The second meaning implies the primacy of the future: the gravitational field of the word shifts from the yesterday that is known to the tomorrow that is yet to be discovered. It is a cluster of new meanings: the pre-eminence of the future, the belief in continuous progress and the perfectibility of the species, rationalism, the discredit of tradition and authority, humanism. All these ideas fuse in that of rectilinear time: history conceived as an onward march. This new cluster of meanings marks the sudden appearance of profane time. Christian time was finite; it began with the Fall and ended in Eternity, the day after the Last Judgment. Modern time, whether revolutionary or reformist, rectilinear or spiral, is infinite.

The change in meaning of the word *revolution* also affects the word *revolt*. Guided by philosophy, it becomes a prerevolutionary activity: it enters the realm of history and the future. The martial word *rebellion*, in turn, absorbs the old meanings of the words *revolt* and *revolution*. Like revolt, it is a spontaneous protest against power; like revolution, it represents cyclical time that ceaselessly reverses top and bottom. The rebel, a fallen angel or a titan in disgrace, is the eternal nonconformist. His action is not engraved upon the rectilinear time of history, the realm of the revolutionary and the reformist, but on the circular time of myth: Jupiter will be dethroned, Quetzalcoatl will reappear, Lucifer will return to heaven. During all of the nineteenth century, the rebel lives on the margin of society. Revolutionaries and reformists look upon him with the same mistrust as Plato passing judgment on poets, and for the same reason: the rebel prolongs the fascination of myth.

THESIS AND THOUGHT

1. Explain the etymological origins of the terms in the title.

2. What distinctions exist among the three key terms and *reformista*, which Paz introduces in paragraph 4?

3. What implications for the future development or direction of human civilization arise from the distinction Paz draws in paragraph 5 between cyclical and rectilinear time?

4. Does Paz merely explain his terms, or does he have some additional purpose? Is the essay controlled by a governing idea or point of view? If so, state it. If not, suggest how one might be created.

STRUCTURE

1. Without a clearly stated thesis and with a final paragraph that does not conventionally "conclude," does this essay have a unifying structural principal or method? Explain.

2. To what extent does Paz depend on comparison-contrast to develop his points? To what extent does he depend on process, particularly historical process?

STYLE

1. Explain whether the use of Spanish (as well as other languages) poses problems that remain unresolved by essay's end.

2. Of the four terms discussed, with which is Paz most sympathetic? Least sympathetic? Justify your responses by referring to specific language in the text, particularly language that creates tone.

CONSIDERATIONS

1. Discuss whether you find that the word *revolution* is overused, misused, or abused, as in "the technological revolution," "the sexual revolution," "the fast-food revolution," and so on.

2. Explain which, if any, of the terms *rebel*, *revolutionary*, or *reformer* you would apply to yourself. If none apply, explain how you perceive your relationship to society or how you propose to deal with social inequities and injustices.

3. The United States prides itself in having been born through revolution (developed through the historical process that Paz describes in para. 3). Jefferson, recognizing that revolutions might subvert their own principles and produce new tyranny, once suggested that periodic revolutions may be beneficial and necessary for the public good. Write an essay explaining why you agree or disagree with Jefferson's proposition, or in which you discuss America's present need for revolution, reform, or rebellion.

4. To what extent do the four terms Paz defines apply to several contemporary or historical figures with whom you are familiar? Explain your responses. Choose one of the figures, and expand your response to several paragraphs or a brief essay. Here are a few suggestions: Thomas Jefferson, Martin Luther King, Jr., Fidel Castro, Moses, Margaret Sanger, Ralph Nader, Jesus, Jomo Kenyatta, Robin Hood, Hitler, Joan of Arc, Malcolm X, Freud, Gandhi, Lenin, Susan B. Anthony, Muhammad, Nelson Mandela, Elvis Presley, Crazy Horse.

───────── **A Question of Equality** ─────────

Kurt Vonnegut, Jr.
(United States; b. 1922)

Kurt Vonnegut is a prolific writer, chiefly of novels, but also of stories, essays, and plays. He was born in Indiana and attended several universities, studying at various times the sciences, engineering, and anthropology. Vonnegut enlisted in the army during World War II, was captured in 1944 by the Germans during the Battle of the Bulge, and spent the duration of the war as a prisoner set to factory work in Dresden. There he witnessed the Allied bombing of 1945 that literally destroyed the city, killing more than one hundred thousand residents. Dresden was not a military target.

Out of his Dresden experience eventually came the novel Slaughterhouse Five *(1969). Published at the height of the Vietnam War, it achieved great popularity as an antiwar protest and helped make Vonnegut's reputation among supporters of the "counterculture." Banned in various places both for its political implications and for its language, the book was made into a film three years later.*

Vonnegut's first broad recognition had come several years earlier with Cat's Cradle *(1963), a novel that debunks scientific and technological "advances" as well as technocratic, religious, and philosophical systems. Such criticism is characteristic of his work, which includes such other novels as* God Bless You, Mr. Rosewater *(1965) and* Hocus Pocus *(1990).*

Among Vonnegut's techniques are humor (including satire) and the devices common to science fiction. One of the questions you might ask yourself as you read is whether the author means simply to describe and fantasize about the future or whether he is essentially focused on the present and criticizing current tendencies.

Harrison Bergeron

THE YEAR WAS 2081, and everybody was finally equal. They weren't only equal before God and the law. They were equal every which way. Nobody was smarter than anybody else. Nobody was better looking than anybody else.

Nobody was stronger or quicker than anybody else. All this equality was due to the 211th, 212th, and 213th Amendments to the Constitution, and to the unceasing vigilance of agents of the United States Handicapper General.

Some things about living still weren't quite right, though. April, for instance, still drove people crazy by not being springtime. And it was in that clammy month that the H-G men took George and Hazel Bergeron's fourteen-year-old son, Harrison, away.

It was tragic, all right, but George and Hazel couldn't think about it very hard. Hazel had a perfectly average intelligence, which meant she couldn't think about anything except in short bursts. And George, while his intelligence was way above normal, had a little mental handicap radio in his ear. He was required by law to wear it at all times. It was tuned to a government transmitter. Every twenty seconds or so, the transmitter would send out some sharp noise to keep people like George from taking unfair advantage of their brains.

George and Hazel were watching television. There were tears on Hazel's cheeks, but she'd forgotten for the moment what they were about.

On the television screen were ballerinas.   5

A buzzer sounded in George's head. His thoughts fled in panic, like bandits from a burglar alarm.

"That was a real pretty dance, that dance they just did," said Hazel.

"Huh?" said George.

"That dance—it was nice," said Hazel.

"Yup," said George. He tried to think a little about the ballerinas. They   10
weren't really very good—no better than anybody else would have been, anyway. They were burdened with sashweights and bags of birdshot, and their faces were masked, so that no one, seeing a free and graceful gesture or a pretty face, would feel like something the cat drug in. George was toying with the vague notion that maybe dancers shouldn't be handicapped. But he didn't get very far with it before another noise in his ear radio scattered his thoughts.

George winced. So did two out of the eight ballerinas.

Hazel saw him wince. Having no mental handicap herself, she had to ask George what the latest sound had been.

"Sounded like somebody hitting a milk bottle with a ball peen hammer," said George.

"I'd think it would be real interesting, hearing all the different sounds," said Hazel, a little envious. "All the things they think up."

"Um," said George.   15

"Only, if I was Handicapper General, you know what I would do?" said Hazel. Hazel, as a matter of fact, bore a strong resemblance to the Handicapper General, a woman named Diana Moon Glampers. "If I was Diana Moon Glampers," said Hazel, "I'd have chimes on Sunday—just chimes. Kind of in honor of religion."

"I could think, if it was just chimes," said George.

"Well—maybe make 'em real loud," said Hazel. "I think I'd make a good Handicapper General."

"Good as anybody else," said George.

"Who knows better'n I do what normal is?" said Hazel.   20

"Right," said George. He began to think glimmeringly about his abnormal son who was now in jail, about Harrison, but a twenty-one-gun salute in his head stopped that.

"Boy!" said Hazel, "that was a doozy, wasn't it?"

It was such a doozy that George was white and trembling, and tears stood on the rims of his red eyes. Two of the eight ballerinas had collapsed to the studio floor, were holding their temples.

"All of a sudden you look so tired," said Hazel. "Why don't you stretch out on the sofa, so's you can rest your handicap bag on the pillows, honeybunch." She was referring to the forty-seven pounds of birdshot in a canvas bag, which was padlocked around George's neck. "Go on and rest the bag for a little while," she said. "I don't care if you're not equal to me for a while."

George weighed the bag with his hands. "I don't mind it," he said, "I   25
don't notice it any more. It's just a part of me."

"You been so tired lately—kind of wore out," said Hazel. "If there was just some way we could make a little hole in the bottom of the bag, and just take out a few of them lead balls. Just a few."

"Two years in prison and two thousand dollars fine for every ball I took out." said George. "I don't call that a bargain."

"If you could take a few out when you came home from work," said Hazel. "I mean—you don't compete with anybody around here. You just set around."

"If I tried to get away with it," said George, "then other people'd get away with it—and pretty soon we'd be right back to the dark ages again, with everybody competing against everybody else. You wouldn't like that, would you?"

"I'd hate it," said Hazel.   30

"There you are," said George. "The minute people start cheating on laws, what do you think happens to society?"

If Hazel hadn't been able to come up with an answer to this question, George couldn't have supplied one. A siren was going off in his head.

"Reckon it'd fall all apart," said Hazel.

"What would?" said George blankly.

"Society," said Hazel uncertainly. "Wasn't that what you just said?"   35

"Who knows?" said George.

The television program was suddenly interrupted for a news bulletin. It wasn't clear at first as to what the bulletin was about, since the announcer like all announcers, had a serious speech impediment. For about half a minute, and in a state of high excitement, the announcer tried to say, "Ladies and gentlemen—"

He finally gave up, handed the bulletin to a ballerina to read.

"That's all right—" Hazel said of the announcer, "he tried. That's the big thing. He tried to do the best he could with what God gave him. He should get a nice raise for trying so hard."

"Ladies and gentlemen—" said the ballerina, reading the bulletin. She 40 must have been extraordinarily beautiful, because the mask she wore was hideous. And it was easy to see that she was the strongest and most graceful of all the dancers, for her handicap bags were as big as those worn by two-hundred-pound men.

And she had to apologize at once for her voice, which was a very unfair voice for a woman to use. Her voice was a warm, luminous, timeless melody. "Excuse me—" she said, and she began again, making her voice absolutely uncompetitive.

"Harrison Bergeron, age fourteen," she said in a grackle squawk, "has just escaped from jail, where he was held on suspicion of plotting to overthrow the government. He is a genius and an athlete, is under-handicapped, and should be regarded as extremely dangerous."

A police photograph of Harrison Bergeron was flashed on the screen upside down, then sideways, upside down again, then right side up. The picture showed the full length of Harrison against a background calibrated in feet and inches. He was exactly seven feet tall.

The rest of Harrison's appearance was Halloween and hardware. Nobody had ever borne heavier handicaps. He had outgrown hindrances faster than the H-G men could think them up. Instead of a little ear radio for a mental handicap, he wore a tremendous pair of earphones, and spectacles with thick wavy lenses. The spectacles were intended to make him not only half blind, but to give him whanging headaches besides.

Scrap metal was hung all over him. Ordinarily, there was a certain 45 symmetry, a military neatness to the handicaps issued to strong people, but Harrison looked like a walking junkyard. In the race of life, Harrison carried three hundred pounds.

And to offset his good looks, the H-G men required that he wear at all times a red rubber ball for a nose, keep his eyebrows shaved off, and cover his even white teeth with black caps at snaggle-tooth random.

"If you see this boy," said the ballerina, "do not—I repeat, do not—try to reason with him."

There was a shriek of a door being torn from its hinges.

Screams and barking cries of consternation came from the television set. The photograph of Harrison Bergeron on the screen jumped again and again, as though dancing to the tune of an earthquake.

George Bergeron correctly identified the earthquake, and well he might 50 have—for many was the time his own home had danced to the same crashing tune. "My God—" said George, "that must be Harrison!"

The realization was blasted from his mind instantly by the sound of an automobile collision in his head.

When George could open his eyes again, the photograph of Harrison was gone. A living, breathing Harrison filled the screen.

Clanking, clownish, and huge, Harrison stood in the center of the studio. The knob of the uprooted studio door was still in his hand. Ballerinas, technicians, musicians, and announcers cowered on their knees before him, expecting to die.

"I am the Emperor!" cried Harrison. "Do you hear! I am the Emperor! Everybody must do what I say at once!" He stamped his foot and the studio shook.

"Even as I stand here—" he bellowed, "crippled, hobbled, sickened—I am a greater ruler than any man who ever lived! Now watch me become what I *can* become!" 55

Harrison tore the straps of his handicap harness like wet tissue paper, tore straps guaranteed to support five thousand pounds.

Harrison's scrap-iron handicaps crashed to the floor.

Harrison thrust his thumbs under the bar of the padlock that secured his head harness. The bar snapped like celery. Harrison smashed his headphones and spectacles against the wall.

He flung away his rubber-ball nose, revealed a man that would have awed Thor, the god of thunder.

"I shall now select my Empress!" he said, looking down on the cowering people. "Let the first woman who dares rise to her feet claim her mate and her throne!" 60

A moment passed, and then a ballerina arose, swaying like a willow.

Harrison plucked the mental handicap from her ear, snapped off her physical handicaps with marvelous delicacy. Last of all, he removed her mask.

She was blindingly beautiful.

"Now—" said Harrison, taking her hand, "shall we show the people the meaning of the word dance? Music!" he commanded.

The musicians scrambled back into their chairs, and Harrison stripped them of their handicaps, too. "Play your best," he told them, "and I'll make you barons and dukes and earls." 65

The music began. It was normal at first—cheap, silly, false. But Harrison snatched two musicians from their chairs, waved them like batons as he sang the music as he wanted it played. He slammed them back into their chairs.

The music began again and was much improved.

Harrison and his Empress merely listened to the music for a while —listened gravely, as though synchronizing their heartbeats with it.

They shifted their weights to their toes.

Harrison placed his big hands on the girl's tiny waist, letting her sense the weightlessness that would soon be hers. 70

And then in an explosion of joy and grace, into the air they sprang!

Not only were the laws of the land abandoned, but the law of gravity and the laws of motion as well.

They reeled, whirled, swiveled, flounced, capered, gamboled, and spun.
They leaped like deer on the moon.

The studio ceiling was thirty feet high, but each leap brought the dancers   75
nearer to it.

It became their obvious intention to kiss the ceiling.

They kissed it.

And then, neutralizing gravity with love and pure will, they remained
suspended in air inches below the ceiling, and they kissed each other for a
long, long time.

It was then that Diana Moon Glampers, the Handicapper General, came
into the studio with a double-barreled ten-gauge shotgun. She fired twice,
and the Emperor and the Empress were dead before they hit the floor.

Diana Moon Glampers loaded the gun again. She aimed it at the musi-   80
cians and told them they had ten seconds to get their handicaps back on.

It was then that the Bergerons' television tube burned out.

Hazel turned to comment about the blackout to George. But George had
gone out into the kitchen for a can of beer.

George came back in with the beer, paused while a handicap signal shook
him up. And then he sat down again.

"You been crying?" he said to Hazel.

"Yup," she said.   85

"What about?" he said.

"I forget," she said. "Something real sad on television."

"What was it?" he said.

"It's all kind of mixed up in my mind," said Hazel.

"Forget sad things," said George.   90

"I always do," said Hazel.

"That's my girl," said George. He winced. There was the sound of a
riveting gun in his head.

"Gee—I could tell that one was a doozy," said Hazel.

"You can say that again," said George.

"Gee—" said Hazel, "I could tell that one was a doozy."   95

Thomas Sowell

(United States; b. 1930)

*A senior fellow of the Hoover Institution at Stanford University, Sowell has
been prominent in conservative economics and politics for more than two
decades. His stands on federally mandated programs such as busing and
affirmative action, and on a variety of issues in education—including African-
American studies programs—have earned him the enmity of liberals in general*

and of mainstream African-American leaders in particular, since Sowell himself is black.

Born in North Carolina and raised there and in Harlem, Sowell attended Stuyvesant High School, a public institution for gifted students, until forced by poverty to leave in tenth grade. He held various jobs, served in the Marine Corps, and upon discharge began to study at Howard University under the GI Bill. Sowell subsequently transferred to Harvard where he received his B.A. magna cum laude, then took an M.A. in economics from Columbia and his doctorate at the University of Chicago, studying under such well-known economists as Milton Friedman.

Since then, Sowell has worked in government (during the Reagan administration), industry, and chiefly education. He has taught at several universities. His stay at Cornell in the 1960s was marked by confrontations with militant African-American students and their many supporters among the nearly all-white faculty on such matters as admissions policy, curriculum, and the easing of academic standards for disadvantaged black students.

Sowell has written widely both in the fields of economics and race relations. Among his works are Black Education: Myths and Tragedies *(1972) and* Race and Economics *(1975). Some of his short pieces have been collected in* Pink and Brown People and Other Controversial Essays *(1981) and* Compassion Versus Guilt and Other Essays *(1987).*

In reading this selection, ask yourself how Sowell's definition of equality differs from more conventional or popular views and whether it has political and social implications.

We're Not Really "Equal"

As A TEACHER I have learned from sad experience that nothing so bores students as being asked to define terms systematically before discussing some exciting issue. They want to get on with it, without wasting time on petty verbal distinctions.

Much of our politics is conducted in the same spirit. We are for "equality" or "the environment," or against an "arms race," and there is no time to waste on definitions and other Mickey Mouse stuff. This attitude may be all right for those for whom political crusades are a matter of personal excitement, like rooting for your favorite team and jeering at the opposition. But for those who are serious about the consequences of public policy, nothing can be built without a solid foundation.

"Equality" is one of the great undefined terms underlying much current controversy and antagonism. This one confused word might even become the rock on which our civilization is wrecked. It should be worth defining.

Equality is such an easily understood concept in mathematics that we may not realize it is a bottomless pit of complexities anywhere else. That is because in mathematics we have eliminated the concreteness and complexities of real things. When we say that two plus two equals four, we either don't say two *what* or we say the same what after each number. But if we said that two apples plus two apples equals four oranges, we would be in trouble.

Yet that is what we are saying in our political reasoning. And we are in trouble. Nothing is more concrete or complex than a human being. Beethoven could not play center field like William Mays, and Willie never tried to write a symphony. In what sense are they equal—or unequal? The common mathematical symbol for inequality points to the smaller quantity. But which is the smaller quantity—and in whose eyes—when such completely different things are involved?   5

When women have children and men don't, how can they be either equal or unequal? Our passionate desire to reduce things to the simplicity of abstract concepts does not mean that it can be done. Those who want to cheer their team and boo the visitors may like to think that the issue is equality versus inequality. But the real issue is whether or not we are going to talk sense. Those who believe in inequality have the same confusion as those who believe in equality. The French make better champagne than the Japanese, but the Japanese make better cameras than the French. What sense does it make to add champagne to cameras to a thousand other things and come up with a grand total showing who is "superior"?

When we speak of "equal justice under law," we simply mean applying the same rules to everybody. That has nothing whatsoever to do with whether everyone performs equally. A good umpire calls balls and strikes by the same rules for everyone, but one batter may get twice as many hits as another.

In recent years we have increasingly heard it argued that if outcomes are unequal, then the rules must have been applied unequally. It would destroy my last illusion to discover that Willie Mays didn't really play baseball any better than anybody else, but that the umpires and sportswriters just conspired to make it look that way. Pending the uncovering of intricate plots of this magnitude, we must accept the fact that performances are very unequal in different aspects of life. And there is no way to add up these apples, oranges, and grapes to get one sum total of fruit.

Anyone with the slightest familiarity with history knows that rules have often been applied very unequally to different groups. (A few are ignorant or misguided enough to think that this is a peculiarity of American society.) The problem is not in seeing that unequal rules can lead to unequal outcomes. The problem is in trying to reason backward from unequal outcomes to unequal rules as the sole or main cause.

There are innumerable places around the world where those who have   10 been the victims of unequal rules have nevertheless vastly outperformed those who are favored. Almost nowhere in Southeast Asia have the Chinese minority had equal rights with the native peoples, but the average Chinese income in these countries has almost invariably been much higher than that of the general population. A very similar story could be told from the history of the Jews in many countries of Europe, North Africa and the Middle East. To a greater or lesser extent, this has also been the history of the Ibos in Nigeria, the Italians in Argentina, the Armenians in Turkey, the Japanese in the United States—and on and on.

It would be very convenient if we could infer discriminatory rules whenever we found unequal outcomes. But life does not always accommodate itself to our convenience.

Those who are determined to find villains but cannot find evidence often resort to "society" as the cause of all our troubles. What do they mean by "society" or "environment"? They act as if these terms were self-evident. But environment and society are just new confused terms introduced to save the old confused term, equality.

The American environment or society cannot explain historical behavior patterns found among German-Americans if these same patterns can be found among Germans in Brazil, Australia, Ireland and elsewhere around the world. These patterns may be explained by the history of German society. But if the words "environment" or "society" refer to things that may go back a thousand years, we are no longer talking about either the casual or the moral responsibility of American society. If historic causes include such things as the peculiar geography of Africa or of southern Italy, then we are no longer talking about human responsibility at all.

This does not mean that there are no problems. There are very serious social problems. But that means that serious attention will be required to solve them—beginning with defining our terms.

THESIS AND THOUGHT

1. According to Sowell, in what way are people equal? In what ways are they not?

2. What "necessitates" the handicapping in "Harrison Bergeron"? How might Sowell respond to both the perceived "need" and the "corrective" action?

3. Describe in your own words the daily life and especially the relationships among members of the Bergeron family. How are these a function of the society in which they live? Support your statements with references to the text.

4. Comment on the idea that the society in "Harrison Bergeron" is a consequence of what Sowell perceives as our failure to define terms reasonably.

5. Having answered the previous questions, describe to what extent the themes of the two pieces overlap. Explain any differences between them.

STRUCTURE

1. Explain how Vonnegut uses process and comparison to define his theme.

2. Identify the conflict(s) upon which Vonnegut's narrative depends.

3. Sowell's essay is clearly about the need for definition, but to what extent does it provide definition itself?

4. Describe Sowell's purpose in using the following kinds of examples, and comment on their effectiveness: fruit (paras. 4 and 8); baseball (paras. 5, 7, and 8); nations or peoples (paras. 6, 10, and 13).

STYLE

1. What elements of humor are present in "Harrison Bergeron"?

2. Although "Harrison Bergeron" is set in 2081, the techniques used to achieve equality are primitive—rubber noses, bags of birdshot, radio noise, "a double-barreled ten-gauge shotgun" (para. 79). Account for the story's insistence on crude devices.

3. "Harrison Bergeron" is developed through numerous brief paragraphs containing both narrative and dialogue. Explain whether their brevity is useful to Vonnegut's development of character and theme.

4. Vonnegut achieves his effects partly through repetition. The word *doozy*, for instance, appears in paragraphs 22, 23, 93, and 95. What other repetitive elements does Vonnegut employ? Why is the repetition significant?

5. Sowell has written for many scholarly journals. "We Are Not Really 'Equal'," however, originally appeared in *Newsweek*. What stylistic elements make the writing appropriate to a mass-circulation magazine as opposed to a specialized academic publication?

CONSIDERATIONS

1. Explain in a substantial paragraph why you agree or disagree with the point of view expressed in either piece or both.

2. Given Sowell's views of equality, inequality, and their causes, explain how he might view affirmative action or similar policies that attempt to establish numerical "equality" or proportional representation for women and racial minorities. Take into account whether the "rules" are equal or unequal in the first place.

3. Although Vonnegut's and Sowell's political opinions are usually perceived as polar opposites, they seem to be in substantial agreement here. Write an essay describing and explaining your own agreement with people or groups whose opinions you normally oppose.

4. Does Vonnegut subscribe to his title character's social vision? Do you? Write an essay on the following topic: "Harrison Bergeron: The Most Dangerous Man in America?"

Donald J. Johnson
(United States; b. 1931)

Jean E. Johnson
(United States; b. 1934)

Leon E. Clark
(United States; b. 1935)

Donald J. Johnson is Director of International Education at New York University. An authority on Asian studies curricula, he teaches courses focused on India and Southeast Asia and also directs summer programs in these two regions and China. As a Fulbright scholar, he worked as an education consultant in New Delhi.

Also a former education consultant in the Indian capital, Jean E. Johnson has taught English and social studies both in New York City and Istanbul. In addition to editing Through Indian Eyes, *from which "What Is Caste?" is taken, Johnson and her husband have co-authored* God and Gods in Hinduism *and* India Through Literature.

General editor of the series of books that includes Through Indian Eyes, *Leon E. Clark is author of* Through African Eyes. *Currently director of the International Education Program at American University, he has had broad experience in education as a high-school and college teacher and as a government consultant in both Africa and Asia. His previous university appointments include one at the University of Mysore.*

What Is Caste?

Editors' Introduction   If you were to ask Ved Mehta's tailor, "What is your caste?" he would probably answer, "I am a tailor." Occupation is one definition of caste in India, but it is not the only one.

In Indian society there are four large classes, called *varnas*, that date back to 1,000 B.C.: Brahmin (priest), Kshatriya (ruler), Vaishya (businessman), and Shudra (worker). Each *varna* had its *dharma*. The Laws of Manu, written at least two hundred years before Christ, describe these four groups as follows:

> For the sake of prosperity of the worlds, he created the Brahmin, the Kshatriya, the Vaishya, and the Shudra . . .
>
> To Brahmins he assigned teaching and studying [the *Veda*], sacrificing for their own benefit and for others, giving and accepting [of alms].

The Kshatriya he commanded to protect the people, to bestow gifts, to offer sacrifices, to study [the *Veda*], and to abstain from attaching himself to sensual pleasures.

The Vaishya to tend cattle, to bestow gifts, to offer sacrifices, to study [the *Veda*], to trade, to lend money, and to cultivate land.

One occupation only the lord prescribed to the Shudra, to serve meekly even these three [other] castes.[1]

But these categories have always been more theoretical than real.

India, from earliest times, had been divided into many small communities, known as *jati*. Today there are over three thousand *jati* in India. Each is distinct because it does not exchange food or intermarry with any other *jati*. But knowing these facts does not fully explain how the caste system functions in Indian society. To understand the complexity of the caste system, consider the following imaginary conversation between an American teacher and an Indian businessman. Does caste seem to be a problem to the Indian? What is caste?

AMERICAN   I appreciate your willingness to explain caste to me. Most   5
Indians tell me I couldn't possibly understand it and can only see caste as a problem. But I want to understand. Is it true that caste began when the light-skinned Aryans came to India and subdued the darker-skinned Dravidians?

INDIAN   Yes and no.

AMERICAN   Do you mean yes or no?

INDIAN   I mean yes *and* no. The early Brahmins were probably Aryans, but many of the very strict Brahmins are in South India, and they are darker than some of the very low-caste people.

AMERICAN   Then caste is not based on color?

INDIAN   That's right. Some high castes are dark, some are light. Low   10
castes also are both dark and light.

AMERICAN   Then race doesn't explain caste. What about rich and poor? Surely the high-caste Brahmins are richer than the low-caste workers—Shudra.

INDIAN   Again, yes and no. Many members of high castes are also well-born, with more education and better jobs, and would be considered "upper class" in your sense. Yet there are many poor Brahmins and rich Shudras. Apu's family in the movie "Pather Panchali" were very poor Brahmins. The night watchman in that office over there is Brahmin. But take the Nadars in South Indian. They were untouchables but are now among the most successful businessmen in the area.

AMERICAN   So caste isn't race or class. Would you agree that it is based on occupation?

[1]**For . . . castes:** Ainslie Embree, *The Hindu Tradition* (New York: The Modern Library, 1966), 79–80. [Au.]

INDIAN   You can guess my answer: yes and no. Occupation is an important feature of caste. Many names are occupational, like your Mr. Potter, Mr. Carpenter, Mr. Smith, Mr. Weaver, Mr. Taylor. Most of our craft groups are also caste groups. Sons follow their fathers' occupations, and daughters marry boys who do the same work as their fathers.

But there are also exceptions. Most Brahmins are not priests. There are   15
villages in North India where most of the farmers are Brahmins. The army is made up of hundreds of castes, and most of them are not from the Kshatriya or warrior group. In Kerela, the Nairs are the dominant caste, and they are not even in the top three *varnas*. Some of India's most important saints came from non-Brahmin castes. Gandhi became a saint, but he was of a commercial caste, and his name means grocer. It's like your John Smith who was a colonizer in America. Did he ever work as a blacksmith? So caste is not based just on occupation.

AMERICAN   It's easier to say what caste isn't than what it is. How about ethnic loyalty? Is caste membership like belonging to a Polish-American or an Italian-American group?

INDIAN   Yes and no. India does have thousands of different ethnic groups, many of which migrated here through the more than 4,000 years of Indian history. You probably know the Aryans, Muslims, and British. But there were also the Bactrians, the Kushans, the Huns, the Parsees, the Afghans, and hundreds of others. Many groups have different physical appearances and claim different histories. How did the Coorgs of South India come here? The Chitpavan Brahmins of Maharastra have blue eyes. Did they come from the Middle East? Are the Jats of North India descendants of white Huns? One of our great anthropologists, Professor Karve, claimed that all caste members were blood-related. She explained caste as an expanded kinship system.

AMERICAN   I give up. Let's say we just don't know why caste groups formed, how they came about, or why.

INDIAN   At last you've said something I can agree with.

AMERICAN   Can we at least learn how many castes there are in India?   20

INDIAN   That depends on whether you mean the large groupings like Brahmins, Jat, Nairs, etc., or the thousands of so-called subcastes.

AMERICAN   Don't tell me you can't answer this either. How many subcastes?

INDIAN   No one has ever counted them, but there are several thousand. There are 550 subcastes of untouchables alone. In the Delhi area, there are hundreds of Brahmin castes.

AMERICAN   This is really getting complicated. Let's forget numbers. Can you tell me how a caste acts—any caste?

INDIAN   Well, behavior, rituals, and taboos are different for each one. I'm   25
a member of the Srivastava community.

AMERICAN   How does that affect your life?

INDIAN   Well, in spite of the fact I live in Delhi, my caste is always a part of my life. My wife, naturally, is a Srivastava. She comes from a family that has known my family for more years than we can remember. Because she is a Srivastava, she knows the food I like, the religious rituals I am used to, she tells our children stories from the *Ramayana,* the same ones I was told as a child. In a thousand unconscious ways, her behavior will echo mine because we are members of the same caste. Marriage almost always takes place within one caste for these reasons. Sometimes women marry into a higher caste, but men hardly ever.

Eating is another thing. My mother, sixty years old now, will not take food from a lower caste. My partner's a Brahmin. In his home I do not ask for food, although we eat in restaurants together. Perhaps this practice came about as a protection from disease. Maybe it's a way to preserve one's culture. You have that in America, don't you? Russian-Americans like their Borscht; Italians prefer their spaghetti; not everyone likes soul food.

Then there's the matter of social life. Most of us prefer to be with members of our own group because we have more in common. We share a history, a tradition; we laugh at the same jokes. Don't you feel more at home with other Northern Europeans like yourself? And don't answer by telling me, "Some of my best friends are black."

Then there's the loyalty. If I'm in trouble I can always count on my family   30
and my community. No matter where I travel in India, I know caste members will accept me. Even when I travel to your country, another Srivastava will take me in. It's good to know you are never alone. Being part of a community really matters; it gives meaning to life, although the community also imposes restrictions on its own members.

AMERICAN How can you tell the difference between a high caste and a low one?

INDIAN It has to do with ritual purity. A Kshatriya king may be powerful and a Vaishya trader may be rich, but their ritual status is lower than that of the poorest Brahmin.

AMERICAN Well, either some castes are higher than others or they aren't.

INDIAN Why must you Americans always insist on things being either one way or another? Things aren't always black or white.

AMERICAN We'll discuss philosophy another time. Now we're discussing   35
sociology.

INDIAN That might be one reason you have trouble understanding India, but, as you say, let's get back to the point. High and low castes have a lot to do with purity—ritual purity. We Hindus have divided everything into pure and impure. That's not the same as sanitary or unsanitary, I might add. For example, meat eating, especially beef, is polluting; alcohol is polluting to some, and so are occupations dealing with the body, like cutting hair. Animal skinning and garbage collecting are also polluting jobs. On the other hand, bathing is ritually purifying; fire can be purifying; the water of the Ganges is purifying. Generally, the more purified daily life, the higher the caste. Less ritually pure behavior means lower caste, although there are exceptions.

AMERICAN How does a low-caste person feel about this? Does he want to move up?

INDIAN Many lower-caste members probably think they are exactly where they should be; that it's a result of deeds done, good or bad, in past lives. Others may think moving up is a good thing. Let me give you one example. The Chamars, people who used to do mainly cow skinning, have a caste tradition that they used to be Brahmins, but long ago one of them was trying to help a cow out of the mud by pulling on its tail and the cow died just as some people were passing by. The Chamars were accused of killing the cow and were polluted by that and condemned to live in a low caste. Caste has never been as rigid as many think. In ancient times people moved up quite often. The scriptures and epics like the *Mahabharata* speak of this a lot. One of our great anthropologists, Prof. Srinivas, has studied this moving up the scale by caste. He calls the process Sanskritization.

AMERICAN What does that mean?

INDIAN It is quite simple, actually. Sanskrit was and is the classical 40
language of India. It is associated with high culture, often Brahmin culture. It's more than a language, really, it's a way of life. Sanskrit culture means the highest culture. When a lower caste imitates the behavior of an upper, often Brahmin, caste, that's called "Sanskritization." It doesn't mean that the lower caste learns to speak Sanskrit.

AMERICAN I can understand moving up as a caste group, but I don't quite understand that way of imitating upper-caste behavior. I thought moving up the scale meant driving a bigger car, getting invited to fancy parties, doing things that were more fun.

INDIAN Don't forget we're talking about India, not America. The upper castes in India are associated with ritual purity. So a caste that makes its move upward often imitates this ritual purity of the Brahmins. If a low caste eats meat, it might become vegetarian when it moves up; it might perform religious rituals more carefully; it might stop drinking alcohol. It might even change its caste name in the hope that other people will think it is a higher caste.

AMERICAN But that's no fun. In America, going up the ladder means you live better.

INDIAN I told you, this is India, not America. Remember the Nadars I spoke of earlier—the untouchable caste that moved up in South India? One of the ways they spent their new money was on building temples. That's because temple building is associated with the upper castes. By the way, didn't your John D. Rockefeller build a cathedral in New York?

AMERICAN Yes, I guess he did. 45

INDIAN There's one more thing. Here in India we hardly ever refer to the "caste system" or to caste at all. "Caste" is a Portuguese word. We speak of our *community* instead. Of course, "community" doesn't mean to us what you mean by the word. It means all the things we've been talking about. And more.

AMERICAN It's certainly complicated.

INDIAN Yes and no. Yes, if you're looking at it from the outside; no, if you're a part of it.

THESIS AND THOUGHT

1. What questions about the nature of caste do you have after reading the selection? Is this in any way a reflection on the limitations of the piece? Having read the selection, can you better define *caste* than you could have before?

2. Based on the editors' introduction and the dialogue, write a brief paragraph that attempts to state affirmatively what caste is.

3. How accurate are the generalizations included in paragraphs 28, 34, and 41? Explain.

4. Comment on the following: "What Is Caste?" is intended more to define the problem of defining caste than to define the phenomenon itself.

STRUCTURE

1. What does the dialogue accomplish that a straightforward essay might not? What, if anything, does it fail to accomplish?

2. How well are paragraphs 1–4 integrated with the dialogue? Could the content have been presented as effectively if it were made part of the dialogue?

3. What is the principal technique used to create the definition?

4. What use does the Indian interlocutor make of comparison?

STYLE

1. Judging from the vocabulary, describe the audience for which "What Is Caste?" was originally intended.

CONSIDERATIONS

1. Based on the reading, what are the essential differences in social mobility between India and the United States? Does such mobility seem to be valued in India at all?

2. Is there any approximation of caste in American society? Is "untouchability" useful as a metaphor in describing the way some groups in the United States are regarded? Explain.

3. Write an essay in which you use dialogue to define a difficult concept.

Sylvia Plath

(United States; 1932–1963)

Sylvia Plath's troubled life ended by suicide in 1963, before her reputation was firmly established. With the posthumous publication of the autobiographical novel The Bell Jar *and the poems in* Ariel *(1965), she came to sudden prominence, partly as a cult figure. In the novel as well as in her poetry, upon which her reputation ultimately rests, emotional distress, depression, domestic discord, psychological abuse, and self-destruction are prominent themes.*

Intellectual as well as artistic, Plath was graduated with honors from Smith College in 1955 and held a Fulbright scholarship to Cambridge from 1955 to 1959. In England, she married British poet Ted Hughes, with whom she had two children. The end of the marriage was among the events and circumstances that led Plath to take her life.

Although "Metaphors" contains none of the themes listed above, readers might sense some self-deprecation beneath the clever and sometimes playful imagery. If you detect any, ask yourself whether it goes beyond what might reasonably be expected given the situation described in the poem.

Metaphors

I'm a riddle in nine syllables,
An elephant, a ponderous house,
A melon strolling on two tendrils.
O red fruit, ivory, fine timbers!
This loaf's big with its yeasty rising.   5
Money's new-minted in this fat purse.
I'm a means, a stage, a cow in calf.
I've eaten a bag of green apples,
Boarded the train there's no getting off.

THESIS AND THOUGHT

1. What is the subject of the poem?
2. What comment on the subject does the poem make?

STRUCTURE

1. What is Plath's principal means of defining her subject?

2. How does the idea of the riddle in the opening line shape the rest of the poem?

3. How do the number of lines, and of syllables within them, help achieve the poem's purpose(s)?

STYLE

1. What do most of Plath's metaphors have in common?

2. Lines 4 and 9 do not seem to conform to the other images. Explain the relevance of each.

3. Which metaphors do you find most effective? Why? Are any of Plath's images **clichés**? Explain.

CONSIDERATIONS

1. How do you react to pregnant women? Consider physical appearance but go beyond it as well. Write an essay either discussing your response or explaining how representative Plath's attitudes are among pregnant women you have known.

2. Choose a physical condition you have experienced and describe it in a series of (preferably related) metaphors.

3. Write a parody of "Metaphors," not necessarily humorous, from the point of view of the fetus.

Jo Goodwin Parker

(United States; birthdate unknown)

Jo Goodwin Parker is a pseudonym for an author who chooses to remain anonymous. Originally a speech, "What Is Poverty?" first appeared in George Henderson's America's Other Children *(1971). Henderson had heard the speech and requested a printed version for use in his book. Parker consented on condition that her identity not be revealed. Although Parker's reasons for maintaining privacy may be purely personal, the very anonymity of poverty—as the public perceives it—may itself be a perversely ironic obstacle to remediation.*

Although a biographic context is often useful to the reader, successful writing must stand on its own merit and be intrinsically compelling or valid. Unlike many other selections in this text, which bear the approving stamp of their authors' deserved reputations, "What Is Poverty?" has itself alone to recommend it.

What Is Poverty?

You ask me what is poverty? Listen to me. Here I am, dirty, smelly, and with no "proper" underwear on and with the stench of my rotting teeth near you. I will tell you. Listen to me. Listen without pity. I cannot use your pity. Listen with understanding. Put yourself in my dirty, worn out, ill-fitting shoes, and hear me.

Poverty is getting up every morning from a dirt- and illness-stained mattress. The sheets have long since been used for diapers. Poverty is living in a smell that never leaves. This is a smell of urine, sour milk, and spoiling food sometimes joined with the strong smell of long-cooked onions. Onions are cheap. If you have smelled this smell, you did not know how it came. It is the smell of the outdoor privy. It is the smell of young children who cannot walk the long dark way in the night. It is the smell of the mattresses where years of "accidents" have happened. It is the smell of the milk which has gone sour because the refrigerator long has not worked, and it costs money to get it fixed. It is the smell of rotting garbage. I could bury it, but where is the shovel? Shovels cost money.

Poverty is being tired. I have always been tired. They told me at the hospital when the last baby came that I had chronic anemia caused from poor diet, a bad case of worms, and that I needed a corrective operation. I listened politely—the poor are always polite. The poor always listen. They don't say that there is no money for iron pills, or better food, or worm medicine. The idea of an operation is frightening and costs so much that, if I had dared, I would have laughed. Who takes care of my children? Recovery from an operation takes a long time. I have three children. When I left them with "Granny" the last time I had a job, I came home to find the baby covered with fly specks, and a diaper that had not been changed since I left. When the dried diaper came off, bits of my baby's flesh came with it. My other child was playing with a sharp bit of broken glass, and my oldest was playing alone at the edge of a lake. I made twenty-two dollars a week, and a good nursery school costs twenty dollars a week for three children. I quit my job.

Poverty is dirt. You can say in your clean clothes coming from your clean house, "Anybody can be clean." Let me explain about housekeeping with no money. For breakfast I give my children grits with no oleo or cornbread without eggs and oleo. This does not use up many dishes. What dishes there are, I wash in cold water and with no soap. Even the cheapest soap has to be saved for the baby's diapers. Look at my hands, so cracked and red. Once I saved for two months to buy a jar of Vaseline for my hands and the baby's diaper rash. When I had saved enough, I went to buy it and the price had gone up two cents. The baby and I suffered on. I have to decide every day if I can bear to put my cracked sore hands into the cold water and strong soap. But you ask, why not hot water? Fuel costs money. If you have a wood fire it costs money. If you burn electricity, it costs money. Hot water is a luxury. I do not have luxuries. I know you will be surprised when I tell you how young I am. I look so much older. My back has been bent over the wash tubs every day for so long, I cannot remember when I ever did anything else. Every night I wash every stitch my school age child has on and just hope her clothes will be dry by morning.

Poverty is staying up all night on cold nights to watch the fire knowing one spark on the newspaper covering the walls means your sleeping child dies in flames. In summer poverty is watching gnats and flies devour your baby's tears when he cries. The screens are torn and you pay so little rent you know they will never be fixed. Poverty means insects in your food, in your nose, in your eyes, and crawling over you when you sleep. Poverty is hoping it never rains because diapers won't dry when it rains and soon you are using newspapers. Poverty is seeing your children forever with runny noses. Paper handkerchiefs cost money and all your rags you need for other things. Even more costly are antihistamines. Poverty is cooking without food and cleaning without soap.

Poverty is asking for help. Have you ever had to ask for help, knowing your children will suffer unless you get it? Think about asking for a loan from a relative, if this is the only way you can imagine asking for help. I will tell you how it feels. You find out where the office is that you are supposed to visit. You circle that block four or five times. Thinking of your children, you go in. Everyone is very busy. Finally, someone comes out and you tell her that you need help. That never is the person you need to see. You go see another person, and after spilling the whole shame of your poverty all over the desk between you, you find that this isn't the right office after all—you must repeat the whole process, and it never is any easier at the next place.

You have asked for help, and after all it has a cost. You are again told to wait. You are told why, but you don't really hear because of the red cloud of shame and the rising cloud of despair.

Poverty is remembering. It is remembering quitting school in junior high because "nice" children had been so cruel about my clothes and my smell. The attendance officer came. My mother told him I was pregnant. I wasn't, but she thought that I could get a job and help out. I had jobs off and on, but never long enough to learn anything. Mostly I remember being married. I was so young then. I am still young. For a time, we had all the things you have.

5

There was a little house in another town, with hot water and everything. Then my husband lost his job. There was unemployment insurance for a while and what few jobs I could get. Soon, all our nice things were repossessed and we moved back here. I was pregnant then. This house didn't look so bad when we first moved in. Every week it gets worse. Nothing is ever fixed. We now had no money. There were a few odd jobs for my husband, but everything went for food then, as it does now. I don't know how we lived through three years and three babies, but we did. I'll tell you something, after the last baby I destroyed my marriage. It had been a good one, but could you keep on bringing children in this dirt? Did you ever think how much it costs for any kind of birth control? I knew my husband was leaving the day he left, but there were no goodbys between us. I hope he has been able to climb out of this mess somewhere. He never could hope with us to drag him down.

That's when I asked for help. When I got it, you know how much it was? It was, and is, seventy-eight dollars a month for the four of us; that is all I ever can get. Now you know why there is no soap, no needles and thread, no hot water, no aspirin, no worm medicine, no hand cream, no shampoo. None of these things forever and ever and ever. So that you can see clearly, I pay twenty dollars a month rent, and most of the rest goes for food. For grits and cornmeal, and rice and milk and beans. I try my best to use only the minimum electricity. If I use more, there is that much less for food.

Poverty is looking into a black future. Your children won't play with my   10 boys. They will turn to other boys who steal to get what they want. I can already see them behind the bars of their prison instead of behind the bars of my poverty. Or they will turn to the freedom of alcohol or drugs, and find themselves enslaved. And my daughter? At best, there is for her a life like mine.

But you say to me, there are schools. Yes, there are schools. My children have no extra books, no magazines, no extra pencils, or crayons, or paper and most important of all, they do not have health. They have worms, they have infections, they have pink-eye all summer. They do not sleep well on the floor, or with me in my one bed. They do not suffer from hunger, my seventy-eight dollars keeps us alive, but they do suffer from malnutrition. Oh yes, I do remember what I was taught about health in school. It doesn't do much good. In some places there is a surplus commodities program. Not here. The country said it cost too much. There is a school lunch program. But I have two children who will already be damaged by the time they get to school.

But, you say to me, there are health clinics. Yes, there are health clinics and they are in the towns. I live out here eight miles from town. I can walk that far (even if it is sixteen miles both ways), but can my little children? My neighbor will take me when he goes; but he expects to get paid, *one way or another*. I bet you know my neighbor. He is that large man who spends his time at the gas station, the barbershop, and the corner store complaining about the government spending money on the immoral mothers of illegitimate children.

Poverty is an acid that drips on pride until all pride is worn away. Poverty is a chisel that chips on honor until honor is worn away. Some of you say that you would do *something* in my situation, and maybe you would, for the first week or the first month, but for year after year after year?

Even the poor can dream. A dream of a time what there is money. Money for the right kinds of food, for worm medicine, for iron pills, for toothbrushes, for hand cream, for a hammer and nails and a bit of screening, for a shovel, for a bit of paint, for some sheeting, for needles and thread. Money to pay *in money* for a trip to town. And, oh, money for hot water and money for soap. A dream of when asking for help does not eat away the last bit of pride. When the office you visit is as nice as the offices of other governmental agencies, when there are enough workers to help you quickly, when workers do not quit in defeat and despair. When you have to tell your story to only one person, and that person can send you for other help and you don't have to prove your poverty over and over and over again.

I have come out of my despair to tell you this. Remember I did not come   15
from another place or another time. Others like me are all around you. Look at us with an angry heart, anger that will help you help me. Anger that will let you tell of me. The poor are always silent. Can you be silent too?

Thesis and Thought

1. What evidence does Parker present for the idea that poverty is not simply the lack of luxuries but of necessities as well?
2. According to Parker, what are the spiritual and moral consequences of poverty—both actual and potential?
3. Has Parker succumbed to the consequences of poverty? Why do you think so?
4. Is Parker's purpose here simply to define her condition? Explain.

Structure

1. What assumption does Parker make about her audience? What is her implicit comparison?
2. How does Parker use "historical context" to define her poverty?
3. How do Parker's numerous examples and illustrations contribute to her definition? Cite three or four that you find particularly effective and explain why they succeed so well.

STYLE

1. Eight of the essay's fifteen paragraphs begin with short, simple sentences: "Poverty is asking for help" (para. 6), "Poverty is remembering" (para. 8), and so on. How does this repetitive technique help achieve Parker's purpose and affect your response to the essay?

2. Brief sentences are characteristic of the piece generally. Here, for instance, is part of paragraph 11:

> Oh yes, I do remember what I was taught about health in school. It doesn't do much good. In some places there is a surplus commodities program. Not here. The country said it cost too much. There is a school lunch program. But I have two children who will already be damaged by the time they get to school.

What tone does such a pattern create? How is it useful to the aims of the essay?

3. What does Parker achieve by addressing the reader directly? In what other ways is the writing informal?

4. Parker employs intense sensory images in paragraphs 2–5 and some vivid metaphors in paragraph 13. How do you react to them? What other emotional appeals does the essay make?

5. Are you convinced that the essay was written by a junior-high-school dropout? Why?

CONSIDERATIONS

1. While we frequently associate poverty with urban settings, Parker's is a case of rural poverty. Why do we seem to hear so little about this aspect of the problem?

2. Reread paragraph 8 for Parker's charitable attitude toward her husband. Is your view of his behavior different from hers? Explain any difference and the reasons for it.

3. Because the essay was first published in 1971, Parker's welfare budget is out of date. Let us, however, assume a 500 percent increase in both assistance and costs since then. Adjusting the figures for family size and composition, how well could you and your family live on such a budget? You might want to bear in mind that the current official poverty line for a family of four is about $14,000 per year.

4. Does Parker see herself as a victim? Do you? Consider, especially, what she says in paragraph 13 about taking action.

5. Using the techniques of Parker's essay, write a personal definition throughout which you explain a significant characteristic of your own existence: what it means to be a commuter, a burger flipper, a new student on campus, disabled, an only child, a single parent, a native of _____ , and so on.

Suggestions for Writing: Definition

I. Write an essay in which you provide an extended definition of one of the following abstractions:

justice	success	culture
evil	power	cute
intellectual	grace	abnormal
courage	education	chaos
ignorance	geek (or one of its synonyms)	

a word from a language other than English requiring definition beyond mere translation, such as *gringo*, *weltschmerz, uhuru, tao, mensch.*

II. Choose one of the following and write an essay in which you define yourself

—as a member of a racial, ethnic, or cultural group

—as a resident of your community

—as a member of a social, civic, political, or academic organization or interest group

—by your occupation (student or other), hobby, or professional aspiration

—by the company you keep

III. Write an extended definition for one of the nonsense words below or for one that you create. Include its denotative meaning and etymology.

helch	plintocracy	labdous
modicient	trobule	quirl
smern	dilpurate	ileofracious
silpitor	nubafrone	chulter

9

Argument and Persuasion

We may convince others by our arguments; but we can only persuade them by their own.

JOSEPH JOUBERT, *Pensées*

"What's for dinner?"

"Meat loaf."

"Again?"

"What do you mean 'again'?"

"We've had it three times this week."

"So?"

"So, a little variety would be nice."

"All right. It's not meat loaf. It's beef à la pay cut. Served with small potatoes."

"Don't get smart on me."

"Somebody has to. You're not very smart on your own."

"Kids like you shouldn't be allowed to drive."

"You cut me off, old man."

"Going all kinds of speeds, running lights."

"I was doing thirty and it was a two-way stop sign—on your street."

"I did stop!"

"How could you tell? I bet you never do over twenty."

"Ever hear of a speed limit? *Limit* means maximum. Unless you're on a highway there's no minimum speed. I've been driving sixty years with a perfect record—till now. I bet you were drinking too. Why, you've still got that brown bag in your hand."

"Would you like a swig of my Yoo-Hoo? Sorry, I'm fresh out of Geritol."

Which of these confrontations best constitutes an argument? A trick question. The answer is neither. They are arguments only in the popular sense of the word meaning *quarrel*. For present purposes, however, an argument is a rational process in which a body of relevant evidence is produced in support of a debatable proposition. Such propositions and evidence are largely lacking in the quarrels above. In the first instance, we might extract two unrelated statements that in other contexts could be propositions: "It is good to vary the menu" and "You are not very smart." Here, however, we have no evidence for either—even if we seem to accept the first (as a premise) without much question. But the true subject of the discussion, the effect of the pay cut, is never dealt with directly. One consequence is emotional rather than rational discourse.

The case of the drivers boils down to each claiming the other is at fault. But there is not enough evidence here for the reader to judge—and what evidence there is, is presented by biased authorities. However, most of the discussion deals with irrelevant stereotyping: the youthful, reckless, drunken driver versus the elderly fuzz-brain who drives at a crawl.

To be sure, even the most rational among us sometimes indulge in irrational confrontation. That paragon of reason, Sherlock Holmes himself, writes to Watson in "The Adventure of the Final Problem" that he and his nemesis, Professor Moriarty, are about to enter "the final discussion" of their differences. The discussion, however, proves to be hand-to-hand combat, which results in their wrestling each other over the Reichenbach Falls, presumably to their deaths.

On the other hand, emotion is not necessarily to be banished altogether from rational discourse. Passion often underlies or accompanies our most firmly held principles, such as democracy, justice, or equality. But it must be remembered that even today, many people as passionately subscribe to principles of authoritarianism and inequality. Ultimately, arguments and their principles must be evaluated according to the light rather than the heat they generate, particularly when someone is trying to convince us to accept them. The danger here lies in the illegitimate use of emotional appeals—to greed, fear, hatred—that too often intrudes on the process of persuasion.

WHAT CAN BE ARGUED

Consider the following list of statements as potential topics for argument:

1. Chocolate is the all-time greatest flavor.
2. Chester A. Arthur was the twenty-first president of the United States.
3. Roger Rabbit is a dumber bunny than Bugs.
4. The United States should surrender part of its sovereignty to the United Nations.
5. Peanut-butter-and-marshmallow sandwiches on date-nut bread are my favorite midnight snack.

6. Eleanor Roosevelt was a tireless worker for the underdog.

7. Cigarette smoking is hazardous to your health.

8. There's nothing like a sunrise in Barbados.

9. Twenty-three million Americans are living below the poverty line.

10. Amy Tan is the author of several best-selling novels.

Of the group, 2, 9, and 10 are not arguable because they are statements of fact. Such statements are either true or false on their face—or upon consultating a simple reference book. Chester Arthur either was or was not the twenty-first president. There is no debate here. Even if the statement is false, simply pointing to a line in an almanac or encyclopedia quells any doubt. Similarly, given a standard and a statistical method, we cannot debate the number of impoverished Americans. There either are or are not twenty-three million. A quick check of the *New York Times* best-seller lists over the past few years will settle any doubts about Amy Tan. The bottom line is that statements of fact are not arguable.

Of the remaining items, 1, 5, and 8 are also not arguable. All of them may be easily rephrased as "I like X, Y, or Z." While it is not strictly true that there is no arguing about taste, it is true that you cannot argue about personal preferences. What, for example, are possible responses to "I like chocolate"? "I like rocky road" or "No, you don't." The first response is neither reply nor comment. It is simply the assertion of another personal preference. The second is ludicrous. We are not yet at the point of experiencing someone else's sensations.

The other statements of preference follow a similar pattern. You cannot deny that someone likes the peanut butter sandwich or the sunrise. You only can offer, by way of polite conversation, your own favorite midnight snack— pickled herring over pork fried rice—or place to watch the sunrise—perhaps Baltimore, Brownsville, or Butte.

By contrast, items 3, 4, and 6 are arguable. None is patently true or false; none is a personal preference. All are debatable—even controversial—and require the presentation of evidence to be convincing. Although some who know the career of Eleanor Roosevelt might regard item 6 as a fact, others require documentation. Which underdogs did she work for? What work did she do? Presented with several pages of such information, we might assent to the initial proposition. The question of surrendering sovereignty, however, is more obviously debatable. As interested readers, we want to know the reasoning behind such a plan, what the goals of such surrender would be, and the evidence that the goals could be achieved. We would also want to hear from opponents who reject the reasoning behind the plan, its goals, and the expectation of success. Although our political preference in this instance might have an emotional base, we are dealing here with something far more complex and cerebral than a preference for chocolate over rocky road. Finally, while the choice between Roger and Bugs looks as if it might be decided on taste, one could in fact establish criteria for "dumbness" and objectively measure each cartoon character against them.

Item 7 concerning the hazards of smoking is a curiosity. Today, the statement would be accepted overwhelmingly as fact. Fifty years ago, the statement would generally have been arguable. Since then, the weight of evidence has established the truth of the proposition.

What the argumentative assertions have in common is that they must be verified and justified—primarily through rational processes.

INDUCTIVE REASONING

Inductive and **deductive reasoning** are two of the principal methods of argument. Induction consists of drawing conclusions from a series of instances or bits of data. For example, suppose you smell a rose and sneeze, smell again and sneeze again, then repeat the process with the same result hundreds of times under varying conditions of geography, season, temperature, and so on. It would not be excessive, at that point, to conclude that every time you smell a rose you sneeze, and (subject to confirmation by laboratory testing) that you are allergic to roses.

The earlier statement "Cigarette smoking is hazardous to your health" was confirmed in precisely this way. Results of various experiments using tobacco, smoke, or their extracts generally indicated risks associated with tobacco use. The effect of the evidence was cumulative. Testing on one or a few subjects or groups of subjects would not have been convincing, nor would three or four sneezes after sniffing roses have confirmed an allergy. Similarly, if Eleanor Roosevelt is to be considered "a tireless worker for the underdog," one must show what she did on behalf of racial or ethnic groups subject to bigotry, for laboring people struggling through the depression, for the oppressed peoples of the world in her capacity as UN delegate, as an educator on the plight of the downtrodden through her newspaper column. All these activities should "add up" to her having been the underdog's ally.

There is nothing very mysterious in the inductive process. We depend on it regularly. If late on a hot summer's afternoon you notice the sky grow dark and the air become oppressively still and heavy, you might say "We're in for a storm." How did you arrive at this conclusion? Year after year you have noticed that the darkness and calm late on a hot summer's day are almost invariably precursors of thunderstorms. Your cumulative inductive experience has led you to make the prediction.

Inductive procedures lie at the heart of scientific method, where the strictures of their application are most severe. For example, sometimes the dark summer afternoon calm passes without a storm breaking. (More accurately, our generalization should have been, "We're *probably* in for a storm.")

But one test of the validity of a scientific experiment is for others to repeat it with identical results. No room here for a storm that doesn't happen. If the results are not duplicated, the proposition is invalidated at once and must be reformulated (if possible) to embrace the deviation.

One of the classical, if crude, experiments in which induction figures prominently was performed by nineteenth-century German biologist August Weismann. Wishing to put to rest the Lamarckian notion that an acquired characteristic may be inherited by subsequent generations, he cut off the tails of mice, which he then bred to see if their offspring would be born without them. None were, thus refuting the idea that acquired characteristics are inherited. Before he was through, Weismann's experiment involved 901 mice over five generations. Had Weismann found a mouse born without a tail, he would have had to alter his conclusions or provide an alternative explanation for the event (e.g., genetic defect or birth accident). His results, however, were flawless.

Beyond such consistency, there are two other considerations for the validity of inductive reasoning. First, the instances have to be representative. The birth of mice without an eye or foot would have been of no significance in Weismann's experiment, for the purpose was to confirm that mice with amputated tails do not produce tailless offspring. Similarly, for purposes of predicting storms on dark, oppressively still summer afternoons, a bright, mild summer afternoon with variable breezes is irrelevant. Second, the number of instances have to be sufficient to warrant a conclusion. Four or five dark, still summer afternoons that precede storms should not lead to a generalized prediction of storms following such conditions. But after years of observing summer storms, you are permitted—even driven—to make the **inductive leap** from individual instances to a general proposition. Such leaps, however, do not necessarily require years of experience. For example, driving to work along Route 96 at 8:00 A.M., someone new in town may realize within a week or two that the road is usually congested at that hour. Again, it is improbable that anyone would stick a finger into an electrical outlet more than twice before concluding that doing so is painful and dangerous. The point at which the leap may be made, therefore, is variable and depends on the phenomenon and your confidence. Still, the adage holds: Look before you (inductively) leap.

DEDUCTIVE REASONING

Deductive reasoning involves arguing from premises or principles, although these, as in the statement that smoking is hazardous, might have originally been established inductively. The simplest form of a deductive argument is called a **syllogism.** It consists of three parts: a major **premise,** a minor premise, and a conclusion. The classical example is as follows:

Major premise: All men are mortal.

Minor premise: Socrates is a man.

Conclusion: Socrates is mortal.

Given the two premises, the conclusion is inevitable. Since Socrates is a member of a class (men) all of whose members are mortal, he necessarily shares in the mortality. This may be illustrated by the following diagram:

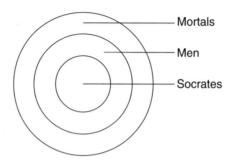

Since men are within the circle of things mortal, and Socrates is within the circle of men, he is also within the circle of things mortal. An argument such as this, in which the conclusion follows logically from the premises, is said to be valid.

There are several pitfalls in reading or writing deductive arguments. One is that the argument might not be valid or that, because of faulty premises, it might be false even if valid. The term **validity** applies to the reasoning process, not the veracity of the individual statements.

Let's return to Socrates and a new formulation.

Major premise: All men are mortal.

Minor premise: Socrates is mortal.

Conclusion: Therefore, Socrates is a man.

Note that each statement here is true but that the argument is invalid. Why? Because based on the premises given one cannot conclude that Socrates is a man:

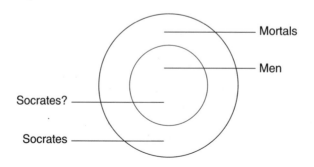

Although men and Socrates are both mortal, Socrates does not necessarily have to be a man to share the mortality.

In this instance, the faulty reasoning is harmless, but the error often takes the insidious form of "guilt" by association:

> Major premise: Liberals support gun control.
>
> Minor premise: Robert Campbell supports gun control.
>
> Conclusion: Robert Campbell is a liberal.

Campbell in fact may be a police officer who favors long sentences and limiting defendants' rights, while opposing foreign aid, social-service programs, and affirmative action. He is likely to resent being labeled "liberal" simply because he shares one "liberal" position.

Here is another example of an invalid conclusion:

> Major premise: Muslims reject the use of alcohol.
>
> Minor premise: Elsa Hinkel rejects the use of alcohol.
>
> Conclusion: Elsa Hinkel is a Muslim.

Perhaps. But she may also be a Methodist, a Mormon, a recovering alcoholic—or none of these. Once more, it is literally unreasonable to identify an individual as a member of a group on the basis of a single shared characteristic.

The following syllogism presents a different problem:

> Major premise: All men are swine.
>
> Minor premise: Socrates is a man.
>
> Conclusion: Socrates is a swine.

In this case, provided that we are using *swine* literally, the argument is *valid but false*. In fact, no men are swine. Because one premise is false, any conclusion drawn from it must also be false. If we are using *swine* figuratively, we might still have difficulties because the premise is subject to challenge—as all premises are—but in this case to invalidate it one need only find a man whose behavior is other than swinish.

To this point we have been dealing with absolute, affirmative categories (all *x* is *y*), but there are other possibilities, such as an absolute negative. Let us switch from Socrates to his much-maligned wife:

> Major premise: No women are immortal.
>
> Minor premise: Xanthippe is a woman.
>
> Conclusion: ?

(Hint: If either premise is negative, the conclusion must be negative as well.)

There are also partial syllogisms. (Some, many, or most *x* is *y*.)

Major premise: Most physics professors are sensitive to student needs.

Minor premise: Helma Ruitenbeek is a professor of physics.

Conclusion: She is probably sensitive to student needs.

IDENTIFYING AND QUESTIONING PREMISES: THE ENTHYMEME

Many, perhaps most, arguments you will encounter or write are unlikely to be presented in full syllogistic form. Major premises, for example, might be implied rather than expressed overtly. A syllogism in which either premise is not stated explicitly is called an **enthymeme.** Because enthymemes are so prevalent, one of your tasks as a reader is to ask yourself on what assumptions an argument is based and whether you can accept them. The success of a deductive argument, in fact, depends upon the acceptability of its premises.

To illustrate, let us consider two arguments frequently raised in the abortion debate. An abortion opponent might claim, "Abortion is murder because it is the wanton taking of a human life." An abortion rights advocate might counter, "Abortion is not murder since a nonviable fetus is neither living nor human." Fundamental to both statements, but unexpressed, are ideas concerning the nature of humanity and life. Two of these are, respectively, the unstated premises "Life begins at conception" and "Life begins when the fetus can survive outside the womb."

Notice that in either case the conclusions are drawn logically from the major premises just given:

1. Since human life begins at conception and since murder is the wanton taking of a human life, abortion is murder.

2. Since human life begins at fetal viability and since murder is the wanton taking of a human life, abortion of a nonviable fetus is not murder.

However, these premises are each subject to question or attack—just as the formulation "Life begins at birth" would be. And so, for this reason, among others, the debate rages on.

The following letter to the editor, urging that a school bond proposal be voted down, provides an opportunity for a more complete analysis of an argument presented as an enthymeme:

When I attended the Allenberry schools there were forty in a class and double sessions. There were no computers, and the library was not a "learning resources center." I did well enough. My dental practice is flourishing and I drive a luxury European car. I achieved this through my own hard work, earning my way through college and dental school in tough times.

There is no reason to spend the hard-earned money of others on educational frills that will simply give each child a personal tutor and contribute further to our "vidiot" culture. Vote the issue down.

(name withheld by request)

It is clear that the good doctor opposes the bond issue. It is not so clear why. The reasons seem to have little to do with sound education practices. But here are some possibilities.

Major *unstated* premise: The public should not pay for educational frills.
Minor *implied* premise: Computers and small classes are educational frills.
Conclusion: Therefore, a bond issue that will pay for computers and small classes should be voted down.

The minor premise is clearly open to attack; another argument, however, that emerges from the letter may be even more objectionable. The writer's single instance (him- or herself) is insufficient to make the case for the unstated claim that people, generally, can do well in the Allenberry schools despite large classes and overcrowding. Would more people prosper, you may reasonably ask, if they went to school elsewhere, or if Allenberry classes were smaller and had access to computers? Question premises.

When writing arguments, you should be equally conscious of the truth (or, at least, supportabilty) of your premises, whether stated or implied, and the validity of the conclusions you draw from them.

ALTERNATIVE APPROACHES TO ARGUMENT

The Toulmin Model

Partly in an effort to unify our perception of the argumentative process, British philosopher Stephen Toulmin has created a vocabulary and analytic model, which includes what we have covered in this chapter about induction and deduction as well as other logical schemes, such as causal analysis. His key terms are **claim, grounds** (or **data**), **warrant,** and backing. The *claim* is the argumentative thesis, the point you hope to establish. *Grounds* are the evidence by which the claim (conclusion or thesis) is supported. The *warrant* is the basis (premise) on which the claim is made; it acts as the intellectual bridge between the claim and data. *Backing* is the support needed to justify the warrant.

That backing is required suggests that warrants are not intrinsically valid or acceptable and that arguments typically function as parts of a linked series, not in isolation. The implication here that warrants (and the reasoning based on them) are not *absolutely* reliable is borne out in Toulmin's introduction of two other terms: *qualifier* and *rebuttal*.

Qualifiers indicate that arguments may be limited by such things as incomplete evidence and the contexts in which they are made. *Rebuttals* are specific exceptions to the "rule" that a particular argument attempts to establish. Such relativism is reinforced by the idea that argumentative claims, grounds, warrants, and backing vary according to discipline or profession.

Let's re-examine in Toulmin terms the argument of the letter to the editor presented in the previous section:

Claim: The bond issue should be voted down.

Grounds: 1. The money would be used for small classes and computers, both of which are educational frills.

2. I achieved academic and material success under the present system.

Warrant: Taxpayers' money should not be used for educational frills in a school system that is already a success.

Here, the warrant is equivalent to a major premise, the claim to a conclusion. Some of the grounds—that computers and small classes are frills and that the present system has succeeded—are parallel to minor premises; other elements—the particular success of the letter writer and that the money would be used for the specified frills—are bits of data that lend inductive support to the claim.

The argument is no less objectionable in this analysis. On the contrary, the Toulmin approach perhaps underscores the argumentative weakness by showing more clearly that the charge concerning frills is itself (literally) an unwarranted assumption in need of its own support. Until such support is provided, the legitimacy of the charge in establishing the claim at hand may be challenged. The single instance of the dentist's success provides only the flimsiest of grounds for accepting the claim.

In addition, there is no backing here for the assertion of general academic success made in the warrant. Perhaps there is less need to back the contention that taxpayers ought not pay for frills. Any such backing would be likely to derive from generally held ethical principles or ideas concerning thrift, but these would also be subject to question. As presented, the argument is unqualified. A more deliberate version might consider such matters as the prosperity of the taxpayers and the competitiveness of Allenberry graduates as compared with graduates of neighboring districts. As for rebuttal, one might suspect (but obviously cannot prove) that our nameless but flourishing dentist is among the minority of students who succeeded under far less than optimal conditions.

In your own thinking about argument, you may use either Toulmin's model or the traditional ones presented earlier. Either will serve most undergraduate academic purposes. Choose the system that enables you to perceive the workings of an argument more clearly.

Rogerian Argument

In recent years the argumentative approach of psychologist Carl Rogers has gained increasing attention. Unlike traditional argumentation, with its assertions, defenses, rebuttals, and refutations, his model is conciliatory rather than adversarial or aggressive. Although the ultimate task is to reach a conclusion, the immediate one is to find areas of agreement between conflicting views or positions in order to establish a degree of unity and to clarify areas of difference. The process is designed to reduce confrontation and to maximize the amount of psychic and intellectual energy devoted to resolving issues.

The advantages of this approach in such matters as labor negotiations or community conflicts are obvious. But even in one-on-one argumentation, acknowledging the (possible) legitimacy of opposing views and underscoring points of agreement need not be merely an ingratiating ploy but an actual means toward achieving a satisfactory conclusion. Even in the case of abortion, opponents can agree on the importance of human life, however bitterly they disagree about defining it. This is also apparent in the similarly troublesome matter of capital punishment. In the context of agreeing on the need for public safety and for criminals to accept responsibility for their actions, one might evaluate the propriety of various punishments with greater calm and less rancor than is usually the case.

In addressing a college faculty on the subject of instituting a foreign-language requirement, an advocate using a Rogerian approach might begin as follows:

> Most of us recognize the importance of foreign languages in an ever-shrinking world with a global economy and instant communication. We also recognize that simply adding requirements to the existing curriculum would lead, eventually, to an unrealistic increase in the time spent as an undergraduate. If we are to require a foreign language, we have several choices. We might eliminate some current requirements or create options among them; we might reduce the number of free electives; we might limit the number of courses in a major; we might credit part of the language study toward fulfillment of the multicultural course requirement—or decide on any combination of these. Despite our reservation, we might even simply increase the number of credits required for graduation.

> There are problems involved with each of these proposals. All of us are zealous to protect our own departments and disciplines; we believe

that academic choice is important to the growth and development of
our students; we fear that, if they are less thoroughly schooled in their
majors, they will be less able to compete for jobs upon graduation. But,
particularly in light of competitiveness, the matter of foreign-language
instruction is pressing. We will have to take some risks and make some
compromises in the best interest of our students—which I am confident
we will ultimately do.

There is no confrontation here. Instead, there is an attempt to acknowledge
various objections and to soothe ill feeling, an attempt to be inclusive, to find
grounds for unity. It is a shared problem, after all, one to be dealt with
communally, not through a battle of wits and a barrage of words. Assuming
the truth of the first sentence, the writer has laid out the common ground of
the need for foreign-language study as well as a series of choices for instituting
it. The discussion from this point should focus not on whether to require a
foreign language but on how best to implement that requirement.

LOGICAL FALLACIES

Arguments that draw conclusions based on inadequate support or that
stray from the issue at hand to discuss irrelevancies are fallacious, that is,
logically flawed.

In the case of two such **logical fallacies,** support is absent altogether.
Begging the question is an error in which the writer or speaker assumes as
fact something that has yet to be proved:

How can we prevent the destruction of human civilization once the
space aliens arrive?

Here, one assumes the existence of the aliens, that they will visit our planet,
and that their arrival will prove disastrous to humans. None of these purported facts has been established.

Perhaps conspiracy charges—unless they are substantiated—are particularly prone to question-begging:

We must radically reconstruct those government agencies that
participated in the plot to kill JFK.

The scheme of white America to destroy African-American youth
is clearly seen in the inner cities, where the flow of drugs goes un-
checked and AIDS proliferates.

In such instances you must be aware of not only whether there is a connection
between the purported cause and the very real effects that it is presumed to
create, but whether the cause itself exists.

A second, related fallacy in which no support is offered is called **circular reasoning.** In this case, a statement seems to offer a rationale but in fact is merely repetitive:

> It's hot today because the temperature is so high.

This not-very-enlightening statement tells us that it's hot because it's hot. But the error crops up in less obvious instances as well:

> A free-market system with few or no controls must be maintained
> if capitalism is to survive.

Translation: Capitalism must be maintained if capitalism is to survive. How true. How circular.

> Reducing the number of foreigners permitted to enter the country
> is the only way to curb immigration.

Translation: Immigration may be controlled by controlling it. No doubt food may be eaten by eating it. This book may be read by reading it. Circular reasoning may be broken by exposing it.

There are times when a thesis (claim) is supported but with insufficient evidence to sustain it. In such instances the thesis is said to be an **overstatement** or **hasty generalization:**

> That Raquel must be a soul-food freak. I saw her yesterday, scarfing
> down half a rack of ribs and a sweet-potato pie.

One such "scarfing" does not a "soul-food freak" make. Perhaps Raquel was eating these dishes for the first time. Perhaps she eats them only occasionally. Perhaps she is, in fact, a broccoli junkie. You need far more than one soul-food sighting to judge Raquel's eating habits.

But you must exercise care in drawing **inferences** even when several pieces of evidence exist.

> Doreen and Max are a hot item. They take three classes together,
> often walk together on campus, carpool together from the same apart-
> ment complex to which both have recently moved, and were seen last
> night sitting side by side and sharing a pizza with two other couples.

Although there might be a stronger case here than for Raquel's diet, the data are suggestive at best. Taking the same classes might be no more than a decision made by the computer or by the dictates of college requirements. Since they do take classes together, it is not surprising that they would be seen on campus going to or from them. Their recent moves might well have been coincidental, and it is certainly reasonable for neighbors with the same destination to share rides. Eating pizza with four other people seems innocuous in itself. Granted, there is circumstantial evidence for some sort of relationship here. Whether it goes beyond simple friendship, however, is questionable, given what we know. Max, incidentally, is gay.

Less doubtful is the following statement about a hypothetical U.S. senator.

> Allison Valdez is one of the most liberal members of the Senate. She has supported gun-control legislation; has voted for every increase and against every decrease for Head Start, Social Security, and Aid to Dependent Children; has supported every piece of civil-rights legislation, including the latest voting-rights act; is in favor of gays in the military; once introduced a bill that would have required redistribution of unearned income, sponsored another to fund civilian police-review boards; and has spoken out in favor of granting asylum to escapees from Latin American right-wing dictatorships. No wonder she is given a 98 percent rating by the Americans for Democratic Action.

Assuming that the word *liberal* applies to the various stands Senator Valdez may have taken, there is certainly sufficient evidence here to back the initial statement. This generalization (thesis) was not made hastily.

One specific form of hasty generalization is **stereotyping.** A stereotype is a belief expressed about a class or group (not necessarily racial or ethnic) that is based on the limited instances of a few of its members. The difficulty with eliminating a stereotype is that its adherents can always point to those few instances in support of it.

Suppose, for example, that you believe that the average athlete has an intelligence level somewhere between a stone and a slug. You point out several athletes who have been academic disasters and were none too bright otherwise. But what about all those athletes who achieved success both in the classroom and in the world beyond? Since a stereotype includes all members of a group—"All jocks are dumb"—a single opposite instance logically destroys it (although the prejudiced adherent tends to dismiss it as an isolated exception).

Let's take two Naval Academy graduates, David Robinson, center for the San Antonio Spurs, and Roger Staubach, former quarterback for the Dallas Cowboys. Suppose we add to them former Philadelphia 76er Julius Erving, who, after raising questions about the laws of gravity, went on to an entrepreneurial career. For good measure, we'll include Althea Gibson, who entered public service once her career in tennis and golf was over, and Dr. Bobby Brown, former president of the American League and New York Yankee third baseman, who earned his medical degree between baseball seasons. You can probably think of dozens of others if you are at all interested in sports. This list by no means proves that all athletes are smart; it merely disproves the idea that all athletes are dumb. If we need to say anything negative about the intelligence of athletes, we can at most support the idea that some athletes are dumb—a not-very-enlightening statement, which could be applied to nearly any group.

Although some of us might regard the stereotyping of athletes (or blonds) as facetious, perpetuating such notions impedes both intellectual processes and, in more sensitive instances, social progress. Preconceptions tend to alter perceptions. If, on meeting a stranger of a group other than our own, we first think (however unconsciously) gangster, alcoholic, cheap, promiscuous, authoritarian, violent, thieving, sneaky, dirty, disrespectful, we have helped erect or reinforce a barrier between us. As a test of how insidious stereotyping can be, examine what racial, ethnic, or other associations you might have just had to the list of characteristics in the previous sentence.

Positive stereotypes are equally illogical and socially offensive in that by defining a group by specific traits they exclude the consideration of other characteristics. Further, what may be "positive" in the eyes of the stereotyper might not be in the eyes of the stereotyped. The image of the title character in Harriet Beecher Stowe's *Uncle Tom's Cabin* is a classic instance. Passive, devout, forgiving, long-suffering Uncle Tom became the paragon of slave nobility to the (white) nineteenth-century abolitionists. In the 1960s, however, most of these traits were disdained by black-activist America and "Uncle Tom" became a contemptuous epithet.

There are several logical fallacies that involve ignoring the question. Among the most common is ***ad hominem*** argument. Meaning "to the man," *ad hominem* avoids the issue by focusing on the person arguing rather than what is being argued:

> Since Blaine is an acknowledged womanizer, you cannot take his call for tax reform seriously.

Here the writer avoids discussing the merit of Blaine's tax proposals by focusing attention on the irrelevant matter of his personal life. The merits of the tax proposal have nothing necessarily to do with the sexual activity of the person who proposed it. Such a diversionary approach, whether *ad hominem* or not, is also called a **red herring.**

> Of course the head of Women's League for Equality supports Olive Gruening for judge. They're both women.

The true issue here is not the gender of either the candidate or her supporter but Gruening's fitness for the bench.

An *ad populam* ("to the people") argument is an appeal to popular prejudices:

> If we want to remain the world's leading military power, if we want
> to keep our nation secure, we must fund the B-92 megabomber.

People generally want to be first or best; they also want to be secure. The statement plays on these desires. Even assuming that the goals are reasonable, the question of whether the B-92 is capable of fulfilling them remains.

In addition to its presence in pseudopatriotic hype, *ad populam* argument often plays upon popular prejudices or fears:

> They [pick a group] don't share our heritage; they don't share our
> values; they shouldn't share our neighborhood.

The statement pays no attention to fair housing laws or to any positive effects of diversity (or even to any negative ones). Instead, it underscores the idea of difference and the fear of the unknown, assumed to be present in the audience.

Bandwagon technique plays upon our insecurities rather than our prejudices—either our desire to be seen as "with it" or our discomfort in being conspicuously different. If "nobody" but you "doesn't like Sara Lee," then you are doubly damned as failing to accept the opinion of the supposed overwhelming majority and as being, in fact, the "nobody." However, there is no necessary connection between reason and majority dictate. Instead, there is often a great deal of pressure to conform: "Everybody thinks (goes to, buys, votes for, does) *x*; why don't you?" Whether you do should depend on rational evaluation of claims and the evidence offered in their support, regardless of who else does or doesn't.

The **straw man** argument is, in a sense, a fusion of *ad hominem* and *ad populam*. Here a writer falsely attributes to an opponent unpopular, easily attacked views and thus sets up a can't-miss target.

> If the American Civil Liberties Union had its way, no criminal
> would ever be convicted, or if convicted, would ever serve a day in jail.

In fact, although it defends the rights of the accused, the convicted, and the condemned, the ACLU neither advocates ignoring crime nor setting justly convicted criminals free. But it is easier and often rewarding for an ACLU opponent to deliberately misstate the organization's actual positions and so avoid having to present a logically legitimate case against the ACLU.

We have already examined the *post hoc* fallacy in chapter 7. To that we might add here the **slippery slope** argument, one in which a series of causes and effects are propounded without necessary, logical connections between them. During the Vietnam War, for example, its supporters claimed that if

South Vietnam fell, then its neighbors, Laos and Cambodia, would follow, then the rest of Southeast Asia, and so on. Although South Vietnam indeed fell, the predicted "domino effect" did not occur. Arguments about predicted effects, such as those presented for and against the decriminalization of "recreational" drugs, are particularly prone to this fallacy, principally because they tend to focus on only one of many possibilities.

Finally, **false dilemma** (either/or reasoning) is similarly narrow, presenting arguments as a polarized choice between two extremes and ignoring all intermediate or alternative positions:

> Either introduce sex-education courses or expect a further spread of HIV.

Sex education might reduce or slow the spread, but even its proponents would not suggest that it would stop the disease in its tracks. Furthermore, the AIDS epidemic might run its course with or without sex education. Or a cure or vaccine might be found. In short, there are possibilities other than the two suggested by the statement.

Many of these fallacies, and others not discussed here, may be covered by the term **non sequitur** ("it does not follow"), a term that may also be applied to any lapse in induction, deduction, or causal analysis.

ARGUMENT AND AUTHORITY

Authorities should be expert or experienced in the matters for which they offer testimony. Improper authority, however, is often employed as a persuasive device, particularly in advertising. Here, what seems to be support is largely irrelevant. If actress June Allyson uses Depends, or if football's Joe Namath wears panty hose or uses Flex-all, a topical analgesic for arthritis pain, they are legitimate authorities only to the extent of their personal experience with the product. However, they have been chosen as spokespeople because of their celebrity status—a condition that is quite beside the point of their limited personal expertise. But how authoritative is one person's paid testimonial? You might want to hear from other users and from scientific experts who will testify to the product's effectiveness and possible risks.

Biased authority is already present to some degree in advertisements such as those in which Allyson and Namath appear. More serious instances would be the president of Philip Morris commenting on the link between smoking and cancer, Ron Popeil reporting on the effectiveness of the food dehydrator he makes and markets, the head of a chamber of commerce touting the advantages of relocating your business to her community, or a university president evaluating the quality of its offerings. All of these are predisposed to favor the products or services they represent. How severely, after all, would President Bullwinkle criticize Whatsamatta U?

Unnamed authorities are always suspect. If nine out of ten dentists surveyed recommend Trident to their patients who chew gum, we want to know how broad and accurate the survey was (assuming it was made at all). How many dentists did not respond? And what do *they* recommend? "Everyone" as in "everyone knows" is also suspect. What "everyone knows" is often grounded in belief, superstition, or prejudice rather than fact. For example, consider the formula "As everyone knows, women can't be. . . . " It is probably invalid for nearly everything but "fathers."

A legitimate authority, ideally, is one that has expertise on the subject and who has no vested interest in making a determination.

ARGUMENT AND ANALOGY

Although analogy may be used legitimately to illustrate an argument or one of its points, it is not a substitute for evidence:

> A school is not very different from a prison. Like inmates, students are processed and regimented. They are confined by established procedures and condemned to predetermined curricula. An authoritarian principal, like the warden, is concerned chiefly that discipline be maintained, and, like guards, teachers see to order in their individual cells. Students and their prisoner counterparts are shuffled from space to space and task to task performing meaningless labor that produces no useful insight, knowledge, or skills.

> Unlike prisoners, however, students must complete their full term; there is no time off for good behavior, no parole.

The passage strongly suggests that schools are restrictive places—according to the last sentence, even more so than prisons. But in truth, most schools have greater flexibility than is suggested here; principals have concerns beyond discipline; after a certain age, students are not compelled to attend. And while enrolled, they get to spend more than three quarters of their time away from school. When we pass from the imagery of confinement to hard facts, the rational limitations of the analogy are exposed regardless of whether it retains emotional impact. "Yes," the reader says, "I understand what you are suggesting about schools. Now, state a claim about the conditions and back it up with concrete evidence."

PERSUASION AND EMOTIONAL APPEALS

As we discovered in discussing definition, language may be emotionally charged. Although argumentation should be largely dispassionate, adding color to the argument through the choice of words often makes for artful and lively writing. There are, however, some provisos: that the charged language does not substitute for argumentative substance and that its use does not violate standards of rational discourse.

One technique to be uniformly avoided is name-calling. This is a species of *ad hominem* argument and therefore fallacious. In addition, its use may well mar an argument that is otherwise coherent. If, for example, you have made a strong case for increasing services to the elderly, carefully pointing out benefits to the recipients and the community and cost effectiveness despite additional expenditure, you would not want to close by calling someone who might oppose your plan, "a heartless skinflint, with no more compassion than a weasel and the intellect of a flea." However, you might end by saying "How could any thinking, compassionate person fail to support this cause?" Because of their positive connotations, the words *thinking* and *compassionate* appeal to the emotions of the audience in such a way as to move them toward sympathy with the cause. Although the implication is that an opponent must be thoughtless and unfeeling, the words, as part of a rhetorical flourish, are well within bounds—particularly since the case for increased services has been well supported.

Similarly, although appeals to beliefs held by the audience usually result in the *ad populam* fallacy, their limited use in a context of sound reasoning may be no more than reinforcing. For example, in a well-reasoned argument to extend the Voting Rights Act, a supporter might refer to the American ideals of equality and representative democracy. The deductive implication is that anyone who accepts such ideals must support the legislation that helps fulfill them. Of course, an opponent might equally allude to the federal principle of government in which the states are to function independently within the union and so strike a sympathetic chord with some constituencies. But merely waving the stars and bars is no more a substitute for argument than waving the stars and stripes.

In any case, we must be alert to any situation in which tone or attitude overwhelms the reasoning. Here, for example, is part of Ralph Nader's introduction to Michael Waldman's *Who Robbed America? A Citizen's Guide to the S&L Scandal:*

> Without doubt, the most telling symbol of . . . wheeling and dealing run amok is the S&L scandal. It is the massive bill, handed to the taxpayers, for Reagan-era zealotry for sweeping deregulation and for a supine Congress in hock to the lobbyists and political action committees (PACs). Washington insiders have known about the S&Ls for years. "There's a lot of sleaze there," they'd say, and shake their heads— as they moved on to the next fund-raiser. Remember when our governmental leaders first let us in on the secret: did you notice that they called it the S&L "crisis" and never the *crime* and looting of the savers' monies it was and is?

Who Robbed America? A Citizen's Guide to the S&L Scandal, p. xiii

Regardless of the possible validity of Nader's charges, what we primarily learn here is that the writer is hostile and enraged, perhaps with a zealotry of his own to match that which he attributes to the Reagan era. At best, the careful reader is forewarned to look beyond the emotionally charged language to any hard data that may be present as well. It is rather ironic that in distinguishing between the words *crisis* and *crime*, Nader himself is sensitive to the manipulation of language by others.

ARGUMENT AND PERSUASION IN ACADEMIC WRITING

Along with analysis and other forms of explanation, argument and persuasion are often central to scholarly pursuits. No experiment in the sciences or social sciences, for example, is without its conclusion based on inductive evidence. Indeed, when scientific debate rages, as in the attempt to determine what killed the dinosaurs, what we have are competing inferences drawn from various, if overlapping bodies of frequently incomplete evidence. Even in literature and the arts, we find argument in the form of interpretation, sometimes emerging from the underlying premises of particular theoretical "schools." Looking at Dostoyevsky's *Crime and Punishment,* for example, the Marxist critic might focus on the ills of an economic system that creates poverty and propels the impoverished victim, like Raskolnikov, toward criminal action. On the other hand, a feminist critic might condemn the patriarchal society in which women, like Sonia, are assigned only the roles of prostitute and saint. Such an approach, for example, underlies Susan Brownmiller's interpretation of some popular fairy tales:

> *Red Riding Hood* is a parable of rape. There are frightening male figures abroad in the woods—we call them wolves, among other names—and females are helpless before them. Better stick close to the path, better not be adventurous. If you are lucky, a *good, friendly* male may be able to save you from certain disaster. . . .
>
> The utter passivity of Red Riding Hood in the teeth of the wolf is outdone by Sleeping Beauty, who lay immobile for one hundred years before she was awakened by the kiss of the prince. . . . Her role is to be beautiful and passive. Snow White in her glass coffin also remains immobile until her prince appears. . . . Thus is female sexuality defined. Beautiful passivity. Wait, just wait, Prince Charming will soon be by; and if it is not Prince Charming but the Big Bad Wolf who stands at the door, then proper feminine behavior still commands you to stay immobile. The wolf is bigger and stronger than you are. Why try to fight back? But don't you worry, little girl. We have strong and kindly huntsmen patrolling these woods.

Against Our Will: Men, Women and Rape, p. 310

The approach is totally in keeping with Brownmiller's view of the significance of power in sexual relations, expressed most forcefully in the statement that rape is "a conscious process of intimidation by which *all* men keep *all* women in a state of fear" (p. 15). As in any argument, you would do well to understand how the writer's premise here affects (or derives from) the support offered, for inductive reasoning is often crucial to the success of an argument, even one based on deductive principles.

In another, less controversial vein, philosopher John Dewey offers inductive support, through a series of representative illustrations, for his contention that practical experience modifies received tradition and belief:

> Gradually there grows up a body of homely generalizations preserving and transmitting the wisdom of the race about the observed facts and sequences of nature. . . . Extravagantly fantastic notions are eliminated because they are brought into juxtaposition with what actually happens.
>
> The sailor is more likely to be given to . . . superstitions than say the weaver, because his activity is more at the mercy of sudden change and unforeseen occurrence. But even the sailor while he may regard the wind as the uncontrollable expression of the caprice of a great spirit, will still have to become acquainted with some purely mechanical principles of adjustment of boat, sails, and oar. . . . Fire may be conceived as a supernatural dragon. . . . But the housewife who tends the fire and the pots . . . will still be compelled to observe certain mechanical facts of draft and replenishment, and passage from wood to ash. Still more will the worker in metals accumulate verifiable details about . . . the operation of heat. He may retain for special and ceremonial occasions traditional beliefs, but everyday familiar use will expel these conceptions for the greater part of the time, when fire will be . . . controllable by practical relations of cause and effect. . . . Technologies of this kind . . . provide not merely a collection of positive facts, but they give expertness in dealing with materials and tools, and promote the development of the experimental habit of mind, as soon as an art can be taken away from the rule of sheer custom.

Reconstruction in Philosophy, pp. 10–12

At times, controversial conclusions drawn from a body of inductive evidence may stimulate further argument to the extent that they are posed as principles or courses of action. For example, conservative policy analyst Dinesh D'Souza, having examined the intellectual, racial, and gender conflicts on American campuses, makes the following proposal under the heading "Nonracial Affirmative Action":

> Universities should retain their policies of preferential treatment, but alter their criteria of application from race to socioeconomic disadvantage. This means that, in admissions decisions, universities would take into account such factors as the applicant's family background, financial condition, and primary and secondary school environment, giving preference to disadvantaged students as long as it is clear that these students can be reasonably expected to meet the academic chal-

lenges of the selective college. Race or ethnicity, however, would cease to count either for or against any applicant.

Ordinarily the admissions policy of selective universities should be based on academic and extracurricular merit. Preferential treatment is justified, however, when it is obvious that measurable indices of merit do not accurately reflect a student's learning and growth potential. Every admissions officer knows that a 1200 SAT score by a student from Harlem or Anacostia, who comes from a broken family and has struggled against peer pressure and a terrible school system, means something entirely different from a 1200 score from a student from Scarsdale or Georgetown, whose privileges include private tutors and SAT prep courses.

Universities seem entirely justified in giving a break to students who may not have registered the highest scores, but whose record suggests that this failure is not due to ability or application but rather to demonstrated disadvantage.

Illiberal Education, p. 251

Coming in the last chapter as it does, the argument is supported by the analysis that precedes it.

Although they regularly include inductive evidence, deductive arguments from principle often dominate works in philosophy and other disciplines when the focus is theoretical rather than experimental. Arguments in disciplines that often devote themselves to formulating public policy—such as education, criminology, political science, and economics—frequently operate within a deductive framework. Because such arguments are often lengthy, complex, and elaborate, it is possible only to suggest their possibilities here.

Education reformer Maria Montessori, for example, offers a series of deductions, which follow from the following initial premise:

If society holds it necessary to make education compulsory, this means that education has to be given in a practical fashion, and if we are now agreed that education begins at birth, then it becomes vitally necessary for everyone to know the laws of development. Instead of education remaining aloof and ignored by society, it must acquire the authority to rule over society. Social machinery must be adapted to the inherent necessities of the new conception that life is to be protected. All are called upon to help. Fathers and mothers must shoulder their responsibilities; and if the home fails for lack of means, then it is required of society not only to give the needed instruction but also the support necessary for bringing up the children. If education signifies a protection of the individual, if society recognizes as necessary to the child's development things that the family cannot provide, then it is society's duty to provide those things. The state must never abandon the child.

The Absorbent Mind, p. 14

Similarly, economist Milton Friedman presents two fundamental principles upon which his lengthy argument is based:

> First, the scope of government must be limited. Its major function must be to protect our freedom both from the enemies outside our gates and from our fellow-citizens: to preserve law and order, to enforce private contracts, to foster competitive markets. Beyond this . . . , government may enable us at times to accomplish jointly what we would find it more difficult or expensive to accomplish severally. However, any such use of government is fraught with danger. We should not and cannot avoid using government in this way. But there should be a clear and large balance of advantages before we do. By relying primarily on voluntary cooperation and private enterprise, in both economic and other activities, we can insure that the private sector is a check on the powers of the governmental sector and an effective protection of freedom. . . .
>
> The second broad principle is that government power must be dispersed. If government is to exercise power, better in the county than in the state, better in the state than in Washington. If I do not like what my local community does, be it in sewage disposal, or zoning, or schools, I can move to another local community, and though few may take this step, the mere possibility acts as a check. If I do not like what my state does, I can move to another. If I do not like what Washington imposes, I have few alternatives in this world of jealous nations.

Capitalism and Freedom, pp. 2–3

Among the conclusions ultimately drawn from these premises is that public housing programs are paternalistic, counterproductive failures and that needless government involvement in basic education could be reduced through implementing a voucher system.

Teacher John Holt is also disturbed by the nature of public education, but on pedagogical rather than political grounds:

> Education is something a person gets for himself, not that which someone else gives or does to him.
>
> What young people need and want to get from their education is: one, a greater understanding of the world around them; two, a greater development of themselves; three, a chance to find their work, that is, a way in which they may use their own unique tastes and talents to grapple with the real problems of the world around them and to serve the cause of humanity. . . .
>
> Schools should be a resource, but not the only resource, from which children, but not only children, can take what they need and want to carry on the business of their own education. Schools should be places where people go to find out the things they want to find out and develop the skills they want to develop. The child who is educating himself, and if he doesn't no one else will, should be free, like the adult, to decide when and how much and in what way he wants to make use of whatever

resources the schools can offer him. If there are an infinite number of roads to education, each learner should and must be free to choose, to find, to make his own. . . .

Unless we have faith in the child's eagerness and ability to grow and learn, we cannot help and can only harm his education.

The Underachieving School, pp. 3–4

This philosophy of education is an underlying premise of Holt's writing as a whole.

One other aspect of academic argument requires attention. Frequently, articles and books are written in whole or part to refute opposing points of view. A general pattern of such **rebuttal** is the exposure of flaws or weaknesses in the rival argument followed by the (supported) presentation of one's own. In his attack on a traditionalist "great books" approach to the college curriculum promoted by Robert Hutchins, philosopher Sidney Hook makes the pattern clear:

To hold up before students the "habitual vision of greatness" is excellent. But . . . this does not mean that the heroes of action and the titans of thought inhabit only . . . the past. Nor does it mean that the study of books, or the study of *great* books, or the study *only* of great books, or the study of great books only of the *past*—to rise in the scale of absurdity—must be central to a liberal education. Great books by all means; but why not also great pictures and symphonies, great plays and cinemas, great social changes and mass movements, as well as the great Armageddons of our own time? We can learn at least as much from the heroic tragedy of Warsaw as from the last stand at Thermopylae. . . .

Even more grandiose is Mr. Hutchins's demand that liberal education deal "with permanent and not shifting conditions, with ultimate and not relative ends." But not very sensible! Slavery, feudalism, capitalism . . . , and technological change . . . [i]ndeed, everything historical would evaporate from the course of study. But if so, then why study *Greek* culture: and if Greek culture, why not American? And if there is something permanent in historical change, why is it privileged over what is not permanent? How can we distinguish which is which, without studying *both* . . . ? Is it true . . . that what are called "ultimate" values have the same meaning . . . in all times, places, and cultures? How can we tell without examining the values of at least some *different* cultures?

Education for Modern Man: A New Perspective, pp. 132–34

Although the arguments you will write as a student are likely to be far more limited than those suggested by the excerpts here, the principles remain essentially the same. In broadest terms, while you are free to offer any proposal, assert any position, or project any point of view, you are absolutely obliged to substantiate it by means of sound evidence presented through rational discourse.

Using Argument and Persuasion

An Appropriate Thesis

Be sure that your thesis is arguable and not a personal preference or a matter of fact. Of the following, only the last is debatable:

1. Soda (pop) tastes like no-frills mouthwash. (personal preference)
2. The simple sugars in soda provide energy but no lasting nutritional benefit and help promote tooth decay. (fact)
3. Soda machines should be removed from the college cafeteria. (argument)

Defined and Consistent Terms

At the outset and as you proceed, define any terms with which your audience may be unfamiliar or which you are using in limited or unusual ways. (See the discussion of stipulative definition on pp. 399–401.)

Be sure that the meanings of your terms are consistent throughout the argument. Otherwise, you may be guilty of equivocation (the misleading use of a word in multiple senses), a tactic that will weaken—if not invalidate—your argument.

For example, if Democratic party leaders chastised the Republican opposition by charging that such opposition was undemocratic, they would be playing fast and loose with their terminology. The right to oppose the views of others is, in fact, inherently *democratic*, though of course *Democratic* leaders would prefer uniform agreement with their own views.

Similarly, if you have defined *education* as a process of gaining intellectual insight through academic study, you cannot go on to include "hard knocks" received on the "mean streets" or any other life experience as part of the curriculum—unless you make it clear when nonacademic learning is introduced that you have now altered or expanded the definition with which you began. If you were arguing that one's education is a lifelong process and that all experience contributes to what we know, you might well begin with the narrow, conventional definition and alter it (acceptably) as the stages of your argument evolve.

Sufficient Support

As in expository writing, be sure that you have sufficient relevant data—illustrations, examples, facts—to support your contentions. If you have too few, or if they are irrelevant, your argument will not stand. Here, for example, is Robert Townsend's commentary on the Harvard Business School:

Don't hire Harvard Business School graduates. This worthy enterprise confesses that it trains its students for only three posts—executive
vice-president, president, and board chairman. The faculty does not
blush when HBS is called the West Point of capitalism.

By design, the "B-School" trains a senior officer class, the nonplay-
ing Captains of Industry. People who, upon graduation, are given a
whirlwind tour of their chosen company and then an office and a
secretary and some work to do while they wait for one of the top three
slots to open up.

This elite, in my opinion, is missing some pretty fundamental
requirements for success: humility; respect for people on the firing line;
deep understanding of the nature of the business and the kind of people
who can enjoy themselves making it prosper; respect from way down the
line; a demonstrated record of guts, industry, loyalty, judgment, fairness,
and honesty under pressure.

I've already applied (no acknowledgment) for the job of guide to
the Harvard Business School in 1995. By that time, tourists will be
wandering around it like Stonehenge, saying, "I wonder what they used
to do here."

Further Up the Organization, pp. 89–90

Of course, this piece is written with tongue at least partly in cheek. But taking
it at all seriously, a reader will want to see documentation of the confession
referred to in the first paragraph; representative examples of those who only
sit and wait and the specific companies for which they work; and illustrations
of the attitudes, personality traits, and assorted ignorance of "this elite."
None, however is forthcoming. The question Clara Peller once asked about
a hamburger of dubious dimension and character applies here as well: Where's
the beef?

Since an argumentative claim is more controversial than the typical
expository thesis, it is likely to require a great deal more evidence—and not
simply casual evidence—to be convincing.

Even when your argument is cast in a deductive mode, as in an argument
from principle, inductive evidence will still be necessary to support it. Consider the following argument arranged as a syllogism:

An outstanding labor leader not only achieves job benefits for the
rank-and-file union members but establishes the justice of their cause
and their human dignity in the minds of the public.

As head of the Brotherhood of Sleeping Car Porters, and as a
tireless advocate of civil rights, A. Philip Randolph improved the working conditions of his members, gained sympathy for their cause from
much of the public, and exerted political power on their behalf.

Surely, Randolph was among the outstanding labor leaders of the
twentieth century.

Assuming the major premise is accepted, the writer's task is to convince the reader of the validity of the minor one. If this is done, through the presentation of data and details, the conclusion (claim) is inescapable.

Moderate Language

Moderate your language. Especially avoid name-calling and substituting the prejudices of your audience (as well as your own) for original ideas. Elevating the language of your epithet does not improve it or your argument. An opponent that you call a "rodent in need of ablution" is still a "dirty rat" and if the term *American* in the Fourth of July speech refers only to "us ever-lovin', blue-eyed, down-home folks" or to the "noble heritage of our ancestors who landed at Plymouth Rock"—and not *them*—then it is merely a euphemistic code word for bigotry.

Except in the most abstract of arguments, you are not expected to eliminate emotionally charged language. But such language must be a means of conveying an argument, not the argument itself. Otherwise your case is reduced to **"rhetoric"** in the most pejorative sense.

> If we cannot cure the social ills that promote such brutal acts as drive-by killing, immolation, and protracted torture, and if we cannot rehabilitate those who commit these atrocities, and if we truly cannot afford to expand our prison system to control the savage offender, then perhaps psychosurgery is a solution to consider.

There are some loaded words here, such as *brutal, atrocities,* and *savage,* and it might be argued that the proposal is as inhumane as the acts it purports to prevent. However, if the possibilities of social cures, rehabilitation, and prison expansion have been thoroughly and dispassionately discussed, the emotional load is tolerable, especially when compared with the oft-heard public cry, "Lock the [expletive deleted] up and throw away the [expletive deleted] key," usually uttered without any semblance of rational context or discourse. While such comments reveal the writer's despair, anger, or disgust, they are irrelevant and antithetical to argument, speaking only to the writer's and, too often, to others' ignorance as well.

Sound Logic

Regardless of their degree of formality, arguments must be logically sound. Not all arguments are complex, however, and even in complex arguments, writers might not explore all the intricacies and will no doubt adjust what they have to say to the perceived ability of their audience to follow. In reality, unless we are specialists, we are likely to encounter or write fewer elaborate, intricate arguments than casual, simpler ones. Arguments may range from the brief, personal letter to the editor to a sober, impersonal document hundreds of pages long in a doctoral thesis or published book.

Some of your college research papers, although tens of pages long rather than hundreds, are likely to be formal. In composing these you will become a specialist on a limited topic, expected to provide as complete support as possible for your thesis or claim, to rebut opposing arguments, to write objectively in third person, and to employ language appropriate to the academic discipline, avoiding such informal usage as contractions and **colloquialisms.**

In many of your short, argumentative (or persuasive) papers, however, where extensive elaboration is impossible, your tone and language might be more relaxed, as you skim across three or four major points and cite a few instances in support of each. Such arguments must still be coherent and avoid logical fallacies, but the requirements for depth and thoroughness are far less stringent. Even so, you are not, in academic terms, simply entitled to hold an opinion. You must back that opinion with reasons why the reader should accept it.

Perhaps the most readily available sources of such informal arguments are the editorial and op-ed pages of a newspaper. Here, letter writers, editors, and columnists express their diverse views, usually in no more than a few hundred words. You would do well to examine these over time, noting both their successes and excesses in emotionally charged language and faulty reasoning. They often provide an especially good exercise in finding the unstated premise or warrant.

An example of a moderately informal (if lengthy) argument, such as you might be required to write for a course in composition, follows:

> We are told from our first year at college that plagiarism is the most heinous of academic crimes. While few are caught and convicted of it, many of those who are guilty fail papers and courses and in some cases are suspended or expelled. In an academic world that reveres intellectual achievement and in a society that fosters integrity, such severity would be understandable. But in a culture that prefers the shortcut to the straight and narrow, the easy buck to ethics, and in an academic environment in which students are often regarded as unavoidable obstacles along the path to promotion and the peddling of pedagogical abstractions, or treated as mere serfs in a professional petty fiefdom, the emphasis placed on plagiarism and other forms of academic dishonesty is both hypocritical and anachronistic.
>
> Society has tended to punish more severely the thug who snatches a purse than one who uses brain power—through fraud or embezzlement, for example. Recently, as in the cases of Wall Street magnates Ivan Boesky and Michael Milken, some select, high-profile, white-collar criminals have been incarcerated—for a year or two—in "country club" minimum-security prisons, then released to perform community service. Their fortunes, however, remain largely intact and the public's fascination with their cases often belies its tacit approval. Lesser fry strike deals

with the IRS and, beyond inconvenience, suffer little penalty at all. The implication is that the true crime was to have gotten caught.

The congressional banking scandal of 1992 is another example of warped values. The short-lived public outcry was largely the result of prior hostility toward Congress, and since (apparently) no criminal acts and no public funds were involved, the furor was more over the bad form of writing overdrafts (later covered) than over substance. At one level, the objections seemed to be based on the question of fairness. Since we, Sue and Steve Citizen, are not permitted to write bad checks, neither should members of Congress. Clearly, the ethical issue of writing such checks was secondary at best.

The public's materialism compounds the problem. Our heroes are too often the lottery winners, the quiz-show champions, the rich and therefore famous whose champagne lifestyles we drool over while choking on our beer budgets. Infomercials touting quick and easy financial schemes are making their way from the wee hours to prime time, and not long ago Hollywood filmed the story of Joey Coyle, a Philadelphia longshoreman who found—and did not return—$1.2 million that had fallen from an armored truck. Our focus is on the ends, not the means. We have had a long romance with the outlaw, from Billy the Kid to the Godfather. If we can't find the pot of gold ourselves, at least we can keep our pittance by playing tax-tag with the IRS.

The moral tone of college and university life is not necessarily higher. Among the student body, illicit drinking and drug use remain serious problems, date rape is undoubtedly present and perhaps widespread, racial conflicts abound—witness the "water buffalo" incident at the University of Pennsylvania, which gained national attention in 1993. Moreover, the student body has already incorporated the ethical views that the public holds toward the Milkens or the Madonnas. Perhaps they have been cheating on tests since grade school, copying "reports" from the *Book of Knowledge* or *Cliff's Notes* with impunity— knowing, in many cases, that teachers are aware of what is going on but that out of indifference or timidity will fail to act. The expectation is that the reactions of their professors will be no different.

In many cases, the expectation is justified. Professors, particularly those without tenure, are not eager to entangle themselves in the snares of the campus judicial process, let alone expose themselves to the possibility of civil law suits. Procedures of this sort are also time consuming and will interfere with their research, some of which involves meeting deadlines.

Professors may have their own ethical baggage. Some of their research might be questionable—as in some experiments involving human or animal subjects, and more to the present point, if it is funded by parties who have a vested interest in the results. Historically, the tobacco industry and what used to be called the military-industrial complex have been generous in providing research funds. Even if nothing was amiss, projects so funded have tended to raise suspicions and have at times called the purpose of the university into question. Is building or engineering a better missile or providing the mathematical or scientific foundation for doing so a legitimate academic pursuit?

But if grants were not forthcoming, the research professors would have to return to their classrooms, perhaps to teach undergraduates, many of whom are regularly taught by graduate assistants. The practice at least suggests some neglect, if not indifference, to undergraduate education at institutions at which it is widespread. At Harvard the practice is so pervasive that in 1993 parents of one undergraduate brought a civil suit against the university, claiming that it was not performing as advertised. Perhaps students perceive that the university does not care and respond by asking, Why should we?

The university administration, of course, contributes to the difficulty. In pressing for research and sanctioning the graduate teaching-assistant system, it has fostered the problems outlined above. And like the professors, administrators wish to avoid any adverse publicity that a fight over a plagiarism case might bring. Princeton, among others, has had such an experience with one of its doctoral students. In addition, administrators are drawn by the dollar. Increasingly, their job is to control costs and acquire income whether from government or private sources, and perhaps they pay less attention than they should to strings attached.

In this sort of academic world, which struggles for power and money, the professor who vigorously prosecutes plagiarism is likely to suffer the fate of a government whistle-blower, shunted aside and looked upon suspiciously even if the student is guilty. Moreover, even among professors themselves, intellectual dishonesty is sometimes a dirty little (if unsubstantiated) secret. "Crowley's name appeared first in the article, but the work is really Fromchuck's." "Baylis has his students do the research, then takes the credit for it." Occasionally, a case becomes public. In 1988, for example, charges of plagiarism against a Harvard psychiatrist made headline news when he was forced to resign from the medical school faculty and an administrative post at a university-related hospital. He later rejoined the hospital staff. Not very different perhaps from Senator Biden's withdrawing from the 1988 presidential primary campaign because of plagiarism, but retaining his position as head of the Senate judiciary committee. Even the (posthumous) discovery of plagiarism in Martin Luther King's doctoral dissertation made only the interior pages of some newspapers, received about twenty seconds of broadcast coverage, and then was never heard of again. Like the others, the event had all the public significance of a bubble bursting on the surface of a boiled pudding.

Neither the public nor academe attaches great significance to white-collar crime—especially to crime in which what is stolen is not even marketable. It is perverse of the university, therefore, to attempt to hold students to an idealistic code of behavior that it regularly undermines by its own example, and the importance of which it most often denies through either neglect or the most minimal of penalties. Students who suffer more serious consequences are simply martyrs to the occasional surge of institutional guilt or remorse, token sacrifices to an ancient god not dead long enough not to be appeased. But in an ambiguous, improvised ethical environment, almost any punishment is excessive. If the severe treatment of plagiarists is to be justified, academia must return actively to its professed ideals. Otherwise, it should abandon altogether the pretense that it takes plagiarism seriously.

If you are nodding or applauding vigorously, stop! This argument is far from flawless. Through its many examples, it does make at least a partial case for the ethical ambiguity on campus and off, and in doing so, takes a step or two toward convincing the reader that any severe punishment for plagiarism is inconsistent with actual values and therefore hypocritical. However, specifics are sometimes lacking, for instance in the paragraph dealing with the purported "ethical baggage" of professors, and the single example of Harvard in the paragraph that follows does not seem sufficient to make the case. In such instances, the argument is overstated and therefore faulty. In addition, evidence that runs counter to the claim is ignored rather than confronted. In 1994, for example, Oxford University revoked a doctorate it had conferred on discovering that the recipient had plagiarized his dissertation.

The writer's string of alliteration in the opening paragraph amounts to stylistic flourish without substance, and the options at the close create a false dilemma. More seriously, the argument either frequently begs the question or at least is based on premises with which fault might well be found. Among these are the blanket statements about the general and academic environments in the opening paragraph, the claim that primary and secondary school teachers ignore cheating, the charge that professors are reluctant to engage in the judicial process, the implication that faculty and administration are indifferent to undergraduate teaching, and the suggestion that university administrators do not pay sufficient attention to any "strings" attached to financial contributions. A proper rebuttal would take many of these and other shortcomings into account.

Unfortunately, the argument is better than some and no worse than many to which you will be exposed. Your task is to read carefully, question critically, and avoid logical lapses in your own work.

Plato

(Greece; ca. 428 B.C.–347 B.C.)

In a sense, Plato and Socrates (ca. 470 B.C.–ca. 399 B.C.), the principal interlocutor of Plato's dialogues and often the principal subject, are a pair of philosophically conjoined twins. Plato was a member of Socrates' intellectual inner circle, and we know Socrates chiefly through Plato's writings; Socrates himself wrote nothing that survives. In addition, scholars have often been hard put to establish where in the dialogues Socrates' ideas end and Plato's begin.

It is possible here to list only a few of the two men's philosophical contributions. First, there is the Socratic method—a series of questions and answers, very like an interrogation, by which the truth of a proposition is arrived at or denied. Second, there is the Platonic idea of "forms," a philosophical construct that proposes an ideal for every object or abstraction. This ideal, however, can never be attained, for the material world can be no more than its weak representation. For instance, a specific book has a fixed number of pages, particular dimensions, typography, and binding, but it is not the essence of "bookness." Third, the soul is immortal, shares in divinity, and, as opposed to the material body, is the source of human qualities. Finally, since government (and all else) is best run by those most knowledgeable, democracy is unacceptable. The ideal government is one strictly organized along class lines with philosopher-kings at the head.

With varying intensity, Plato's writings have been extremely influential in Western thought to our own day. Obviously, his emphasis on hierarchy, the ideal, and the supremacy and immortality of the soul would have been highly acceptable to the Church under whose auspices Western civilization evolved for roughly a thousand years after the fall of Rome.

Four of Plato's dialogues, Euthyphro, The Apology, Crito, and Phaedo, deal specifically with the trial and death of Socrates. Although he had been a dutiful and upright Athenian citizen, Socrates was nevertheless a thorn in the side of the democracy that had been restored in 403 B.C. He had embarrassed many of its leaders intellectually; his philosophical dislike of democracy was well known; and two members of the oligarchy, which had ruled prior to the restoration, had been his close friends. Since political amnesty had been given to those who had cooperated with the former government, Socrates was tried on the trumped-up charges of religious impiety and corrupting Athenian youth.

According to Plato, Socrates insisted on the propriety of his behavior, and conducted his defense without altering his usual provocative tactics. He was convicted by a narrow majority. The jury then had to choose between the death sentence proposed by the prosecution and the nominal fine offered by Socrates. Insulted by Socrates' proposal, many more voted for death than had voted for the original conviction. As Crito opens, we learn that the execution has been delayed a month on religious grounds. Upon the return of the sacred ship, Socrates is to drink the lethal dose of hemlock.

A key to understanding Crito *is to observe the basis for Crito's suggestion that Socrates escape and to compare it with the grounds for Socrates' rejection of the proposal. It is useful to ask, in short, where are they coming from?*

Crito

Persons of the Dialogue

SOCRATES   CRITO

SCENE: The Prison of Socrates

SOCRATES Why have you come at this hour, Crito? it must be quite early?

CRITO Yes, certainly.

SOC What is the exact time?

CR The dawn is about to break.

SOC I wonder that the keeper of the prison would let you in.   5

CR He knows me, because I often come, Socrates; moreover, I have done him a kindness.

SOC And are you only just arrived?

CR No, I came some time ago.

SOC Then why did you sit and say nothing, instead of at once awakening me?

CR Awaken you, Socrates? Certainly not! I wish I were not myself so   10 sleepless and full of sorrow. I have been watching with amazement your peaceful slumbers; and I deliberately refrained from awaking you, because I wished time to pass for you as happily as might be. Often before during the course of your life I have thought you fortunate in your disposition; but never did I see anything like the easy, tranquil manner in which you bear this calamity.

SOC Why, Crito, when a man has reached my age he ought not to be repining at the approach of death.

CR And yet other old men find themselves in similar misfortunes, and age does not prevent them from repining.

SOC That is true. But you do not say why you come so early.

CR I come to bring you a painful message; not, as I believe, to yourself, but painful and grievous to all of us who are your friends, and most grievous of all to me.

SOC What? Has the ship come from Delos, on the arrival of which I am   15 to die?

CR No, the ship has not actually arrived, but she will probably be here today, as persons who have come from Sunium tell me that they left her there; and therefore tomorrow, Socrates, must be the last day of your life.

SOC Very well, Crito; if such is the will of God, I am willing; but my belief is that there will be a delay of a day.

CR Why do you think so?

SOC I will tell you. I am to die on the day after the arrival of the ship.

CR Yes; that is what the authorities say.   20

SOC But I do not think that the ship will be here until tomorrow; this I infer from a vision which I had last night, or rather only just now, when you fortunately allowed me to sleep.

CR And what was the nature of the vision?

SOC There appeared to me the likeness of a woman, fair and comely, clothed in bright raiment, who called to me and said: "O Socrates,

The third day hence to fertile Phthia shalt thou come."[1]

CR What a singular dream, Socrates!

SOC There can be no doubt about the meaning, Crito, I think.   25

CR Yes; the meaning is only too clear. But, oh! my beloved Socrates, let me entreat you once more to take my advice and escape. For if you die I shall not only lose a friend who can never be replaced, but there is another evil: people who do not know you and me will believe that I might have saved you if I had been willing to spend money, but that I did not care. Now, can there be a worse disgrace than this—that I should be thought to value money more than the life of a friend? For the many will not be persuaded that I wanted you to escape, and that you refused.

SOC But why, my dear Crito, should we care about the opinion of the many? The best men, and they are the only persons who are worth considering, will think of these things truly as they occurred.

CR But you see, Socrates, that the opinion of the many must be regarded, for what is now happening shows of itself that they can do the greatest evil to anyone who has lost their good opinion.

SOC I only wish it were so, Crito, and that the many could do the greatest evil; for then they would also be able to do the greatest good—and what a fine thing this would be! But in reality they can do neither; for they cannot make a man either wise or foolish, and they do not care what they make of him.

CR Well, I will not dispute with you; but please to tell me, Socrates,   30 whether you are not acting out of regard to me and your other friends: are you not afraid that if you escape from prison we may get into trouble with the informers for having stolen you away, and lose either the whole or a great part

---

[1]Homer, *Iliad*, ix, 363. [Tr.]

of our property; or that even a worse evil may happen to us? Now, if you fear on our account, be at ease; for in order to save you, we ought surely to run this, or even a greater risk; be persuaded, then, and do as I say.

Soc   Yes, Crito, that is one fear which you mention, but by no means the only one.

Cr   Fear not—there are persons who are willing to get you out of prison at no great cost; and as for the informers, you know that they are far from being exorbitant in their demands—a little money will satisfy them. My means, which are certainly ample, are at your service, and if out of regard for my interests you have a scruple about spending my money, here are strangers who will give you the use of theirs; and one of them, Simmias the Theban, has brought a large sum for this very purpose and Cebes and many others are prepared to spend their money in helping you to escape. I say, therefore, do not shirk the effort on our account, and do not say, as you did in the court, that you will have a difficulty in knowing what to do with yourself, if anywhere else. For men will love you in other places to which you may go, and not in Athens only; there are friends of mine in Thessaly, if you like to go to them, who will value and protect you, and no Thessalian will give you any trouble. Nor can I think that you are at all justified, Socrates, in betraying your own life when you might be saved; in acting thus you are working to bring on yourself the very fate which your enemies would and did work to bring on you, your own destruction. And further I should say that you are deserting your own children; for you might bring them up and educate them; instead of which you go away and leave them, and they will have to take their chance; and if they do not meet with the usual fate of orphans, there will be small thanks to you. No man should bring children into the world who is unwilling to persevere to the end in their nurture and education. But you appear to be choosing the easier part, not the better and manlier, which would have been more becoming in one who professes to care for virtue in all his life, like yourself. And indeed, I am ashamed not only of you, but of us who are your friends, when I reflect that the whole business may be attributed entirely to our want of courage. The trial need never have come on, or might have been managed differently; and this last opportunity will seem (crowning futility of it all) to have escaped us through our own incompetence and cowardice, who might have saved you if we had been good for anything, and you might have saved yourself; for there was no difficulty at all. See now, Socrates, how discreditable as well as disastrous are the consequences, both to us and you. Make up your mind then, or rather have your mind already made up, for the time of deliberation is over, and there is only one thing to be done, which must be done this very night, and if we delay at all will be no longer practicable or possible; I beseech you therefore, Socrates, be persuaded by me, and do not say me nay.

Soc   Dear Crito, your zeal is invaluable, if a right one; but if wrong, the greater the zeal the greater the danger; and therefore we ought to consider whether I shall or shall not do as you say. For I am and always have been one of those natures who must be guided by reason, whatever the reason may be which upon reflection appears to me to be the best; and now that this chance has befallen me, I cannot repudiate my own doctrines, which seem to me as sound as ever: the principles which I have hitherto honoured and revered I still honour, and unless we can at once find other and better principles, I am certain not to agree with you; no, not even if the power of the multitude could let loose upon us many more imprisonments, confiscations, deaths, frightening us like children with hobgoblin terrors. What will be the fairest way of considering the question? Shall I return to your old argument about the opinions of men?—we were saying that some of them are to be regarded, and others not. Now were we right in maintaining this before I was condemned? And has the argument which was once good now proved to be talk for the sake of talking—mere childish nonsense? That is what I want to consider with your help, Crito:—whether, under my present circumstances, the argument will appear to me in any way different or not; and whether we shall dismiss or accept it. That argument, which, as I believe, is maintained by many persons of authority, was to the effect, as I was saying, that the opinions of some men are to be regarded, and of other men not to be regarded. Now you, Crito, are not going to die tomorrow—at least, there is no human probability of this—and therefore you are disinterested and not liable to be deceived by the circumstances in which you are placed. Tell me then, I beg you, whether I am right in saying that some opinions, and the opinions of some men only, are to be valued, and that others are to be disregarded. Is not this true?

CR Certainly.

SOC The good opinions are to be regarded, and not the bad?   35

CR Yes.

SOC And the opinions of the wise are, good, and the opinions of the unwise are evil?

CR Certainly.

SOC And what was said about another matter? Does the pupil who devotes himself to the practice of gymnastics attend to the praise and blame and opinion of any and every man, or of one man only—his physician or trainer, whoever he may be?

CR Of one man only.   40

SOC And he ought to fear the censure and welcome the praise of that one only, and not of the many?

CR Clearly so.

SOC And he ought to act and train, and eat and drink in the way which seems good to his single master who has understanding, rather than according to the opinion of all other men put together?

CR True.

Soc And if he disobeys and disregards the opinion and approval of the 45
one, and regards the opinion of the many who have no understanding, will
he not suffer evil?

Cr Certainly he will.

Soc And what will the evil be, whither tending and what affecting, in
the disobedient person?

Cr Clearly, affecting the body; that is what is ruined by the evil.

Soc Very good; and is not this true, Crito, of other things which we
need not separately enumerate? In questions of just and unjust, fair and foul,
good and evil, which are the subjects of our present consultation, ought we
to follow the opinion of the many and to fear them; or the opinion of the one
man who has understanding? ought we not to fear and reverence him more
than all the rest of the world, and if we desert him shall we not corrupt and
outrage that principle in us which may be assumed to be improved by justice
and deteriorated by injustice?—there is such a principle?

Cr Certainly there is, Socrates. 50

Soc Take a parallel instance:—if, acting against the advice of those who
have understanding, we ruin that which is improved by health and is corrupted by disease, would life be worth having? And that which has been
corrupted is—the body?

Cr Yes.

Soc Is our life worth living, with an evil and corrupted body?

Cr Certainly not.

Soc And will it be worth living, if that higher part of man be corrupted 55
which is improved by justice and depraved by injustice? Do we suppose that
principle, whatever it may be in man, which has to do with justice and
injustice, to be inferior to the body?

Cr Certainly not.

Soc More honourable than the body?

Cr Far more.

Soc Then, my friend, we must not particularly regard what the many
say of us: but what he, the one man who has understanding of just and unjust,
will say, and what the truth will say. And therefore you begin in error when
you advise that we should regard the opinion of the many about just and
unjust, good and evil, honourable and dishonorable.—"Well," someone will
say, "but the many can kill us."

Cr That will clearly be the answer, Socrates; you are right there. 60

Soc But still, my excellent friend, I find that the old argument is
unshaken as ever. And I should like to know whether I may say the same of
another proposition—that not life, but a good life, is to be chiefly valued?

Cr Yes, that also remains unshaken.

Soc And a good life is equivalent to a just and honourable one—that
holds also?

CR Yes, it does.

SOC From these premisses I proceed to argue the question whether it is   65
or is not right for me to try and escape without the consent of the Athenians:
and if it is clearly right, then I will make the attempt; but if not, I will abstain.
The other considerations which you mention, of money and loss of character
and the duty of educating one's children, are, I fear, only the doctrines of the
multitude, who would restore people to life, if they were able, as thoughtlessly
as they put them to death—and with as little reason. But now, since the
argument has carried us thus far, the only question which remains to be
considered is, whether we shall do rightly, I by escaping and you by helping
me, and by paying the agents of my escape in money and thanks; or whether
in reality we shall not do rightly; and if the latter, then death or any other
calamity which may ensue on my remaining quietly here must not be allowed
to enter into the calculation.

CR I think that you are right, Socrates; how then shall we proceed?

SOC Let us consider the matter together, and do you either refute me if
you can, and I will be convinced; or else cease, my dear friend, from repeating
to me that I ought to escape against the wishes of the Athenians: for I am
very eager that what I do should be done with your approval. And now please
to consider my first position, and try how you can best answer me.

CR I will.

SOC Are we to say that we are never intentionally to do wrong, or that
in one way we ought and in another way we ought not to do wrong, or is doing
wrong always evil and dishonourable, as has already been often acknowledged
by us? Are all the admissions we have made within these last few days to be
thrown over? And have we, at our age, been earnestly discoursing with one
another all our life long only to discover that we are no better than children?
Or, in spite of the opinion of the many, and in spite of all consequences
whether for the better or the worse, shall we insist on the truth of what was
then said, that injustice is always an evil and dishonour to him who acts
unjustly? Shall we say so or not?

CR Yes.   70

SOC Then we must do no wrong?

CR Certainly not.

SOC Nor when injured injure in return, as the many imagine; for we
must injure no one at all?

CR Clearly not.

SOC Again, Crito, may we do evil?   75

CR Surely not, Socrates.

SOC And what of doing evil in return for evil, which is the morality of
the many—is that just or not?

CR Not just.

SOC For doing evil to another is the same as injuring him?

CR Very true.   80

Soc Then we ought not to retaliate or render evil for evil to anyone, whatever evil we may have suffered from him. But I would have you consider, Crito, whether you really mean what you are saying. For this opinion has never been held, and never will be held, by any considerable number of persons, and those who are agreed and those who are not agreed upon this point have no common ground, and can only despise one another when they see how widely they differ. Tell me, then, whether you agree with and assent to my first principle, that neither injury nor retaliation nor warding off evil by evil is ever right. And shall that be the premiss of our argument? Or do you decline and dissent from this? For so I have ever thought, and continue to think; but, if you are of another opinion, let me hear what you have to say. If, however, you remain of the same mind as formerly, I will proceed to the next step.

Cr You may proceed, for I have not changed my mind.

Soc Then I will go on to the next point, which may be put in the form of a question:—Ought a man to do what he admits to be right, or ought he to betray the right?

Cr He ought to do what he thinks right.

Soc But if this is true, what is the application? In leaving the prison 85 against the will of the Athenians, do I wrong any? or rather do I not wrong those whom I ought least to wrong? Do I not desert the principles which were acknowledged by us to be just—what do you say?

Cr I cannot answer your question, Socrates; for I do not understand it.

Soc Then consider the matter in this way:—Imagine that I am about to run away (you may call the proceeding by any name which you like), and the laws and the state appear to me and interrogate me: "Tell us, Socrates," they say; "what are you about? are you not going by an act of yours to bring us to ruin—the laws, and the whole state, as far as in you lies? Do you imagine that a state can subsist and not be overthrown, in which the decisions of law have no power, but are set aside and trampled upon by individuals?" What will be our answer, Crito, to these and the like words? Anyone, and especially a rhetorician, will have a good deal to say against the subversion of the law which requires a sentence to be carried out. Shall we reply, "Yes; but the state has injured us and given an unjust sentence." Suppose we say that?

Cr Very good, Socrates.

Soc "And was that our agreement with you?" the law would answer; "or were you to abide by the sentence of the state?" And if we were to express our astonishment at their words, the law would probably add: "Answer, Socrates, instead of opening your eyes—you are in the habit of asking and answering questions. Tell us,—What complaint have you to make against us which justifies you in attempting to ruin us and the state? In the first place did we not bring you into existence? Your father married your mother by our aid and begat you. Say whether you have any objection to urge against those of us who regulate marriage?" None, I should reply. "Or against those of us who after birth regulate the nurture and education of children, in which you also were trained? Were not the laws, which have the charge of education, right in commanding your father to train you in music and gymnastic?" Right, I should reply. "Well then, since you were brought into the world and nurtured and educated by us, can you deny in the first place that you are our child and slave, as your fathers were before you? And if this is true you cannot suppose that you are on equal terms with us in matters of right and wrong, or think that you have a right to do to us what we are doing to you. Would you have any right to strike or revile or do any other evil to your father or your master, if you had one, because you have been struck or reviled by him, or received some other evil at his hands?—you would not say this? And because we think right to destroy you, do you think that you have any right to destroy us in return, and your country as far as in you lies? Will you, O professor of true virtue, pretend that you are justified in this? Has a philosopher like you failed to discover that our country is more precious and higher and holier far than mother or father or any ancestor, and more to be regarded in the eyes of the gods and of men of understanding? also to be soothed, and gently and reverently entreated when angry, even more than a father, and either to be persuaded, or if not persuaded, to be obeyed? And when we are punished by her, whether with imprisonment or stripes, the punishment is to be endured in silence; and if she lead us to wounds or death in battle, thither we follow as is right; neither may anyone yield or retreat or leave his rank, but whether in battle or in a court of law, or in any other place, he must do what his city and his country order him; or he must change their view of what is just: and if he may do no violence to his father or mother, much less may he do violence to his country." What answer shall we make to this, Crito? Do the laws speak truly, or do they not?

Cr I think that they do.

90

Soc Then the laws will say: "Consider, Socrates, if we are speaking truly that in your present attempt you are going to do us a wrong. For, having brought you into the world, and nurtured and educated you, and given you and every other citizen a share in every good which we had to give, we further proclaim to any Athenian by the liberty which we allow him, that if he does not like us, the laws, when he has become of age and has seen the ways of the city, and made our acquaintance, he may go where he pleases and take his goods with him. None of us laws will forbid him or interfere with anyone who does not like us and the city, and who wants to emigrate to a colony or to any other city; he may go where he likes, with his property. But he who has experience of the manner in which we order justice and administer the state, and still remains, has by so doing entered into an implied contract that he will do as we command him. And he who disobeys us is, as we maintain, thrice wrong; first, because in disobeying us he is disobeying his parents; secondly, because we are the authors of his education; thirdly, because having made an agreement with us that he will duly obey our commands, he neither obeys them nor convinces us that our commands are unjust; although we do not roughly require unquestioning obedience, but give him the alternative of obeying or convincing us;—that is what we offer, and he does neither.

"These are the sort of accusations to which, as we were saying, you, Socrates, will be exposed if you accomplish your intentions; you, above all other Athenians." Suppose now I ask, why I rather than anybody else? no doubt they will justly retort upon me that I above all other Athenians have acknowledged the agreement. "There is clear proof," they will say, "Socrates, that we and the city were not displeasing to you. Of all Athenians you have been the most constant resident in the city, which, as you never leave, you may be supposed to love. For you never went out of the city either to see the games, except once when you went to the Isthmus, or to any other place unless when you were on military service; nor did you travel as other men do. Nor had you any curiosity to know other states or their laws: your affections did not go beyond us and our state; we were your special favourites, and you acquiesced in our government of you; and here in this city you begat your children, which is a proof of your satisfaction. Moreover, you might in the course of the trial, if you had liked, have fixed the penalty at banishment; you might then have done with the state's assent what you are now setting out to do without it. But you pretended that you preferred death to exile, and that you were not unwilling to die. And now you have forgotten these fine sentiments, and pay no respect to us the laws, of whom you are the destroyer; and are doing what only a miserable slave would do, running away and turning your back upon the compacts and agreements of your citizenship which you made with us. And first of all answer this very question: Are we right in saying that you agreed to live under our government in deed, and not in word only? Is that true or not?" How shall we answer, Crito? Must we not assent?

CR We cannot help it, Socrates.

SOC Then will they not say: "You, Socrates, are breaking the covenants and agreements which you made with us at your leisure, not under any compulsion or deception or in enforced haste, but after you have had seventy years to think of them during which time you were at liberty to leave the city, if we were not to your mind or if our covenants appeared to you to be unfair. You had your choice, and might have gone either to Lacedaemon or Crete, both which states are often praised by you for their good government, or to some other Hellenic or foreign state. Whereas you, above all other Athenians, seemed to be so fond of the state, and obviously therefore of us her laws (for who would care about a state without its laws?), that you never stirred out of her; the halt, the blind, the maimed were not more stationary in her than you were. And now you refuse to abide by your agreements. Not so, Socrates, if you will take our advice; do not make yourself ridiculous by leaving the city.

"For just consider, if you transgress and err in this sort of way, what good 95
will you do either to yourself or to your friends? That your friends will be in
danger of being driven into exile and deprived of citizenship, or of losing their
property, is tolerably certain; and you yourself, if you fly to one of the
neighbouring cities, as, for example, Thebes or Megara, both of which are
well governed, will come to them as an enemy of their government and all
patriotic citizens will look askance at you as a subverter of the laws, and you
will confirm in the minds of the judges the justice of their own condemnation
of you. For he who is a corrupter of the laws is more than likely to be a
corrupter of the young and foolish portion of mankind. Will you then flee
from well-ordered cities and virtuous men? and is existence worth having on
these terms? Or will you go to them without shame, and talk to them,
saying—what will you say to them? What you say here about virtue and
justice and institutions and laws being the best things among men? Would
that be decent of Socrates? Surely not. But if you go away from well-governed
states to Crito's friends in Thessaly, where there is great disorder and licence,
they will be charmed to hear the tale of your escape from prison, set off with
ludicrous particulars of the manner in which you were wrapped in a goatskin
or some other disguise, and metamorphosed as the manner is of runaways; but
will there be no one to remind you that in your old age, when little time was
left to you, you were not ashamed to violate the most sacred laws from a
greedy desire of life? Perhaps not, if you keep them in a good temper; but if
they are out of temper you will hear many degrading things. You will live, but
how?—fawning upon all men, and the servant of all men; and doing what?—
faring sumptuously in Thessaly, having gone abroad in order that you may get
a dinner. And where will be your fine sentiments about justice and virtue?
Say that you wish to live for the sake of your children—you want to bring
them up and educate them—will you take them into Thessaly and deprive
them of Athenian citizenship? Is this the benefit which you will confer upon
them? Or are you under the impression that they will be better cared for and
educated here if you are still alive, although absent from them; for your
friends will take care of them? Do you fancy that if you have left Athens for
Thessaly they will take care of them, but if you have left it for the other world
that they will not take care of them? Nay; but if they who call themselves
friends are good for anything, they will—to be sure they will.

"Listen, then, Socrates, to us who have brought you up. Think not of life
and children first, and of justice afterwards, but of justice first, that you may
so vindicate yourself before the princes of the world below. For neither will
you nor any that belong to you be happier or holier or juster in this life, or
happier in another, if you do as Crito bids. Now you depart, if it must be so,
in innocence, a sufferer and not a doer of evil; a victim, not of the laws but
of men. But if you leave the city, basely returning evil for evil and injury for
injury, breaking the covenants and agreements which you have made with us,
and wronging those whom you ought least of all to wrong, that is to say,

yourself, your friends, your country, and us, we shall be angry with you while you live, and our brethren, the laws in the world below, will give you no friendly welcome; for they will know that you have done your best to destroy us. Listen, then, to us and not to Crito."

This, dear Crito, is the voice which I seem to hear murmuring in my ears, like the sound of the flute in the ears of the mystic;[2] that voice, I say, is humming in my ears, and prevents me from hearing any other. Be assured, then, that anything more which you may say to shake this my faith will be said in vain. Yet speak, if you have anything to say.

CR   I have nothing to say.

Soc   It is enough then, Crito. Let us fulfil the will of God, and follow whither He leads.

Translated by Benjamin Jowett

THESIS AND THOUGHT

1. What case does Crito make for Socrates' escape?

2. Why does Socrates choose to submit to his death sentence?

3. Evaluate Crito's recommendation and Socrates' choice as courses of principled action.

4. What essential difference is there between the basis of Crito's initial contentions (through para. 32) and the conclusion to which he ultimately comes? Explain why he changes his mind.

5. According to *Crito*, what is the Platonic (Socratic) idea of an individual's political relationship and obligations to society? If you have read the Declaration of Independence, compare Jefferson's view with the one expressed here.

STRUCTURE

1. Outline the series of premises and conclusions that constitute Socrates' argument.

2. To what extent is Crito's argument based on emotional appeals? Socrates' argument? Indicate specific instances.

3. Identify the two analogies with which Socrates is occupied in paragraphs 39–60. Is their use (logically) legitimate?

4. To what extent does *Crito* employ rebuttal? Examine particularly its use by "the laws."

---

[2]**the voice . . . of the mystic:** Socrates took visions and dreams seriously; from childhood he had heard a mystical voice that warned him against specific actions. [Ed.]

STYLE

1. What advantages or disadvantages are there in Plato's use of dialogue to present an argument? What makes Plato's dialogue different from that of a short two-character play? Consider plot development, dramatic conflict, characterization, and theme.

2. What qualitative difference do you observe in the nature of the exchanges between Crito and Socrates after paragraph 33 as compared with those in the preceding paragraphs? Account for the difference in terms of what Plato is attempting to achieve in the two portions of the dialogue.

3. What does Plato (or Socrates) gain by personifying the laws?

CONSIDERATIONS

1. Discuss whether Socrates' acceptance of the vision in paragraphs 21–26 is consistent with his claim in paragraph 33 that he is "one of those natures who must be guided by reason." See also the mystical voice in paragraph 97.

2. Are you as convinced by Socrates' argument as Crito seems to be? Why? What are the premises that underlie your response?

3. Socrates is aware throughout that his position and motives are not those of the masses—Athenian or otherwise. If you agree, explain why you think his view is accurate. If you disagree, state the reasons for your disagreement. Do either in a substantial paragraph.

4. Write a rebuttal (not necessarily using dialogue) to the idea that Socrates is "a victim, not of the laws but of men," and that therefore justice and reason demand his compliance even with a faulty verdict and worse sentence.

5. One of the "arguments" that the laws make to Socrates is a patriotic one— that plays both on Socrates' love for Athens and on the ills of a life lived in exile (para. 95), a choice of sentence that Socrates rejected (para. 94). Focusing primarily on issues of government and law, write an essay in which you consider how you might cope with being banished from your city, state, or country.

Lucius Annaeus Seneca

(Rome; ca. 4 B.C.–A.D. 65)

The son of a rhetorician of the same name, Seneca was born in what is now Cordoba, Spain, then part of a Roman province, and was educated at Rome in both law and philosophy. Having gained a reputation as a speaker, he became a member of the Senate and led a life of political intrigue, particularly during the reign of Nero.

Although he is credited with improving the treatment of slaves and keeping Nero's basest instincts under control, Seneca nevertheless was a party to the conspiracy that resulted in the murder of Agrippina, the emperor's mother. Later, foreseeing his loss of influence and power, Seneca asked for and received permission to retire in A.D. 62. But in A.D. 65 he was accused of conspiring against Nero and condemned to commit suicide. When opening his veins did not suffice, he resorted to suffocation in a steam bath.

Fortunately, Seneca's legacy is literary and philosophical rather than political. His Consolationes *(three essays comforting parents on the loss of their sons) and* Epistulae Morales ad Lucilium *(Moral Epistles to Lucilius) present chiefly a stoic point of view of manners and morals. His philosophical outlook was so compatible with Christianity that early church fathers mistakenly believed he was a Christian. Long after the error was corrected, Seneca's writings continued to be read by influential Christian thinkers.*

Seneca, however, was a playwright as well as a moralist. His nine extant tragedies, of which Medea *is perhaps best known today, are largely dramatic, philosophical poems unsuited to performance. But they were generally familiar to Renaissance playwrights and influenced the many revenge tragedies of the age of Shakespeare.*

Test what Seneca has to say about crowds by asking whether people behave differently as members of a group—particularly a large one—from the way they behave as individuals.

On Crowds

DO YOU ASK ME what you should regard as especially to be avoided? I say, crowds; for as yet you cannot trust yourself to them with safety. I shall admit my own weakness, at any rate; for I never bring back home the same character that I took abroad with me. Something of that which I have forced to be calm within me is disturbed; some of the foes that I have routed return again. Just as the sick man, who has been weak for a long time, is in such a condition that he cannot be taken out of the house without suffering a relapse, so we ourselves are affected when our souls are recovering from a lingering disease. To consort with the crowd is harmful; there is no person who does not make some vice attractive to us, or stamp it upon us, or taint us unconsciously therewith. Certainly, the greater the mob with which we mingle, the greater the danger.

But nothing is so damaging to good character as the habit of lounging at the games; for then it is that vice steals subtly upon one through the avenue of pleasure. What do you think I mean? I mean that I come home more greedy, more ambitious, more voluptuous and even more cruel and inhu-

man,—because I have been among human beings. By chance I attended a
mid-day exhibition, expecting some fun, wit and relaxation,—an exhibition
at which men's·eyes have respite from the slaughter of their fellow-men. But
it was quite the reverse. The previous combats were the essence of compassion; but now all the trifling is put aside and it is pure murder.[1] The men have
no defensive armour. They are exposed to blows at all points, and no one ever
strikes in vain. Many persons prefer this programme to the usual pairs and to
the bouts "by request." Of course they do; there is no helmet or shield to
deflect the weapon. What is the need of defensive armour, or of skill? All
these mean delaying death. In the morning they throw men to the lions and
the bears; at noon, they throw them to the spectators. The spectators demand
that the slayer shall face the man who is to slay him in his turn; and they
always reserve the latest conqueror for another butchering. The outcome of
every fight is death, and the means are fire and sword. This sort of thing goes
on while the arena is empty. You may retort: "But he was a highway robber;
he killed a man! " And what of it? Granted that, as a murderer, he deserved
this punishment, what crime have you committed, poor fellow, that you
should deserve to sit and see this show? In the morning they cried "Kill him!
Lash him! Burn him! Why does he meet the sword in so cowardly a way? Why
does he strike so feebly? Why doesn't he die game? Whip him to meet his
wounds![2] Let them receive blow for blow, with chests bare and exposed to the
stroke!" And when the games stop for the intermission, they announce: "A
little throat-cutting in the meantime, so that there may still be something
going on!"

Come now; do you[3] not understand even this truth, that a bad example
reacts on the agent? Thank the immortal gods that you are teaching cruelty
to a person who cannot learn to be cruel. The young character, which cannot
hold fast to righteousness, must be rescued from the mob; it is too easy to side
with the majority. Even Socrates, Cato, and Laelius might have been shaken
in their moral strength by a crowd that was unlike them; so true it is that none
of us, no matter how much he cultivates his abilities, can withstand the shock
of faults that approach, as it were, with so great a retinue. Much harm is done
by a single case of indulgence or greed; the familiar friend, if he be luxurious,
weakens and softens us imperceptibly; the neighbour, if he be rich, rouses our
covetousness; the companion, if he be slanderous, rubs off some of his rust
upon us, even though we be spotless and sincere. What then do you think the
effect will be on character, when the world at large assaults it! You must either
imitate or loathe the world.

[1]During the luncheon interval condemned criminals were often driven into the arena and
compelled to fight, for the amusement of those spectators who remained throughout the day. [Tr.]
[2]**to meet his wounds!:** until you draw blood. [Ed.]   [3]The remark is addressed to the brutalized
spectators. [Tr.] Generally, the idea of the sentence is that witnessing or participating in brutality,
as in the cries of the spectators, debases the witness or participant. [Ed.]

But both courses are to be avoided; you should not copy the bad simply because they are many, nor should you hate the many because they are unlike you. Withdraw into yourself, as far as you can. Associate with those who will make a better man of you. Welcome those whom you yourself can improve. The process is mutual; for men learn while they teach. There is no reason why pride in advertising your abilities should lure you into publicity, so that you should desire to recite or harangue before the general public. Of course I should be willing for you to do so if you had a stock-in-trade that suited such a mob; as it is, there is not a man of them who can understand you. One or two individuals will perhaps come in your way, but even these will have to be moulded and trained by you so that they will understand you. You may say: "For what purpose did I learn all these things?" But you need not fear that you have wasted your efforts; it was for yourself that you learned them.

In order, however, that I may not today have learned exclusively for myself, I shall share with you three excellent sayings, of the same general purport, which have come to my attention. This letter will give you one of them as payment of my debt; the other two you may accept as a contribution in advance. Democritus says: "One man means as much to me as a multitude, and a multitude only as much as one man." The following also was nobly spoken by someone or other, for it is doubtful who the author was; they asked him what was the object of all this study applied to an art that would reach but very few. He replied: "I am content with few, content with one, content with none at all." The third saying—and a noteworthy one, too—is by Epicurus, written to one of the partners of his studies: "I write this not for the many, but for you; each of us is enough of an audience for the other." Lay these words to heart, Lucilius, that you may scorn the pleasure which comes from the applause of the majority. Many men praise you; but have you any reason for being pleased with yourself, if you are a person whom the many can understand? Your good qualities should face inwards. Farewell.

Translated by Richard M. Gummere

Thesis and Thought

1. What is Seneca's primary objection to crowds? Are his objections strictly moral, or does he have other grounds as well—social class and aesthetics, for example?

2. Why does he single out the Roman "games" for particular disapproval?

3. According to the essay, what is an appropriate basis for human interaction? How widespread is such interaction likely to be? Why? Is it in fact necessary?

STRUCTURE

1. How dependent is Seneca's argument on the weight of authority?

2. What support other than that of the "games," if any, does Seneca provide for his contentions? Is his evidence convincing?

3. Comment on the legitimacy and effectiveness of the following argumentative tactics: the use of the analogy between physical and spiritual well-being in paragraph 1; the implication in paragraph 3 that if we may be adversely affected by individuals, we will be affected to an even greater extent by "the world at large."

4. Seneca makes frequent use of absolute statements (generalizations), the truth of which he apparently assumes to be self-evident: "To consort with the crowd is harmful" (para. 1); "a bad example reacts on the agent" (para. 3); the first five sentences of paragraph 4; and "Your good qualities should face inwards" (para. 5). Does he ever put them to the test? Considering his immediate audience, does he need to? Are you as accepting of these maxims?

STYLE

1. Of what use are the quotations in paragraph 2? Do they enhance Seneca's argument?

2. What is the tone of the quotation that concludes paragraph 2? In the same paragraph, what does the word *voluptuous* mean? What are its connotations? Are other meanings and contexts for its use more prevalent? Consult your dictionary.

CONSIDERATIONS

1. Do you find Seneca's idea about the masses to be elitist? Explain.

2. Assess the difficulty and desirability of maintaining the kind of independence and detachment that Seneca advocates.

3. In response to the statement that the butchered combatant killed a man, Seneca writes in paragraph 2: "And what of it? Granted that, as a murderer, he deserved this punishment, what crime have you committed . . . that you should deserve to sit and see this show?" Do you share his idea that such public spectacles punish the viewer? Write a brief essay in which you explain your position.

4. Does the brutality Seneca describes in paragraph 2 (both between combatants and among spectators) have a counterpart in contemporary American society? Write an essay in which you argue for the abolition of a particularly violent public spectacle.

Christopher Marlowe

(England; 1564–1593)

During his brief life, Marlowe managed to become the foremost playwright in English before the great flowering of Shakespeare and is credited with refining English blank verse as the language completed the evolution from its middle to its modern phase. His life, particularly its end, is clouded in mystery.

Trained for the clergy, Marlowe never took orders but led a double life as playwright and agent in the Elizabethan secret service. He earned a reputation as an atheist or at least an unorthodox believer; but since so much of the politics of the day focused on religion, it is difficult to separate anything Marlowe might have believed from possible impressions he might have deliberately wished to convey in his capacity as secret agent. Marlowe was killed in a tavern brawl. Although his death was ruled self-defense, his killers were of doubtful reputation at the time and one of them, it has since been discovered, was a double agent. That Marlowe was, in fact, murdered is a strong possibility.

Among Marlowe's more notable plays, still occasionally performed, are The Jew of Malta, Edward II, *and* The Tragical History of Dr. Faustus, *all probably written between 1587 and 1592. The last elaborates on the ancient legend of the philosopher so hungry for knowledge that he sells his soul to the devil.*

The lyric reproduced here is typical of the "pastoral" poetry of Marlowe's day, in which sophisticated narrators took on the guise of rural innocents.

The Passionate Shepherd to His Love

Come live with me and be my love,
And we will all the pleasures prove[1]
That valleys, groves, hills, and fields,
Woods, or steepy mountain yields.

And we will sit upon the rocks,   5
Seeing the shepherds feed their flocks,
By shallow rivers to whose falls
Melodious birds sing madrigals.

[1] **prove:** test. [All notes are by the editor.]

And I will make thee beds of roses
And a thousand fragrant posies,   10
A cap of flowers, and a kirtle[2]
Embroidered all with leaves of myrtle;

A gown made of the finest wool
Which from our pretty lambs we pull;
Fair lined slippers for the cold,   15
With buckles of the purest gold;

A belt of straw and ivy buds,
With coral clasps and amber studs:
And if these pleasures may thee move,
Come live with me, and be my love.   20

The shepherds' swains[3] shall dance and sing
For thy delight each May morning:
If these delights thy mind may move,
Then live with me and be my love.

Sir Walter Raleigh
(England; 1554–1618)

Raleigh's career is a history of rising and falling, recovering and failing fortunes. Fighting on behalf of the Protestant cause in both France and Ireland, he came to the attention of Elizabeth I and quickly grew in her favor. He was knighted by 1585 and his various lucrative appointments involving trade in such commodities as cloth, wine, and tin soon made his fortune. But his relationship with Elizabeth Throgmorton (whom he married) enraged the queen and Raleigh was briefly imprisoned in 1592. He never fully returned to Her Majesty's good graces, although his attacks against Spain earned him additional appointments before her death.

James I, however, succeeded Elizabeth in 1603 and, convinced that Raleigh was plotting his overthrow, had him tried for treason. Convicted, Raleigh escaped execution but was confined to the Tower of London until 1616. While imprisoned, he produced his major writing, The History of the World *(1614). Never pardoned, Raleigh was nevertheless released to follow up on his earlier expedition to Guyana in search of Eldorado, a legendary lost city of gold. James granted him permission to discover mines, provided he did not provoke Spain, which had settlements and other interests in the territory. Raleigh failed on both counts and was executed under his original sentence.*

In many ways, Raleigh represents the courtier of his age—egotistical, daring in warfare and exploration, accomplished, even chivalrous: the legend of his

---

[2]**kirtle:** gown.   [3]**swains:** rustic companions.

spreading his cloak over a mud puddle to permit the queen to walk on did not arise accidentally. Writing poetry was itself a courtly grace. Some poems of Queen Elizabeth I survive, as well as several attractive pieces by her father, Henry VIII.

Marlowe's "Passionate Shepherd" was published posthumously in 1599, "The Nymph's Reply" in 1600. Raleigh undoubtedly thought it fitting to take up the literary and philosophical challenge posed by his late friend.

The Nymph's Reply to the Shepherd

If all the world and love were young,
And truth in every shepherd's tongue,
These pretty pleasures might me move
To live with thee and be thy love.

Time drives the flocks from field to fold[1]   5
When rivers rage and rocks grow cold,
And Philomel[2] becometh dumb;
The rest complains of cares to come.

The flowers do fade, and wanton fields
To wayward winter reckoning yields;   10
A honey tongue, a heart of gall,
Is fancy's spring, but sorrow's fall.

Thy gowns, thy shoes, thy beds of roses,
Thy cap, thy kirtle, and thy posies
Soon break, soon wither, soon forgotten—   15
In folly ripe, in reason rotten.

Thy belt of straw and ivy buds,
Thy coral clasps and amber studs,
All these in me no means can move
To come to thee and be thy love.   20

But could youth last and love still breed,
Had joys no date nor age no need,
Then these delights my mind might move
To live with thee and be thy love.

---

[1]**fold:** enclosure. [Ed.]   [2]**Philomel:** the nightingale. [Ed.]

Thesis and Thought

1. How does the worldview expressed in Marlowe's poem differ from that in Raleigh's?
2. How seriously is either poem to be taken?

Structure

1. In what sense is Marlowe's poem primarily persuasive? Raleigh's predominantly argumentative?
2. Evaluate the following statement: Marlowe's poem makes its appeal inductively; Raleigh's is based on deductive reasoning.
3. Show how Raleigh's poem is a rebuttal of Marlowe's.

Style

1. How do Raleigh's stanzaic and rhyme patterns reinforce his argument against "The Passionate Shepherd"?
2. Examine and explain the effect of the following: repetition and parallel structure in Raleigh's fourth stanza; the antitheses in the final lines of stanzas 3 and 4 of "The Nymph's Reply."
3. Although used sparingly in prose, **alliteration** is often found in poetry. Find examples of it in both poems. In which does it seem more abundant? To what effect? Experiment with using alliteration in a substantial prose paragraph.

Considerations

1. Despite the fact that both poems are products of the late sixteenth century, does one poem seem more contemporary in tone than the other? If so, which? In either case, explain why.
2. However innocent, "The Passionate Shepherd" is ultimately a seduction poem. Regardless of your gender or orientation, write a prose paragraph in which, using modern "delights" or temptations, you appeal for someone to live with you, be your love, or both. Then, write another paragraph in which you reject the appeal.
3. Write an essay in which you discuss the present possibility of achieving the idyllic love depicted by Marlowe.

Thomas Jefferson

(United States; 1743–1826)

The inscription on his tombstone is Jefferson's own summary of his life: "Here was buried Thomas Jefferson, author of the Declaration of American Independence, of the Statute of Virginia for religious freedom, and father of the University of Virginia."

The opening passage of the Declaration is representative of his political views. (This will be explored further through the questions that follow the reading.) In religion, he advocated freedom of conscience, proposing the religious-freedom statute to the Virginia legislature during his tenure there (1776–79). Personally, he was a deist, believing in the existence of a God who established the natural law by which the universe was run. Not surprisingly, the "Jefferson Bible" (The Life and Morals of Jesus of Nazareth), published after his death, eliminates the miracles of the New Testament but preserves its teachings.

Education was also one of Jefferson's central concerns. The founding of the University of Virginia was part of a broader plan. He had proposed free elementary education to create an informed citizenry. Qualified students would then be admitted to an upper school, according to their merit, not social or economic class. Of course, as a Virginia planter of his day, he intended the scheme to apply exclusively to whites—and males at that.

On the issues of slavery and race Jefferson was clearly in conflict. Although he kept up to two hundred slaves and freed but five, he was philosophically opposed to slavery, foresaw its moral and political dangers, and twice recommended a program of gradual emancipation combined with repatriation to Africa. As a member of the Continental Congress (1783–84), Jefferson proposed that slavery be barred from the territories after 1800, a proposal that failed by one vote. On the other hand, he believed that whites were superior to blacks—yet even in expressing this belief he includes a number of doubts and reservations. Clearly, on such questions, culture, conscience, and cogitation were at odds.

In addition to politics, Jefferson devoted himself to the study of natural sciences, sociology, and Native American languages—all in the best amateur tradition. His observations are to be found in Notes on the State of Virginia *(1785). He was also an architect, designing and redesigning his residence, Monticello, and influencing the adoption of the neoclassical style. Devoted to books, Jefferson read in Greek, Latin, French, Spanish, Italian, and Old English.*

The Declaration of Independence

In CONGRESS, July 4, 1776.

The Unanimous Declaration of the Thirteen United States of America.

When in the Course of human events, it becomes necessary for one people to dissolve the political bands which have connected them with another, and to assume among the powers of the earth, the separate and equal station to which the Laws of Nature and of Nature's God entitle them, a decent respect to the opinions of mankind requires that they should declare the causes which impel them to the separation.

We hold these truths to be self-evident, that all men are created equal, that they are endowed by their Creator with certain unalienable Rights, that among these are Life, Liberty and the pursuit of Happiness.

That to secure these rights, Governments are instituted among Men, deriving their just powers from the consent of the governed.

That whenever any Form of Government becomes destructive of these ends, it is the Right of the People to alter or to abolish it, and to institute new Government, laying its foundation on such principles and organizing its powers in such form, as to them shall seem most likely to effect their Safety and Happiness. Prudence, indeed, will dictate that Governments long established should not be changed for light and transient causes; and accordingly all experience hath shewn, that mankind are more disposed to suffer, while evils are sufferable, than to right themselves by abolishing the forms to which they are accustomed. But when a long train of abuses and usurpations, pursuing invariably the same Object evinces a design to reduce them under absolute Despotism, it is their right, it is their duty, to throw off such Government, and to provide new Guards for their future security.

Such has been the patient sufferance of these Colonies; and such is now   5
the necessity which constrains them to alter their former Systems of Government. The history of the present King of Great Britain is a history of repeated injuries and usurpations, all having in direct object the establishment of an absolute Tyranny over these States. To prove this, let Facts be submitted to a candid world.

He has refused his Assent to Laws, the most wholesome and necessary for the public good.

He has forbidden his Governors to pass Laws of immediate and pressing importance, unless suspended in their operation till his Assent should be obtained; and when so suspended, he has utterly neglected to attend to them.

He has refused to pass other Laws for the accommodation of large districts of people, unless those people would relinquish the right of Representation in the Legislature, a right inestimable to them and formidable to tyrants only.

He has called together legislative bodies at places unusual, uncomfortable, and distant from the depository of their public Records, for the sole purpose of fatiguing them into compliance with his measures.

He has dissolved Representative Houses repeatedly, for opposing with   10
manly firmness his invasions on the rights of people.

He has refused for a long time, after such dissolutions, to cause others to be elected; whereby the Legislative powers, incapable of Annihilation, have returned to the People at large for their exercise; the State remaining in the mean time exposed to all the dangers of invasion from without, and convulsions within.

He has endeavoured to prevent the population of these States; for that purpose obstructing the Laws for Naturalization of Foreigners; refusing to pass others to encourage their migrations hither, and raising the conditions of new Appropriations of Lands.

He has obstructed the Administration of Justice, by refusing his Assent to Laws for establishing Judiciary powers.

He has made Judges dependent on his Will alone, for the tenure of their offices, and the amount and payment of their salaries.

He has erected a multitude of New Offices, and sent hither swarms of   15
Officers to harass our people, and eat out their substance.

He has kept among us, in times of peace, Standing Armies without the Consent of our legislatures.

He has affected to render the Military independent of and superior to the Civil power.

He has combined with others to subject us to a jurisdiction foreign to our constitution, and unacknowledged by our laws; giving his Assent to their Acts of pretended Legislation:

For Quartering large bodies of armed troops among us:

For Protecting them, by a mock Trial, from punishment for any Murders   20
which they should commit on the Inhabitants of these States:

For cutting off our Trade with all parts of the world:

For imposing Taxes on us without our Consent:

For depriving us in many cases, of the benefits of Trial by Jury:

For transporting us beyond Seas to be tried for pretended offenses:

For abolishing the free System of English Laws in a neighbouring Prov-   25
ince, establishing therein an Arbitrary government, and enlarging its Boundaries so as to render it at once an example and fit instrument for introducing the same absolute rule into these Colonies;

For taking away our Charters, abolishing our most valuable Laws, and altering fundamentally the Forms of our Governments:

For suspending our own Legislatures, and declaring themselves invested with power to legislate for us in all cases whatsoever.

He has abdicated Government here, by declaring us out of his Protection and waging War against us:

He has plundered our seas, ravaged our Coasts, burnt our towns, and destroyed the lives of our people.

He is at this time transporting large Armies of foreign Mercenaries to   30
compleat the works of death, desolation and tyranny, already begun with circumstances of Cruelty & perfidy scarcely paralleled in the most barbarous ages, and totally unworthy the Head of a civilized nation.

He has constrained our fellow Citizens taken Captive on the high Seas to bear Arms against their Country, to become the executioners of their friends and Brethren, or to fall themselves by their Hands.

He has excited domestic insurrections amongst us, and has endeavoured to bring on the inhabitants of our frontiers, the merciless Indian Savages, whose known rule of warfare, is an undistinguished destruction of all ages, sexes and conditions. In every stage of these Oppressions We have Petitioned for Redress in the most humble terms: Our repeated Petitions have been answered only by repeated injury. A Prince, whose character is thus marked by every act which may define a Tyrant, is unfit to be the ruler of a free people. Nor have We been wanting in attentions to our British brethren. We have warned them from time to time of attempts by their legislature to extend an unwarrantable jurisdiction over us. We have reminded them of the circumstances of our emigration and settlement here. We have appealed to their native justice and magnanimity, and we have conjured them by the ties of our common kindred to disavow these usurpations, which, would inevitably interrupt our connections and correspondence. They too have been deaf to the voice of justice and of consanguinity. We must, therefore, acquiesce in the necessity, which denounces our Separation, and hold them, as we hold the rest of mankind, Enemies in War, in Peace Friends.

We, THEREFORE the Representatives of the UNITED STATES OF AMERICA, in General Congress Assembled, appealing to the Supreme Judge of the world for the rectitude of our intentions, do, in the Name and by Authority of the good People of these Colonies, solemnly publish and declare, That these United Colonies are, and of Right ought to be FREE AND INDEPENDENT STATES: that they are Absolved from all Allegiance to the British Crown, and that all political connection between them and the State of Great Britain, is and ought to be totally dissolved; and that as Free and Independent States, they have full Power to levy War, conclude Peace, contract Alliances, establish Commerce, and to do all other Acts and Things which Independent States may of right do.

And for the support of this Declaration, with a firm reliance on the protection of divine Providence, we mutually pledge to each other our Lives, our Fortunes and our sacred Honor.

THESIS AND THOUGHT

1. Especially considering that Britain and the colonists had been engaged in armed conflict since 1775, what were Jefferson's (and the Continental Congress's) purposes in creating and distributing the Declaration?

2. Although many revolutionary manifestos have been issued from Jefferson's day to our own, why was such a declaration particularly significant in the eighteenth century?

3. What indications does Jefferson give that the revolution is a course of last resort? According to paragraph 4, what degree of governmental abuse of authority is sufficient to justify its overthrow? Which of the charges in paragraphs 5–32 might Jefferson have omitted without losing credibility?

STRUCTURE

1. Summarize the Declaration in the form of a simple syllogism, stating a major premise, a minor premise, and a conclusion.

2. Of the premises in your answer to question 1 (or in the Declaration itself), which does Jefferson assume to be unquestionable? Which does he attempt to support?

3. What is the argumentative purpose of the long list of grievances against George III presented in paragraphs 5–32?

4. Is Jefferson's argument deductive, inductive, or both? Explain.

STYLE

1. In light of the atmosphere of crisis in which it was composed, the language of the Declaration is generally restrained. Jefferson, however, sometimes resorts to highly charged language. Find several instances of this and discuss whether they seem to be strategic or spontaneous.

2. Jefferson uses parallel structure liberally in the sentences that begin paragraphs 6–32, and within the last paragraph as well. How does this device serve the purposes of the Declaration? Does Jefferson avoid monotony? If so, how?

3. Occasionally, Jefferson lists items in series, most notably "Life, Liberty and the pursuit of Happiness" in paragraph 1. Other instances of this occur in paragraphs 26, 29, and 34. Explain whether this type of parallelism has effects other than those you named response to in question 2.

CONSIDERATIONS

1. In the phrase "all men are created equal," how inclusive (or exclusive) is the word *men*? Compare what Jefferson might have intended by it with how it is construed today. Even if you perceive it as a synonym for *people* collectively, does it seem sexist to you? Explain.

2. In what limited sense does Jefferson use the word *equal*? Compare the meaning of the word in context with its popular interpretations out of context. (You might want to examine or reread the Vonnegut and Sowell selections in chapter 8.) In light of the fact that Jefferson held slaves, do you find the statement concerning equality surprising? ironic? hypocritical?

3. After two centuries, does the Declaration retain its power as a revolutionary document? Discuss.

4. Assuming that you are a supporter of the crown, write a rebuttal of Jefferson's argument.

5. Recalling a time when you felt oppressed, write a parody of the Declaration aimed at your oppressor.

6. If you accept the major premises of the Declaration, under what conditions would you be willing to join a revolution today or in the future? Write an essay defining your position.

Sojourner Truth
(United States; 1797–1883)

Orator and social reformer, Sojourner Truth was born a slave in New York State. She was originally named Isabella Van Wagener, the surname taken from her final master, who set her free just before New York's abolition law took effect in 1827.

Having had religious visions since childhood, perhaps influenced by her mystical mother, she left for New York City upon emancipation and joined the religious community of Elijah Pierson. In 1843 she took the name Sojourner Truth and became thereafter an itinerant missionary. In the same year, she was introduced to the abolitionist movement in Massachusetts and was soon an advocate for the cause. A dynamic, magnetic speaker, she supported herself through sales of her autobiography.

Later, encouraged by Lucretia Mott, she joined the women's rights movement and became a speaker on its behalf as well. During the Civil War, she collected supplies for black troops and helped integrate public transit in Washington, D.C., where, as a White House guest, she met Lincoln. After the war, Truth served as a member of the National Freedmen's Association, working on behalf of the newly emancipated slaves. She spent her final years in Battle Creek, Michigan.

The racial views of her audience often made her a less-than-welcome speaker. But Truth, a large, deep-voiced, imposing woman, was not easily daunted. Once, her sexual identity questioned, she bared her breasts in defiant challenge to the hostile crowd. Nor is there anything timid in the speech reproduced here.

This selection appears in a reminiscence of Frances D. Gage, who presided over the women's rights convention held in Akron, Ohio, in 1851. After reading it, consider whether you find its argument convincing and whether it appeals primarily to reason or to passion.

A'n't I a Woman?

THE LEADERS OF THE MOVEMENT trembled on seeing a tall, gaunt black woman in a gray dress and white turban, surmounted with an uncouth sun-bonnet, march deliberately into the church, walk with the air of a queen up the aisle, and take her seat upon the pulpit steps. A buzz of disapprobation was heard all over the house, and there fell on the listening ear, "An abolition affair!" "Woman's rights and niggers!" "I told you so!" "Go it, darkey!"

I chanced on that occasion to wear my first laurels in public life as president of the meeting. At my request order was restored, and the business of the Convention went on. Morning, afternoon, and evening exercises came and went. Through all these sessions old Sojourner, quiet and reticent as the "Lybian Statue," sat crouched against the wall on the corner of the pulpit stairs, her sun-bonnet shading her eyes, her elbows on her knees, her chin resting upon her broad, hard palms. At intermission she was busy selling the "Life of Sojourner Truth," a narrative of her own strange and adventurous life. Again and again, timorous and trembling ones came to me and said, with earnestness, "Don't let her speak, Mrs. Gage, it will ruin us. Every newspaper in the land will have our cause mixed up with abolition and niggers, and we shall be utterly denounced." My only answer was, "We shall see when the time comes."

The second week the work waxed warm. Methodist, Baptist, Episcopal, Presbyterian, and Universalist ministers came in to hear and discuss the resolutions presented. One claimed superior rights and privileges for man, on the ground of "superior intellect"; another, because of the "manhood of Christ; if God had desired the equality of woman, He would have given some token of His will through the birth, life, and death of the Saviour." Another gave us a theological view of the "sin of our first mother."

There were very few women in those days who dared to "speak in meeting"; and the august teachers of the people were seemingly getting the better of us, while the boys in the galleries, and the sneerers among the pews, were hugely enjoying the discomfiture, as they supposed, of the "strong-minded." Some of the tender-skinned friends were on the point of losing dignity, and the atmosphere betokened a storm. When, slowly from her seat in the corner rose Sojourner Truth, who, till now, had scarcely lifted her head. "Don't let her speak!" gasped half a dozen in my ear. She moved slowly and solemnly to the front, laid her old bonnet at her feet, and turned her great speaking eyes to me. There was a hissing sound of disapprobation above and below. I rose and announced "Sojourner Truth," and begged the audience to keep silence for a few moments.

The tumult subsided at once, and every eye was fixed on this almost
Amazon form, which stood nearly six feet high, head erect, and eyes piercing
the upper air like one in a dream. At her first word there was a pronounced
hush. She spoke in deep tones, which though not loud, reached every ear in
the house, and away through the throng at the doors and windows.

"Wall, chilern, whar dar is so much racket dar must be somethin' out o'
kilter. I tink dat 'twixt de niggers of de Souf and de womin at de Norf, all
talkin' 'bout rights, de white men will be in a fix pretty soon. But what's all
dis here talkin' 'bout?

"Dat man ober dar say dat womin needs to be helped into carriages, and
lifted ober ditches, and to hab de best place everywhar. Nobody eber helps me
into carriages, or ober mud-puddles, or gibs me any best place!" And raising
herself to her full height, and her voice to a pitch like rolling thunder, she
asked, "And a'n't I a woman? Look at me! Look at my arm! (and she bared
her right arm to the shoulder, showing her tremendous muscular power). I
have ploughed, and planted, and gathered into barns, and no man could head
me! And a'n't I a woman? I could work as much and eat as much as a
man—when I could get it—and bear de lash as well! And a'n't I a woman? I
have borne thirteen chilern, and seen 'em mos' all sold off to slavery, and
when I cried out with my mother's grief, none but Jesus heard me! And a'n't
I a woman?

"Den dey talks 'bout dis ting in de head; what dis dey call it?" ("Intellect,"
whispered some one near.) "Dat's it, honey. What's dat got to do wid womin's
rights or nigger's rights? If my cup won't hold but a pint, and yourn holds a
quart, wouldn't ye be mean not to let me have my little half-measure full?"
And she pointed her significant finger, and sent a keen glance at the minister
who had made the argument. The cheering was long and loud.

"Den dat little man in black dar, he say women can't have as much rights
as men, 'cause Christ wan't a woman! Whar did your Christ come from?"
Rolling thunder couldn't have stilled that crowd, as did those deep, wonderful
tones, as she stood there with outstretched arms and eyes of fire. Raising her
voice still louder, she repeated, "Whar did your Christ come from? From God
and a woman! Man had nothin' to do wid Him." Oh, what a rebuke that was
to that little man.

Turning again to another objector, she took up the defense of Mother   10
Eve. I can not follow her through it all. It was pointed, and witty, and solemn;
eliciting at almost every sentence deafening applause; and she ended by
asserting, "If de fust woman God ever made was strong enough to turn de
world upside down all alone, dese women togedder (and she glanced her eye
over the platform) ought to be able to turn it back, and get it right side up
again! And now dey is asking to do it, de men better let 'em!" Long-continued
cheering greeted this. " 'Bleeged to ye for hearin' on me, and now ole Sojourner han't got nothin' more to say."

Amid roars of applause, she returned to her corner, leaving more than one of us with streaming eyes, and hearts beating with gratitude. She had taken us up in her strong arms and carried us safely over the slough of difficulty turning the whole tide in our favor. I have never in my life seen anything like the magical influence that subdued the mobbish spirit of the day, and turned the sneers and jeers of an excited crowd into notes of respect and admiration. Hundreds rushed up to shake hands with her, and congratulate the glorious old mother, and bid her God-speed on her mission of "testifyin' agin concerning the wickedness of this 'ere people."

THESIS AND THOUGHT

1. To what points is Truth's speech a rebuttal? State in your own words her principal response to each of them.

2. Describe the emotional atmosphere in which Truth delivers her remarks. What effect does the speech have on it?

STRUCTURE

1. Outline Truth's contentions as syllogisms. Are her conclusions validly drawn? Do you question any of her premises? Explain.

2. Defend or oppose the following statement: Truth's speech succeeds primarily through emotion rather than reason.

3. What, if anything, does Gage's narrative framework contribute to the force of Truth's remarks?

STYLE

1. What general impression of Truth does Gage create in describing her? What key words and phrases does she use in doing so? Does Truth's speech reinforce the impression?

2. Identify the various parallel structures and repetitions in paragraph 7 and evaluate their impact on the forcefulness of Truth's presentation.

3. Truth (as Gage records it) speaks in the black dialect of her class and day. Gage writes in the standard English of her own. Is the stylistic contrast helpful to the impact of the whole? Rewrite Truth's speech in conventional English and evaluate its effectiveness in that form.

4. Highly offensive by modern standards, the word *nigger* appears four times in the selection—twice used by whites (paras. 1–2), twice by Truth herself

(paras. 6 and 8). Explain whether there is any difference in the implications of the word as used by Truth and by members of the audience. Is the word, in any instance here, simply denotative? Explain.

CONSIDERATIONS

1. Part of the objection to Truth's speaking is the possible confusion of the issue of women's rights with the issue of slavery. To what extent are the issues of women's rights and civil rights today independent or intertwined?

2. Does Gage present Truth as an individual or as a glorified racial stereotype? Defend your position in a brief essay.

3. Write an impassioned rebuttal to an argument raised against an idea or principle to which you subscribe.

Mark Twain
(United States; 1835–1910)

As "The Lowest Animal" should indicate, Twain is a writer known primarily for his often sharply critical humor. In addition, he helped establish an authentically American literature, independent of European models and themes. The Adventures of Huckleberry Finn, *his most widely acclaimed work, does this most forcefully.*

Born Samuel Langhorne Clemens, Twain was raised in the river town of Hannibal, Missouri. As a young man, he was a pilot on the Mississippi, an activity brought to a halt by the Civil War. Twain served briefly in the Confederate army before deserting to join his abolitionist brother, a Lincoln appointee, in the Nevada territory. There, and later in San Francisco, he prospected unsuccessfully and continued to write, developing the humorous vein he had begun to establish as an adolescent. In 1863 he adopted the name Mark Twain (pilot jargon for "two fathoms deep").

Coming across a story at one of the mining camps, he transformed it into "The Celebrated Jumping Frog of Calaveras County." Reprinted widely, the story earned him an eastern audience. Somewhat later, Twain firmly established his growing reputation as a writer of humorous travel literature with The Innocents Abroad *(1869).*

Meanwhile, during one of his ocean voyages, he had fallen in love with Olivia Langdon, sister of a fellow cruise-ship passenger, through the portrait her brother carried with him. Writing hundreds of letters, Twain wooed her successfully at last, and the couple settled in Hartford, Connecticut. There, for two decades, Twain's talent came to fullest flower. Among the works of this period were Old Times on the Mississippi *(1875),* The Adventures of Tom Sawyer *(1876), and* A Life on the Mississippi *(1883). The Adven-*

tures of Huckleberry Finn *(1884) was written over a period of eight years, some of it during summers in a gazebo study on the grounds of the Langdon family home in Elmira, New York.*

But Twain's unwise investments, particularly in the Paige typesetting machine, brought him to bankruptcy and the brink of financial ruin. Although he regained solvency, Twain's last years were blighted by the loss of his wife and two of his three daughters. He remained, nevertheless, a popular public figure until nearly the end of his life, outspoken and scathing as ever.

In addition to the titles listed above, Twain's writings include The Prince and the Pauper *(1881),* A Connecticut Yankee in King Arthur's Court *(1889),* Pudd'nhead Wilson *(1894),* The Man that Corrupted Hadleyburg *(1900), and* The Mysterious Stranger *(1916).*

Ask yourself as you read how scientific Twain's scientific method is, and whether the essay is primarily argumentative or persuasive.

The Lowest Animal

I HAVE BEEN SCIENTIFICALLY STUDYING the traits and dispositions of the "lower animals" (so-called,) and contrasting them with the traits and dispositions of man. I find the result profoundly humiliating to me. For it obliges me to renounce my allegiance to the Darwinian theory of the Ascent of Man from the Lower Animals; since it now seems plain to me that that theory ought to be vacated in favor of a new and truer one, this new and truer one to be named the *Descent* of Man from the Higher Animals.

In proceeding toward this unpleasant conclusion I have not guessed or speculated or conjectured, but have used what is commonly called the scientific method. That is to say, I have subjected every postulate that presented itself, to the crucial test of actual experiment, and have adopted it or rejected it according to the result. Thus I verified and established each step of my course in its turn before advancing to the next. These experiments were made in the London Zöological Gardens, and covered many months of pains-taking and fatiguing work.

Before particularizing any of the experiments, I wish to state one or two things which seem to more properly belong in this place than further along. This in the interest of clearness. The massed experiments established to my satisfaction certain generalizations, to-wit:

1. That the human race is of one distinct species. It exhibits slight variations—in color, stature, mental calibre, and so on—due to climate, environment, and so forth; but it is a species by itself, and not to be confounded with any other.

2. That the quadrupeds are a distinct family, also. This family exhibits variations—in color, size, food preferences, and so on; but it is a family by itself.

3. That the other families—the birds, the fishes, the insects, the reptiles, etc., are more or less distinct, also. They are in the procession. They are links in the chain which stretches down from the higher animals to man at the bottom.

Some of my experiments were quite curious. In the course of my reading I had come across a case where, many years ago, some hunters on our Great Plains organized a buffalo hunt for the entertainment of an English earl— that, and to provide some fresh meat for his larder. They had charming sport. They killed seventy-two of those great animals; and ate part of one of them and left the seventy-one to rot. In order to determine the difference between an anaconda and an earl—if any—I caused seven young calves to be turned into the anaconda's cage. The grateful reptile immediately crushed one of them and swallowed it, then lay back satisfied. It showed no further interest in the calves, and no disposition to harm them. I tried this experiment with other anacondas; always with the same result. The fact stood proven that the difference between an earl and an anaconda is, that the earl is cruel and the anaconda isn't; and that the earl wantonly destroys what he has no use for, but the anaconda doesn't. This seemed to suggest that the anaconda was not descended from the earl. It also seemed to suggest that the earl was descended from the anaconda, and had lost a good deal in the transition.

I was aware that many men who have accumulated more millions of money than they can ever use, have shown a rabid hunger for more, and have not scrupled to cheat the ignorant and the helpless out of their poor savings in order to partially appease that appetite. I furnished a hundred different kinds of wild and tame animals the opportunity to accumulate vast stores of food, but none of them would do it. The squirrels and bees and certain birds made accumulations, but stopped when they had gathered a winter's supply, and could not be persuaded to add to it either honestly or by chicane. In order to bolster up a tottering reputation the ant pretended to store up supplies, but I was not deceived. I know the ant. These experiments convinced me that there is this difference between man and the higher animals: he is avaricious and miserly, they are not.

In the course of my experiments I convinced myself that among the animals man is the only one that harbors insults and injuries, broods over them, waits till a chance offers, then takes revenge. The passion of revenge is unknown to the higher animals.

Roosters keep harems, but it is by consent of their concubines; therefore no wrong is done. Men keep harems, but it is by brute force, privileged by atrocious laws which the other sex were allowed no hand in making. In this matter man occupies a far lower place than the rooster.

Cats are loose in their morals, but not consciously so. Man, in his descent from the cat, has brought the cat's looseness with him but has left the unconsciousness behind—the saving grace which excuses the cat. The cat is innocent, man is not.

Indecency, vulgarity, obscenity—these are strictly confined to man; he invented them. Among the higher animals there is no trace of them. They hide nothing; they are not ashamed. Man, with his soiled mind, covers himself. He will not even enter a drawing room with his breast and back naked, so alive is he and his mates to indecent suggestion. Man is "the Animal that Laughs." But so does the monkey, as Mr. Darwin pointed out; and so does the Australian bird that is called the laughing jackass. No—man is the Animal that Blushes. He is the only one that does it—or has occasion to. . . .

Man—when he is a North American Indian—gouges out his prisoner's   10
eyes; when he is King John, with a nephew to render untroublesome, he uses a red-hot iron; when he is a religious zealot dealing with heretics in the Middle Ages, he skins his capture alive and scatters salt on his back; in the first Richard's time he shuts up a multitude of Jew families in a tower and sets fire to it; in Columbus's time he captures a family of Spanish Jews and—but *that* is not printable; in our day in England a man is fined ten shillings for beating his mother nearly to death with a chair, and another man is fined forty shillings for having four pheasant eggs in his possession without being able to satisfactorily explain how he got them. Of all the animals, man is the only one that is cruel. He is the only one that inflicts pain for the pleasure of doing it. It is a trait that is not known to the higher animals. The cat plays with the frightened mouse; but she has the excuse, that she does not know that the mouse is suffering. The cat is moderate—unhumanly moderate: she only scares the mouse, she does not hurt it; she doesn't dig out its eyes, or tear off its skin, or drive splinters under its nails—man-fashion; when she is done playing with it she makes a sudden meal of it and puts it out of its trouble. Man is the Cruel Animal. He is alone in that distinction.

The higher animals engage in individual fights, but never in organized masses. Man is the only animal that deals in that atrocity of atrocities, War. He is the only one that gathers his brethren about him and goes forth in cold blood and with calm pulse to exterminate his kind. He is the only animal that for sordid reasons will march out, as the Hessians did in our Revolution, and as the boyish Prince Napoleon did in the Zulu war, and help to slaughter strangers of his own species who have done him no harm and with whom he has no quarrel.

Man is the only animal that robs his helpless fellow of his country—takes possession of it and drives him out of it or destroys him. Man has done this in all the ages. There is not an acre of ground on the globe that is in possession of its rightful owner, or that has not been taken away from owner after owner, cycle after cycle, by force and bloodshed.

Man is the only Slave. And he is the only animal who enslaves. He has always been a slave in one form or another, and has always held other slaves in bondage under him in one way or another. In our day he is always some man's slave for wages, and does that man's work; and this slave has other slaves under him for minor wages, and they do *his* work. The higher animals are the only ones who exclusively do their own work and provide their own living.

Man is the only Patriot. He sets himself apart in his own country, under his own flag, and sneers at the other nations, and keeps multitudinous uniformed assassins on hand at heavy expense to grab slices of other people's countries, and keep *them* from grabbing slices of *his*. And in the intervals between campaigns he washes the blood off his hands and works for "the universal brotherhood of man"—with his mouth.

Man is the Religious Animal. He is the only Religious Animal. He is the   15 only animal that has the True Religion—several of them. He is the only animal that loves his neighbor as himself, and cuts his throat if his theology isn't straight. He has made a graveyard of the globe in trying his honest best to smooth his brother's path to happiness and heaven. He was at it in the time of the Caesars, he was at it in Mahomet's time, he was at it in the time of the Inquisition, he was at it in France a couple of centuries, he was at it in England in Mary's day, he has been at it ever since he first saw the light, he is at it to-day in Crete . . . he will be at it somewhere else to-morrow. The higher animals have no religion. And we are told that they are going to be left out, in the Hereafter. I wonder why? It seems questionable taste.

Man is the Reasoning Animal. Such is the claim. I think it is open to dispute. Indeed, my experiments have proven to me that he is the Unreasoning Animal. Note his history, as sketched above. It seems plain to me that whatever he is he is *not* a reasoning animal. His record is the fantastic record of a maniac. I consider that the strongest count against his intelligence is the fact that with that record back of him he blandly sets himself up as the head animal of the lot; whereas by his own standards he is the bottom one.

In truth, man is incurably foolish. Simple things which the other animals easily learn, he is incapable of learning. Among my experiments was this. In an hour I taught a cat and a dog to be friends. I put them in a cage. In another hour I taught them to be friends with a rabbit. In the course of two days I was able to add a fox, a goose, a squirrel and some doves. Finally a monkey. They lived together in peace; even affectionately.

Next, in another cage I confined an Irish Catholic from Tipperary, and as soon as he seemed tame I added a Scotch Presbyterian from Aberdeen. Next a Turk from Constantinople; a Greek Christian from Crete; an Armenian; a Methodist from the wilds of Arkansaw; a Buddhist from China; a Brahmin from Benares. Finally, a Salvation Army Colonel from Wapping. Then I stayed away two whole days. When I came back to note results, the cage of Higher Animals was all right, but in the other there was but a chaos of gory odds and ends of turbans and fezzes and plaids and bones and flesh—

not a specimen left alive. These Reasoning Animals had disagreed on a theological detail and carried the matter to a Higher Court.

One is obliged to concede that in true loftiness of character, Man cannot claim to approach even the meanest of the Higher Animals. It is plain that he is constitutionally incapable of approaching that altitude; that he is constitutionally afflicted with a Defect which must make such approach forever impossible, for it is manifest that this Defect is permanent in him, indestructible, ineradicable.

I find this Defect to be THE MORAL SENSE. He is the only animal that has   20
it. It is the secret of his degradation. It is the quality *which enables him to do wrong.* It has no other office. It is incapable of performing any other function. It could never have been intended to perform any other. Without it, man could do no wrong. He would rise at once to the level of the Higher Animals.

Since the Moral Sense has but the one office, the one capacity—to enable man to do wrong—it is plainly without value to him. It is as valueless to him as is disease. In fact it manifestly *is* a disease. *Rabies* is bad, but it is not so bad as this disease. Rabies enables a man to do a thing which he could not do when in a healthy state: kill his neighbor with a poisonous bite. No one is the better man for having rabies. The Moral Sense enables a man to do wrong. It enables him to do wrong in a thousand ways. Rabies is an innocent disease, compared to the Moral Sense. No one, then, can be the better man for having the Moral Sense. What, now, do we find the Primal Curse to have been? Plainly what it was in the beginning: the infliction upon man of the Moral Sense; the ability to distinguish good from evil; and with it, necessarily, the ability to *do* evil; for there can be no evil act without the presence of consciousness of it in the doer of it.

And so I find that we have descended and degenerated, from some far ancestor,—some microscopic atom wandering at its pleasure between the mighty horizons of a drop of water perchance,—insect by insect, animal by animal, reptile by reptile, down the long highway of smirchless innocence, till we have reached the bottom stage of development—nameable as the Human Being. Below us—nothing. Nothing but the Frenchman. . . .

THESIS AND THOUGHT

1. What scientific truth does Twain hope (or pretend) to establish? In doing so, what use does he make of the scientific thinking of his day?

2. According to Twain, what is our place in the animal world? What reasons or evidence does he offer for assigning us to this position?

3. How does Twain define humanity's "moral sense"? Why does he regard it as the species' paramount defect?

STRUCTURE

1. Twain purports to use scientific method. Evaluate his procedures (para. 2), his generalizations, premises, or postulates (para. 3), and the experiments of paragraphs 4, 5, 17, and 18. Why does Twain omit the methods by which he reached the conclusions stated in paragraphs 6–16?

2. In what sense is Twain's "argument" inductive?

3. Explain how Twain uses the techniques of comparison, definition, and example to establish his argument.

4. Discuss whether Twain is guilty of stereotyping or of any other logical fallacy.

STYLE

1. Identify several instances of Twain's humor and evaluate their effectiveness in terms of advancing the argument.

2. To what degree does Twain maintain a scientific (i.e., objective) tone? What is his purpose in establishing it? At what point do you realize the pretense? Does he abandon the pretense altogether? Why?

3. Twain uses frequent repetition, of sentence patterns and of words. Examine the repetition in paragraphs 13 and 15 and explain whether Twain avoids monotony.

CONSIDERATIONS

1. In the paragraph subsequent to the last printed here, Twain goes on to explain that the Frenchman also has an "immoral sense." Can you suggest reasons why Twain might have singled out the French from other members of what he calls in paragraph 3 "one distinct species"?

2. Write an essay in which you debunk a widely held or established scientific theory or law, such as gravity, Newton's laws of motion, the existence of the atom or subatomic particles, the mutual convertability of mass and energy, or the germ theory of disease. Be sure to provide strong "evidence" for your contentions.

3. As author (not narrator), does Twain think the human race is redeemable? Write an essay in which you express your own view of human imperfection and possible improvement.

4. This essay was written at the end of the nineteenth century, a century in many ways driven by the idea of an all-but-limitless progress and unbridled confidence in the power of the human mind to discover and control the secrets of nature. Given this context, the antidote Twain provides was probably necessary and perhaps inevitable. Identify an idea that drives society today, and write an essay in which you advocate its opposite.

Sir Arthur Conan Doyle

(England; 1859–1930)

Born in Scotland and educated in England and Austria, Doyle took medical degrees at the University of Edinburgh and established a practice in Southsea, England. But with increasing literary success, including that of two of the longest Sherlock Holmes narratives—A Study in Scarlet, *(1887) and* The Sign of the Four *(1890)—he gradually abandoned medicine for a literary career.*

The popularity of Holmes grew enormously with the publication of shorter pieces in the Strand Magazine. *But by 1893, sick of the character and perhaps concerned that the detective stories would overshadow the historical romances that he regarded as his "serious" fiction, Doyle killed Holmes off. He resisted popular demand to revive the character for nearly a decade, but eventually brought him back.*

Perhaps in his futile attempt to do Holmes in, Doyle sensed that already in 1893 his character was taking on a life of its own. To this day the London post office receives mail addressed to the detective at 221B Baker Street. Holmes societies, such as the Baker Street Irregulars and the Sons of the Copper Beeches—abound. Various theatrical, film, and TV productions have been based on the character or directly on the stories themselves.

Beyond his eccentricities—melancholy and tuneless playing of the violin, keeping tobacco in a Persian slipper, attempting to forget that the earth goes round the sun because the information is useless in his work—Holmes's intellectual trademark is his reasoning, particularly his powers of deduction. At times, as in "Silver Blaze," his thinking seems nearly flawless. But part of Holmes's appeal as a character are his human failings, which sometimes extend to his prejudices and logical lapses. In reading "The Adventure of the Blue Carbuncle," examine carefully the premises upon which Holmes's conclusions are based. Are they acceptable? Are his conclusions validly drawn?

The Adventure of the Blue Carbuncle

I HAD CALLED upon my friend Sherlock Holmes upon the second morning after Christmas, with the intention of wishing him the compliments of the season. He was lounging upon the sofa in a purple dressing-gown, a pipe-rack within his reach upon the right, and a pile of crumpled morning papers, evidently newly studied, near at hand. Beside the couch was a wooden chair, and on the angle of the back hung a very seedy and disreputable hard felt hat, much the worse for wear, and cracked in several places. A lens and a forceps lying upon the seat of the chair suggested that the hat had been suspended in this manner for the purpose of examination.

"You are engaged," said I; "perhaps I interrupt you."

"Not at all. I am glad to have a friend with whom I can discuss my results. The matter is a perfectly trivial one" (he jerked his thumb in the direction of the old hat), "but there are points in connection with it which are not entirely devoid of interest, and even of instruction."

I seated myself in his arm-chair, and warmed my hands before his crackling fire, for a sharp frost had set in, and the windows were thick with the ice crystals. "I suppose," I remarked, "that, homely as it looks, this thing has some deadly story linked on to it—that it is the clue which will guide you in the solution of some mystery, and the punishment of some crime."

"No, no. No crime," said Sherlock Holmes, laughing. "Only one of those   5 whimsical little incidents which will happen when you have four million human beings all jostling each other within the space of a few square miles. Amid the action and reaction of so dense a swarm of humanity, every possible combination of events may be expected to take place, and many a little problem will be presented which may be striking and bizarre without being criminal. We have already had experience of such."

"So much so," I remarked, "that, of the last six cases which I have added to my notes, three have been entirely free of any legal crime."

"Precisely. You allude to my attempt to recover the Irene Adler papers, to the singular case of Miss Mary Sutherland, and to the adventure of the man with the twisted lip. Well, I have no doubt that this small matter will fall into the same innocent category. You know Peterson, the commissionaire?"

"Yes."

"It is to him that this trophy belongs."

"It is his hat."   10

"No, no; he found it. Its owner is unknown. I beg that you will look upon it, not as a battered billycock, but as an intellectual problem. And, first as to how it came here. It arrived upon Christmas morning, in company with a good fat goose, which is, I have no doubt, roasting at this moment in front of Peterson's fire. The facts are these. About four o'clock on Christmas morning, Peterson, who, as you know, is a very honest fellow, was returning from some small jollification, and was making his way homewards down Tottenham Court Road. In front of him he saw, in the gaslight, a tallish man, walking with a slight stagger, and carrying a white goose slung over his shoulder. As he reached the corner of Goodge Street a row broke out between this stranger and a little knot of roughs. One of the latter knocked off the man's hat, on which he raised his stick to defend himself, and, swinging it over his head, smashed the shop window behind him. Peterson had rushed forward to protect the stranger from his assailants, but the man, shocked at having broken the window and seeing an official-looking person in uniform rushing towards him, dropped his goose, took to his heels, and vanished amid the labyrinth of small streets which lie at the back of Tottenham Court Road. The roughs had also fled at the appearance of Peterson, so that he was left in possession of the field of battle, and also of the spoils of victory in the shape of this battered hat and a most unimpeachable Christmas goose."

"Which surely he restored to their owner?"

"My dear fellow, there lies the problem. It is true that 'For Mrs. Henry Baker' was printed upon a small card which was tied to the bird's left leg, and it is also true that the initials 'H. B.' are legible upon the lining of this hat; but, as there are some thousands of Bakers, and some hundreds of Henry Bakers in this city of ours, it is not easy to restore lost property to any one of them."

"What, then, did Peterson do?"

"He brought round both hat and goose to me on Christmas morning,   15 knowing that even the smallest problems are of interest to me. The goose we retained until this morning, when there were signs that, in spite of the slight frost, it would be well that it should be eaten without unnecessary delay. Its finder has carried it off therefore to fulfil the ultimate destiny of a goose, while I continue to retain the hat of the unknown gentleman who lost his Christmas dinner."

"Did he not advertise?"

"No."

"Then, what clue could you have as to his identity?"

"Only as much as we can deduce."

"From his hat?"   20

"Precisely."

"But you are joking. What can you gather from this old battered felt?"

"Here is my lens. You know my methods. What can you gather yourself as to the individuality of the man who has worn this article?"

I took the tattered object in my hands, and turned it over rather ruefully. It was a very ordinary black hat of the usual round shape, hard and much the worse for wear. The lining had been of red silk, but was a good deal discoloured. There was no maker's name; but, as Holmes had remarked, the initials "H. B." were scrawled upon one side. It was pierced in the brim for a hat-securer, but the elastic was missing. For the rest, it was cracked, exceedingly dusty, and spotted in several places, although there seemed to have been some attempt to hide the discoloured patches by smearing them with ink.

"I can see nothing," said I, handing it back to my friend.   25

"On the contrary, Watson, you can see everything. You fail, however, to reason from what you see. You are too timid in drawing your inferences."

"Then, pray tell me what it is that you can infer from this hat?"

He picked it up, and gazed at it in the peculiar introspective fashion which was characteristic of him. "It is perhaps less suggestive than it might have been," he remarked, "and yet there are a few inferences which are very distinct, and a few others which represent at least a strong balance of probability. That the man was highly intellectual is of course obvious upon the face of it, and also that he was fairly well-to-do within the last three years, although he has now fallen upon evil days. He had foresight, but has less now than formerly, pointing to a moral retrogression, which, when taken with the decline of his fortunes, seems to indicate some evil influence, probably drink, at work upon him. This may account also for the obvious fact that his wife has ceased to love him."

"My dear Holmes!"

"He has, however, retained some degree of self-respect," he continued, disregarding my remonstrance. "He is a man who leads a sedentary life, goes out little, is out of training entirely, is middle-aged, has grizzled hair which he has had cut within the last few days, and which he anoints with lime-cream. These are the more patent facts which are to be deduced from his hat. Also, by the way, that it is extremely improbable that he has gas laid on in his house."   30

"You are certainly joking, Holmes."

"Not in the least. Is it possible that even now when I give you these results you are unable to see how they are attained?"

"I have no doubt that I am very stupid; but I must confess that I am unable to follow you. For example, how did you deduce that this man was intellectual?"

For answer Holmes clapped the hat upon his head. It came right over the forehead and settled upon the bridge of his nose. "It is a question of cubic capacity," said he: "a man with so large a brain must have something in it."

"The decline of his fortunes, then?"   35

"This hat is three years old. These flat brims curled at the edge came in then. It is a hat of the very best quality. Look at the band of ribbed silk, and the excellent lining. If this man could afford to buy so expensive a hat three years ago, and has had no hat since, then he has assuredly gone down in the world."

"Well, that is clear enough, certainly. But how about the foresight, and the moral retrogression?"

Sherlock Holmes laughed. "Here is the foresight," said he, putting his finger upon the little disc and loop of the hat-securer. "They are never sold upon hats. If this man ordered one, it is a sign of a certain amount of foresight, since he went out of his way to take this precaution against the wind. But since we see that he has broken the elastic, and has not troubled to replace it, it is obvious that he has less foresight now than formerly, which is a distinct proof of a weakening nature. On the other hand, he has endeavoured to conceal some of these stains upon the felt by daubing them with ink, which is a sign that he has not entirely lost his self-respect."

"Your reasoning is certainly plausible."

"The further points, that he is middle-aged, that his hair is grizzled, that it has been recently cut, and that he uses lime-cream, are all to be gathered from a close examination of the lower part of the lining. The lens discloses a large number of hair-ends, clean cut by the scissors of the barber. They all   40 appear to be adhesive, and there is a distinct odour of lime-cream. This dust, you will observe, is not the gritty, grey dust of the street, but the fluffy brown dust of the house, showing that it has been hung up indoors most of the time while the marks of moisture upon the inside are proof positive that the wearer perspired very freely, and could, therefore, hardly be in the best of training."

"But his wife—you said that she had ceased to love him."

"This hat has not been brushed for weeks. When I see you, my dear Watson, with a week's accumulation of dust upon your hat, and when your wife allows you to go out in such a state, I shall fear that you also have been unfortunate enough to lose your wife's affection."

"But he might be a bachelor."

"Nay, he was bringing home the goose as a peace-offering to his wife. Remember the card upon the bird's leg."

"You have an answer to everything. But how on earth do you deduce that   45
the gas is not laid on in the house?"

"One tallow stain, or even two, might come by chance but, when I see no less than five, I think that there can be little doubt that the individual must be brought into frequent contact with burning tallow—walks upstairs at night probably with his hat in one hand and a guttering candle in the other. Anyhow, he never got tallow stains from a gas jet. Are you satisfied?"

"Well, it is very ingenious," said I, laughing; "but since, as you said just now, there has been no crime committed, and no harm done save the loss of a goose, all this seems to be rather a waste of energy."

Sherlock Holmes had opened his mouth to reply, when the door flew open, and Peterson the commissionaire rushed into the compartment with flushed cheeks and the face of a man who is dazed with astonishment.

"The goose, Mr. Holmes! The goose, sir!" he gasped.

"Eh! What of it, then? Has it returned to life, and flapped off through the   50
kitchen window?" Holmes twisted himself round upon the sofa to get a fairer view of the man's excited face.

"See here, sir! See what my wife found in its crop!" He held out his hand, and displayed upon the centre of the palm a brilliantly scintillating blue stone, rather smaller than a bean in size, but of such purity and radiance that it twinkled like an electric point in the dark hollow of his hand.

Sherlock Holmes sat up with a whistle. "By Jove, Peterson," said he, "this is treasure-trove indeed! I suppose you know what you have got?"

"A diamond, sir! A precious stone! It cuts into glass as though it were putty."

"It's more than a precious stone. It's *the* precious stone."

"Not the Countess of Morcar's blue carbuncle?" I ejaculated.   55

"Precisely so. I ought to know its size and shape, seeing that I have read the advertisement about it in *The Times* every day lately. It is absolutely unique, and its value can only be conjectured, but the reward offered of a thousand pounds is certainly not within a twentieth part of the market price."

"A thousand pounds! Great Lord of mercy!" The commissionaire plumped down into a chair, and stared from one to the other of us.

"That is the reward, and I have reason to know that there are sentimental considerations in the background which would induce the Countess to part with half of her fortune if she could but recover the gem."

"It was lost, if I remember aright, at the Hotel Cosmopolitan," I remarked.

"Precisely so, on the twenty-second of December, just five days ago. John   60
Horner, a plumber, was accused of having abstracted it from the lady's jewel-case. The evidence against him was so strong that the case has been referred to the Assizes. I have some account of the matter here, I believe." He rummaged amid his newspapers, glancing over the dates, until at last he smoothed one out, doubled it over, and read the following paragraph:

" 'Hotel Cosmopolitan Jewel Robbery. John Horner, 26, plumber, was brought up upon the charge of having upon the 22nd inst., abstracted from the jewel-case of the Countess of Morcar the valuable gem known as the blue carbuncle. James Ryder, upper-attendant at the hotel, gave his evidence to the effect that he had shown Horner up to the dressing room of the Countess of Morcar upon the day of the robbery, in order that he might solder the second bar of the grate, which was loose. He had remained with Horner some little time but had finally been called away. On returning he found that Horner had disappeared, that the bureau had been forced open, and that the small morocco casket in which, as it afterwards transpired, the Countess was accustomed to keep her jewel, was lying empty upon the dressing-table. Ryder instantly gave the alarm, and Horner was arrested the same evening; but the stone could not be found either upon his person or in his rooms. Catherine Cusack, maid to the Countess, deposed to having heard Ryder's cry of dismay on discovering the robbery, and to having rushed into the room, where she found matters were as described by the last witness. Inspector Bradstreet, B Division, gave evidence as to the arrest of Horner, who struggled frantically, and protested his innocence in the strongest terms. Evidence of a previous conviction for robbery having been given against the prisoner, the magistrate refused to deal summarily with the offence, but referred it to the Assizes. Horner, who had shown signs of intense emotion during the proceedings, fainted away at the conclusion, and was carried out of court.'

"Hum! So much for the police-court," said Holmes thoughtfully, tossing aside his paper. "The question for us now to solve is the sequence of events leading from a rifled jewel-case at one end to the crop of a goose in Tottenham Court Road at the other. You see, Watson, our little deductions have suddenly assumed a much more important and less innocent aspect. Here is the stone; the stone came from the goose, and the goose came from Mr. Henry Baker, the gentleman with the bad hat and all the other characteristics with which I have bored you. So now we must set ourselves very seriously to finding this gentleman, and ascertaining what part he has played in this little mystery. To do this, we must try the simplest means first, and these lie undoubtedly in an advertisement in all the evening papers. If this fail, I shall have recourse to other methods."

"What will you say?"

"Give me a pencil, and that slip of paper. Now, then: Found at the corner of Goodge Street, a goose and a black felt hat. Mr. Henry Baker can have the same by applying at 6:30 this evening at 221B Baker Street.' That is clear and concise."

"Very. But will he see it?"

"Well, he is sure to keep an eye on the papers, since, to a poor man, the loss was a heavy one. He was clearly so scared by his mischance in breaking the window, and by the approach of Peterson, that he thought of nothing but flight; but since then he must have bitterly regretted the impulse which caused him to drop his bird. Then, again, the introduction of his name will cause him to see it, for every one who knows him will direct his attention to it. Here you are, Peterson, run down to the advertising agency, and have this put in the evening papers."

"In which, sir?"

"Oh, in the *Globe, Star, Pall Mall, St. James's Gazette, Evening News, Standard, Echo,* and any others that occur to you."

"Very well, sir. And this stone?"

"Ah, yes, I shall keep the stone. Thank you. And, I say, Peterson, just buy a goose on your way back, and leave it here with me, for we must have one to give to this gentleman in place of the one which your family is now devouring."

When the commissionaire had gone, Holmes took up the stone and held it against the light. "It's a bonny thing," said he. "Just see how it glints and sparkles. Of course it is a nucleus and focus of crime. Every good stone is. They are the devil's pet baits. In the larger and older jewels every facet may stand for a bloody deed. This stone is not yet twenty years old. It was found in the banks of the Amoy River in Southern China, and is remarkable in having every characteristic of the carbuncle, save that it is blue in shade, instead of ruby red. In spite of its youth, it has already a sinister history. There have been two murders, a vitriol-throwing, a suicide, and several robberies brought about for the sake of this forty-grain weight of crystallized charcoal. Who would think that so pretty a toy would be a purveyor to the gallows and the prison? I'll lock it up in my strong-box now, and drop a line to the Countess to say that we have it."

"Do you think this man Horner is innocent?"

"I cannot tell."

"Well, then, do you imagine that this other one, Henry Baker, had anything to do with the matter?"

"It is, I think, much more likely that Henry Baker is an absolutely innocent man, who had no idea that the bird which he was carrying was of considerably more value than if it were made of solid gold. That, however, I shall determine by a very simple test, if we have an answer to our advertisement."

"And you can do nothing until then?"

"Nothing."

"In that case I shall continue my professional round. But I shall come back in the evening at the hour you have mentioned, for I should like to see the solution of so tangled a business."

"Very glad to see you. I dine at seven. There is a woodcock, I believe. By the way, in view of recent occurrences, perhaps I ought to ask Mrs. Hudson to examine its crop."

I had been delayed at a case, and it was a little after half-past six when I 80 found myself in Baker Street once more. As I approached the house I saw a tall man in a Scotch bonnet, with a coat which was buttoned up to his chin, waiting outside in the bright semicircle which was thrown from the fanlight. Just as I arrived, the door was opened, and we were shown up together to Holmes' room.

"Mr. Henry Baker, I believe," said he, rising from his arm-chair, and greeting his visitor with the easy air of geniality which he could so readily assume. "Pray take this chair by the fire, Mr. Baker. It is a cold night, and I observe that your circulation is more adapted for summer than for winter. Ah, Watson, you have just come at the right time. Is that your hat, Mr. Baker?"

"Yes, sir, that is undoubtedly my hat."

He was a large man, with rounded shoulders, a massive head, and a broad, intelligent face, sloping down to a pointed beard of grizzled brown. A touch of red in nose and checks, with a slight tremor of his extended hand, recalled Holmes' surmise as to his habits. His rusty black frock-coat was buttoned right up in front, with the collar turned up, and his lank wrists protruded from his sleeves without a sign of cuff or shirt. He spoke in a low staccato fashion, choosing his words with care, and gave the impression generally of a man of learning and letters who had had ill-usage at the hands of fortune.

"We have retained these things for some days," said Holmes, "because we expected to see an advertisement from you giving your address. I am at a loss to know now why you did not advertise."

Our visitor gave a rather shamefaced laugh. "Shillings have not been 85 so plentiful with me as they once were," he remarked. I had no doubt that the gang of roughs who assaulted me had carried off both my hat and the bird. I did not care to spend more money in a hopeless attempt at recovering them."

"Very naturally. By the way, about the bird—we were compelled to eat it."

"To eat it!" Our visitor half rose from his chair in his excitement.

"Yes; it would have been no use to anyone had we not done so. But I presume that this other goose upon the sideboard, which is about the same weight and perfectly fresh, will answer your purpose equally well?"

"Oh, certainly, certainly!" answered Mr. Baker, with a sigh of relief.

"Of course, we still have the feathers, legs, crop, and so on of your own   90
bird, if you so wish ———"

The man burst into a hearty laugh. "They might be useful to me as relics of my adventure," said he, "but beyond that I can hardly see what use the *disjecta membra* of my late acquaintance are going to be to me. No, sir, I think that, with your permission, I will confine my attentions to the excellent bird which I perceive upon the sideboard."

Sherlock Holmes glanced sharply across at me with a slight shrug of his shoulders.

"There is your hat, then, and there your bird," said he. "By the way, would it bore you to tell me where you got the other one from? I am somewhat of a fowl fancier, and I have seldom seen a better-grown goose."

"Certainly, sir," said Baker, who had risen and tucked his newly gained property under his arm. "There are a few of us who frequent the Alpha Inn near the Museum—we are to be found in the Museum itself during the day, you understand. This year our good host, Windigate by name, instituted a goose-club, by which, on consideration of some few pence every week, we were to receive a bird at Christmas. My pence were duly paid, and the rest is familiar to you. I am much indebted to you, sir, for a scotch bonnet is fitted neither to my years nor my gravity." With a comical pomposity of manner he bowed solemnly to both of us, and strode off upon his way.

"So much for Mr. Henry Baker," said Holmes, when he had closed the   95
door behind him. "It is quite certain that he knows nothing whatever about the matter. Are you hungry, Watson?"

"Not particularly."

"Then I suggest that we turn our dinner into a supper, and follow up this clue while it is still hot."

"By all means."

It was a bitter night, so we drew on our ulsters and wrapped cravats about our throats. Outside, the stars were shining coldly in a cloudless sky, and the breath of the passers-by blew out into smoke like so many pistol shots. Our footfalls rang out crisply and loudly as we swung through the doctors' quarter, Wimpole Street, Harley Street, and so through Wigmore Street into Oxford Street. In a quarter of an hour we were in Bloomsbury at the Alpha Inn, which is a small public-house at the corner of one of the streets which runs down into Holborn. Holmes pushed open the door of the private bar, and ordered two glasses of beer from the ruddy-faced, white-aproned landlord.

"Your beer should be excellent if it is as good as your geese," he said.   100

"My geese!" The man seemed surprised.

"Yes. I was speaking only half an hour ago to Mr. Henry Baker, who was a member of your goose-club."

"Ah! yes, I see. But you see, sir, them's not *our* geese."

"Indeed! Whose, then?"

"Well, I get the two dozen from a salesman in Covent Garden."   105

"Indeed! I know some of them. Which was it?"

"Breckinridge is his name."

"Ah! I don't know him. Well, here's your good health, landlord, and prosperity to your house. Good night."

"Now for Mr. Breckinridge," he continued, buttoning up his coat, as we came out into the frosty air. "Remember, Watson, that though we have so homely a thing as a goose at one end of this chain, we have at the other a man who will certainly get seven years' penal servitude, unless we can establish his innocence. It is possible that our inquiry may but confirm his guilt; but, in any case, we have a line of investigation which has been missed by the police, and which a singular chance has placed in our hands. Let us follow it out to the bitter end. Faces to the south, then, and quick march!"

We passed across Holborn, down Endell Street, and so through a zigzag   110
of slums to Covent Garden Market. One of the largest stalls bore the name of Breckinridge upon it, and the proprietor, a horsy-looking man, with a sharp face and trim side-whiskers, was helping a boy to put up the shutters.

"Good evening. It's a cold night," said Holmes.

The salesman nodded, and shot a questioning glance at my companion.

"Sold out of geese, I see," continued Holmes, pointing at the bare slabs of marble.

"Let you have five hundred tomorrow morning."

"That's no good."   115

"Well, there are some on the stall with the gas flare."

"Ah, but I was recommended to you."

"Who by?"

"The landlord of the 'Alpha.' "

"Ah, yes; I sent him a couple of dozen."   120

"Fine birds they were, too. Now where did you get them from?"

To my surprise the question provoked a burst of anger from the salesman.

"Now then, mister," said he, with his head cocked and his arms akimbo, "what are you driving at? Let's have it straight, now."

"It is straight enough. I should like to know who sold you the geese which you supplied to the 'Alpha.' "

"Well, then, I shan't tell you. So now!"   125

"Oh, it is a matter of no importance; but I don't know why you should be so warm over such a trifle."

"Warm! You'd be as warm, maybe, if you were as pestered as I am. When I pay good money for a good article there should be an end of the business; but it's 'Where are the geese?' and 'Who did you sell the geese to?' and 'What will you take for the geese?' One would think they were the only geese in the world, to hear the fuss that is made over them."

"Well, I have no connection with any other people who have been making inquiries," said Holmes carelessly. "If you won't tell us the bet is off, that is all. But I'm always ready to back my opinion on a matter of fowls, and have a fiver on it that the bird I ate is country bred."

"Well, then, you've lost your fiver, for it's town bred," snapped the salesman.

"It's nothing of the kind."   130

"I say it is."

"I don't believe you."

"D'you think you know more about fowls than I, who have handled them ever since I was a nipper? I tell you, all those birds that went to the 'Alpha' were town bred."

"You'll never persuade me to believe that."

"Will you bet, then?"   135

"It's merely taking your money, for I know that I am right. But I'll have a sovereign on with you, just to teach you not to be obstinate."

The salesman chuckled grimly. "Bring me the books, Bill," said he.

The small boy brought round a small thin volume and a great greasy-backed one, laying them out together beneath the hanging lamp.

"Now then, Mr. Cocksure," said the salesman, "I thought that I was out of geese, but before I finish you'll find that there is still one left in my shop. You see this little book?"

"Well?"   140

"That's the list of the folk from whom I buy. D'you see? Well, then, here on this page are the country folk, and the numbers after their names are where their accounts are in the big ledger. Now, then! You see this other page in red ink? Well, that is a list of my town suppliers. Now, look at that third name. Just read it out to me."

"Mrs. Oakshott, 117 Brixton Road—249," read Holmes.

"Quite so. Now turn that up in the ledger."

Holmes turned to the page indicated. "Here you are, Mrs. Oakshott, 117 Brixton Road, egg and poultry supplier.' "

"Now, then, what's the last entry?"   145

" 'December 22. Twenty-four geese at 7s. 6d.' "

"Quite so. There you are. And underneath?"

" 'Sold to Mr. Windigate of the " Alpha" at 12s.' "

"What have you to say now?"

Sherlock Holmes looked deeply chagrined. He drew a sovereign from his   150
pocket and threw it down upon the slab, turning away with the air of a man whose disgust is too deep for words. A few yards off he stopped under a lamp-post, and laughed in the hearty, noiseless fashion which was peculiar to him.

"When you see a man with whiskers of that cut and the 'Pink 'Un'[1] protruding out of his pocket, you can always draw him by a bet," said he. "I dare say that if I had put a hundred pounds down in front of him that man would not have given me such complete information as was drawn from him by the idea that he was doing me on a wager. Well, Watson, we are, I fancy, nearing the end of our quest, and the only point which remains to be determined is whether we should go on to this Mrs. Oakshott to-night, or whether we should reserve it for to-morrow. It is clear from what that surly fellow said that there are others besides ourselves who are anxious about the matter, and I should ———"

His remarks were suddenly cut short by a loud hubbub which broke out from the stall which we had just left. Turning round we saw a little rat-faced fellow standing in the centre of the circle of yellow light which was thrown by the swinging lamp, while Breckinridge the salesman, framed in the door of his stall, was shaking his fists fiercely at the cringing figure.

"I've had enough of you and your geese," he shouted. "I wish you were all at the devil together. If you come pestering me any more with your silly talk I'll set the dog at you. You bring Mrs. Oakshott here and I'll answer her, but what have you to do with it? Did I buy the geese off you?"

"No; but one of them was mine all the same," whined the little man.

"Well, then, ask Mrs. Oakshott for it."   155

"She told me to ask you."

"Well, you can ask the King of Prooshia, for all I care. I've had enough of it. Get out of this!" He rushed fiercely forward, and the inquirer flitted away into the darkness.

"Ha, this may save us a visit to Brixton Road," whispered Holmes. "Come with me, and we will see what is to be made of this fellow." Striding through the scattered knots of people who lounged round the flaring stalls, my companion speedily overtook the little man and touched him upon the shoulder. He sprang round, and I could see in the gaslight that every vestige of colour had been driven from his face.

"Who are you, then? What do you want?" he asked in a quavering voice.

"You will excuse me," said Holmes blandly, "but I could not help over-   160 hearing the questions which you put to the salesman just now. I think that I could be of assistance to you."

"You? Who are you? How could you know anything of the matter?"

"My name is Sherlock Holmes. It is my business to know what other people don't know."

"But you can know nothing of this?"

"Excuse me, I know everything of it. You are endeavouring to trace some geese which were sold by Mrs. Oakshott, of Brixton Road, to a salesman

---

[1]**Pink 'Un:** According to W. S. Baring-Gould, this is "a sporting journal, printed on pink paper, not unlike the American *Police Gazette*" (*The Annotated Sherlock Holmes*, vol. 1, p. 462). [Ed.]

named Breckinridge, by him in turn to Mr. Windigate, of the 'Alpha,' and by him to his club, of which Mr. Henry Baker is a member."

"Oh, sir, you are the very man whom I have longed to meet," cried the 165
little fellow, with outstretched hands and quivering fingers. "I can hardly explain to you how interested I am in this matter."

Sherlock Holmes hailed a four-wheeler which was passing. "In that case we had better discuss it in a cosy room rather than in this wind-swept market-place," said he. "But pray tell me, before we go further, who it is that I have the pleasure of assisting."

The man hesitated for an instant. "My name is John Robinson," he answered, with a sidelong glance.

"No, no; the real name," said Holmes sweetly. "It is always awkward doing business with an *alias*."

A flush sprang to the white cheeks of the stranger. "Well, then," said he, "my real name is James Ryder."

"Precisely so. Head attendant at the Hotel Cosmopolitan. Pray step into 170
the cab, and I shall soon be able to tell you everything which you would wish to know."

The little man stood glancing from one to the other of us with half-frightened, half-hopeful eyes, as one who is not sure whether he is on the verge of a windfall or of a catastrophe. Then he stepped into the cab, and in half an hour we were back in the sitting-room at Baker Street. Nothing had been said during our drive, but the high, thin breathings of our new companion, and the claspings and unclaspings of his hands, spoke of the nervous tension within him.

"Here we are," said Holmes cheerily, as we filed into the room. "The fire looks very seasonable in this weather. You look cold, Mr. Ryder. Pray take the basket chair. I will just put on my slippers before we settle this little matter of yours. Now, then! You want to know what became of those geese?"

"Yes, sir."

"Or rather, I fancy, of that goose. It was one bird, I imagine, in which you were interested—white, with a black bar across the tail."

Ryder quivered with emotion. "Oh, sir," he cried, "can you tell me where 175
it went to?"

"It came here."

"Here?"

"Yes, and a most remarkable bird it proved. I don't wonder that you should take an interest in it. It laid an egg after it was dead—the bonniest, brightest little blue egg that ever was seen. I have it here in my museum."

Our visitor staggered to his feet, and clutched the mantelpiece with his right hand. Holmes unlocked his strong-box, and held up the blue carbuncle, which shone out like a star, with a cold, brilliant, many-pointed radiance. Ryder stood glaring with a drawn face, uncertain whether to claim or to disown it.

"The game's up, Ryder," said Holmes quietly. "Hold up, man, or you'll be   180
into the fire. Give him an arm back into his chair, Watson. He's not got blood
enough to go in for felony with impunity. Give him a dash of brandy. So! Now
he looks a little more human. What a shrimp it is, to be sure!"

For a moment he had staggered and nearly fallen, but the brandy brought
a tinge of colour into his cheeks, and he sat staring with frightened eyes at his
accuser.

"I have almost every link in my hands, and all the proofs which I could
possibly need, so there is little which you need tell me. Still, that little may
as well be cleared up to make the case complete. You had heard, Ryder, of this
blue stone of the Countess of Morcar's?"

"It was Catherine Cusack who told me of it," said he, in a crackling voice.

"I see. Her ladyship's waiting-maid. Well, the temptation of sudden
wealth so easily acquired was too much for you, as it has been for better men
before you; but you were not very scrupulous in the means you used. It seems
to me, Ryder, that there is the making of a very pretty villain in you. You knew
that this man Horner, the plumber, had been concerned in some such matter
before, and that suspicion would rest the more readily upon him. What did
you do, then? You made some small job in my lady's room—you and your
confederate Cusack—and you managed that he should be the man sent for.
Then, when he had left, you rifled the jewel-case, raised the alarm, and had
this unfortunate man arrested. You then ————"

Ryder threw himself down suddenly upon the rug, and clutched at my   185
companion's knees. "For God's sake, have mercy!" he shrieked. "Think of my
father! Of my mother! It would break their hearts. I never went wrong before!
I never will again. I swear it. I'll swear it on a Bible. Oh, don't bring it into
court! For Christ's sake, don't!"

"Get back into your chair!" said Holmes sternly. "It is very well to cringe
and crawl now, but you thought little enough of this poor Horner in the dock
for a crime of which he knew nothing."

"I will fly, Mr. Holmes. I will leave the country, sir. Then the charge
against him will break down."

"Hum! We will talk about that. And now let us hear a true account
of the next act. How came the stone into the goose, and how came the
goose into the open market? Tell us the truth, for there lies your only hope of
safety."

Ryder passed his tongue over his patched lips. "I will tell you it just as it
happened, sir," said he. "When Horner had been arrested, it seemed to me
that it would be best for me to get away with the stone at once, for I did not
know at what moment the police might not take it into their heads to search
me and my room. There was no place about the hotel where it would be safe.
I went out, as if on some commission, and I made for my sister's house. She
had married a man named Oakshott, and lived in Brixton Road, where she

fattened fowls for the market. All the way there every man I met seemed to me to be a policeman or a detective, and for all that it was a cold night, the sweat was pouring down my face before I came to the Brixton Road. My sister asked me what was the matter, and why I was so pale; but I told her that I had been upset by the jewel robbery at the hotel. Then I went into the back-yard, and smoked a pipe, and wondered what it would be best to do.

"I had a friend once called Maudsley, who went to the bad, and has just   190 been serving his time in Pentonville. One day he had met me, and fell into talk about the ways of thieves and how they could get rid of what they stole. I knew that he would be true to me, for I knew one or two things about him, so I made up my mind to go right on to Kilburn, where he lived, and take him into my confidence. He would show me how to turn the stone into money. But how to get to him in safety? I thought of the agonies I had gone through in coming from the hotel. I might at any moment be seized and searched, and there would be the stone in my waistcoat pocket. I was leaning against the wall at the time, and looking at the geese which were waddling about round my feet, and suddenly an idea came into my head which showed me how I could beat the best detective that ever lived.

"My sister had told me some weeks before that I might have the pick of her geese for a Christmas present, and I knew that she was always as good as her word. I would take my goose now, and in it I would carry my stone to Kilburn. There was a little shed in the yard, and behind this I drove one of the birds, a fine big one, white, with a barred tail. I caught it and, prying its bill open, I thrust the stone down its throat as far as my finger could reach. The bird gave a gulp, and I felt the stone pass along its gullet and down into its crop. But the creature flapped and struggled, and out came my sister to know what was the matter. As I turned to speak to her the brute broke loose, and fluttered off among the others."

" 'Whatever were you doing with that bird, Jem?' says she.

" 'Well,' said I, 'you said you'd give me one for Christmas, and I was feeling which was the fattest.'

" 'Oh,' says she, 'we've set yours aside for you. Jem's bird, we call it. It's the big, white one over yonder. There's twenty-six of them, which makes one for you, and one for us, and two dozen for the market.'

" 'Thank you, Maggie,' says I; 'but if it is all the same to you I'd rather   195 have that one I was handling just now.'

" 'The other is a good three pound heavier,' she said, 'and we fattened it expressly for you.'

" 'Never mind. I'll have the other, and I'll take it now,' said I.

" 'Oh, just as you like,' said she, a little huffed. 'Which is it you want, then?'

" 'That white one, with the barred tail, right in the middle of the flock.'

" 'Oh, very well. Kill it and take it with you.'   200

"Well, I did what she said, Mr. Holmes, and I carried the bird all the way to Kilburn, I told my pal what I had done, for he was a man that it was easy to tell a thing like that to. He laughed until he choked, and we got a knife and opened the goose. My heart turned to water, for there was no sign of the stone, and I knew that some terrible mistake had occurred. I left the bird, rushed back to my sister's, and hurried into the back-yard. There was not a bird to be seen there.

" 'Where are they all, Maggie?' I cried.

" 'Gone to the dealer's.'

" 'Which dealer's?'

" 'Breckinridge, of Covent Garden.'   205

" 'But was there another with a barred tail?' I asked, 'the same as the one I chose?'

" 'Yes, Jem, there were two barred-tailed ones, and I could never tell them apart.'

"Well, then, of course, I saw it all, and I ran off as hard as my feet would carry me to this man Breckinridge; but he had sold the lot at once, and not one word would he tell me as to where they had gone. You heard him yourselves to-night. Well, he has always answered me like that. My sister thinks that I am going mad. Sometimes I think that I am myself. And now—and now I am myself a branded thief, without ever having touched the wealth for which I sold my character. God help me! God help me!" He burst into convulsive sobbing, with his face buried in his hands.

There was a long silence, broken only by his heavy breathing, and by the measured tapping of Sherlock Holmes' finger-tips upon the edge of the table. Then my friend rose, and threw open the door.

"Get out!" said he.   210

"What, sir! Oh, Heaven bless you!"

"No more words. Get out!"

And no more words were needed. There was a rush, a clatter upon the stairs, the bang of a door, and the crisp rattle of running footfalls from the street.

"After all, Watson," said Holmes, reaching up his hand for his clay pipe, "I am not retained by the police to supply their deficiencies. If Horner were in danger it would be another thing, but this fellow will not appear against him, and the case must collapse. I suppose that I am commuting a felony, but it is just possible that I am saving a soul. This fellow will not go wrong again. He is too terribly frightened. Send him to gaol now, and you make him a gaolbird for life. Besides, it is the season of forgiveness. Chance has put in our way a most singular and whimsical problem, and its solution is its own reward. If you will have the goodness to touch the bell, Doctor, we will begin another investigation, in which also a bird will be the chief feature."

THESIS AND THOUGHT

1. As in most mystery stories, motives, methods, and the sequence of events in this one are not fully revealed until the end. Using strict chronological order and beginning with the scheme to steal the jewel, write a brief summary of the plot of "The Adventure of the Blue Carbuncle."

2. Can the story reasonably be said to have a theme? Explain. What seems to be Doyle's principal purpose?

STRUCTURE

1. On what basis does Holmes assume or conclude that the hat belongs to Mrs. Henry Baker's husband? Is such reasoning valid or complete? What possibilities does Holmes fail to consider? Ignore the fact that his surmise is correct.

2. Holmes's inferences concerning Henry Baker are the rational centerpiece here. Among his conclusions are the following:

   a. he is "highly intellectual"
   b. his financial position has declined in the last three years
   c. the foresight he once had is now diminished
   d. he has undergone a moral retrogression and drinks excessively
   e. his wife "has ceased to love him"
   f. he "leads a sedentary life"
   g. he is middle-aged
   h. he has recently had his hair cut
   i. he is not likely to have had "gas laid on in his house"

   Examine the basis for each of these conclusions (which Holmes himself supplies to Watson in paras. 31–46), and evaluate the soundness of the reasoning.

3. There are several less elaborate instances of Holmes's reputed powers of reason in the story. One involves his wager with Breckinridge (paras. 128–150) and the premise on which it is based. Examine the latter and determine whether Holmes is guilty of stereotyping here. What, by the way, prompts Holmes to bet that the bird is "country bred"?

4. In confronting Ryder, Holmes seems to reconstruct the chain of events leading to the robbery (para. 184). How much of this reconstruction depends upon facts in hand and how much upon inferences based on those facts? Identify the latter and show how Holmes must have drawn them.

5. Identify and discuss the sources of conflict in the narrative.

6. Does the story seem to be a well-unified, well-proportioned whole? Consider, for example, the space devoted to the character of Henry Baker, the necessity of Ryder's account, and the propriety of the conclusion.

STYLE

1. The story is more than a hundred years old. What in Doyle's language indicates its age? Supply several examples.

2. What can be deduced about Holmes's character from the way he addresses others, including Watson? Support your points with references to the text.

3. The following words are foreign to contemporary American vocabulary: *commissionaire* (para. 7), *billycock* and *jollification* (para. 11), *Assizes* (para. 60), *bonny* (para. 71), and *ulsters* (para. 99). Check their meaning and usage in a standard American dictionary. Look up those marked *British* or *Scots* in the *Oxford English Dictionary* and observe their origin and evolution. Are the words referred to in this question still in use today?

4. Explain Breckinridge's reference to having one goose left (para. 139) and Holmes's reference to "a bird" in the final paragraph.

CONSIDERATIONS

1. In its way, "The Adventure of the Blue Carbuncle" is a Christmas story. How does this fact shape its conclusion? Might the story have ended differently had it taken place in July? Should it have ended differently?

2. In paragraph 71 Holmes delivers a brief lecture on the temptations and ill effects of precious stones. What, other than jewels and vast sums of money, provides similar temptations and consequences today? Choose one example, then write a paragraph explaining its seductive appeal and the evils perpetrated in order to obtain it.

3. We are given the impression that the reward for recovering the carbuncle will go to Peterson. But the stone was found in the goose that belonged to Baker, and Holmes himself is responsible for identifying it. Write an argument in which you make a case for any of the three, or any combination of them, receiving the reward.

Suggestions for Writing: Argument and Persuasion

I. Write an argumentative essay based on one of the propositions below. You are free to take an opposing position or any other between the extremes. With your instructor's approval, you may choose either a conventional or Rogerian approach. Before you begin, make sure your premises are clear, that you provide appropriate evidence or support for your contentions, and that your conclusion is valid. Be particularly careful when working with one of the more whimsical topics.

—A term of public service should be required of all citizens.

—Death is preferable to loss of liberty.

—Looking out for number one should be a person's first priority.

—Groundhog Day should be declared a national holiday. (You may substitute Sadie Hawkins Day, Millard Fillmore's birthday, or some other similarly frivolous event for Groundhog Day.)

—Public execution should be restored.

—No law should govern the sexual activity of consenting adults.

—Biology is destiny.

—Print literacy is largely superfluous in an age of media images and instant communication.

—We rely too heavily on the private automobile and not enough on public transportation.

—The United States is a land of unlimited opportunity.

—The ideal of the traditional family is little more than unrealistic nostalgia.

II. While adhering to sound principles of argument and without lapsing into logical fallacy, write a paper in which you persuade

—a customer to purchase a real or imaginary product

—a constituent to vote for a political candidate

—a legislative body to enact a specific bill

—a bank to lend money or issue a credit card to you

—Alfred E. Neuman to worry

—an administration to change a policy (e.g., visiting privileges in the dorm or discounted fares for the elderly)

—terrorists not to commit a specific act of violence

—someone to accept you as a date

III. Write an essay in which you propose and argue for a solution to a problem of public concern on campus or in the larger community. Your paper should define the problem; outline its causes and consequences; examine alternative solutions and explain their limitations; present evidence for the effectiveness of the solution you propose; and anticipate any objections that might be raised against it.

Glossary of Rhetorical Terms

Abstract/Concrete

Abstract terms present feelings, concepts, and characteristics that are intangible and otherwise unavailable to sensory experience. *Fear, fanaticism,* and *finesse* are abstractions. Concrete language, on the other hand, refers to objects that are subject to sense perception: "Tonisha was stricken with fear. Her body trembled, and her skin was bathed in cold sweat." The second sentence, which enlivens the abstraction *fear* by describing what can be seen and touched, is concrete. Similarly, we might make the intellectual construct *fanaticism* more accessible by pointing to particular behavior—such as a soccer-match riot in Liverpool or the bombing of the World Trade Center in New York—as perceptible evidence of excessive zeal. *Finesse* might be described by the deft handling of a sword, the delicacy of playing an arpeggio, or the speaking of a quiet word to defuse an argument. Concrete language, as you can see, is used to clarify and vivify writing. Writing that depends too heavily on abstraction is likely to be vague.

Alliteration

Alliteration is the repetition of consonants in close proximity, particularly at the beginning of words, in order to create special—often musical—effects and to establish, reinforce, or maximize meaning through the repeated sound. Modest alliteration, as in the previous sentence, is sometimes found in prose, but it is chiefly a device of poetry. "Peter Piper picked a peck of pickled peppers," is alliterative, as are Shakespeare's, "When I do count the clock that tells the time," (sonnet 12) and Shelley's, "O wild West Wind, thou breath of Autumn's being," ("Ode to the West Wind").

Allusion

A passing (often indirect) reference to a person, place, event, or phenomenon, which writers use to illustrate or clarify their points. Its success depends on the reader's recognition of the reference. "Spacious, opulent, elegant, the mansion was a miniature Versailles," and, "A latter-day Robinson Crusoe, he lived in self-sufficient isolation," are examples of allusion.

Analogy

A kind of limited comparison that finds similarity between entities that are essentially different, as in the sentence, "Picture the earth as an apple: spherical,

545

with flattened ends, a tough exterior, and a central core." In this instance, analogy is legitimately used for illustration. However, it is often fallacious when used as a substitute for genuine argument, as in, "A mother who controls what her child reads or watches on TV is no different from a Fidel Castro or a Chairman Mao." An extended analogy may be used as a rhetorical pattern. See chapter 5.

Brainstorming

A method of thinking about a writing topic, which involves jotting down notes for ideas and their support as they come to mind.

Claim

An argumentive thesis; that is, the central idea that an argument purports to establish.

Cliché

A word, phrase, or idea so often repeated that it lacks impact as well as originality. "That chili dog was *awesome*," and, "Abe Lincoln was a *truly excellent dude*," are examples, but clichés are not restricted to contemporary overused slang. Conventional political formulas, such as "our great and glorious nation," are little more than stock expressions. "Dead" metaphors, such as those in "put your shoulder to the wheel" and "dead as a doornail" (neither any longer evokes an image), are also clichés.

Clustering

The process of grouping related items (generated by **brainstorming**) for the purpose of discovering related ideas and supporting details useful to a potential piece of writing.

Coherence

The principle that sentences within paragraphs and paragraphs within essays should evolve fluently, with clear connections among them.

Colloquialism

A casual expression, which in writing creates an air of informality. Colloquialisms include contractions and words such as *clobber* and *buddy*.

Concrete

See ABSTRACT/CONCRETE.

Connotation

As distinct from **denotation,** that aspect of meaning that depends upon the associations and emotional charge a word might bear. You can, for example, either *savor* or *scarf* a meal. Both are ways of eating, but the first word might imply refinement, sensuality, and delicacy, whereas the other could suggest gluttony and perhaps crudeness.

Data

See GROUNDS.

Deductive Reasoning

A method of argument by which conclusions are drawn from principles or premises. More broadly, it is also the process of reasoning that applies generalizations to specific instances.

Denotation

The literal, "dictionary" definition of a word without regard to any psychological associations or emotional charge.

Diction

The words and their arrangement that a writer selects with regard to such matters as sophistication, fluency, emotional impact, and formality. *See also* COLLOQUIALISM, JARGON, and SLANG.

Dominant Impression

In descriptive writing especially, the cumulative effect produced by recurrent and related words and images.

Enthymeme

A deductive argument based on a **syllogism** in which either of the two premises is not stated explicitly.

Essay

A work of nonfiction, usually brief, devoted to a single principal idea and topic. Created by Michel de Montaigne in the sixteenth century, the form was intended to have broader appeal than a learned dissertation. This holds true today, although the essay may be formal or informal, detached or personal. In this text the range is reflected by Sam Gill's scholarly "Disenchantment" (chapter 3) and Jo Goodwin Parker's first-person, impassioned "What Is Poverty?" (chapter 8).

Etymological Definition

The root meaning of a word as derived from its linguistic origins and historical evolution.

Euphemism

An expression designed to soften, weaken, or obscure the meaning or emotional impact of what is being communicated. *Private parts* used instead of *genitals* (which, depending on context, might itself be seen as avoiding mention of specific organs by name) is one example. *Re-education* for *indoctrination*, and *police action* for *war*, are more dangerously deceptive.

Exposition

Writing that explains, as distinct from narration (typically), description, and argumentation. Various patterns of exposition are presented in chapters 3–8.

Figurative Language (Figures of Speech)

The imaginative rather than literal use or application of language, intended to increase vividness or emotional impact. See the following specific figures included in the glossary: **hyperbole, metaphor, personification, simile,** and **understatement.**

Freewriting

A process used to generate ideas and support, which requires continuous, uncensored, unedited writing for a specified (brief) period of time. The technique may also be used to relieve writer's block.

Grounds

In the Toulmin system of argumentation, the evidence presented in support of a **claim.** Also called data.

Hyperbole

Deliberate exaggeration to heighten the effect or emphasize the magnitude of what is being described or discussed. "He offered her the moon," and, "A thousand doubts crossed her mind," are hyperbolic expressions.

Inductive Leap

In **inductive reasoning,** the intellectual passage from observation of specific instances or data to a general inference or conclusion, sometimes as the result of sudden insight or perception.

Inductive Reasoning

A logical process through which one reaches a conclusion by discovering a relationship among assembled pieces of information, provided these are sufficient, relevant, and representative of the matter under consideration; in science, the experimental process by which a hypothesis (tentative conclusion) is either invalidated or confirmed.

Inference

The process of drawing conclusions from either **premises** or evidence; also the conclusion so drawn.

Invention

The process of generating writing ideas and then discovering matter to support them. Some techniques of invention are described in the introduction to this text.

Irony

Verbal irony is the use of language to suggest disparity or opposition between what is stated and what is actually meant: "Gyrating in her underwear and inch-thick makeup, Madonna was the very model of demure virginity." When the tone of such irony passes from wry to bitter, the result is *sarcasm:* "Looking up at Sven from her burnt steak, soggy string beans, and half-raw potato, Deirdre exclaimed, 'My, you're a marvelous cook!' " In situational or dramatic irony, people or characters unwittingly behave in a manner contrary to their own best interests. In *Oedipus Rex*, for instance, Oedipus, ignorant of his own guilt, condemns to disgrace and exile whoever has brought the current plague upon Thebes—a fate he ultimately (and *ironically*) suffers himself. *See also* UNDERSTATEMENT.

Jargon

Originally (and still) the language specific to a trade or profession. This form of jargon should not be used when addressing the uninitiated unless its terms are explained. In another sense, of greater immediate interest to writers, jargon describes various abuses of language—wordiness, excessive abstraction, obscurity, needlessly "elegant" diction, circumlocution, and other ways of avoiding clear, direct expression. This form of jargon should not be used at all.

Logical Fallacy

Faulty reasoning, which may result from either basing conclusions on insufficient information or from avoiding the question at hand altogether, often by resorting to illegitimate emotional appeals. Chapter 9 discusses several specific logical fallacies in detail (see pp. 468–473).

Metaphor

A form of figurative language, which creates a comparison by identifying one word or phenomenon with another, as if they were interchangeable entities. "You are the light of my life," and Hamlet's less-conventional "sea of troubles" illustrate the technique.

Paradox

A figure of speech in which an apparently self-contradictory statement is nevertheless meaningful. For example, in the verse "Rich man dies to live so well" the words "dies" and "live" are paradoxical. But the religious context of the song in which the line appears makes it clear that "dies" refers here to spiritual death.

The term also applies to similar discrepancies between conflicting qualities or characteristics and between ideas and actions.

Parallelism (Parallel Structure)

The arrangement of equally important elements in sentences or paragraphs in grammatically equivalent form. The sentence, "Simone is trying to decide among careers in law, medicine, or whether to teach" is not parallel. Here are two versions that are:

> Simone is deciding among careers in law, medicine, and teaching.

> Simone is deciding whether to teach or to practice law or medicine.

Parallelism creates fluency and can also produce powerful rhetorical effects, as may be seen in this quotation from Winston Churchill, British prime minister during World War II:

"We shall fight on the beaches, we shall fight on the landing grounds, we shall fight in the fields and in the streets, we shall fight in the hills; we shall never surrender."

Personification

The figurative attribution of human characteristics to inanimate objects, abstractions, and, in less restrictive application of the term, to nonhuman creatures as well. The device is regularly found in poetry, as in these concluding lines from William Collins's "Ode to Evening," which personifies several abstractions, including the seasons and the subject addressed:

> While Spring shall pour his show'rs, as oft he wont,
> And bathe thy breathing tresses, meekest.Eve!
> > While Summer loves to sport
> > Beneath thy ling'ring light;
> While sallow Autumn fills thy lap with leaves;
> Or Winter yelling thro' the troublous air,
> > Affrights thy shrinking train,
> > And rudely rends thy robes;
> So long, sure-found beneath the sylvan shed,
> Shall Fancy, Friendship, Science, rose-lipped Health,
> > Thy gentlest influence own,
> > And hymn thy fav'rite name!

However, personification is also at home in prose: "Threatening at first, the belligerent thunder retreated to abashed silence, like a loud-mouthed bully subdued."

Point of View

The perspective from which a fictitious narrative is told. This focus helps shape the reader's understanding of events, and attitude toward characters and their motivation, since different narrators may have their own biases and limited perceptions. In nonfiction, the term may be applied to either the writer's "angle" on the subject or to opinions expressed or implied.

Post Hoc Fallacy

An error in reasoning that falsely assumes a causal relationship between events based on chronological sequence alone, without considering whether essential, necessary connections also exist between them. A recent advertising campaign, for example, maintained that people (as photographed) never smiled before there were Hershey bars, implying (illogically) that smiles thereafter were the result of the product's creation. In full form, the term is *post hoc, ergo propter hoc*, Latin for "after this, therefore because of this."

Premise

The idea or principle on which a deductive argument, particularly a **syllogism,** is based. More generally, it is the assumption that underlies any written presentation.

Rebuttal

A response to an argument that first points out the argument's defects and then (or in the process) presents a counterargument.

Rhetoric

Here, the art or study of effective writing (or speech) and its various techniques. In other contexts, the word may sometimes have negative connotations. Phrases like "mere rhetoric" and "empty rhetoric" suggest a discrepancy between words and meaning or a lack of significant meaning altogether. Such rhetoric, of course, should not occur in sound writing.

Simile

A figure of speech, which uses *like* or *as* in establishing an imaginative comparison: "The soft wind rose like a whispered prayer."

Slang

Occasionally used as a synonym for **jargon,** slang is more usually part of the informal vocabulary of particular social or cultural (rather than occupational) groups. Generally inappropriate in formal writing, this typically short-lived vocabulary is dropped and replaced as it becomes more widely known outside its group of origin. Slang expressions such as "the cat's pajamas," "hubba-hubba," "groovy," and "totally tubular" are among those on the ash heap of linguistic history. Decent!

Stipulative Definition

A limited meaning assigned to a term in a specific context: "For purposes of this study, *peer* refers to those who belong to the same economic class, without regard to age or ethnicity."

Structure

The overall organization or design of a piece of writing, including the rhetorical pattern on which it might be based.

Style

The combination of elements such as word choice, sentence structure, degree of development, attitude, and organization that defines the aesthetic of a piece of writing.

Syllogism

A basic pattern in deductive reasoning in which a conclusion is logically drawn from explicit major and minor premises:

> Major premise: Politicians are not to be trusted.
>
> Minor premise: Ralph Royster is a politician.
>
> Conclusion: Royster is not to be trusted.

The logic here is flawless. However, it is possible to argue the truth of the major premise. *See also* VALIDITY.

Symbol

Something (word, gesture, object) that suggests or represents an entity or idea beyond its literal self. In the broadest sense, all language is symbolic.

More narrowly, however, three specific types of symbols are generally acknowledged:

1. Universal symbols are those recognized in nearly all cultures. The sea and sun (or other sources of light), for example, often represent life. We know at once what a flickering, then extinguished, candle beside a sickbed means.

2. Conventional symbols are agreed upon by the social groups that created them. National flags, stars of David, the clenched-fist salute are conventional symbols, as are leprechauns and shamrocks.

3. Personal or private symbols depend, of course, upon one's individual experience and almost invariably need to be explained if alluded to in writing. A broomstick, for instance, might represent terror to someone who was regularly beaten with one, but unless the writing context makes its significance clear, the reader is unlikely to interpret it correctly.

Writers, particularly of fiction and poetry, employ symbols to enhance, vivify, even structure their writing. The road in Bosch's "The Woman" (chapter 1), Melville's "The Isles at Large" (chapter 2), the title character in Peretz's "Bontsha the Silent" (chapter 3), and Merwin's "Unchopping a Tree" (chapter 4) are examples of how symbols might be created and employed.

Thesis

The main idea of a piece of writing, whether stated or implied.

Tone

The attitude writers express toward their subjects, usually manifested through their choice of language. Tone may vary as widely as human emotions themselves, and range, therefore, from detached to impassioned, from humorous to dour, and from sarcastic to sentimental.

Topic Sentence

The sentence that establishes or describes the key point of a paragraph, about which other sentences unite and cohere.

Transition

The movement between statements or ideas, either within or between paragraphs. Transitions are achieved most frequently by signal words or phrases (e.g., *nevertheless, in addition, after, finally*) or by repeated words and their variants or substitutes, such as synonyms and pronouns. If a paragraph, for example, ends with, "The employees refused to form a union," the next might begin with *"Instead, having chosen to go their separate ways, the workers* negotiated individual arrangements." The italicized words and phrases are transitional. *Instead* signals a contrast with what has just been said; *having . . . ways* restates the idea that the union was rejected; *workers* is, of course, a synonym for *employees*.

Understatement

Deliberate minimizing of what is being described or discussed, often with humorous intent, designed to emphasize by contrast the actual magnitude of the subject: "Barry's meal was a modest affair, a light lunch consisting of only two burgers, half a pizza, a large order of fries, and just a medium shake, all of which he barely managed to finish for lack of appetite." Twain's cable message to the Associated Press, "The reports of my death have been greatly exaggerated," is a rather more subtle example.

Unity

The principle that a piece of writing should focus on a single subject and dominant idea.

Validity

In deductive argument, the principle of logical connection among **premises** and conclusions. Note that logical validity does not imply truth. See chapter 9.

Warrant

In the Toulmin system of argumentation, the intellectual connection between **grounds (data)** and **claim.** This is roughly parallel to the premise or underlying assumption of a traditional argument.

Chapter 4

Chapter 5

S. Robert Ramsey. "China, North and South," from *The Languages of China* by S. Robert Ramsey. Copyright © 1987 by Princeton University Press. Reprinted by permission of Princeton University Press.

Chapter 6

Thucydides. "The Glory of Athens (Pericles' Funeral Oration)," from *The Peloponnesian War,* in *Great Books of the Western World.* Copyright © 1952, 1990 by Encyclopaedia Britannica, Inc. Reprinted by permission of Encyclopaedia Britannica, Inc.

Maria Luisa Bombal. "Sky, Sea and Earth," from *Landscapes of a New Land: Fiction by Latin American Women.* Copyright © 1989, 1992 by White Pine Press. Reprinted by permission of White Pine Press.

Desmond Morris. "Territorial Behaviour," from *Manwatching* by Desmond Morris. Copyright © 1977 by Harry N. Abrams, Inc., New York. Reprinted with permission of Harry N. Abrams, Inc. All Rights Reserved.

John S. Mbiti. "The African Concept of Time," from *African Religions and Philosophy* by John S. Mbiti. Copyright © 1969 by John S. Mbiti. Reprinted by permission of Heinemann Publishers, Ltd.

Raymond Chang and Margaret Scrogin Chang. "Four Treasures of the Study," reprinted by permission of W. W. Norton & Company, Inc. from *Speaking of Chinese* by Raymond Chang and Margaret Scrogin Chang. Copyright © 1979 by W. W. Norton & Company. Excerpt from *Written on Bamboo and Silk* by Tsuen-hsum Tsien. Copyright © 1962 by The University of Chicago Press. Reprinted by permission of The University of Chicago Press.

Chapter 7

Yoshido Kenkō. "On Drinking," from *Essays in Idleness,* trans. Donald Keene. Copyright © 1967 by Donald Keene. Reprinted by permission of Columbia University Press.

Emily Dickinson. "After Great Pain, a Formal Feeling Comes," from *The Complete Poems of Emily Dickinson,* ed. Thomas H. Johnson. Copyright 1929 by Martha Dickinson Bianchi and renewed © 1957 by Mary L. Hampson. Reprinted by permission of Little, Brown and Company.

Sadeq Hedayat. "Davud the Hunchback," from *Sadeq Hedayat: An Anthology,* ed. E. Yarshater, *story* trans. H. S. G. Darke. Copyright © 1979 by Bibliotheca Persica. Reprinted by permission of Bibliotheca Persica.

Maurice Shadbolt. "Who Killed the Bog Men of Denmark? And Why?" from the June 1977 edition of *Reader's Digest.* Copyright © 1977 by The Reader's Digest Assn., Inc. Reprinted by permission of The Reader's Digest Assn., Inc.

Stanley Milgram. "The Dilemma of Obedience" (text p. 375), from *Obedience to Authority: An Experimental View* by Stanley Milgram. Copyright © 1974 by Stanley Milgram. Reprinted by permission of HarperCollins Publishers, Inc.

Beth L. Bailey. "Calling Cards and Money," from *Front Porch to Back Seat: Courtship in Twentieth-Century America* by Beth L. Bailey. Copyright © 1988 by The Johns Hopkins University Press, Baltimore/London. Reprinted by permission of The Johns Hopkins University Press.

Chapter 8

Barbara Lawrence. Excerpt from "Four-Letter Words Can Hurt You" by Barbara Lawrence. Originally appeared in the October 27, 1973 edition of *The New York Times.* Copyright © 1973 by The New York Times Company. Reprinted by permission.

Liu Hsiang. "The Mother of Mencius" is reprinted by permission of The Free Press, a division of Macmillan, Inc., from *Chinese Civilization and Society,* ed. Patricia Buckley Ebrey. Copyright © 1981 by The Free Press.

Jacob Bronowski. "The Reach of Imagination," from *A Sense of the Future* by Jacob Bronowski. Copyright © 1977 by Jacob Bronowski. Reprinted by permission of the MIT Press.

Index of Authors and Titles

(Headings of paired or grouped readings appear as small caps.)